T0326547

Diagnosing the Indonesian Economy

Diagnosing the Indonesian Economy

Toward Inclusive and Green Growth

Edited by H. Hill, M. E. Khan, and J. Zhuang

A copublication of the Asian Development Bank and Anthem Press

Anthem Press   Asian Development Bank
www.anthempress.com   *www.adb.org*

This edition first published in 2012 by

ANTHEM PRESS   and
75–76 Blackfriars Road,   Asian Development Bank
London SE1 8HA, UK   6 ADB Avenue, Mandaluyong City, 1550
or PO Box 9779, London SW19 7ZG, UK   Metro Manila, Philippines
and 244 Madison Ave. #116, New York, NY
10016, USA

British Library Cataloguing-in-Publication Data
A catalogue record for this book is available from the British Library.

Library of Congress Cataloging-in-Publication Data
A catalog record for this book has been requested.

ISBN-13: 978 0 85728 447 1 (Hbk)
ISBN-10: 0 85728 447 9 (Hbk)

Foreword

I ndonesia has had a good performance on the economic and poverty fronts in recent years. Its economy has also managed the effects of the recent global economic crisis well, and has grown at relatively high rates compared with other major economies in Southeast Asia. Nevertheless, the country's development challenges remain daunting. Indonesia lags far behind Malaysia and Thailand in terms of per capita gross domestic product (GDP), and will need about two decades to double it if the economy maintains the average annual GDP growth rate recorded in the 2000s. The pace of poverty reduction needs to be accelerated for Indonesia to deliver on the targets set in the country's development plans. Deteriorating trends in the use of natural resources and the environment need to be checked and reversed. Studies indicate that over 5 million hectares of forest was lost during 2000–2005 and that over two-thirds of the country's coral reefs had lost at least half of their living corals by 2005.

This book presents findings of a country diagnostic study on Indonesia, a collaborative effort among the Asian Development Bank (ADB), the Government of Indonesia, the International Labour Organization, and the Islamic Development Bank. The study embodied a new paradigm on development planning, centered on the premise that the economic and political environments differ a great deal among countries, and there is no "one-size-fits-all" solution to development problems; thus, identifying the binding constraints to development and sequencing policy priorities contingent on country-specific circumstances are critical for igniting and sustaining growth and accelerating the pace of poverty reduction.

This study aimed to identify critical impediments to inclusive and sustainable economic growth in Indonesia and to recommend policy options that may stand a good chance of overcoming the impediments. To this end, the study commissioned several background papers on the Indonesian economy to undertake diagnoses in wide-ranging areas, including macroeconomic management, human capital, employment and labor markets, infrastructure, industrial transformation, governance, environment, and poverty and social development. This book presents both an overview of the results and several of the papers and their findings.

I hope that the book will be of value to a wide spectrum of readers—policy makers, academics, development partners, nongovernment organizations, civil society, students of development and economics, and the general public, especially those who care about and are interested in Indonesia and its prosperity.

Changyong Rhee
Chief Economist
Asian Development Bank

Preface

I ndonesia has experienced sharply fluctuating fortunes for the last half century. In the early 1960s, the economy was stagnating, and hyperinflation threatened to further erode living standards. The country, described in the leading development economics textbook as a "chronic economic dropout," was disengaging from the international economic community. Then, in a remarkable turnabout following the regime change of 1965–1966, the new administration signaled a return to economic orthodoxy, and economic growth accelerated. Over the next three decades the economy quadrupled in size, and poverty incidence fell rapidly. However, Indonesia's socioeconomic progress was threatened again by the Asian financial crisis of 1997. It was the worst affected country during the crisis period, principally because it experienced twin crises—both economic and political. In 1998, not only did the modern financial sector and the exchange rate collapse, but there was also a brief episode of hyperinflation and the very real possibility of territorial disintegration.

However, Indonesia navigated these crises with great success. It is now the world's third most populous democracy, having completed two rounds of nationwide elections for the national government and the approximately 500 subnational units of government. The new institutional arrangements for government are in place and are becoming firmly embedded through enthusiastic democratic participation. The country survived the global financial crisis of 2008–2009 with little growth deceleration and is currently enjoying record terms of trade. Indonesia is firmly in the middle-income developing economies group. As a member of the G20 group of leading economies, its international profile is rising.

The timing of this volume is therefore propitious. Its purpose is to draw on the analytical development economics literature and the country's past development experience to set out a policy agenda for sustained growth and poverty reduction. To do so, the diagnostics frameworks developed by Hausmann, Rodrik, and Velasco and by the Asian Development Bank (ADB) were employed in the studies presented here.

The Indonesia country diagnostic study that resulted in this volume was led by ADB and jointly undertaken with the International Labour Organization (ILO) and the Islamic Development Bank (IDB). The work at ADB was headed by Muhammad Ehsan Khan; Deputy Chief Economist Juzhong Zhuang of Economics and Research Department provided the oversight and overall direction. ILO's work on the study was coordinated by Duncan Campbell, and IDB's was coordinated by Areef Suleman. Contributors to the chapters include Priasto Aji, Haryo Aswicahyono, Rizaldi Boer, Maria Rowena M. Cham, Kazutoshi Chatani, Edimon Ginting, Hal Hill, Chris Hope, Zafar Iqbal, Muhammad Ehsan Khan, Niny Khor, Imelda Maidir, Deswanto Marbun, Dionisius Narjoko, Tariq H. Niazi, Yoko Niimi, Umbu Reku Raya, Jindra Nuella Samson, Areef Suleman, Suphachol Suphachalasai, Asep Suryahadi, Athia Yumna, and Juzhong Zhuang. Abuzar Asra, Duncan Campbell, and Patrick Daru provided valuable contributions. The authors are grateful for research assistance provided by Vincent Greco, Lawrence Nelson C. Guevara, and Paulo Rodelio M. Halili. The preparation of the volume was assisted by Amador Foronda, Marife Bacate, Damaris Yarcia, Broderick B. Garcia, Lea Ortega, and Juliet Vanta. The report was edited by Jill Gale de Villa; layout and typesetting were by Michael Cortes.

The study followed a consultative process. Several workshops provided the medium for exchange of information and views among the key stakeholders, including the Government of Indonesia, academic and research institutions, civil society, development partners, and the private sector. Feedback received during the workshops greatly assisted the volume's preparation.

We are grateful for the support provided by the Government of Indonesia. In particular, we thank Vice Minister Lukita Dinarsyah Tuwo, National Development Planning, for his keen interest in the study and guidance in completing this work. We are also grateful for the support and feedback from Dr. Mohamad Ikhsan, Dr. Erna Witoelar, Dr. Prasetijono Widjojo, Mr. Mahendra, Mr. Bambang Sapto Pratomosunu, Dr. Imron Bulkin, Dr. Endah Murniningtyas, Mr. Kennedy Simanjuntak, Mr. M. Donny Azdan, and Dr. Indrajit Kartorejo. We also thank the civil society and private sector representative organizations that participated in the workshops for their support and interest in preparation of this volume.

Hal Hill   Muhammad Ehsan Khan   Juzhong Zhuang

Author Profiles

Priasto Aji is an economist at the Asian Development Bank (ADB) Indonesia Resident Mission, Jakarta. He is a regular contributor to *Asian Development Outlook* and *Asian Development Outlook Updates*. Previously, he worked at the Association of Southeast Asian Nations (ASEAN) Secretariat as a technical officer responsible for macroeconomic surveillance. He received a master's of business economics from the University of Strathclyde, Glasgow, and a master's in economics from the University of Siena, Italy. He is currently pursuing a PhD in economics from the University of Siena.

Haryo Aswicahyono is a senior economist specializing in trade and industry at the Centre for Strategic and International Studies (CSIS), Jakarta. He is also a lecturer at the Faculty of Economics of the University of Indonesia and at the Prasetiya Mulya Business School. His research interests cover trade and industrialization, industrial organization, competition policy, and economic development. He received his civil engineering degree at the Bandung Institute of Technology in 1983 and joined CSIS in 1985. He has a master's degree in economics and a doctorate from the Australian National University (ANU). He has published a number of journal articles, book chapters, and working papers on trade and industrialization in Indonesia.

Rizaldi Boer is director of the Center for Climate Risk and Opportunity Management in Southeast Asia and the Pacific at Bogor Agriculture University. He has been working in the area of climate variability and climate change since 1979 at the national, regional, and international levels. He has a PhD from the University of Sydney, with research focus on climate risk management.

Maria Rowena M. Cham is an economics officer in the Economics and Research Department at ADB and has worked at the National Economic and Development Authority and the Power Sector Assets and Liabilities Management Corporation. She has participated in a number of country diagnostic studies, and has contributed to their reports. She coauthored chapters in *Diagnosing the Philippine Economy: Toward Inclusive Growth* and has published journal articles on various aspects of the Philippine economy. She has a master's in economics from the University of the Philippines and is pursuing a PhD in economics from the same university.

Kazutoshi Chatani is a technical officer (economist) in the International Labour Organization (ILO) Office for Indonesia and Timor-Leste. He is ILO's liaison officer to ASEAN. He served as a research economist in the Economic and Labour Market Analysis Department of the ILO headquarters. His publications include ILO's annual report, *Labour and Social Trends in Indonesia*. He engaged in formulating the National Employment Strategy for Timor-Leste.

Edimon Ginting is senior country economist at the ADB Indonesian Resident Mission. He has worked as an economist at the International Monetary Fund (IMF); a research economist at the Productivity Commission, Australia; adviser to the Budget Committee of the Indonesian Parliament; and researcher and lecturer at the Institute for Economic and Social Research, Faculty of Economics, University of Indonesia. He received his PhD in economics from Monash University, Australia.

Hal Hill is the H.W. Arndt Professor of Southeast Asian Economies, ANU. He headed ANU's Indonesia project for 12 years and edited the *Bulletin of Indonesian Economic Studies*. His general research areas are the ASEAN economies, especially Indonesia and the Philippines; industrialization and foreign investment in East Asia; and Australia's economic relations with the Asia and Pacific region. He has authored or edited 16 books (including *The Indonesian Economy since 1966*, Cambridge, 2000) and about 140 articles, book chapters, and papers. He is an occasional contributor to Australian and Asian newspapers and magazines, and a radio and television commentator. His consultancies have included work for ADB, the Australian and Indonesian governments, United Nations agencies, and the World Bank. He holds visiting appointments at Columbia University, Gadja Mada University, the Institute of Southeast Asian Studies, the Tinbergen Institute, the International University of Japan, the National University of Malaysia, the University of Oxford, and the University of the Philippines. He serves on the editorial board of 13 academic journals.

Chris Hope is reader in policy modeling at the Judge Business School. He was a lead author and review editor for the Third and Fourth Assessment Reports of the Intergovernmental Panel on Climate Change, which was awarded a half share of the Nobel Peace Prize in 2007. He was the specialist adviser to the House of Lords Select Committee on Economic Affairs inquiry into aspects of the economics of climate change, and an adviser on the PAGE model to the Stern Review on the Economics of Climate Change. In 2007, he was awarded the Faculty Lifetime Achievement Award from the European Academy of Business in Society and the Aspen Institute. His research interests involve numerical information in public policy and the integrated assessment modeling of climate change, and he has published extensively in books and peer-reviewed journals. He has recently completed PAGE09, the latest version of the PAGE integrated assessment model. He has a PhD in the economic modeling of renewable energy from the University of Cambridge.

Zafar Iqbal is lead economist in the Country Department, Islamic Development Bank. He has worked as a senior economist in the IMF Resident Mission, Islamabad, Pakistan, and as a research economist in the Pakistan Institute of Development Economics, Islamabad. His recent areas of research are member country partnership strategies, growth diagnostics, infrastructure development, international trade, and development economics.

Muhammad Ehsan Khan is principal economist in ADB's Economics and Research Department and has served as a project economist in ADB's Southeast Asia Department. He is leading ADB's work in the area of growth diagnostics and has been editor of and contributor to publications on the country diagnostic studies of Indonesia, Nepal, Papua New Guinea, and Philippines. He is a coeditor of *Diagnosing the Philippine Economy: Toward Inclusive Growth* (2009).

Niny Khor is an economist in ADB's Economics and Research Department. Her current research focuses on understanding the sources of growth of enterprises and households in Asia, as well as the patterns of employment and exports in Asia. Prior to joining ADB, she was a postdoctoral fellow at the Stanford Center for International Development. She obtained her master's and PhD degrees in economics from Stanford University, where she researched topics on labor economics and development, including how income mobility may affect income inequality in the People's Republic of China and the United States.

Imelda Maidir is a researcher in the Department of Economics, CSIS, Jakarta. Her research interests include trade and industrialization, competition policy, and public economics. Her research areas include industrial competitiveness and the assessment of multilateral and regional economic arrangements. She is an occasional contributor to *The Jakarta Post*. She received her master's degree in public policy from the National University of Singapore.

Deswanto Marbun is public policy practitioner and researcher at the Social Monitoring and Early Response Unit (SMERU) Research Institute. His research projects with SMERU include business enabling environments, social protection policies, poverty measurement, and the impact of the global financial crisis. He has a master's in development management from the Institute for Development Policy and Management, University of Manchester.

Dionisius Narjoko is researcher at the Economic Research Institute for ASEAN and East Asia. His expertise is in industrial organization, Indonesian manufacturing, trade and investment, and applied econometrics. He has written and coauthored numerous articles and papers. He has a PhD in economics from ANU.

Tariq H. Niazi is principal public management specialist at ADB. He has more than 15 years of operational experience in multiple aspects of public sector management and financial sector development, including public finance, fiscal decentralization, legal and judicial reform, and public-private partnerships. Before joining ADB, he worked for the World Bank's Poverty Reduction and Economic Management Unit in the East Asia and Pacific Department. He has worked in many countries across Asia and East Europe and has published on topics including fiscal decentralization and taxation issues.

Yoko Niimi is an economist in ADB's Economics and Research Department. Her current research focuses on development issues in Asia, including inclusive growth, poverty and inequality, and quality of life measurements. She has been working extensively on country diagnostic studies, including for Bhutan, Indonesia, Nepal, and Papua New Guinea. Prior to joining ADB, she consulted for the Development Research Group of the World Bank. She obtained her PhD in economics from the University of Sussex in 2007.

Umbu Reku Raya is a PhD fellow in the Arndt-Corden Department of Economics, Crawford School of Economics and Government, ANU. Prior to his PhD work, he was a researcher at the SMERU Research Institute, Jakarta, and lecturer at the University of Nusa Cendana, West Timor. His research interests include the roles of governance and social return to education in accelerating the reduction of multidimensional poverty in Indonesia. He has a master of arts in development studies from the Institute of Social Studies, The Hague, and a master of science in management from the University of Indonesia, Jakarta.

Jindra Nuella Samson is an economics officer at ADB. Prior to joining ADB, she was an assistant scientist at the International Center for Tropical Agriculture, where she worked in agriculture, rural development, and participatory methodology development. She has also worked with nongovernment organizations in conducting environmental impact assessments in the Philippines. She graduated from the University of the Philippines with a bachelor's degree in economics and a master's degree in environmental science.

Areef Suleman is the division manager: policy development in the Economic Research and Policy Department, Islamic Development Bank. He worked as an international expert on several assignments for the United Nations Industrial Development Organization in Africa prior to heading the Support Programme for Industrial Innovation in South Africa. His recent areas of interest are growth diagnostics, food security, and policy development.

Suphachol Suphachalasai is an economist at ADB, specializing in the economics of climate change. He is leading ADB's technical project that supports Southeast Asian countries in low-carbon economic planning. He is the technical lead on the economics of climate change research in ADB's subregions and supports ADB's clean energy operations. Prior to joining ADB, he was an environmental economist at the World Bank in Washington DC, where he contributed to the World Bank's Strategic Framework for Development and Climate Change; India Strategies for Low Carbon Growth; Climate Change Impacts in Drought and Flood Affected Areas of India; and several country environmental analyses. He has a PhD in economics from the University of Cambridge.

Asep Suryahadi is the director of the SMERU Research Institute in Jakarta, Indonesia. His research interests cover the areas of poverty, social protection, labor, health, and economic development. His current research topics include the impacts of unconditional cash transfers on social welfare, of child labor on health and education outcomes, and of television penetration on fertility. His latest publications include articles in *Education Economics*, the *Journal of Development Economics*, and *Food Policy*. He holds a PhD in economics from ANU.

Athia Yumna is a researcher at the SMERU Research Institute. Her research interests include poverty analysis, development and health economics, and social protection. She has a master's in economics from the University of Warwick.

Juzhong Zhuang is the deputy chief economist in ADB's Economics and Research Department. He has served as assistant chief economist, and as principal economist and senior economist in ADB's Office of Regional Economic Integration. His recent areas of research are inclusive growth and growth diagnostics, early warning systems for financial crises, and the economics of climate change. He is the editor, author, and coauthor of numerous books and articles.

Abbreviations and Acronyms

ADB	—	Asian Development Bank
AFC	—	Asian financial crisis
AIBEP	—	Australia-Indonesia Basic Education Program
APO	—	Asian Productivity Organization
ASEAN	—	Association of Southeast Asian Nations
Bappenas	—	Badan Perencanaan Pembangunan Nasional (National Development Planning Agency)
BGP	—	Bundesanstalt für Geowissenschaften und Rohstoffe (German Federal Institute for Geosciences and Natural Resources)
BLK	—	balai latihan kerja (public vocational training institution/center)
BLT	—	Bantuan Langsung Tunai (Direct [unconditional] Cash Transfer)
BKM	—	Beasiswa Keluarga Miskin (Scholarships for Poor Households)
BKPM	—	Badan Koordinasi Penanaman Modal (Investment Coordinating Board)
BNSP	—	Badan Standar Nasional Pendidikan (National Education Standards Board)
BOS	—	Bantuan Operasional Sekolah (School Operational Assistance)
BPJT	—	Badan Pengatur Jalan Tol (Toll-Road Regulatory Agency)
BPK	—	Badan Pemeriksa Keuangan Republik Indonesia (Audit Board of the Republic of Indonesia)
BPN	—	Badan Pertanahan Nasional (National Land Agency)
BPS	—	Badan Pusat Statistik (Statistics Indonesia)
BRI	—	Bank Rakyat Indonesia
BRTI	—	Badan Regulasi Telekomunikasi Indonesia (Telecommunication Regulatory Agency of Indonesia)
BSM	—	Beasiswa Siswa Miskin (Scholarships for Poor Students)
Bulog	—	Badan Urusan Logistik (National Logistics Agency)

BUMD	—	badan usaha milik daerah (enterprise owned by regional government)
CBT	—	competency-based training
CDM	—	Clean Development Mechanism
CG	—	central government
CMNP	—	PT Citra Marga Nusaphala Persada
CMS	—	PT Citra Margatama Surabaya
CO_2	—	carbon dioxide
DAK	—	Specific Allocation Fund (Dana Alokasi Khusus)
DAU	—	General Allocation Fund (Dana Alokasi Umum)
DG	—	directorate general
DGR	—	Directorate General of Railways
DPD	—	Dewan Perwakilan Daerah (Regional Representatives Council)
DPOD	—	Dewan Pertimbangan Otonomi Daerah (Regional Autonomy Advisory Council)
DPR	—	Dewan Perwakilan Rakyat (People's Representative Council/Assembly, or house of representatives, elected nationally)
FAO	—	Food and Agriculture Organization (United Nations)
FDI	—	foreign direct investment
FY	—	fiscal year
GDP	—	gross domestic product
GDS	—	Government and Decentralization Survey
GFC	—	global financial crisis
GHG	—	greenhouse gas
GR	—	general regulation
IDB	—	Islamic Development Bank
IDD	—	international direct dialling
IEA	—	International Energy Agency
IFC	—	International Finance Corporation
ILO	—	International Labour Organization
IMD	—	International Institute for Management Development
IMF	—	International Monetary Fund
IMT-GT	—	Indonesia-Malaysia-Thailand Growth Triangle
IPCC	—	Intergovernmental Panel on Climate Change
IPP	—	independent power producer
IPRSP	—	Interim Poverty Reduction Strategy Paper
ISIC	—	International Standard Industrial Classification
JETRO	—	Japan External Trade Organization
JICA	—	Japan International Cooperation Agency
JPS	—	Jaring Pengaman Sosial (Social Safety Net)

JPS-BK	—	Jaring Pengaman Sosial Bidang Kesehatan (Social Safety Net for Health)
KPK	—	Komisi Pemberantas Korupsi (Corruption Eradication Commisssion)
KPMK	—	Komiti Penyempurnaan Managemen Keuangan (Financial Management Reform Committee)
KPPOD	—	Komite Pemantauan Pelaksanaan Otonomi Daerah (Regional Autonomy Watch)
KPPU	—	Komisi Pengawas Persaingan Usaha (Commission for Supervision of Business Competition)
KUR	—	Kredit Usaha Rakyat (People's Business Credit)
LG	—	local government
LPEM-FEUI	—	Lembaga Penyelidikan Ekonomi dan Masyarakat-Fakultas Ekonomi Universitas Indonesia
MNE	—	multinational enterprise
MOE	—	Ministry of Environment
MOF	—	Ministry of Finance
MOHA	—	Ministry of Home Affairs
MONE	—	Ministry of National Education
MOT	—	Ministry of Transportation
MSMEs	—	microenterprises and small- and medium-sized enterprises
NAPFD	—	National Action Plan for Fiscal Decentralization
NCCC	—	National Council on Climate Change
NGO	—	nongovenment organization
NO_2	—	nitrogen dioxide
NTT	—	Nusa Tenggara Timur (East Nusa Tenggara)
ODA	—	official development assistance
OECD	—	Organisation for Economic Co-operation and Development
PAD	—	Pendapatan Asli Daerah (local own-source revenues; regional governments' own revenues)
PAKTO	—	Paket Oktober (October package)
PFM	—	public financial management
PISA	—	Programme for International Student Assessment
PKH	—	Program Keluarga Harapan (Hopeful Family Program)
PKPS-BBM	—	Program Kompensasi Pengurangan Subsidi Bahan Bakar Minyak (Fuel Subsidy Reduction Compensation Program)
PLN	—	PT Perusahaan Listrik Negara (Indonesia's state electricity firm)
PNPM	—	Program Nasional Pemberdayaan Masyarakat (National Program for Community Empowerment)

PPK	—	Program Pengembangan Kecamatan (Kecamatan Development Program)
PPP	—	public-private partnership
PRC	—	People's Republic of China
PTKA	—	PT Kereta Api (Indonesian Railways)
REDD	—	reducing emissions from deforestation and forest degradation
RG	—	regional government
Rp	—	Indonesian rupiah
RPJMN	—	Rencana Pembangunan Jangka Menengah Nasional (National Medium-Term Development Plan)
SBI	—	Sertifikat Bank Indonesia (Bank Indonesia Certificate)
SIKD	—	Sistem Informasi Keuangan Daerah (Regional Financial Information System), Directorate of DG Fiscal Balance in MOF
SITC	—	Standard International Trade Classification
SJSN	—	Sistem Jaminan Sosial Nasional (National Social Security System)
SMEs	—	small- and medium-sized enterprises
SMK	—	sekolah menengah atas (vocational secondary school)
SNPK	—	Strategi Nasional Penanggulangan Kemiskinan (National Poverty Reduction Strategy)
SPKD	—	strategi penanggulangan kemiskinan daerah (regional poverty reduction strategy)
SO_2	—	sulfur dioxide
SOE	—	state-owned enterprise
TFP	—	total factor productivity
TI	—	Transparency International
TKPK	—	Tim Koordinasi Penanggulangan Kemiskinan (Coordinating Team for Poverty Reduction)
TNP2K	—	Tim Nasional Percepatan Penanggulangan Kemiskinan (National Team for the Acceleration of Poverty Reduction)
TVET	—	technical and vocational education and training
UNCTAD	—	United Nations Conference on Trade and Statistics
UNDP	—	United Nations Development Programme
UNESCO	—	United Nations Educational, Scientific, and Cultural Organization
UNFCCC	—	United Nations Framework Convention on Climate Change
US	—	United States
USGS	—	United States Geological Survey
USO	—	universal service obligation

VAT	—	value-added tax
VoIP	—	voice-over-internet protocol
WDI	—	World Development Indicators
WEC	—	World Energy Council
WEF	—	World Economic Forum
WGI	—	Worldwide Governance Indicators
WHO	—	World Health Organization
WRI	—	World Resources International

Weights and Measures

°C	—	degrees Celsius
bcm	—	billion cubic meters
cm	—	centimeter
ha	—	hectare
kb/d	—	thousand barrels per day
km	—	kilometer
kWh	—	kilowatt hour
mb/d	—	million barrels per day
$MtCO_2$	—	metric tons of CO_2
Mtce	—	metric tons of carbon equivalent
Mtoe	—	million tons of oil equivalent
ppm	—	parts per million
tCO_2	—	ton of carbon dioxide

Contents

1. Introduction

Hal Hill, Muhammad Ehsan Khan, and Juzhong Zhuang

1.1. Objectives

The Indonesian economy has performed well in recent years. It recovered from the 1997 Asian financial crisis and grew at an average of 5.2% during 2001–2008, which compared favorably with other major Southeast Asian economies. Despite the global economic crisis, the economy posted a growth rate of 4.5% in 2009—one of the highest in Southeast Asia. Nevertheless, the challenges faced by the economy remain formidable. The rate of economic growth in recent years has not been at par with the average the country achieved between 1967 and 1997. The pace of poverty reduction has slowed, and the poverty incidence, at 14.2% in 2009, was only 3.5 percentage points lower than that in 1996. Income and non-income disparities across the country's regions and across the urban–rural divide remain wide. In addition, the expected fall in commodity prices, continued uncertainty about the recovery of the global economy, and tightening of domestic credit further threaten investment and private consumption and in turn hamper the pace of economic growth and poverty reduction.

The Indonesian government is committed to sustaining and improving the growth it has attained in recent years. This commitment is embodied in the current medium-term development plan and will be carried forward in succeeding ones. The creation of a prosperous Indonesia through economic and social development is one of the current plan's three major agenda items. The plan lays out policy directions for changing the high-cost economic structure by improving the investment climate and enhancing industry's competitiveness.

This report has two interrelated objectives. The first is to identify the critical constraints to medium-term economic growth and poverty reduction, and to equitable regional development in Indonesia. The second is to provide some recommendations that policymakers can consider in addressing these constraints so as to achieve broad-based growth and the plan's targets.

1.2. Methodology

The study's framework is based on the inclusive growth concept presented in Figure 1.1. Inclusive growth is growth that not only generates economic opportunities, but also ensures equal access to them by all members of a society. Growth is considered to be inclusive only when it allows all members of a society to participate in and benefit from the growth process on an equal basis regardless of their individual circumstances (Ali and Zhuang 2007). Hence, a development strategy based on the inclusive growth concept is anchored on two pillars: one is to create and expand economic opportunities through high and sustained growth, and the other is to broaden access to opportunities for all members of a society (Zhuang 2008). Several requirements need to be met to satisfy each pillar of the inclusive growth strategy. Hence the study attempts to diagnose the constraints that may be curtailing efforts to generate high and sustained growth to create jobs and opportunities, and to make the growth inclusive. The study employs the growth diagnostic framework to diagnose constraints to high and sustained growth, and the poverty and inequality reduction diagnostic framework to diagnose constraints that may be limiting the pace of poverty reduction and inclusiveness of the economic growth.

Figure 1.1: Inclusive Growth Concept

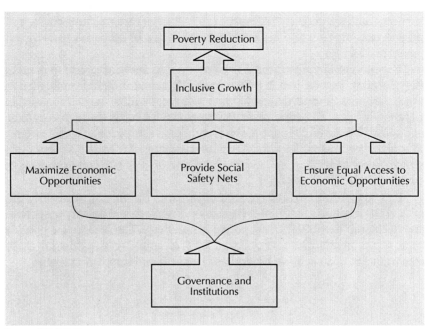

Source: ADB (2007).

Countries at an early stage of development may not have adequate capacity to implement a wide array of policy reforms at the same time. With the diagnostic approach, reforms can start with easing a few critical areas that truly constrain growth. The approach thus offers a practical tool for policymakers and development planners to use in formulating country-specific growth strategies. The application of growth diagnostics is one of the efforts in the search for new approaches to growth strategy after the Washington consensus was questioned in recent years.

The growth diagnostics approach starts with a set of proximate determinants of growth, investigates which of these pose the greatest impediments or are the most critical constraints to higher growth, and figures out specific distortions behind the impediments. The point of departure of the inquiry is a standard endogenous growth model in which growth depends on the social return to accumulation, private appropriability of this social return, and the cost of financing. Each of these three broad determinants of growth is in turn a function of many other factors, which can be presented in a problem tree (Figure 1.2).

Figure 1.2: Growth Diagnostics Framework

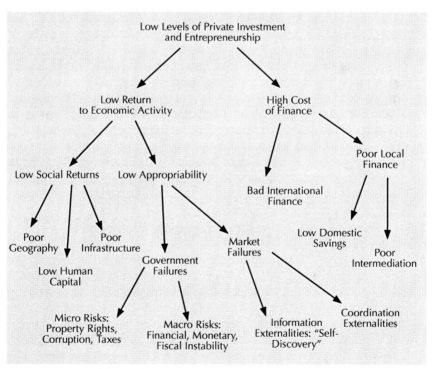

Source: Hausmann, Rodrik, and Velasco (2005).

3

The problem tree provides a framework for diagnosing critical constraints to growth. The diagnosis starts by asking what keeps the level of private investment and entrepreneurship low. Is it low social return to investment, inadequate private appropriability of the social return, or high cost of financing? If it is low social return, is that due to insufficient levels of complementary factors of production—in particular, human capital, technical know-how, and/or infrastructure? If the impediment is poor private appropriability, is it due to macro vulnerability, high taxation, poor property rights and contract enforcement, labor–capital conflicts, information and learning externalities, and/or coordination failures? If high cost of finance is the problem, is it due to low domestic savings, poor intermediation in the domestic financial markets, or poor integration with external financial markets?

At each node of the problem tree, the diagnosis looks for signals that could help answer the question. The two types of diagnostic signals that one can look for are price signals and nonprice signals. Examples of price signals are returns to education, interest rates, and cost of transport. For example, if education is undersupplied, returns to skills/education would be high and unemployment of skilled people would be low. If investment is constrained by savings, interest rates would be high and growth would respond to changes in available savings (for example, inflows of foreign resources). If poor transport links are a serious constraint, bottlenecks and high private costs of transport would be evident. The use of nonprice signals is based on the idea that when a constraint binds, the result is activities designed to get around it. For example, high taxation could lead to "high informality" (e.g., under-reporting of income, resulting in lower tax revenues); poor legal institutions could result in high demand for informal mechanisms of conflict resolution and contract enforcement; and poor financial intermediation could lead to internalization of finance through business groups. Cross-country and cross-period benchmarking and results of business surveys are useful means to gauge whether particular diagnostic evidence signals a binding constraint for the country concerned.

1.3. Poverty and Inequality Diagnostic Framework

Although the growth diagnostics approach was developed to identify the binding constraints to growth and associated policy priorities, the approach can also be applied to other areas of policy analysis, such as identifying critical constraints to the inclusiveness of growth. Inclusive growth not only addresses the inequality issue, but also enhances the poverty reduction agenda (Figure 1.3). Despite a steady decline in poverty in Indonesia in recent years, the pace of reduction has been much lower than before the

Figure 1.3: Diagnostic Framework for Constraints to Reducing Poverty and Inequality

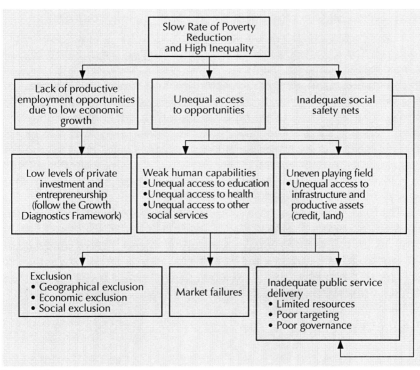

Source: Authors.

1997 Asian financial crisis. There is also a great geographical disparity in poverty across the country, and the vulnerability of Indonesian households to poverty remains high. The limited reduction in poverty and persistent inequality can be caused by the lack of economic opportunities due to poor growth, unequal access to opportunities, and/or the absence of effective and adequate social safety nets.

Within the inclusive growth conceptual framework presented in Figure 1.1, the availability of productive employment opportunities is a key to a household's ability to improve its livelihood. However, even if the economy succeeds in creating productive and decent employment, this would not automatically lead to poverty reduction unless there is equal access to the opportunities. Inequitable access to economic opportunities can be attributable to weak human capabilities and/or an uneven playing field, both of which can prevent people from participating in and contributing to the growth process on an equal basis.

5

Certain groups of people may have weaker human capabilities than others, partly due to unequal access to education, health, and/or other social services, including clean water and sanitation systems. Inequity in accessing opportunities may also be caused by unequal access to infrastructure and productive assets, such as land and credit. For example, in geographically challenged countries like Indonesia, infrastructure plays a key role in promoting inclusiveness.

Promoting equal access to opportunities also requires the government to provide social safety nets to mitigate the effects of external and transitory livelihood shocks as well as to meet the minimum needs of the chronically poor (Zhuang 2008). The importance of social safety nets cannot be overemphasized in countries like Indonesia where a large percentage of the population is clustered around the poverty line, indicating their vulnerability to unforeseen crisis. The inadequate provision of social safety nets can thus be a constraint to reducing poverty and inequality.

The framework also suggests that each of the above issues (weak human capabilities, uneven playing field, and inadequate social safety nets) can, in turn, be due to a number of factors, including market failures, government failures to deliver adequate public services, and/or social exclusion. The key role of the government in promoting inclusiveness is to address these market, institutional, and policy failures.

1.4.   Organization of the Book

Chapters 2–4 comprise Part A, the Overview and Synthesis of the studies for diagnosing the Indonesian economy. Part B, Issues and Challenges, provides more in-depth information on specific areas diagnosed.

Chapter 2, by Hal Hill and Maria Rowena Cham, provides a broad overview of Indonesia's development performance and policy since the 1960s. The authors highlight the episodic nature of the country's economic development, from the stagnation and hyperinflation in the first half of the 1960s, when the country was written off as a "chronic economic dropout," to the rapid growth during the Suharto era, followed by the deep Asian financial crisis of 1997–1998, and reasonably quick return to economic growth, albeit at a somewhat slower rate and in a very different institutional and political context. The authors' economic overview notes that per capita incomes have risen almost six-fold since the mid 1960s, while rapid structural change has seen the once dominant agriculture sector shrink to less than 15% of the economy. However, while the country's growth has been similar to that of its lower income Southeast Asian neighbors, it has never consistently achieved the extremely high growth record of Japan and the newly industrializing economies in an earlier period, and the People's Republic of China currently.

Estimates of total factor productivity growth confirm this conclusion. Indonesia's growth has been reasonably broad-based in that all the major regions have benefited and poverty has fallen quickly, as highlighted in Chapter 9.

The policy settings that have underpinned this record display both continuity and change. The former include a consistent commitment to reasonably prudent macroeconomic management (except briefly at the peak of the crisis in 1998), a broadly open economy, and concern about equity, at least in the official discourse. However, policy making processes changed dramatically with the country's transition from authoritarian to democratic rule in the late 1990s, with a more assertive legislature, a less cohesive executive, a more powerful judiciary and civil society, and greatly increased authority for the subnational tiers of government. Investors, both domestic and foreign, are still adjusting to this fluid institutional environment, which is one of the reasons why investments have not yet recovered to the pre-crisis levels.

Chapter 3, by Muhammad Ehsan Khan, Juzhong Zhuang, Maria Rowena Cham, Niny Khor, and Imelda Maidir, and Chapter 4, by Yoko Niimi and Kazutoshi Chatani, provide the analytical framework for the study, focusing respectively on the critical constraints to growth and poverty reduction. This framework, developed by Hausmann, Rodrik, and Velasco (2005), attempts to identify the most binding constraints to economic growth, and therefore the major policy and reform priorities. A strength of this approach is that it recognizes that there is no one-size-fits-all approach to economic development, and that an understanding of country-specific circumstances is critical.

Commencing with a set of proximate determinants of growth, the resulting "problem tree" attempts to diagnose the barriers to private investment and entrepreneurship, ranging from the absence of complementary inputs, to macroeconomic vulnerabilities and insecure property rights. In turn, each of these constraints can be further disaggregated into what may broadly be termed price and nonprice signals. This framework can also be applied to addressing the critical constraints to social inclusiveness. The latter include not only the creation of productive employment opportunities but also ensuring that these opportunities are distributed widely across the community. In addition, non-income measures of deprivation and the vulnerability of the near poor to adverse exogenous shocks are highlighted in this framework. These elements also lead on to a policy reform agenda for accelerating both growth and poverty reduction.

Chapter 5, by Edimon Ginting and Priasto Aji, examines macroeconomic management since the Asian financial crisis. In the immediate aftermath of the crisis, the government was preoccupied with controlling inflation and managing the very high level of public debt. The government was effective in both respects, contributing to the economy's resilience. In particular, fiscal deficits and public debt are very modest, easing the task of monetary policy.

But the authors emphasize that there are significant challenges going forward. Inflation is under control, but is generally higher than that of Indonesia's major trading partners and neighbors. The government is ambivalent in its response to the large and volatile capital inflows. Central bank independence is legally assured but is still a work in progress in some respects. Inevitably, the real effective exchange rate will continue to appreciate as long as commodity prices remain buoyant. A greater array of fine-tuning monetary policy instruments is also required.

Chapter 6, by Haryo Aswicahyono, Hal Hill, and Dionisius Narjoko, analyzes Indonesia's industrial transformation. The authors highlight the country's latecomer status, with an extremely small formal industrial sector in the mid 1960s, followed by very rapid industrial growth during the 32-year Suharto period, initially through import-substituting catch-up and then, following the successful 1980s reforms, export-oriented industrialization.

The Asian financial crisis was, however, a watershed in several respects. Industrial growth fell sharply, and has never subsequently returned to the earlier high growth rates. Manufactured export performance has been indifferent. Firm-level mobility appears to have declined, possibly owing to financial constraints. Moreover, industrial employment growth has been less responsive. The result of both slower output growth and the declining output–employment elasticity is the phenomenon of "jobless industrialization," with important implications for the pace of poverty decline.

The infrastructure challenge is the subject of Chapter 7, by Areef Suleman and Zafar Iqbal, an issue of great importance given that Indonesia is the world's largest archipelagic state. Emphasizing the importance of physical infrastructure to modern, internationally integrated economies, the authors conclude that Indonesia lags in several respects. Most investor surveys highlight infrastructure issues as among their major concerns. Again, the Asian financial crisis constituted a turning point, with the current level of infrastructure investment—about 3.5% of GDP—being about half that of the pre-crisis period. The problems are manifold, and evident in most sectors, except where there have been major policy liberalizations—notably cellular telecommunications and civil aviation. The problems include the difficulty of land acquisition, poor governance, weak human and institutional capacities, and financial constraints. The award of monopolies to private infrastructure providers has often attracted controversy. Civil servants are reluctant to sign off on major projects for fear of corruption allegations. Since the 2001 decentralization, coordination issues between the three main tiers of government have complicated decision making processes.

Chapter 8, by Kazutoshi Chatani, examines the state of human capital in Indonesia. The country has achieved major educational advances since the 1970s. Enrollments have risen rapidly at all levels, with near universal primary school enrollment, and the government's objective of universal junior high school completion within reach. Gender differentials have narrowed appreciably, and interregional inequalities are less than in other very large developing countries. However, Indonesia generally lags behind its neighbors according to most comparative indicators, particularly those that attempt to measure the quality of educational outcomes. Notwithstanding the quantitative expansions, the availability of scholarships and other measures to advance educational opportunity for the poor is limited. Universities are underfunded, overregulated, and somewhat isolated from the regional mainstream. Inadequate teacher remuneration is a barrier to quality. The vocational system is generally not closely aligned to industry needs. Although surveys of firms do not report skill shortages as a major bottleneck, they are beginning to emerge in some key export sectors and are likely to intensify as the country loses its comparative advantage in low-wage activities and attempts to upgrade its economic structure.

Chatani addresses the links among economic growth, employment creation, and poverty alleviation, noting in Chapter 9 the key role that the labor market plays in translating increased economic activity for the benefit of the poor. As in other developing countries, youth unemployment is a serious problem in Indonesia. The problem was exacerbated by the Asian financial crisis and the subsequent anemic industrial employment growth. In fact, most of the employment growth since the late 1990s has come from the service sector, with agriculture, manufacturing, and mining contributing very little. Improved educational outcomes will be needed to support higher productivity and wage levels.

The system of labor relations has changed significantly since the Suharto era, with increased worker rights, including the freedom to organize. There is some debate about the impact of the significantly tighter labor market regulations over the past decade. Minimum wages have been increased, and now are more likely to be enforced, while Indonesia's severance laws are among the most restrictive in developing Asia.

Indonesia's record on poverty alleviation is the subject of Chapter 10, by Asep Suryahadi, Athia Yumna, Umbu Reku Raya, and Deswanto Marbun. The very high incidence of poverty in the 1960s began to decline steeply with the onset of rapid economic growth, and the country's poverty alleviation record during the period 1966–1997 is widely recognized. The 1997 Asian financial crisis represented the first major setback to this impressive record, with the poverty incidence jumping significantly from 17% to 24%.

After reviewing the historical experience, the authors then examine the record during 1998–2010 in more detail. Two features receive particular emphasis. The first is the trends in poverty during this period, where the authors show that the resumption of economic growth led to a return to the pre-crisis incidence by about 2004. However, the poverty decline was slower during the period, owing to slower economic growth, and most likely also the sluggish employment expansion, as noted in chapters 6 and 10. Also, reducing the incidence of "hard-core"' poverty is likely to be more difficult, and cannot be addressed by economic growth alone. This leads to the second main issue—the initiatives introduced in the wake of the crisis as social protection measures for the poor. The initiatives include public works programs, subsidized food, and incentives to keep the children of poor families in school. These measures have been introduced in the context of the country's rapid and largely successful transition to democracy, with the implication that the programs' success depends on community participation and empowerment.

In the transition to democracy in the late 1990s, the government introduced a "big bang" decentralization, which became effective from January 2001. This reform was long overdue, as the earlier model of Jakarta-centric, top-down administration for the world's largest archipelagic state was hardly appropriate. The reforms resulted in a major devolution of administrative and financial authority, which, combined with local-level elections, has transformed the country's institutional landscape. A decade after the reforms were introduced, Chapter 11, by Tariq Niazi, provides a detailed examination of processes and outcomes. The decentralization has broadly worked, in the sense that the essential services of government have been maintained, and the earlier worries of the possibility of territorial disintegration have been averted. However, much work remains to put the new system firmly in place. The splintering of administrative units (*pemekaran*) has continued, coordination among the three main tiers of government—national, provincial and subprovincial—has been unwieldy, the quality of local governance has been highly variable, and there is not yet clear evidence that the reforms operate in a manner that rewards the better governed regions. To this end, the author lays out a reform agenda to consolidate the progress and fine-tune the relationship between central and local government.

Finally, Chapter 12, by Suphachol Suphachalasai, Juzhong Zhuang, Jindra Nuella Samson, Rizaldi Boer, and Chris Hope, provides a detailed investigation of the state of Indonesia's environment and its natural resource management. The challenges are daunting. As in most of its neighboring countries, successive Indonesian governments have accorded low priority to the environment. This has resulted in one of the most rapid deforestation rates in the developing world. The country's fragile marine ecology has also deteriorated sharply. The large mining industry has generally paid scant attention to local environmental concerns. Much of the country's internationally unique flora and fauna is endangered. Large areas of three of the country's major cities are projected to be below sea level on current trends, while air quality levels are poor. This environmental degradation also has international implications. The smoke haze has resulted occasionally in poor air quality in neighboring Malaysia and Singapore. Indonesia is variously estimated to be the third or fourth largest emitter of carbon dioxide, principally as a result of rapid deforestation. Global problems require coordinated international action, and there is some prospect of substantial external funding for the country in exchange for greater attention to its environmental amenities. The authors also observe that there is a growing awareness of these problems, and they lay out a reform agenda that includes providing incentives to modify past practices, highlighting the need for greater country-specific research and development, raising public awareness of the issues, engaging the private sector and the international community, and providing greater certainty of land tenure and for land use management.

References

Ali, I. and J. Zhuang. 2007. Inclusive Growth Toward a Prosperous Asia. *ERD Working Paper* No. 97, Economics and Research Department. Manila: Asian Development Bank.

Asian Development Bank (ADB). 2007. *Philippines: Critical Development Constraints.* Manila

Hausmann, R., D. Rodrik, and A. Velasco. 2005. *Growth Diagnostics.* Cambridge, MA: John F. Kennedy School of Government, Harvard University.

Zhuang, J. 2008. Inclusive Growth toward a Harmonious Society in the People's Republic of China: Policy Implications. *Asian Development Review* 25(1 and 2). Manila: ADB.

2. Development Policies and Performance

Hal Hill and Maria Rowena M. Cham

2.1. Introduction

During the past half century, Indonesia has experienced pronounced swings in its development policies, priorities, processes, and outcomes, on a scale matched by few other developing countries. For these reasons, economic historians tend to characterize its development as one of missed opportunities (Booth 1998, Dick et al. 2002). The key dates are March 1966, signaling the transition from Sukarno to Suharto, and May 1998, when Suharto stepped down in the face of widespread public protests and the country abruptly swung from authoritarian to democratic rule.

Thus, from 1960 to 2010 there were three distinct periods. The first of these, the remaining years of the "Guided Economy," is not covered in any detail in this volume, but it is useful to be cognizant of them. They were characterized by economic stagnation, hyperinflation, and growing political instability. The country was increasingly isolated regionally and internationally. The government withdrew from most international organizations, vowed to crush the newly formed state of Malaysia, and saw its priorities increasingly aligned to the so-called "Beijing–Pyongyang–Ha Noi–Phnom Penh–Jakarta axis" and other "new emerging forces." The leading economic development textbook of the period characterized the country as a "chronic economic dropout," and saw little prospect for economic development (Higgins 1968).[1] Gunnar Myrdal's (1968) *Asian Drama* offered a similarly gloomy prognosis. The country's development plan for the period 1960–1968 had 1,945 paragraphs, 17 chapters, and 8 volumes to symbolize the country's independence date. The central bank's note printing facility broke down under the pressure to print ever more worthless bank notes.

This chapter is organized around two main sections. Section 2.2 provides a broadly chronological narrative of economic development and the policy settings, drawing attention to both the changes and the continuities,

---

[1] This judgment was authoritative, as the author worked in Indonesia for several years in the 1950s.

and distinguishing between the Suharto and post-1998 periods. Section 2.3 examines several dimensions of this development record, including structural change, regional (subnational) development, and comparative outcomes.

2.2. A Development Narrative

2.2.1. The Suharto Era

The Suharto era constituted the first period of sustained economic growth in the country's recorded history. Rudimentary estimates of 20th century economic growth in Indonesia prepared by van der Eng (2002) indicate that the country's per capita gross domestic product (GDP) in 1966 was about 80% of what it was in 1913, when the first national accounts estimates were prepared. Thereafter, under Suharto, per capita income more than quadrupled (Figure 2.1), and Indonesia became one of the "East Asian miracles" (World Bank 1993). Under Suharto, the constants were a commitment to growth, prudent macroeconomic management, concern with equity, and a more "orderly" process of government. The administration emphasized the *trilogi pembangunan*—the "development trilogy" of growth, stability, and equity. Five-year plans were developed, beginning in 1969, and five-yearly elections followed, commencing in 1971.

Figure 2.1: Indonesia's Economic History—Per Capita Real GDP (1961–2008, Rp million)

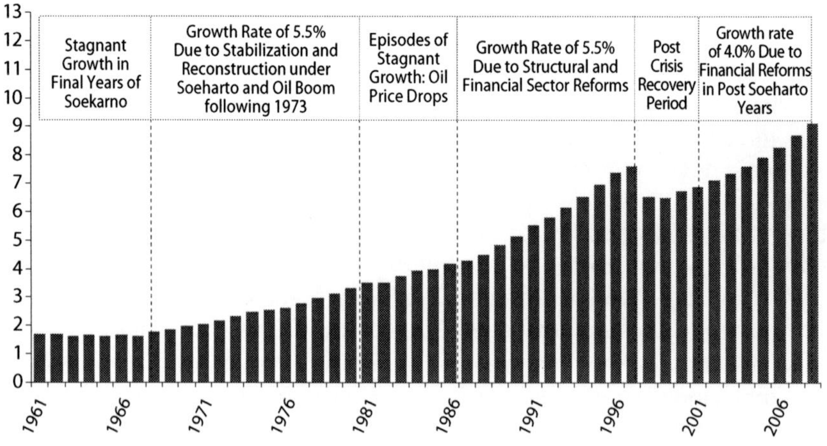

GDP = gross domestic product.
Source: World Bank, WDI, accessed 25 March 2010.

Notwithstanding the constants, the Suharto era was also episodal in some respects, as a result of its own policies and priorities, and international developments over which it had no control. These 32 years are conventionally divided into subperiods, corresponding to particular development challenges and emphases. It is important to emphasize that these periods do not accord with the five-year plans. In fact, most of the plan documents were quickly overtaken by external events. The plans, known as Repelitas (an abbreviation of *rencana pembangunan lima tahun*—five-year development plans), therefore should be regarded primarily as broad statements of philosophical intent at the time they were drafted.

Rehabilitation and Recovery: 1966–1971. The government had four broad objectives during these years. The first was to bring the government's finances under control, and hence extinguish the soaring inflation that had arisen from the monetization of its deficits. The government was remarkably successful at this goal, with inflation returning to single digits by 1969. The multiple foreign exchange rates, which had been a source of endemic corruption, were also progressively removed, and in 1971 the government took the bold step of opening the international capital account. Second, the government adopted a very welcoming attitude toward domestic and foreign investment. The foreign investment law of 1967 provided generous investment incentives and few restrictions. The government also announced its intention to return the foreign property that had been appropriated during the 1958–1965 period. A domestic investment law followed in 1968 with similarly generous provisions. It was directed particularly to the dominant ethnic Chinese business community, whose members had left the country in increasing numbers during the preceding years.

The third objective was to reengage with the West. The government dropped its objections to the formation of Malaysia and severed ties with the communist bloc. It rejoined the International Monetary Fund (IMF) and the World Bank, and quickly developed major programs with both institutions. For several years it was in fact the World Bank's largest borrower. It also reengaged with Japan and the United States (US). Propelled by the cold war, and the fear of falling Asian "dominoes," both quickly became major donors and investors. For many years to follow, Indonesia was to be Japan's largest recipient of both foreign direct investment and official development assistance (ODA). The fourth objective was the restoration of the country's infrastructure, including roads, power, ports, telecommunications, and irrigation, all of which had been badly run down during the previous decade and more, and for which much of the newly received development assistance was mobilized.

The Oil Boom: 1972–1980. The economy was already growing strongly in the early 1970s, and it received a massive boost as the international price of oil and other commodities began to increase rapidly. The quadrupling of oil prices transformed the country's near-term prospects. With aid and foreign investment flows already at record levels, the country's fiscal and

15

balance-of-payment constraints were effectively removed. Agriculture was also growing very rapidly, owing to the delayed but successful adoption, from the late 1960s, of high-yielding rice varieties and the government's vigorous promotion of them through rural infrastructure and generous input subsidies. The government also announced ambitious heavy industry projects in fertilizer, steel, cement, and petrochemicals; as a result, the state-owned enterprises (SOEs), which the government had hitherto been divesting, received renewed emphasis.

As is often the case, however, the resource boom proved to be a mixed blessing. In early 1976, Pertamina, the state-owned oil company, which had been given authority to manage the country's oil resources and had been operating more or less independently of the government, announced that it was about to default on its overseas borrowings to finance its many ambitious investment projects. It had accumulated debts of over $10 billion, then equivalent to about one-third of the country's GDP. Inflation was also rising again, to an annual rate of about 40%, resulting in a sharp appreciation of the real exchange rate given that the nominal rate remained pegged to the US dollar. Thus the non-oil tradable sectors were under great competitive pressures. In response to these concerns, and fearing that the oil boom period was about to end, in November 1978 the government depreciated the currency by 45%. However this decision was also overtaken by external events, with the oil prices again rising sharply in response to renewed conflict in the Middle East.

Adjusting to Lower Oil Prices: 1981–1985. Oil prices remained high until the early 1980s, but then began to fall sharply. This factor, combined with rising global interest rates in response to US monetary policies and reckless investment projects in many resource-rich economies, precipitated the third world debt crisis of the 1980s and led to a "lost decade" for many of them. There was every prospect that Indonesia would join their ranks. Although not possessing petroleum resources on the scale of the Middle Eastern economies, Indonesia was in some respects a "petroleum economy." In the early 1980s, three-quarters of its merchandise exports and two-thirds of its government revenues came from oil and associated energy products. By this period also, the government had embarked on many ambitious investment projects, particularly in heavy industry, and so its external debt was rising quickly.

That Indonesia did not succumb to the debt crisis is testimony to the government's adept economic management. The initial response took the form of several macroeconomic measures: the government trimmed its own spending, postponed major investment projects, devalued the currency in 1983, and sought emergency relief from donors. These measures ensured that the economy was not engulfed by the first-round effects of the debt crisis. However, the government's microeconomic response was muted, and the needed reforms in that area were not undertaken.

Low Oil Prices and Decisive Reform: 1986–1990. It took another round of declining commodity prices, in 1985, to push the government into further reform. The effective macroeconomic policy and another large currency depreciation in 1986 were now accompanied by the much-needed microeconomic reform: the government liberalized the trade regime significantly; enacted regulatory reforms, particularly removing the complex barriers to import–export procedures; simplified the foreign and domestic investment regimes; promulgated a major tax reform; and introduced banking reforms (too quickly, in retrospect). As a result, non-oil exports began to grow very quickly and, aided by the massive relocation of labor-intensive manufacturing activity from Northeast Asia, for the first time in its history Indonesia became a major exporter of labor-intensive manufactures. The reforms also had the beneficial effect of accelerating the reduction in poverty incidence, which had already been declining rapidly owing to fast growth and rapidly rising agricultural incomes.

The 1980s decade was, therefore a period of great achievement for Indonesia. It was one of the few resource rich developing economies to avoid a debt crisis, as is clearly illustrated in the comparative analysis of Gelb and Associates (1988). Indonesia achieved rice self-sufficiency, only a decade after being the world's largest rice importer. And most social indicators improved rapidly, from poverty incidence to education and nutrition, while expenditure inequality remained relatively low.

Slowing Reform and Growing into Crisis: 1991–1998. There seemed every prospect that this development momentum would be maintained as Indonesia entered the 1990s. Growth and investment levels were buoyant, and there was great business confidence. But, as in the good times of the 1970s, problems began to emerge. President Suharto downgraded the role of the technocrats in his 1993 cabinet and promoted his technology minister (and later, briefly, president), B.J. Habibie, and his ambitious high-tech projects. As a result, the reform momentum slowed markedly. In fact there were no major policy reforms during this period. The technocrats were now effectively sidelined and unable to complete many of the major 1980s reforms, including in the finance sector. Corruption appeared to worsen, and was centered mostly around the egregious business empires of the Suharto children. Investment inflows were at record levels, but productivity and export growth began to slow. With growing disaffection toward President Suharto, the country was not well prepared to manage the contagion that inevitably spread quickly from Thailand in mid-1997.

2.2.2. The Asian Financial Crisis and the Transition to Democracy

This brings us to the second key turning point in the country's post-independence period, in 1998, in the wake of, and triggered by, the country's deep economic crisis. Indonesia was the most severely affected by the Asian financial crisis, with the economy contracting by over 13% in 1998. Moreover, like the Philippines in the mid-1980s, it experienced twin crises. The economy contracted sharply, the currency became almost worthless, the banking system imploded, and the country very reluctantly entered into negotiations with the IMF. At the same time there was political and institutional collapse, with a long-serving, authoritarian leader suddenly exiting. Indonesia then entered a highly fluid and uncertain period. It had five presidents in 6 years, its territorial integrity was threatened (and the province of East Timor opted for independence in bloody circumstances in 1999–2000), there were nasty ethnic disputes in several regions off-Java, and some major terrorist incidents erupted. The literature of the time reflected the prevailing pessimism: "From showcase to basket case" was one of the titles (Pincus and Ramli 1998).

In the event, economic growth was restored quite quickly, albeit at a slower rate than under Suharto, and an effectively functioning democracy was established remarkably quickly. By 2010, Indonesia's economic policy landscape had changed dramatically. The following are the key differences compared with the Suharto era with respect to policies, processes, and priorities:

The Presidency. First, the presidency is at once both empowered by the mandate and legitimacy of direct elections and is operationally weaker because there are many more checks and balances on the exercise of authority, and the president's party cannot expect to have a majority in the Parliament—the People's Representative Assembly (Dewan Perwakilan Rakyat—DPR). The inability to directly control the DPR in turn leads to a second difference, namely a "rainbow coalition" in cabinet (*kabinet pelanggi*); as the president builds a coalition of parties to constitute a working majority, the quid pro quo is an allocation of cabinet portfolios to the other parties. Thus, unlike the Suharto era, although the cabinet is appointed by the president, it rarely speaks with one voice. It now consists typically of three groups: those loyal to the president, as members of his party or closely aligned to it; technical nonparty ministers in a few key portfolios (such as finance, foreign affairs, and trade); and members from coalition parties, who have at best short-term loyalty to the administration. Overt differences of opinion are quite common.

The Executive Branch. The nature of the executive has also changed. During the Suharto era, it was accountable primarily to the all-powerful presidency, and largely immune to civil society pressures. In the democratic era, the executive is far more accountable. Senior bureaucrats are regularly called before the DPR. Ministers may have to spend up to one-third of their time there to get important bills passed. These bureaucrats also have to be responsive to civil society, especially the press and nongovernment organizations. Many have been subject to legal action; a substantial number have been incarcerated, including ministers and heads of key statutory authorities such as the central bank (Bank Indonesia) and the Corruption Eradication Commission (Komisi Pemberantas Korupsi—KPK). The result is that the bureaucracy has become extremely cautious and hesitant to take key decisions that may result in corruption allegations (for example concerning major infrastructure projects).

The Legislature. The role of the legislature has also changed fundamentally. During the Suharto era, it operated as a rubber stamp, run by the government's Golkar Party, with only two timid, loyalist "opposition parties" allowed to participate, and heavily scripted general elections with predictable results. Since 1999, however, Indonesia has quickly made the transition to a vibrant democracy. Although there are no major ideological differences between the parties, they are free to establish, organize, and engage in political activities. New parties have emerged on the scene, most prominently, President Yudhoyono's own Partai Demokrat, now the largest single group in the DPR, albeit well short of a majority. These parties are frequently unpredictable. Lacking a coherent ideology, personal and regional loyalties together with blatant money politics are the keys to the passage of legislation.

The Judiciary and Independent Authorities. A fourth tier of governance is the judiciary. Here too the changes have been dramatic. During the Suharto era, the judiciary was essentially irrelevant in determining the outcome of any significant case: political (and often military) power was the principal arbiter of outcomes. In 1998, however, the institutional vacuum created by the regime collapse put great pressure on a legal system completely unprepared to resolve many pressing cases. Most of the corporate and financial workouts required a legal resolution, but the courts were generally unable to function effectively. Many major corruption cases that had been ignored or shelved resurfaced, as did complaints toward the police and military. Ethnic violence flared in several regions, and there were "payback" cases (i.e, the settlement of unresolved grievances, sometimes through extra-judicial means) over land and other disputes. The fear was that, without an adequately functioning legal system, the "parliament of the streets" would become the forum for dispute resolution, with all the dangers inherent in such a system. Hence, the development of an effective, trusted, clean legal system became a high priority, but one where progress has understandably been slow (Lindsey 2004).

Related, there have been attempts to establish independent authorities that are designed to operate free from daily political interference, and to act as a check on government. Thus, for example, Bank Indonesia is now an independent agency, an anticorruption commission has been established, and a competition commission (Komisi Pengawas Persaingan Usaha—KPPU) has been created. Here too it will take time for these agencies to become operationally effective. Bank Indonesia is regarded as a reasonably credible body, but it has had difficulty holding inflation down to that of Indonesia's major trading partners, and some of its governors and senior executives have been the subject of legal action. The KPPU had some early successes in handling complex competition cases, but its recent appointments have become politicized. The KPK has instituted some high profile (and highly popular) cases, but it too has become embroiled in controversy, and its director has been imprisoned (see Chapter 5).

Decentralization. A fifth major difference concerns decentralization. Indonesia was a highly centralized state under Suharto, with little scope for local authority and autonomy. Then, in a dramatic initiative, in May 1999 the government announced a "big bang" decentralization, to take effect from 1 January 2001. The scheme was radical in its intent, with major revenue and administrative authority being passed down to the subprovincial levels of government—the municipalities (*kotamadya*) and districts, also termed "regencies" (*kabupaten*) (Brojonegoro 2004). The fear of territorial disintegration, involving Aceh, Maluku, Papua, Timor, and other outlying regions, was undoubtedly a key motivation for the hasty action. The reforms were to be accompanied by democratization, with direct elections for local leaders as well as the assemblies. As a result, Indonesia now has elections for all 500 of its national, provincial, and subprovincial authorities. The decentralization has more or less worked, in the sense that the nation's territorial integrity has been preserved, and the functions of government have been maintained. But major challenges remain, in the proliferation of subprovincial jurisdictions, in coordinating the many local governments, and in the highly variable quality of local governance (see Chapter 11, and Fengler and Hofman 2009).

The Press, Civil Society, and International Finance Organizations. A sixth difference between the democratic and Suharto eras concerns the role of extra-government actors. Two in particular stand out. First, civil society, long suppressed during the Suharto period, has sprung to life. Indonesia has a vibrant, if unpredictable, press and civil society. Thus, the checks on government, at the national and local level, are now much greater. However, it is not yet obvious that the quality of public administration is any better. Here too, it takes time for these relationships to mature. A second actor is the international development community. As noted, relations between the development community and the Suharto regime were generally very close.

A consortium known as the Consultative Group on Indonesia met annually. In times of crisis, prior to the mid-1990s, Jakarta turned to the international financial institutions and (especially) to Japan. This relationship has cooled considerably since the late 1990s. The Consultative Group on Indonesia has since been abolished, at Indonesia's instigation. The Indonesian government has a rather cool official relationship with the IMF in particular. Its program with the World Bank has been scaled back, and the country is now repaying more (on past loans) that it receives in new money. The Jakarta–Tokyo nexus is much less significant, on both sides. With ODA now just 0.4% of GDP, and probably declining, this is likely to become a permanent feature of the institutional landscape.

2.2.3. Some Continuities

Having drawn attention to the differences between the Suharto and current eras, it is important by way of conclusion to mention the similarities across the entire period since 1966. At least four warrant mention.

Prudent Macroeconomic Management. First, as outlined in Chapter 5, macroeconomic management has continued to be reasonably prudent. On the fiscal side, under Suharto a de facto "balanced budget" rule applied, meaning that the government could spend no more than the sum of its own revenues and international development assistance. Since 2003, a fiscal law has applied, with a broadly similar effect. Indonesia has effectively adopted—and, unlike the European Union, has consistently implemented—the Maastricht principle, that deficits should not exceed 3% of GDP, and public debt should be less than 60% of GDP (Boediono 2005). This has also made Bank Indonesia's task of monetary policy management a good deal more manageable, and inflation has therefore rarely gotten out of control.

A Broadly Open Economy. Second, Indonesia has remained a broadly open economy for the entire period. As noted, the pendulum has swung between more and less open postures, and there has been considerable reservation toward liberalism and globalization in influential community opinion. In some respects, the country might be precariously open (Basri and Hill 2004), but it seems reasonable to assume that this state of affairs will continue. Being surrounded by open economies helps in this respect, as do the various regional agreements, most important the Association of Southeast Asian Nations (ASEAN) Free Trade Area agreement.

Slow Administrative Reform and Institution Building. Third, the process of administrative reform and institution building has been a very slow one. There has yet to be a major reform of the civil service, for example. Its remuneration structures remain highly complex, and uncompetitive at senior levels. The link between performance and reward is weak. Mobility and opportunities for long-term professional development are limited

21

(McLeod 2005). Moreover, SOE reform has proceeded very slowly. There is powerful resistance to divesting the SOEs, even though it is well known that they are highly politicized and inefficient. The absence of reform has also complicated the task of combating corruption. All available evidence suggests that corruption is just as serious in its magnitudes as it was in the Suharto era. The only difference, perhaps, is that it has been "democratized and decentralized," as press commentary frequently remarks. This has resulted in a more "disorganized" form of corruption, which by its nature increases commercial uncertainty, compared with the Suharto era practices, where the parameters were clearly defined (McLeod and MacIntyre 2007).

Equity Outcomes. A fourth continuity is that Indonesia performs reasonably well with regard to equity outcomes. Expenditure inequality has not risen appreciably since it was first measured fairly accurately in the early 1970s (Chapter 9).[2] Access to basic education and (to a lesser extent) health services has been expanded (Chapter 8). The country performed surprisingly well with regard to the rapid introduction of social protection measures in the wake of the Asian financial crisis, especially given the severe fiscal crisis and weak institutions then prevailing (Manning and Sudarno 2011). Moreover, in spite of the very large regional differences, all available evidence suggests that interregional inequality has remained fairly stable since the 1970s, in notable contrast to the People's Republic of China in particular and other large developing nations (Hill, Resosudarmo, and Vidyattama 2008).

2.3. Dimensions of Development

2.3.1. The Comparative Record

This section looks more closely at various aspects of Indonesia's growth dynamics. In comparative perspective, Indonesia's growth record resembles that of its neighbors in some respects (Tables 2.1 and 2.2). After lagging in the 1960s, it grew strongly in the 1970s; grew moderately fast in the 1980s (with a dip in the middle of the decade); and maintained positive growth in the 1990s, notwithstanding the deep crisis. For the latest period, Indonesia actually recorded the highest growth among the original five members of ASEAN,[3] reflecting the fact that it was the least affected by the global financial crisis. These growth rates are reflected in the relative per capita incomes over time. Thus for example, in 1980 Indonesia's per capita income was about half that of Thailand and almost one-fifth that of Malaysia. By 2009, these relativities were broadly similar. At current growth trends, Indonesia will take about 23 years to catch up to Thailand's current per capita income.

---

[2]   However, income inequality, which is not well measured, has probably increased.

[3]   Indonesia, Malaysia, the Philippines, Singapore, and Thailand.

Table 2.1: Per Capita GDP (in 2000 $)

Country	1980	1990	2000	2001	2002	2003	2004	2005	2006	2007	2008
Indonesia	397	612	800	818	844	872	904	943	983	1,033	1,083
Malaysia	1,919	2,608	4,030	3,965	4,096	4,251	4,455	4,609	4,789	5,009	5,155
Philippines	989	901	977	975	999	1,028	1,073	1,106	1,143	1,202	1,225
Singapore	9,043	14,658	23,019	21,869	22,571	23,704	25,651	26,886	28,234	29,185	27,991
Thailand	789	1,400	1,968	1,991	2,072	2,193	2,305	2,387	2,490	2,594	2,645

GDP = gross domestic product.
Source: Estimates based on World Bank, WDI, accessed 25 March 2010.

Table 2.2: Annual Average Growth Rate of Real Per Capita GDP (%)

Period	Indonesia	Malaysia	Philippines	Singapore	Thailand
1951–1960	4.0	3.6	3.3	5.4	5.7
1961–1970	1.9	3.5	1.8	7.4	5.0
1971–1980	5.4	5.3	3.1	7.2	4.4
1981–1990	4.5	3.2	-0.8	5.0	6.0
1991–2000	2.9	4.6	0.8	4.7	3.6
2001–2008	3.9	3.1	2.9	2.6	3.8

GDP = gross domestic product.
Source: Estimates for 1951–1960 based on IMF, IFS, accessed 25 March 2010 and for other years, World Bank, WDI, accessed 25 March 2010.

The one major difference concerns the Philippines. In 1980, Indonesia's per capita income was less than half that of its archipelagic neighbor. But, owing to the latter's deep 1980s crisis, Indonesia had actually overtaken it by the mid-1990s, before succumbing to the Asian financial crisis. By 2009, the two countries' per capita incomes were very similar.

2.3.2. Structural Change

Indonesia's rapid economic growth has resulted in major structural change. While agriculture, industry, and services have all expanded, consistent with the theory of economic development, agriculture's share of GDP has fallen sharply (Figure 2.2). At the onset of rapid growth in the mid-1960s, agriculture accounted for almost 60% of GDP and employed an even larger share of the workforce. The rest of the economy was about evenly distributed between the industry and services sectors. By 2009, industry was the largest sector of the economy, followed by services. Agriculture had shrunk to just 15% of GDP.

Figure 2.2: Sector Shares in GDP (1960–2008)

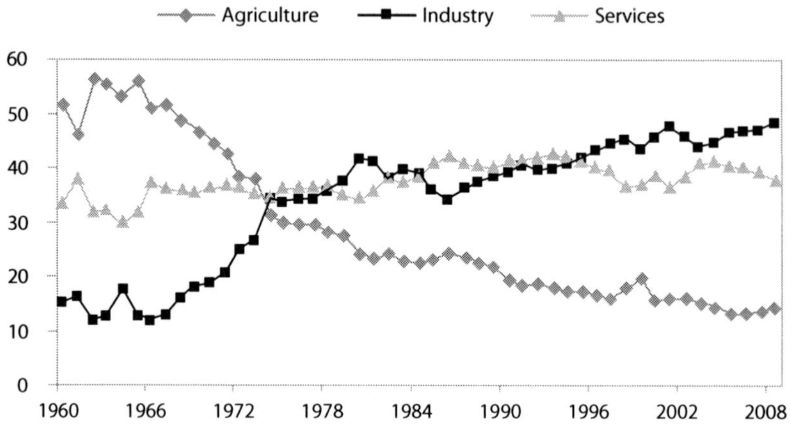

GDP = gross domestic product
Source: World Bank, WDI, accessed on 25 March 2010.

Notwithstanding this major structural change, all economic sectors have expanded. Table 2.3 shows average sectoral growth rates by decade, and each sector's contribution to aggregate economic growth. Table 2.4 shows the same data for manufacturing, the most dynamic sector in the 1970s and 1980s, together with nonmanufacturing industries.

Table 2.3: Annual Average Real GDP Growth and Contribution of Major Production Sectors to GDP Growth (%)

Period	GDP Growth Rate	Agriculture		Industry		Services	
		Growth Rate	Contribution to GDP Growth	Growth Rate	Contribution to GDP Growth	Growth Rate	Contribution to GDP Growth
1961–1970	4.1	2.8	30.4	7.2	43.3	3.5	26.3
1971–1980	7.9	4.5	16.8	10.3	44.5	8.7	38.6
1981–1990	6.4	3.7	14.5	7.4	21.9	7.1	61.8
1991–2000	4.2	2.0	9.0	5.4	57.9	4.0	34.2
2001–2008	5.2	3.4	10.1	4.0	35.0	7.0	54.8

GDP = gross domestic product.
Source: Estimates based on World Bank, WDI, accessed 25 March 2010.

Table 2.4: Annual Average Real GDP Growth and Contribution of Manufacturing and Nonmanufacturing Industry Subsectors to GDP Growth (%)

Period	Manufacturing			Nonmanufacturing Industry		
	Growth Rate	Share in GDP	Contribution to GDP Growth Rate	Growth Rate	Share in GDP	Contribution to GDP Growth Rate
1961–1970	4.6	7.2	7.2	8.2	15.9	41.5
1971–1980	14.0	9.5	18.8	8.7	26.1	26.8
1981–1990	12.2	17.8	35.0	3.6	20.5	12.0
1991–2000	6.6	25.2	41.7	3.8	19.1	16.0
2001–2008	4.7	27.8	24.8	2.9	16.8	9.5

GDP = gross domestic product.
Source: World Bank, WDI, accessed May 2010.

Agriculture grew strongly in the 1970s and into the 1980s, boosted by the rapid adoption of high-yielding varieties, the major investments in rural infrastructure, and generous input subsidies. It also grew quite strongly in the 2000s, with the main driver on this occasion being high prices for tropical cash crops, particularly palm oil. Thus, agriculture has always been a significant driver of Indonesia's economic growth. Even in the most recent decade, when agriculture's share had shrunk, it contributed 10% of the growth.

Manufacturing grew at double-digit rates almost continuously throughout the Suharto era, with the result that its share of GDP more than tripled. During the 1970s, as noted in Chapter 6, import substitution was the main driver, whereas export orientation became increasingly important during and after the 1980s. In the 1980s, manufacturing became the major engine of economic growth, contributing over one-third of the country's economic expansion and rising to over 40% in the crisis decade that followed. However, manufacturing has failed to regain its dynamism since the late 1990s, and for the past decade it has expanded at only about one-third of the rate in the boom decades of the 1970s and 1980s. The industry sector of which it is part grew more slowly for most of the period. That is, the mining, construction, and utilities subsectors grew more slowly in all decades after the 1960s.

The services sector grew steadily throughout the period, with the fastest growth evident in the oil boom decade of the 1970s and through to the 1980s, as the proceeds were distributed into sectors such as telecommunications, transport, finance, trade, and the government. The services sector's growth accelerated again in the 2000s as major liberalizations resulted in rapid

25

growth of telecommunications, transport, and trade. In the 2000s, services contributed almost half the aggregate economic expansion.

Indonesia's structural change is more or less comparable with that of its middle-income neighbors, adjusting for differences in per capita incomes. Its share of agriculture, averaging about 15% during the 2001–2009 period, is higher than in Malaysia and Thailand, but lower than in the Philippines and Viet Nam (Figure 2.3). Its industry share, at 44%, is similar to Malaysia and Thailand, being boosted by the larger mining sector, and is higher than the shares of the other two countries.

Figure 2.3: Average Shares of Major Production Sectors in GDP (2001–2008, %)

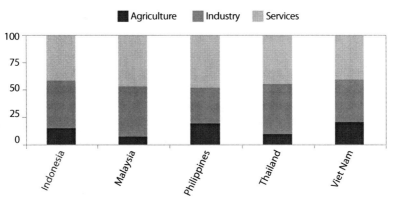

GDP = gross domestic product.
Notes: Based on current market prices. Estimates for Malaysia, Thailand, and Viet Nam are for 2001–2007.
Source: Estimates based on World Bank, WDI, accessed 25 March 2010.

2.3.3 Major Expenditure Components

There has been some variability in expenditure shares, driven by growth, crises, and exogenous shocks. Consumption has been the major expenditure component throughout the period, in the range of 48%–60% of GDP (Tables 2.5 and 2.6). In the wake of economic slowdowns, consumption has generally risen, as expected, thus explaining the higher figure in the 2000s and the decline in the 1970s as compared with the previous decade. During the crisis decade of the 1990s, consumption contributed to most of the growth, as investment fell sharply. The government share has been consistently in the 7%–10% range, rising slightly in the 1980s in the wake of the oil boom.

Investment and exports have displayed greater volatility. The share of investment grew strongly as economic growth took root, with the 1980s share more than triple that of the 1960s. However, it fell sharply following the Asian financial crisis and has recovered very slowly thereafter. The

Table 2.5: Share of Expenditure Components in GDP (%)

Period	Consumption Growth Rate	Consumption Share of GDP	Government Growth Rate	Government Share of GDP	Investment Growth Rate	Investment Share of GDP	Exports Growth Rate	Exports Share of GDP	Imports Growth Rate	Imports Share of GDP
1961–1970	4.3	55.8	0.7	6.4	8.3	9.2	4.0	45.7	5.6	–13.1
1971–1980	6.3	48.0	13.1	7.8	17.7	19.5	9.2	60.1	17.4	–28.1
1981–1990	7.8	56.4	5.3	9.9	8.4	30.2	0.9	35.7	4.3	–32.8
1991–2000	5.9	55.7	0.8	7.4	–0.3	31.9	6.6	39.0	5.2	–33.2
2001–2008	4.7	60.0	8.1	7.6	6.1	23.0	7.7	43.3	8.8	–33.9

GDP = gross domestic product.
Source: Estimates based on World Bank, WDI, accessed 25 March 2010.

Table 2.6: Contribution to GDP Growth by Expenditure Component (%)

Period	Consumption Growth Rate	Consumption Contribution to GDP Growth Rate	Government Growth Rate	Government Contribution to GDP Growth Rate	Investment Growth Rate	Investment Contribution to GDP Growth Rate	Exports Growth Rate	Imports Growth Rate	Net Exports Contribution to GDP Growth Rate
1961–1970	4.3	54.1	0.7	3.0	8.3	14.6	4.0	5.6	33.5
1971–1980	6.3	40.1	13.1	14.0	17.7	43.5	9.2	17.4	8.1
1981–1990	7.8	42.2	5.3	7.5	8.4	41.3	0.9	4.3	11.7
1991–2000	5.9	84.6	0.8	0.5	–0.3	–9.8	6.6	5.2	21.6
2001–2008	4.7	53.3	8.1	11.2	6.1	25.2	7.7	8.8	10.4

GDP = gross domestic product.
Source: World Bank, WDI, accessed March 2010.

export share has been volatile, peaking in the 1970s oil boom at 60% of GDP, but then falling to almost half this share in the next decade as oil prices collapsed. The share has gradually risen since the late 1990s in response to high commodity prices.[4]

These shares are also broadly comparable to those of Indonesia's neighbors during the last decade (Figure 2.4). The consumption and investment shares are close to the regional norm, above the share for Malaysia and below that for the Philippines, the regional outliers. That Indonesia's share of net exports is lower than Malaysia's reflects the fact that Malaysia is running a very large positive trade balance, in contrast to the negative net trade balance for Viet Nam.

---

[4] These volatile export shares serve as a reminder that this conventional indicator of economic openness can produce very misleading results for Indonesia. The 1970s, for example, coincided with the imposition of increasingly restrictive trade and investment regulations, as previously noted.

Figure 2.4: Average Shares of Major Expenditure Components in GDP (2001–2008, %)

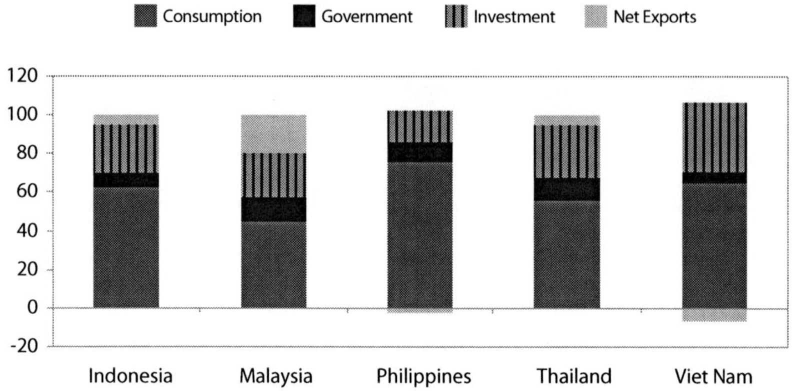

GDP = gross domestic product.
Notes: Based on current market prices. Estimates for Malaysia, Thailand, and Viet Nam are for 2001–2007.
Source: World Bank, WDI, accessed on 25 March 2010.

2.3.4. Regional Diversity

Any analysis of Indonesian growth dynamics has to take account of the country's regional diversity. This chapter follows the conventional approach of classifying the country according to its five major island groups: Java–Bali, Kalimantan, Sulawesi, Sumatra, and the rest of Eastern Indonesia.[5] Java–Bali dominates Indonesia's economy, with 61%–62% of GDP (Table 2.7) and a similar share of the population. Because the six provinces that constitute this grouping have grown faster than the country as a whole in recent years (indeed since the 1970s), their contribution to GDP growth is somewhat higher. The shares for Sumatra and Kalimantan have been about 22% and 9%, respectively. The natural resource sector is a larger share of these regional economies, and thus their growth, and therefore their contribution to national growth, has fluctuated. Sulawesi and the other Eastern provinces account for about 7%–8% of the national economy. Here also the contribution to national economic growth has been variable owing to the natural resource sector, particularly that of Papua.

---

[5]   Official definitions of Eastern Indonesia typically add Sulawesi and sometimes the eastern parts of Kalimantan to Nusa Tenggara, Maluku, and Papua.

Table 2.7: Regional Contributions to GDP and GDP Growth (%)

Year	Sumatra	Bali and Java	Kalimantan	Sulawesi	Eastern Provinces (Maluku, Nusa Tenggara, and Papua)
GRDP: Regional Shares					
2000	22.6	60.1	9.6	4.2	3.5
2001	22.2	60.3	9.6	4.3	3.6
2002	22.6	60.3	9.6	4.3	3.3
2003	22.5	60.3	9.4	4.3	3.5
2004	22.2	60.9	9.3	4.3	3.2
2005	21.9	61.2	9.2	4.4	3.4
2006	21.9	61.5	9.0	4.5	3.1
2007	21.7	61.8	8.9	4.5	3.1
2008	21.6	62.0	8.8	4.6	3.0
GRDP: Contribution to Growth					
2000–2001	11.8	65.9	10.8	5.4	6.2
2001–2002	31.7	58.0	9.2	4.7	−3.6
2002–2003	21.0	60.9	5.4	4.6	8.0
2003–2004	15.5	76.4	6.7	5.7	−4.3
2004–2005	14.8	65.1	6.8	5.1	8.2
2005–2006	22.2	68.0	6.7	5.8	−2.7
2006–2007	19.1	67.1	5.6	5.4	2.8
2007–2008	19.1	65.0	8.3	6.2	1.3

GDP = gross domestic product, GRDP = gross regional domestic product.
Source: Estimates based on BPS Website, accessed March 2010.

2.3.5 Productivity Growth

Estimates of Indonesia's total factor productivity (TFP) vary according to the methodologies and data bases employed, but they typically show that the trends follow that of the GDP. Table 2.8 reports one set of estimates for Indonesia and its middle-income ASEAN neighbors prepared by the Asian Productivity Organization for the period 1980–2000. The estimates suggest that much of Indonesia's growth was input driven, with positive TFP growth only in the 1990s. The other Southeast Asian countries are estimated to have registered positive growth for most of the period, except obviously for the Philippines. However, comprehensive and updated estimates prepared recently (OECD 2008) show a brighter picture, with TFP growth being positive in most years and following that of GDP quite closely (Figure 2.5). In particular, TFP appears to have been responsive to the 1980s reforms, with strong growth in 1986–1996. Growth in the 2000s was similarly positive and quite strong for most of the decade.

Table 2.8: Contribution of Total Factor Productivity to GDP Growth (%)

Period	Indonesia	Malaysia	Philippines	Thailand	Viet Nam
1980–1984	−0.32	−0.03	−2.34	0.37	—
1985–1989	−0.47	0.20	0.49	3.66	2.09
1990–1994	0.82	3.36	−1.68	2.14	4.31
1995–1999	3.67	0.32	1.03	−2.16	3.36
1980–2000	−0.80	1.16	−0.37	1.00	3.41

— = not available, GDP = gross domestic product.
Notes: The analysis for Malaysia is for 1981–2000; Thailand, for 1980–1999; and for Viet Nam, 1986–2000.
Source: APO (2004).

Figure 2.5: Trends in GDP and Total Factor Productivity Growth Rate (1980-2006, %)

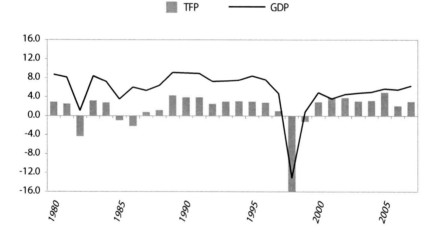

GDP = gross domestic product, TFP = total factor productivity.
Sources: GDP from World Bank, WDI, accessed 25 March 2010. Others from OECD (2008).

References

Asian Productivity Organization (APO). 2004. *Total Factor Productivity Growth: Survey Report.* Tokyo.

Badan Pusat Statistik (BPS). Badan Pusat Statistik Website. http://www.bps.go.id

Basri, M.C. and H. Hill. 2004. Ideas, Interests and Oil Prices: the Political Economy of Trade Reform during Suharto's Indonesia. *The World Economy,* 27(5): 633–56.

Boediono. 2005. Managing the Indonesian Economy: Some Lessons from the Past. *Bulletin of Indonesian Economic Studies,* 41(3): 309–24.

Booth, A. 1998. *The Indonesian Economy in the Nineteenth and Twentieth Centuries: A History of Missed Opportunities.* London: Macmillan.

Brodjonegoro, B. 2004. The Effects of Decentralization on Business in Indonesia. In M.C. Basri and P. van der Eng (eds), *Business in Indonesia: New Challenges, Old Problems.* Singapore: Institute of Southeast Asian Studies, Singapore

Dick, H., V. Houben, J. Lindblad, and K.W. Thee. 2002. *The Emergence of a National Economy—An Economic History of Indonesia, 1800–2000.* Sydney: Allen & Unwin.

van der Eng, P. 2002. Indonesia's Growth Performance in the Twentieth Century. In A. Maddison et al. (eds), *The Asian Economies in the Twentieth Century.* Cheltenham: Edward Elgar.

Fengler, W., and B. Hofman. 2009. Indonesia. In S. Ichimura and R. Bahl (eds), *Decentralization Policies in Asian Development.* Singapore: World Scientific.

Gelb, A. and Associates. 1988. *Oil Windfalls: Blessing or Curse?* New York: Oxford University Press.

Higgins, B. 1968. *Economic Development,* 2nd edition. New York: W.W. Norton.

Hill, H., B. Resosudarmo, and Y. Vidyattama. 2008. Indonesia's Changing Economic Geography. *Bulletin of Indonesian Economic Studies,* 44(3): 407–35.

International Monetary Fund (IMF). International Financial Statistics (IFS) Online. Washington, DC. http://www.imfstatistics.org/imf/imfbrowser.aspx?branch=ROOT (accessed September 2009 to May 2010).

Lindsey, T. 2004. Legal Infrastructure and Governance Reform in Post-crisis Asia. *Asian-Pacific Economic Literature,* 18(1): 12–40.

Manning, C. and S. Sudarno (eds). 2011. *Indonesia Update 2011.* Singapore: Institute of Southeast Asian Studies.

McLeod, R. 2005. The Struggle to Regain Effective Government under Democracy in Indonesia. *Bulletin of Indonesian Economic Studies*, 41(3): 367–86.

McLeod, R., and A. MacIntyre (eds). 2007. *Indonesia: Democracy and the Promise of Good Government*. Singapore: Institute of Southeast Asian Studies.

Myrdal, G. 1968. *Asian Drama*. Lincoln: Penguin.

Organisation for Economic Co-operation and Development (OECD). 2008. Indonesia: Economic Assessment. *OECD Economic Surveys*, 2008 17: i–131. Paris.

Pincus, J., and R. Ramli. 1998. Indonesia: From Showcase to Basket Case. *Cambridge Journal of Economics*. 22(6):723–34.

World Bank. 1993. *The East Asian Miracle: Economic Growth and Public Policy*. Washington, DC.

——. World Development Indicators (WDI) Online. http://ddp-ext. worldbank.org/ext/DDPQQ/member.do?method=getMembers&u serid=1&queryId=6 (accessed October 2009 to May 2010).

3. Critical Constraints to Growth

Muhammad Ehsan Khan, Juzhong Zhuang, Maria Rowena M. Cham, Niny Khor, and Imelda Maidir

I ndonesia's investment level was 30%–32% of gross domestic product (GDP) during 1990–1997 but the level plummeted to 11% of GDP in 1999 following the Asian financial crisis. The investment level has since recovered somewhat and was about 25% of GDP in 2007 and 2008 (Figure 3.1). However, as in the case of GDP growth, the recovery fell well short of the level that prevailed prior to the crisis. Moreover, it does not compare favorably with the region's faster growing economies—e.g., Viet Nam's 41.1% of GDP and Thailand's 28.8% in 2008.

Figure 3.1: Investment Rate/Gross Domestic Capital Formation (% of GDP)

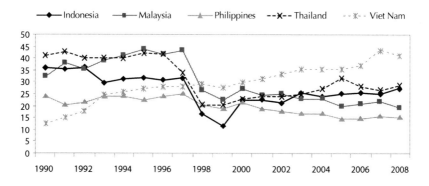

GDP = gross domestic product.
Source: IMF, IFS, accessed May 2010.

Attaining the pre-crisis pace of GDP growth may not be possible unless investment is revived to that period's level. The private sector will need to be the driver of growth in the medium to long term. Public investment will also need to be boosted to address constraints related to the availability, reliability, and efficiency of infrastructure, and to meet the human capital needs. This chapter looks at the factors that may be constraining the Indonesian economy from attaining its pre-crisis levels of investment and growth. Specifically, the chapter asks if Indonesia's investment and growth are being constrained by high cost of finance, low social return to investment, and/or low appropriability of that return.

3.1. Cost of Finance

A comparison with other major economies in Southeast Asia suggests that Indonesia's domestic real interest rate is relatively high. Since the 1997 Asian financial crisis, Indonesia's real lending rate has remained higher than the rates of the region's other major economies except during the period of high inflation from late 2005 through early 2006. In December 2009, Indonesia's real domestic lending rate stood at 10.9%, compared with 3.8% in Malaysia, 3.8% in the Philippines, 6.1% in Singapore, and 2.3% in Thailand (Figure 3.2). Two possible reasons for the high cost of borrowing are a low level of domestic savings and inefficient financial intermediation.

Indonesia's level of aggregate domestic savings is relatively low compared with its regional peers, but may not be a constraint to growth. A low level of domestic savings, in the presence of high demand, could push up the interest rate. Indonesia's gross domestic savings as a percentage of GDP, after peaking at about 38% in 1992, fell to 31.5% in 1997 and to below 20% in 1999. The level has since recovered and was recorded at 30.6% in 2008. This, while comparable to the pre-1997 Asian crisis level, is relatively low when compared with regional peers: in 2008, Malaysia's savings rate was 42.3% and Thailand's was 33.2% (Figure 3.3).

Figure 3.2: Real Domestic Interest Rates (%)

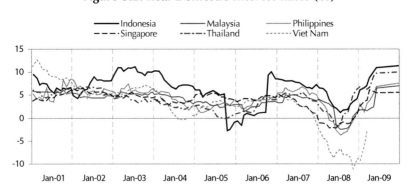

Note: Real domestic rate is the domestic interest rate net of inflation.
Source: Estimates based on IMF, IFS, accessed May 2010.

Figure 3.3: Gross Domestic Savings (% of GDP)

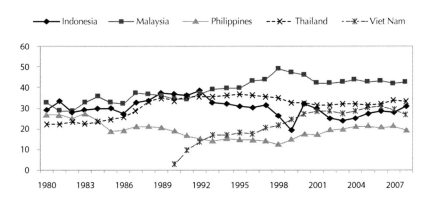

GDP = gross domestic product.
Source: IMF, IFS, accessed May 2010.

Low domestic savings may constrain growth only if they fall short of investment requirements in the economy. Comparing the trend of domestic savings with that of domestic investment suggests that such a constraint may not be operating in Indonesia. Figure 3.4 indicates that, while the level of domestic savings may have constrained investment in the years leading up to the Asian financial crisis, investment has remained short of domestic savings since then. In 2008, gross domestic capital formation was reported at 27.8% of GDP and gross domestic savings at about 30.6%.

Figure 3.4: Domestic Savings and Investment Rates (% of GDP)

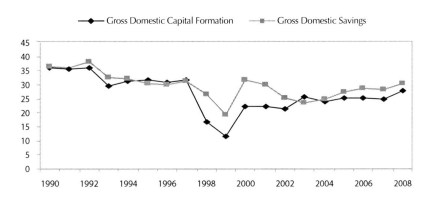

GDP = gross domestic product.
Source: IMF, IFS, accessed May 2010.

Indonesia's domestic financial intermediation is among the least efficient in Southeast Asia. Inefficient financial intermediation can increase the cost of financing for investors. In 2008–2009, the banking sector accounted for more than 80% of the financial sector assets and was the largest source of domestic financing for the corporate sector, at about 48%. A useful indicator for assessing the efficiency of the banking sector is the size of the spread between the lending and deposit rates, with a higher spread indicating less inefficient financial intermediation and vice versa. In Indonesia, this spread, after narrowing to less than 2 percentage points in the run-up to the Asian financial crisis, rose to 7.7 percentage points in 2004 before declining to 5.1 percentage points in 2008 (Figure 3.5). Moreover, the spread is among the highest in the region. In 2009, the percentage point spread was 3.0 for Malaysia, 4.9 for Thailand, and 5.1 for Singapore. Indonesia's spread also exhibits larger and more frequent fluctuations than the spreads in the other countries.

Growth in real domestic credit has not recovered since the 1997 Asian financial crisis. The volume of domestic credit in real terms, which was climbing steadily prior to the crisis, has been somewhat stagnant since then. In 2008, the volume of real domestic credit was only about 85% of the 1997 level, a trend similar to that in the Philippines and Thailand. The decline in domestic credit seems even more pronounced when expansion in the economy is taken into account. In 2008, domestic credit as a percentage of GDP was 36.7%, compared with 59.6% in 1997 and 62.1% in 1999 (Figure 3.6). This decline was observed in other Southeast Asian countries as well. Between 1997 and 2008, the real domestic credit to GDP ratio fell in Thailand from 177.6% to 105.1%, in Malaysia from 163.4% to 115.2%, and in the

Figure 3.5: Spreads between Deposit and Lending Rates (percentage points)

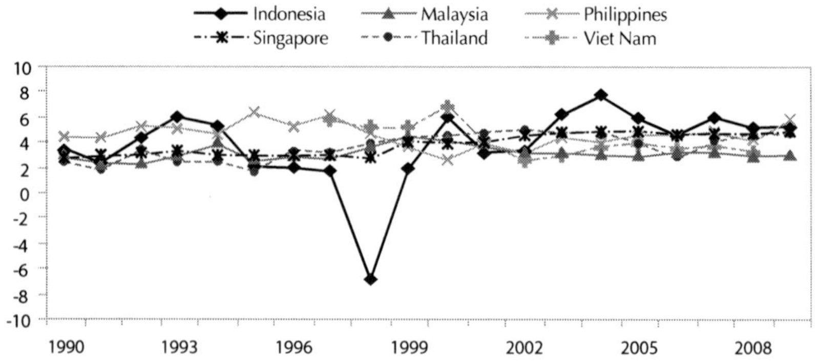

Source: IMF, IFS, accessed May 2010.

Figure 3.6: Ratio of Domestic Credit to GDP (%)

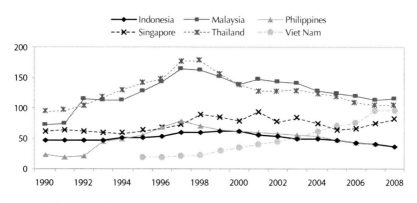

GDP = gross domestic product.
Source: IMF, IFS, accessed May 2010.

Philippines from 78.5% to 40.9%. Prior to the onset of the recent global economic crisis, Singapore and Viet Nam were the only major economies in the region that had been experiencing growth in real domestic credit.

Stagnation or decline in the level of financial intermediation or the degree to which the banking sector puts its deposits back into the economy could be due to a number of factors. One could be that the banks lack funding sources. This does not seem to be the case in Indonesia for two reasons: First, the banking sector has excess liquidity and is holding reserves in excess of Bank Indonesia's statutory requirements (Figure 3.7). Between July 2009 and March 2010, the level of actual reserves was 55%–72% higher than the required level.

Figure 3.7: Excess Local Currency Reserves with Banks (Rp billion)

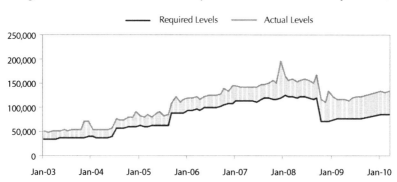

Source: Bank Indonesia, Bank Weekly Report, Table 6, accessed May 2010.

37

Second, the health of Indonesia's banking sector has been improving. Nonperforming loans as a percentage of total loans declined from a high of 48.6% in 1998 to about 3.8% at the end of 2008, which compares favorably with about 2.2% in Malaysia (Figure 3.8). Indonesia's capital adequacy ratio has also improved substantially and was reported at 16.7% at the end of 2008—well above the benchmark level of 12%—and compares well with 9.1% in the pre-crisis period and a low of –15.7% in 1998. The capital adequacy ratio also compares favorably with Malaysia's 12.1% and Thailand's 14.2%. The banks' rate of return on assets has been improving too, and was at 2.3% at the end of 2008, compared with a pre-crisis rate of 1.4% and a low of –18.8% in 1998.

Figure 3.8: Health of the Banking Sector (%)

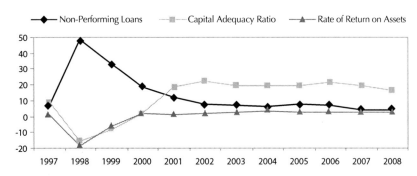

Source: Data for the capital adequacy ratio and return on assets are from IMF, Global Financial Stability Report; data for nonperforming loans are from the Bank Indonesia website.

Another factor that may explain the stagnation in real domestic credit growth is the lack of investors' appetite for bank credit, as they may have access to more attractive financing sources for their investments. This explanation is reasonable, given that Indonesian spreads between lending and deposit rates are high, which may make borrowing from the banks less attractive. This view also draws support from a recent International Monetary Fund (IMF) study that found the real demand for credit to be significantly lower than the supply during most of the 2000s (IMF 2007). The trend in bank credit growth also seems to be consistent with the findings of other studies indicating that the corporate sector increased reliance on bonds and equity markets for Indonesia's financing needs (IMF 2008).

Access to international financial markets is limited, but it may not constitute a critical constraint. Prior to the onset of the global economic crisis, investors had increasingly been tapping into international financial markets. The cost to access the international markets, however, seems high.

The sovereign spreads are substantially larger for Indonesia than for the other major Southeast Asian economies (Figure 3.9). Moreover, the spread has spiked since the onset of the global economic crisis, even though the Indonesian economy weathered the crisis better than other economies in the region. Between mid-2007 and late 2008, the spread rose by about 1,000 basis points. The high sovereign spread, despite extensive reforms or substantial improvements in the economy, has been the focus of a number of studies. A new study concluded that the recent spikes in the sovereign spread had several causes, including external factors, political stability, and macroeconomic management (IMF 2009).

Figure 3.9: Sovereign Spreads ('00 basis points)

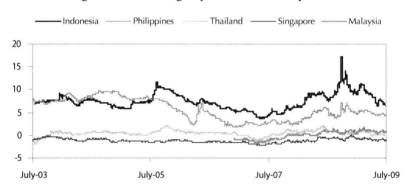

Source: IMF, IFS, accessed September 2009.

Although the cost of accessing the international financial markets is high, Indonesia has increasingly relied on them. The country's source of international financing has predominantly been loans from foreign banks, but its use of offshore bonds has grown substantially in recent years. An IMF study notes that, while foreign loans reported to Bank Indonesia grew at just about 1% per annum between 2003 and 2007, the volume of outstanding offshore bonds more than tripled during the same period (IMF 2008). At the end of 2007, outstanding offshore bonds accounted for about 10% of the total corporate nonfinancial financing and were five times the volume of the domestic (onshore) bonds.

Although the access to and cost of finance do not seem to constitute a critical constraint to private investment overall, small and medium-sized enterprises (SMEs) find it difficult to access finance. Recent surveys support the view that investors do not consider either the access to or cost of finance as a major constraint to doing business in Indonesia. In an investment climate survey in 2007, firms ranked cost of finance 12th in the list of constraints, a drop from 6th in a similar survey in 2003 (ADB and World Bank 2005, LPEM–FEUI 2007). Similarly, investors ranked access to finance 20th in the list of top constraints in 2007, down from 16th in 2003. The situation may have changed with the onset of the global economic crisis. Recent studies indicate that the impacts of the crisis on the economy are already starting to be reversed and, along with other aspects, the access to finance is also improving to the pre-crisis level.

While financing for larger corporate investors does not seem to be constrained, SMEs may have difficulties in accessing finance. Given the SME sector's greater reliance on the banking sector, cost of financing may be a larger concern for such enterprises. In addition, a recent IMF study notes that the global economic crisis' impact on SMEs was disproportionately large, with new lending for them declining more significantly than that for larger investors (IMF 2009).

3.2. Social Returns to Investments

Low economic growth can also be explained by low returns to economic activity, which in turn can be on account of low social returns to investment and/or low private appropriability of the returns. Social returns (or returns to society) can be affected by the level of investment in human capital, infrastructure, and other public goods that complement private investment. Inadequate investment in these complementary factors can lead to low social returns by dampening the productivity of factors of production and increasing the cost of doing business, which in turn lower the returns to investment. A comparison of social returns across the major Southeast Asian

Figure 3.10: Social Returns to Investment in Selected Countries (%)

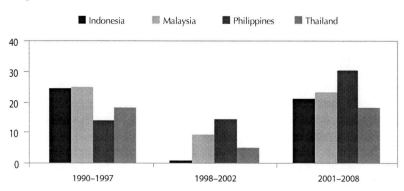

Note: Estimated as the ratio of gross domestic product (GDP) growth rate and gross capital formation as a percentage of GDP.
Source: World Bank, WDI, accessed May 2010.

economies suggests that, while Indonesia's social return to investment is at a level similar to the pre-crisis situation, it is lower than that of Malaysia and the Philippines (Figure 3.10). A low level of social returns could be a symptom of deficiencies in human capital and/or infrastructure.

3.2.1. Human Capital

Investment in human capital development is lower than required. The overall educational attainment of Indonesian workers has improved remarkably in recent years. Indonesia, however, still faces a challenge to equip its workers with marketable skills. More than two of every three workers have not completed high school education (Table 3.1). One reason for this is insufficient investment in education in the past. Public investment in education as a percentage of GDP or of total government expenditure lagged behind that of other major economies in the region, such as Malaysia and Thailand (UNDP 2007). Though the government has increased the budget allocated to education in recent years, evidence suggests that the low level of investment has hampered the improvement of quality in education. In addition, due to the country's vast size and varied geography, access to education is difficult in remote areas. Workers who have obtained only a low level of education tend to engage in low-productivity activities. Household survey results unveil the intergenerational transmission of poverty through a vicious cycle of low educational attainment of parents, low household income, and low investment in children's education. (See section 4.3.1.1.)

Table 3.1: Share of Labor Force by Age Group and Educational Attainment (age 15+, %)

Age Group/ Gender	Junior High School or Below		General High School		Vocational High School		Diploma Academy (college)		University	
	2004	2008	2004	2008	2004	2008	2004	2008	2004	2008
Men										
20–24	61.7	57.6	22.8	24.6	13.1	13.8	1.5	2.3	0.9	1.7
25–29	63.2	60.1	20.2	19.9	10.2	11.7	2.5	3.2	3.9	5.1
Age Total	72.4	69.4	14.8	16.2	7.5	8.2	2.2	2.2	3.2	4.1
Women										
20–24	56.9	49.9	24.4	27.5	12.4	11.9	3.9	6.7	2.4	4.0
25–29	65.1	57.6	16.5	17.9	8.0	8.3	4.5	7.1	5.8	9.0
Age Total	80.0	72.4	10.8	13.2	5.9	5.9	2.8	4.1	0.6	4.5

Source: Data from BPS, Sakernas.

An international survey by the Organisation for Economic Co-operation and Development (OECD) indicates that low public spending on education appears to have compromised the quality and outcome of education in Indonesia (OECD 2007). The Programme for International Student Assessment surveyed key competencies and cognitive skills of 15-year-old students. Table 3.2 shows the student's 2006 mean scores for literacy, mathematics, and science. The results revealed that Indonesian students on average performed below Thai students and students from non-OECD middle-income economies. These results may stem from the fact that 57.4% of teachers did not meet minimum teaching requirements in Indonesia (MONE 2008). On a positive note, the mean scores of Indonesian students improved considerably between 2000 and 2006. This is in stark contrast to results of other non-OECD economies that participated in the survey, whose achievements tended to decline. The vocational education and training system also has considerable room for improving the effectiveness of the curricula, increasing the number of qualified training instructors, enhancing capacity, providing training equipment, and forging more links between training providers and provision and the private sector's demand for skills (Chatani and Kim 2009).

Investors do not consider the scarcity of human capital as a priority constraint, but the returns to some categories of highly skilled workers have increased at disproportionately high rates, suggesting skills shortages in

Table 3.2: Quality of Education

	Mathematics	Science	Reading
Mean PISA Scores, 2006			
OECD Average	498	500	492
27 Middle-Income Economies	437	443	425
Thailand	417	421	417
Indonesia	391	393	393
Share of Students below Proficiency Levels, 2006 (%)			
OECD average	21.3	19.3	20.1
Thailand	53.0	46.1	44.6
Indonesia	65.7	61.6	58.3

OECD = Organisation for Economic Co-operation and Development, PISA = Programme for International Student Assessment.
Note: The 27 middle-income economies are Argentina; Azerbaijan; Brazil; Bulgaria; Chile; Colombia; Croatia; Estonia; Hong Kong, China; Indonesia; Israel; Jordan; Kyrgyz Republic; Latvia; Liechtenstein; Lithuania; Macao, China; Montenegro; Qatar; Romania; Russian Federation; Serbia; Slovenia; Taipei,China; Thailand; Tunisia; and Uruguay.
Source: OECD (2007).

some industries. Feedback from the investment climate survey suggests that business is not constrained by the availability of skilled workforce (LPEM–FEUI 2007). Indonesia has a substantial labor surplus, and young workers are willing to move in search of better income opportunities (Sziraczki and Reerink 2004). Hence most investors who are willing to pay "efficiency wages"[1] will not find it difficult to recruit workers, except for highly skilled workers in certain occupations. Although the share of the workforce with at least high school education is low, the absolute number of high school graduates is substantial. Investment climate surveys thus do not usually detect underlying issues of human capital and skills supply.

Caveats apply to the seemingly sufficient supply of skills in the Indonesian labor market, as opinion surveys often fail to reflect potential investors' views. The perception of managers of existing companies constitutes only a partial picture of the investment climate, because their views are not necessarily the same as those of managers who decided not to invest in Indonesia. Indeed, certain types of investment depend heavily on skills availability. For example, call center businesses and information technology industries may prefer to invest in India or the Philippines, where relevant skills are more available. This suggests that, due to the low availability of a skilled workforce, Indonesia is missing opportunities for growth and employment creation.

Another indication of possible skills shortages is that the returns to education have been rising constantly since the 1997 Asian financial crisis, and the gap between wages for workers with primary education and those with university education has been widening (Figure 3.11). The ratio of wages for workers with university education to that for workers with primary school education increased from 3.5 in 1998 to 4.4 in 2008.

The increasing return to education may also reflect structural changes in the composition of industry. While service sectors recorded above average growth of output and (consequently) jobs (Figure 3.12), the manufacturing sector, especially labor-intensive manufacturing, has been slowing down. Obviously, demand in the labor market has been increasing for highly skilled workers. If this trend continues, skill shortages may constrain economic growth in the future. In addition, Indonesia has not successfully improved the export performance of technology- and skills-intensive, high value-added activities despite the loss of international competitiveness in labor-intensive manufacturing (Islam and Chowdhury 2009). Rigorous investments in human capital may be needed if the manufacturing sector is to meet the challenge of gradually moving to products with higher value addition.

---

[1] "Efficiency wages" are above-market rates paid to get the skills and abilities desired.

3.2.2. Infrastructure

Inadequate infrastructure is a constraint to growth and private investment, at both national and subnational levels. Poor availability and quality of infrastructure can reduce the economic returns to (and thereby deter) investment. The low quality of physical infrastructure is a major problem of the Indonesian economy (see Chapter 7). The 2010 World Economic Forum Report ranked Indonesia 96th among 133 countries (Figure 3.13) due to the poor state of various components of its infrastructure (WEF 2009). In contrast, Malaysia was ranked 27th and Thailand 36th. However, Indonesia performed marginally better than the Philippines, at 98th, and Viet Nam, at 111th. Poor infrastructure negatively affects Indonesia's global competitiveness. The 2010 World Economic Forum Report ranked Indonesia 54th in global competitiveness, which compared unfavorably with Malaysia (24th) and Thailand (36th), but was better than the Philippines and Viet Nam.

Figure 3.11: Hourly Nominal Wages by Educational Attainment (Rp)

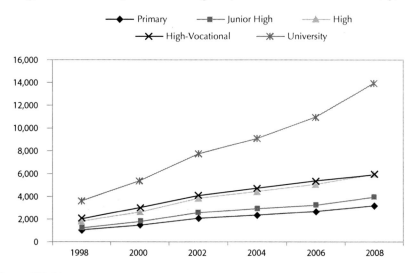

Source: BPS, Sakernas.

Poor infrastructure and its impact on competitiveness are also reflected in the investor feedback in the World Competitiveness Yearbook 2009, which ranked the lack of adequate infrastructure as the second most problematic factor for doing business in Indonesia (IMD 2009). In terms of adequacy of infrastructure, Indonesia was ranked 55th among 57 countries, which was a slip from 53rd in 2008 and was far behind Malaysia (26th) and Thailand (42nd).

Figure 3.12: Sectoral Output and Employment Growth (2004–2008, annual %)

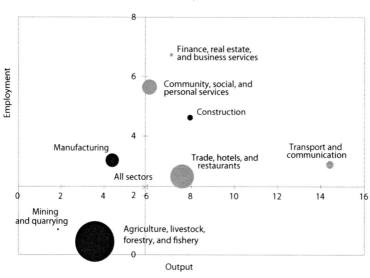

Note: The size of each bubble represents its sector's share of employment in total employment.
Source: Based on BPS, Sakernas.

Figure 3.13: Quality of Infrastructure and Global Competitiveness

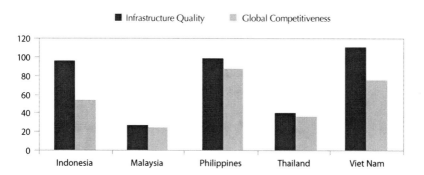

Note: Rankings are for 133 countries. The lower the ranking, the better the infrastructure quality and higher the global competitiveness.
Source: WEF (2009).

In 2008 the Japan External Trade Organization surveyed Japanese firms with active or planned investments outside Japan. Of the respondents, 28.4% considered inadequacies in infrastructure to be a major constraint to investment in Indonesia (JETRO 2009). That this is 4.5 percentage points higher than the 2007 level is a matter of concern. These findings

45

are an important gauge of the potential foreign investors' perception of the attractiveness of investing in Indonesia, as businesses that have not yet invested there have greater options to locate elsewhere than do those who have already invested in the country.

Among the key infrastructure subsectors, investors consider poor transport networks and inadequate electricity supply to be the most critical. The Global Competitiveness Report 2009–2010 ranked Indonesia far behind Malaysia and Thailand in the quality of the road network, port and air transport infrastructure, and electricity supply (Figure 3.14). These findings are consistent with the feedback received by investment climate surveys in 2003, 2005, and 2007 (ADB 2005, LPEM–FEUI 2007). The 2007 survey found poor transport the second most binding constraint to doing business in Indonesia, with 49% of the respondents identifying it as a major constraint—up from 29% in 2003 and 42% in 2005 (Figure 3.15). Of

Figure 3.14: Quality of Key Infrastructure (rank among 133 countries)

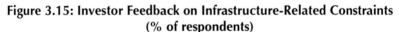

Note: A lower rank implies better infrastructure.
Sources: WEF (2009).

Figure 3.15: Investor Feedback on Infrastructure-Related Constraints (% of respondents)

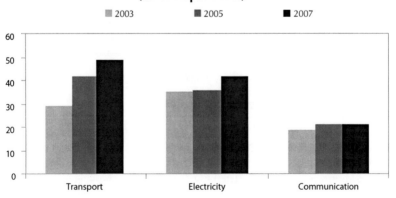

Sources: ADB and World Bank (2005), LPEM–FEUI (2007).

particular concern is the spike in the number of respondents who consider transport a major constraint, as this may indicate how fast the infrastructure is deteriorating. The availability of electricity was ranked 6th on the list, with 42% of the respondents identifying it as a major constraint—up from 35% in 2003 and 36% in 2005. On the other hand, respondents did not consider telecommunications as a critical constraint and ranked it 21st among 22 constraints.

3.2.3. Transport Network

Road Network. Indonesia had over 396,000 kilometers (km) of roads at the end of 2007. Of that, 75% was paved—56% asphalted and 19% gravel surfaced. The country's road density is among the lowest in Southeast Asia. This is true whether in terms of the length per 100 people or per square kilometer, and whether one looks at all roads or paved ones (Figure 3.16).

Figure 3.16: Road Network Coverage (km)

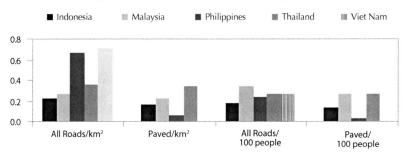

km = kilometer, km² = square kilometer.
Notes: Latest data available for Indonesia are for 2007; Malaysia, 2006; Philippines, 2003; Thailand, 2006; and Viet Nam, 2004. Data on paved roads are not available for Viet Nam.
Sources: ADB staff estimates based on data from BPS (2008) and World Bank, WDI, accessed in October 2009.

Another concern is that 36% of the road network was either damaged or severely damaged at the end of 2007 (BPS 2008). Most of the damaged roads were under the purview of the district governments, and 39% of the 322,000 km of roads under the district governments' responsibility was considered damaged or severely damaged.

Seaports. Most container cargoes in Indonesia are processed through the three main container terminals: Tanjung Priok in Jakarta, Tanjung Perak in Surabaya, and Tanjung Emas in Semarang. Tanjung Priok, with a total peak throughput of 4.2 million 20-foot equivalent units, is the country's largest international container terminal. However, Tanjung Priok's performance lags behind that of most other major ports in Southeast Asia. In volume of container handling, Tanjung Priok ranked 25th of the 50 major ports in the

47

2008 World Port Rankings (Fossey 2008). In comparison, the Singapore port ranked 1st, Port Klang of Malaysia, 14th; and Laem Chabang of Thailand, 20th. The only major port ranked below Tanjung Priok was Manila Port of the Philippines, at 37th. Other comparisons suggest that Tanjung Priok is also less competitive in terms of the length and number of bureaucratic processes for clearance, waiting time, and port access.

The performance of smaller ports catering mainly to interisland cargoes is also poor. Table 3.3 highlights the underlying problems at the specific ports and shows that the low productivity may be due to the lack of equipment, inefficient work methods, limited berth lengths, and shallow routes.

Railroad Network. Compared with other countries in the region, Indonesia has the largest and most intensively used railway network. Of its 5,824 km of railways, 4,337 km are operational. The network, however, is mainly single track and limited to Java and Sumatra. The network's operational performance is considered to be generally poor, with delays in passenger and cargo traffic caused by multiple factors, including institutional problems, weak management, inadequate infrastructure, old and unreliable rolling stock, and outdated signaling and telecommunication systems.

Air Transport. As of 2008, Indonesia's air transport infrastructure comprised 182 regional and international airports. Deregulation of the airline industry in 1999 opened the sector to private airline companies, which led to lower fares in real terms and more scheduled flights to existing and new destinations. During 1999–2006, the annual passenger traffic grew from about 7 million to 34 million—almost a five-fold increase during a period of 7 years. The passenger load factor averaged 70% during 2002–2006. The freight load factor increased significantly, from 31.9% in 2002 to 56.0% in 2006 (BPS 2008). International aircraft arrivals also increased significantly, from 23,000 in 1990 to 48,000 in 2007, an average annual increase of 5.2%.

Table 3.3: Conditions of Regional Ports in Indonesia (2006)

Ports	Draft (m)	Problems
Banjarmasin	4–9	Congestion and shallow route
Batam	9–10	Underdeveloped
Belawan	7–9	Congestion and lack of loading/unloading facilities
Palembang	4–8	Shallow route
Pontianak	4–6	Congestion and shallow route
Samarinda	6–7	Congestion
Makassar	3–12	Congestion

m = meter.
Source: JICA (2006).

Similarly, aircraft departures rose from 23,000 to 49,400, an annual growth of 5.4% during the same period. Cargo arrivals increased annually by 11.9% and departures grew by 5.6% during 1990–2007 (BPS various years).

The entry of low-cost operators was a major reason for the rapid expansion in air traffic, and is widely credited with major social benefits, given the geographical spread and archipelagic nature of Indonesia. At the same time, this has led to severe stress on the infrastructure, and Indonesia now has overcrowded airport terminals and inadequate air traffic control. Air transport safety is also a significant concern. The country's rate of fatal civil aviation accidents was 15 times higher than the world average (BPS 2008). A government-sponsored study on flight safety in March 2007 reported that none of the country's airlines were fully compliant with international safety standards. The Ministry of Transport acted quickly on the report's findings and introduced more stringent controls over domestic flights.

3.2.4. Electricity

Indonesia's electricity sector is characterized by a low electrification rate, a low consumption level, and high inefficiency in transmission and distribution (Box 3.1). The electrification rate climbed from 55% in 2003 to about 61% in 2007, and varied widely, from 21% in East Nusa Tenggara at one extreme to 88% in Jakarta Province. In comparison, the electrification rate in 2003 was 97% in Malaysia, 84% in Thailand, 81% in Viet Nam, and 79% in the Philippines (ADB and World Bank 2005). Per capita electricity consumption in Indonesia was about 566 kilowatt-hours (kWh) in 2007, compared with 3,667 kWh in Malaysia, 2,055 kWh in Thailand, 728 kWh in Viet Nam, and 586 kWh in the Philippines (World Bank, WDI). The system transmission and distribution losses of more than 11% in 2007 were also among the highest in the major Southeast Asian economies.

Indonesia had an installed generation capacity of about 44.5 gigawatts at the end of 2007, about 57% of which was owned by the state-owned PT Perusahaan Listrik Negara (PLN). Of the privately-held generation capacity, 14.8 gigawatts were owned by about 10,000 industrial and manufacturing units that had to generate power on their own because the PLN supplies were not available at their location or were not reliable. Self-generation of electricity is not easy, especially, for SMEs and commercial and residential consumers.

Indonesia's residential and industrial power tariffs are among the lowest in the region and are below cost recovery levels, which limits PLN's ability to invest in and expand generation capacity and networks and is a strong disincentive to private investment in the sector. The low power tariffs for industries may not reduce their power bills, because many large industrial units have to rely on their own diesel generators, which is expensive.

Box 3.1: One Step Forward, Two Steps Backward— Second Time Around?

Electricity Law No. 20 of 2002 was intended to reform the electricity subsector and encourage private investment in it by introducing market competition; unbundling Perusahaan Listrik Negara (PLN), the state electricity agency; establishing a regulatory agency; increasing the role of regional governments in provision of social electricity and price setting to noncompetitive regions; and encouraging private sector participation in the sector. The law was a breakthrough, and its implementation would have put Indonesia at par with other countries in the region that had initiated similar reforms. However, the law was annulled by the Constitutional Court of Indonesia in December 2004 on the grounds that it was not in line with Article 33 of the Indonesian Constitution of 1945, which states that "sectors of production which are important for the county and affect the lives of the people shall be controlled by the state." The court interpreted the term "control" as to regulate, facilitate, and operate such facilities. The court decision was a major blow to the reforms in the subsector and the possibility of private sector participation.

Annulment of the law meant that the country had reverted to Electricity Law 15 of 1985. The court decision implied that private ownership of electricity was not in the people's best interest, and the efficiency gains envisaged through unbundling the industry into seven proposed areas (generation, transmission, distribution, market operator, system operator, retail, and wholesale) were not to be achieved.

To formulate and enact a new law took nearly 5 years from the court decision and 8 years since passage of the 2002 law. The Indonesian Parliament passed the Electricity Law of 2009 (Law 30 of 2009) on 9 September 2009. The new law, although not as ambitious as the 2002 law, introduces changes that would allow entities other than PLN to participate in electricity supply and aims to redefine PLN's roles and mandates. The law's implementing rules and regulations, however, are yet to be issued. Due to opposition from different sections, especially within PLN, there are fears that a long time may pass before the intent of the law can be put into action. Another concern is that the new law could also be struck down in court. The country has already lost 8 years by not implementing the 2002 law, and the losses from the delay must be monumental in economic terms. Hopefully, any interventions by the Constitutional Court, if warranted, will work in favor of the general public's welfare.

continued on next page

Box 3.1 continued

Main Provisions of Indonesia's Electricity Laws

Electricity Law 15/1985	Electricity Law 20/2002	Electricity Law 30/2009
The Government of Indonesia is responsible for regulating the electricity sector. Private companies are allowed to participate in the electricity business; however, PLN is the single buyer of electricity and controls both transmission and distribution functions	The law established a competitive electricity market through multiple power generators and by restructuring and unbundling PLN's functions. The law also provided the mechanism for adjusting electricity tariffs, rationalized the mechanism for power purchase for the private sector and established a regulatory mechanism for the sector.	PLN will no longer have the monopoly on supplying and distributing to end customers. Independent power producers will be allowed these functions, particularly in the regions, although subject to a "right of first priority" provided to PLN.

Sources: World Bank (2005), ALB Business News, Purra (2010).

3.2.5. Telecommunications

Although the business community did not consider telecommunications to be a major constraint, Indonesia lags behind other major Southeast Asian countries in this aspect too. This is evident in

- a low level of teledensity, driven by low investment in and unequal distribution of the infrastructure;
- low internet penetration;
- lack of competition in the sector; and
- lack of consistent and independent regulations on telephony and internet services.

3.2.6. Irrigation

Irrigation infrastructure is inadequate and poorly maintained, and may constrain growth, especially in the outer islands, which are highly dependent on agriculture. On some of the outer islands, agriculture accounts for a large share of gross regional domestic incomes. Productivity and choices of crops, however, are limited in these areas because of low availability of irrigation services and inefficient irrigation infrastructure. While the exact figures are not readily available, estimates suggest that less than 10% of land areas suitable for irrigation in Kalimantan, Maluku, and Papua had access to irrigation in 2004. In individual provinces, only 26% of the irrigable land in Central Kalimantan, 30% in Papua, and 40% in East Kalimantan had been utilized in 2004 (ADB 2006). Reliability and functionality of the irrigation schemes are also low due to poor management and lack of adequate investment in maintenance.

As a result of inadequate irrigation, crop productivity in the outer provinces is substantially lower than that in Java and Sumatra. For example, while the irrigated rice yield in Kalimantan, Maluku, and Papua was 2.8–3.5 tons per hectare, in Java it was 5.4–5.5 tons per hectare (ADB 2006).

3.2.7. Regional Disparity in Infrastructure

Inadequacy in infrastructure is more severe outside Java and Sumatra. There is large disparity in the availability of infrastructure and infrastructure services between Indonesia's islands and provinces. The access to safe drinking water ranged from 87% of households in Java to 66% in Sumatra and about 50% in Kalimantan in 2007. In electricity supply, the disparity is also large, with 37%–73% of households having access. Access to asphalt roads ranged from 40% to 72% of the villages within the individual provinces. There are similarly wide disparities in teledensity.

The disparity in access to key infrastructure and services has had implications for poverty and inequalities (see Chapter 4) and for investment patterns and economic growth. For example, Java received over 91% of the total foreign direct investment (FDI) and about 60% of the total domestic investment in 2008, while Sumatra accounted for just under 7% of the FDI and about 24% of the domestic investment (BKPM 2009). The imbalances in the investment flows suggest that the outer islands, Kalimantan, and Sulawesi will continue to lag behind, and the gap between them and Java and Sumatra will continue to widen.

Regional disparity in infrastructure can also limit Indonesia's ability to benefit from important regional initiatives such as the Indonesia-Malaysia-Thailand Growth Triangle (IMT–GT) and Brunei Darussalam-Indonesia-Malaysia-Philippines–East ASEAN Growth Area. The IMT–GT, in particular, with a potential consumer base of 70 million and possible interregional trade of $16.7 billion per annum, is designed to develop economic corridors that can lead to synergies and cooperation in furthering growth in the member countries. The IMT–GT has identified economic connectivity corridors that cover 10 provinces in Sumatra (Figure 3.17). To fully benefit from the IMT–GT and the preferential trade access, Indonesia would need to boost investments in manufacturing and services in the 10 provinces. However, it could be difficult to attract investment unless the transport networks and electricity supply in the provinces can be significantly improved. As of 2007, only 56% of the roads in the 10 provinces were paved and only 65% were in

Figure 3.17: IMT–GT Economic Connectivity Corridors

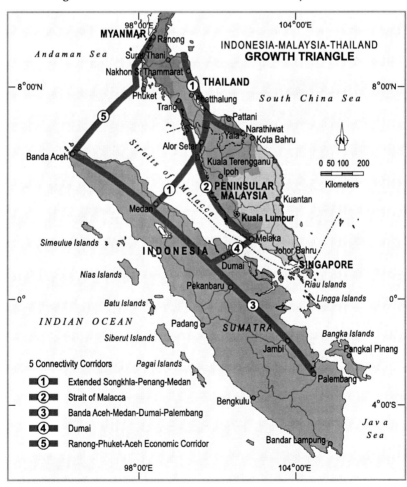

IMT–GT = Indonesia-Malaysia-Thailand Growth Triangle.
Source: IMT–GT Secretariat and ADB (2007).

53

good to moderate condition (BPS 2008). Moreover, the regional ports are too small and lack facilities to handle increased volumes of trade. Electricity supply is also constrained, and investors in manufacturing and services would have additional costs if they must provide their own generation capacities.

3.2.8. Key Constraints to Infrastructure Investment

A survey of key stakeholders active in the infrastructure sector in Java district in November and December of 2009 identified a number of critical constraints to infrastructure investment in the country (IDB 2010). The constraints include, in order of severity, (1) difficulty in land acquisition, (2) weak human and institutional capacity, (3) poor governance, and (4) shortage of financing. These results were validated by an in-depth analysis of the key components of infrastructure—roads, railways, seaports and airports, electricity, and communications.

In addition, the survey identified impediments unique to several infrastructure subsectors. In road infrastructure, the lack of bankable projects in toll roads warrants particular mention. For seaports, the regulatory framework increases rent-seeking opportunities and encourages monopolistic behavior, thereby hindering competition and hampering the sector's efficiency. New investment in air transport infrastructure is discouraged by perceived low returns.

Investment in electricity infrastructure is hindered by social tariff-setting that is below cost recovery levels. Further compounding the problem is the lack of an appropriate risk-sharing mechanism with independent power producers. New investment in the telecommunications sector is discouraged by the monopolistic environment and anticompetitive behavior such as practices in interoperator charges.

Difficulty with Land Acquisition. Since 1993, the Indonesian government has promulgated various regulations on land acquisition.[2] However, the inability and reluctance to strictly enforce legislation on the fast-track land acquisition process has created uncertainty in project implementation schedules, which adversely affects rates of return. The difficulty has discouraged investment in infrastructure, particularly in roads and electricity, where land is a key component. Further, some of the pertinent laws are not mutually supportive,[3] and legislation to address speculative

---

[2] Presidential Decree No. 55 of 1993; Presidential Decree No. 36 of 2005; Presidential Decree No. 65 of 2006; BPN Regulation No. 3 of 2007; and Presidential Regulation No. 13 of 2010.

[3] For example, the Land Expropriation Act No. 20 of 1961 (issued under the Basic Agrarian Act 1960) and Forestry Law 41 of 1999 have objectives that do not support each other. These laws are not well-defined and often cause disputes with the National Land Agency (BPN).

activity is not adequately enforced. This indicates weak institutional capacities and, to some extent, lack of strong political will to enforce land acquisition laws, which are needed to facilitate rapid resolution of disputes over land prices. Inefficiencies in spatial planning have also compounded the problem of land acquisition.

Weak Human and Institutional Capacity. Weaknesses in human and institutional capacity are evident in the paucity of bankable projects prepared by the government, and by the slow physical and financial progress of projects as they are implemented. The problem is aggravated by the dissipation of power through decentralization, the lack of coordination and of clarity on roles, and delegation of authority and/or responsibility. This is exacerbated by the laws and regulations that at times explicitly and implicitly discourage private investment in certain sectors. Consequently, the private sector has found interacting with various layers of government to be frustrating and time consuming.

Poor Governance. The lack of institutional and human capacity has been compounded by poor governance. Discussions with the private sector in Indonesia indicate that investors usually factor the cost of rent seeking into their project planning and financing, and view the expense as part of normal business running costs. Rent-seeking activities adversely impact project viability, and, in some instances, result in quality being compromised. Poor governance is also evident in the complex public procurement procedures and their weak and nontransparent implementation. The issue of governance is covered in more detail in section 3.3.2.

Shortage of Financing. By their very nature, infrastructure projects require long-term financing, which the private sector identifies as being in short supply. Short-term financing is not a major constraint for the public or private sector in Indonesia.

3.3. Appropriability of Returns to Investments

Private parties will invest only when they expect to capture adequate returns from their investments. Anything that weakens or lowers such returns discourages investment and, ultimately, slows economic growth. Risks to such appropriability can emanate from government or market failures. Government failures increase macro or micro risks. The macro risks may include fiscal and financial crises; the micro risks may be bad governance such as corruption, weak rule of law, overly burdensome taxation, and labor–capital conflicts. Market failures affecting appropriability normally reflect information and learning externalities and coordination failures.

3.3.1. Macroeconomic Risks

Indonesia's macro management is sound, with low levels of fiscal deficit, a current account surplus, and manageable levels of debt and inflation. Indonesia's policy framework has evolved significantly. Gains in the economic front since 2001 have been due to sound macroeconomic management and some key economic reforms. Since 2000, the fiscal position has improved, the current account has been in surplus, domestic and external debts have halved, and inflation is at a manageable level.

Fiscal Position. Indonesia has been recording fiscal deficits since the 1997 Asian financial crisis. The fiscal position, however, has gradually improved from a deficit of 2.5% of GDP in 1999 to a deficit of 0.1% in 2008 (Figure 3.18). Improvements in the fiscal position have been driven by a reduction in untargeted fuel and electricity subsidies and an increase in government revenues.

On the revenue side, the level improved from about 15% of GDP in 2001 to nearly 19% in 2008 (Figure 3.19). Improvements in the level of revenues, although comparable with other major Southeast Asian economies, were partly on account of high commodity prices and may not be sustainable when commodity prices start to subside. The tax collection effort, too, has been improving. But, at 13.3% of GDP in 2008, the level was still lower than in most of the region's other major economies: 15.3% for Malaysia, 15.2% for Thailand, and 14.1% for the Philippines (Figure 3.20).

Inflation. Inflation has historically hovered between 8% and 10% (Figure 3.21). At the time of the 1997 Asian financial crisis, inflation climbed to 58%, but then declined to 20% in 1999 and to 4% in 2000. Inflation again breached the 10% level in 2001 and 2002 due to rising fuel and food prices. As a result, monetary policy was directed at achieving a target

Figure 3.18: Fiscal Position of the National Government (% of GDP)

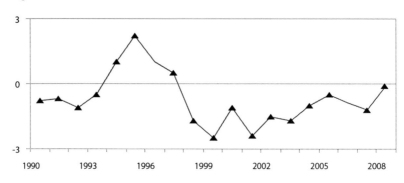

GDP = gross domestic product.
Source: ADB (2009).

Figure 3.19: National Government Revenue (% of GDP)

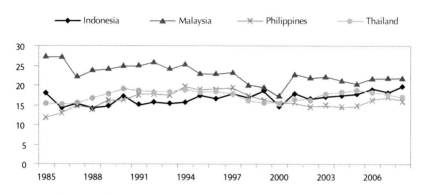

GDP = gross domestic product.
Source: ADB, SDBS, accessed October 2009.

Figure 3.20: Tax Revenues in Selected Southeast Asian Countries (% of GDP)

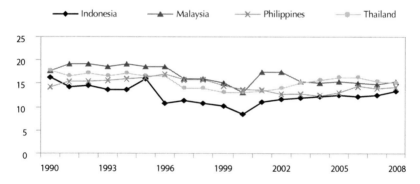

GDP = gross domestic product.
Source: ADB, SDBS, accessed October 2009.

inflation rate. In 2005, the monetary policy was shifted toward full-fledged inflation targeting, which helped the economy tackle the fuel and food price rises during 2005–2008. Inflation in 2008, at about 9.2%, was higher than the levels in some other major economies in Southeast Asia. Recent data, however, indicate that the inflation rate dropped further and was at about 4.9% by the end of 2009 (BPS Website).

Current Account Balance. The current account has been in surplus since the 1997 Asian financial crisis (Figure 3.22). Factors contributing to the surplus include good export performance due to high commodity prices and strong demand, a stable rupiah, and large remittances from overseas workers. The current account position weakened somewhat in 2004–2005

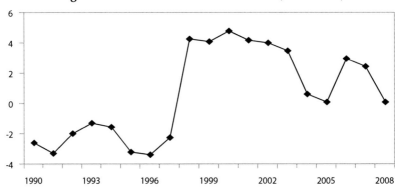

Figure 3.21: Inflation (%)

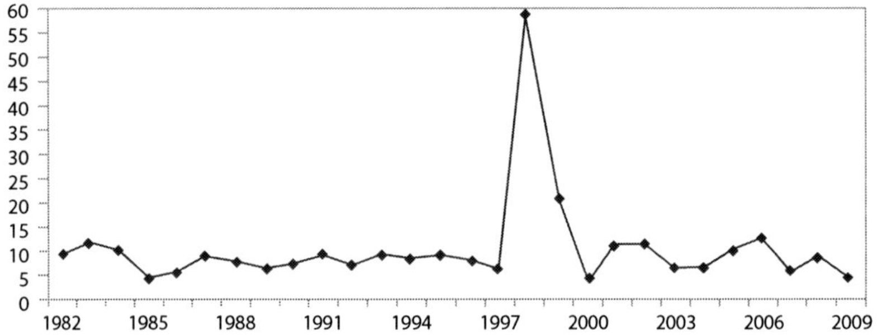

Sources: World Bank, WDI, accessed October 2009 and BPS website, accessed October 2009.

Figure 3.22: Current Account Balance (% of GDP)

GDP = gross domesticproduct.
Source: ADB (2009).

(partly because of increased freight costs and taxes and duties adversely affecting exports) and came under pressure again more recently, due to the global economic crisis. Nevertheless, the current account was able to post a small surplus in 2008, which increased to 2% of GDP in 2009 (ADB 2010).

Public debt is at a manageable level, and has been steadily declining. Consistent with the improved fiscal position and good growth performance, public sector debt as a share of GDP declined from 80% in 2000 to 35% in 2008 (Figure 3.23). Other contributing factors included passage and implementation of Law No. 17 of 2003 (the Fiscal Law), which introduced caps on the budget deficit and public debt levels. At the same time, the share of interest payments in total government spending also fell, from 25% in 2001 to about 10% in 2009, on account of lower interest rates, a stable stock of debt outstanding, and appreciation of the rupiah (Bank Indonesia Website).

Figure 3.23: Debt to GDP Ratio (%)

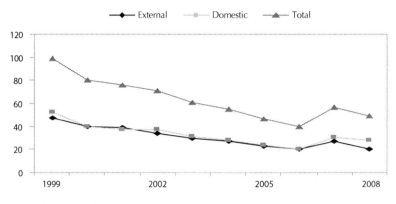

GDP = gross domestic product.
Source: Bank Indonesia, Indonesia Economic Monetary Statistics Weekly Report.

Despite improvements in the macroeconomic policy framework and in growth performance, macroeconomic instability remains a key investor concern. In a 2007 survey, more than 50% of responding firms considered macroeconomic instability and 40% considered uncertainty in economic policies to be major constraints (LPEM–FEUI 2007). The findings were an improvement on those of the 2003 investment climate survey, where nearly 80% of responding firms identified macroeconomic instability and uncertainty in economic policies to be a major constraint (ADB and World Bank 2005). Divergence between investor perceptions and the recent track record of the Indonesian economy and its management tends to suggest that investors have not forgotten the 1997 Asian financial crisis. However, that Indonesia was one of the best-performing countries in Southeast Asia during the recent global economic crisis may help investors regain their faith in the economy and its management.

Budget allocations for key development sectors have been declining while those for public services have been rising. Compared with other major economies in Southeast Asia, Indonesia's development expenditure has been low; as a result it has not been able to fully meet investment needs of key sectors—particularly infrastructure, health, and education—that may be essential for faster economic growth (Figure 3.24). Budget allocations have been dominated by general public services, which include salaries and recurrent expenditures and have accounted for nearly three-fourths of the total budget allocations since 2001. While the share of economic services has increased somewhat since 2004, current allocations remain well below the vast amount required to improve and expand infrastructure and meet other development needs.

Figure 3.24: Government Expenditure by Type of Services (%)

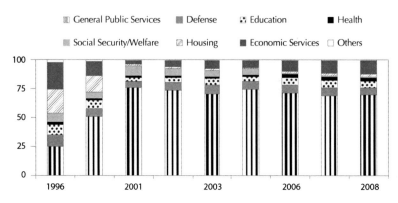

Source: ADB (2009) and BPS (various years).

3.3.2. Governance

3.3.2.1. Control of Corruption

Corruption is perceived to be high in Indonesia, and may be constraining the entry of new businesses and investments. In terms of control of corruption, Indonesia has fared rather poorly compared with some other major economies in the region. The World Bank's Governance Indicators rated Indonesia at 34% in control of corruption in 1996, lower than most neighboring countries, including Malaysia, Philippines, Singapore, and Thailand (Figure 3.25). Indonesia's rate declined sharply to below 10% in the aftermath of the 1997 Asian financial crisis and the transition from the "New Order" regime to a democratic setup. The decline also suggests that the introduction of decentralization through the "big bang" approach in 1999 may have weakened the efforts to control corruption in the country (Box 3.2).

Comparison with other major Southeast Asian countries suggests that Indonesia ranked much lower in control of corruption than Malaysia and Thailand in 2008, although it fared better than the Philippines and Viet Nam (Figure 3.26). Other international surveys paint similar pictures. Transparency International's 2007 Corruption Perceptions Index placed Indonesia, together with Gambia, the Russian Federation, and Togo, 143rd among 179 countries. In 2008, the ranking improved to 126th out of 180 countries, which was better than the Philippines at 141, but far behind Malaysia at 47, Thailand at 80, and Viet Nam at 121 (TI Surveys and Indices).

Figure 3.25: Control of Corruption Rank (various years, %)

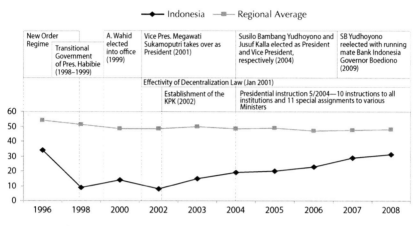

KPK = Komisi Penbarantas Korupsi (Corruption Eradication Commission).
Note: The regional average is for Indonesia, Malaysia, Philippines, Singapore, Thailand, and Viet Nam.
Source: World Bank Governance Matters VIII.

Box 3.2: A Move in the Right Direction with Unexpected Results

Typical outcomes expected from decentralization of government roles would include improvements in governance and service delivery. However, the experience from Indonesia suggests that decentralization resulted in major dents in the quality of governance in the country. In particular, quality of government effectiveness and control of corruption plummeted in the early years of decentralization.

One major change brought about by decentralization was, the way that the national and regional governments planned and interacted. Not only did local governments have full autonomy to plan, but they were also not required to report to the national government on their yearly achievements and performance. Venues and forums for coordination became weak and led to situations wherein national and local level initiatives overlapped. In some cases, the full benefits of investments could not be achieved due to lack of complementary investments from the national or local governments. An example is the Surabaya-Gempol toll road in East Java, which ended up competing with provincial roads that were upgraded and improved in parallel. On the other hand, the Waru-Juanda toll road in East Java could not deliver the envisaged benefits due to poor connectivity with other major roads in the vicinity.

continued on next page
continued on next page

Box 3.2 continued

Empowered to enact local-level laws and regulations, the local legislative bodies literally went on a spree of enacting regulations. Perdana and Friawan (2006) noted that the districts had been enacting, on average, 30 laws and regulations a year. Studies point out that these laws and regulations often were not consistent with national laws and regulations, which created additional hurdles to investment. Given that most local governments were facing a resource crunch and the roles pertaining to revenue generation were not clearly defined, it was of little surprise that a majority of these new laws and regulations were focused on generating new revenue. Perdana and Friawan noted that as much as 60% of the new regulations introduced new levies and taxes, which added to the cost of doing business, in terms of both money and time. An ADB study (2004) found that trucks transporting fresh oranges from North Sumatra to Jakarta had to stop at 16 weigh stations operated by different district governments and had to pay Rp268,500–Rp1,008,500 (about $25–$100) at each station.

Decentralization also resulted in fragmentation of corruption, and made the efforts to control it even more difficult. The flurry of new local laws and regulations also created new opportunities for rent seeking. Where the businesses were used to having to pay one or two officials, now they were expected to pay off officials at district, provincial, and national levels in every district where they operated or through which they transported their goods. A 2008 Asia Foundation study found that, on nine of the surveyed routes, trucks were stopped on average four times and had to pay Rp17,582 in illegal payments to police and other groups.

In part, the unexpected outcome may have been due to the transformation to decentralization through the "big bang" approach with little or no prior preparation at the local government levels. Recognizing this, the government introduced several measures to correct for this; nevertheless, aspects of governance have not been able to climb back to the levels that prevailed in 1996.

Source: Asia Foundation (2008).

A 2007 investment climate survey found that corruption in national institutions, such as tax and customs administration, continued to be a major constraint on investment (LPEM–FEUI 2007). Of the 420 responding firms that had to deal with the customs administration, 86% acknowledged having to make informal payments and bribes to officials, which averaged 6.1% of firms' annual production costs. The survey also found that firms'

Figure 3.26: Control of Corruption Indicators of Major Southeast Asian Countries

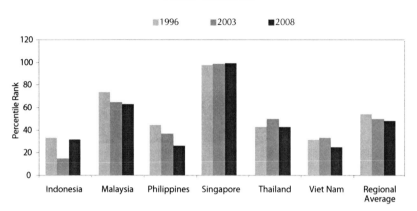

Source: World Bank Governance Matters VIII.

senior management had to spend 5.9% of their time dealing with government officials in 2006. The survey found that government officials visited firms frequently, and 50% of respondents reported that they were expected to provide gifts or bribes during the visits. Visits by security agencies (police and military) were reported to be the most frequent, averaging about six per year.

In response, the government has taken several steps. An example is establishing the Corruption Eradication Commission in 2002, which has proven highly effective in investigating and prosecuting bribery and graft-related cases. After coming to power in 2004, President Yudhoyono's administration acknowledged corruption as a major menace to society and a constraint to growth and made the fight against corruption a key government priority. The government took several initiatives in this regard, including launching an anticorruption program directly led and overseen by the President's office; issuing and implementing Presidential Instruction 5 of 2004; and enacting the National Action Plan for the Eradication of Corruption, which sent a strong signal to the bureaucracy and the public about the government's commitment to fight corruption.

The government also focused on preventing corruption through reforms relating to public procurement and transparency, and to education of the civil service and society. The Ministry of State Apparatus Reform amended the procurement regulations and introduced reforms such as public disclosure of procurement plans and prequalification results through websites and the national media. The Public Procurement Policy Development Agency was established. Moreover, the government has started e-procurement and e-announcements.

Measures such as these have greatly enhanced control of corruption. During 2004–2008, perceptions of the prevalence and control of corruption in Indonesia improved, and the country's ranking in the World Bank's Control of Corruption index improved from 19% to 31%. Similarly, in recent surveys by Transparency International for the 2009 Global Corruption Barometer, 74% of respondents assessed the government's actions in the fight against corruption as "effective," which compares with 21% for the Philippines and 28% for Malaysia and Thailand (TI 2009).

3.3.2.2. Government Effectiveness

Despite recent improvements, Indonesia compares unfavorably with most other major economies in the region in terms of government effectiveness. 1996–2002 was a very tumultuous period in Indonesia's political and economic history, during which government effectiveness seemed to have declined quite substantially. The World Bank Governance Indicators record that Indonesia's government effectiveness plummeted from a high of 63.03 in 1996 to a low of 19.43 in 1997 (Figure 3.27). The drastic decline was largely brought about by the 1997 Asian financial crisis, which was also instrumental in delegitimizing the political power of an otherwise strong New Order regime, leading to President Suharto's resignation (Perdana and Friawan 2007) in May 1998. President Suharto's departure ushered in an era of transition from a centralized and autocratic government setup to a democratic and pluralist one. His successor, President B. J. Habibie, in his short term, introduced critical reforms, including granting press freedom, revising the electorate law to allow for a multiparty election, and reducing the number of seats in Parliament allocated to the military and police (Perdana and Friawan 2007).

The 1999 election, Indonesia's first multiparty election, had 48 parties participating. The Indonesian Democratic Struggle Party won. Abdurrahman Wahid was sworn in as President, and the party's Chairperson Megawati Sukarnoputri became Vice President. The change in government and other key related steps helped restore the ranking in government effectiveness to some extent, but the recovery was short-lived. The government effectiveness level dropped with the introduction of key decentralization reforms.

After the initial adjustment period, however, government effectiveness started to improve with a stable government at the national level and improvements in decentralization laws and capacities of the decentralized governments at the local level. The OECD (2008) reported that the decentralization put the local governments at the forefront of service delivery and implementation of public investment programs. This, the report argued, brought the provision of services "nearer" to the people and helped improve the perception of government efficiency.

Figure 3.27: Government Effectiveness in Indonesia (percentile rankings)

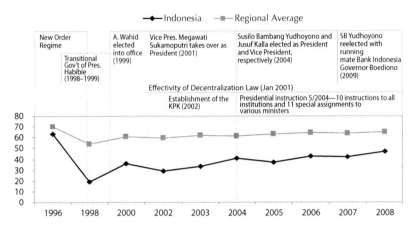

KPK = Komisi Pembaratasan Korupsi (Corruption Eradication Commission).
Note: The regional average is for Indonesia, Malaysia, Philippines, Singapore, Thailand, and Viet Nam.
Source: World Bank Governance Matters VIII.

While the perceived quality of Indonesia's effectiveness in providing goods and services has improved in recent years, it is still behind most other major economies in Southeast Asia (Figure 3.28). The World Bank Governance Indicator for government effectiveness scored Indonesia at 47.3 in 2008, Singapore at 100, Malaysia at 83.8, Thailand at 58.7, and the Philippines at 54.9. Only Viet Nam, at 45.4, scored below Indonesia.

Major issues with government effectiveness at the subnational levels seem to stem from the process of decentralization, which has, in some cases,

Figure 3.28: Government Effectiveness in Selected Southeast Asian Countries

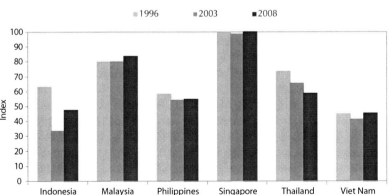

Sources: World Bank Governance Matters VIII.

caused difficulties in the delivery of government services. For example, human resource capacities (such as skilled planners, managers, and government officials), technology, and financial resources are not evenly distributed across the regions. Some of the poorer districts lack appropriate personnel, making it difficult for them to deliver high-quality services and infrastructure. Another major concern is the lack of effective coordination between and among the district, province, and national levels of government. This is especially significant in sectors such as transport and energy, where connectivity with existing and planned national- and provincial-level infrastructure is crucial.

A survey in 2008 by two nongovernment organizations—the Regional Autonomy Watch (KPPOD) and The Asia Foundation—found that across 243 districts and cities, 35% of the business units surveyed picked problems related to infrastructure and 14% cited access to land as the most important constraint to their business activities. Studies have also noted that decentralization led to overregulation at local levels, which often added significantly to difficulties in and costs of doing business. Similarly, the KPPOD–Asia Foundation report noted that 85% of the 5,140 companies surveyed indicated that attending and responding to demands (legal and illegal) of local government officials accounted for 2%–10% of their production costs. Although Law 34 of 2000 restrained the establishment of new local taxes and levies, it is often hard to overturn local regulations enacted before the law came into effect, given that they were approved by local-level parliaments.

3.3.2.3. Political Stability

The perception of political stability and absence of violence is generally poor, with high vulnerability to conflict, violence, and terrorism. Indonesia's rank in the World Bank's Governance Indicator for Political Stability and Absence of Violence has remained in the lowest 20% since the inception of the indicators in 1996 (Figure 3.29). Although Southeast Asia's rank as a whole has declined over the years, Indonesia's score has been substantially lower. It declined from about 19% in 1996 to about 10% in 1998 as a result of the civil and political unrest that led to the resignation of President Suharto. Frequent changes in the administration and other threats to political stability led to continued deterioration in the index until the low of about 4% in 2003. The downward trend, however, was reversed in 2004 with the onset of a period of stability brought about by President Yudhoyono's administration, which helped raise Indonesia's score to 15.7% by 2008. The reelection of President Yudhoyono for a second term of 5 years in 2009 through a peaceful process should help further lift the perceptions of stability and improve investor confidence in the economy in the medium term.

Figure 3.29: Political Stability and Absence of Violence Indicators (percentile rankings)

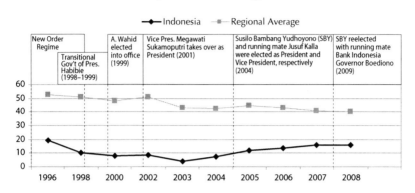

Note: The regional average is for Indonesia, Malaysia, Philippines, Singapore, Thailand, and Viet Nam.
Source: World Bank Governance Matters VIII.

Indonesia's low rank in measures for political stability may be attributed to incidences of terrorism, social violence, and civil riots rather than to a lack of political strength in the current administration. While political stability at the national level is a key factor monitored by the World Bank's Political Stability and Absence of Violence Indicator, it also covers the presence of separatist movements and insurgencies and violence.

Terrorism is another challenge to the country, with occasional incidents serving as reminders of the seriousness of the threat. Operations of Al Qaeda-linked groups such as Jemaah Islamiyah have had an extremely adverse impact on investors' perception of security in Indonesia. Some high-profile terrorist attacks have targeted areas and establishments frequented by western tourists and businessmen. A review of trends in FDI inflows and the World Bank's Political Stability and Absence of Violence Indicator suggests that the incidences of violence and terrorism have substantially discouraged FDI and depressed the ranking of political stability and absence of terrorism (Figure 3.30).

3.3.2.4. Global Competitiveness and Ease of Doing Business

Investors' perception of Indonesia's global competitiveness and ease in doing business has generally been poor. The 2009 Doing Business Survey ranked Indonesia 129th out of 181 countries based on the ease of doing business, placing it behind some of its neighbors (Table 3.4). Indonesia ranked very poorly (171st out of 180) in the ease of starting a business—lower than Malaysia, Philippines, and Thailand. The survey indicated that an investor needed to go through 11 procedures, requiring up to 76 days, to start a business.

Figure 3.30: Annual Net Foreign Direct Investment Flows and Political Stability Rank of Indonesia (1990–2007)

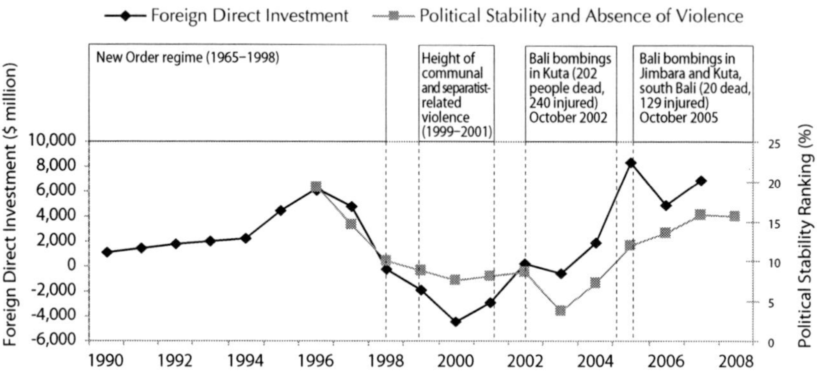

Sources: World Bank Governance Matters VIII and UNCTAD (2009).

Table 3.4: Cost of Doing Business (selected ASEAN countries, 2009)

Country	Overall Ranking	Starting a Business			Registering Property			Enforcing Contracts			Closing a Business	
		Procs.	Days	Cost (% of income)	Procs.	Days	Cost (% of property value)	Procs.	Days	Cost (% of claim)	Years	Cost (% of estate)
Indonesia	129	11	76	77.9	6	39	10.7	39	570	122.7	5.5	18
Malaysia	20	9	16	14.7	5	144	2.5	30	600	27.5	2.3	15
Philippines	140	15	52	29.8	8	33	4.3	37	842	26	5.7	38
Singapore	1	4	4	0.70	3	9	2.8	21	150	25.8	0.8	1
Thailand	13	8	33	4.9	2	2	1.1	35	479	14.3	2.7	36

ASEAN = Association of Southeast Asian Nations, Procs. = procedures.
Source: World Bank and IFC (2008).

Another measure considered in the Doing Business Survey is the cost and procedures needed to register property. For this measure too, Indonesia ranked low and was 107th in 2009, down from 101st in the previous year. The survey estimated that it takes about 39 days and 6 procedures to register a property, adding up to 10.7% of the property value in terms of cost. Indonesia's ranking is again poorer than that of other Association of Southeast Asian Nations countries, such as Malaysia, Philippines, and Thailand.

In terms of contract enforcement, the Doing Business 2009 survey ranked Indonesia 140th out of 181 economies in "Enforcing a Contract" (with 1 being the best). The survey showed that it takes 570 days to enforce a contract in Indonesia (for filing and service, trial and judgment, and enforcement of judgment)—one of the lengthiest processes in the region. The cost of enforcing a claim is estimated at 122.7% of the amount of the claim and is much higher than in other countries in the region (in the Philippines, it is 114%; Lao Peoples' Democratic Republic, 111%; Malaysia, 59%; and Thailand, 29%). The survey found that this issue decreases the number of investments that the firms initiate and that these investments tend to involve only a small group of investors who know each other from previous dealings. Other studies also note that contract enforcement in Indonesia is uncertain, unpredictable, and costly, undermining the adequacy of the law (Booz Allen Hamilton 2007).

Closing a business is also a lengthy process, requiring up to 5.5 years, and it is costly, amounting to 18% of the value of the estate and a recovery rate of $0.137 per dollar invested. Indonesia ranks better in this aspect than the Philippines and Thailand but worse than Malaysia, Singapore, and Viet Nam. According to the World Bank and IFC (2008), bottlenecks in bankruptcy cut into the amount claimants can recover.

3.3.2.5. Other Aspects of Governance

Indonesia's performance in other governance-related aspects is improving. Some of the aspects reported by the World Bank's Governance Indicators 2008 include voice and accountability, regulatory quality, and rule of law (Figure 3.31). In all these aspects, the country's rankings either declined after 1996 or remained stagnant but have recently been improving. In voice and accountability, the transition to democracy and implementation of decentralization have meant major improvements for the country, which is now ranked as a leader in the region. Improvements in regulatory quality

Figure 3.31: Other Governance Indicators (percentile rankings)

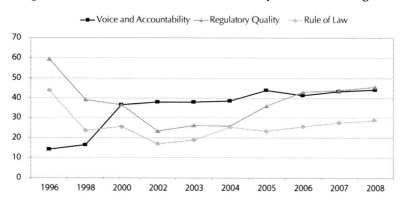

Sources: World Bank Governance Matters VIII.

and rule of law are significant, although they are not equally impressive and have not yet reached their 1996 levels.

Tax rates are comparable to those of other major countries in the region, but paying taxes is a cumbersome process. Indonesia compares favorably with other Southeast Asian countries in its personal and corporate income and value-added tax rates (Table 3.5). In personal income tax, the rate for the highest bracket is higher in the Philippines, Thailand, and Viet Nam than in Indonesia. Similarly, rates for corporate income tax are higher in the Philippines and Thailand than in Indonesia. Indonesia's value-added tax rates are higher than those in Singapore and Thailand but comparable to or lower than those in other major Southeast Asian economies. Thus, the tax rates alone may not make investing in Indonesia less attractive than in the region's other major economies.

Table 3.5: Tax Rate in Southeast Asia (%)

Country	Personal Income Tax Rate	Corporate Income Tax Rate	Value-Added Tax Rate
Indonesia	5–30	28	10
Malaysia	0–27 (Progressive and if resident)	25	...
Philippines	5–32 (Progressive)	30	12
Singapore	3.5–20 (Progressive)	0–18 (depending on profits	7
Thailand	10–37 (Progressive)	2–30 (depending on type of business)	7
Viet Nam	5–35 (Progressive)	25	10

... = Data not available.
Sources: For Indonesia and Viet Nam, Tax Rates Around the World; for Thailand, Revenue Department; for Singapore, AsiaBiz and Janus Corporate Solutions; for Malaysia, Malaysian Industrial Development Authority; for Philippines, Bureau of Internal Revenue.

However, the cumbersome process of paying taxes may deter some investment. Doing Business 2009 reports that, on average, a business has to make 22 tax payments a year, requiring about 344 hours of work (Table 3.6). The report ranks Indonesia 104th among 181 countries for overall payment of taxes, substantially worse than the rank for Singapore (5th), Malaysia (21st), and Thailand (82nd).

Tax rates or cumbersome procedures relating to paying taxes do not seem to be of a critical nature. Firms responding to an investment climate survey ranked the tax rates 8th and tax administration 10th in the list of 22 top constraints to investment (LPEM–FEUI 2007). Similarly, a survey by the Japan External Trade Organization in 2008 indicated that only about 10.4%

Table 3.6: Paying Taxes in Southeast Asian Countries

Country	No. of Payments (per year)	Time Spent (hours per year)	Total Tax Rate (% of profit)	Overall Rank
Indonesia	22	344	44.2	104
Malaysia	12	145	34.5	21
Philippines	47	195	50.8	129
Singapore	5	84	27.9	5
Thailand	23	234	37.8	82
Viet Nam	32	1050	40.1	140

Source: World Bank and IFC (2008).

of the Japanese firms with overseas operations considered tax-related risks and issues as a constraint to doing business in Indonesia (JETRO 2009).

While the Indonesian labor markets are perceived to be rigid, this may not be a critical constraint to investment. Indonesia strengthened labor regulations in the early 2000s. The Manpower Act of 2003 that was introduced to govern severance pay reined in the use of contract workers and regulated minimum wages. The Trade Union Act of 2001 stipulated basic labor rights. Critics of these labor regulations argue that rigid regulations in the labor market increase the cost of adjustment to demand fluctuations, making Indonesia a less attractive destination for potential investors. They often point out that Indonesia belongs to the group of countries with high firing costs.

Indeed, Indonesian labor market flexibility was not rated well among the 133 economies surveyed by the WEF (2009). Ranked at 98th, Indonesia was among the most rigid economies in labor market regulation and compared unfavorably with many of its neighbors (Table 3.7). Malaysia and Thailand have more flexible labor markets. The index of Economic Freedom shows similar results in labor freedom (Miller et al. 2009).

However, the labor market rigidity does not seem to be a critical constraint to private investment in Indonesia. First, a simple cross-country correlation analysis suggests that the correlation between investment (whether FDI net inflows or gross capital formation as a percentage of GDP) and labor market rigidity is low.[4] Second, according to an executive opinion survey, labor rigidity is not among the top five hindrances to business in Indonesia

---

[4] Using data from the World Bank's World Development Indicators and World Economic Forum's Global Competitiveness Report 2009–2010, the authors ran correlations between labor market efficiency and labor market flexibility, and FDI inflows (% of GDP) and gross capital formation (% of GDP). Correlation values ranged from –0.07 to –0.56, with negative signs signifying that less rigid and more efficient markets are associated with higher investment inflows.

Table 3.7: Rankings of Labor Market Efficiency (of 133 economies)

	Indonesia	Cambodia	Malaysia	Philippines	Thailand	Viet Nam	PRC	India
Labor market efficiency	75	52	31	113	25	38	32	83
A. Flexibility	98	74	28	111	31	68	91	69
Cooperation in labor-employer relations	42	105	19	65	28	49	60	40
Hiring and firing practices	34	36	46	110	29	24	77	103
Flexibility of wage determination	92	75	54	96	89	79	53	44
Firing costs	119	71	96	109	84	104	109	85
Regidity of employment	82	92	14	68	24	35	43	54
B. Efficient use of talent	54	46	47	97	31	27	13	88
Pay and productivity	29	50	9	74	38	6	12	46
Reliance on professional management	55	109	29	48	61	82	46	30
Brain drain	25	51	31	104	32	76	39	41
Female participation in labor force	104	28	107	99	53	14	20	122

The full report is downloaded at http://www.weforum.org/en/initiatives/gcp/Global%20
Competitiveness%20Report/index.htm
For the methodology, please refer to the Appendix A and section 1.2 of the report.
Source: WEF (2009).

(Miller et al. 2009). Third, a University of Indonesia survey of the country's investment climate confirmed the findings and ranked labor regulation 11th in importance as a business constraint (LPEM–FEUI 2007), with the top three constraints related to macroeconomic instability, transport, and corruption. That companies can circumvent labor regulations by hiring casual employees or by outsourcing, thus avoiding the costs imposed by the regulations, may partly explain employers placing less importance on labor rigidity in Indonesia.

The results of correlation analysis and opinion surveys, however, are not testimonials of a well-functioning labor market in Indonesia. Further, one should not underestimate the impact of the labor rigidity on potential foreign investors, as the opinion surveys reflect the views of business managers already in Indonesia. It has been argued that, together with high costs of capital, and insufficient infrastructure, the labor regulations implemented in the early 2000s may have contributed to the country having "a high-cost economy" and losing international competitiveness (Dhanani, Islam, and Chowdhury 2009).

Labor market reform has been on the Indonesian government's policy agenda for some time. The challenge is that the government, the trade unions, and the employers' organizations must address labor rigidity and weak social security in tandem. The current social protection system places the financial burden of providing income security for the unemployed on the firms that previously provided employment for these workers through generous severance pay. Shifting the burden of protection to a wider pool participated in by more actors in society would facilitate the process of labor market reform.

3.3.3. Market Failures

In Indonesia, industry is the largest sector in terms of contribution to GDP. During 1990–2008, industry's share of GDP rose from about 39% to 48% (BPS, various years). However, within industry, the share of manufacturing has stagnated at about 27% of GDP since 2000–2001.

Factors responsible for the manufacturing sector's poor performance include the constraints discussed in detail earlier in this chapter. Recent literature suggests that market failures such as information and learning externalities and coordination failures could lead to low private appropriability of returns and, therefore, can also deter private investment (Hausmann, Rodrik, and Velasco 2005).[5] Such market failures may be at play in the case of Indonesia's manufacturing subsector and its exports.

The manufacturing subsector is growing slowly and it is low in technological quality. As previously noted, manufacturing's value addition as a percentage of GDP has stagnated, and the size of its contribution to GDP growth has contracted since 2000. In addition, the subsector has low rates of capacity utilization—58% in 2005 compared with about 70% in 1998–1999 (BPS, various years). Capacity utilization rates, however, have varied widely between industries and over the years.

---

[5] "Information externality" refers to the situation when the benefits of successfully introducing new products and/or production processes in a country may spill over to third parties, but in case of failure the cost is borne by the original proponent. "Learning externality" refers to the situation when the benefits from investments in building the capacity of the workforce spill over to third parties if the trained workers switch employers or migrate to other countries. "Coordination failure" refers to a situation where a firm's linkages to upstream and downstream industries are not well developed, or a firm's access to infrastructure, regulation, and other public goods is poor.

The manufacturing subsector's composition has also not changed much (Figure 3.32). Between 1998 and 2008, the only significant changes included an expansion in the share of food and beverages at the expense of wood and wood products, and published and recorded media. To analyze changes in technological or sophistication levels of the manufacturing subsector, the study constructed a technology sophistication index (PRODY) following the Product Space Analysis Methodology.[6] The results suggested that, similar to the composition of the subsector, the changes in technological content were also marginal—average PRODY scores increased from 10,087 in 2001 to 10,388 in 2005 (Table 3.8).

Figure 3.32: Composition of Manufacturing Sector Output (%)

- ⊡ Food and Beverages
- ▦ Tobacco
- ▤ Textiles
- ▩ Wearing Apparel
- ▥ Leather and Related
- ▦ Wood and Products
- ▦ Paper and Products
- ■ Media (print and recorded)
- ▦ Chemicals and Products
- ▨ Rubber and Plastics
- ▨ Nonmetal Minerals
- ☐ Basic Metals
- ▨ Fabricated Metal Products
- ▨ Machinery and Equipment
- ▦ Electrical Machinery
- ▧ Electronic Appliances
- ■ Medical, Waches, Others
- ▥ Automotives
- ■ Other Transport Equipment
- ▦ Furniture and Manufacturing

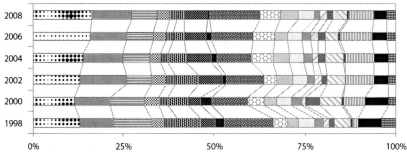

Source: BPS (various years).

Table 3.8: Technological Sophistication of Medium- and Large-Scale Domestic Manufacturing

Industry	PRODY Index	
	2001	2005
Non-Intensive sectors	12,319	12,427
Intensive Sectors	8,629	8,741
Overall	10,087	10,388

Note: A higher score on the PRODY Index implies a higher level of technological sophistication. Nonintensive sectors are those where the country has a revealed comparative advantage of greater than 1.0, while intensive sectors are ones with a revealed comparative advantage of less than one.
Sources: Estimated based on BPS (2005) and SITC and ISIC2 data using concordance methodology provided by Muendler (2009).

---

[6]   The methodology is typically used to analyze exports. In the absence of a detailed distribution of value added for domestic manufacturing, the analysis looked only at the breakdown of value added contributed by medium and large enterprises.

Indonesia's exports have grown in both nominal and real terms; however, the growth rate has been one of the lowest in Southeast Asia. In real terms, the exports grew at an annual average rate of 8.6% between 1990 and 2010 (Figure 3.33). In comparison, over the same period, exports of Malaysia, Singapore, and Thailand grew by 10.0%, 9.6% and 10.8%, respectively. Prior to the 1997 Asian financial crisis, Indonesian exports were growing at rates that were comparable to those of the other major economies in the region. While exports of the other major economies recovered after the crisis, Indonesian exports did not. Indonesian exports declined further in the 1st quarter of 2009—by about 25% on a year-on-year basis. This recent trend, however, is due to the global economic crisis and is consistent with trends in other major Southeast Asian economies.

Figure 3.33: Growth in Exports of Selected Southeast and East Asian Countries (1997=100)

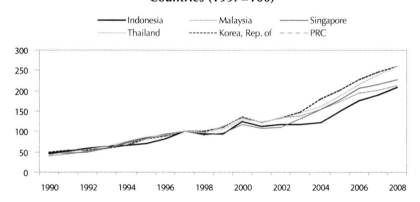

PRC = People's Republic of China.
Source: CEIC, accessed September 2009.

Exports are also not growing in terms of breadth and technological content. In terms of composition of exports, there have been two notable trends during the last three decades (Figures 3.34 and 3.35). First, exports based on mineral fuels, accounting for roughly 40% of total exports in 1990, have declined. Second, the volumes of manufactured exports, after having climbed through the 1990s, declined throughout the 2000s—down to about one-third of the exports in 2008 from being the majority component in 2000. While the decline in exports based on mineral fuels is partly due to rapidly rising domestic demand, the decline in manufactured exports seems to be primarily because the importance of manufacturing is declining in the country.

Analysis of the technological sophistication of Indonesia's exports indicates that they lag far behind those from other major Southeast and East

Figure 3.34: Trends in the Value of the Largest Export Products in Indonesia (1997=100)

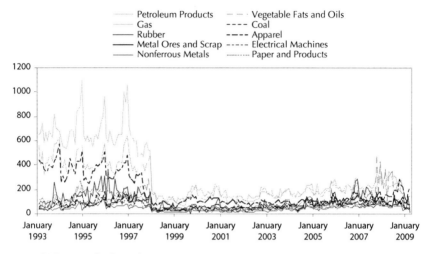

Source: CEIC, accessed in September 2009.

Figure 3.35: Composition of Exports

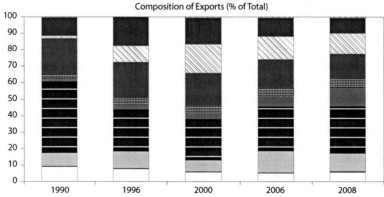

n.e.s. = not elsewhere stated.
Source: BPS Website.

Asian economies. Moreover, the trends suggest a decline in technological sophistication between 2000–2001 and 2005. The PRODY index was around the 8,000 level in 2005 against about 8,800 in 2000. Figure 3.36 compares Indonesian exports with those of other major Southeast Asian countries and provides insights into the lower technological sophistication of Indonesian exports. About 52% of Indonesian exports belonged to group 1 (products with the lowest technological content), while only 4% belonged to the more sophisticated group 3. In contrast, a majority of exports from Malaysia, Philippines, Republic of Korea, and Thailand belonged to group 2.

Figure 3.36: Disaggregation of Exports by Technological Sophistication Group

■ Group 1 (PRODY less than 8,000)   ▨ Group 3 (PRODY 16,001–24,000)
▨ Group 2 (PRODY 8,001–16,000)   ■ Group 4 (PRODY greater than 24,000)

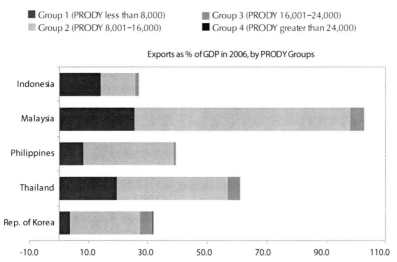

Source: Estimates based on UNCTAD (2009).

What is more worrying is the lack of evidence indicating a change that may lead to a more vibrant manufacturing sector in the near future. Chapter 6 notes that the expansion in exports between 1998 and 2007 was largely in the "old stuff" rather than in the "new stuff" (Figure 6.4). These findings are also supported by an analysis of the export data for the new products that have emerged in pre- and post-Asian financial crisis periods. Table 3.9 indicates that only 69 products that had an export value below $10 million in 2000 rose above $10 million in 2008. In comparison, the export value of 98 products did so between 1990 and 1996. Although the export volume of more products crossed the $100 million threshold between 2000 and 2008 than between 1990 and 1996, the export volume of more products fell below this threshold between 2000 and 2008 than between 1990 and 1996.

Table 3.9: New Products and Export Dynamism

Category	1990–1996	2000–2008
Export Products that Moved Above $10 Million but Were Less than $100 Million		
Number	98	69
PRODY	10,375	11,302
Export Products that Moved Above $100 Million		
Number	37	51
PRODY	11,553	9,824
Products that Regressed to Below $100 Million		
Number	15	27
PRODY	6,686	8,099
Products that Maintained Levels Around $100 Million		
Number	132	113
PRODY	6,851	7,212

Note: A higher score on the PRODY Index implies a higher level of technological sophistication.
Source: Estimates based on UNCTAD (October 2009).

Another point of concern is that the PRODY scores of the products that rose above the $100 million threshold between 2000 and 2008 were lower than those for the products that did so between 1990 and 1996. In other words, the products that rose above the $100 million threshold between 2000 and 2008 were technological less sophisticated than those that rose above the threshold between 1990 and 1996. Further, the products that fell below the $100 million threshold between 2000 and 2008 were more sophisticated than those that did so between 1990 and 1996. The only silver lining is that the products that rose above $100 million between 2000 and 2008 were technologically more sophisticated than those that fell below the threshold during this period.

Stagnation in manufacturing and poor export performance may be partly due to the absence of appropriate and effective industrial and trade policies. A review of industrial and trade policies since the early 1970s suggests that they fostered a protectionist regime aimed at substituting imports rather than promoting exports and rewarding efficiency and innovation. Chapter 6 notes that the country followed a relatively liberal trade regime with little reliance on tariff protection or quantitative import restrictions in the early to mid 1960s. However, prompted by the periods of hyperinflation in the 1960s, the government turned its attention to economic development and embarked on a range of policies that focused on developing its industry by following a protectionist regime. The evolution of industrial and trade policies can be classified into four distinct phases:

1967–1975: The First Phase of Import Substitution. The government provided protection to nascent industries through tariff and duties and sales taxes to discourage imports. Ariff and Hill (1985) noted that tariff protection ranged from 40% to 270% for consumer goods, from 15% to 30% for intermediate goods, and from 0% to 10% for capital goods. They added that this led to an anti-export bias, with the import-substituting industries enjoying a much higher effective rate of protection than the export industries.

1976 to the Mid-1980s: The Second Phase of Import Substitution. Buoyed by increased revenues from rising oil prices, the government pushed for industrialization by promoting upstream industries, including basic, intermediate, and engineering goods industries. A significant difference in this phase from the first one, however, was the greater reliance on nontariff barriers, including import restrictions and bans, local-content regulation (the deletion program), and strict regulation of licensed importers. In addition, nascent industries were protected by strictly regulating and even banning new entrants. Soehoed (1981) noted that these policies led to a widening, rather than a deepening, of the industrial base.

The Mid-1980s to Mid-1990s: Partial Shift to Export Promotion. Deterioration of the balance of payments in the early 1980s due to the decline in foreign exchange earnings from the oil industry hampered the drive toward import substitution and the government took some steps to promote exports. Several of the steps were aimed at reforming taxes and the financial sector, implementing flexible exchange rate policies, and simplifying investment and customs procedures. However, the highly protectionist trade regime, key to establishing inefficient industries, remained largely intact. Rather, a series of quantitative restrictions were introduced on the imports of intermediate inputs needed by the manufacturing industries, thus reinforcing the anti-export bias. In the mid- to late 1980s, the government tried to correct the anti-export bias by providing virtually free trade conditions for industries that exported at least 85% of their output and a duty drawback system to other export industries.

Import controls for the export industries were also relaxed, and a number of nontariff barriers were replaced with tariff barriers. In addition, several specific actions were implemented for the plastic, steel, and textiles industries. Pangestu (1987) noted that these reforms covered a relatively small number of industries, and several important industries were still being regulated through the "approved importers system."

The Post-1997 Asian Financial Crisis Period. The crisis hit the manufacturing sector the hardest. Industries that depended highly on imported inputs, such as transport equipment, footwear, textiles, and plastic and metal industries, were the most affected. Following the crisis, Indonesia initiated a series of wide-ranging reforms that have generally improved the investment climate and competitiveness of the economy. However, the industrial and trade policies continue to target and prioritize selected industries, which may introduce further distortions rather than correcting the existing ones. For example, the 2005–2009 5-year development plan lists industrial clusters that were to receive concerted focus, including the (1) food and beverage industry, (2) fisheries processing industry, (3) textile and textile products industry, (4) footwear industry, (5) oil palm industry, (6) industrial wood products, (7) industrial rubber and rubber goods manufacture, (8) pulp and paper industry, (9) electrical machinery and equipment industry, and (10) petrochemical industry.

However, the impact of recent reforms on promoting the manufacturing sector and exports seems to have been limited at best, indicating that much more needs to be done to correct the distortions and market failures and to overcome constraints to investments identified in the preceding discussions. Moreover, focusing on established rather than emerging industries may not yield intended results in the longer term, and may undermine efficiency and discourage innovation.

Although Indonesia and Malaysia started with similar resource endowments, the development of their manufacturing and exports followed different patterns. Product space analysis of the progression reconfirms the earlier discussions that the industrial and trade policies have not been appropriate and effective in improving Indonesia's manufacturing sector and export performance. In 1985, Indonesia's and Malaysia's export patterns had many similarities (Figure 3.37). Their exports were largely in oil and oil-based products, garments, and forest products. Malaysia had some electronics and machinery-related exports, but these industries were still in the nascent stages. From there on, however, exports in the two countries developed along very different paths. Malaysia shifted its focus from garments and commodity-led exports to more sophisticated industries such as machinery, automotives, and electronics, and by 2000 had positioned itself well to move to an even more sophisticated production base with higher value-added contents. Indonesia, on the other hand, chose to intensify its presence in garments and fish and fishery products. Consequently, Indonesia was trapped in industries with lower levels of technological sophistication and value addition. The impacts of these policies are evident—Malaysia managed to break into more sophisticated industries as early as 2000 and has since strengthened its position in these industries, while Indonesia was unable to enter or sustain a presence in the more sophisticated industries.

A shift toward a more vibrant and efficient manufacturing sector will require concerted efforts to move into industrial clusters that are strategically located in the product space and can provide pathways toward transforming manufacturing into a subsector that is more sophisticated and promises higher levels of value addition. However, a review of the policies enshrined in the recent 5-year development plans does not suggest that this has become a priority. Current policies continue to target existing industries, which presents little opportunity to break into more strategic industries or yield long-term dividends.

Figure 3.37: Export Product Space in Indonesia and Malaysia

A. 1985

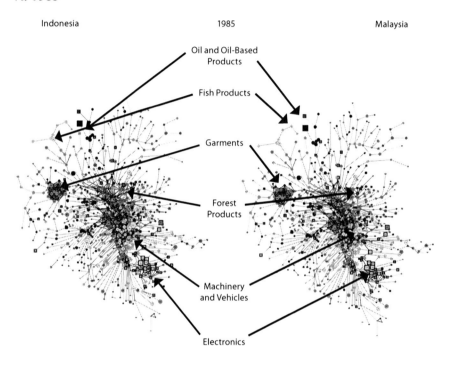

B. 2000

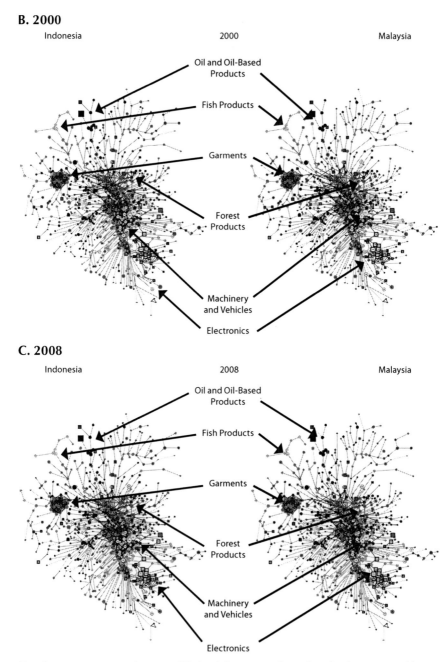

Note: Squares represent actual exports, while the circles represent the products that the country could export but does not. The size of the product's squares or circles represents its global trade volume.
Sources: Global Product Space based on Hidalgo et al. (2007); data for Indonesia and Malaysia are based on UNComtrade (n.d.).

References

ALB Legal News. A Closer Look at the Power Sector in Indonesia—The Latest Initiatives. http://asia.legalbusinessonline.com/industry-updates/indonesia-soemadipradiataher/a-closer-look-at-the-power-sectorin-indonesia-the-latest-initiatives/45834 (accessed 13 May 2010).

Ariff, M. and H. Hill. 1985. *Export-Oriented Industrialization: the ASEAN Experience.* Sydney: Allen and Unwin.

AsiaBiz. Corporate Tax. http://www.asiabizservices.com/singapore-corporate-tax-rate (accessed 3 September 2009).

Asia Foundation. 2008. *Cost of Moving Goods—Road Transportation, Regulation and Charges in Indonesia.* Jakarta.

Asian Development Bank (ADB). 2004. Final Report for TA 3843-INO: Agriculture and Rural Development Strategy Study. Manila.

———. 2005. *Country Environmental Analysis: Indonesia.* Manila.

———. 2006. Indonesia Water Sector Profile. Manila. Unpublished.

———. 2009. Key Indicators for Asia and the Pacific 2009. Manila.

———. 2010. *Asian Development Outlook.* Manila.

———. Statistical Database System (SDBS) Online. http://lxapp1.asiandevbank.org:8030/sdbs/jsp/index.jsp (accessed October 2009).

Asian Development Bank and World Bank (ADB and World Bank). 2005. *Improving the Investment Climate in Indonesia.* Manila: ADB.

Badan Koordinasi Penanaman Modal (BKPM—Investment Coordinating Board). 2009. http://www.bkpm.go.id

Badan Pusat Statistik (BPS—Statistics Indonesia). 2005. Large and Medium Manufacturing Indicators (Indikator Industri Besar Dan Sedang). Jakarta.

———. 2008. Transportation and Communication Statistics 2007 (Statistik Perhubungan 2007). Jakarta.

———. BPS Website. http://www.bps.go.id (accessed October 2009).

———. various years. *Statistical Yearbook of Indonesia (Statistik Indonesia).* Jakarta.

———. Sakernas (National Labor Force Surveys—Survei Tenaga Kerja Nasional). Jakarta.

Bank Indonesia. Indonesia Economic Monetary Statistics Weekly Report. http://www.bi.go.id/web/en/Statistik/Statistik+Ekonomi+Mone ter+Indonesia (accessed May 2010).

———. Bank Indonesia Website. http://www.bi.go.id/web/en/Statistik/ Statistik+Ekonomi+dan+Keuangan+Indonesia/Versi+HTML/ Sektor+Moneter (accessed in October 2009)

Booz Allen Hamilton. 2007. Southeast Asia Commercial Law and Institutional Reform and Trade Diagnostics—Indonesia. Final report prepared for the United States Agency for International Development (USAID). http://www.bizclir.com/cs/countries/asia/indonesia/contractlaw

Bureau of Internal Revenue. National Internal Revenue Code. http://www.bir.gov.ph/taxcode/1900.htm (accessed 3 September 2009).

CEIC. http://www.ceicdata.com (accessed September 2009).

Chatani, K. and K.B. Kim. 2009. *Labour and Social Trends in Indonesia 2009: Recovery and Beyond through Decent Work*. Jakarta: International Labour Organization (ILO).

Dhanani, S., I. Islam, and A. Chowdhury. 2009. *The Indonesian Labour Market: Changes and Challenges*. London and New York: Routledge.

Fossey, J. 2008. *Containerisation International Yearbook 2008*. UK: Informa Maritime & Transport. http://www.iaphworldports.org/world_port_info/statistics/container-4.pdf

Hausmann, R., D. Rodrik, and A. Velasco. 2005. *Growth Diagnostics*. Cambridge, MA: John F. Kennedy School of Government, Harvard University.

Hidalgo C., B. Klinger, A-L Barabasi, and R. Hausmann. 2007. The Product Space Conditions of the Development Nations. Science 317: 482–87.

IMT–GT Secretariat and ADB. 2007. *Indonesia-Malaysia-Thailand Growth Triangle—Building a Dynamic Future: A Roadmap for Development 2007–2011*. Manila: ADB.

International Institute for Management Development (IMD). 2009. *World Competitiveness Yearbook 2009*. Geneva. www.worldcompetitiveness.com

International Monetary Fund (IMF). 2007. Indonesia: Selected Issues. *IMF Country Report No. 07/273*. http://www.imf.org/external/pubs/ft/scr/2007/cr07273.pdf

———. 2008. Indonesia: Selected Issues. IMF Country Report No. 08/298. http://www.imf.org/external/pubs/ft/scr/2008/cr08298.pdf

———. 2009. Indonesia: Selected Issues. IMF Country Report No. 09/231. http://www.imf.org/external/pubs/ft/scr/2009/cr09231.pdf

———. various years. Global Financial Stability Report. Washington DC.

———. International Financial Statistics (IFS) Online. Washington, DC. http://www.imfstatistics.org/imf/imfbrowser.aspx?branch=ROOT (accessed September 2009 to May 2010).

Islam, I. and A. Chowdhury. 2009. Growth, Employment and Poverty Reduction in Indonesia. Geneva: ILO.

Islamic Development Bank (IDB). 2010. Indonesia: Critical Constraints to Infrastructure Development. Jeddah.

Janus Corporate Solutions. Guide Me Singapore: Singapore Goods and Services Tax Guide. http://www.guidemesingapore.com/business/c668-singapore-goods-and-services-tax-gst.htm (accessed 3 September 2009).

Japan External Trade Organization (JETRO). 2009. Survey on International Operations of Japanese Firms (FY 2008). Tokyo.

Japan International Cooperation Agency (JICA). 2006. Study on the Development of Domestic Sea Transportation and Maritime Industry in the Republic of Indonesia (STRAMINDO). Tokyo.

Komite Pemantauan Pelaksanaan Otonomi Daerah (KPPOD—Committee Monitoring the Implementation of Regional Autonomy), United States Agency for International Development (USAID), and The Asia Foundation. 2007. Local Economic Governance in Indonesia, a Survey of Business in 243 Regencies/Cities in Indonesia. Jakarta.

Lembaga Penyelidikan Ekonomi dan Masyarakat–Fakultas Ekonomi Universitas Indonesia (LPEM–FEUI—Institute for Economic and Social Research, Department of Economics, University of Indonesia). 2007. Investment Climate Monitoring. Round IV. Jakarta.

Malaysian Industrial Development Authority. Invest in Malaysia: Taxation. http://www.mida.gov.my/en_v2/index.php?page=taxation-2 (accessed 3 September 2009).

Miller, T., K. Holmes, A. Kim, D. Markheim, J. Roberts, and C. Walsh. 2009. 2009 Index of Economic Freedom. Washington and New York: The Heritage Foundation and Dow Jones & Company.

Ministry of National Education (MONE). 2008. Statistics of Education (Statistik Pendidikan). Jakarta.

Muendler, M. 2009. Converter from SITC to ISIC. University of California, San Diego. http://econ.ucsd.edu/muendler/html/resource.html

Organisation for Economic Co-operation and Development (OECD). 2007. Programme for International Student Assessment (PISA) 2006 Volume 2: Data. Paris. http://www.oecd.org/dataoecd/30/18/39703566.pdf?bcsi_scan_B90AE85AF6AB15C6=0&bcsi_scan_

———. 2008. Indonesia: Economic Assessment. OECD Economic Surveys, 2008 (17): i–131. Paris.

Pangestu, M. 1987. Survey of Recent Developments. Bulletin of Indonesian Economic Studies (April).

Perdana, A., and D. Friawan. 2007. Economic Crisis, Institutional Changes and the Effectiveness of Government: the Case of Indonesia. CSIS Economics Working Paper Series WPI102. Jakarta: Centre for Strategic and International Studies.

Purra, M. 2010. The Indonesian Electricity Sector: Institutional Transition, Regulatory Capacity and Outcomes. Working Paper. Singapore: National University of Singapore.

Revenue Department. Tax Structures. http://www.rd.go.th/publish/6045.0.html (accessed 3 September 2009).

Soehoed, A. 1981. Japan and the Development of the Indonesian Manufacturing Sector. The Indonesian Quarterly. October. Jakarta.

Sziraczki, G. and A. Reerink. 2004. Report of Survey on the School-to-Work Transition in Indonesia. GENPROM Working Paper No. 14. Series on Gender in the Life Cycle. Geneva: ILO. http://www.ilo.org/public/engl

Tax Rates Around the World. http://www.worldwide-tax.com/index.asp#partthree (accessed 3 September 2009).

Transparency International (TI). 2009. 2009 Global Corruption Barometer. Transparency International. http://www.transparency.org/publications/publications/gcb2009

———. Surveys and Indices. http://www.transparency.org/policy_research/surveys_indices/cpi/2007 (accessed May 2010).

UN Comtrade. UN Comtrade Database. http://comtrade.un.org/db/dqQuickQuery.aspx

United Nations Conference on Trade and Statistics (UNCTAD). 2009. FDI Stats. http://stats.unctad.org/FDI/ReportFolders/reportFolders.aspx?sCS_referer=&sCS_ChosenLang=en (accessed October 2009).

United Nations Development Programme (UNDP). 2007. Human Development Report 2007/2008 Fighting Climate Change: Human Solidarity in a Divided World. http://hdr.undp.org/en/media/HDR_20072008_EN_Complete.pdf

World Bank. 2005. Electricity for All: Options for Increasing Access in Indonesia. Jakarta.

———. Governance Matters VIII: Worldwide Governance Indicators, 1996–2008. http://info.worldbank.org/governance/wgi/pdf_country.asp

———. World Development Indicators (WDI) Online. http://ddpext.worldbank.org/ext/DDPQQ/member.do?method=getMembers&userid=1&queryId=6 (accessed October 2009 to May 2010).

World Bank and International Finance Corporation (IFC). 2008. 2009 Doing Business. Washington, DC: World Bank.

World Economic Forum (WEF). 2009. The Global Competitiveness Report 2009–2010. Geneva. http://www.weforum.org/pdf/GCR09/GCR20092010fullreport.pdf?bcsi_scan_B90AE85AF6AB15C6=0&bcsi_scan_filename=GCR20092010fullreport.pdf

4. Critical Constraints to Reducing Poverty and Inequality[1]

Yoko Niimi and Kazutoshi Chatani

Poverty in Indonesia declined significantly during the two decades prior to the 1997 Asian financial crisis (AFC), when the poverty rate surged. The poverty rate has again been decreasing steadily since the crisis. Geographical disparity is an important aspect of poverty in Indonesia, with the poverty headcount rate for Maluku, Papua, and Nusa Tenggara remaining about three times that for Kalimantan. Another important feature of poverty in Indonesia is the dense cluster of population around the poverty line, indicating the vulnerability of Indonesian households to poverty. These observations underline a need for enhancing inclusive growth in order to reduce poverty and inequality. This chapter identifies potential constraints to the inclusiveness of growth using the conceptual framework outlined in Chapter 1.

4.1. Trends in Poverty and Inequality

4.1.1. Poverty

Indonesia's poverty fell significantly during 1976–1996, with the poverty incidence declining from about 40.1% to 11.3% (Figure 4.1). In 1996, the methodology for poverty estimation was revised, and the poverty incidence was estimated at 17.7% based on the new definition. The poverty incidence then shot up to 24.2% in 1998 due to the 1997 AFC. Six years elapsed before the poverty incidence moved below the pre-crisis levels. The poverty incidence then again rose, from 16.7% in 2005 to about 17.8% in 2006 due to the surge in rice prices (World Bank 2006a). The incidence resumed a downward trend when the rice prices subsided and the safety nets were in

---

[1] The editors and publishers gratefully acknowledge the International Labour Organization for contributing to this chapter.

place. As of 2008, the poverty incidence had declined to 15.4%, which was still far from the ambitious target of 8.2% for 2009 set in Indonesia's Mid-Term National Development Plan 2004–2009 (Heriawan 2008). Although the full impact of the global economic crisis is yet to be ascertained, government reports suggest that its impact on the poverty incidence may so far have been marginal.

Figure 4.1: Poverty Trends (1976–2009)

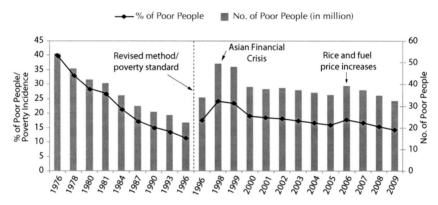

Note: In 1996, the poverty line was adjusted to reflect changes in the consumption patterns of the population, and the coverage was extended for selected nonfood items.
Sources: BPS (various years); Chapter 10 of this volume.

Poverty in Indonesia has been a predominantly rural phenomenon. Although the rural poverty incidence, at 40.4% in 1976, was only slightly higher than the urban poverty incidence of 38.8%, nearly 82% of the poor population was estimated to be residing in rural areas (Figures 4.2 and 4.3). Reduction in poverty during 1976–1996 helped bring the poverty incidence down in both rural and urban areas, with the rural poverty incidence declining to 12.3% and urban poverty incidence to 9.7%—or 19.9% and 13.6%, respectively, based on the new methodology. With the economic recovery, the rural and urban poverty incidences declined, and then both rose with the surge in rice prices in 2006. In 2008, the disparity in poverty incidence between rural and urban areas widened to about 7.2 percentage points from about 1.8 percentage points in 1976. The proportion of poor people living in rural areas declined from about 82% in 1976 to about 64% in 2008.

Figure 4.2: Poverty Headcount Rate: Urban, Rural, and Total (1976–2009, %)

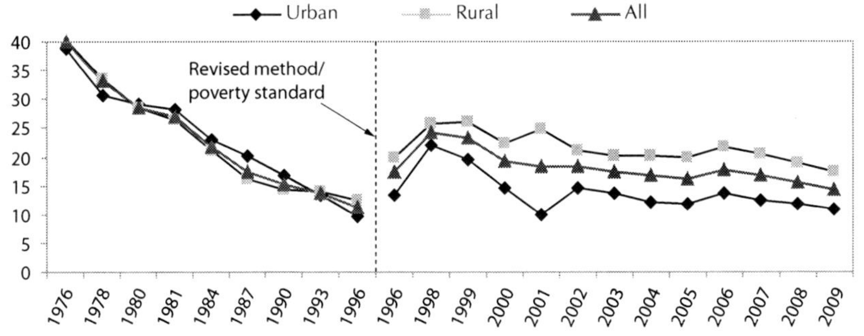

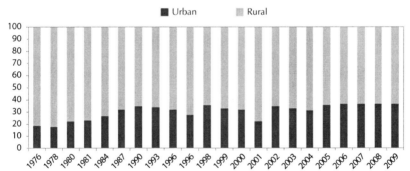

Note: In 1996, the poverty line was adjusted to reflect changes in the consumption patterns of the population and the coverage was extended for selected nonfood items
Sources: BPS (various years); Chapter 10 of this volume.

Figure 4.3: Share of the Poor Population in Urban and Rural Areas (1976–2009, %)

Note: Based on the 1998 revised poverty line.
Sources: BPS (various years); Chapter 10 of this volume.

An important characteristic of poverty in Indonesia is the substantial disparity between regions. Although the poverty incidence declined across all regions during 1996–2008, the reduction was much greater in Kalimantan, Maluku, Nusa Tenggara, and Papua than in other regions (Figure 4.4). Nevertheless, the poverty incidences in Maluku, Nusa Tenggara, and Papua remain significantly high—about three times that of Kalimantan. However, only about 10% of Indonesia's poor live in these regions, while 60% live in the more densely populated islands of Bali and Java (Figure 4.5).

Figure 4.4: Poverty Headcount Rate by Region (1996–2008, %)

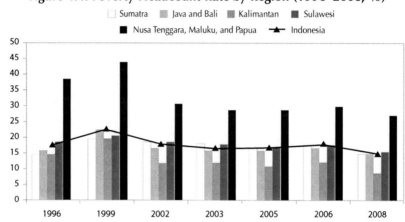

Note: Based on the 1998 revised poverty line.
Sources: BPS (various years); Chapter 10 of this volume.

Figure 4.5: Share of Poor Population by Region (1996–2008)

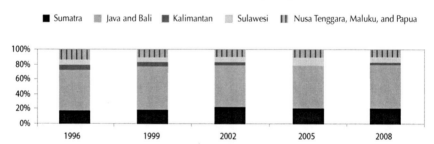

Note: 1996 figures are based on the 1998 revised poverty line.
Sources: BPS (various years); Chapter 10 of this volume.

Another important feature of poverty in Indonesia is the dense cluster of population around the poverty lines. While the level of extreme poverty (i.e., below the $1.25-a-day poverty line) declined significantly—from about 72% in 1981 to about 21% in 2005—more than half of the population was still living below the $2-a-day poverty line in 2005. Table 4.1, which compares Indonesia with other Southeast Asian countries, shows that, although Indonesia's level of extreme poverty is lower than that of the Philippines or Viet Nam, the proportion of its population living below the $2-a-day poverty line is higher than theirs.

Table 4.1: Headcount Indexes Based on Four Poverty Lines in Selected Southeast Asian Countries (2000–2006, %)

Country	Survey Year	Headcount Index			
		$1/day	$1.25/day	$1.35/day	$2/day
Cambodia	2004	26	40	45	68
Indonesia	2005	10	21	26	54
Lao PDR	2002	28	44	50	77
Malaysia	2004	0	1	1	8
Philippines	2006	14	23	26	45
Thailand	2004	0	0	1	12
Viet Nam	2006	12	23	25	50

Lao PDR = Lao Peoples' Democratic Republic.
Source: World Bank, PovcalNet Database.

Furthermore, the percentages of chronically poor (people who were poor in both years) and vulnerable people (those who were poor in one of the years), estimated using the panel data, indicate a relatively high proportion of the vulnerable population even in provinces with a relatively lower percentage of the chronically poor (Figure 4.6).

Figure 4.6: Poverty Dynamics (2005–2007, %)

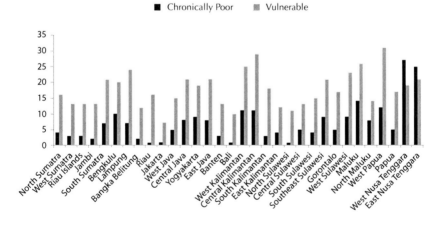

Sources: BPS Susenas Panel Datasets (2005, 2007).

4.1.2. Inequality

Income inequality in Indonesia compares favorably with that in other Southeast Asian countries. During 1981–2007, the Gini coefficient of per capita income hovered at 0.32–0.36. Trends in the Gini coefficient suggest that the inequalities increased during the high-growth period of 1990–1996, declined as a result of the 1997 AFC, and increased with the rise in rice prices in 2006.

4.2. Productive Employment Opportunities

The limited availability of productive and decent employment opportunities is a critical constraint to inclusiveness. Strong economic growth during the last decade helped to lift millions of Indonesians out of poverty. Headcount poverty incidences[2] and the share of the working poor[3] showed a secular decline after a sharp increase in the aftermath of the 1997 AFC (Table 4.2). However, the growth since the 1997 AFC has not been generating sufficient productive and decent employment opportunities to absorb the unemployed, underemployed, discouraged workers (i.e., those who have given up searching for a job), and new entrants to the labor market.

Table 4.2: Poverty and Working Poverty (%)

Year	International Poverty Line—Population Below $1.25/day	International Poverty line—Population Below $2/day	Share of Working Poor at $1.25/day in Total Employment	Share of Working Poor at $2/day in Total Employment
1993	54.4	84.6	65.4	91.2
1996	43.4	77.0	52.5	86.4
1999	47.7	81.5	58.5	91.0
2002	29.3	66.9	37.2	81.4
2005	21.4	53.8	27.8	71.1

Sources: For poverty incidences, World Bank, PovcalNet database; and for the share of the working poor, ILO (2007).

---

[2]   Defined as the share of the population living below international poverty lines ($1.25 and $2 a day, both measured at purchasing power parity).

[3]   The "working poor" are defined as people who are employed, but do not earn sufficient income to meet the basic necessities of life.

Employment growth (31%) fell short of labor force growth (33%) during 1995–2008. As Figure 4.7 suggests, the demographic structure of Indonesia's population is changing, with the working age population increasing in recent years. This is putting further pressure on the economy to generate employment opportunities. The gap between the labor force and employment growth is most pronounced among the youth. The labor force aged 15–24 grew by about 13% (or by 2.4 million) between 1991 and 2008, while employment opportunities for it hardly expanded (Figure 4.8). Without unemployment insurance and other effective social security schemes, most poor people cannot afford a protracted spell of unemployment. In fact, unemployment rates tend to be higher among educated people, as people who can afford higher education are more likely to be able to support themselves during a job search (Table 4.3) than are people with less education. The high incidence of the working poor, therefore, does not necessarily stem from open unemployment.[4] The issue has more to do with the quality of jobs being created in recent years. For example, about 30% of the labor force was estimated to be underemployed in 2009 (Figure 4.9). The share of informal employment also remained high despite the recent economic growth: the share was 63.2% in August 2004 and 61.3% in August 2008. The share increased to 62.1% in February 2009, largely due to the impact of the global economic crisis.

Figure 4.7: Population by Age Groups

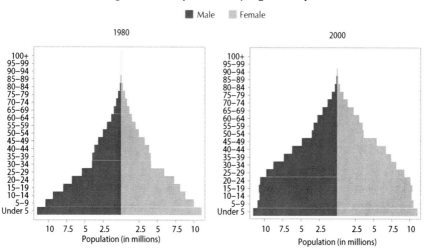

Source: US Census Bureau, accessed 25 March 2010.

---

4   "Open unemployment" refers to unemployment captured by official labor statistics. The term is often used to distinguish official unemployment from discouraged unemployment and other forms of underutilized labor.

Figure 4.8: Population, Labor Force, and Employment Growth Trends (1991=100)

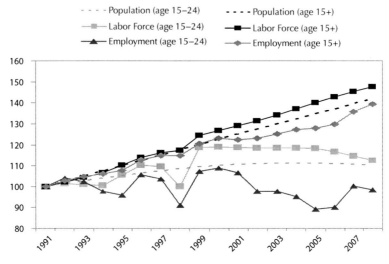

Source: ILO (2009).

Figure 4.9: Share of the Poor Population in Urban and Rural Areas (1976–2009, %)

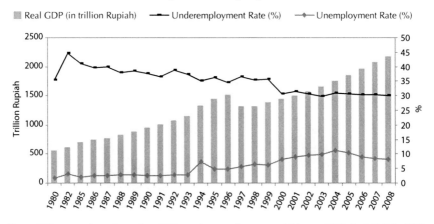

Notes: GDP = gross domestic product. 2009 employment data are as of February 2009. Real GDP for 2008 and 2009 are provisional data. Some changes in the definition of unemployment took place in 1994 and 2001 (see Suryadarma et al. 2006). There was also a change in the definition of economically active age group (i.e., labor force) from population aged 10+ to aged 15+ at the beginning of 1998. While unemployment rates are usually calculated using the annual National Labor Force Survey (Sakernas), the Inter-Census Population Survey (Supas) data were used for the year 1995 as Sakernas was not conducted in that year. Underemployed is defined as an employed person working less than 35 hours a week.
Sources: BPS (various years). For 2009, BPS (2009b).

Table 4.3: Unemployment and Poverty Rates by Educational Attainment (2005, %)

Educational Attainment	Unemployment Rate	Poverty Incidence
Less than Primary	5.5	19.6
Primary	7.0	13.8
Junior Secondary	14.1	9.3
Senior Secondary	19.9	4.4
Tertiary	11.9	0.4

Source: Dhanani, Islam, and Chowdhury (2009).

Meager earnings in the informal economy, especially casual labor in agriculture, leave the working poor vulnerable to shocks (Dhanani, Islam, and Chowdhury 2009). Figure 4.10 confirms this point: the incidence of the working poor is relatively high among casual, unpaid, and own-account workers.[5] According to the labor force survey, the hourly wage of casual workers in the nonagriculture sector was about 59% of employees' wages in 2008.[6] The hourly wage gap was even wider between casual workers in the agriculture sector and employees—the average wage of the former was only about 46% of that of the latter. Increasing decent and productive employment as well as improving the productivity of vulnerable workers is thus a key to reducing poverty.

Figure 4.10: Incidence of Working Poor by Employment Status (2007, %)

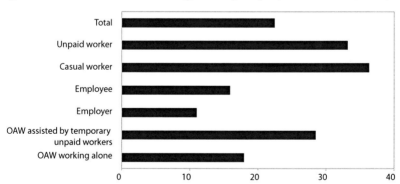

Note: Poverty is measured on a $1.25 per day poverty line. OAW = own-account worker.
Source: Calculations based on BPS.

---

[5] "Own-account workers" are those who work alone or with one or more partners and do not have employees working for them (ILO, International Classification).

[6] "Employees" are all workers who work for an employer and receive remuneration (ILO, International Classification).

Despite a decade of economic expansion, wage employment failed to recover to the level prior to the 1997 AFC. The share of wage employment stood at about 36% in 1997 and declined to 34% in 2007. The majority of workers are own-account and contributing family workers,[7] which constitute a pool of vulnerable workers. The share of vulnerable employment[8] actually went up from 62.8% in 1997 to 63.1% in 2007. The annual growth rate of casual employment is alarming—8.4% (2002–2008 average). The share of casual workers, who are most likely to be part of the working poor, thus increased in total employment—from 8.8% in 2002 to 11.0% in 2008, while that of wage employees remained more or less stable during the same period (Figure 4.11). This trend could undermine Indonesia's efforts to meet the Millennium Development Goal of halving poverty by 2015.

Figure 4.11: Shares in Total Employment by Employment Status (%)

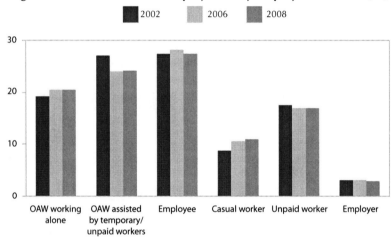

OAW = own-account worker.
Source: Calculations based on BPS, Sakernas.

While Indonesia managed to reduce poverty below the pre-crisis level, that more than 70% of workers live below the $2 poverty line merits further effort to provide them with more productive employment opportunities. A dense distribution of workers earning within the narrow range of $1.25–$2 per day implies that they are highly vulnerable to shocks such as the recent global economic crisis, job loss, injury, or sickness. The discussions in this section suggest that the limited availability of productive and decent

---

[7]   "Contributing family workers" are unpaid family members or relatives engaging in a family business (ILO, International Classification).

[8]   "Vulnerable employment" here is the sum of own-account and contributing family workers.

employment opportunities is a constraint to enhancing the inclusiveness of growth and to reducing poverty and vulnerability. Weak generation of productive and decent employment is, at least partly, a consequence of the slowdown in labor-intensive manufacturing that used to absorb a large number of low- and semi-skilled workers. The pattern of growth has changed since the 1997 Asian financial crisis. Labor-intensive manufacturing lost competitiveness to low-cost producers in the region—the People's Republic of China, India, and Viet Nam—and investment was insufficient. Indonesia has not successfully shifted from labor-intensive manufacturing to high value-adding production (Islam and Chowdhury 2009), as discussed in Chapter 3.

4.3. Access to Opportunities

Even if the economy succeeds in creating sufficient levels of decent and productive jobs, not everyone may benefit if access to the jobs is unequal. In Indonesia, job creation is concentrated in several locations. Rural areas in general lack decent and productive employment opportunities, and people in such areas tend to engage in agriculture or are employed in the informal economy. Figure 4.12 shows that a higher percentage of people are engaged in the informal economy in rural areas (about 76%) than in urban areas (about 42%). Variation is also significant at the provincial level (Figure 4.13). About 83% of people in East Nusa Tenggara work in the informal economy, but the corresponding figure is only 26% in Jakarta. Underemployment rates are also higher in rural areas than in urban areas (Figure 4.12).

Unless workers in rural areas migrate in search of employment opportunities, they are generally less capable than urban residents of earning enough to live above the poverty line. In fact, about 82% of the working poor are in rural areas and about 66% of them are engaged in agriculture.[9] In addition, the migration rate in rural areas, particularly in the Maluku, Papua, and Nusa Tenggara region (Figure 4.14) where the informal employment rate tends to be high, is greater than in urban areas. Both informal employment and underemployment rates vary by the level of education. Figure 4.12 shows that people with primary education or less are more likely to be engaged in the informal economy and/or be underemployed than people who have achieved higher levels of education. And women are more likely to be underemployed than men. The relatively high unemployment rate among the youth is another worrying issue.

---

[9] Calculations by the International Labour Organization (ILO) based on data for 2007 from BPS, Susenas.

Figure 4.12: Unemployment, Underemployment, and Informal Employment Rates (2009, %)

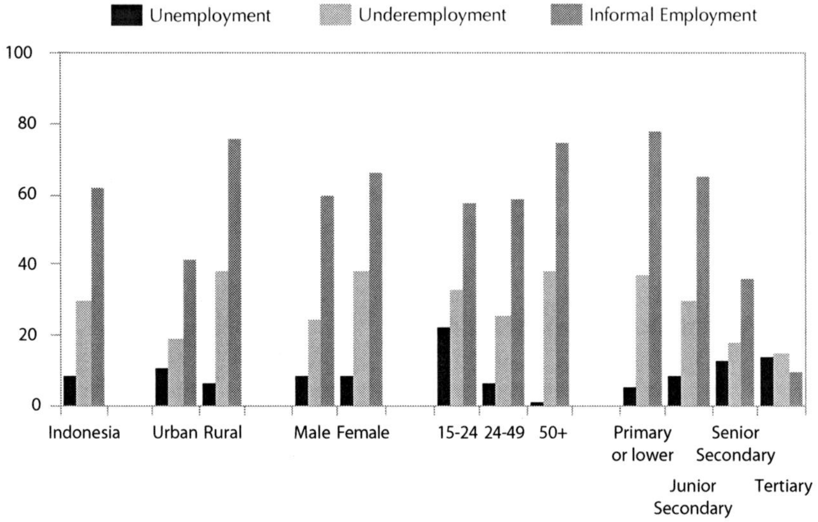

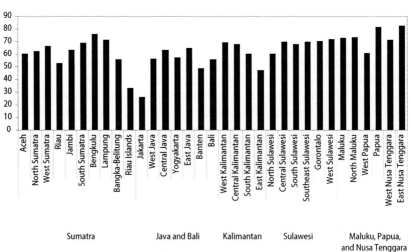

Source: BPS (2009a).

Figure 4.13: Informal Employment Rates (2009, %)

Source: BPS (2009a).

Figure 4.14: Percentage of Households with Migrants (2007, %)

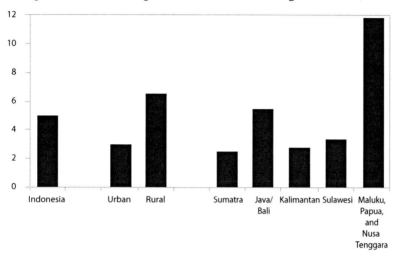

Note: The figure shows the percentage of households with members or former members who are migrants abroad.
Source: Calculations based on BPS.

The evidence presented so far is symptomatic of inequitable access to opportunities. According to the conceptual framework described in Chapter 1, causes that may underlie unequal access to opportunities are (1) weak human capabilities, and (2) uneven playing fields.

4.3.1. Human Capabilities

One reason for the unequal access to opportunities is that some groups of people have weaker human capabilities than others, partly due to unequal access to education, health, and/or other social services such as clean water and sanitation.

4.3.1.1. Education

Links with Employment. Despite the progress in school enrollment, access to secondary and vocational education remains unequal and therefore is a binding constraint to reducing poverty and inequality. One of the most important components of human capabilities is education. Because education is positively linked to access to better employment opportunities (e.g., Card 1999), educational attainment is one of the main vehicles for reducing poverty and enhancing economic growth. Empirical studies show that higher educational attainment (of heads and other members of households) is associated with greater household consumption, and that household welfare in Indonesia is generally correlated with higher levels of education (World Bank 2006c).

In Indonesia, basic education consists of 6 years of primary and 3 years of junior secondary school. After completing junior secondary education, students can choose between general and vocational senior secondary school. The former is the traditional route to academic tertiary education (e.g., universities, academies, or other institutions), while the latter has been the path to vocational tertiary education (e.g., polytechnics or further technical training). Of people who have completed junior secondary education, about 51% go to general secondary schools and about 34% to vocational schools (Riddell 2010). One of the main channels through which education affects a household's welfare is employment. Figure 4.15, for example, illustrates that people who have completed senior secondary education or higher are less likely to be underemployed or in the informal economy than are workers in general. The importance of completing higher levels of education is also supported by a cost-benefit analysis that finds increasing returns to higher levels of education. The rates of social returns[10] to people with junior and senior secondary school levels are estimated to be about 25% and 28%, respectively, while the rate of returns to primary education is low at about 4% (Arze del Granado et al. 2007). The relatively low returns to primary education underline the oversupply of low-skilled workers in Indonesia. Similarly, people who are unemployed are more likely to be discouraged from actively seeking work if they have a lower education background. Of those who had not completed primary education, about 64% were discouraged and about 17% were looking for work, while among those who had completed junior secondary schooling only about 33% were discouraged and 58% were looking for work (MONE 2007).Furthermore, Figure 4.16 illustrates that the wage level varies significantly by educational attainment. The figure shows a relatively large wage gap, especially between employees with junior secondary and those with senior secondary as well as between senior secondary and tertiary education.

---

[10]   Estimates of the returns to education investments are defined as the discount rates that equate a stream of education benefits to a stream of costs for providing education, at different levels, at a given point in time. Education benefits were computed based on wage differentials—additional average earnings from those of the same age group at a previous level of education (see Arze del Granado et al. [2007] for details).

Figure 4.15: Education Level by Employment Status (2009, %)

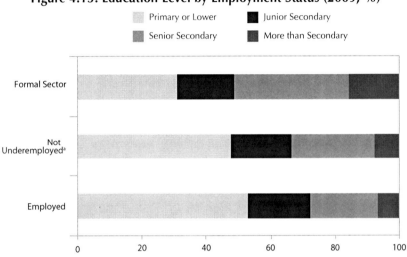

ᵃWorking for 35+ hours per week.
Source: BPS (2009a).

Figure 4.16: Average Wages per Month by Educational Attainment (2009, '000 Rp)

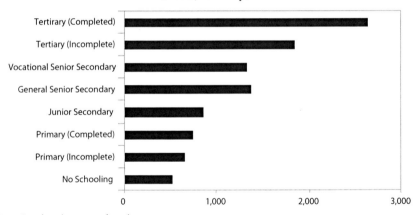

Note: Based on the wages of employees.
Source: BPS (2009a).

The observations noted so far clearly illustrate that people with education beyond the primary level have better access to productive and decent employment opportunities. The education level achieved across age cohorts in Indonesia shows an upward trend over time: only about 20% of people 50 or older completed junior secondary education or higher, while about 70% of those 20–24 did so.[11] However, the distribution of educational attainment across the country and across different expenditure quintiles still shows considerable inequality in access to education—people residing in rural areas and relatively poor people tend to receive less education. The average education level of women is also lower than that of men (Figure 4.17), though the disparity is expected to decrease over time, given the current insignificant gender gap in school enrollment rates (Figures 4.18 and 4.19).

Figure 4.17: Educational Attainment Among People Aged 15+ (2007, %)

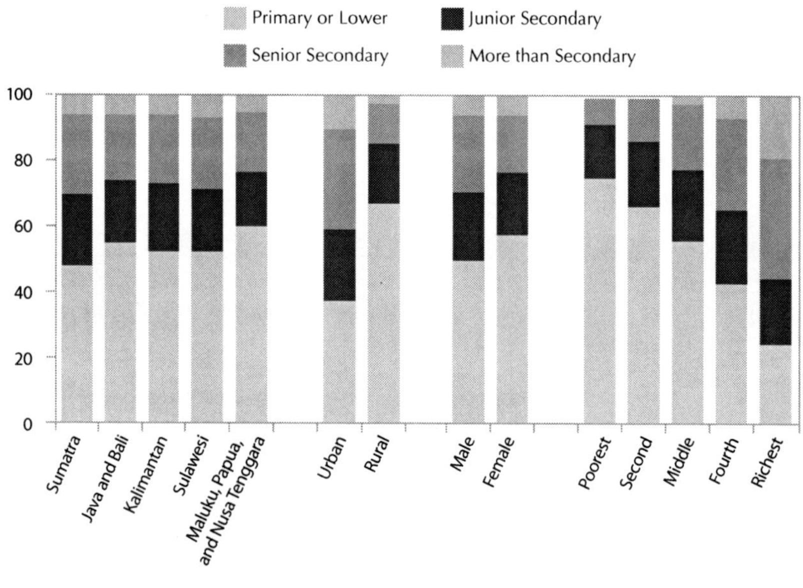

Source: Calculations based on BPS.

Enrollment Rates and Access. School enrollment rates improved at the primary and secondary levels during 1996–2007. The primary school enrollment rate is now uniformly high across the country. In contrast, only about 67% and 45% of children are enrolled in junior and senior secondary school, respectively. This is disappointing, especially given that National Education System Law No. 20 of 2003 proclaims that every child aged 7–15 must attend basic education. Moreover, there is a striking discrepancy in enrollment rates across the country, particularly for senior secondary education. The differences are especially significant between urban and rural children and among expenditure quintiles. For example, only 22% of

---

[11]   Calculations based on data for 2007 from BPS, Susenas.

Figure 4.18: Net School Enrollment Rates for Junior Secondary (%)

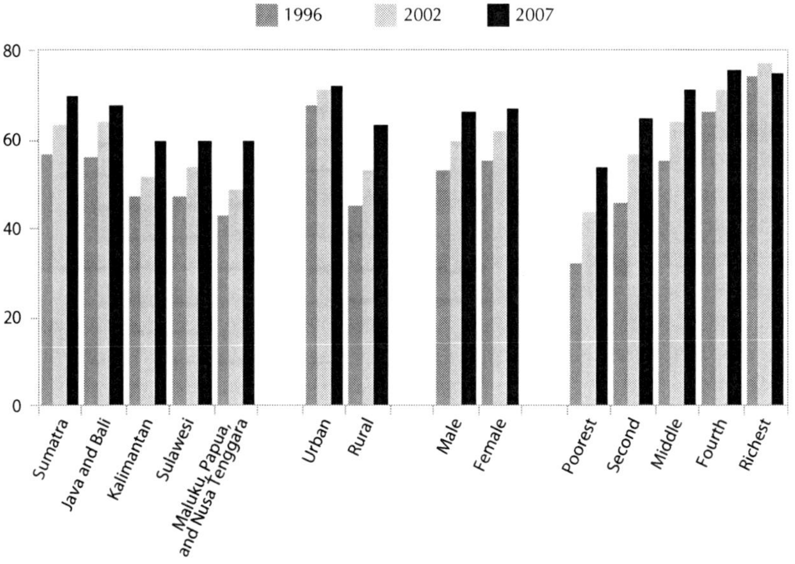

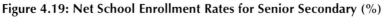

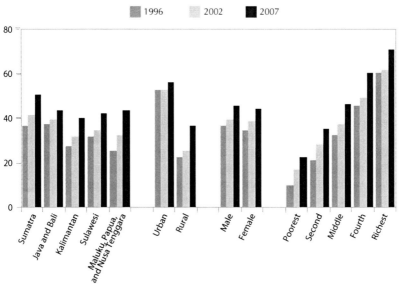

Source: Calculations based on BPS.

Figure 4.19: Net School Enrollment Rates for Senior Secondary (%)

Source: Calculations based on BPS.

children in the poorest expenditure quintile are enrolled in senior secondary school, versus about 70% of children in the richest quintile (Figure 4.19).

Variations in access to education are also observed between and within provinces. Figures 4.20, 4.21, and 4.22 show the provincial average net enrollments (middle points) as well as the minimum (lower points) and maximum (higher points) net enrollment rates at the district level for each province for primary, junior secondary, and senior secondary education. The figures highlight nontrivial variations within provinces. Even for primary education, where Indonesia has achieved high enrollment rates, the net enrollment rate for Papua remains low, at about 81%, compared with the rest of the country, and the lowest rate among districts within Papua is only 51%. The disparity is even more striking for junior secondary education. Papua, again, has the lowest net enrollment rate in the country, about 49%, and the variation within the province is the greatest. Moreover, while East Java has a relatively high provincial average net enrollment rate (about 69%), the rate in its Sampang District, at about 40%, is lower than Papua's provincial average (about 49%).

Figure 4.20: District-Level Net Enrollment Rates: Primary (2007, %)

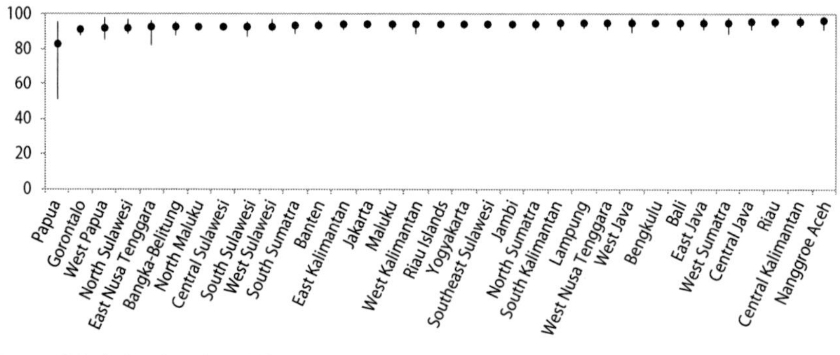

Source: Calculations based on BPS.

Quality. Quality is also an issue in Indonesia's education system. Even if school enrollment rates reach the universal level, this may not contribute to reducing poverty and inequality if the quality of education is poor, because it is likely to affect students' employability and potential earnings, as discussed in Chapters 3, 8, and 9. Some researchers believe that the quality of education in Indonesia needs to be improved (Arze del Granado et al. 2007). The problem of low learning achievement was also

Figure 4.21: District-Level Net Enrollment Rates: Junior Secondary (2007, %)

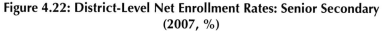

Source: Calculations based on BPS.

Figure 4.22: District-Level Net Enrollment Rates: Senior Secondary (2007, %)

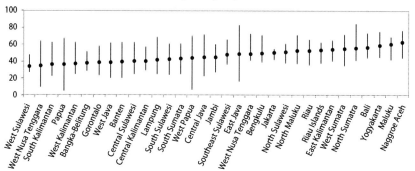

Source: Calculations based on BPS.

found in the Governance and Decentralization Survey (GDS) 2.[12] One of the main problems of education services noted by household respondents was student learning achievements—29% of households thought this needs to be improved; followed by the condition of school buildings and facilities, at 27%; teachers' attention to their students, at 17%; and affordability of the education services, at 8% (Widyanti and Suryahadi 2008).

Improving the quality of teachers is also a challenge in Indonesia. Although National Education Minister Regulation No. 19 of 2005 requires teachers to

---

[12]   The GDS is one of the initiatives that aim to monitor and evaluate the implementation of the governance and decentralization policy in Indonesia. The GDS 2 was undertaken from April to July 2006 in 133 districts. It is an integrated survey of households, public healthcare facilities, private health practitioners, hamlet heads, and district- and village-level officials (Widyanti and Suryahadi 2008).

have a bachelor's degree, teachers at the primary level often fail to fulfill this requirement (World Bank 2009). The Ministry of National Education (2005) notes that only about 55% of teachers at the primary and 73% at the junior secondary levels meet the ministry's minimum qualifications. Arze del Granado et al. (2007) show that, compared with wages of other workers with similar education levels, teachers with relatively low levels of education are overpaid and those with higher levels tend to be underpaid. At the macro level, teachers in Indonesia are significantly underpaid at all levels of schooling compared with teachers in neighboring countries (Jalal et al. 2009). The salary structure provides limited incentives for teachers to improve their academic qualifications; as a result, the quality of education continues to deteriorate. While issues pertaining to the incentives are well known, the significant resources needed to remedy the problem will require substantial incremental budgetary outlays. Law No. 14 of 2005 with National Education Minister Regulation No. 18 of 2007 on the Certification of Practicing Teachers, introducing a new teacher certification requirement that increases their remuneration, is, nevertheless, a welcome step in the right direction.

Senior Secondary and Vocational Education. Another issue related to Indonesia's education is the provision of vocational education. Vocational secondary schools are under the Directorate of Technical and Vocational Education in the Ministry of National Education. In addition, other ministries, such as the Ministry of Manpower and Transmigration and the Ministry of Industry, provide vocational training centers.

While the senior secondary school enrollment rates have increased steadily in recent years, the increase is largely due to the growth in the number of students enrolled in general senior secondary schools (Chen 2009). However, to address high unemployment rates among the educated youth, in 2006 the Ministry of National Education drafted a strategic plan to reverse this trend and increase the number of vocational senior secondary school graduates (MONE 2006).[13] The rationale was that the unemployment rate of vocational school graduates was lower than that of general school graduates.

Empirical evidence across the world on the impact of vocational education on labor market outcomes is mixed.[14] The recent empirical assessments of the effect of vocational education on labor market outcomes, based on the longitudinal household survey data, also do not seem to support the government's strategy (Chen 2009, Newhouse and Suryadarma 2009). Chen finds that attendance at vocational secondary schools results in neither

---

[13]   However, the government will adopt a more balanced approach toward general and vocational senior secondary education (MONE 2010).

[14]   See Newhouse and Suryadarma (2009) for their literature review.

market advantage nor disadvantage in terms of employment opportunities and/or earnings premium. Moreover, Newhouse and Suryadarma find that the returns[15] to public vocational schooling for men have decreased in recent years, and male vocational graduates now face a relatively large wage penalty. Although they cannot directly explore the underlying causes behind this decline, Newhouse and Suryadarma suggest that the declining relevance of technical and industrial skills in an increasingly service-oriented Indonesian economy at least partly explains the declining returns to public vocational education. Nevertheless, the findings of the Newhouse and Suryadarma analysis indicate that vocational schools have a favorable equity effect by improving the opportunity for individuals from disadvantaged socioeconomic backgrounds to be competitive on the job market.

While the government has been enhancing the relevance of vocational education to the needs of businesses in recent years (MONE 2010), the provision of technical and vocational education and training can still be improved. Challenges include improving the effectiveness of the curricula, increasing the number of qualified training instructors, improving training equipment, and enhancing the links between training providers and the private sector to improve the performance of vocational school graduates in the labor market. For example, some public sector training institutions, particularly those under district ownership, are generally in poor condition and severely underused. In addition, some public supervision or control over private sector training providers may be required to improve the quality and relevance of the training they offer.

Indonesia has recently adopted a competency-based training (CBT) system under Regulation No. 31 of 2006 on the National Skills Training System. CBT helps to link training and certification to placement, as the competencies are based on market demand and designed to fit job requirements. The CBT system is supposed to be applied uniformly in the vocational education and training sectors. A speedy implementation of the CBT system remains a challenge. Some training providers face difficulties adopting the system due to the lack of training and management support. In addition, not all training courses are designed to meet local skills demand, and many courses need to be formally assessed.

Financial Burden. Root causes of unequal access to education lie on both the demand and supply sides. On the demand side, financial burden is an issue. Table 4.4 lists the main reasons for school-age children not attending school or dropping out. Financial impediments are by far the main reason—about 57% of school-age children who never went to school or who dropped out gave financial reasons. Not surprisingly, poorer households

---

[15]   The returns are measured in terms of labor market outcomes, including labor force participation, unemployment conditional on participation, formal sector work, and hourly wages (Newhouse and Suryadarma 2009).

are more likely to struggle to secure financial means to send their children to school.

Table 4.4: Reasons for Never Having Attended School or Dropping Out of School (2007, %)

	Financial Reason	Currently Employed	Married / Manages Household	School Is Too Far	Have Enough Education
Indonesia	57.2	7.3	2.5	2.7	5.3
Urban	56.9	9.2	1.7	0.6	6.1
Rural	57.3	6.5	2.8	3.7	4.9
Sumatra	55.4	6.1	1.4	2.8	5.6
Java and Bali	61.2	7.8	2.8	1.6	5.8
Kalimantan	48.9	11.2	2.9	6.6	5.3
Sulawesi	49.8	6.4	2.9	4.6	3.3
Maluku, Papua, and Nusa Tenggara	45.8	5.1	1.9	5.8	3.2
Male	56.3	8.4	0.2	2.6	5.0
Female	58.0	6.2	5.0	2.8	5.6
Expenditure Quintile					
Poorest	60.9	6.2	1.8	3.3	3.9
Second	58.0	7.0	2.3	2.4	5.7
Third	53.9	7.5	3.4	2.4	7.0
Fourth	47.7	10.2	4.2	1.9	7.8
Richest	45.5	15.6	2.4	1.3	5.7

Source: Calculations based on BPS.

Furthermore, the financial burden of secondary schooling seems to be greater than that incurred for primary education (Table 4.5). While about 36% of primary school age children never went to school or dropped out due to financial difficulties, almost 60% of secondary school age children gave financial reasons for not attending school. Suryadarma, Suryahadi, and Sumarto (2006) indeed find that household welfare level is a significant determinant of junior secondary school enrollment in Indonesia. They also find that the availability of local employment opportunities negatively impacts children's continuation to junior secondary school. Paqueo and Sparrow (2006) obtained similar findings. While a similar percentage of urban and rural students cite financial reasons for not attending school, a relatively large share of female children are out of primary and junior secondary school due to financial constraints (Table 4.5).

Table 4.5: Percentage of School-Age Children Who Gave Financial Reasons for Not Attending School, by Education Level (2007, %)

	Primary (7–12)	Junior Secondary (13–15)	Senior Secondary (16–18)
Indonesia	35.8	59.1	59.0
Urban	36.8	58.7	58.1
Rural	35.4	59.3	59.4
Male	34.1	56.6	59.1
Female	38.0	61.9	58.8
Poor	38.4	64.1	66.0
Nonpoor	33.3	56.6	56.9

Source: Calculations based on BPS.

To increase the poor's transition rate from primary to junior secondary education, financial constraints should be eased by further subsidizing junior secondary schooling and/or providing targeted transfers in the form of scholarships or conditional cash transfers to the poor. Conditional cash transfers, in particular, can be used to compensate households for the opportunity cost of schooling (Box 4.1).

Box 4.1: Education, Employment, and Poverty

Education is a key to access productive employment and earn one's way out of poverty. Average wages by educational attainment clearly depict a high return to education in Indonesia as elsewhere. Too many children prematurely withdraw from school and forego opportunities to lift themselves and their future family members out of poverty. Despite the progress in school enrollment rates and the entitlement to education, almost one in five Indonesian children is out of school. The single most important reason is the financial burden faced by families (see Tables 4.4 and 4.5).

Although many children work in Indonesia, comprehensible and reliable data on their numbers and socioeconomic characteristics were missing. In response, the International Labour Organization, in collaboration with Statistics Indonesia (Badan Pusat Statistik), carried out the first Indonesia Child Labour Survey in 2009. The survey found that 4.1 million children aged 5–17, or 6.9% of the total of about 58.8 million, were working children, with 1.8 million classified as "child labor"—i.e., defined for this survey as working children aged 5–12,

continued on next page

children 13–14 who had worked more than 15 hours a week, or 15–17 year-olds who had worked more than 40 hours a week.

Of the total, 41.2% (24.3 million children) were engaged in housekeeping. Surprisingly, 6.7 million children aged 5–17 (or 11.4% of total) were not in school or working. Working children worked on average 25.7 hours per week. The average working hours for those categorized as child labor was significantly longer, at 35.1 hours per week. About 20.7% of working children worked more than 40 hours per week, risking their sound physical and mental development.

The Millennium Development Goals recognize productive employment and decent work as one of the most effective means of reducing poverty. Thus, reducing the number of children who drop out of school prematurely, who work excessive hours, and who are "idle," as well as encouraging and enabling them to pursue education, help reduce poverty. In addition, education helps people avoid or emerge from the vicious intergenerational transmission of poverty.

Source: ILO (2010).

Table 4.6 reports the distribution of education costs across items for primary, junior secondary, and senior secondary school. The table shows relatively large shares of nonfee costs. For secondary schooling, transport actually has the highest share in total education costs. This implies that some households find that schools are too far and/or the cost of transport is too high to send their children to school. Indeed, some provinces, such as Papua, West Kalimantan, and West Sulawesi, have some of the lowest net enrollment rates for junior secondary schooling in the country, while their average travel times taken to go to school are also some of the country's longest. Thus, unequal access to education is not only due to affordability (i.e., the demand side), but also to some supply-side factors.

Public Expenditure. On the supply side, public expenditure on education has trended upward during the last decade except in 2004 (Table 4.7).[16] The increase is due partly to the reallocation of public resources from fuel subsidies to education spending through such programs as the School Operational Assistance Program (Bantuan Operasional Sekolah [BOS]) and conditional cash transfers (World Bank 2009). Thanks to the recent increase, Indonesia's public expenditure has become more comparable to that of other countries in the region (Figure 4.23). However, the largest

---

[16]   The decline in public expenditure on education in 2004 was caused by low budget execution and a crowding-out effect in most social sectors due to increasing fuel subsidies (World Bank 2009).

Table 4.6: Distribution of Education Costs by Education Level (2006, %)

Type of Cost	Primary	Junior Secondary	Senior Secondary
School Fee	7.79	13.05	23.29
Parent Teacher Association Fee	2.72	4.12	6.06
Practical Fee	1.13	1.34	2.57
Student Organization Fee	0.32	0.83	1.12
Examination Fee	0.80	1.25	1.96
Study Material	3.65	3.40	2.88
Uniforms	21.00	14.51	8.42
Textbooks	19.68	15.41	11.53
Stationery	13.44	9.11	5.87
Transport	9.60	21.08	24.35
Other Course/ Training Fee	2.08	2.62	2.31
Other	17.79	13.29	9.65
Total	100.00	100.00	100.00

Source: BPS Susenas Modul Tahun 2006 cited in BPS (2006).

share of national education spending is allocated to the primary level—in 2005, primary education accounted for 47% of total education spending, while junior secondary, senior secondary, and tertiary education received only 27%, 15%, and 12%, respectively (Arze del Granado et al. 2007).

Table 4.7: National Public Expenditure on Education (2001–2008)

Year	2006 Prices (Rp Trillion)	Share of Total National Expenditure (%)	Share of GDP (%)
2001	63.4	11.0	2.8
2002	70.5	14.2	2.7
2003	83.7	14.7	3.1
2004	76.7	13.0	2.7
2005	82.8	13.9	2.6
2006	102.5	15.3	3.1
2007[a]	111.3	15.4	3.0
2008[b]	116.4	13.6	3.0

[a] Estimated subnational budget. [b] Central government budget and estimated subnational budget.
GDP = gross domestic product.
Source: World Bank (2009).

Figure 4.23: Public Expenditure on Education for Selected Countries (% of GDP)

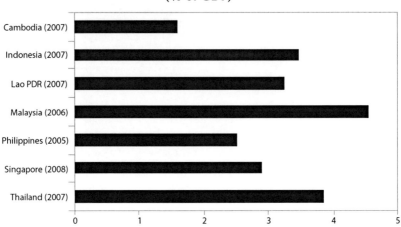

Lao PDR = Lao People's Democratic Republic.
Source: World Bank, WDI, accessed 5 October 2009.

With decentralization, Indonesia has devolved responsibilities for education from the central government to subnational governments. In 2006, for example, about 56% of education expenditure was spent at the subnational level, mostly by district governments (51%) rather than provincial governments (5%). Nevertheless, district government spending on education comprises largely nondiscretionary routine expenditures (about 81% in 2006), while the majority of the development budget is still spent by the central government.[17] Because of the central government's continued dominance in education investments, local governments actually have little discretion in managing funds and shaping the key education sector decisions, even though they are responsible for running, building, and rehabilitating schools. For public spending to be translated into improved performance, the discretion of district governments must be increased and their financial management capacity improved (World Bank 2009).

Another important issue is the allocation of public resources in the education sector. The bulk of routine expenditures at the subnational level is currently allocated to cover the wage bill (about 96% in 2006), which is still set by the central government, with merely 3% for expenditures on goods

---

[17]   However, since 2005, routine and development budget allocations are no longer separated.

and 0.4% for operation and maintenance (World Bank 2009).[18] This pattern needs to be remedied to achieve more efficient and effective use of public spending on education.

Other supply-side issues include the unequal distribution of teachers and, to a lesser extent, schools across the country. As Indonesia has achieved high enrollment rates for primary education, the availability of schools may not be a major concern at the primary level. However, the number of junior and senior secondary schools is much lower—on average, there are five primary schools but only about two junior secondary schools and one senior secondary school per 1,000 school-age children.[19] As a result, secondary schools are still not easily accessible to many school-age children. This partly explains why transport has the highest share in costs of secondary education (Table 4.6). To enhance the transition rate from primary to junior secondary schooling, the availability of schools should be increased in undersupplied areas. The government has recently introduced the One-Roof System (Program Sekolah Satu Atap) in remote areas where the students are few and scattered. The system integrates primary and junior secondary education in one facility and under one management in order to improve access to basic education in underserved areas and to encourage students to move on to junior secondary education.

Distribution of Teachers and Schools. The distribution of teachers across the country is a more problematic issue. In Indonesia, student–teacher ratios are low even by international standards. Comparable ratios for the Asia and Pacific countries are about 31:1 for primary and 25:1 for junior secondary schooling, while Indonesia's ratios are 20:1 and 14:1. However, given the relatively large share of part-time teachers and high absenteeism, class sizes are considerably larger, with 25 students per class at the primary and 37 at the junior secondary levels (Arze del Granado et al. 2007). In addition, among the eight developing countries that participated in surveys on teacher absenteeism, Indonesia ranked third, after Uganda and India, with a 19% absence rate (Usman, Akhmadi, and Suryadarma 2004).

---

18   Many factors are responsible for the large share of teachers' salaries in routine expenditures. First, the perception of an undersupply of teachers in Indonesia has led to increasing their numbers. Based on the teacher employment and deployment survey conducted by the World Bank in 2005, 74 of 276 primary schools that claim to have too few teachers actually show an oversupply. Second, district governments inherited many civil servant teachers who were allocated to schools by the central government prior to decentralization. Finally, because civil servant teachers are employed under the national civil service regulation, district governments have little flexibility in employing and deploying them (World Bank 2009).

19   Calculations are based on the following data sources: the number of schools comes from Departemen Pendidikan Nasional, 2005/2006, cited in the 2008 version of BPS (various years); and the number of school-age children in 2006 is estimated based on BPS, Susenas.

Teacher absenteeism tends to be higher in remote areas. This is mainly because teachers in remote areas have to deal with complex issues, including limited facilities within the schools, difficulties in accessing schools, lack of transport facilities, and high transport costs (SMERU 2010).

Furthermore, teachers are unequally distributed in Indonesia—while some areas have an oversupply of teachers, they are in short supply in remote areas (Figure 4.24). The oversupply of teachers is a problem, as the share of teachers' salaries in routine expenditures is large. And the shortage of teachers is an equally critical issue, particularly in remote areas where the teacher's role is very important, given the limited school facilities and infrastructure (SMERU 2010).

Figure 4.24: Percentage of Primary Schools with Over- and Undersupply of Teachers (2005, %)

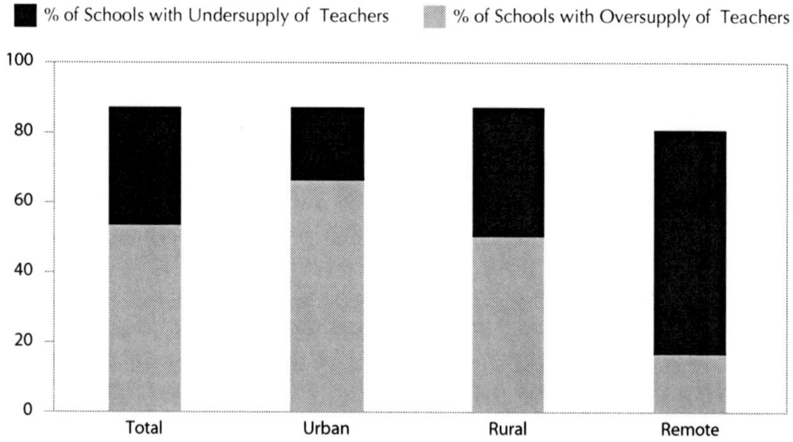

Source: Arze del Granado et al. (2007).

To ensure more equal allocation, incentive schemes are needed for teachers to work in undersupplied areas. The government's new policy of providing financial incentives for teachers working in remote areas, under Law No.14 of 2005 on Teachers and Lecturers, is a first step in the right direction (World Bank 2007). This law was elaborated in various regulations, including National Education Minister Regulation No. 32 of 2007 on Allowances for Teachers in Remote Areas, aiming to motivate teachers to continue teaching in remote areas where they were already working.

In addition, the condition of education infrastructure remains poor in Indonesia. In 2009, the Ministry of National Education classified about 18% of Indonesia's primary school classrooms as heavily damaged and 23% as moderately damaged. The conditions are better at the junior secondary school levels, with 11% and 23% of classrooms classified as heavily and moderately damaged, respectively (MONE 2010). The high ratio of damaged classrooms is not surprising, given the district governments' limited control over development expenditures and the small allocation of public resources for operation and maintenance at the district level. Moreover, essential learning materials, such as textbooks, are not always available.

The BOS program introduced in 2005, through which the central government grants resources directly to primary and junior secondary schools, has enhanced the quality of education, as the majority of the BOS funds have been used for acquiring materials and maintaining school facilities (World Bank 2009). According to the GDS 2, school principals report that the BOS program has had a significant positive impact, particularly on the quality of teaching, availability of books and teaching equipment, quality of school infrastructure, and poor students' access to school (Widyanti and Suryahadi 2008). However, the World Bank (2009) noted that the BOS allocation for assisting poor students is relatively low. In addition, school committee oversight of the BOS allocations needs to be strengthened, and there is considerable room for further involvement of school committees.

Some supply-side factors that are responsible for unequal access to education also affect the quality of education. The factors include the level of teacher qualification, the structure of teacher compensation, teacher absenteeism, classroom quality, and class size (Arze del Granado et al. 2007). Suryadarma et al. (2004) found in their empirical analysis that the student–teacher ratio, quality of school facilities, and teacher absence rate are among the significant determinants of student performance in mathematics and dictation tests among fourth grade children.

4.3.1.2. Health

Health may not be a critical constraint to accessing economic opportunities at present, but Indonesia still lags behind its neighboring countries in some health outcomes, and great disparities exist across the country and socioeconomic groups. Health is also a key component of human capabilities. It is an important determinant of productivity—poor health can adversely affect labor productivity and earnings. It can also impose a financial burden on households and make them vulnerable to poverty. Loss of income due to health-related factors is reported more frequently than loss of income from unemployment (World Bank 2006c).

Indonesia has made progress in improving population health outcomes in terms of life expectancy, maternal and infant mortality rates, and nutritional status, among other things (Bappenas 2010). For example, Table 4.8 presents estimates of infant and child mortality from three demographic and health surveys covering 5-year periods. The table shows that both infant and child mortality rates have declined over time in response to better healthcare and hygiene. Nevertheless, Indonesia still needs to catch up with other neighboring countries (Table 4.9).

Table 4.8: Infant and Child Mortality Rates (Per 1,000 live births)

Period	Infant Mortality Rates	Child Mortality Rates
1993–1997	53	16
1998–2002	44	15
2003–2007	34	10

Source: BPS and Macro International (2008).

Table 4.9: Health Outcomes for Selected Southeast Asian Countries (2007)

Country	Life Expectancy at Birth (years)	Infant Mortality Rate (per 1,000 live births)	Maternal Mortality Rate (per 100,000 live births)
Cambodia	61	70	540
Indonesia	70	34	228
Malaysia	72	10	62
Philippines	71	23	230
Singapore	81	2	14
Thailand	70	6	110
Viet Nam	72	13	150

Note: In case of Indonesia, the figure for life expectancy at birth is for 2009.
Sources: For Indonesia, Bappenas (2010); for other countries, WHO (2009).

Indonesia's achievements in healthcare at the national level have been notable, but significant disparities in health outcomes persist between geographical regions and socioeconomic groups.

Infant mortality rates, for example, vary significantly across provinces (Figure 4.25). While Yogyakarta has an infant morality rate of 19 per 1,000 live births, West Sulawesi's rate is significantly higher—74 per 1,000 live births. The main diseases leading to mortality in children include malaria, pneumonia, diarrhea, and measles (Bappenas 2010).

The prevalence of infectious disease varies significantly across the country. The incidence of malaria, as indicated by the annual parasite index, for example, varies between 0 and about 28 per 1,000 people (Figure 4.26). The index tends to be high in the eastern part of Indonesia, with West Papua being the highest (27.7), followed by East Nusa Tenggara (15.6), and Papua (9.9). Diarrhea is the second leading cause of infant mortality and the fifth

Figure 4.25: Infant Mortality Rates by Province (per 1,000 live births)

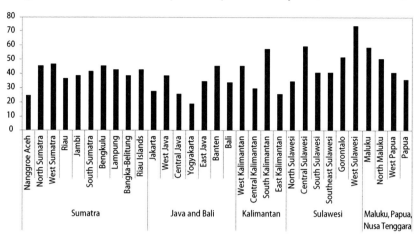

Note: Infant mortality rates are for the 10-year period preceding the survey (i.e., 1998–2007).
Source: BPS and Macro International (2008).

Figure 4.26: Annual Parasite Index (2009, per 1,000 people)

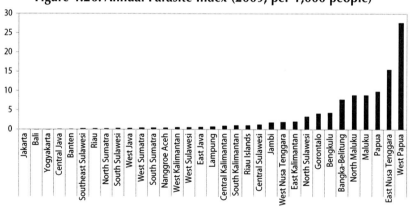

Source: Bappenas (2010).

for all age groups. While about 9% of children under 5 years old had diarrhea in 2007, the incidence of diarrhea varies widely across the country (Figure 4.27). Aceh has the highest rate—about 18.9%—followed by Gorontalo (16.5%) and West Nusa Tenggara (13.2%).

Figure 4.27: Incidence of Diarrhea among Under-5 Children (2007, %)

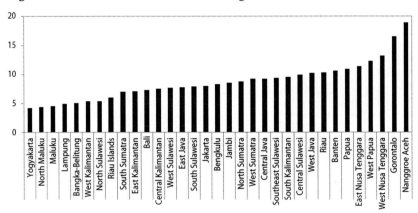

Source: Bappenas (2010).

Limited use of healthcare services, unequal access to healthcare, and unequal access to clean water and sanitation systems affect people's health conditions. A key cause of Indonesia's relatively poor health outcomes is the limited use of healthcare services. Figure 4.28 shows the treatment-seeking behavior among people who had a health complaint during the month prior to the survey. The proportion of people who sought treatment in a healthcare facility has increased somewhat in recent years, partly due to the introduction of the Askeskin program, which was subsequently reformed into the Jamkesmas program. This program provides the targeted poor with free healthcare at community health centers (*puskesmas*) and free inpatient treatment in third class hospital wards. Nonetheless, the figure shows that utilization levels have not yet returned to the pre-crisis level. In addition, access to all types of healthcare facilities, particularly to puskesmas, declined after the crisis, though the trends are reversing in recent years (Figure 4.29).

The utilization of healthcare services varies by geographical region and socioeconomic group (Table 4.10). People living in urban areas, Java, and Bali, and those covered by health insurance are more likely to have visited a healthcare facility than are others. A higher utilization rate of healthcare facilities is also observed among better-off households.

There are great variations in the type of facilities accessed across the country and among expenditure quintiles (Table 4.11). For example, puskesmas are the service most frequently accessed nationwide but the utilization rate is greater among poorer people. In contrast, people living in urban areas and wealthier people are more likely to access other

Figure 4.28: Utilization of Healthcare Services (1993–2007, %)

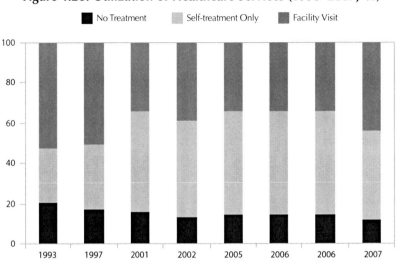

Sources: For 1993–2006, World Bank (2008); and for 2007, calculations based on BPS.

Figure 4.29: Type of Healthcare Facilities Accessed (1997–2007, %)

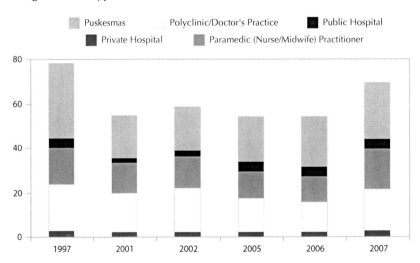

Note: Puskesmas are community health centers.
Source: Calculations based on BPS.

Table 4.10: Utilization of Healthcare Services (2007, %)

	No Treatment	Self-Treatment	Facility Visit
Indonesia	11.7	44.2	44.1
Urban	10.8	43.6	45.6
Rural	12.3	44.6	43.1
Sumatra	13.9	44.0	42.1
Java and Bali	9.9	43.6	46.5
Kalimantan	11.9	51.9	36.2
Sulawesi	13.7	49.0	37.3
Maluku, Papua, and Nusa Tenggara	17.2	38.0	44.8
No Insurance	11.7	46.2	42.2
Has Insurance	11.8	39.4	48.8
Expenditure Quintile			
Poorest	14.7	47.2	38.1
Second	11.7	46.0	42.3
Third	10.7	44.2	45.1
Fourth	10.1	42.1	47.8
Richest	10.6	40.1	49.3

Source: Calculations based on BPS.

Table 4.11: Type of Healthcare Facilities Accessed (2007, %)

	Public Hospital	Private Hospital	Polyclinic/ Doctor's Practice	Paramedic (nurse/ midwife) Practitioner	Puskesmas[a]
Indonesia	4.5	2.7	18.6	18.4	25.1
Urban	5.9	4.5	25.2	11.4	23.0
Rural	3.5	1.3	14.0	23.3	26.5
Sumatra	5.3	3.0	15.3	20.9	24.7
Java and Bali	4.0	3.0	22.4	19.5	22.4
Kalimantan	4.3	1.4	11.7	14.2	25.7
Sulawesi	5.0	1.1	12.0	12.4	29.5
Maluku, Papua, and Nusa Tenggara	5.2	1.3	10.9	11.8	41.5
No insurance	2.9	2.1	18.3	19.8	21.9
Insurance	8.2	4.0	19.4	15.0	32.6
Expenditure Quintile					
Poorest	2.4	0.7	8.3	18.0	28.4
Second	3.0	1.2	13.2	21.6	27.8

continued on next page

	Public Hospital	Private Hospital	Polyclinic/ Doctor's Practice	Paramedic (nurse/ midwife) Practitioner	Puskesmas[a]
Third	4.4	2.0	17.8	21.1	26.2
Fourth	5.6	3.2	24.0	18.8	23.9
Richest	7.9	7.2	34.4	11.0	17.1

[a] Puskesmas are community health centers.
Source: Calculations based on BPS.

healthcare facilities, including public and private hospitals, polyclinics, and doctor's practices.

The use of maternal and child healthcare services varies among wealth quintiles and with the mothers' education level (Table 4.12). The disparities

Table 4.12. Maternal and Child Health-Related Indicators (2007)

	Infant Mortality (per 1,000 live births)[a]	Prenatal Care: 4+ visits (%)[b]	Birth Delivery by a Skilled Provider (%)[c]	Fully Immunized Children (%)[d]
Indonesia	39	81.5	79.4	58.6
Urban	31	89.9	84.3	67.5
Rural	45	75.5	75.9	52.3
Mothers' Education				
No Education	73	44.1	49.5	18.6
Some Primary	51	63.5	69.1	37.3
Complete Primary	44	77.3	79.8	52.1
Some Secondary	35	85.9	82.7	60.6
Secondary+	24	93.1	83.8	72.8
Wealth Quintile				
Poorest	56	61.1	65.0	39.4
Second	47	78.3	79.2	53.0
Third	33	83.4	82.8	58.1
Fourth	29	90.6	86.5	68.0
Richest	26	96.4	86.4	74.9

[a] Infant morality rates are for the 10-year period preceding the survey (i.e., 1998–2007).
[b] Percentage of women who have given a live birth in the last 5 years and had at least four prenatal care visits during pregnancy.
[c] Percentage of live births in the last 5 years assisted by a skilled provider (doctor, nurse, midwife, or auxiliary nurse/midwife).
[d] Percentage of children aged 12–23 months who received tuberculosis (BCG), measles, and three doses each of diphtheria, pertussis, and tetanus (DPT) and polio vaccines.
Sources: For prenatal care, calculations based on BPS, IDHS; and for other indicators, BPS and Macro International (2008).

are particularly striking among mothers' education levels: less than 20% of infants whose mothers received no education were fully immunized, whereas about 73% of infants whose mothers completed secondary schooling or higher were fully immunized. Infant mortality rates are also higher among infants with less educated mothers or from poor families.

4.3.1.3. Other Social Services

Other important social services that could affect health outcomes include the provision of clean water and sanitation systems. Figure 4.30 shows that provinces with relatively low access to clean water and sanitation systems, particularly the latter, tend to have a higher incidence of diarrhea. For instance, in Yogyakarta, where diarrhea in the month prior to the survey was the lowest (1.3% of people), about 73% of people had access to a private toilet facility. In contrast, only about 52% of people had such access in Nanggroe Aceh, where the incidence of diarrhea was the highest (4.0%). Disparities in access to clean water and sanitation systems are also found among different expenditure groups (Table 4.13). Clearly, Indonesia needs to improve the provision of these services, particularly in lagging areas and for the poor.

Figure 4.30: Access to Clean Water and Sanitation, and Incidence of Diarrhea (2007)

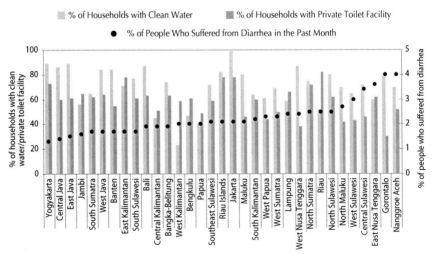

Note: Clean water includes bottled water, tap water, pumped water, protected well water, and protected spring water.
Source: Calculations based on BPS.

Table 4.13: Access to Clean Water and Sanitation (2007, %)

	Households with Access to Clean Water	Households with Access to Toilet Facility Private/Public/ Shared	Private
Indonesia	78.9	77.1	59.9
Urban	92.6	90.5	72.1
Rural	68.5	67.0	50.6
Sumatra	65.3	78.3	65.0
Java and Bali	87.0	78.9	60.0
Kalimantan	50.2	78.1	61.3
Sulawesi	75.9	68.7	53.8
Maluku, Papua and Nusa Tenggara	68.5	62.0	45.9
Expenditure Quintile			
Poorest	67.8	58.8	39.5
Second	73.3	68.0	49.6
Third	77.2	76.8	59.2
Fourth	83.2	86.3	69.9
Richest	92.9	96.0	80.8

Note: Clean water includes bottled water, tap water, pumped water, protected well water, and protected spring water.
Source: Calculations based on BP.

Causes of unequal access to healthcare services are found on both the demand and supply sides. On the supply side, one main issue is the relatively limited allocation of public expenditure to the health sector. Despite a steady increase during the last decade, health spending as a share of gross domestic product remains low (Table 4.14), particularly in comparison with the neighboring countries (Figure 4.31).

Table 4.14: National Public Expenditure on Health (2001–2008)

Year	2006 Prices (Rp Trillion)	Share of Total National Expenditure (%)	Share of GDP (%)
2001	8.3	2.6	0.5
2002	8.8	3.2	0.6
2003	12.1	3.9	0.8
2004	11.8	3.6	0.7
2005	12.2	3.5	0.7
2006	18.0	4.4	0.9
2007[a]	20.9	4.8	1.1
2008[b]	20.3	4.4	1.1

GDP = gross domestic product. [a] = Allocation [b] = Estimated.
Source: World Bank (2008).

Figure 4.31: Public Expenditure on Health for Selected Countries (2006, % of GDP)

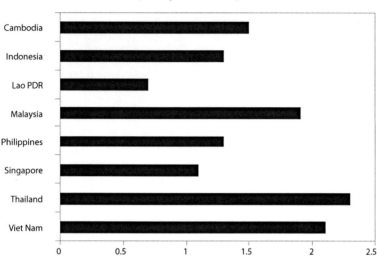

Source: World Bank, WDI, accessed 5 October 2009.

Another issue is that the benefit incidence of public spending on primary healthcare is not particularly pro-poor, but is equally distributed across the income levels. Given the poor's limited use of public hospitals (Table 4.11), better-off households tend to benefit relatively more from secondary healthcare. However, as the lower quintiles' use of healthcare facilities has been increasing since the introduction of the Askeskin program, the benefits of public spending on health are likely to have become more pro-poor in recent years (World Bank 2008).

Along with continued efforts to increase public expenditures for health, the efficiency and effectiveness of budget allocation needs to be improved. As in the education sector, the share spent at the subnational level is larger than that at the central level (though the central level share has been increasing in recent years, largely due to the Askeskin–Jamkesmas program). Nonetheless, the bulk of subnational health expenditure goes for routine expenditure, particularly on personnel. As a consequence, funds allocated to operation and maintenance tend to be limited at the subnational level (World Bank 2008).

The spending structure is reflected in the insufficient provision of healthcare facilities. Despite the impressive expansion of the public health system in the 1970s and 1980s, the growth of public sector health infrastructure has slowed, failing to keep pace with population growth (World Bank 2008). An international comparison of the provision of

124

healthcare facilities and providers highlights Indonesia's insufficient supply (Table 4.15). For example, the Philippines, with a per capita gross domestic product similar to that of Indonesia, performs better on these indicators of healthcare provision.

Table 4.15: International Comparison of Healthcare Facilities and Providers (per 100,000 people)

Country	Hospital Beds Year	No.	Physicians Year	No.	Nurses Year	No.	Midwives Year	No.
Cambodia	2004	1	2000	16	2000	62	2000	23
Indonesia	2002	6	2003	13	2003	57	2003	25
Malaysia	2006	19	2002	71	2002	144	2002	37
Philippines	2006	13	2002	115	2002	436	2002	178
Singapore	2006	32	2003	150	2003	431	2003	9
Thailand	2000	22	2002	31	2002	135	2000	1
Viet Nam	2005	26	2002	56	2002	58	2002	19

Sources: For hospital beds, except for Indonesia and Thailand, WHO, WHOSIS, accessed October 2009; for hospital beds for Indonesia and Thailand, WHO, WHO Regional Office for South-East Asia accessed October 2009; and for other figures, WHO, WHO Global Health Atlas accessed October 2009.

There are also great disparities in the availability of healthcare facilities and providers across the country. More puskesmas, which the poor tend to depend on, are available in poorer provinces than elsewhere. However, in some provinces, such as West Nusa Tenggara, the number of puskesmas per 100,000 people is rather low relative to the poverty rates (Figure 4.32). In general, while community access to health facilities has improved over time—almost 94% of the population can reach basic health facilities within 5 kilometers of their homes (Bappenas 2010)—but the distance to basic health facilities still varies significantly across provinces, as shown in Figure 4.33.

Furthermore, the availability of a doctor at each puskesmas is not guaranteed—on average, 18 of 33 provinces have less than one doctor per puskesmas (World Bank 2008). Indonesia's health sector suffers from high absenteeism among staff—the absence rate in primary health centers is estimated at 40%, and it is higher in poorer areas (Chaudhury et al. 2006). One reason is that many healthcare workers maintain private practices—the government has allowed them to do so outside their normal working hours since the 1970s in recognition of their low public salaries.

Although the wage levels of public doctors, midwives, and nurses, in general compare favorably with those of other workers with a similar level of education, incentives are needed (World Bank 2008). In addition, Indonesia

Figure 4.32: Availability of Puskesmas[a] and Poverty Index (2006)

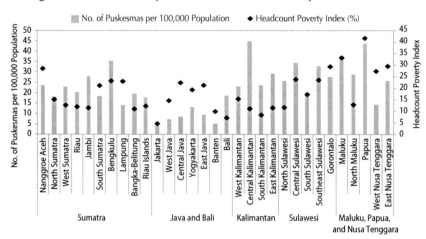

^a Puskesmas are community health centers.
Sources: Calculations based on BPS, Podes for the availability of Puskesmas and on BPS, Susenas Kore for the poverty index.

Figure 4.33: Average Distance to Puskesmas[a] (2006, km)

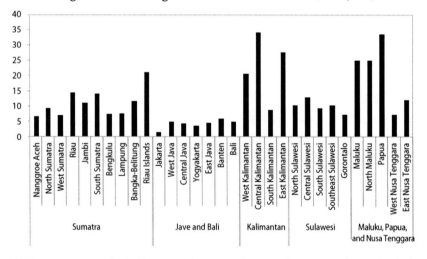

^a Puskesmas are community health centers. The average distance to the nearest puskesmas is calculated among the villages without a puskesmas.
Source: Calculations based on BPS.

needs to strengthen the accreditation and certification system for healthcare staff to improve the quality of healthcare services.

Some demand-side factors are also responsible for unequal access to healthcare. A main issue is the financial burden on individual households.

Given the limited public spending on health, out-of-pocket payments are relatively high and comprise a significant part of health spending in Indonesia (World Bank 2008). In maternal and child healthcare, for example, financial difficulties seem to be the main problem in accessing healthcare services. And poorer households are more likely to have difficulties financing medical treatments (Table 4.16).

Table 4.16: Main Problems in Accessing Maternal and Child Healthcare (2007, %)

	Getting Money Needed	Distance to Health Facilities/ Having to Take Transport	Knowing Where to Go	Concern There May Be No Female Healthcare Provider	Getting Permission to Go/Not Wanting to Go Alone
Indonesia	25	17	5	11	14
Urban	20	8	3	10	10
Rural	29	24	7	11	17
Mothers' Education					
No Education	28	18	8	11	16
Some Primary	22	14	4	11	12
Complete Primary	27	30	5	11	20
Some Secondary	35	26	9	6	18
Complete Secondary (and higher)	39	32	11	11	18
Wealth Quintile					
Poorest	41	34	11	10	24
Second	32	23	7	11	18
Third	28	19	5	11	14
Fourth	24	15	5	11	14
Richest	14	9	4	10	10

Source: Calculations based on BPS, IDHS.

The Askeskin program (which became the Jamkesmas program) was a welcome step toward enhancing access to healthcare. Although the program's coverage needs to be extended and better targeted, Sparrow, Suryahadi, and Widyanti (2008) find that the program has been targeted to the poor and has allocated proportionally more funding to people who are most vulnerable to health shocks. Their analysis also finds that the program has had a positive effect on the use of healthcare services. Furthermore, in November 2009, the Ministry of Health presented a blueprint for a new health insurance scheme targeting universal coverage in 2012 (see section 10.3). If implemented as planned, this is likely to enhance people's access to healthcare services.

However, while Askeskin cardholders increased their use of puskesmas, they did not significantly increase their use of hospital services (World Bank 2008) and the impact of the program for secondary healthcare is greater among the nonpoor (Sparrow, Suryahadi, and Widyanti 2008). Thus, barriers other than financial issues seem to prevent some people from accessing healthcare services. Table 4.16, for example, shows that the distance to healthcare facilities is a main problem in accessing maternal and child healthcare—the distance implies extra cost, which is likely to increase the financial burden, particularly for poor households.

Within households, other obstacles hamper the access of women and children to healthcare services—for about 14% of women, getting permission to go to healthcare facilities and/or not wanting to go alone is a problem. These problems tend to be identified more frequently by less educated women (Table 4.16) and may partly explain why educated mothers are more likely to use services such as immunization, prenatal care, and assisted birth delivery (Table 4.12). Hence, increasing peoples' education levels, particularly of mothers, and increasing the awareness of the potential benefits of modern healthcare, including preventative care, is critical to increasing the utilization of healthcare services in Indonesia.

Unequal access to and limited use of healthcare may also be due to a lack of trust in the public health system. In general, the quality of healthcare services in Indonesia is said to be low, with limited availability of medication, inadequate infrastructure, and often insufficient healthcare personnel. In addition, puskesmas are often reported to have limited access to clean water and electricity (World Bank 2007). The GDS 2 lists the main aspects of healthcare services requiring improvement as the (1) availability of medicines and vaccines (24% of households thought this needs to be improved), (2) affordability of medical services (20%), (3) physical condition of healthcare services (19%), (4) attention and attitude of medical personnel (15%), and (5) waiting time at healthcare service providers (7%). Nonetheless, about 71% of household respondents reported improvements in public healthcare service delivery in recent years (Widyanti and Suryahadi 2008).

4.3.2. Uneven Playing Fields

Unequal access to economic opportunities may also be caused by unequal access to infrastructure and to productive assets such as land and credit.

4.3.2.1. Infrastructure

Good infrastructure, especially high quality roads and reliable electricity supply, can enhance access to key services and to economic opportunities. In geographically challenged countries such as Indonesia, infrastructure plays a key role in promoting inclusiveness. The state of infrastructure affects people's access not only to economic opportunities, but also to public services. Numerous studies illustrate the importance of infrastructure in poverty reduction, income growth, and access to nonfarm economic activities (e.g., Gibson 2009, Gibson and Olivia 2008, Yamauchi et al. 2009, and World Bank 2006c). Poverty diagnostics, for example, show that access to asphalt roads is a key variable associated with increases in household expenditure in Indonesia (World Bank 2006c). The same analysis also illustrates the importance of the quality of roads.

Similarly, based on data from the Indonesia Family Life Survey and the Rural Investment Climate Survey, Gibson (2009) finds that lack of access to and poor quality of infrastructure (such as roads and electricity) constrain nonfarm economic activities of rural households. Furthermore, Gibson finds poor quality of infrastructure, especially roads and electricity, to be a major problem.

Because enhancing nonfarm activities is a key driver for reducing poverty in rural areas, these empirical findings underline the importance of infrastructure for inclusiveness. Land transport is the main system for connecting villages in most provinces. Roads are, therefore, essential for people's livelihoods in Indonesia, although in some areas (e.g., Kalimantan, Maluku, Nusa Tenggara, Papua and West Papua, Riau, and Sumatra) water transport is also a main connectivity system.

Roads. Despite the importance of roads, the supply of good quality roads is limited in many parts of the country. For example, asphalt and concrete roads seem to be concentrated in the Java and Bali region (Figure 4.34), whereas roads in the Kalimantan; Maluku, Papua, and Nusa Tenggara; and Sulawesi regions are in particularly poor condition. Moreover, among the roads managed by the central government, no roads in Jakarta are in damaged condition, whereas more than 60% of such roads in Papua are reported as damaged (Figure 4.35).

Figure 4.34: Type of Surfaces of the Widest Road (2008, %)

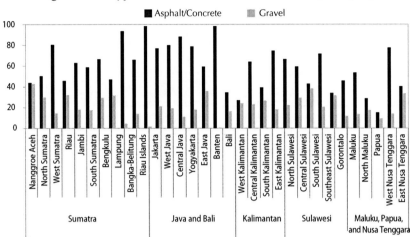

Source: Calculations based on BPS, Podes.

Figure 4.35: Percentage of Damaged Roads (2007, %)

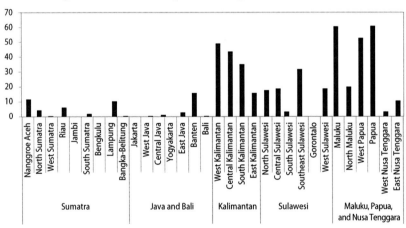

Notes: Based on the roads under the responsibility of the central government.
Source: BPS (2008b).

About 10% of roads are under the purview of provincial governments and 81% are under district governments. Unfortunately, no accurate subdistrict-level data are available on the condition of provincial and district roads. But, at the national level, about 18%, 24%, and 40% of the roads managed by the central, provincial, and district governments, respectively, are in poor condition (BPS 2008). Given the poorer condition of provincial and district roads, the disparity in the quality of roads across the country presented in Figure 4.35 is likely to be an underestimation.

A direct consequence of poor road conditions is increased travel time (and thus also travel costs). For example, in Manggarai District in East Nusa Tenggara, road conditions are much worse and resulting travel times much longer between Manggarai and its main business destinations than from other parts of the country to equivalent destinations—travel over the 140 kilometers from Ruteng to Labuanbajo is usually 3.5–4 hours, whereas it takes only about 1.5 hours to traverse the 128 kilometers from Jakarta to Bandung (World Bank 2006b). Box 4.2 provides details.

There are also great regional discrepancies in accessing markets. Figure 4.36 shows that markets are more commonly found in provinces such as Bali, Jakarta, and Yogyakarta than in the rest of the country. Furthermore, people living in some provinces need to travel long distances to reach the nearest market, particularly in Central Kalimantan, East Kalimantan, Maluku, and Papua (Figure 4.37). As discussed in previous sections, distance to other facilities, such as schools and healthcare centers, also poses a barrier to accessing these key services. Connecting the rural poor through improvements in rural infrastructure should, therefore, be a priority for reducing poverty and inequality.

Figure 4.36: Percentage of Villages with Markets (2008, %)

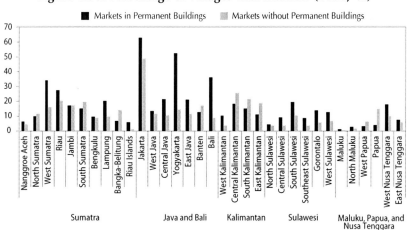

Source: Calculations based on BPS, Podes.

Figure 4.37: Average Distance to Markets (with a permanent building, 2006, km)

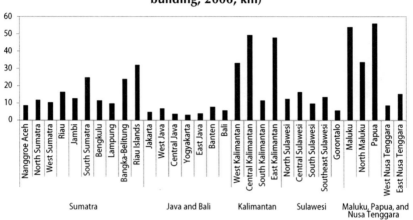

km = kilometer.
Note: The average distance is calculated among the villages without any market.
Source: Calculations based on BPS, Podes.

Electricity. As for electricity, household access does not seem to be very low in many parts of the country, except in provinces such as Papua and West Papua (Figure 4.38). However, because the connection rate at the village level tends to be higher than at the household level, connection within a village seems to be an issue for some provinces, such as East Nusa Tenggara. Moreover, the quality of the electricity provision varies significantly across the country, with outer regions suffering from frequent blackouts (Gibson 2009).

Access. Unequal access to good quality infrastructure is mainly due to insufficient allocation of resources to the poorer regions; limited allocation of expenditures to maintenance; and local governments' limited capacity for planning, budgeting, and executing their spending. Chapter 3 identified several factors that are responsible for the limited availability of infrastructure and for its low quality in Indonesia. This part of the report will raise additional issues that are more specific to the unequal distribution of infrastructure, particularly roads, and disparities in the quality of infrastructure across the country.

Figure 4.38: Access to Electricity (%)

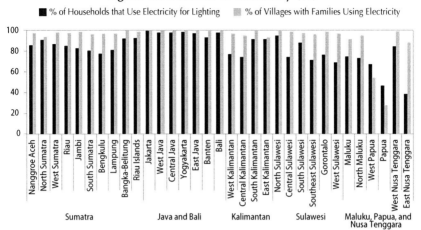

■ % of Households that Use Electricity for Lighting ░ % of Villages with Families Using Electricity

Sources: For the connection at the household level, calculations are based on data for 2007 from BPS, Susenas Kore; and for the connection at the village level, calculations are based on data for 2008 from BPS, Podes.

Box 4.2: Rural Connectivity

Rural connectivity plays a key role in inclusive growth by enhancing people's access not only to economic opportunities, but also to key public services. This is particularly true in remote provinces such as Nusa Tenggara Timur (NTT) with mountainous and island topography that poses transport challenges. Despite its considerable potential for trade-oriented development of value-added activities associated with the primary sector, including agro-food and labor-intensive light industry and services such as tourism, NTT remains one of Indonesia's poorest provinces. Infrastructure deficiency, including port and supporting transport facilities, is one of the most critical constraints to further development in NTT (Roland-Holst and Frielink 2009).

Manggarai District is on Flores Island in NTT. The majority of Manggarai's population is engaged in primary production, and micro and small enterprises make up a large proportion of the off-farm sector, most of which are household-based weaving enterprises or kiosks. The district capital, Ruteng, is approximately 6 hours drive from Manggarai's largest port, Reok, to the north and 4 hours from Labuanbajo, the capital of the neighboring district, Manggarai Barat, from which the majority of sea traffic to Java departs (World Bank 2006a). Despite the importance of rural roads for accessing the district capital and key sea ports, road conditions in Manggarai are very poor.

continued on next page

Table A: Proportion of Villages by Surface Type of Roads (2006, %)

	Type of Surface of the widest road				Passable by Four-Wheel- Drive Vehicles
	Asphalt/ Concrete	Gravel	Soil	Others	
Indonesia	58.0	25.7	15.8	0.5	88.8
NTT	40.6	29.6	29.0	0.8	82.6
Manggarai	21.1	42.6	36.3	0.0	74.1

NTT = Nusa Tenggara Timur.
Source: BPS Podes 2006.

For example, Table A shows that only about 21% of villages in Manggarai District have their widest road surfaced by asphalt/concrete, which is significantly lower than the national (58%) and provincial (41%) averages. As a result, the proportion of villages with their widest roads that are passable by four-wheel-drive vehicles is only about 74%. Thus, in many parts of Manggarai, road transport is unreliable, particularly in rainy season. Moreover, while the majority of roads in Manggarai were classified as district roads (about 79%), about 68% of them were classified as being in bad or very bad conditions in 2003 (World Bank 2006a).

Table B: Comparison between Java and Manggarai

	Java	Manggarai
Travel Time	Jakarta-Bandung Distance: 128 km Time 1.5 hours Speed: 85 km/hour	Ruteng-Labuandajo Distance: 140 km Time: 3.5-4 hours Speed: 35-40 km/hour
Life of a Vehicle	10 years	5 years
Fuel Consumption	1 liter per 4 km	1 liter per 1 km
Maximum Safe Load Limits	17 tons	12 tons

Source: World Bank (2006a)

A major issue arising from poor road conditions is their unfavorable impact on transport time and cost. Table B clearly illustrates that people in Manggarai have to bear longer travel times and greater costs as a result of the poor quality of local roads. The increased travel time and costs, in turn, pose a barrier to local economic development by restricting access to raw materials and potential markets and hence inhibiting the ability of local people to participate in higher value-added activities and diversify their economic activities (World Bank 2006a).

Sources: Authors, BPS Podes (2006), Roland-Holst and Frielink (2009), World Bank (2006a).

Resource Allocation for Infrastructure. One of the main problems for the infrastructure sector in Indonesia is that the allocation of resources does not reflect the needs. Consequently, it tends to exacerbate geographical inequalities in access to and quality of infrastructure. In response to the "big-bang decentralization" in 2001, which marked the post-New Order era, the responsibility for providing basic services was shifted from the central to subnational governments, and it is now funded from the regional budget. Nevertheless, due to the limited ability of many of subnational governments to raise their own revenues, the central government continues to play an important supporting role, particularly in fiscal matters—the central government remains responsible for ensuring the balance of fund allocations among regions (Usman et al. 2008). As a result, the majority of the regional budget consists of transfers from the central government. The main components of the transfers are the General Allocation Fund (DAU), Specific Allocation Fund (DAK), and Shared Revenue Fund. The objective of the transfers is to reduce financial discrepancies between the center and regions as well as among regions, and to reduce interregional disparity in the provision of public services.

The DAU grant is a general purpose grant that is intended to equalize subnational fiscal resources. The current DAU formula has two components: "basic allocation" and "fiscal gap." While the former is made on the basis of the district-level salary bill of the civil service, the latter is allocated to the districts pro rata of their fiscal gap, and this component is the main driver of equalization. While the share of the fiscal gap component is increasing, it comprises only a minor part of the allocation mechanism (World Bank 2007). Even though a poverty variable is included for calculating the fiscal gap component, its share is small. Moreover, the DAU has to be allocated first to cover 100% of the local civil service wage bill. As a result, poorer districts tend to have limited funding to invest even though they have the greater need for maintenance and investment. In contrast, the DAK grant is a special purpose grant. While the DAU is used mostly to cover administrative costs, the DAK is used mainly for capital expenditure and is the main source for the development of physical infrastructure for subnational governments. The DAK's primary objective is to improve the provision of public services that have not met certain standards. In this way, the DAK may ensure that funding is targeted by sector and by region, and thus reduces disparity in growth rates between sectors and regions (Usman et al. 2008).

Nevertheless, the government has not maximized the use of the DAK for addressing the needs of resource-deficient regions and sectors. There are several explanations for the disappointing results. First, the amount of DAK funding available is still relatively small, even though its share has been increasing in recent years (Figure 4.39). This is partly because almost all regional governments receive the DAK, while the fund is supposed to target resource deficit regions. The allocation process has not been entirely transparent either—the allocation mechanisms set forth in the regulations are not yet well understood by many regional governments (Bappenas 2010). Moreover, the DAK has to be allocated to a relatively large number of sectors— in addition to key sectors such as education, health, and infrastructure, it is allocated to public administration infrastructure, agriculture, maritime affairs and fisheries, and the environment.

Figure 4.39: Proportion of Balance Funds in Total Regional Budget Expenditure (2001–2007, %)

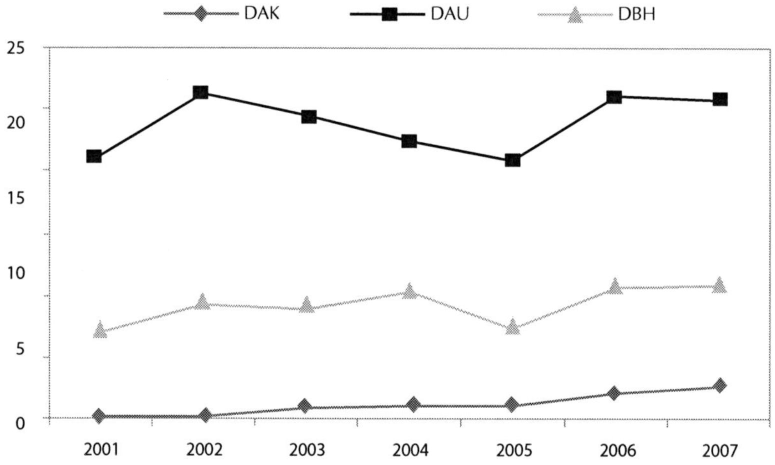

DAK = Specific Allocation Fund, DAU = General Allocation Fund, DBH = Shared Revenue Fund.
Source: Usman et al. (2008).

Second, unlike the DAU and Shared Revenue Fund, no government regulation specifically applies to the DAK. While this makes the DAK a flexible instrument for addressing interregional imbalances, subnational governments cannot be certain about the amount they will receive. Moreover, the timetable for the central government's release of the allocation decisions and of DAK funds often conflicts with the budget preparation. These issues unnecessarily complicate the budget preparation process for subnational governments (Usman et al. 2008).

Another issue is that the central government determines the DAK recipient sectors based on national priorities as set out in the government's work plan.[20] In addition, for each sector, the use of the DAK must follow the centrally determined technical guidelines that set which activities can be funded. For example, according to the technical guidelines, at least 70% of the DAK should be used for periodic maintenance and a maximum of 30% is used for rehabilitation, upgrading, or new road development. Routine maintenance is, in principle, the responsibility of local governments from the regional budget, with exceptions subject to approval from the Ministry of Public Works (Bappenas 2010). However, such guidelines may limit the usefulness of the DAK. For example, Kabupaten Kupang requires a greater allocation of funds for upgrading activities because most of its roads have not been asphalted. This example illustrates the limited scope for subnational governments to design interventions that are most appropriate to local needs and conditions (World Bank 2006c).

The DAK, due to the foregoing issues and despite its potential, is not effectively reducing disparities in the provision of public services across the country. It is important to make the DAK allocation process more transparent, predictable, and fairer to improve the efficiency and effectiveness with which DAK funds are used.

In addition to the general issues discussed so far, some specific issues pertain to road infrastructure. First, district governments do not have control over road user tax, which is still under the control of the central and provincial governments. As a consequence, the districts are unable to raise funds to cover the costs imposed by road users (World Bank 2006b).

Another problem is the relatively low allocation of expenditure to road maintenance, particularly at the subnational level. Road expenditure is biased toward new road construction and upgrading, which, at least partly, is because routine maintenance is less effective in gaining local political support than the construction of new roads. Financial incentives should be provided to subnational governments to ensure adequate road maintenance (World Bank 2007). Thus, in addition to increasing the volume of infrastructure investment, improving the efficiency and effectiveness of spending is also critical.

Other issues include subnational governments' development spending on infrastructure lagging behind their growing revenues (World Bank 2007). This may reflect their limited capacity for planning, budgeting, and executing their spending.

As for electricity, retail tariff levels are below cost and are far below those of other Association of Southeast Asian Nations countries. The current

---

[20] In practice, subnational governments are only asked to send data on the state of regional infrastructure in sectors that receive DAK allocations, and the central government uses the data as a determinant for allocating the DAK by sector and region. The allocation also follows the development priorities laid out in the government's work plan (Usman et al. 2008).

uniform tariff policy provides no incentive to extend the networks and adequately maintain existing assets, particularly in rural and remote areas, where costs tend to be relatively high. Moreover, the consumption subsidy, in the form of low tariffs, encourages excessive consumption and is regressive, because poor households are likely to consume less electricity (or have no connection) than the better-off ones (World Bank 2007).

4.3.2.2. Land

Limited availability of irrigated land constrains poverty reduction in provinces that rely on rice production for livelihoods. Given that a relatively large proportion of poor households work in the agriculture sector, boosting agricultural capability remains important for poverty reduction. Land is one of the main productive assets; equality in accessing productive land is thus important for enhancing the inclusiveness of economic growth. Figure 4.40 illustrates the unequal distribution of irrigated land across provinces. It also highlights the importance of irrigation for increasing agricultural productivity, because land productivity increases with irrigation.

Figure 4.40: Percentage of Irrigated Rice Land and Land Productivity

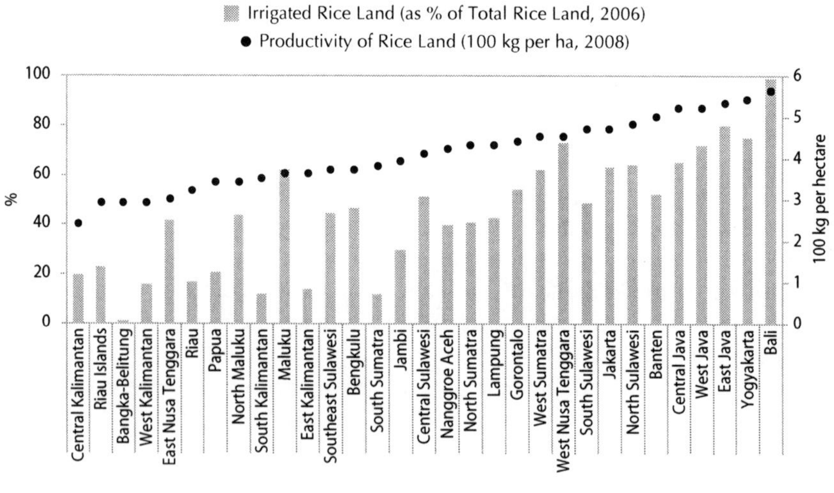

ha = hectare, kg = kilogram.
Sources: For the percentage of irrigated land, calculations based on BPS, Podes and for land productivity, BPS (various years).

Land titling is another issue. The National Land Administration Agency grants titles to nonforest land in Indonesia. Less than 25% of rural landholders have formal land certificates, while almost all farmers possess land-use certificates in the People's Republic of China and Viet Nam and close to 90%

in Malaysia and Thailand (World Bank 2006c). Efforts to hasten the lengthy process of land titling, along with a reallocation of degraded, deforested land to productive uses, are needed to enhance equal access to land.

4.3.2.3. Credit

Despite the successful development of microfinance, access to financial services remains unequal. Accessibility to financial services plays a key role in ensuring equal access to economic opportunities. Along with infrastructure, limited availability of credit can be an obstacle for nonfarm enterprises in rural areas (Ikhwan and Johnston 2009). For poor households, access to financial services can also play a critical role in enabling them to meet their daily needs and cope with crisis. Indeed, both poor and nonpoor households commonly use loans for nonbusiness purposes such as school fees, medical treatment, housing, and daily consumption needs (Johnston and Morduch 2008; Usman, Akhmadi, and Suryadarma 2004).

Indonesia is one of the leading countries in developing microfinance. Bank Rakyat Indonesia (BRI) has the largest microfinance operation among formal financial institutions in the country. In addition to microfinance branches of commercial banks, there are people's credit banks and cooperatives; microfinance institutions established under government programs (including the Rural Credit and Funds Institution in West Java, the Kecamatan Credit Board in Central Java, Credit for Small-Scale Businesses in East Java, and Credit for People's Business); and informal institutions, such as moneylenders (Usman, Akhmadi, and Suryadarma 2004).

The development of microfinance for enhancing access to credit in Indonesia has been a success, but much can still be done to improve the poor's access to credit. A survey of 392 microfinance institutions in 23 countries ranked BRI 7th for market penetration, calculated as a share of borrowers in the total number of poor people in the country.[21] Yet BRI's market penetration is limited to 5.8%. Moreover, there is considerable disparity in the distribution of financial institutions across Indonesia (Figure 4.41). The highest concentration of banks is found in the Jakarta area, and the concentration of even informal microfinance institutions is greatest in the Java and Bali Region.

The unequal access to credit is due to both supply- and demand-side factors. On the supply side, given the limited economic activities and, thus, the relatively small size of the potential market, poor provinces are less likely to attract banks and other financial institutions. Furthermore, the limited network of branch offices and the limited number of credit officers imply the difficulty and high cost of accessing information that allows financial

---

[21]   Source: MIX Market 2006 data cited in ADB and MIX (2008).

Figure 4.41: Access to Financial Institutions (2006, %)

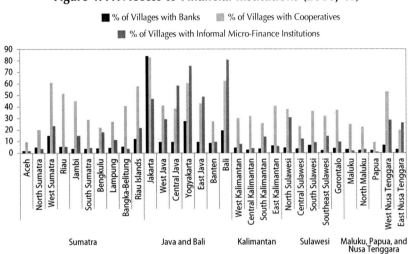

Source: Calculations based on BPS, Podes.

institutions to identify potentially successful borrowers, constraining the provision of loans in rural and remote areas (Ikhwan and Johnston 2009).

On the demand side, BRI's 2002 Microfinance Access and Services Survey[22] revealed that a large proportion of nonborrowing households were unaware that they could qualify for a micro scale loan, indicating a lack of information on whether and from where they could successfully obtain a loan. Although creditworthiness increases with income, nearly 40% of poor households were recorded as creditworthy (Johnston and Morduch 2008).Using data from the Indonesia Family Life Surveys, Okten and Osili (2004) empirically show that social networks help enhance access to credit by playing an important role in the diffusion of knowledge about credit opportunities. These observations suggest that market failures are, at least partly, responsible for unequal access to credit in Indonesia.

Another issue is that some potential borrowers are averse to assuming debt. The Microfinance Access and Services Survey showed that about half of poor households found to be creditworthy would not take loans even if it were possible. The incidence of debt aversion is relatively consistent across all income groups. The prevalence of debt aversion implies that improved availability of credit would not automatically contribute to reducing poverty (Johnston and Morduch 2008).

---

[22] The survey was conducted by BRI during July–August 2002, covering 1,438 households in six provinces: East Java, East Kalimantan, North Sulawesi, Papua, West Java, and West Kalimantan (Johnston and Morduch 2008).

4.4. Social Safety Nets and Poverty Reduction Programs

The provision of adequate social safety nets is one of the three key drivers for promoting inclusive growth (Chapter 1, Figure 1.3). As discussed in Zhuang and Ali (2010), social safety net programs help mitigate the effects of transitory livelihood shocks such as ill health, macroeconomic crisis, industrial structuring, and natural disasters, and meet the minimum needs of the chronically poor. While Indonesia's poverty incidence has been declining steadily over the years, more than 10% of the population is still poor, and a large percentage of households remain vulnerable to poverty. Hence, social safety nets can play an important role in helping poor and vulnerable households improve their welfare and cope with shocks.

Because Indonesia has made good progress in providing social safety net programs since the 1997 AFC, social safety nets may not currently be a critical constraint to the inclusiveness of growth. Indonesia has significantly improved its provision of social safety nets and poverty alleviation programs. The improvement has taken place in two stages: The country first increased the provision of such programs in response to the 1997 AFC, which pushed a great number of households into poverty. To help the poor cope with the economic shock, the government introduced social safety net programs under the Jaring Pengaman Sosial. It was designed as temporary short-term interventions to ensure that the poor had access to food, health, and education.

The Special Market Operation program, which was subsequently renamed the Raskin program, was also introduced in response to the 1997 AFC to help poor households meet their food needs by providing subsidized rice. Another main social safety net program the government introduced was commodity price subsidies, most notably the fuel subsidy. The fuel subsidy was a universal price subsidy and, by fixing fuel prices at subsidized levels, the government aimed to protect households from price fluctuations. However, the subsidy was regressive, and it was a great strain on the government's budget. As a result, the government reduced the fuel subsidy in 2005.

The second phase of the improvement in the provision of social safety net programs came when commodity price crises occurred in the mid-2000s. To mitigate the impact of reducing the fuel subsidy, the government introduced the Compensation for Fuel Subsidy Reductions Program. This was a bold step to make the social safety programs more pro-poor. The program included the Direct (unconditional) Cash Transfer (Bantuan Langsung Tunai) program, the BOS program, the Askeskin program, and the Kecamatan Development Project. The BOS and Askeskin (and later Jamkesmas) programs were aimed at improving access to education and healthcare services, while the Kecamatan Development Project aimed at reducing poverty, improving access to infrastructure and services, and strengthening local governance.

Indonesia has further shifted some of its social safety net programs to conditional cash transfer programs in recent years. The government introduced the Hopeful Family Program (Program Keluarga Harapan) and the National Program for Community Empowerment program for health and education (PNPM Generasi) in 2007, and expanded them rapidly. The former is a conditional cash transfer program directed to households, while the latter is directed to communities. Both are designed to reduce poverty and improve health and education outcomes.

The government has recently formulated the concept of poverty alleviation programs in three clusters—social assistance, community empowerment, and small and microenterprise empowerment—in Presidential Regulation No. 13 of 2009 on the Coordination of Poverty Alleviation. The purpose is to accelerate the poverty reduction programs and give clear guidance for every level of administration (i.e., national, provincial, and district). Furthermore, the National Team for Accelerating Poverty Reduction has been formed under the Vice President on the basis of Presidential Regulation No. 15 of 2010 on Accelerating Poverty Reduction.

As shown in this chapter, Indonesia has made significant progress in providing social safety nets since the 1997 AFC. The recent shift toward conditional cash transfer programs is a particularly welcome step to enhance the effectiveness and efficiency with which limited resources are used. The provision of social safety nets is not currently a critical constraint to promoting the inclusiveness of growth in Indonesia. Nevertheless, there is still scope to improve the programs' coverage and effectiveness. The provision of such programs also needs to be institutionalized so that the government is capable of providing timely and effective social assistance in a crisis.

In expanding the depth and breadth of the social safety nets, continued focus on improving the targeting and monitoring capacity of central and local governments, and on governance is needed. A key challenge Indonesia faces in improving the provision of social safety nets is to address the general weakness of targeting. One issue is that various agencies use different definitions of the poor. It is critical that all the relevant agencies use uniform data on poverty for their programs and activities, especially those that are targeted at the poor, in order to enhance the accuracy of targeting and effectiveness of the programs. A good candidate for the poverty targeting mechanism might be Statistics Indonesia's poverty figures comprising very poor and near poor households based on the results of the 2008 Social Protection Program Data Compilation (Bappenas 2010).

The central and local governments' capacity to implement and monitor welfare programs is also a critical issue, and needs to be strengthened in Indonesia. Olken (2006), for example, examined the extent of corruption in the extensive transfer program, Raskin, under which subsidized rice was distributed to poor households. A comparison between administrative data on the amount of rice distributed and survey data on the amount actually received by households resulted in an estimation that at least 18% of the subsidized rice disappeared. The extent of corruption was also found to be greater in ethnically fragmented and in sparsely populated areas. Such findings suggest that corruption can substantially inhibit the government's ability to implement redistributive programs, especially in rural areas, where monitoring is likely to be challenging.

Other issues include coordination failure among different players and the local governments' and communities' limited involvement in designing and implementing programs (see Chapter 10). Given the multidimensionality of poverty as well as significant variations in the needs of the poor across the country, it is important to enhance the involvement of local governments and communities in designing and implementing social safety net programs by strengthening their capacity for doing so and promoting a participatory decision-making process. In recent years, the government has been undertaking pilot programs (e.g., Pro-Poor Planning and Budgeting) in several regions to increase the planning and budgeting capacity of regional governments and improve the relevancy of the programs to the needs of local poor communities (Bappenas 2010).

The importance of community participation is formally endorsed by Law No. 25 of 2004 on National Development Planning in Indonesia. It institutionalizes multistakeholder consultation forums, commonly known as *musrenbang*, at all levels of government. However, the effectiveness of musrenbang has been limited due, among other things, to insufficient local government support, poor transparency and accountability, and the limited capacity of civil society organizations. Given the great potential of musrenbang to accommodate the voice of the poor in the development planning process and the formulation of poverty reduction program, its involvement should be enhanced.

Finally, social security is still in the early stage of development in Indonesia. With the 2004 National Social Security System Law No. 40 of 2004, Indonesia made landmark progress toward universal coverage. The law's intention is to overhaul the social protection programs and provide universal protection against the risks associated with old age, illness, and work-related injury and death. The implementation of the law, however, has been delayed. A council was nominated to elaborate the law only in early 2009. The most recent data show that only about 17% of employees are covered by social security (ILO and PT Jamsostek, forthcoming). The majority of the people who enjoy the coverage work in the formal sector, and most informal workers, who constituted over 61% of the workforce in 2008, are without social security coverage. The government's efforts to improve the social security system need to be accelerated.

References

Arze del Granado, F., W. Fengler, A. Ragatz, and E. Yavuz. 2007. Investing in Indonesia's Education: Allocation, Equity, and Efficiency of Public Expenditures. *World Bank Policy Research Working Paper* No.4329. Washington, DC: World Bank.

Asian Development Bank (ADB) and Microfinance Information Exchange (MIX). 2008. *2007 Mix Asia 100: Ranking of Microfinance Institutions.* Manila.

Badan Perencanaan Pembangunan Nasional (Bappenas—National Development Planning Agency). 2010. Letter to ADB. 16 July 2010.

Badan Pusat Statistik (BPS). 2006. Statistics of Education. In National Socio-Economic Survey. Jakarta.

———. 2008. Transportation and Communication Statistics 2007 (Statistik Perhubungan 2007). Jakarta.

———. 2009a. *Labor Force Situation in Indonesia.* Jakarta.

———. 2009b. *Trends of the Selected Socio-Economic Indicators of Indonesia October 2009.* Jakarta.

———. various years. *Statistical Yearbook of Indonesia (Statistik Indonesia).* Jakarta.

———. Indonesia Demographic and Health Survey (IDHS) Data 2007. Jakarta.

———. Podes (Village Potential Statistics of Indonesia—Statistik Potensi Desu Indonesia). Jakarta.

———. Sakernas (National Labor Force Surveys—Survei Tenaga Kerja Nasional). Jakarta.

———. Susenas (National Social Economic Surveys). Jakarta.

———. Susenas Panel Datasets. Jakarta.

Badan Pusat Statistik (BPS) and Macro International. 2008. *Indonesia Demographic and Health Survey 2007.* Calverton: BPS and Macro International.

Card, D. 1999. The Causal Effect of Education on Earnings. In O. Ashenfelter and D. Card, eds. *Handbook of Labor Economics* Vol. 3A. Amsterdam: Elsevier.

Chaudhury, N., J. Hammer, M. Kremer, K. Muralidharan, and H. Rogers. 2006. Missing in Action: Teacher and Worker Absence in Developing Countries. *Journal of Economic Perspectives*, 20 (1): 91–116.

Chen, D. 2009. Vocational Schooling, Labor Market Outcomes, and College Entry. *World Bank Policy Research Working Paper* No. 4814. Washington, DC: World Bank.

Dhanani, S., I. Islam, and A. Chowdhury. 2009. *The Indonesian Labour Market: Changes and Challenges.* London and New York: Routledge.

Gibson, J. 2009. The Constraints Associated with Infrastructure Faced by Non-Farm Enterprises at the Kabupatan Level. In N. McCulloch, ed., *Rural Investment Climate in Indonesia*. Singapore: Institute of Southeast Asian Studies.

Gibson, J., and S. Olivia. 2008. The Effect of Infrastructure Access and Quality on Non-Farm Enterprises in Rural Indonesia. *Department of Economics Working Paper in Economics*. No.17/08. Hamilton, NZ: University of Waikato.

Heriawan, R. 2008. *Provision of Macro and Micro Data for Anti-Poverty Program in Indonesia: Challenges and Responses*. Jakarta: BPS.

Ikhwan, A., and D. Johnston. 2009. The Constraints in Accessing Credit Faced by Rural Non-Farm Enterprises. In N. McCulloch ed. *Rural Investment Climate in Indonesia*. Singapore: Institute of Southeast Asian Studies.

International Labour Organization (ILO). 2007. *Key Indicators of the Labour Market*. 5ᵗh edition. Geneva.

———. 2009. *Key Indicators of the Labour Market*. 6th edition. Geneva.

———. 2010. *Working Children in Indonesia 2009*. Jakarta: ILO and Statistics Indonesia.

———. International Classification. http://laborsta.ilo.org/applv8/data/icsee.html

International Labour Organization (ILO) and PT Jamsostek. Forthcoming. Social Security for Informal Economy Workers in Indonesia. ILO.

Islam, I., and A. Chowdhury. 2009. *Growth, Employment and Poverty Reduction in Indonesia*. Geneva: ILO.

Jalal, F., M. Samani, M. C. Chang, R. Stevenson, A. Ragatz, and S. Negare. 2009. *Teacher Certification in Indonesia: A Strategy for Teacher Quality Improvement*. Jakarta: World Bank and Ministry of National Education.

Johnston, D., and J. Morduch. 2008. The Unbanked: Evidence from Indonesia. *World Bank Economic Review*, 22 (3): 517–37.

Ministry of National Education (MONE). 2005. Educational Statistics in Brief 2004/2005. Jakarta.

———. 2006. MONE Strategic Plan (Rencana Strategis Departemen Pendidikan National Tahun) 2005–2009. Jakarta.

———. 2007. EFA Mid-Decade Assessment Indonesia. Jakarta: EFA Secretariat, Ministry of National Education.

———. 2010. Letter to ADB. 16 July.

Newhouse, D., and D. Suryadarma. 2009. The Value of Vocational Education: High School Type and Labor Market Outcomes in Indonesia. *World Bank Policy Research Working Paper*. No. 5035. Washington, DC: World Bank.

Okten, C., and U. Osili. 2004. Social Networks and Credit Access in Indonesia. *World Development*, 32 (7): 1225–46.

Olken, B. 2006. Corruption and the Costs of Redistribution: Micro Evidence from Indonesia. *Journal of Public Economics*, 90:853–70.

Paqueo, V., and R. Sparrow. 2006. Free Basic Education in Indonesia: Policy Scenarios and Implications for School Enrolment. Project Report. Jakarta: World Bank.

Riddell, A. 2010. Indonesia Education Sector Assessment, Development Partner Interventions, Lessons Learned and Opportunities for Investment in Post-Basic Education. Unpublished.

Roland-Holst, D. and B. Frielink. 2009. Trade and Growth Horizons for Nusa Tenggara Timur and Timor-Leste. *Southeast Asia Working Paper Series* No. 4. Manila: ADB.

SMERU. 2010. Remote Area Allowance and Absentee Levels for Teachers in Remote Areas. *Policy Brief*. Jakarta: The SMERU Research Institute.

Sparrow, R., A. Suryahadi, and W. Widyanti. 2008. Public Health Insurance for the Poor in Indonesia: Targeting and Impact of Indonesia's Askeskin Programme. Paper prepared for the Annual Bank Conference on Development Economics (ABCDE Conference), June 2008.

Suryadarma, D., A. Suryahadi, and S. Sumarto. 2006. Causes of Low Secondary School Enrollment in Indonesia. *SMERU Working Paper*. Jakarta: The SMERU Research Institute.

———. Suryadarma, D., A. Suryahadi, S. Sumarto, and H. Rogers. 2004. The Determinants of Student Performance in Indonesian Public Primary Schools: The Role of Teachers and Schools. *SMERU Working Paper*. Jakarta: The SMERU Research Institute.

US Census Bureau. www.census.gov (accessed 25 March 2010).

Usman, S., Akhmadi, and D. Suryadarma. 2004. When Teachers are Absent: Where do They Go and What is the Impact on Students? *SMERU Field Report*. Jakarta: The SMERU Research Institute.

Usman, S., M. Mawardi, A. Poesoro, A. Suryahadi, and C. Sampford. 2008. The Special Allocation Fund (DAK): Mechanisms and Uses. *SMERU Research Report*. Jakarta: The SMERU Research Institute.

Widyanti, W., and A. Suryahadi. 2008. The State of Local Governance and Public Services in the Decentralized Indonesia in 2006: Findings from the Governance and Decentralization Survey 2 (GDS2). *SMERU Research Report*. Jakarta: The SMERU Research Institute.

World Bank. 2006a. *At Loggerheads? Agricultural Expansion, Poverty Reduction and Environment in the Tropical Forest*. Washington, DC.

———. 2006b. *The Impact of Roads Upon Local Small and Medium Enterprises in Manggarai District, NTT Province*. Washington, DC.

———. 2006c. *Making the New Indonesia Work for the Poor*. Washington, DC.

———. 2007. Spending for Development: Making the Most of Indonesia's New Opportunities. *Indonesia Public Expenditure Review 2007.* Jakarta.

———. 2008. *Investing in Indonesia's Health: Challenges and Opportunities for Future Public Spending.* Washington, DC.

———. 2009. *Investing in Indonesia's Education at the District Level: An Analysis of Regional Public Expenditure and Financial Management.* Washington, DC.

———. PovcalNet Database. http://iresearch.worldbank.org/PocalNet/jsp/CChoiceControl.jsp?WDI_Year=2007 (accessed July 2009).

———. World Development Indicators (WDI) Online. http://ddp-ext.worldbank.org/ext/DDPQQ/member.do?method=getMembers&userid=1&queryId=6 (accessed October 2009 to May 2010).

World Health Organization (WHO). 2009. *World Health Statistics 2009.* Geneva.

———. Global Health Atlas. http://apps.who.int/globalatlas (accessed July and October 2009).

———. WHO Regional Office for South-East Asia. Regional Health Situation Country Health System Profile. http://www/searo.who.int/EN/Section313.htm (accessed October 2009).

———. WHO Statistical Information System (WHOSIS). http://www.who.int/whosis/gho/en (accessed July and October 2009).

Yamauchi, F., M. Muto, S. Chowdhury, R. Dewina, and S. Sumaryanto. 2009. Spatial Networks, Labor Supply and Income Dynamics: Evidence from Indonesian Villages. *IFPRI Discussion Papers.* No.894. Washington, D.C.: International Food Policy Research Institute.

Zhuang, J. and I. Ali. 2010. Poverty, Inequality, and Inclusive Growth in Asia. In J. Zhuang ed., *Poverty, Inequality, and Inclusive Growth in Asia: Measurement, Policy Issues, and Country Studies.* London and Manila: Anthem and ADB.

5. Macroeconomic Management

Edimon Ginting and Priasto Aji

5.1. Introduction

The government has navigated the economy through two major economic crises since 1997. In the 1997 Asian financial crisis (AFC), Indonesia was the most severely affected economy in the Asian region, and its economic growth dipped by 13.4% in 1998 (Figure 5.1a). In contrast, Indonesia was among the countries least affected by the recent global financial crisis (GFC), when its economic growth declined only to 4.5% in 2009. The country used the lessons it learned from the AFC to introduce significant economic reforms afterward. This improved Indonesia's macroeconomic management, contributing to the country's resilience during the recent GFC. Indonesia's better performance was attributable to the government's appropriate and swift policy responses, limited exposure to the source of the crisis, and less reliance on exports. Further reforms have also been implemented to reduce vulnerabilities identified during the recent GFC.

However, significant challenges remain. Post-crisis economic management restored economic growth to an average of 5.1% during 2000–2009, but growth remains far below the pre-crisis level of 7%–8%. While poverty and unemployment have declined, they remain relatively high. On average, inflation has declined, but it is still higher and more volatile than in other countries in the region. At the same time, increasing short-term capital inflows complicate the conduct of monetary policies. In this context, the government has set higher targets. To achieve higher and more inclusive growth, Indonesia's new National Medium-Term Development Plan (Rencana Pembangunan Jangka Menengah Nasional [RPJMN] 2010–2014) has adopted a three-pillar development strategy: "pro-growth, pro-jobs, and pro-poor." This will require improving and fine-tuning macroeconomic management beyond the reforms implemented to deal with the recent crisis.

The next section of this chapter presents Indonesia's experience in improving macroeconomic management after the 1997 AFC. Section 5.3

discusses policy responses to deal with the 2008–2009 GFC. Section 5.4 outlines key challenges to broaden the sources of economic growth and improve employment. The last sections discuss ways to enhance the role of both fiscal and monetary policies in achieving higher and more inclusive growth.

5.2. Macroeconomic Management after the Asian Financial Crisis

The government has made substantial progress in improving macroeconomic management. Indonesia was much more severely affected by the AFC than other countries. Output fell drastically, by more than 13.4% in 1998, the sharpest drop in the region, while informal unemployment, inflation, and poverty soared (Thee 2003). This happened notwithstanding reasonable headline macroeconomic indicators prior to the AFC. Indonesia's current account deficit, for example, averaged 2.2% of gross domestic product (GDP) during 1992–1996, versus high deficits in Malaysia (6.0%) and Thailand (6.3%) in the same period. While weak macroeconomic policies did not play a central role in causing the crisis in Indonesia, the pegged exchange rate encouraged excessive private sector foreign borrowing and poor risk management in the financial sector. In 1997, private sector lending was allocated mainly to sectors that earned very little foreign reserves, such as real estate, and short-term external debt stood at about 196.4% of the country's international reserves. At the same time, about 30% of domestic banks' outstanding loans were in foreign currencies, and one-tenth of the loans were to the real sector. The AFC, which led to massive rupiah depreciation, hit the assets and liabilities of the domestic banks.

Macroeconomic management to restore macroeconomic stability in the post-AFC period has been generally sound. Four key elements of macroeconomic policy during this period have been evident. First, to prevent the complete collapse of the financial system, the government decided to recapitalize the banking sector. The policy led to a dramatic increase in the ratio of government debt to GDP, to about 100%. To reduce the government debt, consistent fiscal consolidation was implemented after the banking bailout. The budget deficit was gradually reduced from 2.4% of GDP in 2001 to 0.1% of GDP in 2008 (Figure 5.1b), driven by improved revenue collection, reduced subsidies (especially the untargeted fuel and electricity subsidies), and lowered risk premiums and interest rates. To improve public financial management, the government implemented the Public Finance Law passed in 2003. Reduced deficit, stronger economic growth over the years, and the appreciation of rupiah reduced the debt-to-GDP ratio to 33% in 2008 (Figure 5.1b).

Figure 5.1: Maintaining Macroeconomic Stability
a. Annual Economic Growth

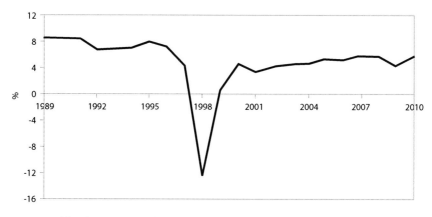

Source: World Bank, WDI, accessed March 2011.

b. Fiscal Indicators

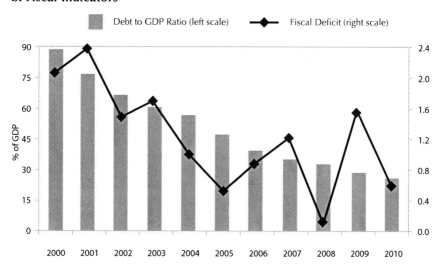

Source: Ministry of Finance, Government Debt Profile, accessed March 2011.

c. Banking Indicators

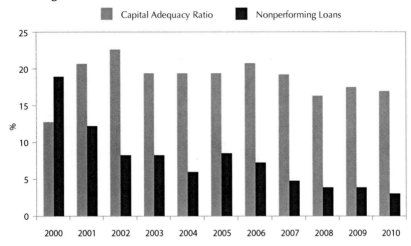

Source: Bank Indonesia, Indonesian Banking Statistics (various years).

d. External Balance

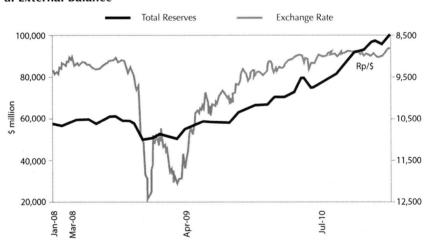

Sources: Total reserves from Bank Indonesia (various editions); exchange rates from Bloomberg, accessed March 2011.

Second, to strengthen the banking sector, the government introduced significant regulatory changes by focusing on risk-based supervision and consolidated supervision of groups rather than traditional monitoring of compliance with regulations by individual banks. This involved a better understanding of banks' risk management and internal control systems, stronger focus on corporate governance and responsibilities of boards of directors and management, stress testing of capital adequacy, and improved off-site monitoring systems. Indonesia has made progress in strengthening supervision capacity, off-site monitoring, early warning systems, corporate governance, and responsibilities of boards of directors and management (Lindgren 2006). Although the efficiency of financial intermediation still needs enhancement, the performance of the banking system continued to improve following a series of regulatory reforms and reforms to supervision practices introduced after the AFC. Nonperforming loans declined to about 3.8% in 2008 from 18.8% in 2000, and the capital adequacy ratio increased to 16.4% from 12.7% in the same period (Figure 5.1c).

Third, inflation surged to about 80% at the peak of the AFC due to the rupiah's depreciation and the open-ended bank recapitalization program. Bank Indonesia managed to restore inflationary pressure quickly to a single digit in 2000. However, inflationary pressure returned shortly thereafter. To improve inflation management, Bank Indonesia adopted an inflation-targeting framework in June 2005. After experiencing double-digit inflation in 2005 and 2006, inflation in Indonesia fell to 6.4% in 2007. The unexpected surge in international food and energy prices pushed domestic inflation to 11% at the end of 2008. As in many countries in the region, inflationary pressure was driven by largely external factors related to the escalating international prices of food and commodities (see section 5.5). Despite inflation targeting, on a number of occasions, inflation still exceed Bank Indonesia's target, due to volatile food prices and fuel price adjustments. Indonesia's inflation being relatively higher than that of its trading partners tends to produce real appreciation of the rupiah, reducing competitiveness of the tradable sectors over time.[1]

Finally, the country's external position has continued to improve. The current account has been in surplus in recent years due to good export performance driven by high commodity prices and strong demand. Consistent with the positive current account position, international reserve holdings increased sharply, to over $65 billion in June 2008. Another factor contributing to the increased reserves is the precautionary motive, pushed by the sharp expansion of trade and capital flows, which are volatile (Ruiz-Arranz and Zavadjil 2008). In addition, the rupiah has become more flexible to changes in the economic fundamentals. This, together with increasing international reserves, has reduced the country's vulnerabilities to external shocks (Figure 5.1d).

---

[1]   Tradable sectors refer to agriculture, mining, and manufacturing; nontradable sectors refer to construction, utility, and services.

5.3. Macroeconomic Management during the 2008–2009 Global Financial Crisis

The global economic downturn, triggered by the collapse of the United States (US) subprime mortgage market, turned into one of the sharpest global economic recessions in modern history. Most developed economies were in deep recession in 2009; the pace of economic growth in developing countries had declined significantly, and in some cases had become negative. Spillovers from the GFC on the Indonesian financial sector—mainly equity markets and the balance of payments—were particularly severe in the last quarter of 2008, more so than in most other regional economies. Equity prices fell by 50% (Figure 5.2a), and investors unbundled financial portfolios, resulting in a decline of $6.5 billion in gross international reserves in the fourth quarter and a 31% depreciation in the rupiah exchange rate from November 2008 to February 2009 (Figure 5.1d). Elevated perceptions about the risks of the Indonesian financial sector and economy have limited Indonesia's access to international credit markets and raised the cost of borrowing. Yields on Indonesian domestic bonds have picked up since mid-2008 and spiked sharply in October to as high as 20% (Figure 5.2a), and spreads on Indonesia's international bonds surged by about 650 basis points. This was due to a rapid increase in domestic lending of about 30%, in part attributable to the squeeze on US dollar lines, and capital outflow and the associated rupiah exchange rate depreciation.

Figure 5.2: Financial Market Performance

a. Stock Index and Bond Yields

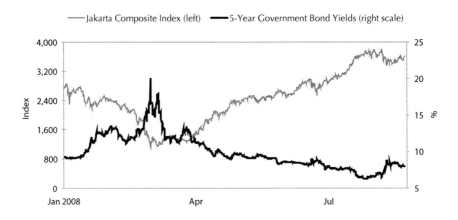

Source: Bloomberg, accessed March 2011.

b. Credit Default Swaps (senior 5 year)

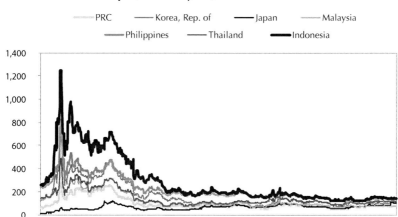

PRC = People's Republic of China.
Source: Bloomberg, accessed March 2011.

While the sources of the GFC and associated risks to the Indonesian economy are different from those of the AFC, subsequent reforms have made the Indonesian economy much more resilient to external shocks. In addition, lessons learned from the AFC were embedded in the handling of the GFC. The government's response was swift and involved proactive measures aimed at reestablishing confidence in the domestic financial sector, increasing liquidity in the banking system, and strengthening Bank Indonesia's lender of last resort facility. These measures included (1) issuing a financial safety net regulation that clearly establishes the roles, responsibilities, and procedures that govern the actions and responses of Bank Indonesia, the minister of finance, and the Deposit Insurance Corporation in the event of the failure of a financial institution; (2) strengthening the role of Bank Indonesia's lender of last resort facility by allowing banks to borrow in the short term from the central bank, backed up by high quality assets such as government bonds and Bank Indonesia Certificates (SBIs); (3) increasing the coverage of the deposit insurance scheme; and (4) easing liquidity in the banking sector through monetary expansion.

On the monetary policy front, Bank Indonesia has broadly operated an appropriate monetary policy stance throughout the crisis. In early 2008, it raised interest rates to counter the threat of second-round inflationary pressures arising from the surge in global commodity prices. It then shifted to an expansionary monetary position at the end of 2008 to provide sufficient liquidity to the banking system against the backdrop of rapidly falling inflation. Policy measures included gradually cutting Bank Indonesia policy rates from 9.5% in December 2008 to 6.5% by August 2009, injecting rupiah liquidity through repurchase agreements, and reducing the reserve requirement for foreign currency deposits. Inflation fell to 2.7% (year-on-year) in July 2009, from its peak of 12.1% in August 2008. Inflation remained benign for the rest of the year, indicative of the slump in domestic economic activity and lower commodity prices.

To strengthen the external position, the government arranged multilateral and bilateral swap arrangements to gain ability to call for more foreign reserves when needed. For example, Indonesia has access to a $14.6 billion swap facility with the People's Republic of China. In this context of slowing exports and waning market confidence, Bank Indonesia has activated its rediscount window for trade receivables, and the government has established an export–import financing agency that will provide trade finance products, including export credit guarantees, and has a mandate to support diversification of export markets and the access of small and medium-sized enterprises to trade finance.

As in most other developing economies, the national government budget does not have automatic stabilizers embedded in the expenditure side of the budget. Empirical evidence for Indonesia suggests that only two budget items have historically exhibited a relation with the economic cycle— government purchases of goods and services, and debt servicing—and the former has exhibited a distinct procyclical response (Baldacci 2009). To allow for a countercyclical fiscal policy, the government projected a wider national government budget deficit of 2.5% of GDP in 2009, up from 1.0% as originally programmed, and up from a 0.1% budget deficit in 2008. Most of the fiscal stimulus package was attributed to one-off or temporary policy measures, which will be reversed once economic recovery sets in. These included the stimulus spending on infrastructure and temporary payroll tax relief to businesses and indirect tax relief to families.

With good initial conditions and swift policy measures, Indonesia weathered the GFC much better than expected. After declining in three consecutive quarters since the fourth quarter of 2008, economic growth began to recover in the third quarter of 2009. With stronger economic activities toward the end of the year, economic growth reached 4.6% in 2009—the third highest among G20 countries. Private consumption contributed the majority of GDP growth in 2009 (2.8 percentage points). It was driven by good harvests (which bolstered rural incomes), low inflation, government cash transfers to poor households early in 2009, election-related spending, and tax cuts (adopted as part of a fiscal stimulus package). Other economic indicators have also been very positive. At 2.8%, inflation was the lowest in 10 years. Unemployment continued to decline thanks to the informal sectors' ability to provide temporary employment for laid-off workers. With the actual budget deficit lower than planned, at 1.6% of GDP, the country's debt-to-GDP ratio fell to 28% in 2009. The banking system remained sound, with a capital asset ratio of 17.4% and gross nonperforming loans at under 4% as of December 2009. The rupiah appreciated against the US dollar by 18.2% in 2009, recovering from a depreciation in late 2008.

In 2010, economic recovery was broader based. While domestic consumption remained resilient and exports expanded by about 32.2%. Investment picked up strongly, supported by increasing foreign direct investment and domestic credit. Yields on government bonds fell significantly to a record level, stock prices climbed, and credit default swaps returned to levels seen before the GFC (Figure 5.2a, b). Indonesia's sovereign ratings were upgraded by all three credit rating agencies in 2010. The upgrades reflect the country's relative resilience during the financial crisis due primarily to its exchange rate flexibility, improved external finances due to foreign reserves accumulation, lowered gross external financing requirements, and a stronger international liquidity position. Standard & Poor's raised its long-term foreign currency credit rating on the country's debt from BB– to BB in March 2010, and Moody's upgraded its rating in January 2011 from Ba2 positive to Ba1 stable. Fitch raised its BB+ rating outlook from stable to positive in February 2011, which suggests an upgrade to investment grade within 12 months.

5.4.   Challenges to Broadening the Sources of Growth

Although economic growth increased to 6.1% in 2010, it is still significantly below the pre-crisis level of 7%–8% (Figure 5.1a). The lower economic growth since the mid-1990s has been accompanied by lower growth in employment (Figure 5.3c). Deeper analysis of the sources of Indonesia's economic growth highlights a number of important facts. First, economic growth after the AFC and economic recovery during the recent GFC has been supported mostly by private consumption (Figure 5.3a). Second, the contribution of investment has remained important but declined significantly after the AFC. The overall share of investment in GDP declined from 26% in 1991–2000 to about 24% in 2001–2009. However, the trend recently reversed, with the investment-to-GDP ratio picking up to 32.2% in 2010. In line with the government's fiscal consolidation efforts, the contribution of government consumption has been relatively small, except in 2009, reflecting the fiscal stimulus. Meanwhile, the contribution of net exports remained positive but varied over time due to its increasing dependence on international commodity prices.

Figure 5.3: Economic Growth and Employment

a. Contributions to Growth by Sources of Demand

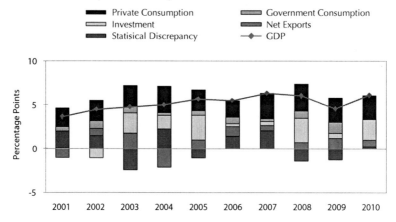

Source: CEIC, accessed March 2011.

b. Contributions to Growth by Tradable and Nontradable Sectors[a]

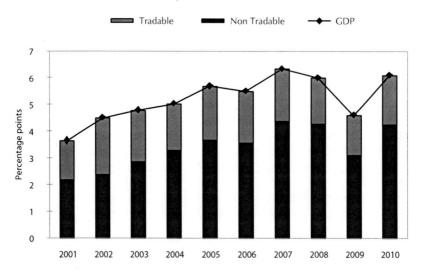

GDP = gross domestic product.
[a] Tradable sectors refer to agriculture, mining, and manufacturing; nontradable sectors refer to construction, utilities, and services.
Source: CEIC, accessed March 2011.

c. Employment Growth by Sectors

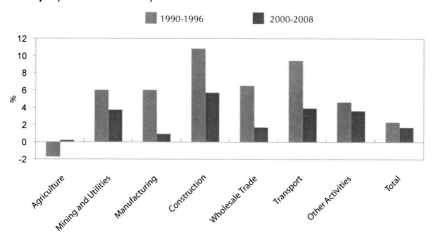

Source: ADB, SDBS, accessed March 2011.

d. Employment Growth by Tradable and Nontradable Sectors

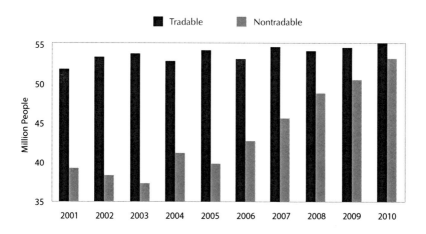

Source: ADB, SDBS, accessed March 2011.

e. Employment by type

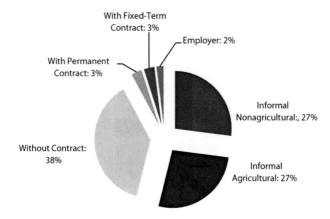

Source: World Bank (2009).

f. Changes in Unemployment and Employment[a]

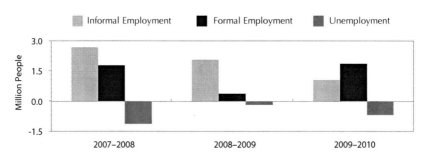

[a] Changes as of February each year.
Source: World Bank (2009).

On the production side, mirroring the dominant contribution of consumption from the demand side, growth was driven mostly by the nontradable sector. The contribution of the tradable sector has stagnated (Figure 5.3b). This is caused partly by the lackluster performance of manufacturing, with its average share in GDP declining from 42% in 1991–2000 to 25% in 2001–2008. Exports of textiles, electronics, footwear, pulp and paper, and wood products stagnated even when the world market expanded, suggesting that Indonesia is becoming less competitive. The country's exports have become more dependent on volatile world markets for mineral and agricultural commodities. Labor-intensive exports growth shrank from 30% a year before 1997 to just 3% a year during 1998–2009 (Papanek and Basri 2010).

Stagnation in the tradable sector resulted in very slow employment creation (Figure 5.3d). In particular, shrinking labor-intensive manufacturing has important employment implications, as Indonesia needs to employ more than 2.5 million workers who enter the labor force every year, and the majority of the workers have inferior jobs in the informal sector (Figure 5.3e). The decline of better employment opportunities in manufacturing tends to increase employment in the informal sector. The recent experience during the GFC, which affected the tradable sectors most severely, illustrates this point very clearly. Although unemployment continued to decline slightly during February 2008 to February 2009, most of employment opportunities (about 2 million) were generated by the informal sector (Figure 5.3f). Only 380,000 formal jobs were generated during the same period.

While the large population and increasing middle class will continue to provide sustainable demand through private consumption, investment and exports must increase significantly to accelerate economic growth over the medium term. Expanded investment to support more productive tradable sectors would be conducive to generating better quality employment. Weakening of the manufacturing sector is attributed largely to declining competitiveness due to the appreciating exchange rate, lack of infrastructure, high logistics costs, and stringent labor market regulations. Indonesia's success at maintaining a healthy macroeconomic environment throughout the GFC boosted the country's ranking in economic competitiveness on the Global Competitiveness Index (Figure 5.4.a) by 10 places to 44 in 2010 (WEF 2009). However, the rank for infrastructure, at 82, is far below the country's overall ranking, implying that infrastructure is a drag on the country's competitiveness (Figure 5.4.b). Indeed, a number of other studies have pointed out that infrastructure has emerged as a major constraint for accelerating economic growth. The government's spending on infrastructure as a share of GDP has fallen by nearly 50% from the first half of the 1990s and is well below that for faster growing Asian economies. Logistics costs in Indonesia are estimated at about 14% of total production costs, compared with only about 5% in Japan (Basri and Hill 2011).

The respectable economic growth achieved in the last 10 years has also contributed to poverty reduction. The poverty rate has fallen by about 1 percentage point per year since 2003, reaching 17.8% in 2006, and falling further to 14.1% in early 2009 and to 13.3% in early 2010. However, poverty remains a serious problem in absolute terms in Indonesia, with over 32 million people below the national poverty line and about 40% of the population vulnerable to falling into poverty if their circumstances suddenly deteriorate (see also Chapters 4 and 10). Higher economic growth is required to accelerate poverty reduction. In addition, some chronic poverty may require a more systematic social protection system over the medium term.

Figure 5.4: The Global Competitiveness Index

a. Macroeconomic Environment Index

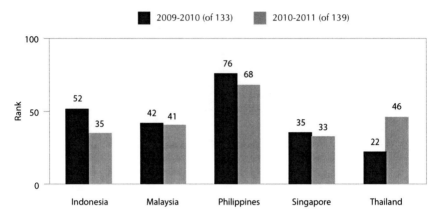

Source: WEF (2010).

b. Indonesia's 2010–2011 Rankings

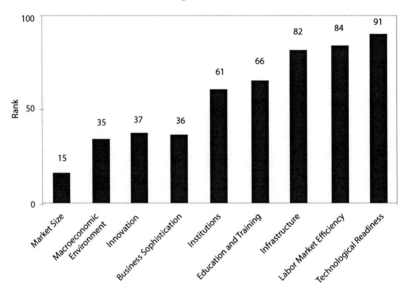

Source: WEF (2010).

5.5.   Improving Macroeconomic Policy to Support More Inclusive Growth

As noted, improved macroeconomic management has been a key story in the country's economic recovery from the AFC and the recent GFC. Despite improved macroeconomic management, economic growth remains below the level achieved before the AFC. Although declining, the poverty incidence is still high. Unemployment declined more slowly than expected, with a large share of employment generated by the informal sector. A key challenge going forward is to make economic growth more inclusive. Ali (2007) defined inclusive growth as growth that creates new economic opportunities and ensures equal access to the opportunities created for all segments of society, particularly the poor. Ali and Son (2007) outlined three key critical measures for achieving inclusive growth (1) creating employment opportunities and promoting higher productivity, (2) developing human capabilities through adequate investment in basic social services of education and health, and (3) providing social safety nets and targeted interventions to help people who are vulnerable and/or suffer from extreme deprivation.

The government has announced its commitment to achieving higher and more inclusive growth in its new RPJMN 2010–2014 through a three-pillar development strategy that is pro-growth, pro-jobs, and pro-poor. In this context, questions arise as to how macroeconomic management could be improved to support the government's objectives of higher and more inclusive growth. This section will discuss how fiscal and monetary policy can be enhanced and fine-tuned to support the government's more inclusive growth strategy.

Regarding fiscal policy, while the fiscal consolidation adopted in the aftermath of the AFC was necessary, it also produced significant underspending in the country's infrastructure and social programs. Infrastructure is regarded as a key bottleneck to accelerating economic growth, and additional spending will be necessary to implement the government's more comprehensive and consolidated poverty alleviation programs. Therefore, significant efforts are needed to create fiscal space to augment spending on infrastructure and poverty alleviation.[2]

Regarding monetary policy, since the introduction of the inflation targeting framework in July 2005, Bank Indonesia's primary objective has been to achieve its inflation target. Available studies suggest that controlling inflation has played a key role in reducing the poverty incidence in Indonesia (World Bank 2006, 2011). On average, inflation has declined significantly

---

[2]   Fiscal space is defined for this chapter as total expenditure minus all compulsory spending such as the public servant salary bill, transfer to the regions, interest payments, and subsidies. Another definition of fiscal space is the room in the budget to fund priority expenditures without undermining fiscal sustainability.

since 2005, but it remains higher and more volatile than inflation in other countries in the region. Although inflation targeting is Bank Indonesia's primary objective, low inflation is a prerequisite for higher and sustainable growth. When inflationary pressure is subdued, monetary policy can help provide countercyclical support to economic growth. However, recent experience suggests that this role has been less effective. The conduct of monetary policy has also been complicated by the recent large inflows of foreign capital.

5.5.1. Increasing Fiscal Space and Improving Budget Execution

Since 1999, fiscal policy has focused primarily on fiscal consolidation and reducing the high public debt-to-GDP ratio. The government has also taken significant steps to reduce spending on domestic fuel subsidies and reorient spending to key priority areas, including education and poverty alleviation programs. To achieve the higher and more inclusive growth set out in the RPJMN 2010–2014, a recent Asian Development Bank study suggests accelerating infrastructure development, improving governance and institutions, and enhancing the access to and quality of education (ADB 2009, 2010). While the government recognizes the need to increase private investment to support its pro-jobs growth strategy, significant additional government spending will be required to achieve the government's higher growth target of above 7% and more significant poverty reduction over the medium term. Increased government spending is key to enticing private investment into the country's lagging infrastructure.

The government will need to increase the fiscal space in the budget to accommodate increased spending for infrastructure and poverty reduction programs. Simple analysis of the government budget suggests that the fiscal space available in the last 5 years remains relatively low at about 4%–5% of GDP (Figure 5.5.a). The contribution of revenues tends to fluctuate (Figure 5.5.b). Overall, the contribution of the improved tax revenue to additional fiscal space has been relatively small, as the tax-to-GDP ratio remained stagnant. In 2009, the tax to GDP ratio declined due to a reduction of tax rates and declining growth caused by the GFC. In addition, the stimulus package introduced to deal with the GFC was dominated by tax measures. The contribution of nontax revenue, which is dominated by fuel and gas royalty, varies with international fuel prices. On the expenditure side, the reduction of interest payments has consistently had a positive contribution (Figure 5.5.c). However, the overall contribution of the expenditure side to fiscal space is dominated by subsidies, which vary depending on the international fuel price. In addition, the government has not been able to use all of the

Figure 5.5: Fiscal Space

a. Fiscal Space: Discretionary Expenditure

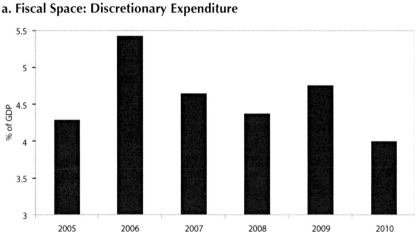

Source: Estimates based on Ministry of Finance, Budget Statistics (various years).

b. Change in Fiscal Space: Revenue Side[a]

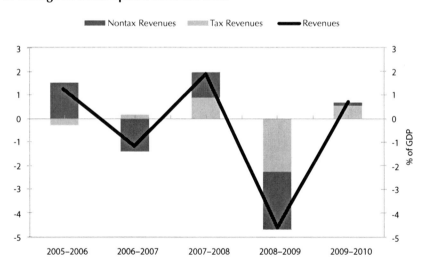

[a] Change between periods; + denotes positive contribution to fiscal space, - denotes negative contribution to fiscal space.
Source: Estimates based on Ministry of Finance, Budget Statistics (various years).

c. Change in Fiscal Space: Expenditure Side [a]

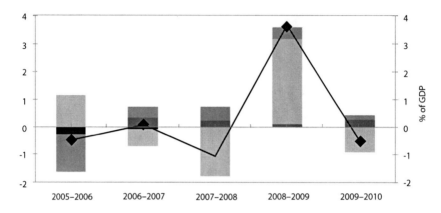

[a] Change between periods; + denotes positive contribution to fiscal space, - denotes negative contribution to fiscal space.
Source: Estimates based on Ministry of Finance, Budget Statistics (various years).

d. Fiscal Space: Projected versus Actual

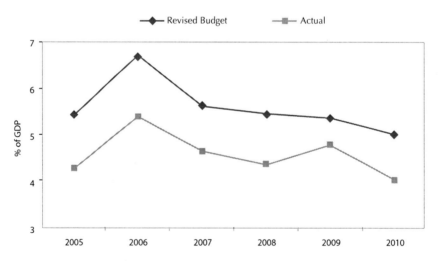

Source: Estimates based on Ministry of Finance, Budget Statistics (various years).

available fiscal space due to the lack of capacity in budget execution. The actual budget deficit has been lower than planned by an average of 1% of GDP annually during 2005–2010.

Several measures can be implemented to create fiscal space at the central government level without increasing the fiscal deficit, as stipulated in the RPJMN 2010–2014. On the revenue side, over the medium term, tax collection could increase through continued reform in the tax administration. The number of taxpayers registered increased from 4.8 million in 2006 to 18.1 million in 2010 and the tax-to-GDP ratio increased by 0.7 percentage point to 11.7%. The effort to reduce tax gaps and introduce new systems and procedures that facilitate a taxpayer-centered approach to improve voluntary compliance should continue. The efforts need to focus on strengthening the self-assessment system and streamlining business processes, improving the quality and integrity of the tax database, introducing risk-based compliance enforcement, improving professionalism and staff integrity, strengthening governance, and increasing the information and communications technology capability to support the entire tax operations.

On the expenditure side, additional fiscal space can be generated from a number of areas. The RPJMN targets continued reduction of the government debt to about 24% of GDP in 2014. This policy, together with continued improvement of economic performance and Indonesia's sovereign rating, will lead to a significant reduction of interest payments. Significant fiscal space can be generated by further reducing untargeted fuel subsidies, which the government has considered through a number of measures for the future. In 2010, spending on fuel subsidies exceeded capital spending and was more than three times social safety net spending (World Bank 2010). The fuel subsidy is highly regressive. The richest 10% of households consume 40% of the total subsidized gasoline, and the top half of households use almost 84% of the total subsidized gasoline. The government has announced its intention to produce budgetary savings in 2011 by reducing spending on lower priority areas. Better coordination across all levels of government to avoid duplication of tasks, including in social and poverty reduction programs, could help generate budget savings. With the major needs to upgrade the country's infrastructure and the slow process of attracting private participation into the sector, there is strong justification to create additional space by relaxing the medium-term budget deficit reduction target.

In addition to increasing fiscal space, continued reform is necessary to improve budget execution. One key feature of current budget execution is that a large proportion of the budget is spent in the last quarter of the year, which can affect the quality of the results. Further, actual budget implementation has consistently been lower than programmed (Figure

5.5d). As a result, fiscal support for economic growth has been suboptimal. To rectify this problem, the government is simplifying the budget execution processes. It has taken measures to allow spending units more authority and flexibility in implementing and managing their budgets to achieve agreed upon outcomes and outputs. Further efforts are also needed to improve the regulatory framework for and capacity in the public procurement system.

To support efforts to make growth more inclusive, the government has developed programs to accelerate poverty reduction. Fragmentation and lack of coordination have limited the effectiveness of the national poverty reduction programs. To address these problems, the government has reorganized the institutional arrangements. It issued Presidential Regulation No. 15 of 2010 to form the National Team for the Acceleration of Poverty Reduction (TNP2K). The team consists of all government agencies responsible for planning, financing, and implementing poverty reduction programs. The TNP2K was established to guide and oversee the reform of poverty reduction policies and programs. Chaired by Indonesia's vice president, the TNP2K will lead the coordination and oversight of all poverty reduction programs under all three clusters of the national poverty reduction strategy: (1) family-based social assistance programs, (2) community empowerment programs, and (3) expansion of economic opportunities for low-income households.

5.5.2. Reducing Inflation and Enhancing Monetary Policy Transmission

Inflation has declined significantly since the formal adoption of inflation targeting in 2005. On average, inflation declined from 12.0% in the 5 years before inflation targeting (2001–2005) to 7.2% during 2006–-2010. However, 5 years after the adoption of inflation targeting, on a number of occasions inflation still occasionally exceeded Bank Indonesia's targets, triggered by significant fuel price adjustments and the surge in international commodity prices, as well as domestic supply shocks. In 2006, large major fuel price adjustments pushed inflation back to double digits. The significant increase in inflation in 2006 also reversed the gain in poverty reduction, with the poverty incidence increasing to 17.6% from 16.0% in 2005. In 2008, inflation reached 12.0%, driven by increased international commodity prices. More recently, food supply disruptions caused by bad weather and by infrastructure weaknesses drove inflation up from 2.8% in late 2009 to 7.0% in December 2010 (Figure 5.6b). Food price inflation surged to nearly 16% late in 2010. Inflation exceeded the central bank's target of 4.0%–6.0% in some months after August 2010.

Figure 5.6: Containing Inflation

a. Headline and Core inflation

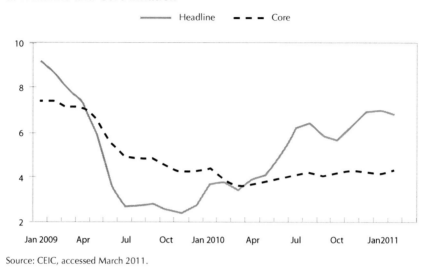

Source: CEIC, accessed March 2011.

b. Contribution to Inflation: Food and Nonfood

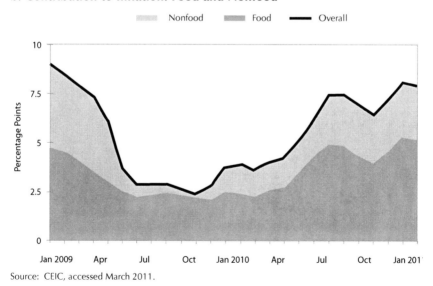

Source: CEIC, accessed March 2011.

c. Contribution to Inflation: Food and Nonfood

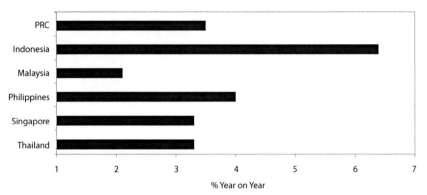

PRC = People's Republic of China.
Source: BPS Website, accessed September 2010.

d. Credit of Commercial Banks Based on Location (December 2010, Rp billion)

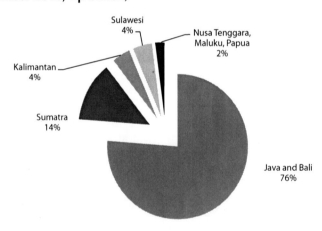

Source: Bank Indonesia (2011).

With this high volatility, inflation in Indonesia tends to be higher than in other countries in the region (Figure 5.6c). Some inflationary pressures are temporary, particularly those originating from volatile food items. An important indicator of temporary pressures is the gap between headline inflation and core inflation (Figure 5.6a). While core inflation increased only by 4.3% in 2010, temporary inflationary pressure was 2.7%; or about 39% of overall inflation. Recent inflationary pressure also has a regional dimension. Regions with positive contributions to national inflation at the end of 2010 are largely outside key business areas in Java (Figure 5.6e).

e. Contributions to Inflation: Regional [a]

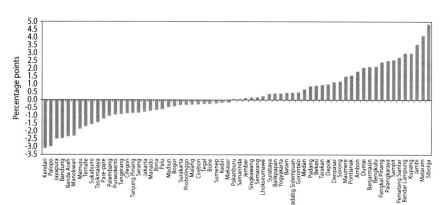

[a] Difference between regional and national year-end inflation in 2010.
Source: Estimates based on BPS Website, accessed March 2011.

This increases the difficulty of implementing monetary policy. As shown by the distribution of credit across the country (Figure 5.6d), many regions that contribute positively to national inflation are financially less developed. Therefore, transmission of monetary policy to these regions will also be less efficient.

As noted earlier, due to the rupiah's real appreciation, higher inflation has eroded the competitiveness of key manufacturing exports. Empirical evidence has identified a negative relationship between GDP growth and the level and volatility of inflation (Judson and Orphanides 1999). One important channel is through a higher cost of capital. Goyal and Ruiz-Arranz (2009) found that the government's domestic and international borrowing costs have been higher than costs of comparable countries largely due to the higher rate of inflation in Indonesia. The government's domestic and international borrowing costs are often used as benchmarks for the cost of private sector lending. Therefore, reducing inflation further is a key for attracting the significant amount of private investment needed to support higher growth.

While a significant part of inflationary pressures is temporary and originates from the supply side and administrative price adjustment, frequent and large deviations of inflation from the stated target could reduce the credibility of monetary policy. Thus, Bank Indonesia and the government have implemented a two-tier strategy for dealing with inflation. First, Bank Indonesia generally uses monetary policy when inflationary pressures persist. Second, to deal with temporary food inflation originating from the supply side, the government sets up a national team involving Bank

Indonesia and several line ministries, headed by the Coordinating Ministry of Economic Affairs.

On the monetary policy front, with the surge in capital inflows into the country, Bank Indonesia initially used quantitative measures by increasing the statutory reserve requirement for commercial banks from 5% to 8%, effective 1 November 2010. The measure is expected to absorb approximately Rp53 trillion (about 3% of total bank lending) worth of liquidity from the banking system. To manage inflation that is expected to increase gradually, Bank Indonesia raised its rate by 25 basis points to 6.75% for the first time since August 2009. On the supply-side response, the interdepartmental team for controlling inflation implemented a number of key measures, including (1) improving food supply in the affected regions; (2) temporarily suspending import duties on 57 key commodities and implementing market interventions; and (3) helping the poor through the Raskin program, which distributes 15 kilograms of rice per month to 17.5 million families.

In conducting monetary policy, Bank Indonesia uses the Bank Indonesia Certificate (SBI) rate as the signal of its policy stance. When inflationary pressure is building, Bank Indonesia raises the SBI rate, then reverses it when inflationary pressure subsides. A number of key reforms have been implemented to enhance the SBI's role as a key monetary policy instrument, including bringing it more in line with the interbank rate. However, the effectiveness of monetary policy depends on how efficiently it is transmitted to affect real economic activities by the banking sectors. Recent data (Figure 5.7a) suggest that the banking sector is very quick in transmitting SBI rate increases to the borrowers, but lags significantly in transmitting interest rate cuts. This implies that the effect of monetary policy is biased toward tightening. Therefore, based on recent experience, monetary policy tends to be insufficiently effective in providing countercyclical support to economic growth. Moreover, the cost of banking intermediation in Indonesia is still relatively high—at 5%–6%, one of the highest in the region (Figure 5.7b). This is explained by several factors, including (1) duopolistic behavior of the banking sector, (2) inefficient financial contract enforcement, (3) high risks associated with more volatile inflation, and (4) relatively low banking penetration in the Indonesian economy. Therefore, further reforms to financial intermediation can help improve the role of monetary policy transmission in supporting economic growth when inflationary pressure is not present.

Figure 5.7:   Enhancing Monetary Policy Transmission

a. Bank Indonesia and Lending Rates

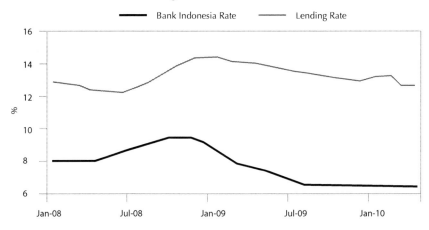

Source: Bank Indonesia, Monetary Policy Reports (various editions).

b. Net Interest Margin

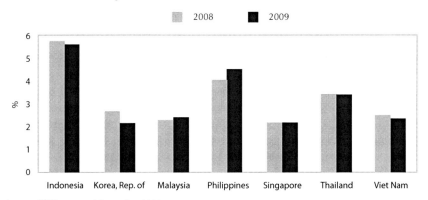

Source: CEIC, accessed December 2010.

5.5.3. Managing Capital Inflows

As noted earlier, the conduct of monetary policy has also been complicated by the recent large inflow of foreign capital. Portfolio inflows surged by 47.1% to $15.2 billion in 2010. Net foreign equity purchases estimated at $23 billion pushed the Jakarta Stock Exchange index of share prices up by

173

46% in 2010 (Figure 5.8a). Foreign holdings of government rupiah bonds increased by 81.3%, equivalent to about $9.8 billion (Figure 5.8b) and their yields fell steeply (Figure 5.2a). Concern over the rise in inflation coupled with international market jitters in early 2011 resulted in some reversal of short-term capital flows. Net foreign purchases in the equity market were negative (–$0.6 billion) in the first 3 months of 2011, while net foreign purchases of government bonds were positive at $1.6 billion. Foreign direct investment rose by 161% to $12.7 billion in 2010, reflecting the better domestic and international investment climate. Gross international reserves climbed by more than $30 billion, to $96.2 billion at year-end, covering 7.1 months of imports and government debt payments. As a result, the rupiah has been under continued pressure to appreciate (Figure 5.1d).

Capital flow in general can bring significant benefits to emerging economies by augmenting limited domestic savings to finance productive investment, promote trade of goods and services, and foster financial market development. However, policymakers in emerging markets are also concerned that the recent surge of capital inflows could cause problems. First, a significant amount of the flows are perceived to be temporary and can be reversed when policy rates in advanced economies return to more normal levels. Second, massive capital inflows complicate macroeconomic management and could lead to excessive exchange rate appreciation that adversely impacts the domestic tradable sector. Third, large capital inflows may lead to excessive foreign borrowing and foreign currency exposure, which can lead to asset price bubbles.

The key policy question therefore is how best to deal with the surge in capital inflows by retaining the benefits while minimizing the potential risks. The options are well known—monetary policy, fiscal policy, exchange rate policy, macro prudential regulation, and capital control. International experience, however, suggests that each policy measure is only a partial solution. Therefore, a policy mix using a combination of measures is generally necessary. In developing the policy mix, policymakers face dilemmas and trade-offs best summarized by the "Impossible Trinity." The Impossible Trinity principle says that an economy can never have all three of the following features at the same time: (1) fixed or semifixed exchange rates, (2) an independent monetary policy, and (3) perfect capital mobility unconstrained by capital controls. In practice, only two of these three objectives can be achieved at a time. The implications are as follows:

- **Principle 1:** If policymakers want an independent monetary policy, in the absence of capital controls, they need to give up fixed exchange rates in favor of a flexible regime.
- **Principle 2:** If policymakers want fixed or semifixed exchange rates, in the absence of capital controls, they lose monetary and credit policy independence.

Figure 5.8: Capital Flows to Indonesia

a. Net Foreign Investment Inflows to Equity

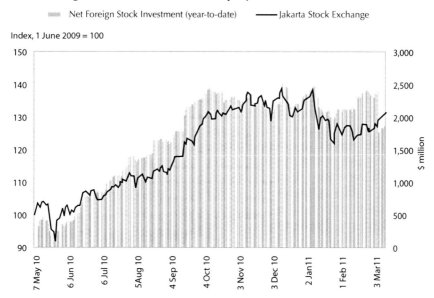

Source: CEIC, accessed December 2010.

b. Foreign Ownership of Government Securities

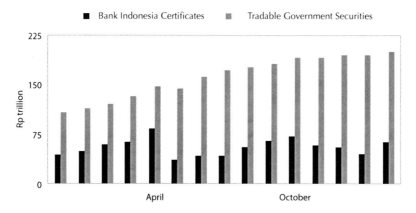

Source: Bank Indonesia Website, accessed March 2011.

- **Principle 3:** If policymakers want to maintain monetary independence while maintaining fixed or semifixed exchange rates, they need to sacrifice perfect capital mobility and use capital controls.

The appropriate policy mix to deal with the surge in capital inflows will depend on the conditions of the economy, including the level of reserves, the level of capacity utilization, the scope for exchange rate appreciation, and the quality of prudential regulations. In responding to a surge of capital inflows, it is important to distinguish between transitory (short-term) capital inflows driven by short-term cyclical factors, and longer term inflows that are supported by long-term factors such as growth differentials and better long-term economic prospects. Longer term capital inflows such as foreign direct investment usually contribute to productivity improvement, which will provide room for gradual appreciation over the medium term.

Bank Indonesia has adopted a policy mix involving (1) sterilizing part of the capital inflow and accumulating international reserves, (2) allowing the rupiah to appreciate moderately, and (3) introducing macro-prudential regulations to reduce the liquidity of SBIs.

Sterilization and Reserve Accumulation. In 2010, Bank Indonesia intervened in the foreign exchange market by purchasing foreign currency surpluses driven by large capital inflows. With the threat of inflation gradually emerging, Bank Indonesia partly sterilized the effect of such foreign exchange intervention on the domestic monetary base through a matching open market operation using SBIs. Learning from experience during the recent GFC and the increasing share of short-term capital inflows, Bank Indonesia used the recent episode of large capital inflows to augment its reserve holdings. Since the end of 2009, the country's gross international reserves increased by about $30 billion to $96.7 billion at the end of December 2010. Sterilization and reserve accumulation continued in early 2011, increasing the country's gross international reserves further to $105.7 billion at the end of March. However, the cost to the Bank Indonesia balance sheet could be significant, given the low returns from Bank Indonesia's foreign reserves investments. This could have implications for Bank Indonesia's ability to independently implement monetary policy to manage expected increases in inflationary pressures. In this context, alternative ways to reduce sterilization costs need to be considered, including introducing instruments other than SBIs. Bank Indonesia is now holding Rp254 trillion of nonmarketable government bonds that pay low interest. Making the bonds more marketable will allow Bank Indonesia to use them in its repurchase operations to absorb liquidity.

Currency Appreciation. Bank Indonesia also allowed the rupiah to appreciate by 4%–5% in 2010 to partly absorb the effect of surging capital inflows. The 2010 International Monetary Fund Article IV Consultation Report notes that the rupiah was broadly in equilibrium, suggesting that further appreciation would reduce the competitiveness of the tradable sector. In addition, due to higher inflation in 2010, the rupiah appreciated against the currencies of other countries in the region. This suggests that there will be less room for the rupiah to appreciate going forward, in particular to accommodate increased short-term capital. However, good export expansion during 2010, despite the rupiah's appreciation, implies that there will be some room for further appreciation without hurting competitiveness.

Monetary Policy. Monetary policy to lower the Bank Indonesia rate will reduce the differentials between Indonesia's interest rates and those in the advanced economies. Starting in the second half 2010, reducing the Bank Indonesia rate was not an option because of the gradual pickup in inflation. With continued inflationary pressure and higher economic growth projected for 2011, there will be less room for Bank Indonesia to reduce the rate. However, as previously noted, inflation in Indonesia is not entirely a monetary phenomenon, and more than half of inflationary pressure is explained by supply-side factors, volatile food prices, and other seasonal dynamics. The latter include festive seasons and large disbursements of government spending in the last quarter of the year. Better efforts to reduce supply-side and seasonal price inflation, including through the efforts of the National Team for Inflation Control, will provide some room to cut interest rates in the medium term.

Macro Prudential Regulation. Given that Indonesia has adopted an open capital account, the government has been very careful in considering capital controls. A feasible policy option has been to introduce macro prudential regulation. Bank Indonesia has imposed a minimum 30-day holding period for SBIs, changed auctions of these securities to monthly from weekly, issued longer maturity SBIs, and introduced a new term deposit facility for commercial banks to reduce the need to issue SBIs. At the same time, Bank Indonesia encourages the increased use of Treasury bills. The central bank introduced higher reserve requirements for foreign currency deposits and stepped up its monitoring and reporting of foreign exchange transactions and capital inflows. In the first quarter of 2011, the central bank limited banks' short-term foreign loans to a maximum of 30% of their capital and decided to increase reliance on 9-month SBIs, further discouraging short-term investments. In April 2011, Bank Indonesia extended the minimum holding requirement for SBIs to 6 months.

Fiscal Policy. Theoretically, a fiscal contraction to reduce domestic demand can help reduce inflationary pressures and hence provide room for interest rate cuts. However, fiscal contraction is not appropriate for Indonesia, given that government spending on infrastructure has been lagging for over 10 years. As a large component of recent inflationary pressure has been attributed to supply-side constraints, increasing and accelerating infrastructure development is required to ease domestic supply constraints. A feasible fiscal policy option is to reorient part of government spending. Government spending on goods and services is generally more inflationary than is other spending. The government has announced its intention to produce budgetary savings in 2011 by reducing lower priority spending. Reorienting this budgetary saving to more productive spending such as infrastructure will reduce demand pressure and help ease supply constraints. In addition, given that monetary policy is likely to be occupied by the need to manage capital inflows and potential inflationary pressure, a higher priority may be merited on fiscal policy to support more inclusive economic growth in the future.

Looking at the composition of overall capital inflows to emerging markets, the share of longer term capital is generally much higher than that of short-term capital. This implies that a larger part of capital inflows to emerging markets is driven by longer term fundamentals rather than cyclical factors. Indonesia could use this trend by increasing opportunities for longer term investment alternatives for foreigners to be channeled to large-scale infrastructure development needs through workable public–private partnerships and other mechanisms. With declining costs of foreign capital, this would enhance the country's growth prospects while reducing associated risks by improving the mix between long-term and short-term capital inflows. In addition, infrastructure development could absorb some of the appreciation pressure through improving productivity and increasing the import of capital goods.

Capital Controls. When the pure macroeconomic responses are not sufficient to deal with the substantial surge in capital inflows, capital controls can be considered as part of the policy mix. For example, when the space for further rupiah appreciation becomes more limited and inflationary pressure requires an increasing monetary policy response, then, as Principle 3 (discussed earlier) states, perfect capital mobility must be sacrificed. This is particularly true for transitory capital inflows, which may drive temporary currency appreciation, but with more permanent negative impacts on the tradable sectors. Other countries have introduced tax instruments to deal with capital inflows. But, because the main concern is "hot money" (short-term, reversible capital inflows), the instrument introduced should focus on short-term capital. A progressive tax based on length of stay would be a productive option, because it would reduce real return differentials between short- and long-term alternatives, although administering such a tax policy is complex. Another option is an equivalent macro prudential regulation that could reduce the volume of capital inflows, such as the extension of the SBI holding period that was introduced in April 2011.

Other Policies. The government proposed measures to Parliament to cushion the local currency government bond market from sudden capital outflows. Under the measures, funds from state-owned enterprises and the budget can be used to buy bonds in the event of a sudden capital reversal. In addition, Bank Indonesia can draw on the country's foreign exchange reserves and bond buyback funds allocated in the 2011 budget to support the bonds.

5.6.   Concluding Remarks

The government has made substantial progress with improving macroeconomic management. Indonesia's resilience during the GFC was attributable to applying the lessons learned from the AFC—the significant economic reforms brought in have improved the country's macroeconomic management. The government's appropriate and swift policy responses, limited exposure to the source of the GFC, and lowered reliance on exports also contributed to the country's good performance. Further reforms have been implemented to reduce vulnerabilities identified during the GFC; however, significant challenges remain. Although post-crisis economic management has restored economic growth to a respectable level, growth remains far below the potential. At the same time employment generation and poverty reduction have been slower than expected, because economic growth after the AFC has been supported primarily by private consumption, with low investment and volatile exports. On the production side, growth was driven mostly by the nontradable sector, while the tradable sector stagnated. In fact, the country's exports have become more dependent on volatile world markets for mineral and agricultural commodities.

Recognizing the need to accelerate economic growth with better employment and poverty reduction outcomes, the government has adopted a three-pillar development strategy aimed at being pro-growth, pro-jobs, and pro-poor. To achieve sustainable, higher, and more inclusive growth, the country will need to overcome several challenges, including through action to (1) diversify the sources of growth, (2) close the development gap between the eastern and western parts of the country, (3) accelerate infrastructure development to encourage connectivity and lower logistics costs, (4) rapidly improve the quality of human resources, (5) manage rapid urbanization, and (6) cope with climate change.

While most of the challenges are beyond macroeconomic management, macroeconomic policy can play an important role in achieving higher and more inclusive growth. On the fiscal policy front, while the fiscal consolidation adopted during 1999–2008 has provided a good fiscal position for the government, it has also led to significant underspending on social programs and infrastructure. Because infrastructure has been regarded as a key bottleneck to accelerating economic growth, significant efforts are required to create the fiscal space needed to augment spending for infrastructure. Lessons from recent international development experience also suggest that improved delivery of social and poverty alleviation programs is important for sustainable growth. Finally, to maximize the government's contribution to the country's growth, public finance management and the public procurement system should be improved.

On the monetary side, although on average inflation in Indonesia has declined significantly since the central bank adopted inflation targeting in 2005, Indonesia's inflation remains higher and more volatile than that in other countries in the region. With stronger economic growth, core inflation has gradually risen and will require appropriate monetary response. Monetary policy can be more effectively transmitted with a more efficient and deeper banking system. However, part of the inflationary pressure is caused by food prices and is often temporary in nature, as seen from the recent large gap between headline and core inflation. For this type of temporary inflation, monetary policy is often not effective. In addition, Indonesia's inflation is often higher in the regions that are remote from Java and Bali, and financially less developed. This suggests that, to lower inflation, monetary policy will need to be supported by supply-side measures, such as better food distribution systems and regional connectivity. The conduct of monetary policy has also been complicated by the recent large inflows of short-term foreign capital. To deal with such inflows, policy options include monetary, fiscal, and exchange rate policies; macro prudential regulation; and capital controls. As each measure is only a partial solution, an appropriate policy mix needs to be developed depending on the degree of capital inflows and on the associated risks.

References

Ali, I. 2007. Pro-poor to Inclusive growth: Asian Prescriptions. *ERD Policy Brief* No 48. Manila: Asian Development Bank.

Ali, I. and H.H. Son. 2007. Defining and Measuring Inclusive Growth: Application to the Philippines. *ERD Working Paper Series* No 98. Manila: Asian Development Bank.

Asian Development Bank (ADB). 2009. *Report and Recommendation of the President to the Board of Directors: Proposed Loan to the Republic of Indonesia for the Second Infrastructure Reform Sector Development Program*. Manila.

———. 2010. *Indonesia: Critical Development Constraints*. Manila.

———. Statistical Database System (SDBS) Online. http://lxapp1.asiandevbank.org:8030/sdbs/jsp/index.jsp (accessed March 2011).

Badan Pusat Statistik (BPS). BPS Website. http://www.bps.go.id

Baldacci, E. 2009. Neither Sailing against the Wind, nor Going with the Flow: Cyclicality of Fiscal Policy in Indonesia. In Indonesia: Selected Issues. *IMF Country Report* No. 09/231. Washington, DC: International Monetary Fund.

Bank Indonesia. 2011. Indonesian Banking Statistics March 2011. 9(4): May 2011. Jakarta.

———. various editions. Indonesian Banking Statistics. Jakarta.

———. various issues. Monetary Policy Reports. http://www.bi.go.id/web/en/Publikasi/Kebijakan+Moneter/Laporan+Kebijakan+Moneter (accessed March 2011).

———. Bank Indonesia Website. http://www.bi.go.id/web/en/Statistik/Statistik+Ekonomi+dan+Keuangan+Indonesia/Versi+HTML/Sektor+Moneter/ (accessed March 2011).

———. Indonesia Economic Monetary Statistics (various editions). http://www.bi.go.id/web/en/Statistik/Statistik+Ekonomi+Moneter+Indonesia, (accessed March 2011).

———. Ownership of Government and BI Securities. http://www.bi.go.id/web/en/Publikasi/Investor+Relation+Unit/Market+Data+dan+Info/Ownership+of+Government+and+BI+Securities

Basri, M. and H. Hill. 2011. Indonesian Growth Dynamics. *Asian Economic Policy Review* 6(1): 90–107.

Bloomberg. http://www.boomberg.com/ (accessed March 2011).

CEIC. http://www.ceicdata.com (accessed December 2010 to March 2011).

Goyal, R. and M. Ruiz-Arranz. 2009. Explaining Indonesia's Sovereign Spreads. In Indonesia: Selected Issues. *IMF Country Report* No. 09/231. Washington, DC: International Monetary Fund.

Judson, R. and A. Orphanides. 1999. Inflation, Volatility and Growth. *International Finance,* (2): 117–38.

Lindgren, C-J. 2006. Banking Integration in the ASEAN Region: An Overview. Manila: Asian Development Bank.

Ministry of Finance. various years. Budget Statistics (various years). Jakarta.

———. various editions. Government Debt Profile. Jakarta.

———. Ministry of Finance Website. http://www.depkeu.go.id/Eng (accessed March 2011).

Papanek, G. and M. Basri. 2010. The Impact of the World Recession on Indonesia and an Appropriate Policy Response: Some Lessons for Asia. In A. Bauer and M. Thant (eds.) *Poverty and Sustainable Development in Asia: Impacts and Responses to the Global Economic Crisis*. Manila: Asian Development Bank.

Ruiz-Arranz, M. and M. Zavadjil. 2008. Adequacy of Indonesia's Foreign Exchange Reserves. In Indonesia: Selected Issues. *IMF Country Report* No. 08/298. Washington, DC: International Monetary Fund.

Thee, K.W. 2003. The Indonesian Economic Crisis and the Long Road to Recovery. *Australian Economic History Review* 43(2).

World Bank. 2006. *Making the New Indonesia Work for the Poor*. Washington, DC.

―――. 2009. *Indonesia Economic Quarterly*, December 2009.

―――. 2010. *Indonesia Economic Quarterly*, June 2010.

―――. 2011. *Indonesia Economic Quarterly*, June 2011.

―――. World Development Indicators (WDI) Online. http://data.worldbank.org/indicator (accessed March 2011).

World Economic Forum (WEF). 2009. The Global Competitiveness Report 2009-2010. Geneva.

―――. 2010. *The Global Competitiveness Report 2010–2011*. Geneva.

6. Industrialization: Patterns, Issues, and Constraints

Haryo Aswicahyono, Hal Hill, and Dionisius Narjoko

6.1. Introduction

The industrial sector is well suited to a study of Indonesia's development constraints. The sector's growth and performance have been highly episodic and variable. Unless one could argue (implausibly) that the growth of variability is explained primarily by external, demand-side factors, then an examination of domestic, supply-side factors will hold the key to understanding the constraints to rapid industrialization, and to economic growth more generally. Industrialization has also been at the heart of practically every major Indonesian policy debate, ranging from the costs and benefits of globalization through to the connections between the development of small and medium-sized enterprises (SMEs), employment growth, and poverty alleviation. Therefore the industrial policy environment is a prism through which the country's broader policy debates and issues may be examined.

This chapter analyzes and explains the patterns and performance of Indonesian industrialization since the 1960s, and connects these outcomes to a range of development constraints, including (1) the availability of complementary inputs, especially infrastructure, to ensure that markets perform effectively; (2) regulatory and other policy impediments to industrial growth; and (3) the rapidly changing international economic context. Of particular importance in the latter category are the changing terms of trade and hence the real exchange rate (relevant for a major commodity exporter such as Indonesia), the rise of the People's Republic of China (PRC) as an industrial superpower, and the growing importance of international production networks and buying chains.

An understanding of the policy and institutional context is crucial to an interpretation of industrial outcomes. The industrial sector's fortunes almost invariably reflect economy-wide fortunes, and Indonesia has industrialized rapidly only when overall economic growth has been rapid. Thus, economy-wide variables—the exchange rate, inflation, trade and investment policies, the state of physical infrastructure, etc.—are by far the most important determinants of industrial policy outcomes. Indeed, the authors would argue that sector-specific policies toward industry have been largely ineffective, and sometimes costly. But there are industry-specific issues and constraints that deserve mention. Some of these flow from the fact that industry is by definition a tradable activity (unless import barriers are prohibitive), and others are related to specific features of the industrial sector.

This study of the industrial sector is enhanced by the country's generally good industrial data base. In particular, the annual survey of manufacturing firms (which extends to firms with at least 20 workers) is available at the firm level over time. This permits an unusually rich range of industrial analyses, which are illustrated with one particular set of applications in section 6.4.

The chapter is organized around three main sections:
- Section 6.2 provides an overview of the industrialization record, including the major episodes of industrial development since the 1960s, the changing industrial structure, and ownership patterns.
- Section 6.3 investigates a range of industrial policy issues and constraints. These include export patterns, trade policy, ownership patterns, competition policy and structure, spatial dimensions, and the broad policy environment.
- Section 6.4 examines the industrial record in the aftermath of the Asian financial crisis (AFC), drawing attention to the impact of and response to the AFC at the firm level, and the marked slowdown in industrial employment growth.

Section 6.5 summarizes the main conclusions and presents key policy recommendations.

6.2. Industrialization Trends and Patterns

6.2.1. An Overview

Indonesia, the fourth most populous nation in the world and the largest economy in Southeast Asia, has an unusual economic and industrial history, with its 66 years of independence dominated by three major episodes. Through to the mid-1960s, Indonesia had barely commenced the process of modern industrialization. It lagged well behind its Asian neighbors, experiencing neither the state-orchestrated heavy industrialization of the PRC and India nor the export-oriented growth then getting under way in the Asian newly industrialized economies. Indonesia's modern industrial sector, such as it was, was dominated by a few large state-owned enterprises (SOEs), which in most cases had been established by Dutch commercial interests before World War II, and were subsequently taken over by the state as part of the 1957–1958 nationalizations.

Then, in a sudden reversal of fortunes, the country began to experience very rapid industrialization from the late 1960s, with annual industrial growth of at least 9% in all but two of the 27 years, 1970–1996 (Hill 1997). Figures 6.1 and 6.2 provide a long-term summary of these trends, for output and exports. Initially this growth was catch-up and import-substituting in nature. There was a decade of oil-driven growth, and the beginnings of a brief and costly heavy industry strategy from about 1973. But from the mid 1980s, a successful transition to labor-intensive, export-oriented industrialization was engineered. Manufactures became the principal driver of export growth during 1980–1995, with the share rising from a minuscule 2% to more than 50%. For the first time in its history, Indonesia became "East Asian" in this important respect. The rapid growth was brought to an abrupt halt in 1997–1998 by the AFC, which resulted in a peak-to-trough growth collapse of more than 20 percentage points. In 1998, the contraction in the manufacturing sector was about the same as for the economy as a whole, at 13%. Thereafter, growth was positive from 1999, but at lower rates than prior to the AFC. For reasons discussed subsequently, the AFC appears to have been a turning point for the industrial sector, with its growth falling below the economy-wide average for the first time since the 1960s. As a result of the earlier rapid growth, from 1965 to 1997 the share of the manufacturing sector in gross domestic product (GDP) more than tripled. Since the crisis, the share of manufacturing has tended to decline slightly, triggering fears of a premature "deindustrialization."

Figure 6.1: Manufacturing Value Added (1960–2009)

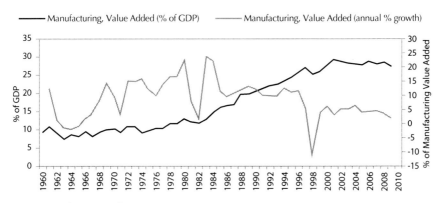

GDP = gross domestic product.
Source: Processed from unpublished national accounts data from Badan Pusat Statistik (BPS—Statistics Indonesia).

Figure 6.2: Exports of Manufactured Goods (1960–2009)

Source: Processed from unpublished export and import data from Badan Pusat Statistik (BPS—Statistics Indonesia).

Returning to Indonesia's latecomer industrial status, Table 6.1 presents a range of industrial indicators for the country and selected middle-income developing Asian economies. The table compares industrial output and manufacturing export levels and growth rates for the PRC, India, Indonesia, Malaysia, Philippines, and Thailand. Although Indonesia's industrial output is larger than that of its smaller Southeast Asian neighbors, and much larger than that of India on a per capita basis, it is dwarfed by the PRC. The more pronounced differences are evident with respect to share of manufactured exports and growth in manufactured exports, with Indonesia's levels and growth rates lagging behind.

6.2.2. Structural Change

Within manufacturing, structural change has been equally rapid (Table 6.2). Since the 1970s, there has been a shift toward a more diversified industrial structure, away from the earlier dominance of simple consumer goods and resource processing. The major labor-intensive and footloose industries[1] grew rapidly during the switch toward export orientation in the mid-1980s. Textiles, garments, and footwear were the major drivers of this export growth. Wood products expanded fast in response to the prohibition on the export of unprocessed timber, before encountering environmental constraints in the 1990s. Heavy industry grew quickly through to the mid-1980s in response to protection and major state investments. Within machinery and equipment, the automotive industry grew rapidly under the impetus of prohibitive

---

[1]   "Footloose industries" are industries that can locate anywhere, without restrictions due to availability of resources, transport, etc.

Table 6.1: Indicators of Manufacturing Value Added and Exports

	Indonesia	Malaysia	Philippines	Thailand	PRC	India
Value Added						
Total MVA (constant 2000 $ billion)[a]	67.6	36.5	22.4	66.0	832.1	132.5
Total MVA (current $ billion)	142.5	49.2	32.9	89.9	1691.2	195.8
MVA per capita (current $)	619.8	1791.7	357.6	1326.4	1270.1	169.5
Total MVA (% of GDP)	27.2	25.5	20.4	34.1	33.9	15.9
MVA growth 1990-latest observation (%)	5.6	6.4	2.9	6.8	12.3	6.9
Exports						
Total manufactured exports (current $ billion)	48.5	110.1	33.0	113.8	1124.3	108.7
Total manufactured exports per capita (current $)	210.8	4007.0	359.1	1679.5	844.4	94.0
Manufactured exports (% of total exports)	40.6	69.9	85.9	74.6	93.6	66.8
Manufactured exports growth 1990-2009 (%)	9.2	10.7	13.3	11.4	18.5	12.0

GDP = gross domestic product, MVA = manufacturing value added, PRC = People's Republic of China.
[a] Data are for 2008 except for Thailand and PRC, which are for 2007.
Source: World Bank, WDI, accessed March 2011.

protection for most of the Suharto period, but collapsed in 1998–1999. Electronics has become increasingly important and export-oriented, but has never been as prominent as in neighboring East Asian economies.

Indonesia became a significant industrial exporter from the mid-1980s, as shown in Figure 6.2 (Hill 2000). The 1980s was a crucial period in Indonesian economic history. At the beginning of the decade, as oil prices first tapered off and then fell sharply, the country was highly exposed to the international oil market. Oil, gas, and related minerals provided about two-thirds of government revenue and almost three-quarters of merchandise exports. Indonesia could well have followed other major developing members of the Organization of the Petroleum Exporting Countries—notably Mexico and Nigeria—into a debt crisis.[2] Instead, the decline in oil prices triggered

---

[2]   See Gelb and Associates (1988) for a comparative assessment of the management of the 1970s oil boom in selected developing countries. Indonesia emerges as the country that most effectively recycled its windfall oil boom revenues, and that adjusted most quickly to the downturn in prices.

Table 6.2: Changing Structure of Manufacturing Output (% of total manufacturing output)

	1975	1980	1985	1990	1995	2000	2005	2009
Food, Beverages, and Tobacco	44.4	38.2	32.6	23.0	22.3	21.2	24.7	25.3
Textiles, Leather Products, and Footwear	10.7	13.3	14.0	19.7	17.8	16.1	11.9	12.6
Wood and Wood Products	2.4	5.7	8.7	12.1	8.2	5.4	3.9	2.3
Paper and Printing	4.7	4.0	3.8	4.7	4.8	6.3	7.7	6.8
Fertilizers, Chemicals, and Rubber	22.4	18.0	16.0	12.8	13.1	14.8	17.2	20.5
Cement and Nonmetallic Minerals	2.6	4.2	5.0	3.8	3.6	3.5	5.1	5.0
Iron and Basic Steel	0.7	3.1	7.2	8.0	7.5	3.6	2.7	3.4
Transport Equipment, Machinery, and Apparatus	12.1	13.4	12.5	15.5	21.9	27.0	24.8	21.9
Other Manufacturing Products	0.1	0.1	0.2	0.5	0.7	2.1	1.9	2.2

Source: Processed from unpublished Statistik Industri data from Badan Pusat Statistik (BPS—Statistics Indonesia).

a major reassessment of trade and industry policy. The political economy pendulum swung in favor of the technocrats and their supporters, who advocated a more liberal economic agenda, including reduced protection, a more open posture toward foreign investment, and simplified export procedures (Basri and Hill 2004).

Initially, manufactured exports were concentrated in resource-based activities, especially plywood, reflecting the country's natural resource endowments and the prohibition against exporting unprocessed commodities (Table 6.3). Indonesia's industrial export base began to widen significantly as the reforms took hold, with textiles, garments, footwear, electronics, furniture, sporting goods, and toys registering rapid growth. The share of labor-intensive products in total manufactured exports increased in the wake of the 1980s reforms, from about 44% in 1980 to 70% by 1990. These reforms worked in the sense that there was the strong and immediate export response just noted. Indonesia grew quickly out of the mid-1980s recession and, although external debt rose sharply, debt-to-GDP ratios remained comfortable and started declining from the end of the decade. The reforms were also good for equity, as employment expanded significantly in the new export-oriented factories on Java. For the first time in its history, Indonesia became "East Asian" in the sense of emerging as a major industrial exporter.

Table 6.3: Manufactured Exports by Factor Intensity (1980–2010)

	1980	1985	1990	1995	2000	2005	2010
Definition 1							
Value ($ million)							
Unskilled, labor- intensive	171	663	4,201	10,573	13,429	13,787	18,378
Resource-based, labor-intensive	77	957	3,084	4,722	3,414	2,905	2,566
Resource- based, capital-Intensive	115	242	998	2,406	4,749	5,975	11,233
Electronic	97	81	205	2,944	9,072	10,050	11,949
Footloose, capital intensive	39	101	553	2,311	4,576	7,448	14,294
Total Value	**499**	**2,044**	**9,041**	**22,957**	**35,241**	**40,165**	**58,419**
Share (%)							
Unskilled, labor-intensive	34.2	32.5	46.5	46.1	38.1	34.3	31.5
Resource -based, labor-intensive	15.4	46.8	34.1	20.6	9.7	7.2	4.4
Resource-based, capital-Intensive	23.1	11.8	11.0	10.5	13.5	14.9	19.2
Electronic	19.5	4.0	2.3	12.8	25.7	25.0	20.5
Footloose, capital intensive	7.7	4.9	6.1	10.1	13.0	18.5	24.5
Definition 2							
Value ($ million)							
Resource-based manufactures	3,889	2,867	2,010	2,583	3,268	2,899	3,053
Low-technology manufactures	161	596	3,833	10,038	13,497	14,249	19,459
Textiles, garments, and footwear	126	505	2,996	7,131	9,042	9,316	12,728
Other low technology	35	91	837	2,907	4,455	4,933	6,730
Medium-technology manufactures	91	246	1,394	5,002	7,575	11,350	19,753
Automotive products	4	1	39	321	486	1,289	2,719

continued on next page

	1980	1985	1990	1995	2000	2005	2010
Medium-technology process industries	80	222	1,170	2,714	3,721	4,590	7,603
Medium-technology engineering industries	7	23	185	1,967	3,367	5,471	9,432
High-technology manufactures	14	34	69	199	277	309	614
Electronics and electrical products	96	81	159	1,593	7,105	6,942	7,812
Total Value	**4,251**	**3,825**	**7,465**	**19,414**	**31,722**	**35,749**	**50,691**
Share (%)							
Resource-based manufactures	91.5	75.0	26.9	13.3	10.3	8.1	6.0
Low-technology manufactures	3.8	15.6	51.3	51.7	42.5	39.9	38.4
Textiles, garments, and footwear	3.0	13.2	40.1	36.7	28.5	26.1	25.1
Other low technology	0.8	2.4	11.2	15.0	14.0	13.8	13.3
Medium-technology manufactures	2.1	6.4	18.7	25.8	23.9	31.7	39.0
Automotive products	0.1	0.0	0.5	1.7	1.5	3.6	5.4
Medium-technology process industries	1.9	5.8	15.7	14.0	11.7	12.8	15.0
Medium-technology engineering industries	0.2	0.6	2.5	10.1	10.6	15.3	18.6
High-technology manufactures	0.3	0.9	0.9	1.0	0.9	0.9	1.2
Electronics and electrical products	2.3	2.1	2.1	8.2	22.4	19.4	15.4

Source: Processed from unpublished Statistik Industri data from Badan Pusat Statistik (BPS—Statistics Indonesia).

Since about 1990, export performance has been more erratic. Export growth began to slow in the early 1990s as a result of increased competition in export markets, a slackening in the reform momentum, slower productivity growth, and the real rupiah appreciation. In the post-AFC era, export growth has also generally slowed, around an increasingly volatile trend, for reasons to be discussed shortly. Notably, in 2000–2010, neither the labor-intensive nor the high-tech (but mostly labor-intensive electronics) manufactures performed well. The fastest growing segment has been medium-technology manufactures, much of it resource-based in nature.

Indonesia's ownership patterns are unusual in some respects. The concentration of ownership has changed very little since 1990, as measured by the share of the four largest firms in each industry's output (Table 6.4). These concentration shares are generally high, with figures of at least 60% in more than half the industry groups. Such levels are typical for developing economies at a relatively early stage of industrialization. More detailed estimates of industrial concentration are now dated, and relate to the pre-1997 period, but are still broadly indicative of the patterns. There are high levels of ownership concentration, both in the sense of corporate conglomeration and seller concentration. Claessens, Djankov, and Lang (2000) documented the former, finding that Indonesia exhibited the highest level of corporate concentration in East Asia in 1996, with the top 10 families owning 57.7% of listed corporate assets (in terms of the shares of its leading conglomerates in output and capitalization).[3] In terms of plant-level industrial concentration, Bird (1999) found high levels of concentration, typical of those in relatively small, late-industrializing economies. During 1975–1993, concentration levels were declining steadily, though in the latter year the simple average four-firm concentration ratio was still 54%. Concentration ratios were significantly lower once allowance is made for imports.

---

[3] However, the mid-1990s data were dominated by Suharto-linked conglomerates that have since been largely dismantled, and thus the figure would be lower now. That is, the major actors have almost certainly changed. Dobele et al. (2006) in Indonesia's 40 Richest, Forbes Asia, provide a more recent listing of Indonesia's richest individuals and their business interests. The listing is at best indicative, and there are no consistent longitudinal data.

Table 6.4: Concentration and Foreign Ownership by Sector (1990–2005)

	1990	1993	1996	1999	2002	2005
Concentration (share, in %)						
Food, beverages, and tobacco	59	69	59	57	56	60
Textiles, clothes, and leather industry	29	32	28	29	30	42
Wood and wood products	22	24	26	25	29	33
Paper and paper products	61	57	61	70	73	64
Chemicals and chemical products	58	58	57	63	59	56
Nonmetallic mineral products	61	59	59	63	66	66
Basic metal industries	80	73	79	79	74	66
Fabricated metal, machinery, and equipment	74	75	74	67	69	71
Other manufacturing industries	61	66	61	62	73	79
Unskilled labor-intensive	30	33	29	30	32	43
Resource-based, labor-intensive	48	57	51	50	51	57
Resource-based, capital-intensive	65	62	64	67	66	61
Electronics	74	68	68	57	55	67
Footloose, capital-intensive	73	78	78	75	72	72
Non-Oil and Gas Manufacturing	54	56	56	54	57	58
Foreign Ownership (share, in %)						
Food, beverages, and tobacco	8.5	9.7	14.0	15.8	9.4	24.9
Textiles, clothes, and leather industry	17.8	21.8	29.3	37.4	32.1	32.8
Wood and wood products	10.1	11.7	22.9	15.8	11.6	11.2
Paper and paper products	30.2	14.9	33.8	23.5	46.4	29.0
Chemicals and chemical products	33.1	36.6	43.0	44.8	29.7	26.3
Nonmetallic mineral products	18.0	23.3	33.4	34.6	28.3	35.9
Basic metal industries	24.8	35.3	24.3	43.1	29.4	30.5
Fabricated metal, machinery, and equipment	46.1	36.4	42.4	58.0	67.6	68.3
Other manufacturing industries	19.5	44.4	51.9	56.1	33.7	46.9
Unskilled, labor-intensive	16.2	21.1	27.3	35.4	28.8	30.0
Resource-based, labor-intensive	9.0	10.2	16.8	15.9	9.8	22.8
Resource-based, capital-intensive	29.5	32.5	35.9	40.0	34.9	29.9
Electronics	41.7	43.0	48.7	82.4	71.5	68.9
Footloose, capital-intensive	47.2	34.7	39.5	44.0	66.0	68.1
Non-Oil and Gas Manufacturing	21.9	23.4	30.9	35.5	33.5	37.2

Notes: Breakdown is based on ISIC 2-digit categorization. "Concentration" refers to the share of the four largest firms in each industry. "Foreign ownership" refers to the percentage share of firms with any foreign equity in each industry's total output.
Source: Processed from unpublished Statistik Industri data from Badan Pusat Statistik (BPS—Statistics Indonesia).

Indonesia's industrial ownership patterns reflect the interplay of history, policy, and industrial organization factors. In the mid-1960s, no foreign capital was present, and the "commanding heights" of the economy were in state hands. SOEs continued to be important throughout the Suharto era. The oil boom period financed a major expansion in SOEs, initially in heavy industry, and later in several costly high-tech projects. Meanwhile, foreign investment returned to the country from the late 1960s in response to the newly liberal policy regime and generous fiscal incentives. As is the case in most countries, domestic firms are the major players in Indonesian industry, accounting for more than 50% of manufacturing value added in most 2-digit industries, under the International Standard Industrial Classification (ISIC). Among domestic firms, SOEs are important in certain industries that the government considers to be of strategic importance, such as fertilizer, steel, and cement, together with some firms that were inherited from the pre-1966 nationalizations (e.g., sugar processing) and never subsequently relinquished. During the AFC, the SOE sector in general contracted, especially the prestige projects, which depended heavily on direct government support.

Foreign ownership has risen steadily since the economy was opened up in the late 1960s. The share of these firms in non-oil and gas manufacturing value added rose from about 23% in 1975 and 22% in 1990 to 37% in 2005 (Table 6.4). The share rose in the wake of the crisis, in response to policy liberalizations and the opportunity for foreign firms to buy distressed local assets. Moreover, as is documented in the following text, foreign firms have been better able to endure the crisis. As is evident in the 2-digit ownership data, and consistent with industrial organization theory, multinational enterprises (MNEs) are important in the category dominated by electronics and the automotive industry. They are also important in basic metals (principally steel and related products), the chemical industries, and a few labor-intensive activities (textiles, garments, footwear, and miscellaneous manufactures) where knowledge of export markets is important.

One issue that continues to be of concern is whether Indonesia is reaping the benefits of this substantial MNE presence, in terms of knowledge and technological spillovers, over and above the direct benefits of increased economic activity, employment, exports, and tax payments. MNEs introduce a highly productive package of inputs, and the question is whether Indonesia—its workers, entrepreneurs, investors, and policymakers— benefits from this. The usual manner of addressing this question is via the "spillovers" methodology, which attempts to measure the impact of foreign direct investment (FDI) on subsequent productivity and performance of domestic firms, especially those in the same industry and neighborhood. Inevitably there will be "backwash" effects, from the additional competition that foreign investors introduce, for final products and resources. But do the spillovers outweigh these negative effects?

There is considerable literature on this subject for Indonesia, precisely because of its comprehensive firm-level data base. Lipsey and Sjoholm (2011) provide a detailed review of this literature, and Temenggung (2008) presents a representative recent study for Indonesia. The general conclusion is that, although Indonesia has benefited from the MNE presence, it could have attracted more FDI and extracted greater benefit. The authors support this conclusion with reference to the uncertain regulatory climate, barriers to international trade and investment, and supply-side bottlenecks. One notable area in which FDI plays a particularly important role is global electronics and automotive production networks—where Indonesia has lagged behind its major Southeast Asian neighbors.

6.2.3. Deindustrialization?

The pronounced slowdown in industrialization and the consequent declining share of manufacturing in GDP has prompted widespread concern that Indonesia may be experiencing premature deindustrialization. Is this a valid concern? First, as noted below, sectoral shares in any economy are not of great normative significance. The original Chenery formulation posited a relationship between the shares of the agriculture, mining, and service sectors and per capita income. But these were of course average shares, and countries will obviously be distributed around this average depending on a range of country-specific factors, including natural resource endowments, size, degree of export orientation, and industry policies.

In fact, according to this formulation, Indonesia was actually "over-industrialized" prior to the AFC, in that, like many of its East Asian neighbors, its manufacturing share was actually larger than what would be expected on the basis of its per capita income. Figure 6.3 shows the manufacturing share of Asian and Pacific economies (in logarithmic terms, excluding the PRC) according to the level of development, the latter represented by the logarithm of GDP per capita. The figure shows a typical pattern of development: the manufacturing share increases with the level of income, plateaus at a certain income level, and then declines. As can be seen in the figure, Indonesia's manufacturing share has been higher than the international average since 1986, when the income per capita at constant 2000 dollars was about $500. The 1980s reforms, combined with the declining mining sector in the wake of low commodity prices, were the primary driver of this above-average manufacturing share. Hence, the assertion of deindustrialization is evidently false, at least according to this criterion.

Figure 6.3: Manufacturing Share by Level of Development, Asian and Pacific Economies

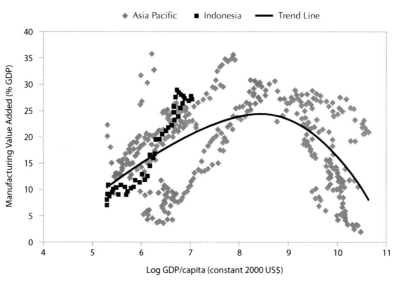

Source: Processed from unpublished Statistik Industri data from Badan Pusat Statistik (BPS—Statistics Indonesia).

To repeat, the industrial slowdown and declining sectoral share may be cause for concern, to the extent that it is linked to declining competitiveness and regulatory obstacles. But declining shares per se are not necessarily cause for concern, and Indonesia's industrial shares are broadly normal.

6.3. Industrialization—Issues and Constraints

This section examines aspects of the industrialization record and the industrial policy environment—export structure and performance, trade policy, ownership and concentration, spatial dimensions of industrialization, and the general regulatory environment.

6.3.1. Export Structure and Performance

As Indonesia liberalized in the 1980s, it became a more trade-exposed economy. From 1979–1980 to 2005–2006, Indonesia's share of global non-oil exports almost doubled, from 0.5% to 0.9%, at about the rate for Southeast Asia as a whole (from 3.0% to 6.9%).[4] In the immediate post-crisis

---

[4]   Unless otherwise indicated, the comparative export data are sourced from Athukorala and Hill (2010), based on UN Comtrade data.

period, exports responded significantly to the exchange rate depreciation, with a lag. However, despite buoyant commodity prices in the early years of the 21st century, export growth since 1998 has been sluggish, compared with neighboring East Asian economies and with the country's pre-AFC record. The data refer to growth and shares in nominal dollar exports. For manufactures, they therefore obviously understate the growth in domestic currency terms and in volumes. For total exports, by contrast, the nominal price data overstate the volume growth from 2001, because the growth rates are inflated by increased international prices for commodities (Athukorala 2006a). Thus, the overall picture for manufactured exports is a clear "bounce" in the wake of the sharp exchange rate depreciation in 1997–1998, followed by a growth rate trend that is substantially lower than the decade after the mid-1980s reforms.

As discussed in the previous section, manufactured exports are classified into five main categories, broadly corresponding to factor intensity groupings (Table 6.3 and Box 6.1): unskilled, labor-intensive; resource-based, labor-intensive; resource-based, capital-intensive; footloose, capital-intensive; and electronics. Electronics is a separate category owing to its size and the

---

Box 6.1: The Five Main Categories of Manufactured Exports

The five categories are based on the following International Standard Industrial Classification (ISIC) groups (and corresponding Standard International Trade Classification groups for export statistics): (1) unskilled, labor-intensive: ISIC 32 (textiles and garments), 332 (furniture), 342 (printing and publishing), and 39 (other manufacturing); (2) resource-based, labor-intensive: ISIC 31 (food and beverages) and 331 (wood products); (3) resource-based, capital-intensive: ISIC 341 (paper and paper products), 35 (chemicals, rubber, and plastics), 36 (nonmetallic minerals), and 37 (basic metals); (4) footloose, capital-intensive: ISIC 381 (metal products), 382 (nonelectrical machinery), 384 (transport equipment), and 385 (professional and scientific equipment); and (5) electronics: ISIC 383 (electrical machinery). Note that electronics is typically classified as a high value-added (research and development-intensive) activity. However, it is one of few industries whose factor intensity ranking clearly shifts between low- and high-income countries. In countries like Indonesia, electronics exports are dominated by labor-intensive assembly and packaging activities. Lall (2000) provides further discussion of this issue.

Source: Authors.

ambiguity of its factor proportions. In each case, the four largest exports at a disaggregated Standard International Trade Classification (SITC) level are identified. There are significant differences in performance across these major product groups, reflecting the interplay of external and domestic policy factors. The two labor-intensive product groups have performed very poorly. The resource-based group, mainly wood products, shrank for most of the period, reflecting mainly supply mismanagement. For the footloose group, export growth was also slowing before the crisis, but there was no recovery in response to the large exchange rate depreciation. The declining growth rates were evident in products constrained by quotas (for example, most garments) and products for which quotas do not apply (such as footwear). Thus, the outcome points to a general competitiveness problem.

Indonesian electronics exports have grown erratically from a very small base in the early 1990s, and broadly following the global electronics cycle since 2000. There was some interruption to supply during the crisis, as MNE export and import operations were disrupted, and some foreign investors avoided the country owing to political instability. In any case, Indonesia is a minor player in this, the fastest growing nonresource-based sector of international trade until the current global financial crisis. Indonesia's difficulties in the sector are due to the country's inability to adapt to the industry's specific operational requirements, particularly efficient cross-border logistics, infrastructure, and a predictably open FDI environment (Athukorala 2006b, Kimura 2006). As a result, Indonesia's share of global parts and components exports (defined as SITC 75–77), the best proxy indicator for participation in these global factory networks, was just 0.6% in 2005–2006, compared with the Southeast Asian and East Asian shares of 10.5% and 39.7%, respectively.

Paradoxically, Indonesia's export performance after the AFC has been strongest where it was least expected—in the moderately capital-intensive sectors. Both the resource-based and footloose segments have performed quite well. In the case of the former, high commodity prices are the primary explanation and have sufficed to overcome the increased commercial risk of operating in this sector. Among the footloose products, there has been a remarkably rapid adjustment in the automotive industry. Historically, it has been the most heavily protected of Indonesia's major manufacturing sectors. Yet, when protection was reduced during the AFC, the major auto firms were able to rationalize their production quite quickly, dropping uneconomical production lines, concentrating on products in which they were already quite competitive (for example, utility vehicles and auto parts), and (among those with foreign equity participation) shifting increasingly to exports (Aswicahyono, Basri, and Hill 2000). Petrochemicals and related products have also performed well.

The slow change in export composition and the slow pace of "export discovery" are also adduced in support of the argument that Indonesia's industrial competitiveness is sluggish. In Figure 6.4, the change in manufactured exports over 1998–2007 is decomposed into three categories: "extensive new," "intensive margin," and "extensive exit." Intensive margin can be defined as the volume of existing exported products. "Extensive margin" can be defined as the number of exported products. Expanding the intensive margin implies expanding the volume of currently exported products, while expanding the extensive margin implies increasing the number of exported products, that is, introducing new exported products. In other words, the methodology provides an indication of whether the export growth (or contraction, and hence "exit") is due primarily to increased exports of existing export items, or to expansion into new export lines

Figure 6.4: Change in Manufactured Exports (1998–2007)

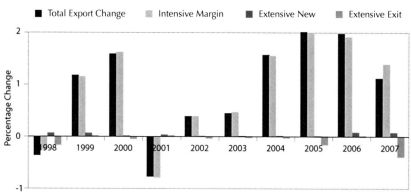

Source: Processed from unpublished Statistik Industri data from Badan Pusat Statistik (BPS—Statistics Indonesia).

Since the late 1990s, the growth of Indonesian exports has been driven mainly by the expansion in the volume of trade of established exports, rather than by the introduction of new manufactured goods. As evident in Figure 6.4, a decomposition of export growth during 1998–2007 shows that the expansion of the intensive margin (so-called "old good stuff") dominates over the expansion of extensive margin in manufacture. That is, new products have not played a major role in the growth. Furthermore, a key part of this intensive margin growth has been driven by price increases rather than increases in exported volumes. For example, four-fifths of the growth in Indonesia's commodity exports during 2005–2007 is the result of price increases rather than of an increased volume of exports. Perhaps these results are no great surprise: in an era of high commodity prices and the PRC's very strong domination of economic growth in Asia and the Pacific, the outcomes are more or less as expected. As in the 1970s, the challenge for Indonesia is to be prepared for the inevitable softening in these commodity prices, ushering in an era when competitiveness will be the major arbiter of export success.

6.3.2. Trade Policy

Indonesia was a broadly open economy as the AFC hit (Fane and Condon 1996). Average levels of import protection had declined since the major 1980s reforms, and most sectors received quite low protection, except where politically influential lobby groups and individuals were able to resist the liberalization (Basri 2001). There was further liberalization in 1998–1999 as part of the letter of intent with the International Monetary Fund (IMF). Although the country has exited the program, there has been no major backtracking since then, even though protectionist pressures have intensified in certain agricultural products. Thus, the Fane and Condon projection estimates still provide the best summary picture. It is quite extraordinary, and indicative of lack of interest among policymakers, that the key empirical tool of industrial policy analysis—effective protection by the industrial sector—pertains to the mid-1990s, and that more recent protection estimates have not been undertaken.

In passing, it is useful to dwell on the political economy reasons as to why Indonesia did not turn inward after the AFC, even with the resurgence of strongly nationalist sentiment.[5] This is an important issue, because it partly explains the economy's underlying resilience at that time. At least six factors appear to be relevant. First, in the immediate post-AFC period, the IMF letter of intent played a role, and some of the dismantling of protection (e.g., Suharto-linked monopolies) was popular. Second, the very large depreciation of the rupiah provided some exchange rate protection for tradables. Moreover, recovery depended on the growth of the export sector, which is politically empowered, and of course opposed to protection. Third, finance ministries are typically central to the resolution of a crisis, and these agencies are generally more likely to favor lower protection. Fourth, the major 1980s liberalizations were still a recent memory at the time of the AFC, and thus an unwinding of successful reforms was likely to be resisted. Fifth, the global trend toward liberalization now has strong intellectual appeal, particularly with the example of the increasingly open Asian giants, the PRC and India, and in contrast to the earlier appeal of Northeast Asian-style guided, export-oriented, industry policy. Finally, at the margin, Indonesia is a signatory to various trade agreements—the World Trade Organization and the Association of Southeast Asian Nations Free Trade Area in particular— that provide a mild barrier to increased protectionism.

---

[5] Basri and Hill (2004, 2008) discuss this issue.

Although Indonesia has remained open since the crisis, there are a number of serious trade policy challenges. First, the principal source of protectionist pressure now emanates from the agriculture sector, in contrast to earlier periods, when manufacturing was the main beneficiary of protectionism. With democratization, rural votes matter, and politicians are able to exploit this factor along with appeals to sentimental notions of food self-sufficiency. Successive agriculture ministers since the AFC have become among the most vocal and populist supporters of protection, especially for rice, ostensibly on the (mistaken) grounds that it constitutes an antipoverty strategy. Moreover, it is now easier to introduce protection for agriculture than manufactures owing to various loopholes (quarantine, etc.) and because the northern countries of the Organisation for Economic Co-operation and Development are extremely slow to liberalize their own agricultural protection. Thus, on balance, the trade regime now arguably taxes the manufacturing sector.

A second challenge may be termed "trade plus" issues. This refers to the proposition that liberalization is a necessary but not sufficient condition for successful internationally oriented growth. Aspects of Indonesia's commercial policy environment are discussed shortly. Two key factors relevant for the export story since the AFC have been the increasingly complex export–import procedures (the sweeping 1980s reforms have been undone) and the exodus of FDI. The latter is particularly important in rapidly expanding industries such as electronics, dominated by vertically integrated MNEs (Athukorala 2006b, Kimura 2006).

One consequence of the mixed reform record is the growing popularity of export zones, which offer simpler administrative procedures and (sometimes) freer trade. Their proliferation should be interpreted as reflecting the difficulty policymakers have in achieving further "first-best," economy-wide liberalization.

Third, the making of trade policy remains in an institutional vacuum. The ad hoc interdepartmental Team Tariff sets tariffs on an informal basis, without reference to clear objectives and rigorous analytical research, and in a largely nontransparent manner. The team has no control over other trade barriers, principally nontariff barriers, and the more protectionist line ministries (mainly agriculture and industry) seek to bypass the team using nontariff barriers. This ambiguity has resulted in mixed trade policy outcomes: tariffs have continued to fall, whereas nontariff barriers—thus far relatively mild, apart from some agricultural and heavy industry products—have proliferated.[6]

Finally, domestic trade barriers have emerged as just as important as international barriers, if not more so (McCulloch 2009). The domestic barriers take the form of arbitrary, ad hoc, and often illegal charges to

---

[6]   For further discussion, see Bird, Hill, and Cuthbertson (2008).

internal trade. Some are simply opportunistic exactions levied on passing traffic by the military and police. Some local authorities in coastal regions have in effect introduced their own, privatized customs services. Other charges have been introduced by the local governments following the 2001 decentralization. Some of the charges may be legal, but many are not, and there is a tendency for local authorities to simply snub Jakarta. These barriers reflect the weakened authority of the central government and the absence of a clear framework for center–regional fiscal responsibilities and authority. While in aggregate these charges may not be large, they increase the sense of unpredictability in the commercial environment, and the revenue losses are large relative to local government resources.

6.3.3. Market Structures and Competition

Section 6.2 observed that, reflecting Indonesia's political economy structures and its still relatively small modern sector economy, the country has high levels of corporate conglomeration and seller concentration, and that evidently there has been very little change since about 1990.

The AFC deeply affected Indonesia's modern financial and corporate sectors, and there were major changes in Indonesia's political economy and institutions during 1997–1999. Both have had important implications for market structures and levels of competition. Although detailed micro-level data are lacking, some general conjectures are nevertheless relevant. In particular, at the economy-wide level, competitive pressures are likely to have increased since the AFC for at least five reasons. First, this has been a period of corporate volatility and restructuring. As noted, the huge Suharto-linked business empires (Bimantara, Humpus, etc.) have collapsed, while many of the major private sector conglomerates have experienced significant changes, related either to financial work-outs, to the loss of crony privileges, or to both. Foreign ownership shares have increased in most major industries, and this has generally (though not always) led to increased competition. A second factor is that levels of import protection are generally low and have remained so since the AFC.

Third, there has been some, though limited, additional deregulation in key sectors, many of them SOE-dominated. Notable examples include domestic civil aviation and telecommunications. Moreover, the establishment of the Commission for Supervision of Business Competition (Komisi Penga-was Persaingan Usaha) in 1999 has probably increased competition. The Commission has maintained active scrutiny of collusive arrangements, and in general has operated apolitically, particularly in its earlier years, and more effectively than many observers had expected.[7] Fourth, although corruption is probably as serious a problem now as in the Suharto era, there

---

7 See Thee (2006) for an early assessment of its operations.

is arguably less entrenched, systemic, and blatant "palace corruption" of the type that proliferated in the late Suharto era. In effect, corruption has been "decentralized and democratized."

Finally, the decentralization initiative of 2001 has shifted power away from the center, and with it the concentration of regulatory authority and bureaucratic rents. The effects are probably thus far quite limited, and local monopolies may have meanwhile increased. But, over time, there is likely to be increased competition for business investment among regions, and this will, on balance, probably be conducive to increased competition in aggregate. That is, there is no longer a centralized monopoly dispenser of rents. For example, the authority to issue business licenses has been transferred to regional (*kabupaten*) and municipal (*kotamadya*) governments.

One would not want to overstate the importance of these developments, but they all point in the direction of a modest increase in competitive pressures.

6.3.4. Spatial Dimensions

Indonesia is the world's largest archipelagic state, and therefore any review of its industrialization patterns needs to include the spatial dimension. In view of the country's highly uneven human settlement, with almost 60% of the population living on the island of Java, which accounts for only 7% of the nation's land area, the location of industrial activity is also therefore likely to be highly uneven. Three broad sets of factors have shaped the spatial patterns of industrialization.

The first factor is proximity to the local market, which, combined with access to industrial infrastructure and labor, explains why the country's two great industrial clusters are in and around (1) the two largest cities of Jakarta and Surabaya (East Java); and (2) the next tier of major cities— Bandung (West Java), Semarang (Central Java), and Medan (North Sumatra). Second, as the export drive became increasingly important, location in relation to export facilities—harbors, airports, export zones— became increasingly important. This reinforced the pivotal role of the cities (except for Bandung), while also introducing new players. Two in particular have become important: the Riau Islands (principally Batam), which have become enmeshed in Singapore's export-oriented electronics industry; and Bali, where there have been significant spillovers from tourism to a range of labor and fashion-intensive manufactures, including garments, fashion accessories, and handicrafts. The third factor has been natural resource endowments, which has influenced the location of resource-based industries such as wood products and pulp and paper. The availability of energy supplies, principally coal and gas, has also been a factor in the location of some heavy industries, such as fertilizer and mineral processing. Kalimantan has been the center of much of this resource-based industrialization.

As a result of these locational and natural resource pulls, Indonesia's spatial industrial patterns are surprisingly diverse, more so than, for example, in the Philippines and Thailand, with their heavy concentrations around their capitals. Figure 6.5 summarizes these regional patterns with three sets of industrial indicators for the Indonesia's provinces.[8] Three general patterns stand out. First, Java dominates manufacturing. The major industrial provinces are, in order of size, West Java, East Java, Jakarta, and Banten. The combined industrial output of West Java, Banten (which were historically one province), and Jakarta accounts for about half of national production. Outside these regions, only Central Java, Riau Islands, and North Sumatra have industrial output on any national scale. There is almost no manufacturing of any scale in the eastern provinces in Sulawesi, Maluku, Papua, and Nusa Tenggara.

Figure 6.5: Distribution of Industry among Provinces

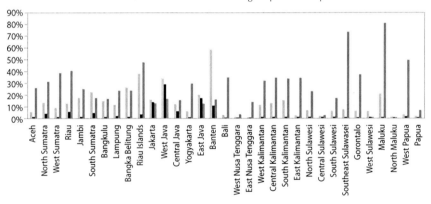

GRP = gross regional product, MVA = manufacturing value added.
Source: Processed from unpublished regional accounts data from Badan Pusat Statistik (BPS—Statistics Indonesia).

Manufacturing features prominently in several provinces. Here, also, the Java provinces—Banten and West Java in particular—are the most industrialized. But the share of manufacturing exceeds 20% of the national

---

[8] A more elaborate picture would emerge from an analysis of the country's 460 second-level units—regions and municipalities—or some combination of industrial clusters that extend across several regions. Such an analysis is beyond the scope of the current study, however, and the broad conclusions from the province-level analysis would still hold.

economy in several other provinces. These are mostly natural resource processing, which does not register significantly on a local scale. Examples include South Sumatra—and its off-shoot, Bangka-Belitung Islands—and Maluku.

The third variable in the figure shows the percentage of manufacturing output that is exported. Here, there is much less correlation with the scale of provincial output. As expected, the figures are high for Batam and Bali. They are also high for much of Kalimantan and the eastern provinces, and several Sumatra provinces. This reflects the fact that much of the manufacturing is resource processing—mostly timber products—for export.

6.3.5. The Regulatory and Commercial Policy Environment

Any discussion of Indonesia's regulatory and policy environment has to start with the observation that the country has had an unhappy experience with industry policy. There has been a history of expensive showcase projects that have contributed little to the country's industrialization. The Ministry of Industry has been dominated by an engineering approach to industrialization that favors output targets rather than efficiency, and has tended to be captured by protectionist interests, including the SOEs directly under its purview. The Investment Board (Badan Koordinasi Penanaman Modal) has sought to employ fiscal incentives and has chased large projects but lacks the analytical capacities to manage industry policy. Policies toward SMEs have tended to be welfare oriented and "distributionalist" in emphasis. Thus, industry policy generally takes place in a vacuum, with no agreed upon overall industrial strategy. For example, little benefit came from the estimated $3 billion that former technology minister and later President B.J. Habibie allocated to his prestigious, high-tech projects for two decades (although there was a significant training element). The government has rarely had success in "picking winners." Most industries that received assistance were dominated by politically influential individuals (Basri 2001) and have tended to underperform by the usual benchmarks. Meanwhile, the government has underinvested in education and, with the partial exception of agriculture, most extension and research and development support programs have had little effect.

Since the regulatory and commercial policy environment tends to be economy-wide in nature, and not sectoral, we conclude this section with a general analysis of its key features. As discussed in Chapter 3, Indonesia's business regulatory regime remains complex, opaque, and costly. Most comparative business surveys now rank Indonesia quite poorly, by East Asian and international yardsticks. Corruption levels are high, licensing procedures are lengthy and unpredictable, and Indonesia ranks poorly in the World Bank's 2009 Doing Business Survey.

Similarly, according to all available (and admittedly patchy) evidence, corruption is as serious a problem now as it was during the Suharto era. In some cases it has been documented to be worse, as in illegal logging (Resosudarmo 2005). The key difference is that the corruption now occurs in the context of slower economic growth and is less predictable. That is, abstracting from considerations of morality, and following Shleifer and Vishny (1993) and others, businesses are likely to be deterred by a system where there is greater uncertainty regarding the likely returns from corrupt payments. Under Suharto, especially during the second half of his tenure, the rules of the game were generally clear, in that the points of payment, or the preferred business partners, were well known. Thus, the business climate is now considerably less attractive, owing to slower economic growth; greater unpredictability; and other challenges, notably labor regulations and worsening infrastructure constraints.

These developments have three implications. First, investment is a good deal lower than pre-AFC levels. Foreigners are less interested in the country. The state has less capacity to maintain its large SOE sector, although it continues to block privatization, especially when influential stakeholders are affected. But, and most important, domestic investors are holding back.

A second implication is that the composition of investment has changed. Investors are now tending to eschew longer term projects in favor of short-term investments that can be more easily liquidated. For example, the Jakarta stock exchange index has increased more quickly than FDI (evidence of a preference for portfolio investment), and real estate and shopping mall projects have boomed in recent years. Meanwhile, there has been much less interest in major sectors with longer time horizons. Two notable examples are infrastructure and mining. As noted in Chapter 7, the government has had little success in attracting private sector interest in infrastructure, despite major, high-profile summits on the subject. Serious doubts remain concerning the projects, ownership modalities, pricing, legal redress in the event of dispute, the attitude of local governments, and land acquisition. Several high-profile disputes with foreign infrastructure providers in the wake of the AFC have also served as a deterrent. Mining investment remains anemic in spite of record commodity prices. During the Suharto era, Indonesia attracted over 5% of global mining exploration investment, whereas it now attracts less than 0.5%. International surveys of the mining investment climate (for example by the Canadian-based Fraser Institute) rank Indonesia among the lowest in the world, not far above Zimbabwe and Venezuela.

A third implication concerns policy. Attempts to overcome these constraints have inevitably focused on the second best. A notable example is in trade policy where, despite a generally open economy, exporters experience difficulties with customs, labor, and infrastructure. This has led to recent initiatives to extend the operation of special economic zones that, apart from Singapore-connected Batam–Bintan, have never worked as successfully as in neighboring countries.

Another example concerns privatization of the country's large and inefficient SOE sector. Here the best hope for policymakers is probably, as in the PRC, to enforce a hard budget constraint, make the subsidies visible, and ensure that the SOEs have to compete against private firms and without special favors. Over time, and with private sector growth, the share of the SOE sector will decline, even if it remains about the same size in absolute terms. As noted, the most effective reform avenue has been deregulating SOE–dominated industries, so they are forced to compete with new private sector entrants. Direct privatization has thus far been resisted, not least by the ministry responsible for the supervising these firms. In fact, SOEs are now arguably just as blatant a vehicle for political patronage as was the case during the Suharto era, and political parties have actively vied to control the ministry.

Reform of the business environment requires first and foremost political leadership. But bureaucratic reform is also a prerequisite. In McLeod's (2005) phraseology, the struggle to develop a more effective civil service continues. Democracy has rendered the bureaucracy more accountable, at least to the "parliament of the streets." But it has often had the effect of freezing government procedures because public servants, long accustomed to having to cut corners (sometimes legitimately) to implement policy, are now apprehensive, lest they become embroiled in anticorruption allegations. Post-Suharto governments have thus far found it too difficult to institute the badly needed fundamental reforms. Recruitment is a complex process, and is confined mostly to base-grade entry. The capacity to recruit specific skills required by a department is circumscribed. Interservice mobility is rare. Promotion is dominated by seniority, while performance counts for little. Staff functions are ill-defined. Official salaries at the middle and senior levels are not competitive with the private sector, and as a result are supplemented by a range of nontransparent allowances. Meanwhile, the transfer of large numbers of civil servants to the regional governments has been a costly and disruptive process.

These regulatory weaknesses are compounded by a legal system that, as noted in the comparative surveys (see Chapter 3), also ranks poorly. Foreign investors and creditors have traditionally had little faith in resolving disputes through formal legal mechanisms in Indonesia (Lindsey 2004). For example, since the AFC, (1) domestic parties in dispute with their foreign partners or creditors have been able to use the legal system to thwart the latters' contractual claims; and (2) Indonesian partners have often refused to go to arbitration, even when it was stipulated in their letters of agreement, and have rather used local courts to overrule the arbitration provisions. There are also cases of local partners persuading the courts to overrule the arbitration award in the belief that they will receive more favorable treatment from local courts and judges (Butt 2008).

6.4. The Asian Financial Crisis and its Aftermath

This section examines in more detail the firm-level impacts and the employment effects of the AFC, including the deep but short-lived growth collapse, the general slowdown in the manufacturing sector, and indifferent export performance.

6.4.1. Firm-Level Responses and Adjustment[9]

A feature of rapid industrialization and well-functioning product and factor markets is high levels of firm mobility across size groups. An earlier study of Indonesian industrialization found considerable evidence of this mobility, in particular of firms graduating to larger size groups (Aswicahyono, Bird, and Hill 1996). This phenomenon was examined through very detailed firm-level analysis, made possible because each firm in the annual survey is identified by a consistently designated code that enables the firm to be traced over time. The analysis demonstrated that the widely discussed phenomenon that the share of small firms in industrial output was apparently declining could actually be interpreted positively, not as a sign that these firms were being pushed out in the process of rapid industrialization (the commonly held perception at the time) but rather that they were graduating to larger groups. This result was shown by comparing the share of total output by firm size in the "current year," the basis for the gloomy conclusion, and in the "initial year," the basis for the positive interpretation.

This chapter repeats the exercise for the period 1990–2005, and assigns each firm to a size group. The groups are chosen arbitrarily but plausibly as firms with 20–99, 100–499, and 500 or more workers.[10] Output is then estimated (and employment, though not shown here) by the three groups, based on each firm's size in the current year and the initial year, with the latter being either 1990 or the year the firm commenced operation. The results are presented in Table 6.5. There is little change in the size share based on current size, with the share of small firms rising slightly before the AFC, then falling somewhat, while the largest firms were most affected by the AFC. However, based on size in the initial year, the small firm share rose quite quickly through to the AFC, but then began to decline from 2001.

---

[9]   This subsection draws on Aswicahyono, Hill, and Narjoko (2010).

[10]   That is, approximately corresponding to small, medium, and large firms. Experimentation with different size groups revealed that the general conclusions are not sensitive to the definition of size groups.

Table 6.5: Manufacturing Output by Size Group (1990–2005)

Year	Current Size (% value added)		
	Small	Medium	Large
	L=20-99	L=100-499	L=500-
1990	7	27	66
1991	6	28	66
1992	7	28	64
1993	7	23	70
1994	7	23	70
1995	7	22	71
1996	7	21	73
1997	8	27	65
1998	8	24	68
1999	7	25	68
2000	7	24	68
2001	9	24	68
2002	7	24	69
2003	6	23	70
2004	6	25	69
2005	5	25	70
Year	Initial Size (% value added)		
	Small	Medium	Large
	L=20-99	L=100-499	L=500-
1990	7	27	66
1991	7	28	65
1992	10	31	59
1993	10	31	58
1994	11	29	60
1995	13	29	59
1996	12	31	57
1997	14	38	48
1998	14	32	54
1999	12	33	54
2000	13	31	56
2001	15	31	54
2002	13	31	56
2003	13	31	56
2004	13	32	55
2005	12	33	55

L= size of labor force.
Source: Processed from unpublished Statistik Industri data from Badan Pusat Statistik (BPS—Statistics Indonesia).

Thus the AFC and its immediate aftermath appear to have marked a turning point in this process of firm mobility. Until the AFC, smaller firms continued to display the dynamism evident in the pre-AFC period. However, afterward, the pace of graduation slowed, and the small firm share in both series declined. These results are not necessarily cause for concern, as they could simply reflect a longer term process of industrial consolidation. They may also reflect the effects of the AFC, from which smaller firms experienced greater adjustment difficulties, or the increased competitive pressures that occurred as firms sought to survive.

General data to support the latter proposition are lacking, but there is presumptive evidence to advance the hypothesis that the barriers for smaller firms increasing their scale have risen since the AFC, particularly in access to finance. This is due to the credit rationing devices that are commonly put in place after crises, which invariably support larger firms with better collateral and credit histories (Stiglitz and Weiss 1981). The underlying argument is that banks have had more difficulty differentiating between "good" and "bad" loan applicants after the AFC and, as a result, banks are more likely to adopt more stringent lending policies, favoring firms that were able to provide more collateral and/or an established credit history. There is some evidence from East Asia in the late 1990s supporting this view. As Gosh and Gosh (1999) and Ding, Domac, and Ferri (1998) argued, credit was rationed during the AFC, and SME firms were more adversely affected than larger ones.

Indonesia's banking sector was the most severely affected among the East Asian crisis economies, resulting in a significant renationalization of banks and reform of the regulatory regime. However, as Rosengard et al. (2007: 87) note, these reforms have had the unintended consequence of limiting the access of small enterprises to formal sector financial institutions. Based on the questionable premise that larger financial institutions are less likely to fail than smaller ones, the country's small, community-based institutions have been instructed to merge with larger, centralized units, and among the latter "... innovative microfinance services were viewed with suspicion and hostility."

Transition matrixes of the size distribution of firms support the conclusion that the speed of firm mobility slowed after the AFC. These matrixes are computed for the pre- and post-AFC periods, defined here as 1992–1996 and 2001–2004 (Table 6.6). They show the distribution of firms for the same three size groups according to the initial and final year of each subperiod. Thus, of the small firms in 1992, by 1996, 90.6% were still small, while 8.8% had graduated to the medium group and 0.6% to the large group. A clear result over the two subperiods is that there is less mobility: more small firms remained small after the AFC than before it. A similar conclusion holds for the medium-sized firms.

Table 6.6: Transition Matrixes

Firm size	S=20–99	M=100–499	L=500+
a. Distribution of Plants (% of total plants), 1992 and 1996			
	1996		
1992 S=20–99	90.6	8.8	0.6
M=100–499	13.1	75.4	11.5
L=500+	1.9	13.1	85.1
b. Distribution of Plants (% of total plants), 2001 and 2004			
	2004		
2001 S=20–99	96.1	3.7	0.1
M=100–499	10.9	84.3	4.8
L=500+	0.9	11.8	87.3

L = large, M = medium, S = small.
Source: Computed from unpublished BPS Statistik Industri data of 1992, 1996, 2001, and 2004.

The analysis of firm-level dynamics can be extended by examining two additional aspects: the patterns of firm-level entry and exit, and the rates of expansion and contraction for surviving firms. Here, too, this analysis is done by tracking the history of each firm enumerated in the survey. An earlier study by Narjoko (2006) examined these patterns in the pre-AFC and AFC periods. This analysis extends the examination through to 2004, by which time manufacturing output had returned to pre-AFC levels and was growing moderately strongly. Specifically, the section examines two interrelated phenomena: the entry and exit rates of firms over time and, among the survivors, expansion and contraction rates.

First, with respect to entry and exit rates, the analysis can be conducted with reference to the number of plants, employment, or value added. The story is broadly similar, and so results are presented only for the rates by number of firms. (The additional data for other variables are available from the authors on request.) The following definitions are used for entry and exit rates for industry j and time periods t and t-1:

$$\text{Entry rate}_{j,t} = \frac{\text{NEP}_{j,t}}{\text{NTP}_{j,t-1}}$$

$$\text{Exit rate}_{j,t} = \frac{\text{NXP}_{j,t}}{\text{NTP}_{j,t-1}}$$

Where:

$NEP_{j,t}$ = total number of plants that enter industry j between t and t-1,

$NXP_{j,t}$ = total number of plants that exit industry j between t and t-1, and

$NTP_{j,t-1}$ = total number of plants in industry j in t-1.

The four subperiods are pre-AFC (1993–1996), AFC (1996–1999), early post-AFC (1999–2002), and return to growth (2002–2004). Before the AFC, as would be expected, there were high plant entry rates, and these were almost double the exit rates (Figure 6.6). However, consistent with industrial dynamism, the exit rates were significant. As the AFC hit, entry rates fell to approximately half the pre-AFC figure, while exit rates rose and began to exceed entry rates. These trends applied to practically all industry groups, but especially to textiles, clothing, and footwear; wood products; and nonmetallic minerals (respectively, ISIC 32, 33, 36). They also applied to most firm and ownership groups, though with considerable variations (Narjoko 2006, Narjoko and Hill 2007).

Figure 6.6: Firm Entry and Exit Rates Relative to the Asian Financial Crisis (%)

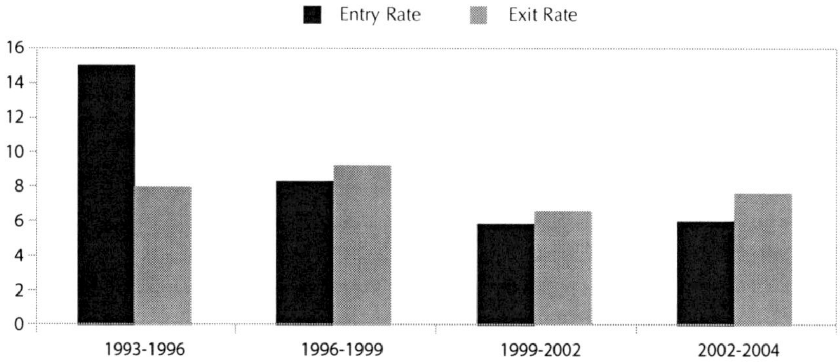

Source: Computed from unpublished Statistik Industri data from Badan Pusat Statistik (BPS—Statistics Indonesia).

While this response is expected, some trends are puzzling. In particular, the immediate crisis response of exit rates exceeding entry rates persisted through to 2004, by which time positive economic growth had resumed for 4 years. Moreover, entry rates continued to decline, in contrast to what might have been the expected outcome of a sharp decline during a crisis and recovery thereafter. At least two conjectures are plausible here. One is a delayed response of firms: the initial adjustment is to reduce output, switch output composition, extend credit lines, live off past capital, and so on, in the hope that the firm can trade through the difficulties. Especially for well-established firms, such strategies can endure for several years. Hence, the exit rates are spread out over several years, as illustrated in Figure 6.6, rather than a single large reduction in the crisis period. The second conjecture relates to the extended decline in entry rates, for 5 years after the AFC. Here the likely explanation is that potential new entrants were holding back and observing the continuing exit process, in addition to high levels of excess capacity following the crisis. The difficulties in accessing finance and rising competitive pressures have arguably resulted in increased barriers to entry.

What happened to firms that survived the crisis? The analysis follows the usual definitions of expansion and contraction rates (see for example Davis, Haltiwanger, and Shuh 1996), with reference to employment in industry j and time period t:

$$\text{Expansion rate}_{j,t} = \frac{\text{EMPL\_POS}_{j,t}}{\text{EMPL\_T}_{j,t-1}}$$

$$\text{Conraction rate}_{j,t} = \left| \frac{\text{EMPL\_NEG}_{j,t}}{\text{EMPL\_T}_{j,t-1}} \right|$$

Where:

$\text{EMPL\_POS}_{j,t}$ = total employment of plants that expanded between t and t-1,

$\text{EMPL\_NEG}_{j,t}$ = total employment for plants that contracted between t and t-1, and

$\text{EMPL\_T}_{j,t}$ = total employment in year t.

Here, too, as would be expected, expansion rates exceeded contraction rates prior to the crisis (Figure 6.7). During the crisis, expansion rates declined but contraction rates increased, and the two rates converged. Thereafter, the pre-AFC pattern of expansion exceeding contraction resumed, although the gap between the two narrowed—that is, the net expansion rate was lower. There were also differences among major industry groups, with a similar division as for the entry and exit rates. In particular, growth originated more from the expansion of existing plants than the entry of new ones in the resource-based and capital-intensive industries, such as food products and processing, paper products, chemicals, and machinery and equipment (ISIC 31, 34, 35, and 38).

Figure 6.7: Firms' Expansion and Contraction Rates (%)

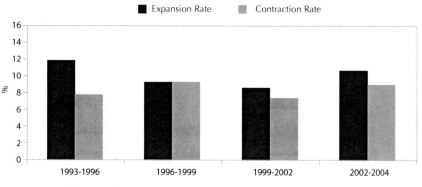

Source: Computed from unpublished Statistik Industri data from Badan Pusat Statistik (BPS—Statistics Indonesia).

The picture for firm dynamics can be summarized by decomposing employment growth into that due to entry and exit on the one hand, and expansion and contraction on the other. The analysis is conducted with reference to employment effects rather than plants, and thus the terms are referred to as "Entry rate 2" and "Exit rate 2" to differentiate them from those above. That is:

$$\text{Entry rate } 2_{j,t} = \frac{\text{EMPL\_EN}_{j,t}}{\text{EMPL\_T}_{j,t-1}}$$

$$\text{Exit rate } 2_{j,t} = \frac{\text{EMPL\_EX}_{j,t}}{\text{EMPL\_T}_{j,t-1}}$$

Where:

$\text{EMPL\_EN}_{j,t}$ = total employment of plants that entered industry j between t and t-1, and

$\text{EMPL\_EX}_{j,t}$ = total employment of plants that exited industry j between t and t-1.

So,

Employment growth decomposition$_{j,t}$ = Entry rate $2_{j,t}$ + Expansion rate$_{j,t}$ + Exit rate $2_{j,t}$ + Contraction rate$_{j,t}$

Figure 6.8 presents the results of the decomposition. The results show that, since the AFC, expansion has become more important than entry for employment over time. The inference is that, in the wake of the AFC, most of the growth originated from firms that were able to survive the crisis and adapt more quickly to the significantly altered policy and commercial environment. As Narjoko (2006) demonstrated for the period through

213

to 2000, specific firm attributes were commonly associated with these outcomes, in particular prior export orientation and foreign ownership. In addition, firms that maintained credit lines or had low debt generally survived and were able to respond more quickly to the economic recovery from 2000. Potential new entrants were apparently deterred by real or perceived barriers to entry, including the more unpredictable business and political environment, and a much more cautious financial sector.

Figure 6.8: Firm Dynamics (1993–2004)

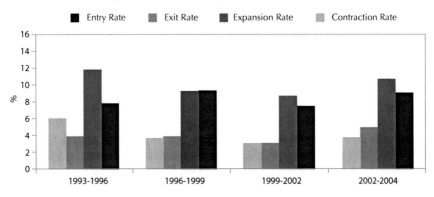

Source: Computed from unpublished Statistik Industri data from Badan Pusat Statistik (BPS—Statistics Indonesia).

6.4.2. Jobless Industrialization?[11]

At the same time as firm mobility and dynamics appeared to have declined, output growth since the AFC has become considerably less employment-elastic, resulting in the formerly major engine of Indonesian employment growth becoming much less significant. Three sets of calculations are used to probe this relationship: the relationship between output and employment growth in Indonesia by sector before and after the AFC, the Indonesian employment manufacturing record in the comparative Asian perspective, and Indonesia's industrial employment dynamics among the major firm size groups.[12]

First, employment growth is the outcome of a simple identity—the product of output growth and the elasticity of employment growth with respect to output growth. Hence:

---

[11]   This subsection draws on Aswicahyono, Hill, and Narjoko (2011).

[12]   In the paper on which this section draws, the authors also present estimates of employment–output and employment–wage elasticities. These results generally confirm those from the more aggregated sectoral estimates.

$\Delta N = \Delta Y (\Delta N / \Delta Y)$.

To understand employment growth, the left-side variable in the equation, we therefore need data on the two right-side variables. The analysis commences with the aggregate picture for the major sectors in Indonesia, before and after the AFC, followed by a comparison of the industrial sectors for Indonesia and several neighboring economies. Since the focus is on longer term trends and the AFC years were so atypical, data are presented for two subperiods: 1990–1996, corresponding to the later years of the long Asian boom, and 2000–2008, by which time the immediate impacts of the AFC had been resolved and economic growth had resumed, but before the global financial crisis had any major impact.

Table 6.7 shows output and employment growth for the two periods, together with the implied output–employment elasticities. Also, for each sector the differences between the two periods are presented for the three series, and the rankings of these differences.

Aggregate output growth was considerably slower in the second period, at about two-thirds of that in 1990–1996. However, the slowdown was not uniform across sectors. In fact, the data point to major changes in the drivers of Indonesian economic dynamism before and after the AFC. Two sectors actually grew faster: agriculture, reflecting generally buoyant commodity prices and competitive exchange rates, and transport and telecommunications, driven by technological changes and substantial deregulations.

By contrast, there was a major slowdown in three sectors: mining and utilities, manufacturing, and construction, with growth rates in the second period less than half those of the first. The explanations for this outcome are both sector specific and economy-wide. Construction growth prior to the AFC was at unsustainable levels, and it was hard hit by the crisis. Growth since then has been subdued, owing in part to financing constraints and reduced public sector investments. The latter factors also explain slower utilities growth, while mining growth has been slow as a result of the uncertain exploration and taxation environment, and notwithstanding historically high commodity prices.

The slowdown in manufacturing growth, from well above the economy-wide average to just below it, is the most puzzling result. As a tradable goods sector, like agriculture it benefited from the competitive boost of a depreciating exchange rate in the wake of the AFC. Moreover, the sector faced no significant demand-side constraints until the recent global financial crisis. Global manufacturing growth was rapid; there was a continuous relocation of the industry to developing economies; and, unlike in agriculture, there have been no major external trade barriers.

The picture is similarly varied for employment growth, except that the slowdown was less pronounced than that of output. That is, employment

Table 6.7: Indonesia - Sectoral Output and Employment Growth (1990–2008)

	1990–1996	2000–2008	Ranking
GDP Growth (%)			
Agriculture	3.1	3.9	2
Mining and Utilities	5.3	1.5	5
Manufacturing	11.2	5.2	6
Construction	13.7	6.5	7
Wholesale Trade	8.9	5.8	4
Transport	8.2	10.1	1
Other Activities	6.4	5.8	3
Total	7.9	5.3	
Employment Growth (%)			
Agriculture	–1.7	0.2	1
Mining and Utilities	6.0	3.7	3
Manufacturing	6.0	0.9	5
Construction	10.8	5.7	6
Wholesale Trade	6.5	1.7	4
Transport	9.4	3.9	7
Other Activities	4.6	3.6	2
Total	2.3	1.7	
Implied Output Elasticities			
Agriculture	–0.6	0.1	2
Mining and Utilities	1.1	2.6	1
Manufacturing	0.5	0.2	5
Construction	0.8	0.9	3
Wholesale Trade	0.7	0.3	6
Transport	1.1	0.4	7
Other Activities	0.7	0.6	4
Total	0.3	0.3	

Source: ADB SDBS, accessed March 2011.

growth in the second period was about three-quarters of that in the first, and this in a context where aggregate labor supply is anyway gradually beginning to decline. Here, too, there is considerable variation across sectors. The two major differences are the turnaround in agriculture, to slightly positive growth compared with the earlier contraction, and the collapse in manufacturing growth. Employment in all the other sectors grew more slowly, in some cases by a significant margin. Some of these outcomes reflect a continuation of significant labor-saving technological changes, such as the major transformation in trade patterns, from traditional petty trade to modern malls and retail outlets, in addition to the ubiquitous cellular telecommunications revolution, and the rapid growth of civil aviation and motorized land transport.

The bottom third of Table 6.7 presents the implied output elasticities. These indicate whether the slowdown in nonagricultural employment is due mainly to slower output growth or less employment-elastic output growth. The aggregate picture is that output elasticity rose slightly. However, the increase is almost entirely due to the change in agriculture, from labor shedding to slightly positive growth. With the exception of mining and utilities, which employ few workers, and a slight increase in construction, the general picture is less elastic employment growth. In particular, the elasticities fell sharply in three major employers of labor—manufacturing, trade, and transport and communications. The explanation in the case of the latter two is clear: there was a major change in the technology with which the services were provided, owing to the proliferation of modern shopping malls, rapidly expanding civil aviation, and so on. Even in a low-wage economy like Indonesia, all these activities are much more capital intensive than the services they replaced. However, no such exogenous labor-displacing technology swept through manufacturing. The explanation for the declining output–employment elasticities in manufacturing, therefore, has to lie elsewhere, in the commercial environment and factors affecting the willingness of employers to hire labor.

It is useful to compare these results with outcomes in neighboring developing economies, to ascertain whether any of these trends are evident. Here, also, pre- and post-AFC periods are analyzed with respect to output and employment growth, and the implied elasticities. Table 6.8 presents the results.

Table 6.8: East Asian Manufacturing Output and Employment Growth (1988–2008)

	1988–1996	2000–2008	Change	Reverse Ranking
Employment Growth (%)				
Indonesia	7.6	0.9	-6.7	3
Malaysia	8.6	-1.4	-10	1
Philippines	2.4	0.7	-1.7	4

continued on next page

	1988–1996	2000–2008	Change	Reverse Ranking
Thailand	9.9	2	-7.9	2
Korea, Republic of	0.2	-1	-1.1	5
Implied Output Elasticities				
Indonesia	0.67	0.2	-0.47	4
Malaysia	0.62	-0.32	-0.94	1
Philippines	0.78	0.17	-0.62	2
Thailand	0.88	0.33	-0.55	3
Korea, Republic of	0.02	-0.16	-0.18	5

Source: ADB SDBS, accessed March 2011.

In the pre-AFC period, the pace of Indonesian industrialization was similar to that in its rapidly industrializing neighbors, Malaysia and Thailand, and much faster than in the Republic of Korea and the Philippines. Industrial growth in the three Southeast Asian growth economies— Indonesia, Malaysia, and Thailand—slowed sharply after the AFC, most of all in Malaysia and least in Thailand. The Philippine growth rate accelerated slightly, from a weak base, while Korean growth slowed somewhat. Thus, from a growth perspective, Indonesia is well within Southeast Asian norms.

The employment picture is also broadly similar. The three Southeast Asian economies experienced a very sharp growth slowdown. Malaysian manufacturing employment actually shrank, reflecting the fact that this higher wage economy has been progressively shedding its labor-intensive segments. Employment growth in Thailand was slightly stronger, but the absolute growth decline was sharper than in Indonesia. Korean and Philippine employment growth was anemic throughout, contracting in the former case since 2000. Thus, here, also, Indonesia does not emerge as a regional outlier.

The output elasticities declined significantly in all five economies. As noted, they turned negative for the Republic of Korea and Malaysia. The rates of decline are broadly similar for Indonesia, the Philippines, and Thailand. In fact, although Thailand's output elasticity remains the highest of the five, the rate of decline in Indonesia is the lowest among the Southeast Asian sample.

To sum up so far, on the basis of the aggregated sectoral data, Indonesia has experienced a pronounced slowdown in industrial employment growth since the AFC. Manufacturing was the only sector to experience both a marked deceleration in output growth and a major decline in output elasticity. This therefore suggests that sector-specific factors were at work in the country's industrial labor market. However, in comparative East Asian terms, the Indonesian industrial record is not an outlier. Other fast-industrializing middle-income developing countries registered similar declines in both output growth and output elasticities. Among the four comparators, the Thai experience is arguably the most relevant. The Republic of Korea has clearly moved out of the labor-intensive phase of industrialization, while Malaysia is in transition. In both cases, very low or even negative employment-output elasticities are not surprising. Growth in the Philippines has been slower throughout. The widespread presumption in Indonesia is that the country's tighter labor market regulation since 2000 is the principal explanation for the sharp drop in its output elasticity. Yet, although Thailand's output and employment growth remain somewhat higher, its output elasticity has fallen just as fast, even though the Thai labor market is not as heavily regulated as Indonesia's and has not been subject to regulatory tightening since the AFC. In other words, more general factors appear to be affecting the patterns of Southeast Asian industrialization and employment, in addition to labor market policies.

The more disaggregated Indonesian industrial census data shed light on these issues. Indonesia has two main industrial statistics series: the annual survey of establishments with at least 20 employees, known as Statistik Industri, and the decennial economic census of all industrial establishments (Sensus Ekonomi). Results from the Sensus Ekonomi series are presented because, although conducted only once every decade, they are more comprehensive in scope, covering all firms with at least five employees, than the Statistik Industri, which covers firms of 20 and more employees. The Sensus Ekonomi data are probably also more reliable.

The Sensus Ekonomi surveys were conducted in 1986, 1996, and 2006. These periods thus neatly coincide with major subperiods—1986–1996 was the decade of reform and rapid growth, and 1996–2006 encompasses the AFC and return to slower growth. To investigate the impacts across firms of different size, establishments are classified into three (arbitrary) groups: "large" (100+ employees), "medium" (20–99), and "small" (5–19). Other size classifications do not affect the results. The disaggregation by size is relevant, as the authors conjecture that scale may influence firm responses to economic events and regulations. For example, smaller firms may be more resilient to adverse economic shocks, and they may fall outside the regulatory net. The industrial statistics are examined at the 2-digit ISIC level of industrial classification, and the industries are combined into a broader factor intensity group, "labor-intensive" (ISIC 32, 33, 39), "resource-based" (ISIC 31, 34, 35), and "capital-intensive" (ISIC 36-38), because industries within these groups share some similar characteristics and response patterns.[13]

The raw data on manufacturing employment are revealing. Table 6.9 summarizes the results for the three Sensus Ekonomi size groups. Employment grew quite rapidly during the whole period 1986–2006, by 7.3% per annum. However, there was a marked slowdown between the two subperiods, with growth declining from 10.1% in the first decade to just 4.6% in the second. There were also some significant compositional shifts. In both 1986 and 1996, large firms accounted for just over half of employment, whereas by 2006 small firms had become the dominant employer. The medium firm share declined throughout the period. Employment in both large and small firms grew rapidly in the first decade, by 10.3% and 11.4%, respectively. But from 1996 to 2006, large firm employment barely increased, at just 1% per annum, whereas small firm employment continued to expand quickly, by 8.8%. Medium firm employment growth also declined, but not to the same extent as in large firms.[14]

Thus there was clearly a sharp slowdown in the growth of Indonesia's industrial employment since the AFC, especially compared with the "reform decade," 1986–1996. This occurred because of the slower industrial growth, and most particularly because of the much lower output–employment elasticity. Among the sectors, manufacturing is unusual in this respect, in that there was both slower output growth and lower employment elasticity. This growth slowdown appears to have occurred across all major manufacturing sectors. There were also significant compositional shifts since the AFC, with almost all of the industrial employment growth coming from small firms. Firms in the "factory sector," with 20 plus workers, seem to have virtually stopped hiring during this period.

The explanation for these outcomes is broadly as follows: Immediately after the crisis, there was a major boost to competitiveness from the rapidly depreciating nominal exchange rate. But this did not translate into

---

[13]   The labor-intensive industries are textiles, garments, and footwear; wood products and furniture; and miscellaneous manufactures. The resource-based industries are food and related products; paper products; and chemical, rubber, and plastic products. The capital-intensive group includes nonmetallic minerals; steel products; and metal and machine goods, electronics, and automobiles. More elaborate classifications could be employed, such as the foregoing, but they are unlikely to affect the results significantly. If Indonesia were a major participant in global electronics production networks (which it is not), then, strictly speaking, the components assembly industry should be classified as labor-intensive.

[14]   One caveat to these results is that the employment data are all "head count" estimates. Data on the intensity of work, that is hours worked, by firm size, are not available. While the estimates for large and medium firms are likely to closely resemble some "full-time equivalent" employment figure, that for the small firms could well be lower, owing to seasonality factors and more variable output and work patterns. Hence, it is possible, but not certain, that the rising small share is an overstatement.

Table 6.9: Indonesian Manufacturing Employment by Firm Size (1986, 1996, and 2006)

	Large	Medium	Small	Total
Total ('000)				
1986	1,331	345	770	2,446
1996	3,545	609	2,273	6,427
2006	3,921	823	5,297	10,041
Composition (% of total)				
1986	54	14	32	100
1996	55	10	35	100
2006	39	8	53	100
Growth (annual average, %)				
1986–1996	10	6	11	10
1996–2006	1	3	9	5
1986–2006	6	4	10	7

Source: Computed from BPS, Susenas (1986, 1996, 2006).

employment growth, because much of the formal sector of the economy was incapacitated by corporate debt workouts, foreign investors were leaving, and the financial markets were freezing up. Also, regulatory and policy uncertainty increased in the transition from authoritarian to democratic rule, and the major decentralization initiative of 2001. The latter especially affected access to natural resources, on which several Indonesian manufacturing activities depend. Intensified labor market regulation and infrastructure constraints emerged as serious problems after 2000. From about 2003, rising commodity prices and the return of foreign capital began to put pressure on the exchange rate, with significant real appreciation commencing around 2005. By then, all the earlier competitiveness advantages from the exchange rate depreciation had been eroded. These events occurred in the context of intensified international competition, particularly from the PRC, but also from other lower wage competitors, notably Viet Nam.

These factors operated as economy-wide influences, in addition to sector-specific effects. For example, tighter labor market regulations had an adverse effect on the traditional labor-intensive sectors—textiles, clothing, and footwear—in addition to the breakdown in the formerly effective operation of the import drawback facility for export-oriented firms. The more cumbersome export–import procedures and a less inviting foreign investment regime meant that Indonesia has been a relatively minor participant in the rapidly expanding global production networks centered on "fragmentation trade." Activities based on natural resources were affected by interruptions of reliable raw material supplies.

Does this slower manufacturing employment growth matter? The answer to this question depends on the explanation for the slower growth. The growth of employment in manufacturing is of concern to the extent that a major link in the transmission mechanism from growth to poverty reduction has been weakened. That is, fewer Indonesian workers are now drawn into the relatively better paid jobs in the manufacturing sector. Moreover, most of the industrial jobs now being created are in small firms, where employment conditions are generally inferior to those in larger firms, especially to the extent that smaller firms are able to evade labor protection measures. As argued above, the much slower job growth is principally the result of Indonesia's declining international competitiveness, underlining again the crucial link between macro-level economic reform and poverty reduction.

Nevertheless, it is important not to overstate the problems, for at least two reasons. First, Indonesia's record is not that different from that of its neighbors, including the traditionally dynamic Thai economy, where labor market regulation has not intensified. This suggests that the changes are part of a generalized regional phenomenon, in which rising competition from the PRC and the demise of very labor-intensive segments are important factors explaining slower employment growth.

Second, more jobs are being created in other sectors. The fastest growth has occurred in several service sectors, reflecting technological advance, deregulation, and (at the margin) the switch to nontradables as a result of the appreciating real exchange rate since about 2003. Agriculture has reversed the earlier decline, reflecting buoyant commodity prices, and drawing attention to Indonesia's resource-based economic diversity. While the assertion that Indonesia is experiencing premature deindustrialization may be an overstatement, industrial deceleration is evident and seems to have become a permanent feature of Indonesia. Is this structural shift in employment patterns a cause for concern? "Industrial fundamentalists" would assert that it is, on the grounds that greater externalities are associated with industrialization, such as interindustry linkage creation and skill formation. But such views are of dubious validity, as shown by the existence of many high-income service and resource-based economies in the world.

6.5. Conclusions and Policy Recommendations

The major conclusions can be stated as follows. Indonesia has achieved rapid industrialization since 1967, and especially during 1967–1997, when average annual industrial output growth was almost 10%. Initially this growth was supported by the general adoption of "orthodox" economic policies, and was import substituting in nature. In the first half of the 1980s, as global commodity prices fell sharply, the sweeping policy reforms facilitated the effective transition to a more export-oriented strategy. The AFC introduced a third major episode in industrialization, with growth slowing significantly. This slower growth was also accompanied by declining firm-level mobility and slower employment growth, especially in the formal factory sector. The record since 1999 has triggered widespread concern about premature deindustrialization, in the sense of a declining industrial share, even though industrial output has continued to expand.

There is also considerable, and unresolved, debate about the causes of the slowdown and its origins, in particular, whether the main causes are the strengthening real exchange rate (occasioned by rising terms of trade), restrictive labor market regulations, deteriorating infrastructure, regulatory complexities, or a failure to keep up with faster reforming competitors. As this chapter has shown, all of these factors have been present since about 2000. These factors also contain the elements of a reform agenda for going forward, an agenda that has general relevance and is specifically directed at the manufacturing sector.

Three general areas are of paramount importance. The first is investing in the supply side, or at least providing an environment conducive to investments from the private sector. The most important is all aspects of physical infrastructure—roads, rail, seaports, airports, and utilities. Education and industrial extension are also emerging as constraints. Indonesia has been underinvesting on the supply side since the AFC, and all major surveys of the investment climate point to them being a critical constraint to future development. This constraint relates both to the levels of investment and to the policy environment that governs the investments. That is, investments without a clear pricing and competitive framework will be ineffective.

The second relates to more open policies toward trade, investment, human capital, and technology flows. Although Indonesia is a broadly open economy, there are important unreformed sectors, notably agriculture and heavy industry, and the lobby groups in the political arena and the bureaucracy that support this status quo. The investment regime remains ambivalent toward foreign equity, especially as majority investors. Thus, Indonesia has missed out on profitable investment areas, such as rapidly growing service activities and the global electronics industries. Policies toward the rapidly globalizing international education industry and the employment of skilled labor are also unduly restrictive.

Third, regulatory reform in all its dimensions is proceeding very slowly. The complex task of civil service reform has hardly commenced. As many investment surveys have demonstrated, Indonesia's licensing regime is one of the most complex and costly in developing Asia. Restrictive labor market regulations have stymied employment growth. The state enterprise sector is largely unreformed. Legal sector reform is proceeding very slowly. International surveys of government effectiveness and corruption rank Indonesia rather poorly. Admittedly, these reforms are difficult and politically sensitive. But, a decade after the restoration of democracy and decentralization, and well into the second term of an administration that received a clear public mandate for reform, there is little sign of major progress. In the absence of a clear reform agenda, industrial growth will remain respectable but well below its potential. Moreover, second-best measures to promote industry, such as the recently announced fiscal incentives program for major industries, are likely to be ineffective.

References

Asian Development Bank (ADB). Statistical Database System (SDBS) Online. https://sdbs.adb.org/sdbs/index.jsp

Aswicahyono, H., M.C. Basri, and H. Hill. 2000. How not to Industrialize?: Indonesia's Automotive Industry. *Bulletin of Indonesian Economic Studies*, 36 (1): 209–41.

Aswicahyono, H.H., K. Bird, and H. Hill. 1996. What Happens to Industrial Structure when Countries Liberalise? Indonesia since the mid 1980s. *Journal of Development Studies* 32(3): 340–63.

Aswicahyono, H., H. Hill, and D. Narjoko. 2010. Industrialisation after a Deep Economic Crisis: Indonesia. *Journal of Development Studies*, 46(4): 1084–108.

———. 2011. Indonesian Industrialization: Jobless Growth? In C. Manning and S. Sumarto (eds), *Indonesia Update 2011*. Singapore: Institute of Southeast Asian Studies.

Athukorala, P-C. 2006a. Post-crisis Export Performance: the Indonesian Experience in Regional Perspective. *Bulletin of Indonesian Economic Studies*, 42(2): 177–211.

———. 2006b. Product Fragmentation and Trade Patterns in East Asia. *Asian Economic Papers*, 4(3): 1-28.

Athukorala, P-C. and H. Hill. 2010. Asian Trade: Long-Term Patterns and Key Policy Issues. *Asian-Pacific Economic Literature*, 24(2): 52–82.

Badan Pusat Statistik (BPS—Statistics Indonesia). National Socioeconomic Survey (Susenas).

———. Website. http://www.bps.go.id

Basri, M. 2001. *The Political Economy of Manufacturing Protection in Indonesia, 1975-1995*. Canberra: Australian National University. Unpublished PhD thesis.

Basri, M. and H. Hill. 2004. Ideas, Interests and Oil Prices: the Political Economy of Trade Reform during Soeharto's Indonesia. *The World Economy* 27(5): 633–56.

————. 2008. Indonesia—Trade Policy Review 2007. *The World Economy* 31(11): 1393–408.

Bird, K. 1999. Industrial Concentration in Indonesia. *Bulletin of Indonesian Economic Studies*, 35(1): 43–73.

Bird, K., H. Hill, and S. Cuthbertson. 2008. Making Trade Policy in a New Democracy after a Deep Crisis: Indonesia. *The World Economy*, 31(7): 947–68.

Butt, S. 2008. The Constitutional Court's Decision in the Dispute between the Supreme Court and the Judicial Commission: Banishing Judicial Accountability? In R.H. McLeod and A. MacIntyre (eds), *Indonesia: Democracy and the Promise of Good Governance*. Singapore: Institute of Southeast Asian Studies.

Claessens, S., S. Djankov, and L.H.P. Lang. 2000. The Separation of Ownership and Control in East Asian Corporations. *Journal of Financial Economics* 58: 81–112.

Davis, S.L., J.C. Haltiwanger, and S. Shuh. 1996. *Job Creation and Destruction*. Cambridge, MA: MIT Press.

Ding, W., L. Domac, and G. Ferri. 1998. Is there a Credit Crunch in East Asia? *World Bank Policy Research Working Paper* 1959. Washington DC: World Bank.

Dobele, J., C. Vorasarun, and Forbes Indonesia Staff. 2006. Indonesia's 40 Richest, *Forbes Asia*, 18 September.

Fane, G., and T. Condon. 1996. Trade Reforms in Indonesia, 1987–1995. *Bulletin of Indonesian Economic Studies*, 27(1): 105–25.

Fraser Institute. www.fraserinstitute.org

Gelb, A. and Associates. 1988. *Oil Windfalls: Blessing or Curse?* New York: Oxford University Press.

Gosh, S.R. and A.R. Gosh. 1999. East Asia in the Aftermath: Was there a Crunch? *IMF Working Paper* No. 38. Washington DC: International Monetary Fund.

Hill, H. 1997. *Indonesia's Industrial Transformation*. Singapore: Institute of Southeast Asian Studies.

————. 2000. *The Indonesian Economy,* 2nd edition. Cambridge: Cambridge University Press.

Kimura, F. 2006. International Production and Distribution Networks in East Asia: 18 Facts, Mechanics, and Policy Implications. *Asian Economic Policy Review* (1): 346–47.

Lall, S. 2000. The Technological Structure and Performance of Developing Country Manufactured Exports. *Oxford Development Studies* 28(3): 337–69.

Lindsey, T. 2004. Legal Infrastructure and Governance Reform in Post-Crisis Asia: The Case of Indonesia. *Asian-Pacific Economic Literature* 18(1): 12–40.

Lipsey, R. and F. Sjoholm. 2011. Foreign Direct Investment and Growth in East Asia: Lessons for Indonesia. *Bulletin of Indonesian Economic Studies* 47(1): 35–63.

McCulloch, N. (ed). 2009. *The Rural Investment Climate in Indonesia.* Singapore: Institute of Southeast Asian Studies.

McLeod, R. 2005. The Struggle to Regain Effective Government under Democracy in Indonesia. *Bulletin of Indonesian Economic Studies,* 41(3): 367–86.

Narjoko, D. 2006. Indonesian Manufacturing and the Economic Crisis of 1997/98. Canberra: Australian National University. Unpublished PhD thesis.

Narjoko, D. and H. Hill. 2007. Winners and Losers during a Deep Economic Crisis: Firm-Level Evidence from Indonesian Manufacturing. *Asian Economic Journal* 21(4): 343–68.

Resosudarmo, B. (ed). 2005. *The Politics and Economics of Indonesia's Natural Resources.* Singapore: Institute of Southeast Asian Studies.

Rosengard, J. et al. 2007. The Promise and the Peril of Microfinance Institutions in Indonesia. *Bulletin of Indonesian Economic Studies* 43(1): 87–112.

Shleifer, A. and R. Vishny. 1993. Corruption. *Quarterly Journal of Economics* 108(3): 599–617.

Stiglitz, J. and A. Weiss. 1981. Credit Rationing in Markets with Imperfect Information. *American Economic Review,* 71(3): 393–410.

Temenggung, D. 2008. Foreign Direct Investment and Productivity Spillovers in Indonesian Manufacturing. Canberra: Australian National University. Unpublished PhD thesis,

Thee, K.W. 2006. Indonesia's First Competition Law: Issues and Experiences. In C. Lee and C.M. Fong (eds), *Competition Policies and Deregulation in Asian Countries.* Kuala Lumpur: University of Malaya Press.

World Bank. World Development Indicators (WDI). http://data.worldbank.org/data-catalog/world-development-indicators

7. Infrastructure Development: Challenges and the Way Forward[1]

Areef Suleman and Zafar Iqbal

7.1. Overview

In this era of globalization and international competitiveness, sustainable socioeconomic development and poverty reduction cannot be achieved without adequate and efficient infrastructure. Several studies have examined the relationship between infrastructure and economic growth in Indonesia. For example, Mawardi (2004) showed that infrastructure had a positive impact on Indonesia's economic growth. A recent empirical study by Mustajab (2009) estimated that a 1% increase in infrastructure investment contributes 0.3% to Indonesia's gross domestic product (GDP). This supports the contention that adequate infrastructure is a major driver of sustainable economic growth and poverty reduction in Indonesia.

However, the current state of Indonesia's infrastructure is far from encouraging, and it came as no surprise that the business community identified inadequate infrastructure (in terms of both quantity and quality) as the second biggest impediment to doing business (compared with 10th in Malaysia and Thailand). The slow pace of infrastructure development and its poor quality are attributable to the low level of investment by both the public and private sectors in Indonesia. The situation has deteriorated since the 1997 Asian financial crisis—current investment in infrastructure is about 3.5% of GDP versus the pre-crisis level of approximately 8% in 1997 (Figure 7.1).

[1] The editors and publishers gratefully acknowledge the Islamic Development Bank for contributing this chapter.

Figure 7.1: Infrastructure Investment in Indonesia, 1996–2006

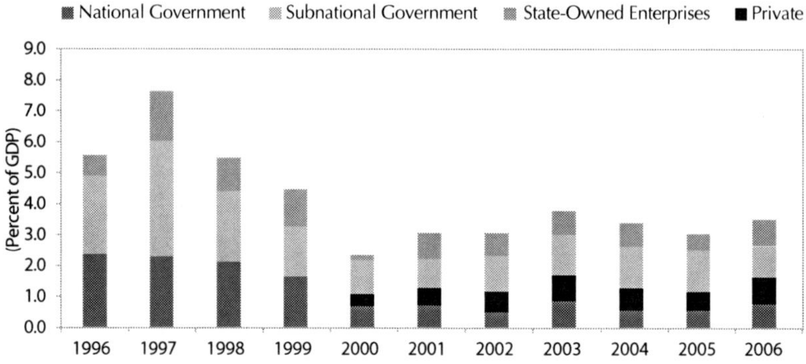

■ National Government   ▨ Subnational Government   ▨ State-Owned Enterprises   ■ Private

Source: Data from Asian Development Bank, Jakarta.

Foreign direct investment (FDI) is an important source of financing for the infrastructure sector. Like domestic private investment, FDI flows have been recovering slowly in recent years but remain lower than the pre-crisis level. The data indicate a huge gap between approved and realized FDI, particularly in 2007. In 2003, the gap was about $10 billion, which rose to nearly $30 billion by 2007. Close to one-third of the FDI in 2007 went to transport, storage, and communication (Table 7.1). The rising gap

Table 7.1: Approved and Realized Foreign Direct Investment, 2003–2007[a]

	2003	2004	2005	2006	2007
Approved FDI ($ million)	16,305	10,471	13,640	15,665	40,146
of which (% of total): Electricity, gas, and water supply	2.2	2.6	0.2	7.5	3.6
Construction	5.5	9.2	12.4	16.3	4.3
Transport, storage, and communication	28.2	5.6	22.8	1.9	12.0
Realized FDI ($ million)	5,445	4,572	8,911	5,992	10,341
of which (% of total): Electricity, gas, and water supply	1.4	0.1	0.8	1.8	1.2
Construction	1.9	8.4	10.3	2.4	4.3
Transport, storage, and communication	49.0	2.3	33.1	10.8	32.0
Gap Between Realized and Approved FDI ($ million)	−10,860	−5,899	−4,729	−9,673	−29,805

FDI = foreign direct investment.
[a] Excludes FDI in oil and natural gas projects, banking, nonbank financial institutions, insurance, leasing, mining, as well as household investment.
Sources: Indonesia, Offering Memorandum (April 2009), and Indonesia's Investment Coordinating Board (BKPM), cited in IDB (2010).

between approved and realized FDI in infrastructure is a cause for concern for the investment community and its impact on the country's business environment.

In terms of adequacy of infrastructure, Indonesia slid from its 53rd ranking in 2008 to 55th in 2009 (of 57 countries), significantly behind Malaysia (26th) and Thailand (42nd) but slightly ahead of the Philippines (IMD 2009). In addition, the World Economic Forum Report ranked Indonesia's overall infrastructure quality 96th (of 133 countries studied), and 54th in global competitiveness (Figure 7.2). This is a cause for concern, because the state of infrastructure is inextricably linked to a country's global competitiveness (i.e., better quality infrastructure facilitates higher levels of competitiveness). It is, therefore, not surprising that Indonesia's poor infrastructure quality has negatively impacted its global competitiveness ranking.

Figure 7.2: Rankings of Quality of Overall Infrastructure and Global Competitiveness, 2009–2010 (of 133 countries)

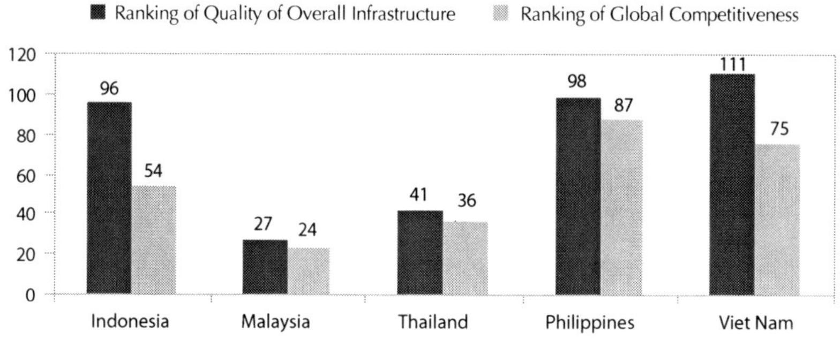

Note: The lower the ranking, the better the infrastructure quality and more competitive the economy.
Source: WEF (2009).

The poor quality of infrastructure becomes more apparent on examining the disparities among provinces. Given the vastness of the country and its limited financial resources, it is not surprising that there are regional imbalances in terms of availability and access to infrastructure. For example, teledensity of fixed-line telephones is low on average, and ranges from a peak of about 25 in Greater Jakarta, to 11–20 (medium densities) in other big cities, and a low of about 0.2 in rural areas in Eastern Indonesia (BPS Podes 2008). The share of households with access to safe drinking water also varies significantly across provinces. In 2007, close to 66% of households in Sumatra and 87% in Java had access to safe drinking water, while in Kalimantan only about 50% of households enjoyed that facility.[2]

---

[2]   BPS National Socioeconomic Survey (Susenas) 2007, cited in IDB (2010).

Access to infrastructure and productive assets is also low and unequal across regions. The share of families with electricity ranged from 37% to 73%, and the percentage of villages with access to an asphalt/concrete road varied from 40% to 72% in 2007.

The imbalance is due mainly to low investment in infrastructure in regions outside Java and Sumatra (Box 7.1). In 2008, Java received 91.2% of realized FDI and 60.1% of domestic investment, while Sumatra had 6.8% of FDI and 23.8% of domestic investment.[3] This is not surprising, because returns on investment will be higher where populations are denser. Under the National Medium-Term Development Plan 2010–2014, the government intends to allocate more public investment to regions that are clearly unattractive to the private sector. The regional imbalances will need to be carefully assessed

Box 7.1: Reducing Regional Disparities Should Become a Long-Term Priority

There are high levels of disparities between the different regions in Indonesia from several perspectives. For example, gross domestic product per capita ranges from Rp2.4 million ($262) in Gorantalo to Rp36.7 million ($4,014) in Jakarta; population density varies from only 5 people per square kilometer in Papua to 13,560 in Jakarta. The regional disparities are also evident in the extent of investment flows and infrastructure at the regional level.

Regional Variations in Investment, Output, and Population (2007)

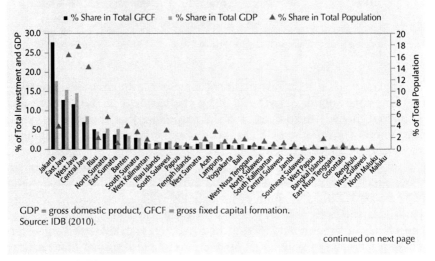

GDP = gross domestic product, GFCF = gross fixed capital formation.
Source: IDB (2010).

continued on next page

---

[3]   Source: Indonesia Investment Coordinating Board (BKPM), cited in IDB (2010).

The disparities are attributable to low levels of investment in some regions, which is driven by decisions pertaining to the financial and social returns on investment. An example is the provision of electricity, for which the cost of services varies from approximately Rp1,000 to Rp 4,000 per kilowatt and, because prices are fixed and uniform across the country, serving a few people in sparsely populated areas results in high losses. Therefore, the more densely populated areas tend to have more infrastructure (transport, communications, and electricity) that is also of a higher quality.

Given the limited human and institutional capacity within the government, and the overall business and investment climate, the government may not be able to address simultaneously the requirements of achieving regional balance and lessening the constraints limiting growth of the whole economy. In the short term, by focusing on relaxing the binding constraints, the government can create a conducive environment for higher levels of investment, move the country onto a higher growth trajectory, and thereby improve the living standards of a vast majority of the population. If, however, the government focuses on addressing regional disparities in the short term, it risks not being able to make an impact on both disparities and economic growth.

Thus, the government should weigh the opportunity costs of acting on a populist decision to reduce regional disparities as opposed to pursuing economic growth. Confronting regional disparities and the binding constraints to economic growth simultaneously may lead to paralysis, with no progress on either issue. Hence, it would be prudent to focus on economic growth in the short term (by relaxing the binding constraints) and on regional disparities in the long term.

in order to maximize the impact of government expenditure and to assure that all regions are included in the development process.

Clearly, development of adequate infrastructure is vital for the country's economic growth and for improving the quality of its people's lives. However, both the quality and quantity of Indonesia's infrastructure, along with the regional imbalances, require much work for the country to achieve higher levels of inclusive and sustainable growth.

7.2.   Framework for Diagnosing Critical Constraints to Infrastructure Development

Using the growth diagnostic approach developed by Hausmann, Rodrik, and Velasco (2005), a diagnostic framework for the infrastructure sector was developed (Figure 7.3). The the role of all stakeholders (public and private sectors, public–private partnerships [PPPs], and foreign investors) in infrastructure development was added to the framework, as opposed to focusing purely on private investment. The framework provides a consistent approach to identifying the most binding constraints to infrastructure development. The approach offers a practical tool for policymakers to use in formulating a strategy for the sector, and may assist the international development community toward providing funding aimed at removing the binding constraints and thus maximizing the developmental impact on the country.

Figure 7.3: Critical Constraints to Infrastructure Development

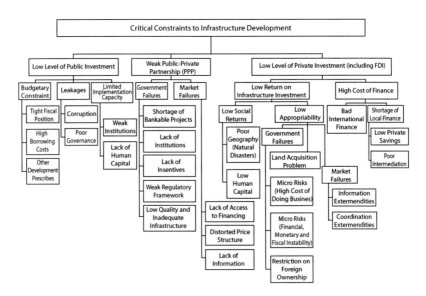

FDI = foreign direct investment.
Source: Authors.

Critical constraints to infrastructure development in Indonesia are attributed to three broad factors: low levels of public investment, low levels of private investment, and weak PPPs. To determine the underlying causes for the low levels of investment, the issues and drivers behind them are examined:

- Diagnosis of the low level of public investment in infrastructure starts by examining the cause: Is it budgetary constraint, limited implementation capacity, and/or corruption or poor governance?

- The diagnostic framework looks into what is hampering the level of private investment in the sector: Is it low because of micro risks (i.e., high cost of doing business) or macro risks (i.e., financial, monetary, and fiscal instability)?
- Diagnosis of weak PPPs explores the main factors limiting them in infrastructure: Are PPPs weak due to a shortage of bankable projects or an insufficient regulatory framework?

Impediments. The obstacles to infrastructure development are verified in greater detail on the basis of a primary survey and by using the latest available data and information. This allows determination of the binding constraints within each category, and facilitates the development of specific solutions for each subsector. Based on the diagnostic framework, the following hypotheses have been developed and tested:

(1) regarding public investment in infrastructure:
- the government has limited institutional and human capital, which has adversely impacted its ability to identify and implement suitable infrastructure projects; and
- the government's ability to increase public investment in new infrastructure while maintaining and rehabilitating existing infrastructure is constrained by limited financial resources;

(2) regarding private investment in infrastructure:
- private investment, particularly in roads, toll roads, and electricity, is constrained by land acquisition problems;
- the low level of private investment is due largely to poor governance and corruption, exacerbated by the decentralization of power, which has resulted in additional rent-seeking activities;
- lack of long-term financing is constraining private investment in infrastructure projects, which generally take a long time to complete; and
- micro risks, specifically around the cost of doing business, coupled with weak institutional and human capacity, result in poorly prepared bankable infrastructure projects, making it difficult to attract private investors to the sector; and

(3) regarding PPPs, they are inhibited by a shortage of bankable projects, lack of institutional capacity, weak regulatory framework, and/or provision of low quality and inadequate infrastructure.

Key Issues. The following subsections examine the constraints affecting public and private investment, and PPP in the country. To tackle the infrastructure bottlenecks, the government has developed a medium-term infrastructure plan for 2010–2014, with an estimated financing requirement of Rp1,429 trillion ($157 million).[4] The government target is to increase the

---

[4]   Exchange rates used in this chapter are year averages from ADB (2011).

share of infrastructure investment to 5% of GDP (Figure 7.4). It also plans to initiate reforms to attract domestic and foreign investors to the sector. In this regard, the government has published a PPP book that contains plans for the infrastructure projects to be offered to the private sector (Bappenas 2010). The PPP book identifies 100 projects with a total cost of $47.3 billion, mostly in toll roads, water supply, railways, and power. The medium-term plan for infrastructure indicates that the central government can finance only 47% of the infrastructure needed; the gap is to be covered by local governments (28%) and PPP (25%).[5]

Figure 7.4: Funding for the Medium-Term Infrastructure Plan in Indonesia (2010–2014, Rp billion)

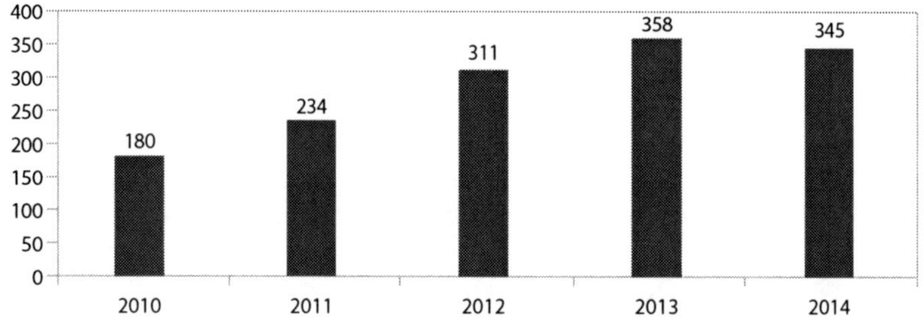

Source: Bappenas (2010), cited in IDB (2010).

Despite concerted government efforts,[6] public–private investment in infrastructure has not been forthcoming to the desired extent. Therefore, the impediments to private sector participation in infrastructure must be analyzed. In addition, projects must be packaged so that they are attractive to private sector participation. To accomplish this, the capacity of relevant institutions for implementing PPP projects will need to be strengthened in

---

[5]   Minister for National Development Plan Agency. Dedy Priatna, 17 December 2009, cited in (IDB 2010).

[6]   For example, from an institutional perspective, in addition to the existing agencies dealing with infrastructure, in 2005 the government revitalized the National Committee for the Acceleration of Infrastructure Provision to better integrate efforts to cope with the increasing demand for infrastructure. A number of supporting units, such as the Risk Management Unit and Government Investment Agency under the Ministry of Finance, were established along with a number of PPP nodes, the Center for Government-Private Coordination, and the Public Service Board. Activities to encourage private investment in infrastructure, such as the 2005 Infrastructure Summit and 2006 Infrastructure Forum, were also initiated. In 2006, the government launched the Invesment Policy Package aiming to boost institutional capacity and coordination among line ministries dealing with infrastructure development and regulations. The 2008 Budget Law also indicated the government's increased support for infrastructure development.

areas such as preparing and marketing bankable projects to attract long-term domestic and foreign funds.

7.3.   Key Factors Affecting Infrastructure Investment in Indonesia

7.3.1.   Primary Survey of Infrastructure Stakeholders

The Islamic Development Bank (IDB) undertook a primary survey of selected stakeholders active in Indonesia's infrastructure sector in November and December 2009 in Java district, to gain first-hand knowledge of the impediments to infrastructure investment in the country (IDB 2010). The survey indicated that investors viewed macroeconomic stability positively and that private savings did not seem to be a critical constraint to investment in infrastructure. The key broad constraints the survey found were difficulty acquiring land, weak human and institutional capacity to implement projects, poor governance, and unavailability of long-term financing. Table 7.2 shows the major constraints that the respondents identified, with their ranking.[7] The survey results are also validated by an in-depth subsectoral

Table 7.2: Ranking of Factors Adversely Impacting Infrastructure Development in Indonesia

Major Constraints	Scarcity		Cost		Impact		Overall Rank [b]
	% of Respondents	Rank [a]	% of Respondents	Rank [a]	% of Respondents	Rank [a]	
Difficulty in Land Acquisition	52	2	69	1	61	1	1
Weak Human and Institutional Capacity [c]	55	1	48	4	45	3	2
Poor Governance	...	...	58	2	58	2	3
Shortage of Financing	45	3	49	3	34	4	4

... = not available.
[a] The rank of 1, 2, 3, and 4 is based on the percentage of respondents noting the items as major constraints.
[b] The overall ranking is based on the weights (50% for scarcity, 30% for cost, and 20% for impact,
[c] This factor is the underlying issue behind the negative perspective on several areas including: government coordination, bankable projects, implementation capacity, interface with the government, and legal and regulatory framework.
Source: IDB (2010).

---

[7]   These findings are comparable to those of the Global Competitiveness Report 2009–2010 (IMD 2009), wherein inefficient government bureaucracy (equivalent to weak human and institutional capacity) was the most frequently cited problem, with corruption, access to financing, and labor and tax regulations ranking 4th, 5th, 6th, and 7th, respectively.

analysis and the underlying reasons for all of these constraints emerge from the discussion in the following sections.

7.3.2. Validation of the Infrastructure Survey Findings

The survey focused on the infrastructure subsectors that are most critical for sustainable and inclusive growth in Indonesia. Thus, this study is restricted to analyzing the transport (roads, toll roads, railroads, air transport, and ports), electricity, and communication subsectors, which are critical for sustainable and inclusive growth.

In 2008, the quality of infrastructure in Indonesia was far below that in Malaysia and Thailand, but at par with that in the Philippines and Viet Nam. Table 7.3 shows that the area in which Indonesia fares the worst is the quality of electricity supply, ports, and roads. Of particular concern is that in 1991 and 2000, Indonesia's infrastructure was considered superior to that of the Philippines and Viet Nam. However, since 2005 these two countries have been at par with Indonesia, while Thailand and Malaysia have been improving their infrastructure (Bhattacharyay 2009:10). Thus, Indonesia has not been upgrading its infrastructure quality at the same pace as its regional comparators.

Table 7.3: Quality of Infrastructure by Subsector in Indonesia and Neighboring Countries (2008)

	Indonesia	Malaysia	Philippines	Thailand	Viet Nam
Quality of Roads	94	24	104	35	102
Quality of Railroad Infrastructure	60	19	92	52	58
Quality of Port Infrastructure	95	19	112	47	99
Quality of Air Transport Infrastructure	68	27	100	26	84
Quality of Electricity Supply	96	39	87	41	103
Telephone Lines	79	72	102	84	36

Note: The lower the ranking, the better the infrastructure quality.
Source: WEF (2009).

7.3.3. Constraints of Transport and Electricity

At the country level, transport is the second main obstacle to entrepreneurship identified by the business community in the 2003, 2005, and 2007 investment climate surveys, and electricity was rated as the 6th most important obstacle to their businesses. The share of respondents perceiving transport as a business constraint increased from 29% in 2003 to 49% in 2009 (Figure 7.5), further validating the results of deteriorating infrastructure found in the Global Competitiveness Report 2009–2010 (IMD 2009).

Figure 7.5: Indonesia's Main Business Constraints (%)

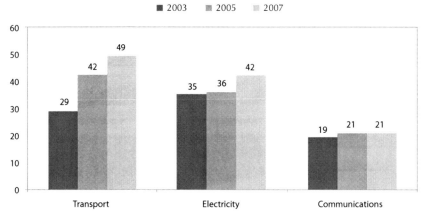

Sources: IDB (2010).

7.3.4. Investment Levels as a Constraint to Infrastructure Development

The poor performance of infrastructure is directly attributable to the low levels of investment in it. An effective and efficient transport system, which is the foundation for a competitive economy (especially for countries wishing to pursue an export-led growth strategy), requires sustained high levels of investment. In Indonesia, investment at the subsector level has been relatively low, below 1.5% of GDP per annum for transport and communications. Electricity, which has also been identified as a constraint to business, has had less than 1% of GDP invested into it since 2000 (Figure 7.6). This does not bode well for the long-term sustainable growth of the economy, which depends on reliable, uninterrupted power supply. Power outages have become a regular phenomenon, and the situation is likely to deteriorate because of the declining performance of the existing aging power plants.

Figure 7.6: investment in Infrastructure Subsectors (1996–2006)

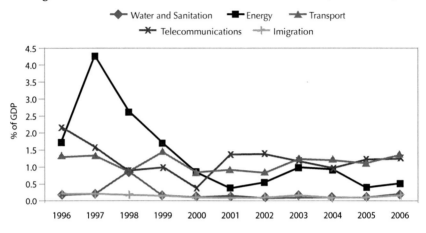

Source: ADB, ILO, and IDB (2009).

7.4.   Transport Infrastructure

Although Indonesia is a big archipelago, interisland and coastal shipping accounts for only 7% of freight and passenger movements, while roads carry 92% of total freight and 84% of passenger traffic. Rail accounts for about 1% freight and 7% of passenger movement, with inland waterways and air transport carrying the remaining traffic (ADB 2004).

7.4.1.   Roads

As indicated in Figure 3.16 (Chapter 3), Indonesia's road density (the ratio of total road network length to the area of the country) is 0.20, which is low compared to densities in Viet Nam (0.68), the Philippines (0.67), Thailand (0.35), and Malaysia (0.28). Although roads are critical for Indonesia's development, their expansion has not kept pace with population increase. What is worrisome is that the demand for better road transport has been growing at a faster pace than GDP for nearly a decade. This trend is anticipated to continue in the foreseeable future, with traffic expected to increase at 1–1.5 times GDP growth rates—roughly 7%–10% per annum (World Bank 2006). Another key concern is that 36% of the road network was either damaged or severely damaged at the end of 2007 (BPS 2007). Most of the damaged or severely damaged roads were under the purview of the district governments, and 39% of the 322,000 kilometers (km) of road under the district governments was considered damaged or severely damaged. The inefficiency, unreliability, and high cost of road transport is a key constraint to Indonesia's economic development.

7.4.1.1. Public Sector Investment in Roads

Investment in and maintenance of the road network are funded predominantly through the central government budget, including financial support from bilateral and multilateral banks. The national budget is not supplemented by vehicle purchase and ownership taxes, which are appropriated by the local governments and are thus not available for national road maintenance and investment. However, the two taxes could be used for maintaining and investing in provincial and district roads.

The Ministry of Public Works, through the Directorate General of Highways, significantly increased the road budget, from Rp7.5 trillion ($818 million) in 2006 to about Rp20 trillion ($1.92 billion) in 2009, with expenditure in 2010 estimated at more than Rp24 trillion ($2.6 billion). The problem of poor quality roads is attributed to an appalling shortage of annual budget for road maintenance, which, up to 2004, was less than Rp1 trillion ($112 million) versus the required Rp20 trillion. However, the situation has been improving in recent years, with the government increasing the allocation for road maintenance from Rp3.8 trillion ($415 million) in 2006 to Rp12.1 trillion ($1.32 billion) in 2009 and a budgeted Rp14.4 trillion ($1.58 billion) for 2010. The bulk of the national road budget (60.8%) was spent on maintenance in 2009, followed by 26.1% on investment. This highlights the government's commitment to maintaining the infrastructure. However, the country also needs additional infrastructure, and this should be addressed by providing new investment in roads.

Key constraints to public investment in road infrastructure are weak institutional capacity, lack of human capital, and unsustainable public funding. Due to decentralization, the responsibility for project implementation now rests with the local governments. Capacity constraints at the local government level have hindered the use of budget allocations and project delivery. The lack of skills and limited operational capabilities within local government have led to delayed project implementation. Capacity constraints appear more prevalent in project design and development, resulting in implementation delays. Responding to these constraints, the Directorate General of Highways (especially for externally funded projects) is

- implementing a capacity development program by providing management support to the local government staff,
- using standardized bidding documents for both national and international competitive bidding procurement, and
- implementing an electronic procurement system.

While the large-scale and long-term impact of these efforts remain to be seen, they are intended to mitigate the negative impact of decentralization.

Regarding funding, allocations for road projects (preservation, capacity expansion, and extension of the road network) have been inadequate since the 1997 Asian financial crisis (AFC) and started increasing only in 2007–2009. This is particularly true for regional roads. The funding approved by the Parliament (through the national budget and allocation of regional budgets) is expected to remain below the expenditure requirements for 2011 on.

In addition, the prevalent public perception that road maintenance and development should be covered by the central government budget needs to be changed. The government should embrace the concept that cost for preserving and expanding the road network should be recovered from road users.

Underfunding problems are compounded by unpredictability in the level of funding. To ensure adequate and sustainable financing of roads, the government should consider establishing a road fund financed directly from road user charges. The discussion on a road fund has been ongoing, and, to address the underinvestment in road infrastructure, it is imperative that the appropriate legal framework be established so the fund can be implemented.

7.4.1.2. Private Sector Investment in Road Infrastructure

The first private investment in road development was in 1990 for a toll road. The investment was made through a build-operate-transfer scheme between private operators and Jasa Marga, the state-owned toll road operator. The government is increasingly relying on private sector investment for developing toll roads; however, 20 of the 24 toll road projects that have signed concession agreements are being delayed by the land acquisition process (with some delays dating back to 1996). Hence, a key concern in developing toll roads is land acquisition. The responsibility for acquiring land for any public infrastructure rests with the government. For infrastructure projects undertaken as PPPs, the regulation requires that, prior to the tendering process, the government will prepare, finance, and execute a land acquisition plan. However, in practice this has not been fully implemented due to limited government budget allocations and the complexity of the acquisition process. Theoretically, the schedule for land acquisition is agreed on in advance in the concession contract, with the government responsible for acquiring the land, and the private sector responsible for financing the acquisition. The pre-agreed land cost would be paid by the private investors after the land has been cleared completely for construction. This would give private investors full control over the start and completion of construction work, knowing in detail when they could expect to start commercial operation. However, in reality, the government acquisition process takes a lot longer than anticipated, resulting in financial loss and implementation delays for the private investors.

Key constraints in PPPs and private investment in roads are difficulties with land acquisition, a lack of "bankable" projects, and a lack of long-term financing.

Land Acquisition. The core issue in land acquisition is reaching agreement on a suitable price. The negotiations are conducted between the government and the landowners. The negotiations are usually lengthy and frustrating, involving local government, landowners, nongovernment organizations providing advocacy to the affected people, and land speculators profiting from price escalation. This obviously exposes private investors to substantial risks of project implementation delays and cost overruns. Because banks have been very reluctant to lend money for land acquisition due to uncertainties surrounding the costs and acquisition period, toll road developers depend on equity to finance land acquisition. This arrangement is especially risky for investors in urban toll road projects, where land cost can be as much as 50% of the total project cost. Due to the lengthy and risky land acquisition processes, many road projects have stalled or experiencing significant cost overruns, adversely impacting returns on investment, profitability, and long-term commitment to the project (Box 7.2).

Box 7.2: Delayed and Costly Land Acquisition Makes Projects Unviable

PT Citra Marga Nusaphala Persada (CMNP) is the first private toll road operator in Indonesia, with two operating projects: (1) the Jakarta Intra Urban Toll Road section Cawang–Tanjung Priok–Jembatan Tiga, and (2) Waru–Juanda in Surabaya. CMNP also holds a concession for the Depok–Antasari toll road south of Jakarta, which is currently in the land acquisition phase. The construction of the Depok–Antasari toll road has been problematic due to delays in land acquisition. The land acquisition cost was initially budgeted at about Rp700 billion ($72 million), but has escalated to about Rp1.8 trillion ($198 million). The costs have risen to such an extent that the financial viability of the project is being questioned. CMNP is in discussion with the Toll-Road Regulatory Agency and its bankers to seek government assistance in paying part of the land acquisition cost and renegotiating the concession agreement. In addition, CMNP will need to develop a new business plan and prepare a new feasibility study for its financiers.

Source: IDB (2010).

"Bankability." The government has had difficulty preparing "bankable" projects. In 2007, the Toll-Road Regulatory Agency (BPJT) invited tenders for 13 toll road projects under its "Batch II" package, but received only six bids. The tenders were subsequently cancelled due to lack of interest, and BPJT considered restructuring the projects to be more attractive to private investors. Discussions with potential private sector investors indicated that the lack of interest was because the lands rights of way had not been acquired for any of the 13 toll roads tendered, and the proposed concession agreements were not regarded as bankable. Hence, investors considered the risks too high to attract their interest.[8]

Under the "Batch III" package, the Solo–Kertosono toll road project was highlighted as a model PPP, wherein the government committed to take the responsibility for land acquisition. This also failed to elicit interest from investors when it was tendered in 2007 (only one bid was received). Although the risk of land acquisition rested with the government, the project had low returns on investment, and was not considered viable unless the government was willing to bear more of the construction costs. The government is now entering into direct negotiation with the sole bidder on the concession agreement.

As of 2010, no further tenders for new toll road projects were under way. The BPJT is focusing on resolving the problems with toll road projects awarded prior to the AFC. Resolution of these projects entails the same issues: land acquisition and the type and amount of government support required to facilitate financial viability and closure.

Long-Term Financing. The other key constraint is that the long-term financing needed for road infrastructure projects is not available. Commercial banks in Indonesia are willing to provide financing for a period of only up to 7 years, and state-owned banks may go up to 12 years, but road infrastructure projects require financing beyond that time. Hence, the lack of long-term financing is due largely to the mismatch between the time horizon for funding and that of financing requirements for infrastructure projects. Thus, it is important that banks diversify their funding sources to include longer term financing, by developing a domestic bond market (the preferred option), issuing global bonds, or long-term borrowing from international banks.

7.4.2. Seaports

Sea transport is vitally important to Indonesia, which is the largest archipelago in the world. The country's sea area is approximately 7.9

---

[8] These issues were highlighted in discussions with key stakeholders in the infrastructure sector in July–November 2009 (IDB 2010).

million square kilometers, about four times its land area. Thus, Indonesia is heavily dependent on maritime transport for international and domestic trade. Patunru, Nurridzki, and Rivayani (2007) indicated that about 90% of Indonesia's external trade is conducted through seaports. Interisland and coastal shipping accounts for about 7% of total national freight and passenger movements, second after road transportation. Thus, the development of shipping and port services throughout the country is one of the government's top priorities.

Most container cargo in Indonesia is processed through the three main container terminals: Tanjung Priok in Jakarta, Tanjung Emas in Semarang, and Tanjung Perak in Surabaya. Tanjung Priok, with a total peak throughput of 3.8 million 20-foot equivalent units, is the country's largest international container terminal. However, Tanjung Priok's performance lags behind that of most other major ports in Southeast Asia. In volume of container handling, Tanjung Priok ranked 24th of the 50 major ports in the 2005 World Port Rankings (Containerisation International 2008). In comparison, Singapore port was ranked 1st, Port Klang in Malaysia 14th, and Laem Chabang in Thailand 20th. The only major port ranking below Tanjung Priok was Manila Port in the Philippines, at 31st. Other performance comparisons suggest that Tanjung Priok is also uncompetitive in terms of length and number of bureaucratic process for clearance, waiting time, and port access (IDB 2010).

The performance of smaller ports catering mainly to interisland cargo is also poor. Their productivity related to loading and unloading of vessels is relatively low, with all Indonesian ports having a berth occupancy rate of about 58%. Port efficiencies can also be judged from the average turnaround times of 3–5 days, with loading and unloading taking up to 35% of the time in the port. Table 7.4 highlights problems at specific ports and shows that the low productivity may be due to the lack of equipment, inefficient work methods, limited berth lengths, and shallow channels.

Table 7.4: Conditions of Regional Ports in Indonesia (2006)

Ports	Draft (meters)	Problems
Banjarmasin	4–9	Congestion and shallow channel
Batam	9–10	Underdeveloped
Belawan	7–9	Congestion and lack of loading/unloading facilities
Makassar	3–12	Congestion
Palembang	4–8	Shallow channel
Pontianak	4–6	Congestion and shallow channel
Samarinda	6–7	Congestion

Source: JICA (2006), cited in IDB (2010).

7.4.2.1. Public Sector Investment

Key constraints to public sector investment in ports infrastructure are weak human and institutional capacity, labor regulations, corruption, and geographic issues.

Table 7.5 summarizes the findings of the Ministry of Transportation and Japan International Cooperation Agency (2005) study on port productivity and service levels in Indonesia. In addition, labor regulations effectively institutionalize underutilization of port facilities and limit the potential for efficiency improvements. In many ports, only one shift of labor is provided, and opportunities for overtime are limited. Nathan Associates (2001) observed that this results in the loss of 6 hours of productivity in each 24 hours of operation, because the break times are not staggered to ensure continuous servicing of vessels.

Table 7.5: Issues with Service at Seaports

Findings	Underlying Reasons
Low productivity and poor service	• Inefficient work methods • Lack of personnel integrity • No transparency • Lack of use of information technology
Long delay for importation	• Long bureaucratic and inefficient process
Small cargo throughput	• Low export volume • Low country competitiveness
Congested and low quality port access road	• Poor planning • Poor transportation management • Low investment on access roads

Source: JICA (2005).

Another cause of poor port performance is corruption. Patunru, Nurridzki, and Rivayani (2007) noted that "informal payments" are frequently used to speed queuing time resulting from the lack of key infrastructure facilities such as gantry cranes and storage space. A broad range of informal payments is also required at the ports for export and import procedures (IDB 2010).

Indonesia has very few natural deepwater harbors, and its river system is prone to serious siltation, which restricts port depth. Ray (2008) noted that port depth appears to be a major problem at almost every port in Indonesia. To operate normally, many ports have to undertake continuous dredging, which is expensive. Depth issues are especially acute for the main ports on the northern coast of Java, which service the country's most populous and industrialized regions. The seabed and coastal soil are mainly alluvial and unstable, and the coastal waters are shallow. Hence, finding appropriate sites for new ports is difficult.

7.4.2.2. Private Investment and PPPs

Private investment in ports has had mixed results. PPPs in ports started in 1995 with the concession granted to Hutchison Whampoa to rehabilitate and operate Koja Container Terminal for 20 years. Full private investment has been successful for bulk supply terminals serving coal miners, such as by Adaro Energy and Dermaga Prakasa Pratama in Kalimantan. Both terminals are serving the domestic and international coal markets, which are growing. To raise financing during the AFC, the government embarked on additional PPPs through partial privatization by selling 52% of Jakarta International Container Terminal to Hutchison Whampoa and 49% of Tanjung Perak Container Terminal to P&O (DP World), both in 1999. These joint ventures have not been fully successful, with the private investors accused of not achieving target performance and failing to attract sufficient traffic to the port.

Key constraints in private investment and PPPs have been the weak regulatory framework and institutional capacity, lack of bankable projects, and low return on investment. Private investment has shied away from port infrastructure due to the lack of a clear and predictable regulatory environment. Prior to the issuance of the new maritime law (Law 17 of 2008), state-owned port operators (Pelindos) were acting both as a landlord and an operator under PPP contracts. This deterred private investment, as potential investors in PPP projects were not receiving fair treatment. Law 17 of 2008 revoked the Pelindos' monopoly powers, making them ordinary port operators, and the role of landlord was vested in a port authority, which would act on behalf of the government. This structure aims to clarify the division of responsibilities between the public authority and private investors in PPP contracts and to remove the conflict of interest.

Regarding institutional capacity and bankability, government officials at the Ministry of Transportation (MOT), for national port projects, and at regional levels, for regional ports, do not have the required capacity to structure internationally acceptable bankable PPP projects. Historically, the contracting authority's role was performed by a Pelindo, with the government responsible for policy making. Hence, skills were not developed within the government to function as a contracting authority. To resolve this problem, MOT requested assistance from the Project Development Facility of the PPP Center Unit within the National Development Planning Agency (Bappenas). This is intended to recruit experienced transaction advisers aimed at helping MOT and regional governments prepare attractive port projects and bankable port concession agreements.

However, as of 2010, no bankable project had been offered to investors. Partial privatization of Tanjung Priok and Tanjung Perak in 1999 were primarily a government fund-raising effort during the AFC, rather than for using private investors' expertise to increase port productivity. Subsequent efforts to offer Bojonegara Port in West Java and Lamong Bay Port in East Java did not materialize, as the government was still structuring the deals to be attractive to private investors (e.g., establishing the port authority and acquiring the land). Preparing the two projects for tender has been ongoing since 2006, but the process has been agonizingly slow due to weak institutional capacity.

Regarding returns on investment, under the new sea transport law, the government retains control over tariffs for PPP port projects. The tariffs are set by the port authority after consultation with MOT. This may be expected, as ports have substantial geographic monopoly and there would be no competition between ports. However, private investors would expect port tariffs to be determined through a competitive bidding process during the selection of a port investor. Application of a cost-of-service or rate-of-return regulation would generally result in tariffs too low to generate interest from investors.

7.4.3. Railways

Indonesia's rail network is limited to Java and Sumatra. Of the network's total 5,824 km of track, only 4,337 km are operational. Java has a larger rail network than Sumatra, with major rail corridors being Jakarta–Bandung, Jakarta–Semarang–Surabaya–Banyuwangi (the "North Route"), Bandung–Kroya–Yogyakarta–Surabaya (the "South Route"), and the connector route of Cirebon–Purwokerto–Kroya. Most of the railway system is single track, but due to the growing demand for mass urban transport, the government intends to improve the capacity and quality of the Jabotabek railways network, which comprises nearly 266 km of double track. The expansion of the railways continues to be plagued by land acquisition issues. Millions of passengers in Greater Jakarta use rail for relatively short distances, while in Sumatra, the railways are mainly used for coal and commodity transport. Among its neighboring countries, Indonesia has the longest (4,337 km) rail network and the most intensive use (25.5 billion-passenger-km) of railways, as indicated in Table 7.6).

Table 7.6: Key Railways Statistics in Indonesia and Neighboring Countries (2006)

	Indonesia	Malaysia	Philippines	Thailand	Viet Nam
Rail Lines (km)	4,337	1,667	491	4,044	3,147
Passengers (million-passenger-km)	25,535	2,075	144	9,195	4,333
Freight (million-ton-km)	4,698	1,572	...	4,037	3,447

... = not available, km = kilometer.
Source: World Bank WDI.

7.4.3.1. Key Constraints to Public Investment in Railway Infrastructure

The key constraints to public sector investment in railways are weak human and institutional capacity, land acquisition problems, and a low return on investment. Under the railway law of the previous New Order regime, development and implementation of the railway services were conducted predominantly by Indonesian Railways (PT Kerata Api—PTKA), with policy making and tariff regulations under the domain of MOT. This arrangement resulted in PTKA having 23,000 staff, compared with the newly established Directorate General of Railways (DGR) under MOT, which has only about 300 full-time staff. At the local government level (province or district), this number drops to zero in some instances. The lack of sufficient competent staff will need to be addressed if DGR is to carry out its policy and regulatory functions efficiently and effectively. To strengthen DGR's performance requires transferring staff from PTKA to DGR, effective resource management, and an extensive capacity development program.

Land acquisition is the most critical impediment to investment in expanding the rail infrastructure. The National Land Agency and an interministerial coordination group under the Coordinating Ministry of Economic Affairs have been established to develop laws and regulations appropriate for simplifying and accelerating the land acquisition process. It is a major constraint for the network in Greater Jakarta, stalling railway expansion. The government anticipated that the land acquisition would be completed by the end of 2009, with construction of the project finished by 2012. The key problem is procurement of land (which is owned by a PTKA retiree).

Because train fares are determined based on social considerations, returns on railway investments are low. This often hampers the sustainability of services and has resulted in dependency on government budget for subsidizing operating costs.

7.4.3.2. Key Constraints to Private Investment and PPPs in Railways Infrastructure

Under the railway law of the New Order regime, the private sector could participate in railways through joint ventures with PTKA, but did not do so due to lack of transparency in the financial arrangements between the government and PTKA. Hence, the only partnership in the existing railway network is between PTKA and the state-owned Angkasa Pura II, which is bidding for the PPP rail link connecting Sukarno–Hatta Airport with downtown Jakarta.

As with other transport sectors, new laws and regulations were developed, but they still lack clarity for PPPs. Although the law mandated that the playing field between PTKA and private sector operators would be level, PTKA's monopoly would be maintained, and private investment in railways would be limited to a minority shareholding in the national railways company, with the private sector not allowed to operate its own rolling stock (IDB 2010).

Regarding institutional capacity, the contracting responsibilities for railways infrastructure are held by MOT, which lacks the experience, resources, and capacity to prepare and structure a PPP project. This weakness was evident during the preparation and implementation of the PPP Sukarno–Hatta Airportrail link project. Because the project was structured without government support, the result was in a nonbankable project agreement (Tempo Interaktif 2009). For the next planned PPP project on coal railways in Kalimantan, MOT and the Provincial Government of Central Kalimantan, with the help of Bappenas, are working with transaction consultants to market and tender the project. This opportunity for on-the-job training with experienced international consultants may accelerate the learning process while simultaneously achieving successful PPP project implementation.

Regarding return on investment for the private sector, under the new railways law, the government controls track access charges through MOT. The regulation for calculating and setting the charges has not been enacted yet. The details of the charges are very important to a PPP, as they determine project viability. If an arrangement similar to that with PTKA is applied, the private sector may perceive that the rate of return is too low to justify participation.

7.4.4. Airports

Given the geographical extent of Indonesia, the expansion of low-cost air travel is seen as a major contributor to social development and economic growth. Although the economic prospects for the aviation industry appear positive, overcrowded airport terminals (especially in regional hubs like

Polonia Medan and Djuanda Surabaya), inadequate air traffic control, and safety issues could hinder its growth (ADB 2006).

Compared with its neighbors, on a per capita basis, Indonesia's passenger traffic (13 passengers/100 inhabitants) is marginally higher than Viet Nam (8) and the Philippines (10), but significantly lower than Malaysia (80) and Thailand (33). In terms of airfreight, Indonesia is ahead of the Philippines and Viet Nam but far below Malaysia and Thailand. However, in terms of registered carrier departures worldwide and passengers carried, Indonesia is ahead of all its neigboring countries (Table 7.7).

Table 7.7: Key Air Transport Statistics in Indonesia and Neighboring
Countries (2007)

Indicator	Indonesia	Malaysia	Philippines	Thailand	Viet Nam
Registered Carrier Departures Worldwide ('000)	358	185	65	130	60
Passengers carried ('000)	30,406	21,326	8,818	21,192	7,194
Airfreight (million ton-km)	485	2,662	286	2,455	258
Population (million)	225.6	26.5	87.9	63.8	85.2
Passengers/100 inhabitants	13	80	10	33	8

km = kilometer.
Source: World Bank, WDI.

While private airlines have responded quickly to market liberalization, airport infrastructure, which is still largely under the public domain, has grown at a slower pace. Due to government-determined domestic airport tariffs (which are low), services provided are not profitable. Only major hubs (e.g., Bali, Jakarta, Medan, and Surabaya) with significant international traffic are able to break even in their operations.

Funding policy and mechanisms are not established for how the central and local governments, airports, and private sector can finance new airport projects. The use of foreign loans from multilateral or bilateral agencies to finance expansion of major airports is restricted, because most of the airports are used for both civilian and military purposes.

7.4.4.1. Constraints to Public Investment

Key constraints to public investment in infrastructure are weak human and institutional capacities and weak capacity to fund commercial airports. The weak human and institutional capacities are manifested in the high rate of air accidents. The National Transportation Safety Committee indicated that 70%–80% of the accidents resulted from inadequacies in human capacity (errors by pilots, air traffic controllers, and maintenance crews). Institutional weaknesses are also apparent in the limited supervision for flight-worthiness tests and procedures. The new aviation law requires the creation of a single air traffic controller, which will assume the roles currently handled by the airports and MOT. The law does not stipulate that the new air traffic controller must be staffed by civil servants (as in the case for the establishment of port authority in the maritime law). Public investment in the air traffic controller and other safety-related institutions is crucial for the sector's growth.

Large and profitable airports are operated by the airports themselves, and they have brought in professionalism and customer-oriented services. However, unprofitable remote airports are operated by MOT, which depends on the national budget to cover expenses. This arrangement has made it difficult for MOT to build capacity and resources to adequately maintain facilities or invest in new ones.

7.4.4.2. Private Investment and PPPs in Airport Infrastructure

Private sector participation in airport development and management is limited to the airports subcontracting terminal services. The government has considered privatizing the airports or PPPs in some major hubs, but no significant progress has been made along these lines. Until the new aviation law becomes effective (through the issuance of the implementing regulations), viable PPPs in airport operation are limited to joint ventures with the airports, which have been offering partnerships in terminal operation or rail access. As noted previously, so far there has been only one PPP, the Sukarno-Hatta Airport link with downtown Jakarta (between the airport and the state-owned railway operator PTKA).

Key constraints to private investment and PPPs include the weak regulatory framework, weak institutional capacity, and low returns on investment. The lack of equal access and opportunities and of a clear and predictable regulatory and investment environment is the primary deterrent to private sector investment in airport infrastructure. In addition, the provision of certain services is restricted to the public sector. Under the previous law, commercial airport operations were conducted by the airports, which limited options for PPP transactions to the provision of terminal services while keeping the lucrative air-side business for themselves. Although the new law separates the air traffic control function from the airports, they are well positioned to maintain and expand their market share in the airport businesses. The new law would also transfer the contracting power to MOT and local governments, whose detailed jurisdiction and authority to run airports are yet to be established. The regulation laying the legal foundation for the airport contracting authority is still being drafted. Until the legal and regulatory framework is determined, private investors are unlikely to become involved in the airports.

MOT and the local governments lack experience, resources, and capacity to prepare and structure PPP projects. For example, the Project Development Facility in Bappenas has been asked to prepare and transact the PPP for the West Java International Airport in Kertajati.

Under the new air transportation law, the government maintains control of airport service charges through consultation with MOT. Because there is no independent regulatory body, political considerations could affect the determination of airport fees and thereby adversely impact the return on investments.

7.5. Electricity

Irregular and poor quality of electricity supply is a key constraint to business growth, as stated by 43% of Indonesian businesses surveyed (OECD 2008). This is not surprising, given that the electricity sector is characterized by

- low-levels of electrification ranging, from 21% in East Nusa Tenggara to 88% in the capital city of Jakarta—the country's electrification rate increased from 55% in 2003 to 65% in 2009;
- persistent high transmission and distribution losses of over 11% since 1997;
- unsustainable subsidized nationwide uniform electricity tariffs that are set below cost-recovery levels (set by the President after consulting with Parliament); and
- suppressed demand—new connections cannot be established quickly due to lack of supply to maintain a safe level of reserve margin.[9]

Regionally, Indonesia has the lowest industrial tariff for electricity, due largely to heavily subsidized electricity (below operational costs). This has discouraged the state-owned provider PT Perusahaan Listrik Negara (PLN) from increasing capacity (because the more electricity it produces and sells, the greater are its losses). And PLN's transmission and distribution losses (10% in 2009) are higher than those in Malaysia (7.2%) and Thailand (7.3%), while comparable to those in the Philippines and Viet Nam. IDB (2010) notes that, in 2009, Indonesia's electrification rate (66%) was significantly lower than those of Thailand (99%), Malaysia (98%), Viet Nam (97%), and the Philippines (79%).

---

[9] Reserve margin is a measure of power system reliability, i.e., the electricity power system's unused capability at peak load as a percent of its total capability.

7.5.1. Key Constraints to Public Investment in Electricity Infrastructure

Public investment in electricity in Indonesia faces six key constraints: land acquisition issues, low tariffs, lack of policy and regulatory coordination, inefficient allocation of limited resources, supply constraints, and low load factors.

Land Acquisition. When land has to be acquired to build power plants and set up transmission and distribution lines, PLN has to negotiate directly with the landowner. If the landowner is asking an exorbitant price, the legal process to acquire the land is protracted, resulting in PLN paying a premium for the land. Although legislation to expedite land acquisition is in place, the government appears unwilling to implement unpopular decisions. Hence, acquiring land to establish new infrastructure is a major constraint to further investment in the sector.

Electricity Tariffs. Electricity tariffs are below cost recovery levels, and tariffs are uniform nationwide. Hence, the expansion of electricity production capacity has been hampered by concerns of profitability and sustainability, adversely impacting PLNs ability and willingness to invest in new power generation capacity. Given the sensitivity of electricity pricing, political will is required, as well as a revision of the subsidy schemes to achieve social and economic objectives.

Policy and Regulatory Coordination. The World Bank study on rural electrification in Indonesia, "Electricity for All," found that many players in the country were working on various rural electrifications programs (e.g., central government, local governments, PLN, nongovernment organizations, cooperatives) with government departments (the Ministry of Energy and Mineral Resources, Ministry of Cooperatives Development, and State Ministry for the Development of Underdeveloped Areas) with different agendas, procedures, and financing sources (IDB 2010). Unfortunately, there is no effective coordination among the players. There are also legal and regulatory ambiguities surrounding the responsibility for rural electrification. It is unclear whether the responsibility is given to the Social Electrification Unit within the Ministry of Energy and Mineral Resources or to PLN. As a result, PLN disbanded its Rural Electrification Unit in 2001, and the rate at which the electricity network was expanding slowed further.

Allocation of Limited Resources. The decision to maintain oil price subsidies compounds the problem, hampers other energy programs, and remains a barrier to energy diversification and conservation. The subsidies have made it less viable to explore investment in alternative sources of energy, created economic inefficiencies, and diverted limited state resources from the provision of other important social and physical infrastructure. In 2009, approximately 4% of GDP was allocated for fuel subsidies. Approximately half of this went to the electricity subsector (Figure 7.7)—this is higher than the investment made in the electricity subsector, which was less than 1% of GDP per annum during 2000–2006.

Supply Constraints. Part of PLN's electricity generation business depends on natural gas supplies. PLN has had difficulty obtaining adequate supplies of natural gas to meet its demand, due to its suppliers' inability to deliver contracted volumes. Since 2003, the shortage has resulted in PLN shutting down certain power plants and switching fuel in some dual-fired plants. In addition, some of the natural gas fields from which PLN receives supplies are being depleted. Because supply agreements are medium term (about 5 years), PLN could switch to other energy sources or alternative suppliers of natural gas. But, until such changes can be effected, PLN will have to procure natural gas from suppliers far away. While PLN continues to negotiate with suppliers and is expanding its generation network to reduce its dependence on natural gas, whether it will be able to secure sufficient additional gas supplies for its existing plants or to implement its growth strategy remains unsure.

Figure 7.7: Oil and Electricity Subsidies in Indonesia

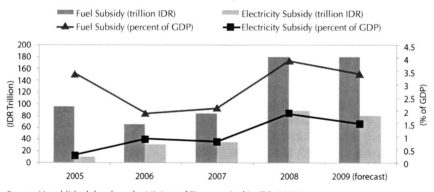

Source: Unpublished data from the Ministry of Finance, cited in IDB (2010).

Part of PLN's electricity generation depends on coal suppliers, and Indonesia has abundant coal reserves. To increase the number of power plants, a stable long-term supply of coal must be secured at reasonable prices. This would allow PLN to expand capacity and establish new coal-fired power plants.

Low Load Factor. The average power system load factor in Indonesia in 2007 was approximately 59.6%. This varied significantly between regions, ranging from 30% in Central Java to 84% in Riau (eastern part of Sumatra). The low load factor has made it difficult for PLN to expand its base load generation capacity. Due to the vast land area and many islands, a national grid is not a viable option.

7.5.2. Private Investment and PPPs in Electricity Infrastructure

Independent power producers (IPPs) have been operating in Indonesia since 1994, when licenses were issued to IPPs to generate electricity to be sold to PLN. As of 2009, IPPs contribute approximately 15% (4,568 megawatts) of the total capacity. As of 2009, 20 IPPs were operating, 16 were under construction, 30 were securing financing, and 6 were finalizing power purchase agreements. Under these circumstances, all outstanding matters on the 30 projects in the financing stage must be resolved expeditiously so that generation capacity can improve substantially.

Due to Indonesia's vulnerability to macroeconomic shocks and the drawbacks of corruption and a weak judicial system (see Chapter 3), the country is not an attractive destination for investment in the electricity sector, particularly in today's challenging environment. The three key constraints to private investment and PPPs in electricity infrastructure are land acquisition, power purchase pricing, and lack of government support.

Land Acquisition. For private sector-driven projects, the responsibility for resolving land acquisition issues rests solely with the private sector. Private sector investors are often forced to pay premium prices or risk long delays in acquiring land, adversely impacting project timing, planning, costs, and start-up.

Power Purchase Pricing. PLN's price for purchasing electricity has been one of the most significant barriers to IPPs, especially for renewable energy resources. PLN was required to purchase electricity based on a formula that used the nationwide uniform tariff as a reference. As a result, small-scale and renewable energy IPPs were not viable, because they could not produce energy at the price PLN offered. New reference prices based on local cost of supply were introduced in November 2009 to overcome this problem.

Government Support and Risk Sharing. Due to the lack of government support, several IPP projects failed to achieve financial closure. Risk should be allocated to the party that is in the best position to address and mitigate it, and the government is best suited to manage risks related to country, political, and/or government actions and events, while the distributor is most suited to carry risks related to network operation (including demand and supply risk, and grid failure), and private investors and lenders should bear risks related to constructing, operating, and maintaining independent power plants. By offering an appropriate and conservative risk-sharing structure, the government and PLN would be in a better position to promote tariff competition among private investors in the sector and encourage investment within a stable and consistent framework. There are also significant delays in the IPP procurement process (Figure 7.8).

Figure 7.8: Envisaged IPP Procurement Process and Time Frame

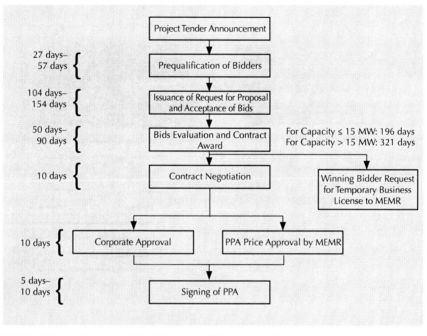

MEMR = Ministry of Energy and Mineral Resources, PPA = power purchase agreement.
Source: MEMR as cited in IDB (2010).

7.6. Telecommunications

The telecommunications sector is dominated by three large players (Excelcomindo; Indosat; and Telkom, which is predominantly government-owned), with strong barriers against entry by others. It is, therefore, not surprising that affordable access to telecommunications and internet infrastructure is limited. However, telecommunications infrastructure in Indonesia was not identified as a major constraint to economic growth. In a recent economic survey (OECD 2008), only 21% of firms surveyed reported availability of telecommunications as a business constraint, compared with 49% for transport and 43% for electricity infrastructure. However, compared with other Asian countries, Indonesia's telecommunications infrastructure lags, as is evident by the

- low level of teledensity (driven by underinvestment and unequal distribution of telecommunications infrastructure);[10]

---

[10] "Teledensity" refers to the number of landline telephones in use for every 100 individuals living in an area.

- low internet penetration;
- lack of competition in the fixed-line telecommunication business; and
- lack of consistent and independent regulations on telephony and internet services.

7.6.1. Key Constraints to Private Investment in Telecommunications Infrastructure

Lack of Bankable Projects. A substantial proportion of projects available in the telecommunications sector for PPPs are based in rural areas. The cost of rolling out projects in these areas is high, while the tariff for telecommunication fixed-lines is not set independently by the regulator, and is based on sociopolitical considerations. Thus, rural tariffs have to be in line with national tariffs, and not higher to defray the additional infrastructure costs. This discourages investors from developing new subscriber networks, including the implementation of projects with universal service obligations (USOs—i.e, projects that deliver communications access needed by all people regardless of ability to pay). In addition, the maintenance of completed USO networks is problematic, because the tariff barely covers operation and maintenance costs. This could be addressed either by subsidy (not a good alternative, due to the fiscal impact) or by increasing the local fixed-line tariffs. However, historically the government refused to raise telephone call tariffs in 2006 due to what it considered as unfavorable socioeconomic conditions.

Weak Human and Institutional Capacity. This is best illustrated by the USO and Palapa Ring Projects. In USO projects, the call for tenders failed to attract sufficient qualified bidders in 2007, probably due to the inability to prepare bankable projects that would attract quality bidders. As a result, the tender process had to be repeated a year later. In the Palapa Ring Project, due to concerns abut transparency in the selection of members of the project consortium, some members decided to leave the consortium. The funding commitment from the remaining three members (Telkom, Indosat, and Bakrie Telecom) was insufficient to cover the project costs, with the government having to allocate some resources to finance the project.

7.6.2. Private Investment in Telecom Infrastructure

Private investment in the telecommunication sector has been encouraged by selling more Telkom and Indosat shares on the international and domestic capital markets, reducing Telkom's monopoly, and auctioning licenses to private sector operators. This has increased private sector participation, particularly in cellular telecommunications.

Recent analysis by Credit Suisse as cited in IDB (2010) asserted that price competition and the combination of high capital expenditure (for coverage and capacity) with lower-than-expected revenues translates into a low return on invested capital in Indonesia's telecommunications industry—estimated at only 6% in 2010, down from the initial projection of 8.4%. This is below the cost of capital for the telecommunications industry, and is significantly lower than the current country risk-free rate (the yield of local currency government bonds in early October 2009 was approximately 10%). Although Telkom was corporatized in 1985, PPPs in the sector commenced 10 years later, in 1995.

Two issues emerge as the key constraints on private investment in telecommunications: the monopolist environment and the weak legal and regulatory situation. The dominance by the state-owned Telkom has discouraged competition and investment in the telecommunications sector. Telkom's anticompetitive behavior (e.g., restricting interconnection to Telkom's network) has made interoperator telecommunication expensive for consumers. Interconnection charges were negotiated bilaterally between operators and Telkom, and there is no standard reference (contract terms and pricing). This has produced anticompetitive practices that are discriminatory and lack transparency. Interconnection fees Telkom has charged Telkomsel (Telkom's cellular subsidiary) may be lower than to the fees charged other cellular operators (Rasyid 2005). Telkom's dominance of fixed-line access has also affected the business of competitors, such as Indosat. For example, Indosat preferred to enter into a revenue-sharing mechanism with its potential business partners rather than incur direct capital and operating expenses to expand its fixed-line network. This is not an attractive investment, and thus Indosat's fixed-line business portfolio remains small, below 9% of its total revenue.

The Telecommunications Regulatory Agency (Badan Regulasi Telekomunikasi Indonesia—BRTI) is chaired by the Director General of Post and Telecommunication of the Ministry of Communication and Informatics. Although BRTI is well established, comprising knowledgeable and experienced commissioners, it does not have the authority to issue its own directives and regulations. BRTI's regulatory jurisdiction is limited to network provision and basic telecommunication services, while value-added services such as voice-over-internet protocol, and other multimedia services are still regulated by the Ministry of Communication and Informatics. This has resulted in BRTI becoming somewhat ineffective, especially in terms of the legal and regulatory framework. Consequently, BRTI's institutional set-up, including its authority and jurisdiction, is currently being examined with a view to making it a strong and independent regulatory body that complies with international best practices. An example of the weak legal and regulatory environment is the case of Indosat's international direct dialling business (Box 7.3).

Box 7.3: Indosat's International Direct Dialling

Indosat's international direct dialling (IDD) business directly connects Indonesia to more than 260 countries and destinations worldwide. Indosat operates four international gateway exchanges, in Batam, Jakarta, Medan, and Surabaya. The Jakarta gateway serves the Jakarta metropolitan region and the West Java and Central Java provinces, accounting for approximately 64% of the company's international traffic.

During 2001, IDD traffic dropped by 7.5%, which was attributed to the increased use of the internet (via the voice-over-internet protocol—VoIP) for international calls. Use of the internet was estimated to have captured 5%–10% of the international telephone market by the end of 2001. Although VoIP licenses were officially issued by the government to five operators (Atlasat, Gaharu, Indosat, Satelindo, and Telkom), several unlicensed VoIP operators continue business. Despite the attempt to eliminate illegal VoIP operators, the numbers kept increasing. In 2002, Indosat's IDD traffic dropped a further 20%, and it claimed that illegal VoIP inflicted a loss of about Rp245 billion ($27 million) per year.

Indosat's IDD business deteriorated further when, in 2004, Telkom received an IDD license from the government. Telkom claimed that it held a 52% share of the IDD services market at the end of April 2005. Currently, Indosat's IDD and fixed-line businesses account for only 9.7% of total revenue.

Sources: Gatra Akibat VOIP Illegal Indosat Rugi, January 19, 2009; Mandiri Sekuritas Debt Research, November.

7.7. Consolidation of Survey Results and Reasons for Key Constraints

The results of the primary survey suggest that most constraints hindering the pace of infrastructure development in Indonesia, in order of severity, are (1) difficulty in land acquisition, (2) weak human and institutional capacity, (3) poor governance, and (4) shortage of financing. The survey also indicates that macroeconomic stability has been maintained and viewed positively by investors, and this has not adversely impacted infrastructure-related business. Further, the survey shows little improvement in the return on infrastructure investment during 2005–2010.

An in-depth analysis of three major infrastructure subsectors—transport, electricity, and communications indicates the constraints to investment in them. With regard to components of the transport subsector, difficulty in land acquisition appears to be the most binding constraint, followed by the weak institutional and human capacity within the government (manifested in the inability to prepare bankable projects and implement government regulations); poor governance; and shortage of long-term funding. Table 7.8 indicates the breakdown of the major impediments by subsector. The status of Indonesia's infrastructure also hampers its ability to profit from its participation in the Indonesia-Malaysia-Thailand Growth Triangle. For example, electricity is in short supply, which prevents investors from setting up manufacturing; roads are few and in poor shape, adding to the costs of doing business; and inefficient and underdeveloped ports hamper the shipment of goods to the region (Box 7.4).

Table 7.8: Major Constraints to Infrastructure Development in Indonesia (based on in-depth analysis of subsectors)

| Major Constraints | Transport | | | | Electricity | Telecommu-nications |
	Roads	Railways	Seaports	Airports		
Difficult Land Acquisition	✓	✓			✓	
Weak Human and Institutional Capacity [a]	✓	✓	✓	✓	✓	✓
Poor Governance	✓	✓	✓	✓	✓	✓
Long-term Funding not Available	✓	✓	✓	✓	✓	
Perceived Low Return on Investment			✓			
Social Electricity Tariff Setting Below Cost Recovery					✓	
Inefficient Allocation of Limited Resources					✓	

✓ = major constraint.
[a] Consistent with the survey definition, this factor is the underlying issue behind the negative perspective on several areas including government coordination, bankable projects, implementation capacity, interface with the government, and legal and regulatory framework.
Source: From IDB (2010).

Box 7.4: Indonesia-Malaysia-Thailand Growth Triangle: Major Constraints to Infrastructure Support and Connectivity of Subregions

Weak and inadequate infrastructure has adversely affected the Indonesian economy's connectivity with its neighbors, particularly Malaysia and Thailand. This is underscored by the slow implementation of the Indonesia-Malaysia-Thailand Growth Triangle (IMT–GT) Initiative, which aims to accelerate private sector-led economic growth and help facilitate the development of the subregion as a whole.[a]

Since its formation in 1993, IMT–GT activities and scope have grown. It could improve both intra- and interregional growth and equity. Strengthening cross-border transport and logistics linkages would expand market size and economic opportunities that could be exploited by the bordering provinces in each of the three countries. In turn, this would reduce disparities within each country. The IMT–GT has identified economic connectivity corridors that cover 10 provinces in Sumatra. To fully benefit from the IMT–GT and its preferential trade access, Indonesia needs to boost investments in manufacturing and services in the 10 provinces. However, investment will be difficult to attract unless the transport networks and electricity supplies in the provinces can be significantly improved.[b]

The IMT–GT Roadmap 2007–2011 was prepared with a strong infrastructure bias. In terms of population, land area, and employment opportunities, Indonesia stands to gain the most among the three countries. However, the country's infrastructure imbalances limit its ability to benefit from this important regional initiative. Needless to say, the constraints identified as part of this infrastructure diagnostic study (weak human and institutional capacity, coordination failures, and shortage of financing) also plague the IMT–GT.

A key thrust of the IMT–GT subregion is to "strengthen infrastructure linkages and connectivity" through the IMT–GT Roadmap 2007–2011. The high priority areas for infrastructure development identified in the IMT–GT Roadmap include (1) improving cross-border infrastructure and transport service connections, (2) facilitating road transport in the IMT–GT subregion through mutual recognition of vehicle documentation, (3) developing shipping services and facilities to support cross-border trade and investment activities, (4) improving and developing transport infrastructure in the North–South corridor in Sumatra to enhance economic linkages with Malaysia and Thailand of the IMT–GT subregion, (5) improving and developing IMT–GT air

continued on next page

services and facilities, and (6) developing a strategy and program for IMT–GT cooperation in energy.

Since 1993, progress on implementing the IMT–GT Initiative has been significantly below expectation, specifically with regard to strengthening roads, railways, airports, seaports, and electricity infrastructure at the inter- and intraregional levels. The underlying impediments to progress, consistent with the findings of this infrastructure growth diagnostic study are as follows:

- **Weak human and institutional capacity** has been apparent from the disconnect between strategies, programs, and projects. Too many flagship projects were identified without considering the implementation capacity of the three government levels, particularly at the local level. Furthermore, limited analytical work has been undertaken to guide project formulation. The weakness in human and institutional capacity is also evident in project information gaps and inadequate project monitoring systems. The success of development corridors such as the IMT–GT hinges on private sector participation. However, the paucity of bankable projects prepared by the government has resulted in minimal participation by the private sector and by domestic and international financial institutions.

- **Coordination failures** including weak coordination at all tiers of Indonesia's government, contributed to slow implementation of the IMT-GT Roadmap. In particular, there has been minimal ownership at the local government level, which is not actively engaged in project preparation and identification. In addition, the interface between public and private sectors is weak.

- **Lack of financing** has hampered the implementation of the IMT–GT Roadmap, which requires $15 billion to $20 billion over a 10-year period, which is not a substantial amount of money for the three fast-growing economies (e.g., compared with Indonesia's $200 billion 2010–2014 medium-term infrastructure plan). Under the IMT–GT Initiative, no proper financial plan was prepared, and none of the three governments have provided sufficient funding for the projects. This indicates a lack of political will from all three governments.

The objectives of the IMT–GT Roadmap, in particular reducing regional disparities, cannot be achieved in the remaining 2 years. A detailed diagnostic study encompassing all three countries to identify the binding constraints to the successful roll-out of the IMT–GT is

continued on next page

merited. Unless such an exercise is carried out, and a strategy to relax the most binding constraints is developed and implemented, progress on the IMT–GT will not be forthcoming, to the detriment of both growth and equity.

[a] The IMT–GT is a subregional cooperation initiative started in 1993 by the governments of Indonesia, Malaysia, and Thailand, with objectives of accelerating and sustaining economic growth, reducing poverty, improving the quality of life, and establishing peace and stability in the subregion by enhancing trade and investment.

[b] Despite the higher cost of generating their own power (30%–50% more expensive than power from the state-owned electricity company), many industrialists in Sumatra have resorted to self-generation due to the erratic supply of electricity. This adversely impacts their competitiveness and willingness to invest further in the area.

Source: Indonesia-Malaysia-Thailand Growth Triangle Website.

7.7.1. Land Acquisition Difficulties

Difficulty in land acquisition is arguably the most binding constraint on public and private investment in infrastructure, and on PPPs in transport, electricity, and telecommunications. Given the vastness of Indonesia, the question is why the cost of land is so prohibitive? The primary reasons center around landowners' desire to receive the highest price possible for their property, corruption, and government lack of will to enforce pertinent legislation.

Discussions with private investors revealed that a number of projects were delayed due to problems with land acquisition, especially for toll roads. Speculative activity and breach of confidentiality regarding development plans adversely impact the financial viability of projects. Examples provided included privately owned land changing hands before being officially earmarked for specific infrastructure projects, leading to land prices increasing well over the price estimated in the project plan. Landowners often inflate prices of land needed for infrastructure projects—65% of the 196 land acquisition problems that have occurred since 1970 were related to conflict over compensation.

Although Indonesia has legislation to address speculative activity, the law is not adequately enforced, and the government appears to lack the will to do so. This is to avoid the appearance of authoritarianism and being anti-poor. Moreover, discussions with the private sector indicated that some of the land speculators were related to members of the bureaucracy, partly explaining why there was lack of appetite to address the issue. Consequently, the onus of settling land acquisition issues often falls on the private sector participants in a project.

Presidential Regulation 65 of 2006 and other regulations limit the legal options available to property owners to challenge government efforts to acquire land for infrastructure projects. Despite the regulations (Box 7.5), the government is extremely reluctant to acquire land through domain-type legal proceedings. To tackle this challenge, the government recently established a revolving land acquisition fund managed by the Ministry of Public Works. The fund could play an important role in breaking the current deadlock over land acquisition for toll roads and other infrastructure projects. This is an important consideration for land-intensive toll road development. Potential investors have long sought such a revolving fund to finance land acquisition to limit or remove this risk for investors. In general this acquisition risk, which currently rests with the investor, should be addressed by the government prior to the investment decision, or be borne by the government.

Box 7.5: Weak Formulation and Implementation of Land Acquisition Regulations

Presidential Decree No. 55 of 1993, Land Acquisition for the Development of the Public Interest, specifies grievance procedures for landowners; defines public interest for development purposes; separates private projects, which should use regular land purchase arrangements; places more emphasis on community consultation and reaching agreement with people affected on the form and the amount of compensation; and presents expanded options for compensation including cash, substitute land, formal land title, and resettlement. This decree laid down the rules on how the government could exercise the state's inherent power of eminent domain.

Presidential Decree No. 36 of 2005, Provision of Land for Realizing the Development for Public Interests, amended the earlier Presidential Decree No. 55 of 1993 and provided forms of compensation for private assets needed to pursue government development projects. This decree became controversial, because the power of eminent domain was being used to allow private entities to profit, and it received a lot of criticism from the public.

Presidential Decree No. 65 of 2006, The Procurement of Land for Realising Development for Public Interest, was issued in June 2006 to amend the previous regulation on land acquisition (36 of 2005), correcting it by restricting the use of eminent domain for government development projects only. The legislation aims at shortening the land acquisition process and capping land costs. It provides the legal basis for the government to acquire land for infrastructure projects from landowners by providing compensation in the form of money, substitute

continued on next page

land, and/or resettlement or other forms of compensation agreed to by the parties. By and large, however, both Presidential Decrees 65 of 2006 and 36 of 2005 are similar, merely introducing refinements to the provisions of Presidential Decree No. 55 of 1993. The government has been extremely reluctant to acquire land through these eminent domain-type legal proceedings.

BPN Regulation No. 3 of 2007, Land Acquisition Implementation Guideline of Presidential Decrees 36 of 2005 and 65 of 2006. The Regulation of the State Minister of Agrarian Affairs and National Land Agency No. 1 of 1994, Operational Directives of the Decree 55 of 1993 was the enabling regulation for implementing Presidential Decree 55 of 1993. This regulation was replaced by National Land Agency (Badan Pertanahan Nasional—BPN) Regulation No. 3 of 2007. BPN, an independent agency under the President, is the central government unit empowered to acquire land for public purposes.

Presidential Regulation 13 of 2010, Financing under Public-Private Partnership Schemes, deals with land-related issues. This regulation affirms that no public–private partnership projects may be offered without ensuring that the required land is available.

Unsupportive Regulations: other laws related to land acquisition, particularly the Basic Agricultural Law (1960) and the Forestry Law (41 of 1999) do not support each other. Under the Forestry law, the Ministry of Forestry has the power to acquire land for public purposes, but only forestry area, and local governments are allowed to acquire only up to 2 hectares of land for public purposes. Under the Land Expropriation Act No. 20 of 1961, issued under the Basic Agrarian Act of 1960, if there is no agreement with the landowners, the state can take land by force, provided the land is required for the public interest. However, expropriation must be used only as a last resort. These laws are not well-defined, which often causes disputes with BPN.

Source: IDB (2010)

The problem of land acquisition is compounded by inefficient spatial planning. At the regional and provincial government levels, rules and regulations for determining areas for housing, infrastructure, and industry have not been finalized. This process requires coordination at the central level among the relevant institutions, because spatial planning cannot be made by a single ministry, such as the Ministry of Public Works. In addition, greater coordination is needed between central and local governments on the delegation of authority in order to avoid complications at the implementation stage. The lack of clear rules and regulations related to spatial planning has resulted in slow progress on infrastructure development in most provinces.

7.7.2. Weak Human and Institutional Capacity

Devolution of power through decentralization and a lack of coordination have resulted in inefficient decision making, due mainly to lack of clarity about roles, authority, and responsibility. The plethora of institutions and authorities dealing specifically with infrastructure development has raised the issue of effective and efficient coordination among institutions. Policy making, decision taking, implementation, monitoring, and evaluation require considerable coordination among government agencies at the central and regional and provincial levels. Uncertainty over which level of the government is responsible for providing services persists, due to unclear assignments of functions. In some cases, local and regional government's regulations are not consistent with national regulations. As a result of these issues, it is a frustrating and time-consuming exercise for the private sector to interaction with the government (Box 7.6).

Box 7.6: Coordination Failures within the Government Adversely Impact Infrastructure Investment

When the private sector has invested in infrastructure, the lack of communication and coordination within government have compromised project viability. This has damaged business confidence in the government's ability, and made investors wary of undertaking infrastructure projects. The lack of a holistic planning environment with long-term strategic interregional development plans results in incomplete networks and lower than projected demand. The point is best illustrated by the two toll road projects, Surabaya–Gempol Toll Road (completed in 1986) and Waru–Juanda Toll Road (completed in 2008).

Waru–Juanda Toll Road. The Waru–Juanda toll road is part of the Surabaya Eastern Ring Road Toll Project (which commenced in 1997). Based on a potential traffic volume of 53,000 vehicles per day, PT Citra Margatama Surabaya (CMS), had invested about Rp1.5 trillion by 2008 (twice the original value estimated in 2002). However, when the toll opened, actual traffic was only 23.6% of the estimated volumes, resulting in CMS experiencing substantial losses. The lower volume of traffic was attributed to poor networking of the Waru-Juanda toll road. The initial traffic projection of 53,000 vehicles is achievable if the road network around the Waru-Juanda toll road is improved. The feasibility study had

continued on next page

---

indicated the Waru-Juanda toll road would be integrated with both the Surabaya East Ring Road and the Surabaya-Gempol toll road, and with the Surabaya-Mojokerto road in the west. In addition, the alternative road to Juanda Airport was upgraded and opened shortly before the toll road was completed, and captured a significant portion of the traffic that would otherwise have used the toll road, clearly reflecting coordination failures on the part of the government.

Surabaya-Gempol Toll Road. The Surabaya-Gempol road connects Surabaya in the north and Gempol in the south of East Java, has been operating since 1986, and was the main access road for Surabaya–Malang and Surabaya–Pasuruan (Pasuruan is one of the main industrial regions in East Java). The traffic volumes were much below the projected level due to improvements on alternate routes by the provincial government, which diverted traffic away from the Surabaya-Gempol toll road, indicating weak coordination among the tiers of governments.

Challenges. Planning and coordination of infrastructure implementation at all levels of government have posed even greater challenges since decentralization in 2001. In addition, coordination failures within government show the government's weak human and institutional effectiveness, which is behind that of regional comparators. Ultimately, coordination failures and ad-hoc approaches to infrastructure development have increased scepticism about public–private partnership projects offered by the government, shaking investor confidence and deterring private investment.

Source: IDB (2010).

The problem is compounded if there is delay in transferring funds to regions.[11] The responsibility for infrastructure development lies largely with the regional authorities, whose capacity to implement is weaker than that of the national government. Some local governments were unable to undertake the required expenditure due to limited skills and operational capabilities. The most severe capacity shortage is in project design and development, leading to delayed implementation. Thus, the problem is exacerbated both by delays in fund transfers and by lack of technical ability to undertake projects. As indicated in Table 7.9, capacity constraint at the local government level has taken a toll on infrastructure development (OECD 2008).

---

[11]   Funds are meant to be transferred at the beginning of the fiscal year but are usually transferred after first quarter due to the slow budgeting process.

**Table 7.9: Infrastructure Spending for Public Works
(2005-2009, % of total allocation)**

Infrastructure	2005	2006	2007	2008	To 8 Sept. 2009
Water Resources	88.9	93.4	77.9	92.7	37.4
Roads and Bridges	99.3	93.8	88.3	96.2	43.1
Water and Sanitation	98.3	93.6	92.1	95.3	36.0
Total	98.4	93.6	85.4	95.0	39.9

Source: Data provided to the authors by the Ministry of Public Works, Jakarta, Indonesia
(4 October 2009).

Further, infrastructure projects funded by the multilateral development banks have been delayed, in some cases up to 5 years, due to weak human and institutional capacity (Box 7.7).

Box 7.7: Delays in Project Implementation in Indonesia

Projects financed by multilateral development banks have experience significant delays due to factors related mainly to weak human and institutional capacity in Indonesia. These delays increase costs, lead to poor project performance, and slow the delivery of benefits.

Completion reports of a number of infrastructure projects financed by the Islamic Development Bank reveal delays of 3–5 years in project implementation. The delays are attributed to difficulties in financing import of parts for the project components, price escalations due to devaluation of the rupiah, and national regulation matters. Further, due to the decentralization process in Indonesia, the procedures for loans to regional governments from multilateral development finance institutions have yet to be established.

The World Bank (2008) estimated that, of 35 ongoing projects in 2008, more than 50% were delayed by 1–5 years. The main reasons cited were procurement delays at the central level, late releases of budget to regional governments and subsequent delayed disbursements, and delays in the procurement of equipment.

Project completion reports of the Asian Development Bank during 2008–2009 for Indonesia show that 11 of 13 projects were delayed 1–6 years. The major reasons were slow procurement, weak capacity at the local government levels, inadequacy of trained field personnel,

continued on next page

early termination of the services of the international consultants, land acquisition and resettlement, delayed selecting and fielding of the consultants, lack of counterpart funds, and poor contractor performance.

Source: World Bank (2008).

The lack of institutional and human capacity is further evident in the quality of bankable projects being prepared by the government. A case in point is the *Public-Private Partnerships Infrastructure in Indonesia* (commonly known as the PPP Blue Book), wherein project costs for roads vary significantly, from $4.7 million to $19.8 million per kilometer, with no explanation given for the variation, although terrain might play a huge role in costs (Bappenas 2010). Moreover, all road projects between 7.5 and 135 km long are expected to take 2 years for land acquisition and 2 years to build, although negotiations for land acquisition may take 3–7 years or more. The low level of interest the private sector has shown in government tenders reflects the poor quality and lack of bankability of the projects prepared.

Lack of government capacity to implement legal and regulatory changes is impeding infrastructure investment. Although legislation was promulgated to improve the investment climate, several of the laws are not being enforced, especially those pertaining to land acquisition.

Lack of hierarchical authority makes coordination difficult. The transfer of functions and financial resources to the lowest levels of local government has led to provincial governments lacking authority over rural districts and urban municipalities, resulting in low levels of coordination among them. Heads of lower level governments are not accountable to provincial governments, giving rise to weak regional coordination, and jeopardizing the benefits of decentralization.

Short-term focus on the local level stifles long-term infrastructure projects. Decentralization has put the local governments at the forefront of service delivery, including in public investment programs. However, capacity constraints have resulted in a backlog of investment projects. At the same time, the Ministry of Home Affairs' tardiness in approving local government budgets delays their implementation. The short-term, calendar year budgeting focus makes it difficult for local governments to carry out and finance large-scale multiyear investment projects.

7.7.3. Poor Governance

Rent-seeking activities adversely impact infrastructure investment and project costs. Governance indicators in Indonesia have improved but are still weak. The country ranks 126th of 180 countries in Transparency International's Corruption Perception Index (2009). In the infrastructure sector, poor governance is related to rent-seeking activities by officials dealing with projects. Poor governance was the second highest constraint on investment noted in the IDB survey. This finding is consistent with that of previous studies, especially in relation to the impact of the decentralization initiated in 2001. Decentralization has increased the number of officials with discretionary power over economic activities, has made regulations more complex, and has increased opportunities for rent-seeking (OECD 2008: 63). The World Bank estimated that corruption can add up to 20% to the cost of doing business in Indonesia.[12] This results in a high-cost economy, leading to low incentives to invest in infrastructure.

Increased autonomy has resulted in higher costs and lower effectiveness. The decentralization program granted local governments considerable autonomy to issue business regulations, including licenses, and to levy fees and user charges for the provision of local services. Based on this prerogative, most jurisdictions have introduced several levies, often without the approval or even knowledge of the central government, as a means of raising revenue. Central government efforts to tackle this problem have so far yielded mixed results. The human and institutional capacity at the local level requires strengthening. To achieve the anticipated efficiency gains, the current decentralization process requires stronger and more effective coordination among tiers of government and requires accountability mechanisms (Aswicahyono and Friawan 2007: 149).[13] Another important aspect of decentralization that is thwarting infrastructure development is the inconsistency in rules and regulations between regional and central governments.

Government effectiveness lags behind that of key regional comparators. Indonesia scored 47.3 on the World Bank's Governance Indicator for government effectiveness, compared with Singapore at 100, Malaysia at 83.8, Thailand at 58.7, and the Philippines at 54.9. Only Viet Nam, at 45.4, scored below Indonesia (World Bank WGI). Decentralization compounded the difficulties in delivering government services, largely due to the lack of skills and capacity and the unequal distribution of resources across regions. Lack of coordination between the tiers of the government and the different lines of functions further complicates the issue.

---

[12] Business Monitor International Ltd., Indonesia Infrastructure Report Q1 2010 cited in IDB (2010).

[13] Aswicahyono and Friawan (2007: 149) list some problems with the decentralization process that cause inefficiency, such as unclear assignment of government functions; lack of minimum standards of service delivery; and shortcomings of the new intergovernmental fiscal system.

In terms of anticorruption measures, Indonesia has fared poorly compared with some other major economies in the region. The World Bank's Governance Indicators 2008 rated Indonesia (31%) lower in control of corruption than Malaysia (63%) and Thailand (43%) in 2008, although it fared better than the Philippines (26%) and Viet Nam (25%). Other international surveys paint similar pictures. Evidence also suggests that, as a result of decentralization, corruption has become fragmented and unpredictable, as it involves more players (Perdana and Friawan 2007).

President Yudhoyono's administration has acknowledged corruption as a constraint to growth and the fight against corruption as a key government priority, and has introduced initiatives to curb corruption. The Corruption Eradication Commission, formed in 2002, appears effective in investigating and prosecuting bribery and graft-related cases. Additional measures include reforms relating to public procurement and transparency, and education of the civil service and society. These initiatives have yielded positive results, with perceptions of the prevalence and control of corruption in Indonesia improving between 2004 and 2008.

However, anecdotal evidence suggests that deficiencies in public procurement and tighter oversight in the context of the authorities' ongoing anti-corruption initiatives have made local government officials wary of executing budgetary commitments for fear of prosecution. This may be an unavoidable short-term cost of anticorruption efforts toward ensuring accountability at all levels of the government. The amount of unspent budgetary appropriations, especially those financed through revenue sharing with the natural resource-rich jurisdictions, has increased over time, taking a toll on the government's ability to implement investment projects.

7.7.4. Shortage of Financing

Short-term and domestic financing is not a major constraint, but long-term financing is. In reviewing the 2008 budget, the government recorded a cash surplus of $7.2 billion (1.4% of GDP). In addition, the budget deficit amounted to only 0.1% of GDP, compared with the target of 2.1% (the budget deficit in Malaysia was 4.7%; in Thailand, 1.8%; and in the Philippines, 1% in 2008), highlighting Indonesia's fiscal strength. Further, if the governments at the national and provincial levels are not exhausting their infrastructure budget allocations due to capacity constraints, domestic financing cannot be viewed as a binding constraint to infrastructure development in the public sector.

However, the private sector has difficulty securing long-term financing for infrastructure projects. Banks will provide financing of only 7 (for commercial banks) to 12 (for government banks) years duration,[14] whereas infrastructure projects require financing in excess of 12 years, which is currently unavailable locally.[15] Currently, 90% of local banks' sources of finance are savings accounts and demand and time deposits, and only 1% from long-term bonds. The funding structure is, therefore, inadequate to fund long-term investments in infrastructure, where the time-horizon is in excess of 12 years. Further, uncertainty regarding the time and cost involved in land acquisition and the perceived lack of local banks' confidence in funding long-term investments have made international financiers wary of providing funding to the private sector for long-term projects.

References

Asian Development Bank (ADB). 2004. Transport Sector Strategy Study for Indonesia. Manila.

———. 2006. Indonesia Country Strategy and Program 2006–2009. Manila.

———. 2011. *Key Indicators for Asia and the Pacific 2011*. Manila.

ADB, International Labour Organization (ILO), and Islamic Development Bank (IDB). 2009. *Indonesia: Critical Development Constraints.* Manila.

Aswicahyono, H. and D. Friawan. 2007. Infrastructure Development in Indonesia. Chapter 5 in *International Infrastructure Development in East Asia—Towards Effective and Balanced Regional Integration.* Economic Research Institute for ASEAN and East Asia.

Badan Perancanaan dan Pembangunan Nasional (Bappenas—National Planning Development Board). 2010. Public-Private Partnerships, Infrastructure Projects in Indonesia, 2010-2014. Jakarta

Badan Pusat Statistik (BPS—Statistics Indonesia). 2007. Statistik Perhubungan 2006. Jakarta.

———. 2008. Village Potential Statistics (Podes). http://www.rand.org/labor/bps/podes.html

Bhattacharyay, B. 2009. Infrastructure Development for ASEAN Economic Integration. *ADBI Working Paper 138.* Tokyo: Asian Development Bank Institute. http://www.adbi.org/working-paper/2009/05/27/3011.infrastructure.dev.asean.economic

Containerisation International. 2008. Containerisation International Yearbook 2008. Informa UK Ltd.

---

[14]   Discussions held with senior commercial bank officials in September 2009.

[15]   Domestic private sector investors confirmed and emphasized this constraint in detailed discussion held during September 2009.

Hausmann, R., D. Rodrik, and A. Velasco. 2005. *Growth Diagnostics.* Cambridge, MA: John F. Kennedy School of Government, Harvard University.

Indonesia-Malaysia-Thailand Growth Triangle Website. http://imtgt.org

International Institute of Management Development (IMD). 2009. World Competitiveness Yearbook (2009). Geneva. www.world competitiveness.com

Islamic Development Bank (IDB). 2010. Indonesia: Critical Constraints to Infrastructure Development. Jeddah.

Japan International Cooperation Agency (JICA). 2005. Study on the Development of Domestic Sea Transportation and Maritime Industry in Indonesia (STRAMINDO). Tokyo.

Lembaga Penyelidikan Ekonomi dan Masyarakat–Fakultas Ekonomi Universitas Indonesia (LPEM–FEUI—Institute for Economic and Social Research, Department of Economics, University of Indonesia). 2007. Investment Climate Monitoring. Round IV. Jakarta.

Mawardi, D.R. 2004. Hubungan Antara Infrastruktur Ekonomi dan Pertumbuhan PDRB di Jawa Timur dengan Menggunakan Pendekatan Model Persamaan Produksi Cobb–Douglas. Thesis/ Dissertattion. Petra Christian University, Surabaya, Indonesia.

Mustajab, M. 2009. Infrastructure Investment in Indonesia: Process and Impact. PhD dissertation. Rijksuniversiteit. Netherlands.

Nathan Associates, 2001. Indonesian Shipping and Port Sector Review. Jakarta: USAID.

Organisation for Economic Co-operation and Development (OECD). 2008. Indonesia: Economic Assessment. *OECD Economic Surveys.* Paris.

Patunru, A. Nurridzki, N and Rivayani, 2007. Port Competitiveness: A Case Study of Semarang and Surabaya, Indonesia. Institute for Economic and Social Research (LPEM), University of Indonesia, and Asian Development Bank Institute (ADBI).

Perdana, A. and D. Friawan. 2007. Economic Crisis, Institutional Change and the Effectiveness of Government: The Case of Indonesia. Center for Strategic and International Studies (CSIS). Indonesia.

Rasyid, A. 2005. Indonesia: Liberalization at the Crossroad, Impact on Sector Performance, Teledensity, and Productivity. Communication and Strategies No. 58, 2nd Quarter 2005. Bandung.

Ray, D. 2008. Indonesian Port Sector Reform and the 2008 Shipping Law. Jakarta: USAID.

Tempo Interaktif. 2009. Pemerintah Batal Ambil Alih Proyek Kereta Bandara Sukarno-Hatta, (Government Cancelled Plan to Take-Over Sukarno-Hatta Rail-link Project). 29 June.

Transparency International (TI). 2009. 2009 Global Corruption Barometer. http://www.transparency.org/publications/publications/gcb2009

World Bank. 2006. Strategic Road Infrastructure Project, Project Appraisal Document. Jakarta

———. 2008. Doing Business. Washington, DC.

World Bank. Governance Matters VIII: Worldwide Governance Indicators (WGI). http://info.worldbank.org/governance/wgi/pdf_country. asp

World Bank. World Development Indicators (WDI) Online. http://ddpext. worldbank.org/ ext/DDPQQ/member.do?method=getMembers& userid=1&queryId=6

World Economic Forum (WEF). 2009. Global Competitiveness Report 2009–2010. Geneva. http://www.weforum.org

8. Human Capital and Economic Development[1]

Kazutoshi Chatani

This chapter examines whether human capital, as evidenced by the availability of skilled workers, constrains growth in Indonesia. The chapter gives an overview of the skills level of the workforce using educational attainment as a proxy. Although the chapter notes an overall improvement in the skills level of young Indonesian workers (age 15–24) in recent years, Indonesia lags behind regional comparators. Though investment climate surveys do not detect human capital as a hindrance to business, labor market indicators suggest that a skills shortage has been affecting Indonesia's competitiveness in the region. The judgement as to whether the available human capital constitutes a constraint to growth depends on development strategies and blueprints for the growth of Indonesia's industry. With the launch of the master plan for six economic corridors, the country is aiming at a medium- and long-term growth scenario of moving up the production ladder from light industry and natural resources exploitation to a more sophisticated manufacturing production and knowledge-based economy. Under this scenario, human capital is likely to constitute a constraint to growth; therefore, improving the access to and quality of secondary and tertiary education could help achieve the growth scenario.

8.1. Education and Skills Level of the Workforce

Overall, the educational attainment of Indonesian workers has been improving remarkably in recent years (World Bank 2010). The share of

---

[1]   The editors and publishers gratefully acknowledge the International Labour Organization for contributing this chapter.

workers with tertiary education and above has increased, with the trend most pronounced among women (Table 8.1).

Table 8.1: Share of Labor Force by Age Group and Educational Attainment (age 15+)

	Junior Secondary School or Below		General Senior Secondary School		Vocational High School		Diploma Academy (college)		University	
	2004	2010	2004	2010	2004	2010	2004	2010	2004	2010
Men										
20–24	61.7%	54.0%	22.8%	25.3%	13.1%	16.5%	1.5%	1.9%	0.9%	2.3%
25–29	63.2%	55.9%	20.2%	20.6%	10.2%	13.8%	2.5%	3.4%	3.9%	6.3%
All Ages	72.4%	66.8%	14.8%	16.7%	7.5%	9.6%	2.2%	2.2%	3.2%	4.7%
Women										
20–24	56.9%	45.2%	24.4%	29.4%	12.4%	14.1%	3.9%	6.2%	2.4%	5.1%
25–29	65.1%	51.8%	16.5%	18.9%	8.0%	9.8%	4.5%	8.6%	5.8%	10.9%
All Ages	80.0%	69.4%	10.8%	13.6%	5.9%	7.1%	2.8%	4.2%	0.6%	5.8%

Sources: BPS, Labor Force Situation in Indonesia (various years); author's calculations.

The younger workers have been driving the shift toward higher educational attainment of the workforce.[2] For example, between 2004 and 2010, the share of workers aged 25–29 who had university education increased by 62% for men and 87% for women. Indeed, in 2010, 44.1% of male workers and 48.2% of female workers in that age bracket had at least either general high school education or vocational high school education, versus only about 30% of workers of all ages. The transition rates between education levels are moving upward (World Bank 2010). This trend is expected to continue, because the government is discussing implementing compulsory 12-year education by 2014 (Franken 2010).

The increasing educational attainment of younger people is undoubtedly a favorable outcome of poverty reduction and policy interventions since the mid-1980s. Indonesia has achieved a significant reduction in abject poverty, and increased household incomes have improved the likelihood that children will enroll in school. On the policy side, mandatory education was extended through junior secondary school in 1994, and has contributed to the improved transition rate from primary to junior secondary education (World Bank 2010). In addition, that workers with higher education receive higher salaries has provided students with an incentive to pursue university

---

[2]   A similar trend is observed across emerging Asia (Lee and Francisco 2010).

education. Also, the bleak prospects of finding employment after completing secondary education might have helped drive decisions to pursue higher education (see Chapter 9 on employment).

8.2. Skills Levels of the Workforce Lag behind Regional Comparators

Despite the laudable improvement in the educational attainment of the Indonesian workforce in recent years, the hard fact is that the country still lags behind regional comparators in this sphere (Table 8.2). The proportion of the Indonesian workforce with tertiary education is low, at 6.5%, compared with other selected countries in the region. Malaysia, the Philippines, and Singapore boast relatively well-educated workforces, with 20.3%, 27.7%, and 23.7%, respectively, having achieved a college diploma or higher. A similar trend in the same countries can be seen in the workforce shares that completed senior secondary education, whereas the share of Indonesia's workforce having less than high school education is much higher than that of the other neighboring countries.

Table 8.2: Share of Workforce by Education (2007, % of total)

Country	Below Senior Secondary Education	Senior Secondary Education	Tertiary Education
Indonesia	72.9	20.6	6.5
Malaysia	23.4	56.3	20.3
Philippines	33.6	38.7	27.7
Singapore	27.7	48.6	23.7

Source: World Bank, World Databank.

The relatively low educational attainment of the Indonesian workforce versus that in other regional comparators is an outcome of constraints on the access to and quality of education in Indonesia (see Chapter 9). While Indonesia has nearly achieved universal primary education (as have its comparators in the region), student enrollment drops significantly from primary to junior secondary school (World Bank 2010). To its credit, Indonesia has shown steady and rapid progress in improving its junior secondary school enrollment rate in recent years, after the government implemented compulsory 9-year education in 1994 (Table 8.3)—the net enrollment rate for senior secondary school rose 11.9 percentage points from 1994 to 2009. Nevertheless, in 2009, one-third of Indonesian children did not enroll in junior secondary school despite the legal obligation to do so. Although the net enrollment rate in senior secondary education has been rising steadily, less than half of the children of senior secondary school age attended such schools in 2009. The net enrollment rate for secondary education in Indonesia was estimated at 58%, versus about 75% in Malaysia. The Philippines, Thailand, and Viet Nam were also ahead of Indonesia in net secondary enrollment rate (UNDP 2007).

Table 8.3: Time Trends in Net Enrollment Rate in Indonesia (1994–2009)

Year	1994	1997	2000	2003	2006	2009
Primary school	92.1	92.3	92.3	92.6	93.5	94.4
Junior secondary school	50.0	57.8	60.3	63.5	66.5	67.4
Senior secondary school	33.2	36.6	39.3	40.6	43.8	45.1
University/diploma/ academy	7.9	7.7	8.0	8.6	8.9	10.3

Note: "Diploma: and "academy" are nondegree programs after senior secondary school.
Source: BPS, Labour Force Situation in Indonesia (various years).

Recent studies shed light on the causes of the drop in enrollment rates during the transition between primary and secondary education. The SMERU Institute used longitudinal household survey data to statistically test the causes of the attrition (Suryadama, Suryahadi, and Sumarto 2006). Using a regression analysis, they found that household wealth had a statistically significant effect on secondary school enrollment. Indeed, 57.2% of school-age children who had never attended school or who had dropped out of school cited financial reasons (see Chapter 4, Tables 4.4 and 4.5).

School density in rural areas significantly affects the access to secondary education. In fact, a breakdown of education cost reveals that fees other than for tuition account for the lion's share of secondary education's cost. For example, transport consumes 21.1% of the cost of junior secondary and 24.4% of that of senior secondary education. Primary schools are located even in remote villages, but secondary schools may not be. The Badan Pusat Statistik (BPS) Village Potential Census indicated that, in 2008, 57.5% of villages that had a primary school did not have a junior secondary school, and only 18.2% of villages had both primary and general senior secondary schools (cited in BPS 2009). The majority of students from rural villages have to commute to secondary schools in a nearby town or live in a boarding house to pursue secondary education. Obviously, this is costly for low-income households. And residents on Indonesia's small islands are at a disadvantage in their access to secondary education.

The SMERU Institute study also found that increased availability of jobs, indicated by a reduced unemployment rate, increased the dropout rate in a statistically significant way.

For Indonesia to upgrade the educational attainment of its workforce is desirable for several reasons. First, education can serve as an important input in improving labor productivity and subsequently increasing output. Second, upgrading education can catalyze change by giving the labor market the ability to adopt and develop new technology. Indonesia enjoyed several decades of sustained high economic growth via the expansion of the manufacturing industry, notably of labor-intensive manufacturing, and a significant increase in employment opportunities for workers with modest educational background. However, this growth model has been largely characterized by a substantial increase in capital and labor inputs, rather than gains in total factor productivity (Firdausy 2005: 7). Indonesia's low factor productivity can be partly attributed to the relatively low skill levels of its workforce.

There are several causal links between workers' low educational attainment and industrial development. First, workers (and a workforce) that have low levels of educational attainment generally must rely primarily on the agricultural and trade sectors as their main sources of employment, and approximately 40% of Indonesia's workers were employed in agriculture in 2009. Additionally, less educated workers are much more likely to seek employment outside the formal economy. Over 60% of the labor force worked in the informal economy during 2000–2009. On average, workers in the informal sector earn much less than employees in the formal sector. Moreover, informal workers often do not receive nonwage benefits such as medical care and other social security arrangements. Second is the issue of structural weakness that is inherent in having a workforce with low education levels. In particular, jobs in the manufacturing and service sectors have become increasingly difficult to fill due to a lack of qualified workers (Firdausy 2005).

The Indonesian government is committed to improving education and has been allocating an increasing budget share to this end. While public expenditure on education was estimated at 14.2% of total government expenditure in 2004, this had increased to 17.9% in 2008 (UNESCO Data Centre). Although Indonesia still lags behind Thailand and Viet Nam in education's share of government expenditure, it surpassed Malaysia and the Philippines in 2008. As a result, current school-age Indonesian children are expected to receive 12.7 years of education on average, provided that the current patterns of age-specific enrollment rates remain constant. The expected years of schooling of Indonesian children is now comparable with those in other countries of the region, exceeding Malaysia, where per capita income is more than three times that in Indonesia. However, as Indonesia implemented 6-year mandatory primary education relatively late[3] in the region, the country has many undereducated adults—the mean length of schooling of adults was 5.7 years in 2010, which was among the lowest in the region (Table 8.4).

Table 8.4: Education in Selected Southeast Asian Countries

	Public Expenditure on Education (% of GDP)	Public Expenditure on Education (as % of total public spending)	Mean Years of Schooling (of adults)	Expected Years of Schooling (of children)	GDP per Capita, PPP (constant 2005 international $)
Year	2008	2008	2010	2010	2008
Cambodia	1.6 (2007)	12.4 (2007)	5.8	9.8	1,802
Indonesia	2.8	17.9	5.7	12.7	3,689
Lao PDR	2.3	12.2	4.6	9.2	1,960
Malaysia	4.1	17.2	9.5	12.5	13,163
Philippines	2.8	16.9	8.7	11.5	3,240
Thailand	3.8	20.5	6.6	13.5	7,469
Viet Nam	5.3	19.8	5.5	10.4	2,578

GDP = gross domestic product, Lao PDR = Lao People's Democratic Republic, PPP = purchasing power parity.
Source: Public expenditure on education: UNESCO, Data Centre (accessed 24 March 2011); other data: UNDP Human Development Indicators (accessed 24 March 2011).

Government spending on education as a percentage of gross domestic product (GDP) varies significantly in the seven Association of Southeast Asian Nations (ASEAN) countries in the comparison, ranging from 1.6% in Cambodia to 5.3% in Viet Nam. GDP per capita among the countries also shows significant divergence: per capita income in Malaysia is about 7.3 times that of Cambodia. As a result, public education expenditure per capita varies significantly, ranging from $29 in Cambodia to $540 in Malaysia. Malaysia, Thailand, and Viet Nam spent 5.2, 2.7, and 1.3 times, respectively, as much as Indonesia did on education per person. Because the demographic composition of populations differs from country to country, per capita public expenditure on education is not comparable in the strict sense. In addition, public expenditure on education does not imply the quality of or outcome from education. Some caution may be merited in interpreting the data,

---

[3]   Presidential Instruction Decree No. 10 of 1973 mandated the government to implement compulsory education for school age children (age 7–12). The government implemented this decree in 1984.

because they do not include private education. But, as private education does not match the scale of public education, Table 8.4 reveals by and large a comparative picture of the investment in education by Indonesia and its regional comparators.

8.3. Indicators of the Quality of Education

In addition to relatively low enrollment rates in secondary and tertiary education, the quality of education in Indonesia leaves ample room for improvement, as implied by students' poor performance on international exams measuring cognitive skills. According to an international study, the Programme for International Student Assessment (PISA),[4] which surveyed key competencies and cognitive skills of 15-year-old students, Indonesian students did not fare well on average compared with students in other middle-income countries, let alone students in high-income countries. Table 3.2 (Chapter 3) shows a time series of PISA mean scores in mathematics, science, and reading of students from Indonesia, Thailand, 27 middle-income economies, and the Organisation for Economic Co-operation and Development average. Indonesian students' scores in each subject were among the lowest of the middle-income countries (OECD 2007). While Indonesian students' reading skills improved during 2000–2009, their math skills stagnated and the decline in science scores is worrying.

In addition to the low PISA scores, Indonesian students have also fared poorly on measures of mathematics and science competencies according to the Third International Mathematics and Science Study, which tests the performance of 8th grade students. In 2003, Indonesian students ranked 34th in mathematics and 36th in science of the 45 countries surveyed. In this same exam in 2007, Indonesia's position remained virtually the same, showing little improvement in these critical competency areas (Jalal et al. 2009). These results suggest that improving the quality of education remains a challenge in Indonesia.

On a positive note, Indonesia is probably going to improve outcomes from education in the coming years. In general, education outcomes measured by standardized examinations and per capita income are positively correlated. This is because the higher the income the more people can afford education. Higher tax revenues also allow the government to implement reforms in education. Indonesia is a new member of the lower middle-income countries, and its income has been increasing rapidly, at 3.8% per year (OECD PISA [various years]). Together with the government's commitment to improve education and increase the enrollment in secondary education, the income effect on education will gradually kick in to favor better education outcomes.

---

[4]   The PISA is conducted by the Organisation for Economic Co-operation and Development.

8.4. Education Reforms Needed

An important reform to improve the quality of Indonesian secondary schools involves the qualification of teachers and incentives given to them. Teachers in Indonesia have relatively low levels of academic qualifications compared with teachers in other countries in the region. Jalal et al. (2009) noted that only 73% of teachers in secondary schools had the minimum qualifications specified by the Ministry of National Education (MONE), and more than 60% of them did not have the equivalent of a 4-year bachelor's degree.

A significant determinant of the low quality of teachers in Indonesia is the relatively low pay university graduates receive for teaching compared with other jobs. In contrast to other professions in Indonesia, the teachers' level of education is not positively correlated with salary levels. Analyzing the labor force survey administered in 2004, Arze del Granado et al. (2007) showed that, compared with other jobs in Indonesia, teachers with low levels of educational attainment were actually generously remunerated, while teachers with high levels of education were underpaid—qualified teachers' salaries were 21% below those of employees in different jobs with the same academic qualifications.

Table 8.5 compares teachers' salary ranges by education level in Indonesia, Malaysia, and Thailand. Because the salaries are not directly comparable due to different income levels, the table shows teachers' starting and top salaries as a percentage of per capita income. The starting salaries for teachers in the three countries are more or less comparable in proportion to the country's per capita income. Secondary school teachers' starting salaries are relatively higher in Indonesia than in Thailand, but top salaries for Indonesian teachers are significantly lower. Experienced teachers are much worse off in Indonesia than teachers in Malaysia and Thailand, creating a disincentive for young university graduates to pursue a teaching career. Overall, the pay scale suggests difficulties in attracting university graduates to teaching because wages for university graduates have been rapidly rising in the Indonesian labor market. The government, therefore, has initiated reforms in teachers' remuneration.

Table 8.5: Teachers' Salaries by Level of Education (% of GDP per capita at PPP)

	Year	GDP per Capita (at PPP, constant 2005 international $)	Primary School Starting Salary	Primary School Top Salary	Junior Secondary School Starting Salary	Junior Secondary School Top Salary	Senior Secondary School Starting Salary	Senior Secondary School Top Salary
Indonesia	2005	3,217	85.0	122.5	90.6	133.1	104.9	147.8
Malaysia	2004	11,363	73.8	165.4	102.8	273.1	102.8	273.1
Thailand	2005	6,751	87.4	409.8	87.4	409.8	87.4	409.8

GDP = gross domestic product, PPP = purchasing power parity.
Source: Teachers salaries: UNESCO (2007): Table 5.h.i., p. 144; GDP per capita: World Bank, World Databank; author's calculations.

The imbalance in teacher deployment also merits education reformers' attention. Indonesia has a relatively low student-to-teacher ratio (Figure 8.1), with more teachers per student on the payroll than other regional countries. For example, there is one teacher for every 12 students in senior secondary schools on average, which is the lowest ratio among the countries in comparison. This has produced very low marginal returns and served as a significant cost burden on secondary schools. As noted in Arze del Granado et al. (2007), a student-to-teacher ratio of 30:1 is an optimal level to produce adequate returns. The oversupply of teachers in Indonesia may be partly responsible for the relatively low remuneration per teacher. Arguably, having an adequate number of qualified teachers would serve education better rather than having too many underqualified teachers.

Figure 8.1: Student-to-Teacher Ratios

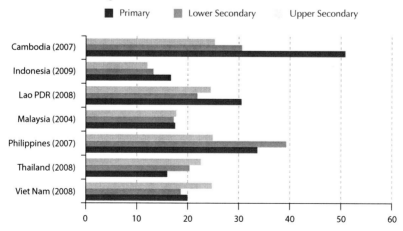

Lao PDR = Lao People's Democratic Republic.
Source: UNESCO, Data Centre.

A caveat applies to this general picture: although the student-to-teacher ratio in Indonesia is far below optimal at all education levels, schools in remote areas critically need more qualified teachers. The deployment of teachers is geographically biased to the disadvantage of students in remote rural areas. Therefore, additional incentives are needed to entice qualified teachers to work in remote places in order to address the geographical imbalance. Some provincial governments provide incentives to teachers who are deployed in remote areas, e.g., in Gorontalo and Papua.

8.5. Vocational Education and Skills Training

In addition to general education, technical and vocational education and training (TVET) plays a vital role in developing human capital. A main objective of TVET is to supply the labor market with skilled workers that meet industry's needs. Various types of institutions provide vocational education and skills training: vocational high schools (SMKs), public vocational training centers (BLKs), community learning centers and other nonformal educational institutions, and companies. These institutions offer vocational education and/or skills training to different target groups at various stages of people's career development. This section describes these TVET institutions and discusses challenges that confront them and the government's response to the challenges. Then it turns to more general issues of skills recognition in the labor market.

8.5.1. Types of Vocational Education

Vocational High Schools. The SMKs provide post-junior high school formal vocational education, and their program is managed by MONE. SMKs aim to prepare students for a wide range of occupations, from agribusiness, animal husbandry, and fisheries to office management and banking. Some SMK courses combine classroom teaching and apprenticeship in enterprises. MONE tallied over 855,000 students being educated at over 6,700 SMKs in school year 2007/08.

Public Vocational Training. BLKs provide nonformal vocational education and training for diverse trainees, including SMK graduates, dropouts from general senior secondary schools, and job seekers. BLKs are under the jurisdiction of the Ministry of Manpower and Transmigration. Of the 162 BLKs operating in 32 provinces in 2006, 11 were managed directly by the central government and the rest by provincial or district governments since decentralization. Partly because local governments lack understanding about the importance of vocational training and due to scarce funding, BLKs have suffered from insufficient maintenance. As a result, their facilities and equipment have deteriorated, with 59% of BLKs needing revitalization (Table 8.6 and World Bank 2010: Table 7). The central government intends to revamp BLKs and allocated Rp164 billion ($18.2 million) to this end (ILO 2010) out of the fiscal stimulus package that the government implemented in 2009 as a response to the global financial crisis.

Table 8.6: Condition of Public Vocational Training Centers (2006)

Location Condition	Western Provinces (102 BLKs)	Central Provinces (52 BLKs)	Eastern Provinces (8 BLKs)	Total (162 BLKs)
Good	16%	4%	0%	11%
Fair	37%	19%	0%	30%
Poor	47%	77%	100%	59%

BLK = public vocational training center.
Source: Ministry of Manpower and Transmigration, cited in World Bank (2010): Table 5-2.

The polytechnic institution is the highest level for formal vocational education. Polytechnics are classified as higher education and are under the jurisdiction of MONE. The vast majority of polytechnics are private institutions. Graduates of both general and vocational senior secondary schools can enter polytechnics and acquire technical vocational skills in various fields. Graduates of polytechnics are considered skilled workers and take relatively well-remunerated occupations such as line management in factories and engineering.

Community Learning Centers. Community learning centers and private institutions are other important providers of nonformal education. MONE supervises these institutions, which provide diverse training courses such as tailoring, embroidery, computer skills, and cosmetology. Overall, these institutions rest on relatively feeble financial footing, because they rely on government subsidies and/or tuition payments from participants.

Corporate Training. Companies often provide hands-on training to their employees, which play an important role in enhancing the efficiency and competitiveness of a company. On-the-job training builds job- or company-specific skills aiming to improve productivity at the company level. Some large companies run their own TVET centers. Although business establishments are important actors in skills training, it is difficult to have a complete picture of enterprises' contribution to human capital development in Indonesia, largely due to a lack of reliable and comprehensive data. Only about 24% of Indonesian firms offer a formal training program, which is well below the level in countries such as Bangladesh, the People's Republic of China (PRC), and India, which have labor-intensive manufacturing (ADB and World Bank 2005).

The Economic Census of 2006 indicates that the vast majority of enterprises in Indonesia operate informally: in Indonesia, microenterprises accounted for 83.3% of business establishments, small enterprises accounted for 15.8%, and 43.0% of all enterprises did not have permanent business premises. Training activities in such establishments are not well documented.

8.5.2. Enhancing Technical and Vocational Education and Training

In 2006, MONE drafted a strategic plan to expand the number of vocational schools across the country. According to the strategic plan, the primary goal was to increase the number of school leavers who are ready to work, particularly those who do not continue to tertiary education (Newhouse and Suryadarma 2009). MONE's policy is based on statistics indicating that the unemployment rate of vocational graduates is lower than that of general education graduates. Hence, increasing the share of vocational graduates should result in a lower overall unemployment rate.

Proponents of vocational education argue that, in addition to enhancing students' employability, vocational schools boost equity by providing an opportunity for individuals from underprivileged backgrounds to be competitive in the job market. Newhouse and Suryadarma (2009) use father's education as a proxy for family background and find that children of highly educated parents are more likely to attend general than vocational school (in a statistically significant manner). Additionally, their regression model finds that workers from disadvantaged backgrounds obtain the largest benefits from vocational education, while school type has no statistically significant effect on labor market outcomes for individuals with fathers that have at least a secondary degree. Proponents of TVET have also argued that modern technology has led to production processes that require highly specialized skills (Tilak 2002). Hence, vocational education can serve an important role in providing specialized training to workers in the industrial and service sectors.

The arguments against expanding vocational education have focused primarily on the economic implications. Opponents have argued that vocational education inhibits the socioeconomic attainment of students by reducing their future access to tertiary education (Chen 2009). Moreover, the returns to general education exceed those of specialized training, because general education is transferable across economic sectors, while vocational education tends to be job-specific (Blaug 1973). Hence, general education is advantageous in a flexible labor market that promotes significant labor mobility across sectors and occupations.

Turning to the empirics, recent World Bank studies have focused on the effects that TVET have on labor market outcomes in Indonesia (Chen 2009,

Newhouse and Suryadarma 2009). The studies used longitudinal household survey data to track cohorts of students entering both vocational and general schools. Both studies found no market advantage or disadvantage in terms of employment for vocational school students. The studies did find a large drop in the wage premium for the most recent cohort of vocational school graduates (Figure 8.2), which suggests that the technical skills taught in the vocational programs may not translate well to the job market. The drop in wage premium may result from the fact that vocational graduates enjoy only a short-term advantage over general education students at the onset of employment. Vocational graduates have job-specific skills that allow them to start work immediately without significant on-the-job training. Over time, however, general school graduates find it easier to upgrade their skills and thus enjoy higher rates of return, because they are better able to adapt to employers' skills demands. Additionally, the lower wage premium of vocational graduates may also indicate the relative short lifespan of their job skills in the current labor market. The quality of vocational education may have deteriorated to the point that the skills taught are not adequate to meet employers' needs.

Figure 8.2: Wage Ratio between Vocational and General Senior High School Graduates (general senior high school =100)

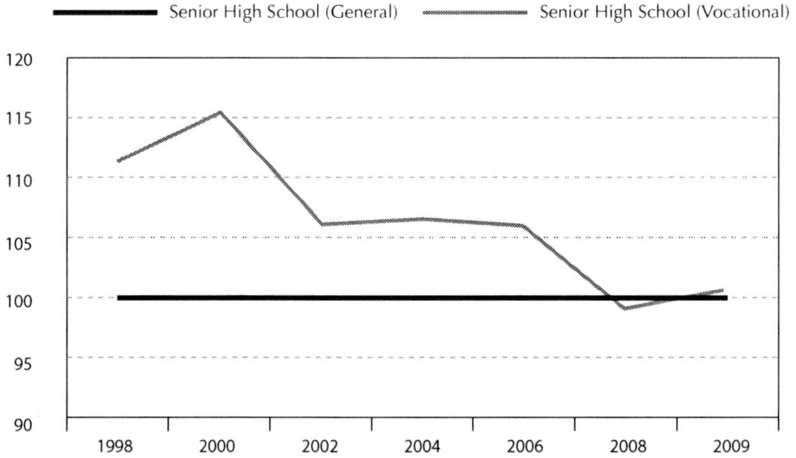

Sources: BPS, *Labor Force Situation in Indonesia* (various years); author's calculations.

8.5.3. Recognizing Skills

The ultimate purpose of TVET is to increase labor market outcomes of trainees, and skills recognition is a key to improving their ability to find employment. Therefore the Indonesian government has been promoting competency-based training and national skills certification and has established the National Education Standards Board (BNSP) to set competency requirements for key occupations and help certify workers' skills. BNSP is an independent nongovernment body, although some training officers of the Ministry of Manpower and Transmigration are seconded to the agency. BNSP verifies and endorses competency standards developed by sector associations and government agencies. After vocational education and/or training, trainees can take skills assessment tests at accredited assessment centers. The centers have skills assessors certified by BNSP. If a candidate passes the assessment, then the center recommends that an appropriate professional certification institution issues a corresponding national skills certificate. The professional certification institution is often a private institution established by chambers of commerce and licensed by BNSP.

The skills certification system in Indonesia needs enhancement. First, from the trainees' perspective, assessment centers are not always accessible physically and/or financially, as they are usually located in large cities such as provincial capitals.[5] Travelling to the capital city is expensive for most people of average income. Second, not all assessment centers have assessors to cover all the occupations. Third, not all trainees can afford the assessment fee. Last but not the least, the "signalling effect" of national skills certification has not been proven effective, partly because employers are not always aware of skills certificates.[6]

8.6. Human Capital, Investment, and Growth

As noted in Chapter 9 on employment, investment climate survey results indicate that business is not constrained by a lack of skilled workers. Indonesia has a substantial labor surplus, and young workers are willing to move in search of better income opportunities (Sziraczki and Reerink 2004). Hence, most investors who are willing to pay "efficiency wages" (wages that are higher than determined by the market)[7] will not find it difficult to recruit production workers, except for highly skilled workers in certain occupations. Although the share of the workforce with at least high school education is relatively low in Indonesia, the absolute number of high school graduates is substantial. The investment climate surveys thus do not detect availability of workforce as a hindrance to investment.

---

[5] For example, the average Indonesian province is over 57,000 square kilometers, which is far larger than Switzerland.

[6] Interview with Srinivas Reddy, ILO skills development specialist, on 25 March 2011

[7] Some employers prefer to pay "efficiency wages" to buy effective units of labor and reduce shirking and absenteeism.

Caveats apply to the seemingly sufficient supply of skills in the Indonesian labor market, because opinion surveys often fail to reflect potential investors' views on the availability of human capital. Perceptions of managers of companies that currently operate in Indonesia constitute only a partial picture of the investment climate, because their views are not necessarily the same as those of companies that decided not to invest in Indonesia. The availability of the types and levels of skills in a country may dictate the kind and the volume of investment in the country. A variety of factors, such as infrastructure, government efficiency, business regulations, and industrial relations, affect investment decisions. Skills availability is undoubtedly one such factor. Further, certain types of investment weigh heavily on skills availability. For example, call center business and information technology industries would invest in India or the Philippines, where workers with necessary skills are available. This example implies that Indonesia is missing opportunities for growth and employment creation due to a lack of sufficient skills in its workforce. Higher skills among Indonesian workers would be likely to induce more investment, although this cannot be shown quantatively.

Indonesia's rich natural resources attract investment. However, mining (including oil) companies often bring skilled workers from abroad, and investment in mining is heavily capital intensive and generally has a very modest employment effect.

Some evidence suggests skills mismatch (or a shortage of skilled workers) in the Indonesian labor market.[8] The Indonesian labor market has an overabundance of lower end skills, while advanced expertise in fields such as management and some professions remain in scarce supply (di Gropello 2011). The widening wage gaps between workers with primary education and those with a university degree indicate that the supply of skills may not match the demand in the market. The ratio of wages for workers with university education to workers with primary school education increased from 3.5 in 1998 to 4.4 in 2008. The average hourly wage for workers with a university diploma is more than triple that for workers with junior secondary school education and more than double the average remuneration for workers with senior secondary education.

Skills mismatch can constrain economic growth in two ways. First, lack of an appropriately and sufficiently skilled workforce deters a structural shift from low-productivity production to more value-added activities. In fact, skills endowment is a determining factor for the structure of the economy at the macro level. Figure 8.3 plots 77 countries for which data are available on a skill level versus industry structure diagram. The horizontal axis indicates the share of workers with secondary education or above, and

---

[8]   Skills mismatch refers to the gap between skills supply (types, levels, and quantity) and skills demand in a labor market.

Figure 8.3: Skills and Agriculture's Share in GDP

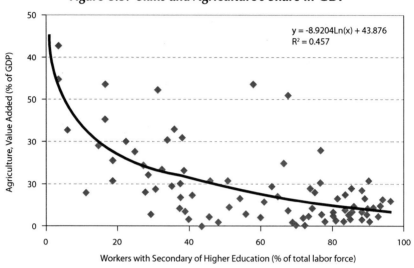

Sources: World Bank, World Databank; author's calculations.

the vertical axis represents the share of value added of agriculture in GDP. The figure shows that as the share of workers with secondary education or above increases, agriculture's share in value added of the economy declines. In other words, an economy's growth to emphasize industry and services appears to be correlated with an increasing share of educated people in its workforce. Although this statistical analysis does not purport to show a causal relation between the two variables, one can argue that skills availability is a precondition for a country to depart from an agriculture-based economy to a more capital- and knowledge-intensive one.

Second, lack of a skilled workforce prevents an economy from swiftly adopting new technologies and productivity-enhancing innovation. Even where economic structure remains constant, increased productivity pushes up the sum of value added in the economy, thus accelerating growth, and skills catalyze this process. At the micro level, having the requisite skills permits enterprises to integrate available technologies into their production. Figure 8.4 shows a positive correlation between the skills level of the workforce and the level of production technology. The logarithm of the number of technicians in research and development per million people was used as a proxy for technology levels of production. Clearly, the higher the skills level of the labor force, the more companies can adopt technology in their production. Figure 8.4 implies the importance of human capital for an economy to move to more value-added production. Because higher skills levels lead to more value-added production and thus higher income, the skills level of the labor force and income level (i.e., GDP per capita) are positively correlated.

Figure 8.4: Skills and Technology Adoption

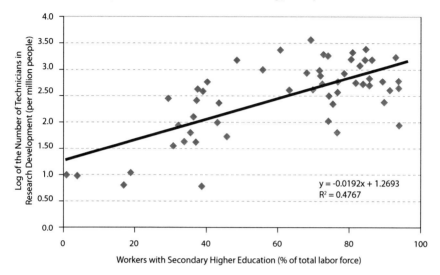

y = -0.0192x + 1.2693
R² = 0.4767

Sources: World Bank, World Databank; author's calculations.

8.7. Human Capital and Economic Structure

This and the following sections examine to what extent Indonesia's current human capital endowment contributes to the country's economic growth through shifts in economic structure and labor productivity. Regarding human capital and economic structure, a structural change in the composition of industry has been taking place in Indonesia since the mid-1990s (Chapter 6). The share of agriculture output in Indonesia's GDP declined from 19.4% in 1990 to 15.3% in 2009 (Figure 8.5), whereas the shares of industry and services increased. Because GDP per employee is higher in industry and services than in agriculture, the shift in industry composition and employment has been conducive to economic growth. The recent improvement in education undoubtedly contributed to the shift. The more educated, younger workers are increasingly employed in secondary and tertiary industries (ILO 2009).

Figure 8.5: Annual Growth Rate of Output and Employment by Sector (2000–2009, %)

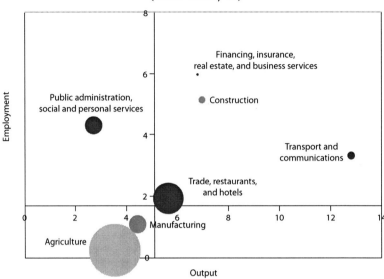

Note: The size of the bubble indicates the share of employment in the sector in 2009.
Sources: Employment: BPS, Labor Force Situation in Indonesia; Output: ADB (2010); author's calculations.

The shift from agriculture to industry and services has altered the Indonesian labor market's demand for skills and thus the education required to produce them. Nearly 70% of workers in the growing service sector have senior secondary education or above (Figure 8.6), which is considerably higher than that in manufacturing, at about 40% (World Bank 2010). One question is whether the current education and TVET systems have been successfully generating enough workers with the skills demanded by employers. The widening wage gaps by education, or (more precisely) the increasing wage premium for university graduates, have been partly driven by the change in skills demand triggered by structural changes in the composition of the Indonesian economy. The wage trend implies that the labor market demand for highly skilled workers has been increasing, but Indonesia's education and skills development systems have not fully responded to the demand. If the structural shift in the economy continues and the skills shortage deepens, then economic growth may be capped by a deficiency in skills.

Figure 8.6: Share of Workers by Education and Sector (%)

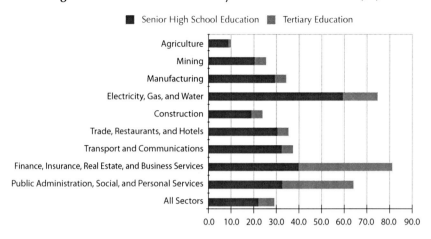

Sources: BPS, Labor Force Situation in Indonesia; author's calculations.

8.8. Human Capital and Labor Productivity

Turning to human capital and sector productivity growth, when compared with other countries in the region, one can find evidence that suggests human capital does constrain Indonesia's economic growth. Indonesia's productivity increased during 2000–2009, but its performance was mediocre in the region, and available data indicate skills constraint as a cause. Figure 8.7 presents GDP per worker by sector in 2000 and 2009 in Indonesia. All sectors gained productivity, to varying degrees. Communications charted notable productivity growth, at 9.1% per year between 2000 and 2009. The productivity of the trade, restaurants, and hotels subsector in 2009 was nearly 40% higher than in 2000. Various factors contributed to the economy-wide productivity gain, and human capital is undoubtedly one.

Compared with other regional countries, Indonesia's seemingly high performance in enhancing labor productivity does not appear very spectacular. After all, Indonesia is one of the fast-growing emerging Asian nations. Figure 8.8 shows trends in labor productivity of ASEAN member states less Brunei Darussalam, Myanmar, and Singapore, plus the PRC. Malaysia had a head start in 1960 and continuously and quite rapidly lifted its productivity. Indonesia has generally charted a sustained progression in labor productivity since 1960. In the early 1990s, Indonesia's productivity growth picked up, but the gain was reversed due to the Asian financial crisis. In the 2000s, Indonesia experienced an economy-wide productivity gain, as discussed earlier, and almost caught up with the Philippines' level of labor productivity.

293

Figure 8.7: Labor Productivity by Sector (million rupiah at 2000 constant market prices)

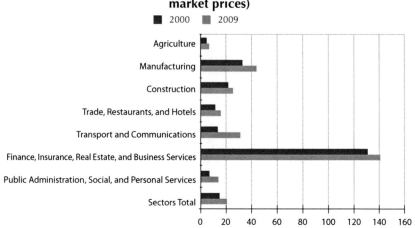

Sources: GDP by sector: ADB, Statistical Database System, accessed 25 March 2011; Employment: BPS, Labor Force Situation in Indonesia (2000 and 2009); author's calculations.

High economic growth in some Asian countries has been underpinned by increased human capital and productivity. Productivity trends in Thailand and Indonesia were more or less the same between the mid-1960s and early 1980s. Then Thailand experienced rigorous productivity growth as a result of industrialization, leaving Indonesia far behind. The level of productivity in the PRC had long been below that of Indonesia until the early 2000s. The PRC's productivity growth picked up in the 1990s and accelerated significantly in the last decade. The PRC's GDP per person employed in 2010 was 1.55 times that of Indonesia. Rapid productivity growth in the PRC and Thailand was a consequence of a set of successful policies including investment attraction, infrastructure development, and industrial policies. It is not a coincidence that the PRC, Malaysia, and Thailand emphasized education more than Indonesia did in the past.

Figure 8.9 illustrates the trends in manufacturing value added per worker in selected ASEAN countries during the 1990–2009 period. Indonesia's manufacturing labor productivity increased steadily, but lagged behind that of the Philippines. Malaysia and Thailand succeeded in industrialization, and their manufacturing productivity grew faster, at 5.1% and 3.1% per year between 1990 and 2008, than that of Indonesia, at 2.9%. Malaysia's manufacturing value added per worker in 2009 was nearly 3.8 times Indonesia's in the same year.

To explain the slow growth of Indonesia's manufacturing labor productivity, Islam and Chowdhury (2009: 115) pointed out a failure of Indonesian manufacturers to invest in "upgrading technology and

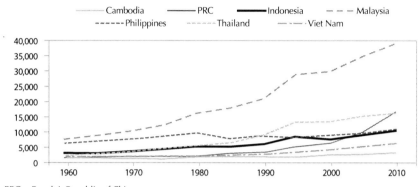

Figure 8.8: GDP per Person Employed (in 2010 $ at PPP)

PRC = People's Republic of China.
Source: Conference Board Total Economy Database.

Figure 8.9: Labor Productivity in Manufacturing (constant 2000 $)

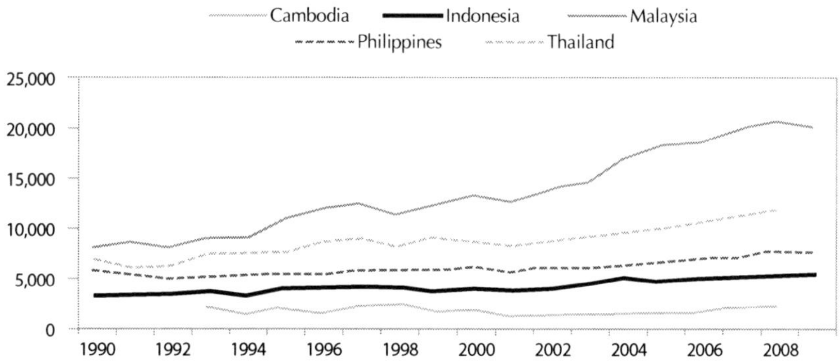

Sources: ADB (2010); ADB, SDBS; Author's calculation

manufacturing capabilities and retraining the labour force." Indonesia has generally been unable to strengthen its position regionally in the industrial technology sector (ADB and World Bank 2005, Thee 2006). The 2004–2005 Global Competitiveness report ranks Indonesia consistently below its regional neighbors in indicators that measured technological readiness and institutional capabilities for adopting new technology (WEF 2004). Traditionally, Indonesia maintained regional competitiveness by relying on its comparative advantage of having a large labor surplus for labor-intensive manufactured goods. However, other Asian nations—the PRC and Viet Nam in particular—have emerged as strong competitors in the same low-skill labor-intensive products. Recent trends in real wages for production workers are downward, leaving virtually no room for suppressing wages.

With the strong rupiah, Indonesia's ability to expand its economy based on labor cost competitiveness has been undermined, as other low-cost producers in the region have strengthened their competitiveness. Hence, improved technological capabilities and a gradual moving to more value-added products have become an extremely important strategic initiative to maintain competitiveness in the manufacturing sector.

A significant roadblock to Indonesia's technological development is the inability of the workforce to effectively adapt to innovative and complex technologies. A key factor in the failure is the lack of adequate human capital within the workforce. In workforce surveys, international firms have consistently cited the shallow and backward technological base and the inability of the workforce to adapt to complex and new technologies as key impediments to technological advances. The investment climate survey reported that 53% of firms in Indonesia rated the skill and education levels of labor in large firms as a moderate to severe obstacle to business (LPEM–FEUI 2007). In an investment climate survey of Japanese firms, 75% of respondents agreed that human resource development and staff enhancement was important to improve competitiveness in Indonesia (JETRO 2009). In addition to demands for better skilled employees on the factory line, firms expressed concern over the abilities of local managers to oversee production processes: almost 40% of Japanese firms surveyed stated that it was difficult to recruit local middle managers.

Hence, a well-trained and better educated workforce is essential for improving the competitiveness of the Indonesian industry sector. Indonesia's education system has been ineffective at providing the skills necessary for workers to succeed in industry. Critics have argued that the general secondary education system relies too much on rote learning and does not adequately develop a mastery of literacy or mathematical skills that are important for creativity and adaptability (Thee 2006: 351). The interaction effect between the workforce's limited formal training and relatively low level of education is not conducive to productivity growth and competitiveness. Thus, a renewed focus on educational attainment and improved skills training is recommended for Indonesia to adequately compete in the high-quality product market.

8.9. Conclusions and Policy Options

In recent years, Indonesia has made significant strides in improving the educational attainment of its workforce. The number of workers with a primary school education has risen, and, recently, the number with secondary and tertiary level education has also increased. However, Indonesia's progress has lagged behind that of regional countries, which has probably affected Indonesia's competitiveness in the region. Before the

Asian financial crisis, Indonesia was able to achieve high levels of growth without a significant increase in human capital by focusing primarily on labor and capital inputs. The economy was structured predominantly around agriculture and labor-intensive manufactured goods. At the time, Indonesia maintained a comparative advantage in the region due to the relatively low labor costs involved in production. As a result of this market advantage, the government focused mainly on raising the level of children enrolled in primary schools, and fewer resources were invested in education programs beyond the primary level.

This pattern of economic growth and the human capital development strategy have proved costly to the long-term growth prospects of the economy, mainly since Indonesia started to lose its comparative advantage in labor-intensive goods. Unfortunately, the country has been unable to successfully make a transition to more sophisticated manufacturing production and a knowledge-based economy. Indonesia's struggles to restructure the economy can be attributed largely to the difficulty in developing stocks of human capital adequate to facilitate this economic transition. The current weak base of human capital has significantly constrained economic growth. The failure of the workforce to create and absorb complex technologies has hampered efficiency gains in the manufacturing sector.

The policy implications of Indonesia's human capital deficiencies are that the country needs to address several demand-side factors, including the inequity in educational opportunities at higher levels of education and the provision of adequate incentives for individuals to continue schooling beyond the primary level.

The importance of demand-side factors to secondary school enrollment has several policy implications. Similar to the pro-poor policies enacted to improve enrollment in primary school, the government may wish to increase spending on secondary school programs in order to improve enrollment rates and reduce the effect that household income has on attendance. To achieve this, the government needs to do a better job of effectively targeting scholarship programs for low-income households, especially in rural areas, where secondary school density is low. Under the current scholarship scheme, funds are given only to children who are already enrolled in school (Suryadama, Suryahadi, and Sumarto 2006). Hence, there are no incentives for dropouts to return to school.

Additionally, the quality and efficiency of the education institutions need improvement. In particular, several important supply-side determinants of educational quality and efficiency that need to be addressed include the oversupply of teachers, the level of teacher qualification, the scarcity of qualified teachers in secondary schools and in rural areas, and the structure of teacher compensation. The oversupply of underskilled teachers and the inadequacy of the current school curricula do not appear conducive to improving the performance of students in basic mathematics and science. The current teachers' remuneration scheme does not appear attractive to qualified university graduates, given the high demand for their skills and subsequent wage raises that workers with university education receive elsewhere. Additional incentives for qualified teachers who are willing to teach in remote areas may merit consideration.

The problem of quality is also prevalent outside the general school system. TVET has struggled to adequately equip students with viable, lasting technical skills for the labor market. Moreover, the economic returns to vocational training have dropped considerably in recent years, indicating that it is not in tune with the demands of the labor market. Revitalizing public vocational training institutions calls for attention of policymakers and adequate resource allocation. Enhancing the relevance of TVET courses to the needs of the industry must be an integral part of future reforms of the system. Moreover, the skills recognition scheme needs to be made more accessible and affordable. Raising awareness of the national competency standards and skills certifications among employers remains as a challenge.

Overall, it is recommended that the Indonesian government set education policy as a key strategic initiative in the coming years to offset the potential constraining effects of human capital. By increasing education levels in the workforce, the economy can move away from manufacturing labor-intensive goods, which is an important move for sustained economic growth. Additionally, increasing educational attainment will bring significant efficiency gains via the adoption of new technologies. Thus, for Indonesia to effectively compete in the global economy and achieve long-term growth, the promotion of human capital must become a top priority among policymakers.

References

Arze del Granado, F., W. Fengler, A. Ragatz, and E. Yavuz. 2007. Investing in Indonesia's Education: Allocation, Equity, and Efficiency of Public Expenditures. *World Bank Policy Research Working Paper*. No.4329. Washington, D.C.: World Bank.

Asian Development Bank (ADB). 2010. *Key Indicators for Asia and the Pacific 2010*. Manila.

———. Statistical Database System (SDBS) Online. http://www.adb.org/statistics/sdbs.asp (accessed in March 2011).

Asian Development Bank (ADB) and World Bank. 2005. *Improving the Investment Climate in Indonesia*. Manila.

Badan Pusat Statistik (BPS—Statistics Indonesia). 2009. *Statistical Yearbook of Indonesia (Statistik Indonesia)*. Jakarta.

———. various years. *Labor Force Situation in Indonesia*. Jakarta.

————. various years. *Laborer Situation in Indonesia*. Jakarta.

Blaug, M. 1973. *Education and the Employment Problem in Developing Countries*. Geneva: International Labour Organization.

Chen, D. 2009. Vocational Schooling, Labor Market Outcomes, and College Entry. *World Bank Policy Research Working Paper* No. 4814. Washington, DC: World Bank

Conference Board Total Economy Database. http://www.conference-board. org/data/economydatabase (accessed January 2011)

di Gropello, E. 2011. *Skills for the Labor Market in Indonesia: Trends in Demand, Gaps, and Supply*. Washington, DC: World Bank.

Firdausy, C. 2005. Productivity Performance in Developing Countries: Indonesia. *UNIDO Country Case Studies,* November 2005. Vienna: United Nations Industrial Development Organization (UNIDO).

Franken, J. 2010. Analysis: Indonesia's 12-Year Compulsory Education Program. *The Jakarta Post,* 28 June.

International Labour Organization (ILO). 2009. *Labor and Social Trends in Indonesia 2009: Recovery and Beyond through Decent Work.* Jakarta.

————. 2010. *Global Jobs Pact Country Scan: Indonesia.* Geneva.

Islam, I. and A. Chowdhury. 2009. *Growth, Employment and Poverty Reduction in Indonesia.* Geneva: ILO.

Jalal, F., M. Samani, M. C. Chang, R. Stevenson, A. Ragatz, and S. Negare. 2009. Teacher Certification in Indonesia: A Strategy for Teacher Quality Improvement. *World Bank Policy Research Working Paper* No. 48578. Washington, DC: World Bank.

Japan External Trade Organization (JETRO). 2009. Survey on International Operations of Japanese Firms. Tokyo.

Lee, J-W., and R. Francisco. 2010. Human Capital Accumulation in Emerging Asia, 1970–2030. *ADB Economics Working Paper Series* No. 216. Manila: ADB.

Lembaga Penyelidikan Ekonomi dan Masyarakat–Fakultas Ekonomi Universitas Indonesia (LPEM–FEUI—Institute for Economic and Social Research, Department of Economics, University of Indonesia). 2007. Investment Climate Monitoring. Round IV. Jakarta.

Newhouse, D. and D. Suryadarma. 2009. The Value of Vocational Education: High School Type and Labor Market Outcomes in Indonesia. *World Bank Policy Research Working Paper.* No. 5035. Washington, DC: World Bank.

Organisation for Economic Co-operation and Development (OECD). 2007. Programme for International Student Assessment (PISA) 2006 Volume 2: Data. Paris. http://www.oecd.org/dataoecd/30/18/39703566. pdf?bcsi_scan_B90AE85AF6AB15C6=0&bcsi_scan_

————. various years. Programme for International Student Assessment. http://www.pisa.oecd.org

Suryadarma, D., A. Suryahadi, and S. Sumarto. 2006. Causes of Low Secondary School Enrollment in Indonesia. *SMERU Working Paper*. Jakarta: The SMERU Research Institute.

Sziraczki, G. and A. Reerink. 2004. Report of Survey on the School-to-Work Transition in Indonesia. *GENPROM Working Paper* No. 14. Series on Gender in the Life Cycle. Geneva: ILO. http://www.ilo.org/public/engl

Thee, K. W. 2006. Policies Affecting Indonesia's Industrial Technology Development. *ASEAN Economic Bulletin* 23(3): 341–59.

Tilak, J. 2002. Vocational Education and Training in Asia. In J. Keeves and R. Watanabe (eds.), *The Handbook on Educational Research in the Asia Pacific Region*. Norwell, MA: Kluwer.

United Nations Development Programme (UNDP). 2007. *Human Development Report 2007/2008 Fighting Climate Change: Human Solidarity in a Divided World*. http://hdr.undp.org/en/media/HDR_20072008_EN_Complete.pdf

———. Human Development Indicators Database. http://hdr.undp.org (accessed 24 March 2011).

United Nations Educational, Scientific, and Cultural Organization (UNESCO) Institute for Statistics. 2007. *Education Counts: Benchmarking Progress in 19 WEI Countries: World Education Indicators 2007*. Paris.

———. Data Centre. http://stats.uis.unesco.org/unesco/TableViewer/document.aspx?ReportId=143&IF_Language=eng (accessed 24 March 2011).

World Bank. 2010. *Education, Training, and Labor Market Outcomes for Youth in Indonesia*. Jakarta.

———. World Databank (online world development indicator database). http://databank.worldbank.org/ (accessed January 2011)

World Economic Forum (WEF). 2004. *Global Competitiveness Report 2004–2005*. Geneva. http://www.weforum.org

9. Economic Growth, Employment Creation, and Poverty Alleviation[1]

Kazutoshi Chatani[2]

9.1. Introduction

This chapter focuses on linkages between economic growth, employment creation, and poverty alleviation. Broadly speaking, the fruit of economic growth is distributed through income opportunities and social policies that redistribute income, such as progressive taxation and social security, and that enhance economic opportunities of the deprived, such as education and public health. Because of limited space, the chapter's scope of discussion is confined to economic growth and poverty alleviation through employment. The chapter focuses on employment, not other forms of income opportunities, because employment is often the only reliable means of income for most citizens and the deprived. It is increasingly accepted that realizing high economic growth alone does not necessarily guarantee poverty alleviation. The economic and labor market performances in Indonesia during the decade after the Asian financial crisis (AFC), corroborate this observation, and similar evidence abounds elsewhere in the world. This chapter thus sheds light on the relations between economic growth, employment creation, and poverty alleviation in Indonesia in order to gain insight into strengthening the linkages.

The effect of economic growth on poverty reduction depends largely on the employment parameter that connects the two. Creation of employment can be considered as a function of economic growth, but the relation is not linear, because many variables affect the capacity of the economy to

---

[1]   The editors and publishers gratefully acknowledge the International Labour Organization for contributing this chapter.

[2]   The author is grateful to Duncan Campbell for his helpful comments.

generate employment, which will be discussed in the first half of this chapter. The relation between employment creation and poverty reduction is also not straightforward, because the quality of employment and the access of disadvantaged groups of workers to employment opportunities influence the relation, which will be the focus of the second half of this chapter. Figure 9.1 presents the conceptual framework of the chapter.

Figure 9.1: Conceptual Framework of This Chapter

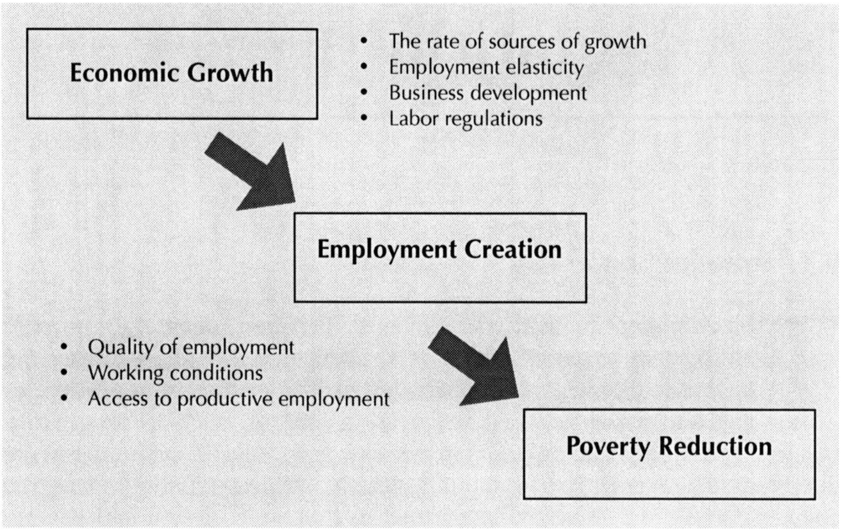

| Economic Growth | • The rate of sources of growth
• Employment elasticity
• Business development
• Labor regulations |

Employment Creation

• Quality of employment
• Working conditions
• Access to productive employment

Poverty Reduction

Source: Author.

9.2. Growth and Employment Creation

This section examines the growth–employment nexus in Indonesia. It analyzes the capacity of the Indonesian economy for generating employment, with a particular focus on the rate and sources of economic growth and employment elasticity to economic growth. The section first highlights a slowdown in labor-intensive manufacturing and a decline in infrastructure investment in explaining stagnant employment growth after the AFC; it then turns to the business environment and employment creation, because growth of enterprises is a key to employment generation. The section pays particular attention to business regulations and access to capital. Following this, a shift in economic structure and its implications for employment are examined. Finally, the section evaluates the impact of labor regulations on employment growth, referring to available empirical evidence.

9.2.1. Slowdown in Employment Growth after the Asian Financial Crisis

Employment growth, more precisely the growth of productive employment, fell short of workforce growth after the AFC, which that erupted in 1997. Figure 9.2 shows the growth trends of the workforce and employment of two age groups. If one takes the entire age cohort (age 15 and above), it is evident that workforce growth outpaced the expansion of employment opportunities, as the two lines started to diverge and the gap widened in the post-crisis period between 2000 and 2006. Remarkably, employment growth stagnated after the AFC until it picked up again in 2007, which created a stark contrast to the steady upward trend of workforce growth. That employment recovery lags behind economic recovery by several years was repeatedly observed in past crises (ILO 2009a). Overall, the workforce grew by 49.0%, whereas employment grew by 41.7% during 1991–2009.

Figure 9.2: Labor Force and Employment Growth Trends (1991 = 100)

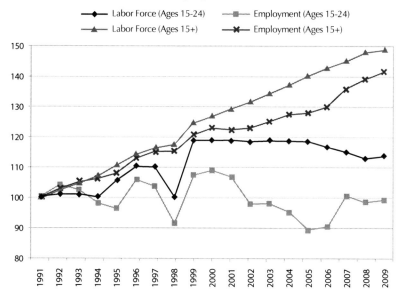

Sources: ILO 2009c; BPS Sakernas

The growth gap between the workforce and employment during the post-crisis period was more pronounced among the youth (age 15–24). The youth workforce and employment trends in Figure 4.8 (Chapter 4) depict three salient issues that confront young workers and jobseekers in Indonesia. First, employment of the youth is much more vulnerable to an external shock than employment of older workers. The sharp dip in employment in the aftermath of the AFC corroborates this point: youth employment shrank by 8.9% (for a loss of 1.9 million jobs) during the crisis. Many young workers withdrew from the labor market, because hopes of finding jobs were dim. With relatively less professional experience and skills, young workers are often among the first who suffer from weak labor demand. Youth employment realized a V-shaped recovery; however, it proved vulnerable to weak labor demand during the protracted period of labor market recovery from the tremendous external shock. Youth employment opportunities kept shrinking after 2001 until they fell below the record of 1998 in 2005. In fact, youth employment between 2002 and 2006 was below the level recorded in 1991 despite sustained economic recovery since the AFC. Second, partly relating to the first point, youth employment fluctuates far more widely than total employment (age 15+). This highlights the susceptibility of youth employment to the business cycle. Job opportunities for those who leave school depend on the economic conditions of the time. This is explained by the labor adjustment procedure of enterprises, which halt new recruitment before laying off staff. The downward trend of youth participation in the workforce—from 54.1% in 2004 to 50.3% in 2009—indicates that the youth are being discouraged from seeking work by the difficulty of finding jobs. The decline in workforce participation is partly a result of improved enrollment of the youth in higher education (see Chapter 8 on human capital). Throughout the period between 1991 and 2009, the workforce of people aged 15–24 grew by 13.4% (or by 2.4 million youths) while employment opportunities for them shrank by 1.0%.

9.2.2. Rates and Sources of Growth

One reason for the slow growth of employment after the 1997 AFC is slower economic growth. Between 1989 and the run-up to the crisis, the Indonesian economy was expanding at 7.2%–9.0% annually, a rate of growth the country never achieved again after the crisis. In fact, the average annual gross domestic product (GDP) growth rate between 2000 and 2005 was 4.6%. Lower rates of economic growth generally depress employment growth rates, all else being equal. As the section illustrates later, employment elasticity to output also declined in the post-crisis period. In addition, the sectoral composition of the Indonesian economy changed, which also affected labor market outcomes.

Throughout the 1990s and 2000s, approximately half of Indonesia's economic growth originated from private consumption. Another motor of economic growth has been investment, which contributes about 25%–30% of growth (Table 9.1). This pattern of contribution to GDP growth has been consistent, although the rates have been slower since the AFC. A notable change is a decline in the contribution of net exports to growth in the post-crisis period. The thrust of the export-led growth model that Indonesia pursued in the 1980s and until the onset of the AFC weakened thereafter, partly due to a slowdown in the labor-intensive manufacturing sector. The chapter will turn back to this point later. In addition, Indonesian exports, of which goods are the majority, increasingly rely on natural resource exploitation. In fact, the share of agricultural raw materials, ores and metals, and fuel increased by nearly 10 percentage points, from 33.9% in 2000 to 43.5% in 2008 (Table 9.2). Unlike agricultural plantations, which generate job opportunities, mining is capital-intensive and has a modest employment effect. Regarding the second motor of economic growth, namely gross fixed capital formation, 72.7% of investment was in buildings in 2008 (Table 9.3). Much of the rest comprises imported machinery, equipment,

Table 9.1: National Accounts (at 1993, 2000 constant prices)

	Annual Growth Rate (1990–1996, %)	Contribution to Growth (1990–1996, %)	Annual Growth Rate (2000–2009, %)	Contribution to Growth (2000–2009, %)
Private Consumption	8.8	45.6	4.3	49.8
Government Consumption	2.9	2.2	8.9	13.4
Gross Fixed Capital Formation	10.8	26.5	7.1	29.8
Net Exports (exports less imports)	12.9	28.1	4.8	9.8
Increase in Stocks	−10.1	−2.4		−2.6
Statistical Discrepancy				−0.1
Gross Domestic Product	7.8	100.0	5.1	100.0

Sources: ADB, SDBS online; author's calculations.

Table 9.2: Composition of Exports (% of merchandise exports)

Export Category	2000	2002	2004	2006	2008
Agricultural Raw Materials	3.6	4.3	5.0	6.4	6.4
Ores and Metals	4.9	5.3	6.4	10.0	8.0
Food	8.9	11.5	12.3	11.7	17.7
Fuel	25.4	24.4	25.8	27.2	29.1

Sources: BPS Website; author's calculations.

**Table 9.3: Composition of Gross Fixed Capital Formation
(at constant market prices, 2008)**

Category	Billion rupiah	Share (%)
Buildings	86,301.9	72.7
Domestic Machinery and Equipment	3,447.6	2.7
Imported Machinery and Equipment	16,562.6	14.2
Domestic Transport Tools	1,612.3	1.4
Imported Transport Tools	4,456.5	5.1
Domestic Others	2,831.2	2.3
Imported Others	1,987.3	1.6
(imported, total)	(102,992.8)	(20.9)
Gross Domestic Fixed Capital Formation	117,199.5	100.0

Sources: BPS Website; author's calculations.

and transport tools. Such imported fixed capital enhances productivity and benefits industries, thus contributing to employment creation; however, the direct and immediate employment effect of the investment is negligible in Indonesia.

9.2.3. Output and Employment Growth

Table 9.4 compares output and employment growth rates between pre-crisis (1990–1995) and post-crisis (2000–2005) periods. It is remarkable that the pace of output growth declined by more than half in the manufacturing and construction sectors after the crisis. The impact on employment was particularly evident in manufacturing. Manufacturing employment had grown by 5.8% per year during 1990–1995, but plummeted to 0.5% per year a decade later. As this chapter will discuss later, the stagnation of job creation in manufacturing can be partly ascribed to the slowdown in labor-intensive manufacturing. Employment opportunities in the construction sector kept expanding in the post-crisis period, but the rate of expansion was much lower than prior to the crisis, largely due to a reduction in public infrastructure investment, as this chapter points out later. By comparison, the agriculture sector maintained its pace of expansion over the two periods, with agricultural productivity rising prominently in the pre-crisis period. The return of workers to agriculture in the post-crisis period is explained by the weak growth of employment in other sectors. Growth has gathered momentum in the communications sector in the post-crisis period thanks to large investments in communications infrastructure, but this had only

Table 9.4: Annual Output and Employment Growth Rates (%)

Sector	Pre-crisis (1990–1995)		Post-crisis (2000–2005)	
	Output	Employment	Output	Employment
Agriculture	3.1	-3.5	3.2	0.3
Mining and Quarrying	5.9	4.3	-0.3	14.9
Manufacturing	11.1	5.8	5.0	0.5
Electricity, Gas, and Water	11.3	9.9	6.7	22.5
Construction	13.9	12.9	6.2	5.5
Trade, Restaurants, and Hotels	9.0	4.8	5.5	-0.6
Transport and Communications	8.1	8.4	10.9	4.4
Financing, Insurance, Real Estate, and Business Services	9.8	6.6	6.9	5.3
Community, Social, and Personal Services	2.1	5.7	1.2	1.5
Total	**7.9**	**1.3**	**4.6**	**0.9**

Sources: Output: ADB (2010); employment: BPS, Labor Force Situation in Indonesia (various years); author's calculations.

a moderate contribution to employment growth, which suggests that the sector's growth is highly capital-intensive.

In addition to the lower rates of economic growth, employment elasticity to output has declined since the AFC. Islam and Chowdhury (2009) applied a panel data regression approach to workforce survey data and regional accounts in order to estimate sectoral employment elasticity with the following model specification:

$$\ln E_{it} = \beta_0 + \beta_1 \ln Y_{it} + \beta_2 \ln RW_{it} + \beta_3 \ln E_{it-1} + \beta_{it,}$$

where:
E = employment by sector,
Y = output (sectoral GDP),
RW = real wage (sectoral nominal wage deflated by sectoral real GDP deflator),
i = province,
t = year.

Table 9.5 presents the resulting estimated employment elasticity to output. The results show a considerable decline in employment elasticity in all sectors but mining, electricity, gas, and water, and finance. Although the lower employment elasticity may suggest gains in labor productivity, the slow employment growth in the post-crisis period can be a result of growth that has not generated a concomitant number of jobs (Islam and Chowdhury 2009).

Table 9.5: Estimates of Employment Elasticity to Output

Sector	Pre-crisis (1993–1997, except 1995)		Post-crisis (2000–2006)	
Agriculture	1.37	*	0.68	*
Mining, Electricity, Gas, Water	−0.15		0.23	***
Manufacturing	0.86	***	0.12	***
Construction	1.60	***	0.63	***
Trade, Restaurants, and Hotels	2.99	***	0.81	***
Transportation and Communications	1.98	***	0.48	***
Finance	0.59		0.67	**
Services	0.89	***	0.17	***

Note: ***, **, and * denote statistical significance at the 1%, 5%, and 10% levels, respectively.
Source: Islam and Chowdhury (2009): Table 1.18.

9.2.4. Slowdown in Labor-Intensive Manufacturing

To understand the slow growth of employment in the manufacturing sector during the first decade of the millennium, it is helpful to look at the path along which Indonesia's manufacturing has developed. Indonesia's manufacturing sector started to expand rapidly in the late 1960s and maintained high growth until the AFC disrupted the trend with slower growth during 1981–1986 (Table 9.6). The sustained growth doubled the share of Indonesia's manufacturing output during the 1970s and 1980s. At the onset of this expansion, Indonesia adopted an import substitution strategy, imposing high tariffs on imports while providing subsidized capital to infant industries from state-owned banks. The country then changed its policy to export expansion in the mid-1980s. Various policy interventions, such as currency devaluation, reductions in tariffs on imports needed by exporters, and incentives for exporters, embodied the export-oriented industrial growth policy. The result was remarkable growth in manufacturing, especially in labor-intensive subsectors such as textiles, garments, footwear, and furniture. The annual growth rate of labor-intensive exports reached 44.6% between 1985 and 1990. Given the labor surplus in Indonesia, the shift of workers from low productivity agriculture to labor-intensive manufacturing induced productivity gains and income growth. The growth

Table 9.6: Sectoral Growth Rate and Contribution to Growth, 1960–2008 (%)

	Agriculture		Manufacturing		GDP Growth Rate	GDP per Capita Growth Rate
	Growth Rate	Contribution to Growth	Growth Rate	Contribution to Growth		
1960–1967	1.4	37.5	2.0	8.5	2.0	−0.1
1967–1972	4.4	26.8	10.1	11.2	7.9	5.8
1972–1981	4.2	20.3	12.1	21.9	7.0	4.6
1981–1986	2.8	16.7	7.3	21.9	4.1	2.1
1986–1997	2.9	7.1	13.1	32.4	7.9	6.1
1997–2008	2.4	12.3	2.8	27.7	2.8	1.4

GDP=gross domestic product.
Note: Because of changing weights as a result of using series in different base years, the GDP growth rate calculated as the weighted average of sector growth rates, used here, differs slightly from the total GDP growth rate normally shown.
Source: Papanek 2009: Table 1.

of manufacturing expanded employment opportunities in the sector and in related sectors through backward and forward linkages (Papanek 2009).

The growth of manufacturing output slowed considerably after the AFC of 1997/98, negatively affecting employment generation. Prior to the crisis (1990–1995), manufacturing employment was growing at 5.8% annually; however, between 2000 and 2005, this growth plummeted to 0.53% per year (Table 9.7). The drop had a considerable impact on low-skilled workers, aggravating youth unemployment.

The large decline in agricultural employment and simultaneous increase in employment in other sectors during the pre-crisis period indicated a shift of workers from the low-productivity agriculture sector to modern high-productivity sectors. However, the shift reversed somewhat between 2000 and 2005, as suggested by an increase in agricultural employment and a slowdown in absorption of labor in the other sectors.

Researchers pointed out several factors that account for the slowdown in manufacturing output and employment growth. First, the financial sector was wrecked by the AFC and failed to fuel the expansion of businesses and provide funds for manufacturers to upgrade their technology and to innovate in the years following the crisis. This coincided with a remarkable rise of competitors in the region, notably the People's Republic of China (PRC). The PRC's labor productivity surpassed that of Indonesia in the early 2000s.[3] Second, labor costs rose rapidly in foreign investors' currency due to the rupiah's appreciation. High interest rates, high yield of Indonesian

---

[3]   Source: Conference Board Total Economy Database.

Table 9.7: Employment Growth by Sector (1990–1995 and 2000–2005)

Sector	1990–1995		2000–2005	
	Employment Growth	Annual Growth Rate	Employment Growth	Annual Growth Rate
Agriculture	-6,549,421	-3.5	629,547	0.3
Mining and Quarrying	120,954	4.3	452,263	14.9
Manufacturing	2,433,208	5.8	311,229	0.5
Electricity, Gas, and Water	80,978	9.9	124,013	22.5
Construction	1,700,138	12.9	1,068,222	5.5
Trade, Restaurants, and Hotels	2,846,721	4.8	-579,858	-0.6
Transportation, Storage, and Communications	1,145,204	8.4	1,098,986	4.4
Financing, Insurance, Real Estate, and Business Services	180,732	6.6	259,252	5.3
Community, Social, and Personal Services	2,922,146	5.7	757,003	1.5
Total	**4,880,660**	**1.3**	**4,120,657**	**0.9**

Sources: BPS, Labor Force Situation in Indonesia (various years); author's calculations.

government bonds, and a commodity boom that started in 2004 induced a significant net inflow of foreign exchange, pushing up the rupiah's value. Bank Indonesia, which is mandated to target inflation, kept its policy rate high until the global financial crisis in order to suppress the inflationary pressure on prices. This monetary policy, however, was rather ineffective at reining in inflation caused by commodity price increases (Islam and Chowdhury 2009). Although a strong currency helped the government and private companies service their debts and contributed to macroeconomic stability, the rupiah's appreciation cost the economy dearly by reducing the competitiveness of Indonesian exports versus imports. Some researchers pointed to the strong Indonesian rupiah and insufficient investment as causes for Indonesia's lowered competitiveness in labor-intensive manufacturing (Islam and Chowdhury 2009, Papanek 2009). Consequently, policymakers and researchers became concerned about the deindustrialization that has been affecting Indonesia (Basri 2009)

Arguably, the increase in labor costs in major foreign currencies and not in nominal wages affected investment and employment creation in Indonesia after the AFC. Many observers ascribe slow job creation to a sharp rise in minimum wages and thus labor costs (World Bank 2010). But real wages have not changed in the last decade. In fact, the trend of real wages has been largely stagnant or downward since 2003, hardly improving living standards and the welfare of workers. Further, factory workers' wages are generally close to applicable minimum wages, but the real wages of production workers below the supervisory level have been on a downward trend since 2005 (Figure 9.3). And, while real wages stagnated or declined, wages in terms of major foreign currencies increased sharply (Papanek 2009). For example, the rupiah strengthened by about 40% against the United States (US) dollar when real exchange rates are applied between 2000 and 2009 (Figure 9.4). During the same period, real wages in Indonesia stagnated. This implies that wages in Indonesia went up significantly in US dollar terms, reducing the cost competitiveness of Indonesia's workforce from the international investors' perspective. Between 2000 and 2009, imports from the US[4] to Indonesia more than doubled, whereas exports from Indonesia to the US increased only by 24.8% (US Census Bureau).

Figure 9.3: Index of Monthly Real Average Wages of Production Workers below Supervisory Level (March 2005=100)

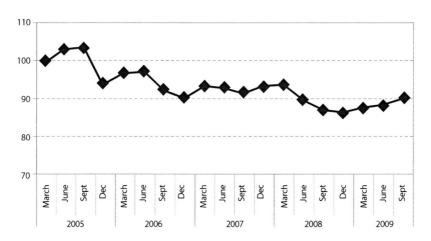

Sources: BPS Website; author's calculations.

---

4 The US was Indonesia's second largest export destination in 2008; Japan was the first.

Figure 9.4: Inflation and Exchange Rates, Indonesia and the United States

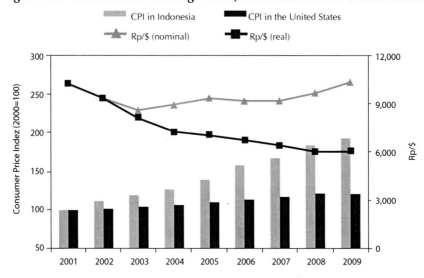

CPI = consumer price index.
Sources: CPI is sourced from IMF, World Economic Outlook Database; exchange rates are from Bank Indonesia.

9.2.5. Infrastructure Investment and Construction Employment

Another factor explaining the sluggish growth of productive employment after the AFC is the diminished growth of construction jobs as a result of lower investment in infrastructure. As well as having an impact on the number of construction jobs, investment in infrastructure influences, through backward and forward linkages, employment opportunities in related sectors—construction materials and transport, trades, business, and sectors stimulated by construction workers' consumption. Public sector spending on infrastructure (which is much higher than private spending on infrastructure), depends on political will and the government's ability to finance infrastructure development projects. The AFC was an unfortunate turning point. Its impact lasted for many years, with public spending on infrastructure, as a percentage of GDP, plummeting from 5.34% in fiscal year (FY) 1993/1994 to 2.33% in FY2002 (Mustajab 2010).

According to estimates based on a 2005 social accounting matrix of Indonesia, Rp1 trillion investment in infrastructure generates about 27,000 full-time equivalent jobs (Chatani and Ernst 2011). But the number of jobs actually generated is much higher than this estimate, because many construction jobs are temporary. Analysis based on an input–output table has limitations, because it assumes a linear relation between input and output (i.e., no scale effect) and it postulates that actors maintain constant behavior. Bearing these shortcomings in mind, a social accounting matrix and an employment satellite account (i.e., a matrix of sectoral employment information per unit of expenditure) can generate a rough estimate of the effect that public expenditure has on employment. An employment satellite account can be disaggregated by gender, age group, and geographical location to gain further insight. A reduction in the ratio of public infrastructure spending to GDP by 3 percentage points in 2002 was equivalent to a budget cut in infrastructure development by Rp54.7 trillion in that year. This might have reduced employment opportunities by about 1.5 million jobs across the economy in 2002 alone. The analysis operates with a margin of error, and thus the figure may not be very precise, but it illustrates well the negative impact of reduced infrastructure spending on employment. If infrastructure's effect on economic activities (e.g., better access to markets) is incorporated into the calculation, the potential job loss and missed opportunities for job creation due to the reduced public spending in infrastructure development will be greater than the estimate.

9.2.6. Business Environment

Another key factor causing weak growth of productive employment is slow creation of enterprises. Table 9.8 compares the number of registered business establishments per 1,000 citizens in selected Association of Southeast Asian Nations countries and other economies. The scarcity of formal businesses

Table 9.8: Number of Registered Businesses per 1,000 Citizens and Poverty Incidence

	2001	2002	2003	2004	2005	2006	Population Below $1.25 a Day (%)	Year	Population Below $2 a Day (%)
Brazil	26.5	27.7	28.6	29.2	30.5	...	5.2	2007	12.7
Hong Kong, China	55.9	56.4	59.1	62.0	65.9	71.7	neg.		neg.
India	0.6	0.6	0.6	0.6	0.7	0.7	41.6	2005	75.6
Indonesia	1.0	1.1	1.1	1.1	1.2	1.2	21.4	2005	53.8
Russian Federation	12.5	14.1	16.0	17.9	20.3	20.8	0.2	2005	1.5
Singapore	20.6	21.0	22.3	23.5	24.1	26.3	neg.		neg.
Thailand	3.6	3.6	3.7	3.9	4.1	4.3	0.4	2005	11.5
Viet Nam	0.2	0.3	0.4	0.5	0.6	...	21.5	2008	48.4

... = not available; neg. = negligible.
Sources: World Bank, World Databank; ILO (2009c); author's calculations.

stands out in India, Indonesia, and Viet Nam compared with other selected economies. Growth in the number of registered businesses between 2001 and 2005 was also nearly flat in India and Indonesia. Indonesia, for example, had merely 0.2 more formal enterprises per 1,000 people in 2005 than in 2001. This does not compare well with the records of other economies. During the same period, the number of formal businesses increased by 3.5 per 1,000 people in Brazil; 4.0 in Hong Kong, China; and 10.0 in Singapore. It is important to note that poverty incidences are considerably higher in countries with a low density of formal businesses. Poverty data are not available for Hong Kong, China and for Singapore, but their poverty incidences are likely to be very low. Although Table 9.8 does not prove a causal relationship between the density of registered businesses and poverty, it strongly indicates that, where formal enterprises are not well developed, a large proportion of workers are forced to engage in low-productivity economic activities in the informal economy, thus resulting in a high probability of workers living in poverty.

A comparison among countries indicates that those with a higher share of formal businesses appear to have an environment that is conducive to establishing new businesses. Table 9.9 shows the share of newly registered enterprises in total enterprises in selected economies. Those that have a high number of formal enterprises per 1,000 people tend to allow easy entrance of new enterprises into the markets. In fact, in 2005, the share of enterprises that were new was 14.7% in Hong Kong, China; 19.0% in Singapore; and 13.0% in the Russian Federation. These economies also had a high density of registered businesses per 1,000 people in the same year, at 65.9, 24.1, and 20.3, respectively. Economies that have higher shares of formal businesses appear to have a more conducive environment for establishing new businesses than other economies. A high rate of new business entrance

Table 9.9: Business Entry Rate (new registrations as % of total)

	2000	2001	2002	2003	2004	2005	2006	2007
Brazil	11.2	10.5	9.0	9.1	8.6	8.7	...	...
Hong Kong, China	10.5	11.1	10.4	12.5	12.4	14.7	15.2	15.4
India	...	3.7	3.8	4.4	5.6	5.3	2.7	...
Indonesia	...	4.6	3.0	3.0	1.7	7.8	7.0	...
Russian Federation	14.0	13.4	12.1	12.7	11.9	13.0	16.3	15.0
Singapore	...	10.0	12.9	14.8	17.5	19.0	18.6	19.4
Thailand	8.2	8.7	9.6	11.1	12.2	12.0	10.5	8.5

... = not available.
Source: World Bank, World Databank.

thus implies that the private sector taps effectively into the latent growth potential of the economy and creates productive employment.

Indonesia's low business entry rate appears to stem in part from the high costs and long time required to start a business. Indonesian entrepreneurs have to spend more days and capital to start a business than entrepreneurs in other selected Asian economies (Table 9.10). Further, regulations on businesses and the business start-up environment vary significantly from province to province because of decentralization. *Doing Business in Indonesia 2010* (World Bank and IFC 2010) compared the ease of starting a business in 14 major Indonesian cities,[5] noting it took 43 days to start a business in even the best performing cities in Indonesia—Bandung and Yogyakarta (Table 9.11). Other Indonesian cities ranked even lower. The two cities ranked

Table 9.10: Time and Cost to Start a Business in Selected Countries (2009)

	Time Required to Start a Business (days)	Cost to Start a Business (% of GNI per capita)
Hong Kong, China	6	1.8
India	30	66.1
Indonesia (Jakarta)	60	26.0
Malaysia	18	15.6
Russian Federation	30	2.7
Singapore	3	0.7
Thailand	32	6.3
Viet Nam	50	13.3

GNI = gross national income.
Source: World Bank, World Databank.

Table 9.11: Time and Cost to Start a Business in Selected Indonesian Cities (2009)

Indicator	Best Performing City (global rank among 183 economies)	Worst Performing City
Days to Start a Business	Yogyakarta and Bandung 43 days (143)	Jakarta 60 days
Cost to Start a Business	Jakarta 26% of income per capita (117)	Manado 38.3% of income per capita

Source: World Bank and IFC (2010).

---

5   Balikpapan, Banda Aceh, Bandung, Denpasar, Jakarta, Makassar, Manado, Pekanbaru, Palangka Raya, Palembang, Semarang, Surabaya, Surakarta, and Yogyakarta.

143rd among the 183 economies. Thus, Indonesian cities are not competitive in terms of cost of starting a business or the time taken to do so.

9.2.7. Access to Capital and Enterprise Development

In addition to onerous business regulations that appear to hamper business development in Indonesia, access to capital constrains the growth of small and medium-sized enterprises (SMEs).[6] Because SMEs are the backbone of the economy and the largest employers in most countries, development of SMEs heavily influences employment creation. In fact, the vast majority of enterprises in Indonesia are SMEs (Table 9.12), with 98.9% of business establishments categorized as microenterprises according to Law No. 20 of 2008 concerning SMEs. Credit distribution by size of enterprise, however, is virtually the reverse picture of this. Large enterprises take the lion's share of bank credit (both working capital and investment); the SMEs' share is merely 15.1% (Figure 9.5); and microenterprises, which are the vast majority of establishments, account for merely 2.8% of bank credit. Only 16.5% of working capital and 11.4% of investment capital were distributed to SMEs in January 2011 (Table 9.13). The skewed credit distribution reflects the risk-averse nature of Indonesia's banks. Given the limited access that SMEs, especially microenterprises, have to credit, it can be safely inferred that entrepreneurs without good track records in business will have very limited access to credit. Anecdotal evidence suggests that banks request substantial collateral from risky borrowers, including entrepreneurs. Incomplete land registration exacerbates the access to capital.

Table 9.12: Distribution of Business Establishments by Size (%)

Size	Share (%)
Micro	98.90
Small	1.01
Medium	0.08
Large	0.01

Source: BPS (2009).

---

6   Law no. 20 of 2008 concerning SMEs classifies enterprises by size as follows:
- microenterprise is a privately owned and/or individual business entity that has a net worth not exceeding Rp50 million (excluding land and building) or has annual sales revenue not exceeding Rp300 million.
- small enterprise is a business entity (not including subsidiaries) that has a net worth of more than Rp50 million but not exceeding Rp500 million (excluding land and building business) or has annual sales of more than Rp300 million but not exceeding Rp2.5 billion.
- medium enterprise is a business entity that has a net worth of more than Rp500 million but not exceeding Rp10 billion (excluding land and building business) or has annual sales of more than Rp2.5 billion but not exceeding Rp50 billion.

Figure 9.5: Credit (Working Capital and Investment) Distribution by Size of Enterprise (%)

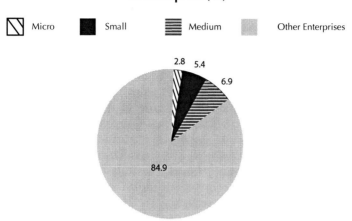

Sources: Bank Indonesia (2011); author's calculations.

Table 9.13: Outstanding Credit by Type and Category of Debtor (January 2011)

	Working capital	Investment
Amount (Rp billion)		
SMEs	282,705	77,960
Large enterprises	1,427,535	606,303
Share (%)		
SMEs	16.5	11.4
Large enterprises	83.5	88.6

Sources: Bank Indonesia (2011); author's calculations.

9.2.8. Shift to Services Employment

While growth of labor-intensive manufacturing has slowed, that of the services sector has gained momentum. The services sector has accounted for over half of Indonesia's economic expansion since 2005 (Figure 9.6). The development of the communications sector has been particularly robust, reflecting rigorous investment in telecommunication infrastructure to support an increasing number of mobile phone and internet users. The annual average growth rates of agriculture and manufacturing between 2004 and 2009 were 3.7% and 3.9%, respectively, which were below the industry's average of 5.6% (Table 9.14). Employment generally reflects this shift in economic structure, as attested by the changes in sectoral shares in employment of the last decade (Table 9.15). The agriculture sector's share of total employment dropped a significant 5.6 percentage points between 2000 and 2009. The share of manufacturing employment declined slightly during 2000–2009. Consequently, employment opportunities have increasingly been created in the services sector.

Education levels of the workforce appear to be a determining factor in the shift from an agrarian to an industry-based economy, and further to a more knowledge-based economy because of the higher skills required by secondary and tertiary industries (see Chapter 8 on human capital). Although Indonesian students increasingly pursue higher education, the level of human capital endowment in the workforce may still constrain a smooth shift from agriculture to services. The skills demand from the growing services sector has increased return from education, widening the wage gap by educational attainment (see section 4.2). This wage trend signals a skills shortage at the higher end of the labor market.

Figure 9.6: Contribution to Growth by Sector (%)

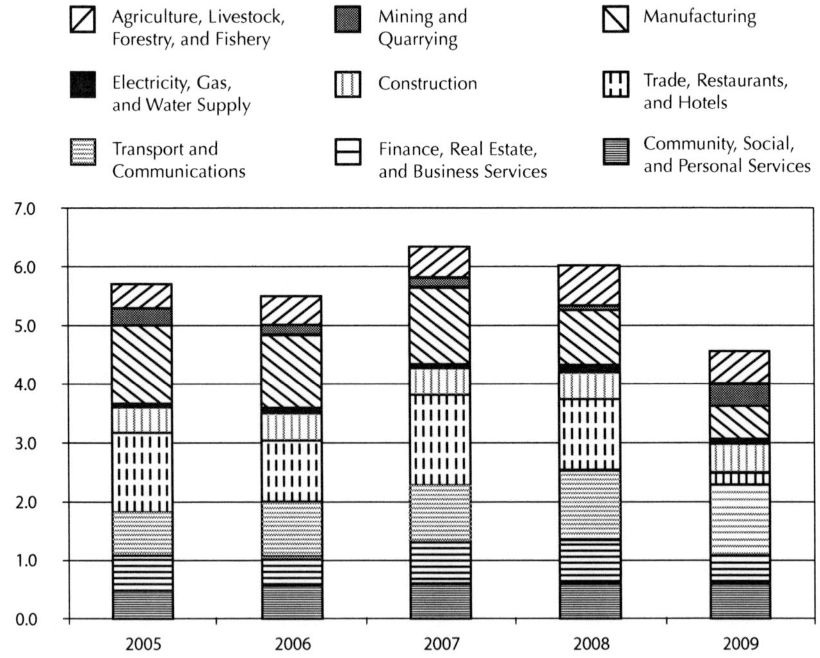

Sources: BPS Website; author's calculations.

Table 9.14: Share and Growth of Output and Employment by Sector (GDP at 2000 constant market prices)

Sector	Sector Share of GDP (2009, %)	Sector Share of Employment (2009, %)	Average Annual Output Growth (2004–2009, %)	Average Annual Employment Growth (2004–2009, %)
Agriculture	13.6	39.7	3.7	0.5
Mining and Quarrying	8.3	1.1	2.4	2.2
Manufacturing	26.2	12.2	3.9	3.0
Electricity, Gas, and Water	0.8	0.2	9.4	-0.5
Construction	6.4	5.2	7.8	3.9
Trade, Restaurants, and Hotels	16.9	20.9	6.3	2.8
Transportation, Storage, and Communications	8.8	5.8	14.6	2.2
Financing, Insurance, Real Estate, and Business Services	9.6	1.4	6.7	5.7
Community, Social, and Personal Services	9.4	13.4	6.1	5.9
Total	**100.0**	**100.0**	**5.6**	**2.3**

GDP = gross domestic product
Sources: BPS Website; author's calculations.

Table 9.15: Sector Share in Employment (%)

Year	2000	2005	2009
Agriculture	45.3	44.0	39.7
Mining and Quarrying	0.5	1.0	1.1
Manufacturing	13.0	12.7	12.2
Electricity, Gas, and Water	0.1	0.2	0.2
Construction	3.9	4.9	5.2
Trade, Restaurants, and Hotels	20.6	19.1	20.9
Transportation, Storage, and Communications	5.1	6.0	5.8
Financing, Insurance, Real Estate, and Business Services	1.0	1.2	1.4
Community, Social, and Personal Services	10.7	11.0	13.4
Total	**100.0**	**100.0**	**100.0**

Sources: BPS, Labor Force Situation in Indonesia (various years).

9.2.9. Labor Regulations, Investment, and Employment Creation

The regulatory framework and labor market institutions underwent substantial change after the AFC. Several important labor regulations were enacted: the Trade Union Act of 2001, the Manpower Act of 2003, the Industrial Dispute Resolution Act of 2004, the Migrant Worker Act of 2004, and the Social Security Act of 2004. Indonesia also ratified five International Labour Organization (ILO) conventions[7] between 1998 and 2000, including the Freedom of Association and Protection of the Right to Organise Convention (C87) in 1998, the Abolition of Forced Labour Convention (C105) in 1999, and the Elimination of the Worst Forms of Child Labour Convention (C182) in 2000. In addition, the upsurge of labor unions fundamentally changed the picture of industrial relations in Indonesia. Another significant factor that has been affecting the regulatory environment governing the labor market is decentralization. Minimum wage setting, industrial relations, and vocational training are largely governed at the local level.

Some observers who evaluated these changes in labor regulations and labor market institutions blamed them, especially the generous severance pay and rapid increase in minimum wages, for stagnant investment and employment growth (Aswicahyono, Hill, and Narjoko 2011; OECD 2008; Suryahadi et al. 2003;). Critics of these labor regulations argue that rigid regulations in the labor market increased the cost of adjustment to demand fluctuations, making Indonesia a less attractive destination for potential investors. For example, the Organisation for Economic Co-operation and Development ascribed a slowdown in job growth, high unemployment among the youth, and widespread informality to the Manpower Act of 2003, which tightened employment protection legislation, and to a rapid rise in minimum wages (OECD 2008).

Indonesia imposes high firing costs. In fact, Indonesian labor market flexibility does not fare well among the 133 economies surveyed by the World Economic Forum (WEF 2009). The country is ranked in 98th position and is among the most rigid labor markets of the eight selected countries in the region (Table 9.16). Malaysia and Thailand are ranked as having flexible labor markets. Though the firing costs in the eight countries compared are

---

[7]   Indonesia has ratified all the core conventions of the ILO: Forced Labour (C29), Freedom of Association and Protection of the Right to Organize (C87), Right to Organize and Collective Bargaining (C98), Equal Remuneration (C100), Abolition of Forced Labour (C105), Discrimination (Employment and Occupation) (C111), Minimum Age Convention (C138), and Elimination of the Worst Forms of Child Labour (C182).

**Table 9.16: Ranking of Labor Market Efficiency
(selected Asian countries, of 133 countries total)**

		Indonesia	Cambodia	Malaysia	Philippines	Thailand	Viet Nam	PRC	India
A	Flexibility	98	74	28	111	31	68	91	69
	Cooperation in labor–employer relations	42	105	19	65	28	49	60	40
	Hiring and firing practices	34	36	46	110	29	24	77	103
	Flexibility of wage determination	92	75	54	96	89	79	53	44
	Firing costs	119	71	96	109	84	104	109	85
	Rigidity of employment	82	92	14	68	24	35	43	54
B	Efficient use of talent	54	46	47	97	31	27	13	88
	Pay and productivity	29	50	9	74	38	6	12	46
	Reliance on professional management	55	109	29	48	61	82	46	30
	Brain drain	25	51	31	104	32	76	39	41
	Female participation in labour force	104	28	107	99	53	14	20	122
	Labor Market Efficiency (A+B)	75	52	31	113	25	38	32	83

PRC = People's Republic of China.
For the methodology, please refer to Apendix A and section 1.2 of the source.
Source: WEF (2009).

generally high, Indonesia leads the group. The index of Economic Freedom[8] shows similar results for labor freedom.

The question is, to what extent does labor market rigidity deter investment in Indonesia? According to the World Economic Forum's *Global Competitiveness Report 2009–2010*, labor rigidity is not among the top five hindrances to undertaking business in Indonesia (Figure 9.7). Survey research by the University of Indonesia confirms the findings, ranking labor

---

[8] The index of economic freedom is compiled by the Heritage Foundation. For details, see http://www.heritage.org/Index/

regulation only 11th as a business constraint (LPEM–FEUI 2007), with the top three constraints related to macroeconomic instability, transport, and corruption. This suggests that labor rigidity is a minor issue versus factors such as insufficient infrastructure and onerous bureaucracy, as documented in the surveys. That employers circumvent onerous and costly labor regulations by hiring contract workers or by resorting to outsourcing might also have affected employers' perceptions of business constraints in Indonesia.

Potential investors examine various aspects of the business environment, including geographic location, infrastructure, political stability, corruption, taxation, availability of labor and its skills level, labor costs, and industrial relations. The rigidity of labor regulations is merely one of the factors that influence investors' decision. Indeed, if the rigidity of labor regulations alone determines investment and employment creation, as critics asserted, then the PRC's recent performance in attracting investment and creating employment opportunities is hard to explain, given that the PRC labor market is nearly as rigid as that in Indonesia.

Figure 9.7: The Five Most Problematic Factors for Doing Business in Indonesia

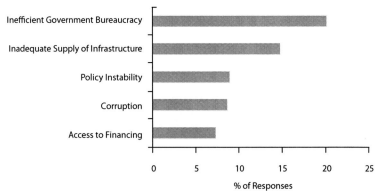

Source: WEF (2009).

Importantly, while labor regulations might be considered rigid, compliance with the regulations, such as the minimum wage and severance payment requirements, is particularly low, although these are the two primary targets of criticism from people who are campaigning for more lenient labor regulations. The low compliance is mostly because of high informality in economic activities and the weak capacity of the labor administration to enforce the law. The share of workers being paid less than the applicable minimum wage has been on the rise (Figure 9.8), reaching 43.7% in 2009. It appears that recent hikes in the minimum wage simply pushed more workers below the minimum, rather than serving as a floor that supports the workers' income above the poverty line. The real wages of workers who could be supported by the minimum wage regulations have been declining since 2005 (Figure 9.3). The minimum wages are set based on living wages (the minimum income that meets a worker's basic needs) for an adult, not for a family. Earning below the applicable minimum wage probably implies that the worker's family is destitute. Similarly, the record of compliance with the severance payment requirement is poor. The vast majority of terminated employees who were entitled to severance payment did not receive part or all of it (Table 9.17). In 2008, only 7% of terminated workers who were eligible for severance payment received it in full.

Figure 9.8: Share of Employees Who Receive Wages Below the Applicable Minimum Wage (%)

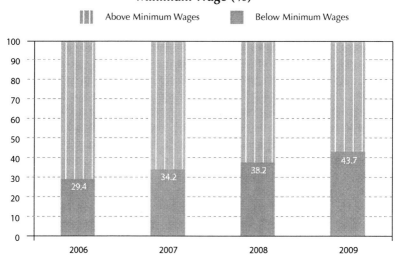

Source: BPS, Labor Force Situation in Indonesia (various years).

Table 9.17: Compliance with Legal Severance Payment Requirements (2008)

Degree of Compliance	Share
Terminated Employees Receiving Full Amount or More	7%
Less than the Entitled Amount	27%
No Severance Pay	66%

Source: World Bank (2010).

The evidence suggests that labor relations alone are not the culprit of suboptimal growth and sluggish employment growth; rather, it is due to a combination of factors such as insufficient development of infrastructure, governance, and human capital (ADB, ILO, and IDB 2010). Companies circumvent regulations by hiring casual employees or by outsourcing, thus avoiding the costs imposed by regulations. Consequently, the labor market regulations might have affected the quality of employment. An increase in the number of people in unstable employment without social protection has certainly affected the capacity of employment opportunities to distribute the fruit of economic growth and thus to reduce poverty. The next section sheds light on the link between employment and poverty reduction.

9.3. Quality of Employment, Access to Productive Employment, and Poverty

This section investigates the employment–poverty reduction nexus. Employment opportunities provide a means of escaping poverty, but the poverty alleviation effect of employment depends on the quality of employment and access to productive employment. Productive employment is defined for the purpose of this chapter as employment that provides workers with sufficient income to escape from poverty. Being in employment does not necessarily mean living out of poverty, as evidenced by the large share of the Indonesian workforce comprising the working poor. Similarly, a low unemployment rate does not always imply a low poverty incidence. The access to employment determines the degree to which the economy efficiently involves the economically active population in production, thus affecting the inclusiveness of growth. The state of access to employment can be observed through the lens of the employment–poverty nexus in developing countries including Indonesia. This is because having access to full and productive employment provides a means to escape from poverty. The following subsections examine poverty trends in Indonesia and relations between employment and poverty.

9.3.1. Trends in Poverty

The economic growth during 1993–2005, except during and in the aftermath of the AFCof 1997, considerably reduced headcount poverty incidences[9] and

---

[9]   "Headcount poverty" is defined as the share of the population living below international poverty lines ($1.25 and $2 a day, both measured on a purchasing power parity basis).

the share of the working poor.[10] The incidence of extreme poverty (the share of the population living below the $1.25 poverty line) was more than halved between 1993 and 2005, from 54.4% to 21.4%. The incidence of poverty as measured by the $2-a-day poverty line also charted a considerable drop, of 30.8 percentage points (Table 9.18). The incidence of working poverty depicts similar trends. The sustained trend of economic growth during 1993–2005 lifted a large proportion of the population and the workforce out of poverty.

Table 9.18: Poverty, Working Poverty, and Income Distribution Inequality

Year	Intn'l poverty Line: Population below $1.25 a Day (%)	Intn'l Poverty Line: Population below $2 a day (%)	Share of Working Poor at $1.25 a day in Total Employment (%)	Share of Working Poor at $2 a day in Total Employment (%)
1993	54.4	84.6	65.4	91.2
1996	43.4	77.0	52.5	86.4
1999	47.7	81.5	58.5	91.0
2002	29.3	66.9	37.2	81.4
2005	21.4	53.8	27.8	71.1

Sources: International poverty line: World Bank, PovcalNet; working poor: ILO (2009c).

Despite the laudable pace of poverty reduction, that more than 70% of Indonesia's workers live below the poverty line of $2 a day warrants further efforts at poverty reduction by creating productive employment and delivering decent work. As this chapter discusses later, the economic expansion of the past decade was not employment rich. A dense income distribution of workers within the narrow range between $1.25 and $2 a day implies that they are highly vulnerable to falling into abject poverty, especially if they are subject to shocks such as a downswing of the economy, job loss, injury, or sickness. The success of poverty reduction in the recent past rests on a fragile foundation. Addressing the vulnerability of the workforce to poverty is also important for sustainable economic growth, given the high share of private consumption in the GDP.

---

[10] The "working poor" is defined as employed people living in a household whose members are estimated to be below the poverty line. The number of working poor can be estimated by taking the product of the poverty rate and labor force aged 15 years and above (ILO 2009b).

9.3.2. Unemployment, Education, and Poverty

The high incidence of working poverty does not necessarily stem from open unemployment.[11] In the absence of unemployment insurance, most poor people cannot afford a protracted spell of unemployment. Table 9.19 reveals a significantly high poverty incidence among the least educated, but higher unemployment among those with higher education. Thus, the causes of the high poverty incidence among workers with relatively less education are not related to unemployment, but rather to the low productivity of their economic activity and thus low earnings.

It appears that poverty incidence and education are negatively correlated. Although unemployment rates for people with senior secondary and tertiary education are relatively high at 19.9% and 11.9%, respectively, their probabilities of being in poverty are significantly lower. This is primarily because the educated people have better access to well-remunerated jobs. As this chapter argued earlier, skills demand has been shifting to reward education as the services sector expands. Figure 9.9 demonstrates that wages are increasingly a function of education. Indeed, in 2009, the average monthly wages for workers with tertiary education were about four times the wages of people with primary education. Comola and de Mello (2009) estimated wage determinants of earnings of Indonesian workers, both formal and informal workers, by applying a multinomial selection model to household survey (Susenas) data from 1996 and 2004. They found that returns to education are more linear than found by estimates using a binomial model. The wage gap between university graduates and other workers has been widening. High remuneration for skills constitutes a factor for the high

Table 9.19: Unemployment and Poverty by Educational Attainment (2005)

Highest Education Attained	Unemployment Rate (%)	Poverty Incidence (%)
Less than Primary	5.5	19.6
Primary	7.0	13.8
Junior Secondary	14.1	9.3
Senior Secondary	19.9	4.4
Tertiary	11.9	0.4

Note: "Less than primary" = did not finish primary school.
Source: Dhanani, Islam, and Chowdhury (2009).

---

[11] "Open unemployment" refers to unemployment captured by official labor statistics. The term is often used to distinguish "official unemployment" from "discouraged unemployment" and other forms of underutilization of labor.

Figure 9.9: Index of Nominal Monthly Wages by Educational Attainment (wages for workers with primary education=100)

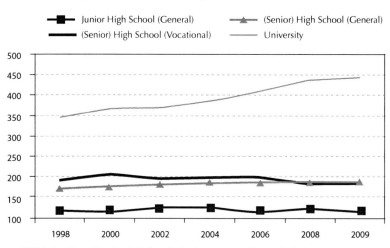

Sources: BPS, Labor Force Situation in Indonesia (various years); author's calculations.

unemployment rate among the educated, because a good job is generally worth waiting for and they can afford to wait.

The Indonesian labor market exhibits a vicious combination of a deficit of formal employment and an abundance of low-skilled workers. This phenomenon works against the access of workers without high educational qualification to formal wage employment. As a result, workers with a modest educational background work predominantly in the informal economy and are often underemployed (Table 9.20). That low unemployment coexists with high incidences of underemployment among workers with poor educational background suggests a limited supply of jobs and income opportunities being shared among numerous poor workers. Table 9.20 also shows a worrying sign: a continuous increase in the incidence of informal employment irrespective of the level of education. Informal employment is a cause of working poor because of meager working conditions: underemployment causes poverty even in the formal economy (Alisjahbana and Manning 2006).

Table 9.21 statistically summarizes the discussion thus far. It shows correlation coefficients between unemployment rates, the share of informal employment[12] in total employment, and headcount poverty index by province. The unit of observation is the province. The table clearly shows a tendency for a high incidence of informal employment in a province to occur with high headcount poverty in the province. As previously discussed,

---

[12]   Badan Pusat Statistik (Statistiks Indonesia) defines informal employment by using a matrix of employment status and main occupation (see ILO 2010).

Table 9.20: Unemployment, Underemployment, and Informal Employment by Education (%)

Category/ Year	Primary or Lower	Junior Secondary	Senior Secondary	Tertiary
Unemployment				
1996	2.3	7.8	14.1	12.0
2002	5.5	12.3	16.8	10.6
2009	4.5	9.4	13.5	13.9
Underemployment				
1996	40.6	29.1	21.1	19.7
2002	37.9	26.1	17.3	21.5
2009	36.8	30.0	17.7	15.5
Informal Employment				
1996	67.1	50.1	24.8	7.1
2002	77.5	59.7	32.1	8.2
2009	78.0	64.6	36.4	9.8

Note: The definition of unemployment was broadened in 2001; thus it requires caution in time series comparison. The three last columns indicate people who have completed those levels.
Sources: Computed using BPS Labor Force Situation in Indonesia (1996, 2002, and 2009).

Table 9.21: Matrix Correlating Agricultural Employment, Unemployment, and Informal Employment

	Share of Agricultural Employment	Unemployment Rate	Informal Employment
Share of Agricultural Employment			
Unemployment Rate	−0.57		
Informal Employment Rate	0.92	−0.57	
Headcount Poverty Index	0.39	0.02	0.44

Sources: Unemployment and informal employment are sourced from BPS, Labor Force Situation in Indonesia (February 2009); headcount poverty index from the BPS Website.

unemployment does not necessarily determine poverty incidences, as implied by the low correlation coefficient (0.02) between the two variables. Outside plantations, most agricultural employment is informal, which explains the high correlation between the share of agricultural employment and informal employment. The agriculture sector tends to absorb surplus labor at the expense of labor productivity, resulting in poverty among agriculture workers.

9.3.3. Geographic Dimensions of the Employment–Poverty Nexus

Analysis of employment and poverty by geographic area reveals that the lack of productive employment opportunities in rural agrarian areas constitutes a key factor for persistent poverty. Table 9.22 reveals that 82.1% of the working poor are in rural areas, where employment opportunities are scarce. Because Indonesia is an archipelago of large and small islands in a vast area, employment opportunities are concentrated in places such as Jakarta, Medan, and Surabaya; this constitutes a geographical dimension of poverty incidence. In addition, the wage gap between urban and rural areas has been widening since 2000 (Table 9.23)—the average rural wages were more than three-quarters of the average urban wages in 2000 but fell to two-thirds in 2009.

Table 9.22: Distribution of the Working Poor by Sector, Geographical Area, and Gender (2007, %)

Sector	Urban	Rural	Male	Female	Total
Agriculture	5.2	60.3	39.3	26.2	65.5
Industry	4.1	9.1	8.8	4.4	13.3
Services	8.5	12.7	12.8	8.4	21.2
Total	17.9	82.1	60.9	39.1	100

Note: The poverty line: $1.25 a day.
Sources: Calculations by International Labour Organization based on BPS, Susenas Kore (various years).

Arguably, people who live far from where numerous employment opportunities are found are disadvantaged in accessing employment and thus are more likely to be among the working poor. The ratio of the number of employees to total workers varies considerably by province, from 0.66 in Jakarta to 0.11 in Nusa Tenggara Timur, with the national average being 0.31. Rural areas in general lack sufficient productive employment opportunities, and most people in such areas engage in agriculture. Figure 9.10 reveals an uneven distribution of formal/informal employment among provinces. Almost three quarters of employment in Jakarta is formal, whereas over 80% of employment in eastern provinces such as Papua and Nusa Tenggara Timur is informal. In sum, productive employment opportunities are unevenly distributed throughout Indonesia, with workers in rural areas generally disadvantaged in their efforts to earn enough to stay out of poverty.

Table 9.23: Monthly Wage Trends

	2000	2003	2006	2009
Monthly Nominal Wages in Rupiah and Weekly Working Hours				
By Sex				
Male	481,308	739,473	905,503	1,191,059
weekly working hours	45	44	44	44
Female	326,035	549,098	693,987	927,745
weekly working hours	42	41	41	41
By Area				
Urban	489,841	804,548	1,004,516	1,341,872
weekly working hours	45	45	46	45
Rural	342,196	498,276	619,321	795,225
weekly working hours	41	40	40	40
Total	430,197	684,915	839,996	1,103,234
weekly working hours	44	43	43	43
Consumer Price Index (2000=100)	100	133.0	176.5	219.8
Monthly Wage Index (2000=100)				
By Sex				
Male	100	118	109	115
Female	100	130	124	133
By Area				
Urban	100	124	114	125
Rural	100	112	105	108
Total	100	123	113	119
Wage Ratio				
Female/Male	0.73	0.80	0.82	0.84
Rural/Urban	0.77	0.70	0.71	0.67

Note: Employee includes employee and casual employee. Wages are adjusted on pro-rata basis to 40 hours of work per week in calculating real wage index and wage ratios.

Sources: Wage data from BPS, Labor Force Situation in Indonesia (various years); consumer price index from World Bank, World Databank; author's calculations.

9.3.4. A Closer Look at Agricultural Employment and Poverty

Table 9.22 also shows that 65.5% of the working poor engaged in agriculture. This concentration is a result of low wages and shorter working hours in the sector. The average hourly wages are significantly lower in agriculture than in other sectors (Table 9.24). For example, hourly agricultural wages were 59.1% of those in industry and 65.4% of those in manufacturing. The wage gaps widen for weekly wages because the average working hours in agriculture are shorter than in the other sectors. Agricultural workers averaged 34 hours weekly, which was about 20% less than for industry. As a consequence, the average weekly wage in agriculture (Rp501,001) is less than half the national average weekly wage for industry total (Rp1,071,886). Shorter weekly working hours in agriculture indicate a lack of full employment and an oversupply of workers in agriculture. Alisjahbana and Manning (2006) noted that agriculture workers are prone to be poor or near poor whether they are fully employment or underemployed, and the households whose breadwinners were underemployed in agriculture were highly likely to live below or near the poverty line.

Table 9.24: Average Weekly Working Hours and Wages by Industry (2008)

Sector	Weekly Working Hours	Weekly Wages (Rp)	Hourly Wage (Rp)
Agriculture	34	501,001	3,401
Mining and Quarrying	46	1,699,374	8,526
Manufacturing	45	1,014,461	5,203
Electricity, Gas, and Water	43	1,913,074	10,268
Construction	46	1,001,215	5,023
Trade, Restaurants, and Hotels	50	1,001,395	4,622
Transportation, Storage, and Communications	48	1,521,501	7,315
Finance, Insurance, Real Estate, and Business Services	45	1,950,236	10,002
Community, Social, and Personal Services	43	1,387,234	7,445
Total	43	**1,071,886**	**5,753**

Sources: BPS, Labor Force Situation in Indonesia (August 2008); author's calculations.

Figure 9.10: Unemployment, Informal Employment, and Headcount Poverty Index by Province (2009)

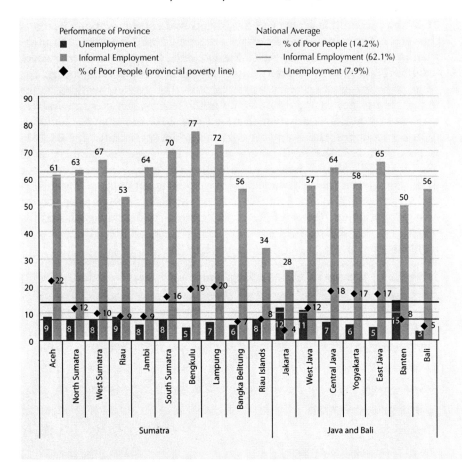

Sources: For the unemployment rate, BPS, Labor Force Survey (accessed August 2010); for informal employment, BPS, Labor Force Survey (accessed February 2010), and for poverty, BPS Website (accessed March 2011).

9.3.5. Employment Status and Poverty

Quality of employment constitutes another facet of the employment–poverty nexus. Certain types of employment status are more highly associated with poverty than others. Figure 9.11 illustrates high incidences of working poverty among casual workers, unpaid family workers, and own-account workers. This concentration reflects the low wages that such workers earn. For example, the average monthly earnings of casual workers in agriculture

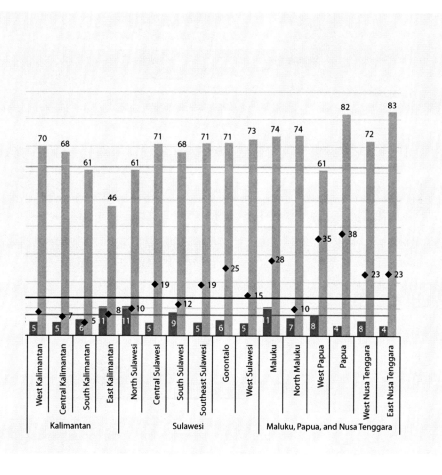

are less than a third that of employees (Table 9.25). The wage gap between casual workers in nonagriculture sectors and wage employees is narrower, but casual workers' earnings are only about 54% of the employees' wages per month. Compared with wage employees, casual workers have more precarious contracts, fewer or no fringe benefits, and less labor and social protection, and they are less likely to be represented by trade unions.

Figure 9.11: Incidence of Working Poor by Employment Status ($1.25 per day poverty line, 2007)

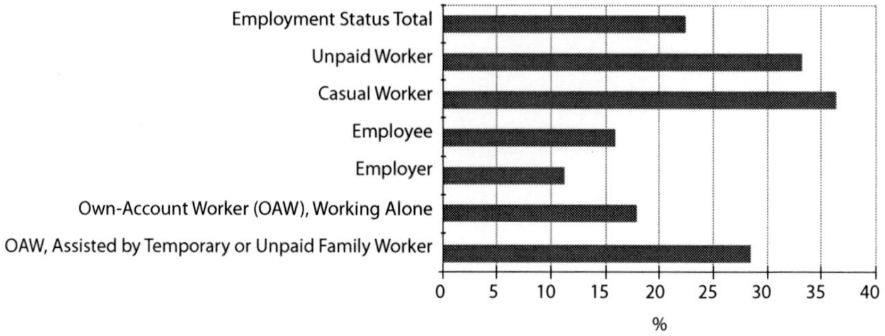

Sources: ILO calculations based on BPS, Susenas (various years).

Table 9.25: Monthly Income and Working Hours by Status in Employment (2010)

Employment	Monthly Income (Rp)	Monthly Income ($)	Weekly Work (hours)
Employee	1,410,982	156.8	45
Casual Employee in Agriculture	451,416	50.2	34
Casual Employee not in Agriculture	762,517	84.7	45

Note: Exchange rate used: $1=Rp9,000.
Sources: BPS, Laborer Situation in Indonesia (2010); author's calculations.

The recent trends of employment growth by employment status are a worrying sign of a slowdown in poverty reduction, as casual employment has been growing rapidly (Table 9.26). The increase of casual employment in agriculture was double that in total employment from 2002 to 2009, and nonagricultural casual employment expanded at an alarming pace of 6.9% annually. Consequently, the share of casual employment increased (Table 9.27). If this trend continues, it will mount a serious challenge to poverty reduction efforts.

Education appears to influence the employment status of workers. Figure 9.12 presents the breakdown of the educational background of workers by employment status. Employees, many of whom are in the formal economy and earn higher wages than workers with other employment status, have higher educational attainment. Close to 58.2% of employees have at least

Table 9.26: Employment Growth by Status in Employment

Employment	2002	2009	Annual Growth Rate (%)
Own-Account Worker	17,632,909	21,046,007	2.6
Employer, Assisted by Temporary/Unpaid Worker	22,019,393	21,933,546	−0.1
Employer, Assisted by Permanent Worker	2,786,226	3,033,220	1.2
Employee	25,049,793	29,114,041	2.2
Casual Employee in Agriculture	4,513,600	5,878,894	3.8
Casual Employee not in Agriculture	3,559,927	5,670,709	6.9
Unpaid Family Worker	16,085,318	18,194,246	1.8
Total	91,647,166	104,870,663	1.9

Sources: BPS, Labor Force Situation in Indonesia (various years); author's calculations.

Table 9.27: Shares in Employment by Status in Employment (%)

Employment	2002	2006	2009
Own-Account Worker	19.2	20.4	20.1
Employer, Assisted by Temporary/Unpaid Worker	24.0	20.9	20.9
Employer, Assisted by Permanent Worker	3.0	3.0	2.9
Employee	27.3	28.1	27.8
Casual Employee in Agriculture	4.9	5.8	5.6
Casual Employee not in Agriculture	3.9	4.8	5.4
Unpaid Family Worker	17.6	16.9	17.3

Sources: BPS, Labor Force Situation in Indonesia (various years); author's calculations.

secondary education, and about one-fifth of them have tertiary education. Conversely, 82.8% of casual employees in agriculture have at best completed primary education. Education, therefore, is a key determinant of the access to productive employment and thus an important driver of reducing poverty on the supply side.

Figure 9.12: Share of Workers by Employment Status and Highest Educational Attainment (2010, %)

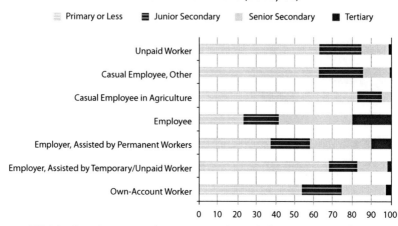

Sources: BPS, Labor Force Situation in Indonesia (2010); author's calculations.

9.4. Conclusions and Suggested Policy Options

This chapter examined the linkages between economic growth, employment creation, and poverty reduction in Indonesia, comparing the two periods before and after the AFC. After the crisis, the labor market recovered less well than economic growth, as the economy did not generate sufficient full and productive employment opportunities for the existing unemployed, underemployed, and discouraged workers, or for new entrants to the labor market.

The second section of this chapter noted several key factors that affected the capacity of the economy to generate employment in the decade after the AFC:

- First and foremost, the growth rate of the economy slowed. Net exports' contribution to growth declined, and the goods Indonesia exports have become increasingly based on exploiting natural resources, which generates little employment.
- Second, the growth of the labor-intensive manufacturing sector lost momentum; although Indonesia has surplus labor, labor-intensive manufacturing lost competitiveness to lower cost producers in the region.
- Third, diminished investment in public infrastructure particularly affected employment growth in the construction sector.
- Fourth, with the slowdown in manufacturing, the source of economic growth and employment creation has been shifting to the services sector; however, the skills level of the workforce does not

adequately support this structural shift (see Chapter 8 on human capital). So far, Indonesia has not successfully shifted from labor-intensive manufacturing to high value-added production (Islam and Chowdhury 2009).

- Fifth, the business environment is not very conducive to job-rich growth via enterprise development, due to onerous business regulations and because SMEs and entrepreneurs have insufficient access to capital.

The chapter also examined whether labor market regulations negatively affect creation of productive employment. Empirical evidence examined in this chapter suggests that addressing labor market rigidity alone will not lead to the creation of increased and more productive employment, because compliance with labor regulations is very low, and changing the regulations to match the reality is unlikely to generate employment. Other factors, such as underdeveloped infrastructure, poor governance, and suboptimal human capital endowments deter investment and employment creation in a significant manner (ADB, IDB, and ILO 2010). Labor regulations alone cannot be blamed for the slow growth of employment. Productive labor market reform must address two issues simultaneously: lack of social security and labor rigidity. The current system relies heavily on formal enterprises to provide income security against unemployment and retirement. Various social programs target the deprived and support them. Policymakers may wish to expand the fiscal space for social security to cover more workers. Constructive social dialogue among the parties concerned would help propel the labor market and social security reform agenda.

The third section of the chapter examined the linkage between employment and poverty alleviation. The Indonesian economy has maintained growth for decades except during the severe economic crisis in the late 1990s. Consequently, many workers have been able to successfully lift themselves above the poverty line.[13] Nevertheless, a large proportion of the workforce remains vulnerable to falling into poverty. Over 70% of workers earned less than $2 a day in 2005. Therefore, efforts to reduce poverty by creating full and productive employment need to be enhanced. Weak educational attainment and geographical remoteness from employment opportunities constrain access to employment, reducing the capacity of workers in rural areas or with low educational qualifications to earn their way out of poverty. As the data in this chapter suggest, underemployment, agricultural employment, and employment in the informal economy are associate with poverty. Casual employment, which is rapidly expanding, is also prone to poverty. To achieve sustainable poverty reduction will require (1) creating

---

[13] The consumption-based poverty indexes (e.g., $1.25 and $2 per day, measured at purchasing power parity) declined.

formal employment outside the agriculture sector, and (2) improving access to education by continuing efforts to increase the enrollment rates and the quality of secondary and tertiary education.

To create more employment in the formal economy, policymakers may wish to improve the business environment in Indonesia. The number of formal businesses per 1,000 people is low, and new business creation is rather sluggish compared with other regional countries. Reducing the time and costs required to start a new business and improving the access of SMEs and entrepreneurs to capital would change this picture and vitalize the private sector, leading to the creation of productive employment. Improved infrastructure and governance would also induce investment and employment creation, as discussed in other chapters.

On the labor demand side, enhancing the level of skills appears to be urgently needed in order to compete with other regional producers and gradually move to higher value-added segments of the market. To shift its industry to more sophisticated, capital- and knowledge-intensive production, Indonesia needs to upgrade the skills of its workforce. For the discussion and policy recommendation on human capital, see Chapter 8.

References

Alisjahbana, A. and C. Manning. 2006. Labour Market Dimensions of Poverty in Indonesia. *Bulletin of Indonesian Economic Studies*, 42(2): 235–61.

Asian Development Bank (ADB). 2010. *Key Indicators for Asia and the Pacific 2010*. Manila.

——— Statistical Database System (SDBS) Online. http://lxapp1.asiandevbank.org:8030/sdbs/jsp/index.jsp (accessed January 2011).

Asian Development Bank (ADB), International Labour Organization (ILO), and Islamic Development Bank (IDB). 2010. *Indonesia: Critical Development Constraints*. Manila.

Aswicahyono, H., H. Hill, and D. Narjoko. 2011. *Indonesian Industrialization: Jobless Growth?* In C. Manning and H. Hill, eds., *Indonesian Update 2011*. Singapore: Institute of Southeast Asian Studies.

Badan Pusat Statistik (BPS–Statistiks Indonesia). 2009. *Statistical Yearbook of Indonesia*. Jakarta.

———. various years. *Labor Force Situation in Indonesia*. Jakarta.

———. various years. *Laborer Situation in Indonesia*. Jakarta.

———. various years. Sakernas (National Labor Force Survey - Survei Tenaga Kerja Nasional). Jakarta.

———. various years. Susenas (National Socioeconomic Survey). Jakarta

———. BPS Website. http://dds.bps.go.id/ (accessed January and February 2011).

Bank Indonesia. 2011. *Indonesian Banking Statistics*. 9(3) February 2011.

Basri, F. 2009. *Deindustrialisasi* [Deindustrialization] Tempo Ed. 30 Nov–6 Dec 2009: 102–3.

Chatani, K. and C. Ernst. 2011. *Fiscal Stimulus Package: Its Impact on Employment Creation*. Geneva: International Labour Organization (ILO).

Comola, M. and L. de Mello. 2009. The Determinants of Employment and Earnings in Indonesia. *Economic Department Working Paper* No. 690. Paris: Organisation for Economic Co-operation and Development (OECD).

The Conference Board. The Conference Board Total Economy Database http://www.conference-board.org/data/economydatabase/ (accessed January 2011).

Dhanani. D., I. Islam, and A. Chowdhury. 2009. *The Indonesian Labour Market: Changes and Challenges*. London and New York: Routledge.

Heritage Foundation. http://www.heritage.org/Index/. (accessed November 2010).

International Labour Organisation (ILO). 2009a. *The Financial and Economic Crisis: A Decent Work Response*. Geneva.

———. 2009b. *Guide to the New Millennium Development Goals Employment Indicators: Including the Full Set of Decent Work Indicators*. Geneva.

———. 2009c. *Key Indicators of the Labour Market 6th Edition*. Geneva.

———. 2009d. *Labour and Social Trends in Indonesia 2009: Recovery and Beyond through Decent Work*. Jakarta.

———. 2010. *Global Jobs Pact Scan for Indonesia*. Geneva.

International Monetary Fund (IMF). World Economic Outlook Database. October 2010. http://www.imf.org/external/pubs/ft/weo/2010/02/weodata/index.aspx (accessed December 2010).

Islam, I., and A. Chowdhury. 2009. *Growth, Employment and Poverty Reduction in Indonesia*. Geneva: ILO.

Lembaga Penyelidikan Ekonomi dan Masyarakat–Fakultas Ekonomi Universitas Indonesia (LPEM–FEUI—Institute for Economic and Social Research, Department of Economics, University of Indonesia). 2007. Investment Climate Monitoring. Round IV. Jakarta.

Mustajab, M. 2010. *Indonesian Infrastructure: Condition, Problem and Policy*. posted on Bappenas blog on 24 December 2010. http://www.bappenas.go.id/blog/?p=63 (accessed 22 April 2011).

Organisation for Economic Co-operation and Development (OECD). 2008. Indonesia: Economic Assessment. *OECD Economic Surveys*. Paris.

Papanek, G. 2009. *Constraints to Growth and Poverty Reduction in Indonesia*. Paper submitted to ADB. Unpublished.

Suryahadi, A., W. Widyanti, D. Perwira, and S. Sumarto. 2003. Minimum Wage Policy and its Impact on Employment in the Urban Formal Sector. In *Bulletin of Indonesian Economic Studies* 39(1): 29–50.

US Census Bureau. U.S. International Trade Data (online statistics). http://www.census.gov/foreign-trade/ (accessed in January 2011).

World Bank. 2010. *Indonesia Jobs Report: Towards Better Jobs and Security for All*. Jakarta.

———. World Databank (online world development indicator database). http://databank.worldbank.org/ (accessed January 2011)

———. PovcalNet. http://search.worldbank.org/all?qterm=povcalnet

World Bank and International Finance Corporation (IFC). 2010. *Doing Business in Indonesia*. Jakarta.

World Economic Forum (WEF). 2009. *The Global Competitiveness Report 2009–2010*. Geneva. http://www.weforum.org/en/initiatives/gcp/Global%20Competitiveness%20Report/index.htm

10. Poverty Reduction: The Track Record and Way Forward

Asep Suryahadi, Athia Yumna, Umbu Reku Raya, and
Deswanto Marbun

10.1. Background

Indonesia, the world's largest archipelago, has over 17,000 islands and is home to 230 million people or 3.4% of the world's population. Despite its abundant resources, Indonesia is among the lower middle-income countries, with only $2,254 per capita income in 2008 (World Bank 2009b, 2009c). Since the 1997 Asian financial crisis, efforts to protect the poor through targeted social safety nets for health, education, and rice consumption as well as the newly introduced community and microenterprise empowerment programs have demonstrated Indonesia's development policy agenda. However, Indonesia's progress toward achieving some of the Millennium Development Goals has not been consistent; issues are especially apparent with goals 1–5 and 6C, for reducing multidimensional poverty, covering extreme poverty, food consumption, universal 9-year education, gender equality, maternal and neonatal health and child survival, and malaria and other communicable diseases.

In the National Medium-Term Development Plan (Rencana Pembangunan Jangkah Menengah Nasional—RPJMN) of 2004–2009, the Yudhoyono administration targeted reducing the proportion of Indonesians living below the poverty line[1] from 17.42% in 2004 to 8.20% in 2009, a 9.22 percentage point decrease in 5 years. The 2009 data, however, show that 14.15% of the population, or 32.53 million people, still live below the national poverty line, which is 5.95 percentage points under the government's target. The newly launched RPJMN 2010–2014 has targeted a poverty rate of

---

[1] The poverty line equals 2,100 kilocalories per capita per day for the food component plus basic nonfood consumption, i.e., housing, apparel, health, education, utilities, and transport. The average composition is 76% for food consumption and 24% for nonfood consumption, with the ratios being 70:30 in urban and 79:21 in rural areas (Avenzora and Haryono 2008).

8% in 2014, working toward integrated and inclusive development that accommodates issues of localities, geography and equality in the distribution of infrastructure and economic development to foster equality in human development (Bappenas 2009).

Indonesia proclaimed its independence in 1945 and has since struggled with improving the national income and eradicating poverty. From 1945 through the 1960s, the country experienced wars against its invaders (Japan and the Netherlands) and local separatism, civil conflicts, and political reconstruction, resulting in the loss of assets and natural resources, injury to and loss of human lives, unstable governments, low gross domestic product (GDP) levels, and high poverty levels. Beginning in the early 1970s, Indonesia enjoyed rapid economic growth, averaging 7% annually, until the 1997 Asian financial crisis ground it to a halt. In 1998, the Indonesian economy contracted by more than 13%. Post-crisis recovery has been relatively quick, but a decade later the economic growth has not returned to the high levels of the era prior to the crisis. Growth since the crisis has averaged about 5% annually (70% of the level prior to the crisis).

The high economic growth during the pre-crisis period was accompanied by improved social indicators. Life expectancy increased, infant mortality rates fell, and school enrollment rates rose. In addition, the provision of basic infrastructure—water supply, roads, electricity, schools, and health facilities—rose substantially. More significantly, even though the total population increased from about 135 million in 1976 to 200 million in 1996, the number of people living below the national poverty line decreased markedly, from about 54 million to 22.5 million people, during the same period (BPS 1997).

However, beginning in mid-1997, Indonesia was struck by a currency crisis, which, by the first half of 1998, had developed into a full-blown economic and political crisis and was exacerbated by an El Niño drought. During this crisis period, the Indonesian currency plummeted to 15% of its pre-crisis value in less than 1 year; the economy contracted by an unprecedented 13.7% in 1998; domestic prices skyrocketed (the general inflation rate was 78% in 1998, and the food inflation rate was 118%); and mass rioting took place in the capital—Jakarta—and a few other cities. This culminated in the fall of the New Order government, which had been in power since the mid-1960s (Sumarto, Suryahadi, and Widyanti 2005).

The social impact of the crisis, particularly on poverty, was substantial. The official estimate is that the national poverty rate increased from about 17.3% in February 1996 to 24.3% in February 1999 (BPS 2002). During the period, the number of urban poor doubled and the number of rural poor increased by 75%. A study by Suryahadi, Sumarto, and Pritchett (2003), which tracks the poverty rate over the course of the crisis, shows that the rate increased by 164% from the onset of the crisis in mid-1997 to the peak of the crisis around the end of 1998.

To reduce the adverse social impact of the crisis, in 1998 the Indonesian government introduced a social safety net (Jaring Pengaman Sosial or JPS) program aiming to prevent the poor from falling more deeply into poverty and reducing the exposure of vulnerable households to risk. From 1998 to 2010, the government shifted its development agenda, not only relying heavily on economic growth but also creating poverty reduction programs to ensure that development goals are achieved. The JPS, which was created to mitigate the impact of the 1997 financial crisis, has evolved into a wider poverty reduction effort, and poverty reduction has become a specific objective that is formally stated in the national development planning documents.[2]

This chapter reviews the government's poverty reduction strategies, policies, and programs during 1998–2010 and suggests pathways to strengthening its poverty reduction efforts. In doing so, the chapter reviews other studies and surveys on poverty dynamics and analyzes the documents pertaining to national and local poverty reduction strategies, policies, and programs.

The rest of the chapter is organized as follows. Section 10.2 reviews the government's poverty reduction strategies and policies. Section 10.3 explores the three clusters of the government's major poverty reduction programs. The final section concludes and offers policy recommendations. The glossary in the Appendix lists the Indonesian abbreviations, acronyms, and short names of programs mentioned in this chapter, their Indonesian and English language equivalents, and some notes, to facilitate reading and comprehension of the chapter..

10.2. Recent Developments in Poverty Reduction Strategies and Policies

10.2.1. Poverty Reduction Strategies and Policies

Although Indonesia very successfully reduced poverty during the 1970s to the mid-1990s, the term "poverty" was not stated as a top priority of the country's development agenda until the early 1990s. The first five 5-year development plans (*rencana pembangunan lima tahun*—Repelitas) and the RPJMNs in the New Order era, did not contain a chapter on poverty. The sixth Repelita (1994/1995–1998/1999) was the first document that mentioned poverty alleviation and equality in development. The two issues were also integrated in other chapters of that document.

---

[2] For example, Poverty Reduction is the first chapter in the RPJMN 2004–2009 section for achieving a prosperous Indonesia. That chapter reflects the National Poverty Reduction Strategy Paper (Strategi Nasional Penaggulangan Kemiskinan, or SNPK, 2005).

Nonetheless, during the pre-crisis high-growth period, the government under President Suharto had carried out a number of poverty reduction programs. For example, in the early New Order era, several departments had programs aimed at poverty reduction: the Department of Home Affairs ran experimental savings and loans projects, the Department of Social Affairs conducted projects focused on increasing the welfare of the poor and needy, and the Department of Agriculture managed programs aiming to increase the income level of small-scale farmers (Leith et al. 2003). Furthermore, in the 1990s, Suharto's administration took important steps toward what later became the inspiration for the National Program for Community Empowerment (PNPM). Poverty reduction initiatives in the late New Order era include the (1) Presidential Instruction on Disadvantaged Villages; (2) Disadvantaged Village Infrastructure Development Program; (3) Urban Poverty Reduction Program (P2KP); (4) People's Prosperity Savings and People's Prosperity Business Credit (Takesra and Kukesra); (5) Small Farmers and Fisherman Income Expansion Project; and (6) Subdistrict Development Program (Leith et al. 2003).

In the post-crisis era, the set of social safety net JPS programs that had started as a response to the Asian financial crisis have been institutionalized in Indonesia's poverty reduction programs. From the onset of the crisis, the government employed a social protection system that was a mixture of universal subsidies and targeted safety net programs. The aims were to prevent the chronic poor from falling more deeply into poverty and to reduce the exposure of vulnerable households to risks.

The JPS had a four-pronged strategy: (1) ensuring the availability of affordable rice; (2) improving household purchasing power by creating employment; (3) preserving access to critical social services, particularly health and education; and (4) sustaining local economic activity through regional block grants and small-scale credit. The JPS program aimed to prevent or at least significantly reduce the worst effects of the crisis (Sumarto, Suryahadi, and Widyanti 2002).

After the crisis, successive administrations maintained some of the JPS programs and attempted to restructure the extremely regressive subsidies on fuel products (mainly kerosene, automotive diesel fuel, and gasoline) and to channel budgetary savings into targeted social protection and poverty reduction programs. The savings were then used to fund social undertakings known in general as the Fuel Subsidy Reduction Compensation Program (Program Kompensasi Pengurangan Subsidi Bahan Bakar Minyak—PKPS-BBM). The PKPS-BBM program has helped to maintain the post-crisis gains despite periodic economic fluctuations and, more importantly, has enabled the central government to make the transition to a more progressive public spending regime (Sumarto, Suryahadi, and Bazzi 2008).

Since the crisis, successive administrations have taken the politically difficult but economically rational and pro-poor step of allocating resources more effectively in sectors that matter to the social welfare. However, Indonesia's budgetary allocations to social and human development priorities as a proportion of gross domestic product (GDP) remain among the lowest in Southeast Asia. Policymakers face a critical trade-off between balancing the state budget and making necessary social investments (Sumarto, Suryahadi, and Bazzi 2008).

Despite the relatively low investment in poverty reduction, politically, the government took an important initiative by preparing and launching the first national grand strategy to reduce poverty across the country. This strategy was formally documented in the Interim Poverty Reduction Strategy Paper (IPRSP). To prepare the IPRSP, the government, under President Abdurahman Wahid, set up an interministerial agency—the Coordination Agency for Poverty Alleviation (Badan Koordinasi Penanggulangan Kemiskinan). That agency was dissolved and changed into the Poverty Reduction Committee (Komite Penanggulangan Kemiskinan) under President Megawati Soekarnoputri. The government finally finished an IPRSP in 2003 (Committee for Poverty Alleviation 2003). This IPRSP sets out a preliminary poverty reduction strategy as a precursor to a full poverty reduction strategy paper, the Strategi Nasional Penanggulangan Kemiskinan—SNPK. To produce the SNPK, the Committee for Poverty Alleviation accommodated inputs from stakeholders including civil society. Nonetheless, commitment to the SNPK, at both the political and bureaucratic levels, remained elusive (Leith et al. 2003).

10.2.1.1. A Road to the National Strategy for Poverty Reduction

The IPRSP completed in March 2003 stated that the national strategy for poverty reduction document should be formulated through several steps: (1) identification of poverty problems, (2) evaluation of poverty reduction policy and programs, (3) formulation of strategy and policy, (4) formulation of the program and its delivery, and (5) evaluation of policy and the program. After completing the IPRSP, the government finished the SNPK in 2004.

While poverty had previously been considered primarily a problem of lack of income and that the poor need have no voice in the development process, the SNPK formulated poverty alleviation programs on a rights-based approach. Poverty is a multidimensional problem involving not only monetary issues but also the vulnerability to moving into and out of poverty and the difficulty the poor face with being involved in the process of forming policies that affect their lives. The assertion of the basic rights of the poor—social, cultural, economic, and political rights—is central to the understanding of how to overcome the poverty problems. The rights-based approach also alters the relationship between the government and the people, especially the poor. In the rights-based view, the state (e.g., government, parliament, military, and all state institutions) has an obligation to respect, protect, and fulfill the basic rights of the poor systematically and in a progressive way.

The SNPK also acknowledged the interrelated factors involved in the poor's powerlessness in and needs for meeting their basic rights, their vulnerability to business competition, their exposure to conflict and violence, demographic problems, gender inequality, and the wide disparity between those who live in the less and the more developed regions. Also, the poverty problem is slightly different in rural, urban, coastal, and less developed areas. The SNPK also acknowledged that the poor face difficulty acquiring assets, especially land and capital; accessing public services, particularly education and health; and participating in the public decision-making process. Moreover, a SMERU (2003) study of participatory poverty assessments showed that limited education and skills, lack of employment opportunities, and lack of access to capital and adequate income are dominant issues.

The SNPK recognized the need to create more opportunities for the poor, strengthen institutions in communities, increase the capacity of communities, improve social protection, and connect to the global partnership for development. These five items are the main strategies in poverty alleviation as formulated in the SNPK. Furthermore, the SNPK action plan emphasized the progressive and systematic realization of the need to respect, protect, and fulfill people's basic rights to (1) food, (2) basic health services, (3) education, (4) job opportunities and business development, (5) housing, (6) clean water and sanitation, (7) land ownership, (8) natural resources and the environment, (9) security, and (10) participation in the decision-making process.

The new understanding that combating poverty is not only the government's concern has produced an initiative to bring all development actors into the effort. Therefore, the success of the poverty alleviation strategy and policy implementation depends on the relationship, partnership, and active efforts of central and local governments, Parliament, the private sector, civil society, academicians, and international agencies. The last but important step in implementing any program is putting in place a sound monitoring and evaluation system. The last chapter of the SNPK highlights this point, acknowledging the importance of monitoring and evaluation of timely, accurate, relevant, complete, and comprehensive data and information.

As seen in Figure 10.1, the SNPK is integrated in the RPJMN. The strategy and action plans of poverty alleviation become one of the main priorities in the RPJMN and comprise a specific chapter in it. Therefore, the SNPK provides major guidance for mainstreaming the policy and program of poverty alleviation in the RPJMN.

Figure 10.1: Poverty Reduction in the Framework of the National Development Plan

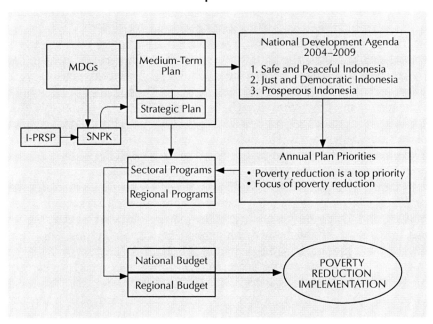

IPRSP = Interim Poverty Reduction Strategy Paper, MDG = Millennium Development Goal, SNPK = poverty reduction strategy paper (Strategi Nasional Penanggulangan Kemiskinan).
Source: Bappenas (2006).

10.2.1.2. Review of the National Medium-Term Development Plan (RPJMN) 2004–2009

The RPJMN provides policy guidance and programs for 5 years for national and local governments, based on the vision and mission of the elected president. The RPJMN 2004–2009 put poverty reduction as a top priority, i.e., reducing the proportion of people who are poor to 8.2% by the end of 2009. Multidimensional poverty reduction was integrated into the RPJMN's three priority agendas:

- **"Safe and Peaceful Indonesia"**: enhancing a sense of safety, security, and peace as reflected in the reduction of tension and threats between groups, and reduction of the crime rate;
- **"Just and Democratic Indonesia"**: improving justice and law enforcement, with a priority on eradicating corruption, improving the implementation of decentralization, and enhancing people's participation in the development process; and
- **"Prosperous Indonesia"**: reducing the number of poor people,

focusing on pro-poor growth and creating employment opportunities, while improving access to quality health and education services, reducing regional disparities, and improving the management of natural resources and the environment.

Figure 10.1 also shows that, to achieve the poverty reduction targets by the end of 2009, the RPJMN was implemented through the annual government work plan (*rencana kerja pemerintah*), sectoral ministry work plans, and district and municipal sectoral plans. The National Development Planning Agency (Bappenas) and the Ministry of Finance propose indicative ceilings at the sector and program level to the Cabinet at the commencement of the budgetary process. The Parliament approves the budget after further discussion with the central and regional governments based on the final annual government work plan.

Chapter 16 of the RPJMN, which is on poverty reduction, articulates the problems of poverty as (1) fulfillment of the basic needs, (2) the population burden, and (3) gender inequality. Other matters discussed in the chapter are the targets of the poverty reduction agenda, policy direction, and development programs, and the chapter is a short explanation of the ideas in the SNPK. The poverty reduction agenda is also part of other chapters in the RPJMN. Poverty is mentioned in the first chapter, the "National Development Agenda." Reducing the poverty rate to 8.2% in 2009 is the first target to meet the Prosperous Indonesia agenda. Poverty is also repeatedly brought up in several chapters, including those on agriculture revitalization, cooperatives and small and medium-sized enterprises (SMEs), employment, macroeconomic stability, rural development, and access to education and health services.

One year after the implementation of the RPJMN 2004–2009, Indonesia vastly improved its targeting for social protection by redefining household qualifications for participation. Despite its poverty reduction programs, Indonesia is still plagued by a high poverty rate, inequality, and vulnerability. The 2009 poverty rate target was 8.2%, but the actual rate was 14.15% of Indonesians living below the national poverty line.

Several factors explain why the 8.2% poverty rate target cannot be achieved. External and internal factors obviously have hampered the poverty reduction process. The most influential recent external shocks to the poverty reduction efforts are the fuel and commodity price surges. Internal issues include the coordination of policy and poverty alleviation programs among sectors and between central and local governments (TKPK 2009). Moreover, the large extent of Indonesia's near poor population that is vulnerable to falling into poverty when subject to economic shock has increased the difficulties of implementing the poverty reduction program.

10.2.1.3. Review of the National Medium-Term Development Plan (RPJMN) 2010–2014

The newly launched RPJMN 2010–2014 tries to sharpen the focus on poverty alleviation, taking advantage of the massive shift from universal to targeted social protection programs during 2005–2009. The new RPJMN targets reducing poverty from 14.15% in 2009 to 12.00%–13.50% in 2010 and 8.00% in 2014. To achieve the targets, the government realizes that the development agenda should consider the five most important weaknesses of the past poverty reduction practices: (1) limited coverage and quality of the social protection schemes, (2) wide welfare disparities between provinces, (3) low access of the poor to basic services, (4) vulnerability of the poor to the negative impact of external forces such as globalization, and (5) increasing vulnerability of the poor due to climate change.

During 2010–2014, poverty alleviation is to be pursued by improving the apparatus or institution responsible for social protection, extending the coverage of social protection, and strengthening the multidimensional pathways to poverty alleviation in which all development sectors should contribute. In other words, the government intends to accelerate poverty reduction by institutionalizing and mainstreaming social protection in all developmental sectors. To create multisectoral harmony on and synergy in the management of poverty alleviation, the central government put forward a new regulation, Presidential Regulation No. 15 of 2010, which puts the authority for the management and practice of national poverty alleviation under the Vice President, who heads the National Team for Accelerating Poverty Reduction (Tim Nasional Percepatan Penanggulangan Kemiskinan—TNP2K). Previously, this authority was under the Coordinating Ministry of People's Welfare.

The central government also issued Presidential Decree No. 3 of 2010 related to poverty reduction. The decree reemphasizes the RPJMN 2010–2014 targets for higher and faster economic growth, major poverty reduction (to an 8% poverty rate), and massive job creation and labor market absorption (to achieve a 5% unemployment rate).

10.2.1.4. Review of the Regional (Local) Poverty Reduction Strategies and Policies

As part of formulating the SNPK, several regions conducted participatory poverty assessments to enhance their understanding of local poverty characteristics and problems. Moreover, in the decentralization era, the regional governments (at provincial and district levels) have increasing roles in the poverty reduction efforts. As a consequence, regional poverty reduction strategies (strategi penanggulangan kemiskinan daerah—

SPKDs) are needed for several reasons (World Bank 2005b). First, many of the responsibilities for addressing multidimensional aspects of poverty have been devolved to the local level and/or are a shared responsibility. Second, diverse conditions—the highest poverty numbers are on Java, but the highest incidence is beyond Java—require poverty diagnosis at the local level. Third, with decentralized planning and budgeting, policies and budget must be influenced at local levels. Furthermore, on the one hand, the SNPK will become the reference for local governments to develop their own poverty strategies—SPKDs (World Bank 2005a), and, on the other hand, the usefulness of national planning documents such as the SNPK will depend on how well their goals and outcomes are reflected and pursued in local plans (World Bank 2004b). Suryahadi and Sumarto (2007) also pointed out that to make poverty reduction efforts effective requires effective program design and implementation at the national and local levels. For that reason, symbiosis as well as pull and push interests exist between local and national strategy papers.

The new framework for multidimensional poverty requires understanding the voice of the poor. And the local governments are required to be strongly involved in formulating poverty strategy, despite their lack of capacity and limited experience in doing so. Participatory poverty assessments provide opportunities for local government to work with poor communities in identifying and discussing the root causes of their poverty problems. Through the assessments, strategies and action plans for poverty reduction that are specific to local situations can be produced based on the poverty problems identified (World Bank 2004a).

Data from the Directorate of Community's Empowerment, Ministry of Home Affairs, in 2007 indicated that implementation of the regional SPKDs is rather slow at the provincial level but more rapid at the local level. Only 14 of 33 provinces had an SPKD, while 316 of the 400 municipalities and cities had one.

There are good examples from 15 municipalities (in nine provinces) that finalized an SPKD with assistance from the World Bank's Initiatives for Local Governance Reform Project, and 8 of the 15 SPKDs have been legalized through a decree of the district head, which has budget implications (World Bank 2005b). As at the national level, the local SPKD is also integrated in the local 5-year regional strategic plan, which is channeled through technical agency programming in subdistrict and district planning discussions, then through the executive budgeting team before approval by the local parliament. The strategic plan has implications for annual planning and budgeting. A result is that the views of some of the poor are being accommodated in local policy, for example:

- Bulukumba government in South Sulawesi committed to provide more incentives for teachers working in isolated areas and formulated policy on the poor's access to capital;

- in Bulukumba (South Sulawesi), Ngawi (East Java), and Bolaang Mongondow (North Sulawesi), regulations on special planning were formulated in a participatory manner to protect communities' interests;
- local regulations and law enforcement on river pollution were formulatefd in Bolaang Mongondow (North Sulawesi) and Bandung (West Java); and
- local regulations on forest management were formulated in Lamongan (East Java).

10.2.2. Institutional Setting of Poverty Reduction

The new paradigm in the poverty alleviation agenda has led to a rethinking of the institutional setting for tackling multidimensional poverty. Experience has shown that to combat poverty requires a comprehensive and integrated approach, which is more complicated after the huge social, economic, and political turmoil in the 1997 crisis (Committee for Poverty Alleviation 2003). The issues raised in the IPRSP are regional autonomy and decentralization, demand for good governance, and globalization. These three issues are related to the involvement in the poverty alleviation program of multiple stakeholders—central and regional government, Parliament, private sectors, nongovernment organizations, other civil society organizations, and the community. Furthermore, in the new paradigm of poverty alleviation, empowerment of the poor becomes a foundation on which to synergize and sharpen policies and programs in poverty alleviation (TKPK 2009).

An initiative to integrate the poverty reduction efforts under one body started in 2001 with the issue of Presidential Decree No. 124 of 2001. Presidential Decree No. 8 of 2002 established the Committee for Poverty Alleviation, led by the coordinating minister of people's welfare and with the coordinating minister of economic affairs as deputy. The committee's main task is to coordinate the formulation and implementation of poverty reduction programs by engaging government institutions and other development actors in each level of government as well as multiple other stakeholders (Committee for Poverty Alleviation 2003, TKPK 2007).

To emphasize the importance of the institutions in the front line of poverty reduction efforts, the government launched Presidential Regulation No. 54 of 2005, the "Coordination Team for Poverty Reduction." The team's main task is to continue the work of the Committee for Poverty Alleviation, emphasizing concrete action to reduce the number of poor more rapidly by coordinating and synchronizing planning and implementation of poverty alleviation policies. This team is led by the coordinating minister for people's welfare. On February 2010, the government issued Presidential Regulation

No. 15 of 2010 about accelerating poverty reduction. Based on this regulation, the name of the poverty reduction body was changed to the National Team for Accelerating Poverty Reduction (TNP2K). The TNP2K has three main tasks—formulating the poverty reduction policy and program, synergizing the poverty reduction activities among ministries and institutions, and monitoring and evaluating progress. The new regulation also highlights a change in organization, as the President made the Vice President the head of the TNP2K.

Coordination between the center and the regions is unchanged. Regional poverty alleviation coordination teams at the province, district, municipal, and city levels should be set up, with the provincial teams responsible to the governor and the national team, and the district, municipality, and city teams reporting to their respective government heads and the provincial team. However, the relationship between the teams at central and regional levels is functional and not subordinate.

10.3. Major Poverty Reduction Programs

Regarding the rights-based approach, the government has formulated the poverty alleviation program in three clusters (Figure 10.2) based on the beneficiaries' segmentation—very poor, poor, and near poor. The first cluster is a social assistance program that aims to fulfill the basic needs in food, health, education, clean water, and sanitation—to enhance the poor's quality of life and decrease their burdens. The second cluster is the empowerment program, which aims to enhance the capacity and income of the poor and involve them in the development process based on empowerment principles. The last cluster is the SME empowerment, which aims to give SMEs access to finance and enhance their sustainability.

The three clusters concept was formulated legally in Presidential Regulation No. 13 of 2009, the "Coordination of Poverty Alleviation." Under this regulation, the government consolidated poverty alleviation into three clusters to accelerate the poverty reduction programs and give clear guidance for every level of administration (national, provincial, and district). However, the three clusters were implemented before the regulation was enacted.

10.3.1. Cluster 1: The Government's Social Assistance for Poverty Reduction

Prior to the 1997 Asian financial crisis, Indonesia had adopted a long-term poverty alleviation strategy via massive investment in public education and health, and public infrastructure. This approach helped to foster human capital accumulation, create a newly educated middle class, and increase economic opportunities for isolated areas. In the 1970s, special measures to

Figure 10.2 : Three Clusters in the Poverty Alleviation Program

Cluster I	Cluster II	Cluster III
Social Assistance Aim: reduce economic cost burden of the poor	**Community Empowerment** Aim: increase the poor's income and affortability	**Microenterprises Empowerment** Aim: increase savings and business sustainability of SMEs
Main Instruments: Raskin, Jamkesmas, PKH, scholarship for the poor **Other Instruments:** Social assistance for disabled, elderly, children, etc. **Targets:** 18.5 million near poor, poor, and very poor households	**Main Instruments:** PNPM Mandiri (PPK, P2KP, PPIP, PISEW, etc.) **Targets in 2009:** 6,408 subdistricts in 465 districts and cities	**Main Instruments:** Credit for the People (KUR) **Targets in 2009:** Rp20 trillion for 4 million microcredit recipients

KUR = Credit for the People program, Kredit Usaha Rakyat; P2KP = Urban Poverty Program; PISEW = PNPM-Social Infrastructure; PKH = Program Keluarga Harapan; PNPM = National Program for Community Empowerment; PPIP = PNPM-Rural Infrastructure; PPK = Kecamatan Development Program; SMEs = small and medium-sized enterprises.
Source: TKPK (2009).

target the poor were hampered by the very high proportion of people living below the poverty line, which, in 1976, was 40.1% or 54.2 million individuals. In the absence of government social protection, the poor rely primarily on traditional risk pooling mechanisms through informal saving or donations from relatives or religious groups; or, when financial markets are accessible, idiosyncratic risk can be insured through borrowing mechanisms.

However, the typical local risk pooling mechanism fails when the whole community is hit by aggregate shock such as the 1997 Asian financial crisis. Exacerbated by the El Niño drought and political instability, the crisis was transformed into unpredictable hyperinflation. The hyperinflation impact was country-wide, paralyzing formal financial institutions and informal local insurance mechanisms. During the crisis, per capita levels of household expenditure declined substantially and poverty rates rose by at least 25%. To mitigate the hyperinflation, households tried to maintain the physical amount of staple food they consumed, but at the cost of health and educational expenditures. This hampered the long-term sustainability of poverty alleviation through human capital accumulation, especially among the poorest households (Frankenberg, Thomas, and Beegle 1999).

Table 10.1: Creation, Development and Recategorization of National Social Protection Programs in Indonesia (1998–2010)

Program Classification	1998/1999	1999/2000	2000	2001	2002	2003
Subsidized Rice	OPK	OPK	OPK	OPK		
					Raskin	Raskin
Social Health Insurance	JPS-BK	JPS-BK	JPS-BK	JPS-BK		
				PKPS-BBM	PKPS-BBM	PKPS-BBM
Educational Support Fund	JPS-Scholarship	JPS-Scholarship	JPS-Scholarship			
	JPS-DBO	JPS-DBO	JPS-DBO			
				BKM	BKM	BKM
Unconditional Cash Transfer						
Conditional Cash Transfer						
Community CCT	KDP	KDP	KDP	KDP	KDP	KDP
Microfinance						

BKM = Beasiswa Keluarga Miskin, Scholarship for Poor Households; BLT = Bantuan Langsung Tunai, Unconditional Cash Transfer, BOS = Bantuan Operasional Sekolah, School Operational Assistance; BSM = Beasiswa Siswa Miskin, Scholarships for Poor Students; CCT = conditional cash transfer; JPS = Jaring Pengaman Sosial, Social Safety Net; JPS–BK = Jaring Pengaman Sosial Bidang Kesehatan, Social Safety Net for Health; JPS–DBO = Jaring Pengaman Sosial Bidang Dana Bantuan Operasional, Social Safety Net for School Operational Assistance Fund; KDP = Kecamatan Development Program; KUR = Kredit Usaha Rakyat, People's Business Credit; OPK = Operasi Pasar Khusus, Special Market Operation; PKH = Program Keularga Harapan, Hopeful Family Program (a conditional cash transfer); PKPS–BBM = Program Kompensasi Pengurangan Subsidi Bahan Bakar Minyak, Fuel Subsidy Reduction Compensation Program; PNPM = National Program for Community Empowerment.

Sources: Authors' analysis; Fiszbein and Schady (2009), Ministry of Social Affairs (2008), Hastuti et al (2009), Sumarto, Suryahadi, and Bazzi (2008), World Bank (2006), Sparrow (2006), Hastuti and Maxwell (2003)

Fiscal Year						
2004	2005	2006	2007	2008	2009	2010
Raskin	Raskin	Raskin	Raskin	Raskin	Raskin	Raskin
PKPS-BBM	PKPS-BBM					
	Askeskin	Askeskin	Askeskin	Askeskin		
				Jamkesmas	Jamkesmas	Jamkesmas
BKM	BKM	BKM				
			BSM	BSM	BSM	BSM
	BOS	BOS	BOS	BOS	BOS	BOS
	BLT	BLT		BLT	BLT	
			PKH	PKH	PKH	PKH
KDP	KDP	KDP	PNPM	PNPM	PNPM	PNPM
			KUR-M	KUR-M	KUR-M	KUR-M

To protect food security, education, health, and employment of the poor households in late 1998, the government initiated the first nationwide social protection scheme for health and education, subsidized rice, and implemented a cash-for-work program for poor households (Sparrow 2006, 2007; World Bank 2006). With some modifications, many of the programs are working; several of them are discussed in the context of the poverty alleviation strategy in post-crisis Indonesia. Table 10.1 summarizes the evolution of social protection in health, education, food, and household financial liquidity.

As seen in the table, the government has continuously adjusted social protection schemes, aiming at better targeting and improved effectiveness of the schemes by slowly moving to a single definition of poverty (i.e., the definition of Statistics Indonesia: Badan Pusat Statistik—BPS) but using multiple instruments through the conditional cash transfer, Program Keluarga Harapan (PKH). The PKH is a multisectoral cash transfer scheme that, due to its conditionality, can replace the targeted education scholarship scheme and complement the existing Jamkesmas program in the health sector.

Households and individuals may receive assistance from more than one social protection scheme, provided they are eligible for the schemes to which they apply. The schemes may be used in three ways.

The first and the most common channel is direct use, wherein the recipient uses the social assistance according to the designed purpose. For example, subsidized rice is consumed by the recipient household, student scholarships are used for the recipients' own education, and health cards are used for the possessors' medical treatment. The second channel is intrahousehold reallocation, in which the recipient household changes its individual or overall consumption pattern due to the availability of subsidized rice, student scholarship, health card, or cash transfer. For example, the National Logistics Agency (Badan Urusan Logistik, which is referred to as Bulog), reported that subsidized rice enables households to switch household expenditure to education expenses (Bulog 2009). Therefore, subsidized rice improves the household's food intake and gives rise to additional educational expenditure, and may thereby improve children's education. The third channel is a between-households spillover effect, where, due to family or social networks, the recipient households share resources with other households. The Bulog report showed that very poor households that were recipients of subsidized rice shared the rice in social gatherings, which they had not done prior to receiving the subsidized rice.

The complete set of current government social assistance is mapped in Figure 10.3. The five programs are (1) Raskin subsidized rice, (2) Jamkesmas social health insurance, (3) scholarships for poor students (BKM and BSM), (4) the school operational assistance (Bantuan Operasional Sekolah—BOS), and (4) the PKH conditional cash transfer for households. In addition, the PNPM Generasi, a conditional cash transfer for poor communities for better health and education is included because, although it is categorized as part of Cluster 2 on community empowerment, in practice it provides direct transport incentives, books, umbrellas, and shoes for poor students as well as transport incentives for pregnant women to visit midwives at the integrated health service post (posyandu)[3] (Febriany, Toyamah, and Sodo 2010).

While the social assistance programs help poor households, one major weakness with the programs is that of targeting. It is commonly argued that targeting can allow the government to reduce poverty more effectively and at a lower cost than providing untargeted assistance; however, targeting can entail expensive hidden administrative cost (van de Walle 1998). Sumarto (2006) revealed that targeting problems plagued all Indonesia's social safety nets programs in 1998. SMERU (2006) showed that the Direct (unconditional) Cash Transfer (Bantuan Langsung Tunai—BLT) program suffered from both leakage and undercoverage problems. Comparing the targeting performance in social assistance programs around the world, Coady, Grosh, and Hoddinott (2004) found that Indonesia is among neither the best nor the worst performers. They showed that the Trabajar public works program in Argentina was able to transfer 80% of program benefits to the poorest quintile, whereas Indonesia's Social Safety Net for Health (Jaring Pengaman Sosial Bidang Kesehatan—JPS-BK), the best-performing Indonesian social assistance program reviewed in the paper, was able to distribute only 33.6% of transfers to the poorest quintile. Furthermore, the World Bank (2009a) demonstrated that the targeting accuracy of social assistance in Central Asia, Europe, and Latin America transferred a very high share of benefits to the poorest quintile.

10.3.1.1. Protecting Staple Food Consumption of the Poor

During the 1997 crisis, the price of rice, the staple food for most Indonesians, skyrocketed. The poor, whose rice consumption made up to a quarter of their total expenditures, were the most negatively affected. Effects of the drop in rice consumption included diminishing health of children under 5 (World Bank 2006), and it appeared that, to smooth consumption, households reduced their investment in children's education and pushed their early entrance into the labor market. To protect the rice consumption of the poor,

---

[3] A *posyandu* or an integrated health service post is a medium for a village or community to provide basic health services for its own members. The main objective is to help reduce under-5 and maternal mortality rates. The services, given by local cadres assisted by a health center (*puskesmas*) medical staff member, include immunization, weight measuring, and general health check for children under 5 as well as general health checks for mothers and the elderly.

Figure 10.3: Current Government Scheme on Protecting Rice Consumption, Education, and Health of Poor Households

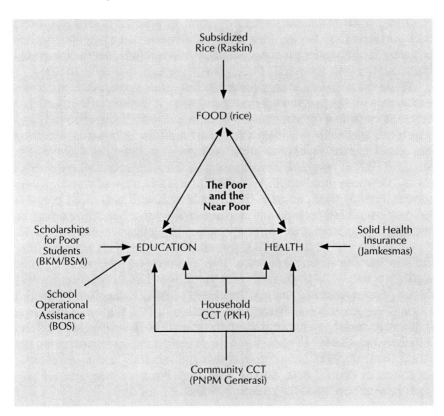

CCT = conditional cash transfer, PKH = Program Keluarga Harapan.
Source: Authors.

in July 1998 the government introduced a subsidized rice scheme, the Operasi Pasar Khusus program, for 1.05 million tons of rice in the program's first fiscal year.

To strengthen the pro-poor targeting message, in early 2002 the name, but not the content, of the program was modified into Raskin (Beras untuk Orang Miskin—Rice for the Poor). The Raskin program distributed up to 3.1 million tons of rice in 2009 (Table 10.2). That the number of recipient households in 2005–2008 was higher than the target indicates targeting inaccuracy and community decision to share the rice equally with the nonrecipients—the poor who were not listed as recipients and nonpoor— due to benevolence among the recipients or to minimize social friction in the community (Hastuti et al. 2009).

Table 10.2: Targets, Recipients, and Amount of Subsidized Rice for Poor Households

Fiscal Year	Program	Number of Poor Households (million)	Number of Targeted Households (million)	Number of Recipient Households (million)	Amount of Subsidized Rice (million tons)	Budget (Rp billion)
1998/99	OPK	...	...	...	1.05	...
1999/00	OPK	...	...	...	2.60	...
2000	OPK	16.00	7.50	...	1.35	...
2001	OPK	15.00	8.70	...	1.50	...
2002	Raskin	15.12	9.79	...	2.35	4.5
2003	Raskin	15.75	8.58	...	2.06	4.7
2004	Raskin	15.75	8.59	...	2.06	5.4
2005	Raskin	15.79	8.30	11.11	1.99	4.97
2006	Raskin	15.50	10.83	13.88	1.62	5.32
2007	Raskin	19.10	15.80	16.74	1.74	6.47
2008	Raskin	19.10	19.10	19.13	3.34	11.66
2009	Raskin	18.50	18.50	...	3.13	12.98
2010	Raskin	17.49	17.09	...	2.73	8.92

... = data not available, OPK = subsidized rice scheme, the Operasi Pasar Khusus.
Note: The criteria for determining the poverty of a household were the National Coordinating Board for Family Planning (Badan Koordinasi Keluarga Berencana Nasional) standard for 1998–2006 (wherein "poor" was termed "pre-prosperous"; the number of poor households from socioeconomic data collected by Statistics Indonesia for 2007; the number of target households from socioeconomic data collected by Statistics Indonesia for 2008–2009; and an estimate for January–December 2010 based on the National Budget.
Sources: Hastuti and Maxwell (2003), Handoko and Patriadi (2005), Hastuti et al. (2008, 2009), Bulog (2008, 2009, 2010).

During 2002–2009, 29.55% of the subsidized rice was distributed to the lowest expenditure quintile and 24.98% to the second lowest expenditure quintile, for a total of 54.53% to the two lowest quintiles. And the two highest quintiles received 24.83% of the subsidized rice, although the higher the expenditure quintile the lower the leakage, with greater improvement during 2007–2009 (Table 10.3). Further examination by Hastuti and Maxwell (2003) and Hastuti et al. (2008) revealed improved effectiveness of the targeting and distribution of the subsidized rice.

Does subsidizing rice alleviate poverty by increasing household consumption above the 2,100 kilocalorie equivalent per capita per day? Sumarto, Suryahadi, and Widyanti (2005), analyzing 1998/99 data, reported that the rice consumption of households participating in the subsidized rice

Table 10.3: Expenditure Quintile of Households Receiving Raskin Benefits (%)

Expenditure Category	2002	2003	2004	2005	2006	2007	2008	2009	Average
Q1 (lowest)	29.11	28.19	28.47	29.19	29.04	30.47	30.62	31.33	29.55
Q2	23.66	23.38	23.37	24.01	23.48	27.23	27.20	27.48	24.98
Q3	19.63	19.88	20.03	19.84	19.83	22.28	22.02	21.68	20.65
Q4	16.37	16.74	16.60	16.06	16.36	14.50	14.80	14.62	15.76
Q5 (highest)	11.22	11.81	11.53	10.90	11.29	5.53	5.36	4.89	9.07
Total	100	100	100	100	100	100	100	100	100

Sources: Hastuti et al (2008); Avenzora and Haryono (2008); BPS (2007, 2009).

program was 4.4% higher than that of the nonparticipant households. With this increase, the recipient households were 3.82% less likely to be poor than their counterparts. The impact of subsidized rice is greater than that of other social protection programs, such as health cards, student scholarships, and workfare programs. The World Bank strongly supported continuing the Raskin program, conditional on improved management of rice distribution (World Bank 2006).

In an in-depth study in East Java, Southeast Sulawesi, and West Sumatra, Hastuti et al. (2008) noted that the main benefits of the subsidized rice program included smoothing out food consumption, reducing the psychological burden due to uncertainty about food availability, and enabling households to switch financial resources to children's education. Therefore, household recipients of the Raskin made direct use of it and used intrahousehold allocation channels.

10.3.1.2. Protecting the Health of the Poor

The first social health program targeted to poor households, the Health Card Program (Kartu Sehat), was started in 1994 and fully institutionalized in 1998 through the JPS. The JPS was funded by the Asian Development Bank (ADB) and ran from 1998 to 2001. The JPS was replaced by the PKPS–BBM, 2001–2005, which used the JPS program management. In 2005, during President Yudhoyono's first term, the scheme's name was changed to Asuransi Kesehatan bagi Keluarga Miskin (Askeskin). Like the JPS, the PKPS–BBM and Askeskin were targeted to poor households. Due to suboptimal performance of the Askeskin, the scheme was reformed into the Jaminan Kesehatan bagi Masyarakat Miskin (Jamkesmas) in 2008. While the Askeskin targeted households, the Jamkesmas targets individuals.

In the JPS scheme, eligible household could apply for a health card that could be used to waive medical expenses for outpatient and inpatient care at subdistrict health centers and third-class public hospital wards. By February 1999, 11% of Indonesians (approximately 22 million people) lived in a household with a health card. Although intended for the poor, only 69.42% of the health cards were allocated to the two poorest quintiles, and 20.51% of the cards were allocated to the two richest expenditure quintiles. Sparrow (2006) argued that the leakage to the middle and upper quintiles was due to managerial error (i.e., lack of quality poverty information). However, given the widespread aggregate impact of the Asian financial crisis at the time the JPS commenced, the leakage can also be understood as a wise coping mechanism of near-poor households to avoid falling into poverty due to health shocks. Such households could request the village head to issue a letter stating that they were poor and thus eligible for a health card. The JPS ended in 2001, and the government introduced the PKPS–BBM for health, in which social health insurance was funded from budgetary saving by reducing the fuel subsidy. The PKPS–BBM used almost the same mechanism as the JPS, in which any poor or near-poor household could apply for a health card through the intercession of the village head.

During 1999–2002, the health card increased outpatient care by 0.11 percentage points (Pradhan, Saadah, and Sparrow 2007). The impact was five times stronger when the availability of budgetary support for public health services was taken into account. Consequently, a mix of demand- and supply-side policies should be implemented at the same time to strengthen the impact on protecting the health of the poor.

During the first year of President Yudhoyono's administration, in March 2005, the government renamed the PKPS–BBM as Askeskin—health insurance for the poor. Still using the budgetary saving from reducing the fuel subsidy, the new scheme was solely managed by PT Asuransi Kesehatan (Askes), the state enterprise that manages health insurance for public employees and their household members. However, due to suboptimal financing and targeting of the program, in 2008 the Ministry of Health limited PT Askes' function to arranging payments and renamed the scheme Jaminan Kesehatan Masyarakat Miskin (Jamkesmas), which translates as "health guarantee for the poor." The Jamkesmas targets individual poor people and is budgeted for about 76.4 million individuals.

The positive impact of the Askeskin and Jamkesmas on health care utilization and (presumably) the health of the poor is mixed due to the negative impact the reduction in fuel subsidy had on the overall livelihood of the poor (Sparrow, Suryahadi, and Widyanti 2010). Due to the reduced fuel subsidy, commodity prices increased sufficiently so that the Askeskin and Jamkesmas were unable to offset the impact on health care utilization, hence undermining the access of the poor to quality health service. Thus, all funding needs and sources should be considered in determining social health policy.

In November 2009, the new minister for health presented a blueprint for a new health insurance scheme targeting universal coverage in 2012. Consequently, social health insurance is likely to be changed again in the near future. However, the major issue for this universal program is the source of funds, which may no longer be the fuel subsidy reduction.

Complementing the state-driven health development, in 2006 the Ministry of Health initiated community-driven health development through the Alert Village Program (Program Desa Siaga),[4] aiming at improving maternal and neonatal health by boosting the demand side of related health services, to complement existing government social health insurance (Ministry of Health, 2006, 2009). The program set a new paradigm in which people shoulder more responsibility for their own health, rather than the health workers. Village people with some understanding of health matters are organized into a network and trained in basic health literacy by health workers, doctors, and motivators. The Alert Village Program first targeted districts and provinces with high maternal mortality and low child survival rates, including East and West Nusa Tenggara.

Raya and Lada (2009) evaluated 34 participating villages in East Nusa Tenggara. They found that the program had been able to form a network and provide data on and notifications about maternal and neonatal health matters, referral transport in emergencies, blood donors, funding, and family planning, thus boosting the demand side of maternal and neonatal care and family health. The program, however, has not been able to significantly improve the supply side, especially the high turnover of midwives in remote villages and the absence or inadequacy of health facilities. Nationally, the Ministry of Health (2006, 2009) aimed to bring 12,000 villages into the program in 2006–2007 and all 70,000 villages in 2009. However, as of 2010 not all villages were participating effectively and efficiently.

Poor households suffer from a greater lack of access to quality health services than do nonpoor households, due to two interrelated factors: the availability of health facilities and workers, and the cost of health services. First, in rural areas, where most Indonesian poor live, the health facilities and health workers are not available or are available to only a minimal extent (Mukherjee 2006). In remote villages, health facilities and workers are likely to be limited to village birth houses and midwives, usually offering only limited services for prenatal, pregnancy, delivery, and neonatal care.

Second, to receive proper medical treatment in health facilities with doctors and nurses, the poor have to travel to subdistrict public health stations or district public hospitals. Thus, they incur costs of transport,

---

[4]   The term *desa siaga,* or "alert village," refers to village-level societies that are capable of identifying their own problems, planning a solution to overcome the problems, and executing the plans and that are constantly alert to health problems, disasters, and emergencies.

medical examination, and medicine, as well as the opportunity cost of time off from productive work.

Even with the widely available Indonesian social health insurance, the Jamkesmas, the out-of-pocket payments for medical treatment are high for the poor (Sparrow, Suryahadi, and Widyanti 2010). Consequently, while the impact of social health insurance is good among the nonpoor, it does not overcome all barriers to healthcare for the poor. An option to make health services more affordable for the poor would be a medically related cash transfer for reimbursing travel costs incurred by poor patients, which would complement the Jamkesmas.

10.3.1.3. Protecting Education of the Poor

Among the immediate impacts of the Asian financial crisis was an increase in drop-out rates, especially among school-age girls from poor rural areas, potentially perpetuating the transmission of poverty to the next generation. In 1998, the first pro-poor targeted JPS on education was introduced together with the JPS on health. The JPS comprised two parts: scholarships and school subsidies. By February 1999, 5% of children aged 10–18 (approximately 2.1 million children) had received a scholarship (Sparrow 2006). From 1999–2002 data, Sparrow found that participation in the scholarships increased the probability that participating children would attend school in the previous week by 1.5 percentage points more than nonparticipants and reduced the incidence of child labor from 14.0% to 10.2%. The effect on labor was higher for students from poor households in rural areas, and for boys. Therefore, the scholarships had helped (1) the poor households to protect their children's enrollment in elementary and junior high school, and (2) to prevent premature entry into the labor market.

The JPS also had the Operational Assistance Fund (JPS—Dana Bantuan Operasional). The Operational Assistance Fund was targeted to improve the supply side of elementary and secondary schools. The fund did not directly target poor students, although poor areas will likely correlate with poor educational quality and infrastructure, and hence higher eligibility for the funds. The same principle applies to the scholarships for poor households (Beasiswa Keluarga Miskin—BKM) and school operational assistance (Bantuan Operasional Sekolah—BOS) funds. Due to the area-wide targeting, it is difficult to analyze the impact of such programs on poverty reduction. Pro-poor schemes of such programs need to be reformulated so that the portion that is directly allotted for the poor can be measured, monitored, and then evaluated.

The Sekolah Satu Atap[5] Project innovatively combines the management of one new junior secondary school one into the management of an existing elementary school, thus expanding its coverage up to a 9-year elementary education and supporting the national objective for 9-year compulsory education in the poorest and most underserved provinces and districts in Indonesia. During 2006–2009, 1,547 new school buildings were constructed and furnished in 14 provinces, under the supervision of the Ministry of National Education. The project also supported the construction and operation of 46 Islamic schools in Java and Sumatra in 2006, operated under the Ministry of Religious Affairs (AIBEP 2007, 2010b). East Nusa Tenggara, South Sulawesi, and West Kalimantan provinces have received the greatest amount of resources from the project, while provinces with a high poverty rate in Papua are not covered, probably due to the high regional income from mining taxes and revenue sharing.

10.3.1.4. Protecting the Financial Liquidity of the Poor

To compensate for the negative impact the reduced fuel subsidy had on the poor, in 2005 the government introduced the BLT, an unconditional cash transfer to enhance the financial liquidity of poor households. Eligible households received Rp100,000 (about $10) per month. The BLT was financed from budgetary savings due to the reduction of the fuel subsidy and covered 19.1 million recipient households.

Among Indonesian social protection programs, the BLT received the greatest public attention due to its management. The program was targeted to poor households based on the Statistics Indonesia standard; however, because the poverty information system was inaccurate, this standard was criticized by nonrecipients who perceived themselves as eligible for the cash transfer. Other criticism came from opposition leaders due to the BLT's poor targeting, timing, and lack of conditionality: Due to poor targeting, the leakage was high and there were undercoverage problems; some people saw the BLT as part of short-term transfers to win the votes of the poor during elections; and, due to the lack of conditionality, the program was seen to "provide a fish rather than a fishhook," and thus could establish a dependency mentality among the poor.

However, policymakers and recipients who favored the BLT perceived it as the right way to enhance household financial liquidity in the midst of the price hike due to the reduced fuel subsidy as, in theory, the BLT money should have contributed to smoothing out household consumption.

---

[5]   *Sekolah satu atap*, or "one-roofed schools," is a term for schools that accommodate more than one level of education (primary school to senior high school, preschool and primary school, etc.) in one building.

The BLT program was terminated in late 2009 and replaced with a conditional cash transfer, the Hopeful Family Program—Program Keluarga Harapan or PKH (Fiszbein and Schady 2009). The PKH was first introduced in 2008 in three pilot provinces with the highest poverty rate, and in 2009 the PKH operated in seven provinces. In 2010, the PKH was implemented in 13 provinces, covering more than 703,000 recipient households. Recipient households that fulfill educational and health requirements are eligible for Rp600,000–Rp2,200,000 per year (Rp50,000–Rp183,000 per month) or around $67–$244 per year (about $5.5–$20 per month). Unfortunately, the PKH covers fewer than 1 million households, compared with the 19.1 million households covered by the BLT or the 17.09 million covered by subsidized rice. The government argues that the PKH targets only the very poor households, to improve their maternal and neonatal health and/or children's education status.

A qualitative study by Febriany, Toyamah, and Sodo (2010) on elementary education revealed that the PKH motivates rural households to maintain their children's enrollment in elementary and junior secondary schools, and hence to increases enrollment rates. But the PKH has not adequately brought dropouts back to school. The study also found the health benefits of the program were strongest in rural poor areas. Nevertheless, the short duration of the program and the supply-side issues in village healthcare have prevented the PKH from reaching its maximum potential contribution to increasing the percentage of births attended by skilled midwives in an adequate health facility.

10.3.2. Cluster 2: Community Empowerment for Poverty Reduction

For the second cluster, the government integrated programs scattered in different ministries and institutions under the umbrella of the National Program for Community Empowerment (Program Nasional Pemberdayaan Masyarakat—PNPM) to empower poor districts and subdistricts. Previously, such programs were inefficient, ineffective, and overlapping. Therefore, in 2006 President Yudhoyono declared a new policy to accelerate poverty alleviation efforts and to extend employment opportunities for the poor by consolidating empowerment programs under the PNPM.

Community empowerment is not a new approach to development in Indonesia. The Inpres Desa Tertinggal and Village Infrastructure Program were implemented before the Asian financial crisis. After the crisis, empowerment was extended into various programs, such as the Empowerment of the Regions to Overcome the Impact of the Economic Crisis, Kecamatan Development Program (Program Pengembangan Kecamatan—PPK), Urban Poverty Reduction Program (P2KP), Farmer and

Fisher's Increasing Income Project, and Economic Empowerment for Coastal Communities.

The PNPM adopted the scheme and mechanism of the PPK. The PPK was initiated before the crisis as a revised Inpres Desa Teringgal and Village Infrastructure Program. The first phase of the PPK (PPK I) started in 1998–1999 and continued to 2002; PPK II was implemented during 2003–2006; and PPK III, during 2006–2007. The PPK provides subdistricts with block grants of approximately Rp500 million to Rp1 billion ($55,000–$110,000), depending on population size. The subdistricts with the poorest rural communities are targeted. The program requires active engagement of communities in a participatory planning and decision-making process to define their development needs and activities. The latest impact evaluation of PPK II (Voss 2008) indicated that the program had a significant impact on poor households and households living in poor subdistricts. Voss also revealed that the PPK II is most effective in poor and remote areas where infrastructure costs prevent local government investment or where government investment is not a priority.

The P2KP is the urban counterpart to the PPK. The P2KP was first started in 1999 to reach urban poor people in Java. It provides revolving capital within a community for sustainable income generation by urban poor groups and individuals. The P2KP will also fund development of basic infrastructure and related employment generation activities selected by communities in low-income urban areas. The P2KP initially targeted the poor in about 60 local government jurisdictions in the northern half of Java, especially in Yogyakarta, Malang, and Bandung, where most of the country's dense urban areas and small-scale industries are located.

The success of the PPK and P2KP programs encouraged the government to advance the PNPM. The harmonization agenda in the PNPM will be continued until 2015 by dividing the program in two parts (Tim Pengendali PNPM Mandiri 2009):

- The PNPM-Inti is the area-based community empowerment program. Its programs include the PPK, P2KP, PNPM-Disadvanteged and Specific Area (P2DTK), PNPM-rural infrastructure (Program Peningkatan Infrastruktur Perdesaan—PPIP), and PNPM-socioeconomic infrastructure (Program Pengembangan Infrastruktur Sosial Ekonomi Wilayah—PISEW) schemes.

- The PNPM-Penguatan is an area- and sector-based community empowerment program, implemented to achieve a particular target. Examples are the PNPM-Rural Agribusiness Development (Pengembangan Usaha Agribisnis Perdesaan—PUAP) and Direct Cash Transfer for Agricultural Investment (Bantuan Langsung Masyarakat Untuk Keringanan Investasi Pertanian—BLM-KIP).

The harmonization agenda is a process of synchronizing and integrating objectives, principles, and policies, from planning and budgeting to implementation and monitoring of the poverty alleviation program, based on empowerment of communities and individuals. The harmonization is crucial for the PNPM to succeed, considering that the programs are under the coordination of different ministries.

The main source for funding the PNPM is ministries' and institutions' budgets. Each ministry and institution allocates budget for the applicable PNPM technical components and cash transfers. Each ministry is also responsible for the use of the PNPM operational budget at the relevant national, provincial, and lower levels. Furthermore, each ministry should coordinate with the governor and head of the regional governments for program implementation. Regional governments can also participate in the budgeting. Funding from local budgets, if needed, can be used to support PNPM activities such as coordination activities, additional cash transfer components, and other technical expenses. Generally, local budgets provide 20%–25% of the PNPM funding, the share depending on each region's fiscal capacity. Funding also comes from multi-and bi-lateral development partners, as grants and loans. This funding is coordinated under the PNPM Support Facility, the head of which is the deputy for poverty, manpower, and SMEs in Bappenas.

The PPK and P2KP achievements in several provinces became a basis for extending the program to all provinces and more districts. The PNPM-Disadvantaged and Specific Area, PNPM-rural infrastructure, and PNPM-socioeconomic infrastructure schemes are not implemented in all provinces, but may be extended in the future.

The poverty reduction program through community empowerment seems to be very effective at increasing the access of poor communities to basic health and education services (Voss 2008; LP3ES 2007). However, for sustaining the projects and post-project services, they should be integrated into the original design of the PNPM. The importance of community capacity, especially the role of the village alert network cadres in increasing community awareness of child and maternal health, is widely acknowledged. Village leaders also have important roles in boosting community participation.

10.3.3. Cluster 3: Microenterprise Empowerment for Poverty Reduction

This cluster is intended to empower the poor and near poor who have an occupation or business that fulfills their basic needs, but who still need to improve their well-being. While the role of microenterprises in eradicating poverty has been widely known for several decades, the 1997 crisis highlighted how microenterprises help the poor to survive and recover from crisis. Most of the poor work in the informal sector, comprising small-scale and microenterprises that produce or distribute goods and services. These enterprises are generally independent, are largely family owned, use low levels of skills and technology, and are highly labor intensive. Microenterprises provide income and employment for significant proportions of workers in rural and urban areas (Harvie 2003). In 2009, Indonesia had about 43 million microenterprises, accounting for more than 50% of national GDP. The data also show that each microenterprise absorbs about 1–5 workers (TKPK 2009).

Harvie (2003) also pointed out that microenterprise development—complemented with proper microfinance support—can help achieve the main social and economic development objectives: poverty reduction, empowerment of women, employment creation, and development of private sector enterprises. Though the four objectives cannot be fully separated, this section focuses on the role of microenterprise empowerment to reach poverty alleviation objectives.

The General Assembly of the United Nations has recognized the positive impact of microcredit on poverty reduction with the launching of General Assembly Resolution 52/194 of 18 December 1997, on the role of microcredit in eradicating poverty. This was reemphasized during the International Year of Microcredit 2005. Indonesia has had a long history of policies and programs to provide microcredit for the poor. Indonesia's first microfinance institution, Badan Kredit Desa, was established more than 100 years ago and by 2005 Indonesia had 50,000 microfinance institutions, among the highest number in the world (Shrader et al. 2006).

Ismawan (2004) noted that, since the early 1970s, massive agricultural credit programs with subsidized interest rates have been implemented to increase agricultural production and farmers' incomes through the adoption of new technologies. Small-scale and microenterprises became a government target in the 1970s with the introduction of the Small Enterprise Development Program. Indonesia's microfinance sector was also influenced by the deregulation of the banking sector in 1983. The deregulation opened the opportunity for fundamental reform of the Bank Rakyat Indonesia Village Unit System, which had suffered from the collapse of the BIMAS (agricultural loan) credit program. A second financial deregulation package, called "PAKTO" —short for *Paket Oktober* or October package— was introduced in 1988 and reduced the barriers to new private banks entering into microfinance. The PAKTO can be considered as a microfinance regulation, as it enabled the entry of new, privately owned microbanks (known as "people's credit banks"). The regulations were consolidated in the banking law in 1992, which mandated the role of microbanks and formally placed them vis-à-vis commercial banks.

After the 1997 crisis, a memorandum of understanding between the Central Bank of Indonesia and the secretary of the Committee for Poverty Alleviation established a financial consultancy to assist microenterprises and small- and medium-sized enterprises (MSMEs) to access banking services. The consultancy provides services to connect MSMEs with banks so the MSMEs can quickly absorb credit, based on the bank's credit business plan. In 2004, the government launched a scheme for microcredit without substitute collateral. This scheme is supported by funding from the state-owned enterprises' partnership and environmental program as credit assurance for microenterprises. Prior to 2004, several microcredit programs operated under various ministries.

Microcredit for the Poor is a government program aimed at empowering microenterprises. The program's main objective is to increase access of the poor to inexpensive capital. Furthermore, the SNPK elaborated the relationship between microenterprises, microfinance, and microcredit in the agenda of poverty alleviation. Policies include creating a conducive business climate, creating employment, improving business capacity, improving entrepreneurship, and enhancing access to productive resources. Particularly related to cluster 3, in late 2007, the government launched for MSMEs and cooperatives a microcredit loan program called Kredit Usaha Rakyat (KUR).

Through the KUR, the government subsidizes 70% of the premium. The KUR's target is microenterprises and cooperatives that have feasible businesses but are not bankable because they lack collateral. The KUR is also accessible by community groups, empowered by the previous program. Up to August 2009, the KUR had benefited more than 2 million businesspeople nationally, with an amount of Rp15.3 trillion.

However, evidence regarding the KUR's effect on poverty reduction is hard to find. The impact of microcredit projects on poverty reduction is hard to measure, as it depends on the design of the project. An ADB (2001) study evaluating ADB's rural credit assistance in several Asian countries, including Indonesia, could only conclude that such projects are an indirect channel for poverty reduction by improving incomes and the acquisition of assets. In doing so, those who give credit assistance have to make sure that the project involves small farmers as well as areas with high incidence of poverty.

MICRA (2007) found similar results. Assessing five microcredit programs in Indonesia, MICRA concluded that poverty targeting in terms of location serves the poor community well—reaching low-income people in relatively poor areas. The use of participatory rural appraisals and statistical data is effective in targeting poor areas and appropriate beneficiaries. However, monitoring and evaluation are lacking. The government tends to focus on directing resources toward reaching the poor but allocates insufficient resources to designing and implementing effective monitoring and evaluation for assessing the program impacts. Achieving an effective and efficient program also requires determining how to measure the program's impact.

10.4. Conclusion and Policy Recommendations

10.4.1. Conclusion

Poverty reduction has become a major policy initiative in Indonesia since the 1997 Asian financial crisis. This is a significant departure from the development approach prior to the crisis. In the first five Repelitas, between 1969 and 1994, poverty reduction was not explicitly stated as an objective of development. Rather, the government aimed at economic growth, stability, and equality. Only in the sixth Repelita, in 1994, did the government aim explicitly for poverty reduction, implemented through a presidential instruction on the "left behind villages program."

When the 1997 financial crisis hit Indonesia, the government grappled with the social impact, including an increase in poverty. The government established the Social Safety Net (JPS) program, covering food security, health, education, employment creation, and community empowerment. The JPS program was the start of various poverty reduction and social protection programs implemented by successive governments in the post-crisis period.

Currently, the government strategy for poverty reduction is formulated by sorting poverty reduction programs into three clusters based on their objectives and targets: (1) social assistance, with the objective of providing direct assistance to poor households to ease their burdens in meeting basic needs; (2) community empowerment, to provide funding that poor communities can use to improve basic social and economic services according to their own priorities; and (3) microenterprise empowerment, to provide microenterprises with access to credit without having to provide collateral.

The expectation is that, over time, poor households that receive cluster 1 programs will graduate and become beneficiaries of cluster 2 programs, and finally can benefit from cluster 3 programs to take them out of poverty. Evaluations of the effectiveness of these programs in achieving their stated objectives have shown mixed results. To increase the effectiveness of poverty reduction programs, the government recently established a national team for accelerating poverty reduction, chaired by the Vice President. This shows the high level of the government's commitment to achieving its target in poverty reduction.

10.4.2. Policy Recommendations

The current development strategy for pro-poor growth through job creation fits well with Indonesia's long-term effort to fight poverty and vulnerability to poverty efficiently and sustainably. However, the newly introduced national management of poverty alleviation and the current poverty database targeting mechanism, as well as program integration and quality, need to be improved. In line with the RPJMN 2010–2014 poverty alleviation target, for addressing these weaknesses, this chapter proposes several key policies that together could enhance the human and financial capital of the chronic and transient poor so they can move out of poverty, and simultaneously safeguard the near poor from falling into poverty.

The three areas of reforms proposed, as summarized in Table 10.4 at the end of the chapter, are

- institutional capacity for managing the reduction of poverty and vulnerability;
- quality of the poverty database and targeting mechanism; and
- better integrated and higher quality social assistance, community empowerment, and microenterprise empowerment programs.

10.4.2.1. Institutional Capacity for Managing the Reduction of Poverty and Vulnerability

The "big bang" decentralization based on Laws 22 and 25 of 1999 brought to the fore the institutional capacity issue in poverty reduction policy. Greater responsibilities and authority, particularly for budget and expenditure management, are acquired of regional governments at provincial and district levels. As reported by World Bank (2006), McCulloch (2009), Patunru, McCulloch, and von Luebke (2009), districts are now more in charge of most service delivery, providing public facilities and infrastructure, and issuing local regulations on social, political, and economic matters.

Other studies reveal the connection between governance and poverty reduction. Bad governance makes poverty reduction efforts ineffective (Blaxall 2000; Eid 2000; Gupta, Davoodi, and Alonso-Terne 1998) if, for example, the money for poverty alleviation projects is misused (Woodhouse 2001). Therefore, the consensus is that good governance is necessary for effective poverty reduction practices in Indonesia.

To improve regional governance and enhance poverty reduction efforts, clear guidelines are needed to ensure appropriate regulation of markets at national and local levels. Furthermore, in the design and implementation of poverty reduction programs, coordination among central government departments and between central and lower level governments needs to be strengthened. This may require a poverty reduction body—either a new body or an existing one—with a strong mandate to coordinate poverty reduction efforts at the central and lower levels. This body would have the power to review and revoke central and lower level government regulations that are counterproductive to poverty reduction efforts. Meanwhile, civil society needs to strengthen its capacity and build a coalition to fight bad governance practices. The poverty reduction body and civil society should become partners to increase the effectiveness of efforts to reduce poverty.

The poverty reduction body would also become the center of the poverty information system. It would be the hub for exchanging all data relevant to poverty reduction efforts. The poverty reduction body would become the depository of all studies on poverty in Indonesia and, therefore, the center for providing lessons learned from poverty reduction programs, from the central and lower level governments.

In the future, every economic policy should be assessed prior to implementation to ascertain its likely impact on the poor. If the assessment shows that a policy would have a negative impact on the livelihoods of the poor, then the policy should be revised or cancelled. However, if the policy is considered as a necessity and has to be maintained as it is, an accompanying policy would have to be formulated to fully compensate the poor for any negative impacts.

Community participation is essential to poverty reduction efforts. The principle of community participation is relevant in the context of a decentralized, democratic Indonesia where voice, transparency, and accountability have become daily practice. However, the community participation will be successful only with the support of the local government and the capacity of civil society organizations to understand the poverty reduction programs and to push for greater transparency.

The poverty reduction body would lead in improving the way poverty reduction programs are designed, implemented, and monitored. Currently, the participation of the poor in most poverty reduction programs is primarily limited to being passive beneficiaries. Although households in general participate in village meetings, the depth of their participation and their awareness of information concerning village activities is low. The poverty reduction body would lead the efforts to effectively involve the poor in designing, implementing, and monitoring poverty reduction programs.

Lessons learned from experience show that schemes managed at the local level might be able to provide services more effectively and efficiently than those managed from the national level, even if the system is developed and owned by the central government. Evidence shows that participation in social protection programs depends highly on the role of local activists or cadres. The cadres have the ability to distribute people's rights in a program comprehensively. They can reduce communication barriers between government officials and the community, and hence reduce the cost of program socialization. The cadres also have extensive knowledge about determining which community members are poor, thus improving the targeting of social protection programs.

10.4.2.2. Quality of Reforms in the Poverty Database and Targeting Strategy

Targeting is an important feature of the design of poverty reduction programs. Targeting can concentrate program expenditures on those who need them most, thus saving money and improving program efficiency. In addition, given budgetary and time constraints facing program implementers, expenditures on social sectors must be fine-tuned and well targeted (Sumarto and Suryahadi 2001).

The two general types of targeting mechanism are (1) administrative targeting (selection by program implementers), and (2) market-based or self-selection targeting (depending solely on the incentive structure inherent in a program to attract potential beneficiaries). Two approaches commonly used in administrative targeting are geographic targeting and household or individual targeting. Indonesia has adopted a combination of the two general mechanisms.

The government, however, has not been particularly accurate in targeting, and evidence from various targeted programs shows they are only slightly pro-poor. Both the undercoverage error (the proportion of the poor that are not included in the program) and the leakage error (the proportion of beneficiaries who are not poor) are high (Sumarto and Suryahadi 2001, World Bank 2006).

Sumarto and Suryahadi (2001) formulated important lessons from Indonesia's experience, aiming to improve the effectiveness of targeting and thus increase the benefits of poverty reduction programs. First, because static administrative targeting is inadequate to catch the newly poor or shocked households, a well-designed, publicly accessible, "real-time" information system is crucial to implementing effective social protection programs. Second, designing and implementing large-scale social safety net programs in a crisis situation requires institutional commitment at the central level, supported by clear objectives and simple design. Third, there has to be some allowance for local flexibility in countries as large and complex as Indonesia.

To address the problem of unaffordable services for the poor, the current policy to rely on conditional cash transfers is in the right direction. The PKH scheme could overcome the problem of unaffordable direct, indirect, and opportunity costs faced by the poor in accessing services. To improve the bargaining power of the poor vis-à-vis service providers, the government could introduce a voucher scheme wherein the poor themselves choose the provider for the services they need, such as education and healthcare, through competitive means. In addition, greater focus is needed on including disadvantaged and marginalized groups in the services provided by the government. Such groups include people who do not have proper identification cards, who are often considered as illegal residents and thus are excluded from government services and programs, and people who live in isolated areas, including indigenous peoples.

Even if the economy achieves strong growth, some sections of the population will remain vulnerable to poverty, and most of them work in the informal sector. Therefore, it is important to develop a comprehensive and integrated social protection system. This social protection system should be able to maintain people's standard of living above a socially and politically agreed minimum level, including guaranteed access of all people to basic levels of services such as education, healthcare, clean water, and sanitation.

Lessons from experience show that the ad hoc poverty reduction programs implemented directly during the 1997 financial crisis lacked integration; were scattered through different institutions,, causing targeting problems; and had issues of monitoring and evaluation. The newer programs apparently have better monitoring and evaluation systems but the impacts of programs are generally infrequently evaluated. Thus, integrating the programs under one umbrella would be complicated. In addition, finding sufficient administrative and fiscal capacity to implement a universal program is a challenge.

10.4.2.3. Toward Integrating and Improving the Quality of Social Assistance, Community Empowerment, and Microenterprise Empowerment Programs

The evolution of names, contents, targeting mechanisms, and delivery of the various social assistance programs (cluster 1) leads to a crucial quest to integrate this cluster into the Indonesian National Social Security System (Sistem Jaminan Sosial Nasional—SJSN). Indonesia has six interrelated programs from which individual households directly benefit (Figure 10.3):
- Raskin (subsidized rice),
- Jamkesmas (social health insurance),
- BKM and BSM (poor student scholarships),
- BOS (school operational assistance),
- PKH (conditional cash transfers for households), and
- part of the PNPM Generasi (conditional cash transfers for communities).

Although by design the direct impact of each program is different, the household-level impact of the six programs should be viewed from an integrated household consumption perspective, as some programs can substitute for, or have spillover effects on, others. If the programs were put together in an intrahousehold decision-making frame, they could be solidified into one or two programs; for example, one scheme for household conditional cash transfers with specific requirements for health status, educational enrollment, and food consumption basket, plus the expanded coverage of Social Health Insurance (Jamkesmas) could fulfill the SJSN law. Reducing the number of social assistance schemes would reduce the administrative costs of the programs (World Bank 2006).

Clusters 1 and 2 should cover separate areas; for example, cluster 2 elements such as the PNPM Generasi should work solely on boosting the supply side and not the demand side. Because cluster 2 is still in a pilot testing phase, timely monitoring and evaluation are needed to continually improve its technical guidance and the effectiveness and efficiency of its implementation practices.

Cluster 3 on microenterprise empowerment needs to be redesigned to have more leverage for the poor and near poor and to link it with local initiatives on poverty reduction, and to provide incentives for smallholders to accumulate productive assets, through a productive asset transfer program.

Table 10.4: Summary of Policy Agenda for Enhancing Poverty Reduction Efforts

		Policy Agenda	
Purpose	Reform Area	Short Term (1–2 years)	Medium to Long Term (2–5 years)
To enhance human and financial capital accumulation by the chronic and transient poor so they can move out of poverty and to safeguard the near-poor from falling into poverty	1. Institutional capacity to reduce poverty and vulnerability to poverty	1.1. Strengthen the capacity of national and regional planning agencies for planning, coordinating, implementing, and monitoring poverty and vulnerability reduction programs	1.3. Strengthen community participation in planning, coordinating, implementing, and monitoring local initiatives on poverty and vulnerability reduction programs
		1.2. Initiate rigorous and external evaluation system for national and local, public and private initiatives for reducing poverty and vulnerability	1.4. Ensure that rigorous and external evaluation is an integral part of every poverty and vulnerability reduction proposal
	2. Quality of poverty database and targeting mechanism	2.1. Redesign the poverty database to ensure accurate targeting of multidimensional poverty problems	2.3. Implement an accurate poverty targeting mechanism for clusters 1 (social assistance), 2 (community empowerment), and 3 (microenterprise empowerment) of poverty reduction programs

continued on next page

Table 10.4: Summary of Policy Agenda for Enhancing Poverty Reduction Efforts

		Policy Agenda	
Purpose	Reform Area	Short Term (1–2 years)	Medium to Long Term (2–5 years)
		2.2. Improve the accuracy of the poverty database to ensure accurate understanding of multidimensional poverty profiles	2.4. Evaluate and improve the accuracy of the newly designed and implemented poverty database and its targeting scheme
	3. Integration and improvement of the quality of social assistance, community empowerment, and microenterprise empowerment programs	3.1. Design the integration of the social assistance programs (cluster 1) to improve the adequacy of the range of services, value for money, and coverage of poor and near-poor individuals and households in combating poverty and vulnerability to poverty	3.5. Evaluate the implementation of integrated social assistance programs as a preliminary move toward fulfilling the National Social Security System law
		3.2. Redesign cluster 2 programs to not overlap or duplicate the related programs of social assistance (cluster 1). For example the PNPM Generasi (cluster 2) could overlap or/and duplicate the Program Keluarga Harapan (PKH) (cluster 1)	3.6. Integrate the national People's Business Credit program with local initiatives for reducing poverty and vulnerability to poverty
		3.3. Redesign the scheme of People's Business Credit initiatives (cluster 3) to provide the poor, near-poor, and smallholders with adequate access to the program	
		3.4. Provide incentives for smallholders to accumulate productive assets, initiated through a program to transfer productive assets	

Appendix: Glossary

Abbreviation, Acronym, or Short Form	Indonesian	English Approximation	Notes
APBN	Anggaran Pendapatan Belanja Nasional	National Budget	
Askeskin	Asuransi kesehatan bagi warga miskin	Health insurance for the poor	
Bappenas	Badan Perencanaan Pembangunan Nasional	National Development Planning Board	
BKD	Badan Kredit Desa	Village Credit Institution	A system of village-owned financial institutions in West, Central, and East Java, and Yogyakarta
BKKBN	Badan Koordinasi Keluarga Berencana Nasional	National Coordinating Board for Family Planning	
BKM	Beasiswa Keluarga Miskin	Scholarships for Poor Households	
BLM-KIP	Bantuan Langsung Masyarakat Untuk Keringanan Investasi Pertanian	Direct Cash Transfer for Agricultural Investment	
BLT	Bantuan Langsung Tunai	Direct (unconditional) Cash Transfer	
BOS	Bantuan Operasional Sekolah	School Operational Assistance	
BPS	Badan Pusat Statistik	Statistics Indonesia	
BSM	Beasiswa Siswa Miskin	Scholarships for Poor Students	
Bulog	Badan Urusan Logistik	National Logistics Agency	
IDT	Inpres Desa Tertinggal	President Instruction on Disadvantaged Villages	
Jamkesmas	Jaminan Kesehatan Masyarakat	Public Health Insurance	Evolved from Askeskin
JPS	Jaring Pengaman Sosial	Social Safety Net	
JPS–BK	Jaring Pengaman Sosial Bidang Kesehatan	Social Safety Net for Health	
JPS–DBO	Jaring Pengaman Sosial Bidang Dana Bantuan Operasional	Social Safety Net for School Operational Assistance Fund	

Appendix: Glossary

Abbreviation, Acronym, or Short Form	Indonesian	English Approximation	Notes
Kukesra	Kredit Usaha Keluarga Sejahtera	People's Prosperity Business Credit	Soft loan given to pre-prosperous and level-1 prosperous rural households that are not listed as beneficiaries of People's Prosperity Savings (Takesra)
KUR	Kredit Usaha Rakyat	People's Business Credit	Microcredit loan program for microenterprises and small and medium-sized enterprises as well as cooperatives
OPK	Operasi Pasar Khusus	Special Market Operation	Government policy aimed at helping the poor by providing subsidized rice
P2DTK	Program Pengembangan Daerah Tertinggal dan Khusus	Disadvantaged and Specific Areas Development Program	Part of the National Program for Community Empowerment (PNPM) aimed at empowering the government and the community for accelerating socioeconomic development in disadvantaged and specific areas

continued on next page

Appendix: Glossary

Abbreviation, Acronym, or Short Form	Indonesian	English Approximation	Notes
P2KP	Program Penanggulangan Kemiskinan di Perkotaan	Urban Poverty Reduction Program	A government program for poverty reduction through the empowerment of communities and other local development actors, including local government and other stakeholders, aimed at developing autonomous poverty reduction and sustainable development movements
PISEW	Program Pengembangan Infrastruktur Sosial Ekonomi Wilayah	Regional Socioeconomic Infrastructure Development Program	Part of the National Program for Community Empowerment (PNPM) aimed at encouraging the synchronization of regional development planning through empowering the capacity of government apparatus and institutions in the community
PKH	Program Keluarga Harapan	Hopeful Family Program	Conditional cash transfer for poor households
PKK	Pemberdayaan Kesejahteraan Keluarga	Empowerment for Family Welfare	
PKPS-BBM	Program Kompensasi Pengurangan Subsidi Bahan Bakar Minyak	Fuel Subsidy Reduction Compensation Program	
PNPM	Program Nasional Pemberdayaan Masyarakat	National Program for Community Empowerment	

continued on next page

Appendix: Glossary

Abbreviation, Acronym, or Short Form	Indonesian	English Approximation	Notes
PNPM Generasi Sehat dan Cerdas		National Program for Community Empowerment for Better Health and Education	Part of government's main poverty reduction program (PNPM Mandiri) especially aimed at accelerating the achievement of three goals of the MDGs: 9-year universal education, reduction in neonatal mortality, and improvement in the health of mothers
PNPM Mandiri		National Program for Community Empowerment	A national government poverty reduction program based on community empowerment
PNPM Perdesaan		National Program for Rural Community Empowerment	Part of government's main poverty reduction program (PNPM Mandiri) especially aimed at improving the welfare of and providing more job opportunities for rural poor communities by encouraging autonomy in decision-making and development program management
PNPM Perkotaan		National Program for Urban Community Empowerment	Also known as P2KP

continued on next page

Appendix: Glossary

Abbreviation, Acronym, or Short Form	Indonesian	English Approximation	Notes
PPIP	Program Peningkatan Infrastruktur Perdesaan	Rural Infrastructure Improvement Program	Part of government's main poverty reduction program (PNPM Mandiri) especially aimed at improving infrastructure in rural areas
PPK	Program Pengembangan Kecamatan	Kecamatan (Subdistrict) Development Program	
PPLS-08	Program Pendataan Perlindungan Sosial 2008	2008 Social Protection Data Collection Program	
PSE-05	Pendataan Sosial Ekonomi Penduduk 2005	Socioeconomic Data Collection	
PUAP	Pengembangan Usaha Agribisnis Perdesaan	Rural Agribusiness Development	
Raskin	Beras untuk Rakyat Miskin	Rice for the Poor	Subsidized rice sold to the poor at affordable price
Repelita	Rencana Pembangunan Lima Tahun	Five-Year Development Plan	Development plan (during the New Order Era, 1969–1998)
RPJMN	Rencana Pembangunan Jangka Menengah Nasional	National Medium-Term Development Plan	
SJSN	Sistem Jaminan Sosial Nasional	National Social Security System	
SKPD	Satuan Kerja Perangkat Daerah	Local Government Work Unit	
SNPK	Strategi Nasional Penanggulangan Kemiskinan	National Poverty Reduction Strategy Paper	
Susenas	Survei Sosial-Ekonomi Nasional	National Socioeconomic Survey	
Takesra	Tabungan Keluarga Sejahtera	People's Prosperity Savings	A program facilitated by Post Indonesia (PT POS), to support rural families, aimed at encouraging savings

continued on next page

Appendix: Glossary

Abbreviation, Acronym, or Short Form	Indonesian	English Approximation	Notes
TKPK	Tim Koordinasi Penanggulangan Kemiskinan	Coordinating Team for Poverty Reduction	
TNP2K	Tim Nasional Percepatan Penanggulangan Kemiskinan	National Team for Accelerating Poverty Reduction	

References

Asian Development Bank (ADB). 2001. *Impact Evaluation Study on ADB's Rural Credit Assistance in Bangladesh, People's Republic of China, Indonesia, Nepal, Philippines, Sri Lanka, and Thailand.* Manila.

Australia-Indonesia Basic Education Program (AIBEP). 2007. Program Manual. Jakarta: Australia-Indonesia Basic Education Program, Australia Indonesia Partnership.

———. 2010a. Achievements: Annual Performance Report 2007. http://www.bep.or.id/index.php?option=com_content&task=view&id=46&Itemid=64

———. 2010b. Basic Education Program—Pilar 1. School Construction. http://www.bep.or.id/index.php?option=com_content&task=view&id=33&Itemid=46

Avenzora, A. and Y. Haryono. 2008. *Analisis dan Penghitungan Tingkat Kemiskinan Tahun 2008* (Analysis and Computation of the Poverty Rate in Year 2008). Jakarta: Badan Pusat Statistik.

Badan Perencanaan den Pembangunan Nasional (National Development Planning Agency—Bappenas). 2006. Poverty Reduction in Indonesia: a Brief Review of Facts, Efforts, and Ways Forward. Paper presented in Forum on National Plans and PRSPs in East Asia in 4-6 April 206, Vientiane http://siteresources.worldbank.org/ INTEASTASIAPACIFIC/Resources/226262-1143156545724/Indonesia_Brief.pdf> (accessed 10 November 2009).

———. 2009. Laporan Penyelenggaraan Musrenbangnas RPJMN 2010–2014 di Jakarta pada Desember 2009. (Minutes of the meeting for the National Development Consultation for the Mid-Term National Development Plan 2010–2014, Jakarta, December 2009). http://musrenbangnas.bappenas.go.id/uploads/Laporan/Laporan_Musrenbangnas_RPJMN_2010_2014.pdf (accessed 26 February 2010).

Badan Pusat Statistik (Statistics Indonesia—BPS). 1997. Statistical Yearbook of Indonesia. Jakarta.

———. 2002. *Dasar-Dasar Analisis Kemiskinan* (The Basics of Poverty Analysis). Jakarta: Statistics Indonesia and the World Bank Institute.

———. 2007. National Socioeconomic Survey (Susenas) Household Panel Data. Jakarta.

———. 2009. National Socioeconomic Survey (Susenas) Household Panel Data. Jakarta .

Badan Urusan Logistik (National Logistics Agency—Bulog). 2008. Rapat Kerja Pengendalian Dan Evaluasi Raskin Semester I 2008 (Coordination Meeting for Monitoring and Evaluation of the Rice for the Poor Program in the First Semester of 2008). http://www. menkokesra.go.id/pdf/rakerpim/rakerpim_sem1_08_ bulog.pdf (accessed 17 November 2009).

———. 2009. Raskin 2009. http://www.bulog.co.id/ (accessed 11 December 2009).

———. 2010. Raskin. http://www.bulog.co.id/ (accessed 21 June 2010).

Blaxall, J. 2000. Governance and Poverty. Paper presented at the Joint Workshop on Poverty Reduction Strategies in Mongolia. World Bank, Ulan Bataar, 4–6 October. http://www.worldbank. org/poverty/strategies/events/ mongolia/gov.pdf (accessed 22 March 2003).

Coady, D., M. Grosh, and J. Hoddinott. 2004. *Targeting of Transfers in Developing Countries: Review of Lessons and Experience.* Washington, DC: World Bank.

Committee for Poverty Alleviation. 2003. *Interim Poverty Reduction Strategy Paper.* Jakarta.

Eid, U. 2000. Good Governance for Poverty Reduction. Paper presented at the Asian Development Bank Seminar on The New Social Policy and Poverty Agenda for Asia and the Pacific. Chiang Mai, 5 May. http://www.uschi-eid.de/docs/000505-poverty.htm (accessed 21 March 2003).

Febriany, V., N. Toyamah, and R. J. Sodo. 2010. Studi Kualitatif Dampak PNPM Generasi dan PKH Terhadap Ketersediaan dan Pemanfaatan Pelayanan Kesehatan Ibu dan Anak dan Pendidikan Dasar: Ringkasan Eksekutif (A Qualitative Study of the Impact of the PNPM Generasi and PKH on the Availability and Utilization of Maternal and Neonatal Health Services and Basic Educational Services: Executive Summary). Jakarta: SMERU Research Institute.

Fiszbein, A. and N. Schady. 2009. Conditional Cash Transfer: Reducing Present and Future Poverty. A World Bank Policy Research Report. Washington, DC: World Bank.

Frankenberg, E., D. Thomas, and K. Beegle. 1999. The Real Costs of Indonesia's Economic Crisis: Preliminary Findings from the Indonesia Family Life Surveys. *Labor and Population Program Working Paper Series* 99-04. Santa Monica, CA: RAND.

Gupta, S., H. Davoodi, and R. Alonso-Terne. 1998. Does Corruption Affect Income Inequality and Poverty? *IMF Working Paper* No. 98/76. Washington, DC: International Monetary Fund.

Handoko, R. and P. Patriadi. 2005. Evaluasi Kebijakan Subsidi Non BBM (Evaluation of Non-Fuel Subsidy). *Kajian Ekonomi dan Keuangan* 9(4) http://www.fiskal.depkeu.go.id/eng/kajian%5Crudi&pandu-4. pdf

Harvie, C. 2003. The Contribution of Micro-enterprises to Economic Recovery and Poverty Alleviation in East Asia. *University of Wollongong Economics Working Paper Series* WP 03-07. Australia.

Hastuti and J. Maxwell. 2003. Rice for Poor Families (RASKIN): Did the 2002 Program Operate Effectively? Evidence from Bengkulu and Karawang. Research Report. Jakarta: The SMERU Research Institute.

Hastuti, S. Mawardi, B. Sulaksono, Akhmadi, S. Devina, and R. P. Artha. 2008. The Effectiveness of the Raskin Program. Research Report. Jakarta: SMERU Research Institute.

Hastuti, S. Usman, S. Mawardi, J. Sodo, D. Marbun, and Ruhmanuytati. 2009. Pemantauan Dampak Sosial Ekonomi Krisis Keuangan Global 2008/09: Peran Program Perlindungan Sosial dalam Meredam Dampak Krisis Keuangan Global 2008/09. Research Report. Jakarta: SMERU Research Institute.

Ismawan, B. 2004. *Managing the Growth of Microcredit Programs: Human Resource Management including Recruiting, Training, and Motivating Staff, the Challenge of Microfinance Growth and Human Resource Management.* Paper presented at 2004 the Asia Pacific Region Microcredit Summit Meeting of Council (APRMS), Dhaka, 16–19 February. http://www.pksf-bd.org/speeches%20&%20 Papers/ Mr.%20Bambang_Ismawan/MANAGING%20THE%20 GROWTH%20OF%20MICROCREDIT%20PROGRAM1.doc (accessed 20 December 2009).

Leith, J., C. Porter, SMERU Institute, and P. Warr. 2003. Indonesia Rice Tariff , Research Report on Poverty and Social Impact Analysis. Jakarta: Government of Indonesia and Department for International Development, United Kingdom.

LP3ES: Institute for Social and Economic Research, Education, and Information. 2007. Qualitative Baseline Survey on PNPM. Final Report. Jakarta: LP3ES.

McCulloch, N. 2009. Introduction. In McCulloch, N. (ed.) Rural Investment Climate in Indonesia. Singapore: Institute for Southeast Asian Studies.

MICRA. 2007. Rapid Evaluation Report on Government Community Development Operations: Microfinance and Microcredit. http://www.micra-indo.org/content/view/69 /72/en (accessed on 26 December 2009).

Ministry of Health. 2006. *Pengembangan Desa Siaga dan Pos Kesehatan Desa* (The Development of Alert Villages and Village Health Center) http://www.litbang.depkes.go.id/download/Lokakarya/LoknasBandung/Desa-Siaga.pdf

———. 2009. *Rancangan Final Sistem Kesehatan Nasional* (Final Design of National Health System). http://www.depkes.go.id/index.php/berita/info-umum-kesehatan/130-rpjpk-dan-sistem-kesehatan-nasional.html

Ministry of Social Affairs. 2008. Efektifitas Bantuan Langsung Tunai 2008 (The Effectivity of Direct Cash Transfer in 2008). http://www.depsos.go.id/unduh/wawancana%20 MENSOS%20vs%20RAMAKO.pdf (accessed 8 November 2009).

Mukherjee, N. 2006. Voice of the Poor: Making Services Work for The Poor in Indonesia: Qualitative Consultation with the Poor at Eight Sites. Jakarta: World Bank. http://siteresources.worldbank.org/INTINDONESIA/Resources/Publication/ 280016-1152870963030/2753486-1165385030085/VOPenglish_cover.pdf (accessed 11 November 2009).

National Poverty Reduction Strategies (PRSP/SNPK). 2005. Indonesia Secretary of Poverty Reduction Strategies Coordination Team. Jakarta: TKPK

Patunru, A., N. McCulloch, and C. von Luebke. 2009. A Tale of Two Cities: The Political Economy of Local Investment Climate in Solo and Manado, Indonesia. IDS—Centre for The Future State, Working Paper 2009(338). http://www2.ids.ac.uk/futurestate/pdfs/Wp338.pdf (qaccessed 12 January 2010).

Pradhan, M., F. Saadah, and R. Sparrow. 2007. Did the Health Card Program Ensure Access to Medical Care for the Poor during Indonesia's Economic Crisis? *World Bank Economic Review*, 21(1): 125–50.

Raya, U. and C. Lada. 2009. Evaluation of Community Empowerment Program for Maternal and Neonatal Health in Alert Villages in 6 Districts of West Timor and Rote Ndao–Nusa Tenggara Timur. Center for Village Development of Nusa Cendana University and GTZ East Nusa Tenggara.

Shrader, L., N. Kamal, W. Darmono, and D. Johnston. 2006. *Youth and Access to Microfinance in Indonesia: Outreach and Options.* Jakarta: MercyCorps and MICRA.

SMERU. 2003. A Consolidation of Participatory Poverty Assessments in Indonesia (Volume I: Understanding the Voice of the Poor: Input for the Formulation of Poverty Reduction Strategy Paper). *Research Report.* Jakarta: SMERU Research Institute.

———. 2006. Evaluation of the Unconditional Cash Transfer in Indonesia. *SMERU Policy Brief.* Jakarta: SMERU Research Institute.

Sparrow, R. 2006. Health, Education and Economic Crisis: Protecting the Poor in Indonesia. PhD Dissertation. *Tinbergen Institute Research Series,* 373. Amsterdam: Vrije Universiteit.

Sparrow, R. 2007. Protecting Education for the Poor in Times of Crisis: An Evaluation of a Scholarship Programme in Indonesia. *Oxford Bulletin of Economics and Statistics,* 69 (1): 99–122.

Sparrow, R, A. Suryahadi, and W. Widyanti. 2010. Social Health Insurance for the Poor: Targeting and Impact of Indonesia's Askeskin Program. *SMERU Working Paper.* Jakarta: SMERU Research Institute. http:// www.smeru.or.id/ report/workpaper/askeskin/askeskin_eng.pdf (accessed 10 June 2010).

Sumarto, S. 2006. Social Safety Nets: Indonesia. *ODI Policy Brief 5.* London: Overseas Development Institute.

Sumarto, S., and A. Suryahadi. 2001. Principles and Approaches to Targeting: With Reference to the Indonesian Social Safety Net Program. *SMERU Working Paper.* Jakarta: SMERU Research Institute.

Sumarto, S., A. Suryahadi, and S. Bazzi. 2008. Indonesia's Social Protection during and after the Crisis. In A. Barrientos and D. Hulme (eds.), *Social Protection for the Poor and Poorest: Concepts, Policies and Politics.* Palgrave Studies in Development. Hampshire: Palgrave MacMillan.

Sumarto, S., A. Suryahadi, and W. Widyanti. 2002. Designs and Implementation of the Indonesian Social Safety Net Programs. *Developing Economis,* 40(1): 3–31.

———. 2005. Assessing the Impact of Indonesian Social Safety Net Programmes on Household Welfare and Poverty Dynamics. *European Journal of Development Research,* 17(1): 155–77.

Suryahadi, A. and S. Sumarto. 2007. The Role of Regional Government in Poverty Reduction. *SMERU Newsletter* No. 21, Jan-Mar/2007. Jakarta: SMERU Research Institute.

Suryahadi, A., S. Sumarto, and L. Pritchett. 2003. Evolution of Poverty during the Crisis in Indonesia. *Asian Economic Journal* 17(3): 221–41.

Team for Poverty Reduction (TKPK). 2007. A Brief History of Poverty Alleviation Coordination Team (TKPK). http://tkpkri.org/ sejarah-singkat-tim-koordinasi-penanggulangan-kemiskinan.html (accessed 15 November 2009).

———. 2009. *Capaian Koordinasi Penanggulangan Kemiskinan 2005-2009* (Achievement in Coordination Poverty Alleviation 2005–2009), Jakarta: Secretariat of Coordination Team for Poverty Reduction (TKPK), the State Ministry of People Welfare.

Tim Pengendali PNPM Mandiri. 2009. *Penjelasan dan Tanya Jawab seputar Program Nasional Pemberdayaan Masyarakat (PNPM) Mandiri* (Explanation and Question and Answer on National Program on Community Empowerment), Sekretariat Tim Pengendali PNPM Mandiri.

van de Walle, D. 1998. Targeting Revisited. *The World Bank Research Observer*, 13 (2).

Voss, J. 2008. Impact Evaluation of the Second Phase of the Kecamatan Development Program in Indonesia. Jakarta: EASIS-World Bank.

Woodhouse, A. 2001. Fighting Corruption in KDP. World Bank, Jakarta. Memo.

World Bank. 2004a. Initiative for Local Governance Reform. Jakarta.

———. 2004b. Poverty Reduction Strategies in Decentralized Contexts: Comparative Lessons in Local Planning and Fiscal Dimensions. Washington DC.

———. 2005a. *Indonesia Initiatives for Local Governance Reform Project: Project Appraisal Document*. Jakarta.

———. 2005b. Initiatives for Local Governance Reform: Decentralized Poverty Reduction Strategy (PRS): Experience from Indonesia. http://siteresources.worldbank.org/INTPRS1/ Resources/383606-111990439 0686/bbl051005_presentation.ppt (accessed 20 November 2009).

———. 2006. *Making the New Indonesia Work for the Poor*. Jakarta.

———. 2009a. Bulgaria: Social Assistance Programs: Cost, Coverage, Targeting and Poverty Impact. Research Report, Human Development Sector Unit Europe and Central Asia Region. Washington DC.

———. 2009b. Gross National Income Per Capita 2008, Atlas method and PPP. http://siteresources.worldbank.org/DATASTATISTICS/ Resources/GNIPC.pdf (accessed 1 March 2010).

———. 2009c. Investing in a more Sustainable Indonesia: Country Environmental Analysis. Jakarta: World Bank. http://www. preventionweb.net/files/11888_507620v20Revis1ox0info10CEA1 english.pdf (accessed 1 March 2010).

11. Decentralization

Tariq H. Niazi

11.1. Introduction

This chapter diagnoses Indonesia's experiences with decentralization. The historical focus is on the period from the commencement of "big bang" decentralization reforms in 1999 until early 2010. The policy focus is on the medium-term period of 2010–2015. The study of decentralization in any country typically involves a complex mix of historical, political, administrative, financial, economic, and governance elements. The study of decentralization in Indonesia in many ways involves even more than the usual range of complexities, because of the volatilities of recent history and politics, the country's highly regulated and complex administrative systems, the widely dispersed geographic nature, and large population of about 235 million people. Indonesia's complexities can lead to generalized national assessments of how decentralization is progressing, but the reality is widely differing experiences across the archipelago.

Much of the emphasis in this chapter is on fiscal and economic aspects of decentralization. However, the chapter also touches on political, administrative, and governance elements that, taken together with financial and economic matters, comprise an attempt to address the broader political economy of decentralization in Indonesia. Commonly stated higher level objectives for decentralization in Indonesia include improved local-level delivery of government services and better social and economic development outcomes (higher regional growth, reduced poverty, increased employment, etc.). While some of these objectives may be beyond the scope and capacities of regional governments (RGs)[1] to deliver, they provide a broad framework as to what this diagnosis covers. The focus is on (1) the political economy of what RGs can be realistically expected to achieve given the existing responsibilities assigned to them, and (2) decentralization-related policy matters that can ultimately make a difference to the living standards of local communities.

The chapter diagnoses the most serious constraints and issues that impinge on the attainment of more effective decentralization outcomes in

---

[1]   In this chapter the term "regional government" refers to a combination of provincial and local governments. The term "local government" refers to a combination of district (*kabupaten*) and city and municipality (*kota*) governments.

Indonesia. After outlining the key constraints and issues and briefly reviewing recent institutional, policy, and program approaches to addressing them, the chapter then summarizes suggestions for reforms that might help to improve decentralization outcomes. Views as to how well decentralization reforms have been designed and implemented since 2001 differ widely. Whatever the range of perspectives, one thing is clear: Indonesia will continue to have decentralized forms of government and service delivery. The debate centers not on whether decentralized approaches should stay or go, but rather on how policies and implementation approaches can be improved to the benefit of communities throughout Indonesia.

11.2. Overview of Decentralization Developments Since the 1999 "Big Bang"

11.2.1. Politics

For more than 30 years during the Suharto era, heavily centralized approaches were taken to political management of affairs in Indonesia's regions. Provincial governors were appointed by the President and were very powerful figures, with their central role being to represent the central government (CG) and, particularly, the President. They in turn were instrumental in appointing mayors as leaders of cities, and *bupatis* as leaders of districts, with the President having considerable control over the local-level leaders through the provincial governors. Local or provincial heads (and parliaments) were not elected during in this era, though village-level government was to some extent conducted through traditionally appointed leaders. The "big bang" decentralization reforms that commenced in 1999 were precipitated by both financial and political crises. The 1997 Asian financial crisis served to catalyze growing political discontent, especially among students and the young, which, along with other rallying forces at the time, eventually forced Suharto's departure. This in turn ushered in a new era of democratic politics at the central level, which quickly flowed through to democratic forms of governance at RG levels.

The basic element of governance established at local and provincial levels was the regional representatives council (*dewan perwakilan daerah*—DPD) and, after a period of RG heads being indirectly elected by DPDs, the provincial and local heads were directly elected by popular vote. Both central and local political systems broadly follow the American presidential approach, with provincial and local government (LG) heads having significant powers, though with checks and balances through power-sharing arrangements with the DPDs: the RG heads and DPDs are provided with joint roles and powers, though often the ultimate powers rest with the head of the RG in the event of unresolved disputes with the DPD.

Figure 11.1 sets out the basic structure of the RG system, with 33 provinces, 95 cities and municipalities (*kota*), 370 districts (*kabupaten*), and about 73,500 rural and urban villages (*desa* and *kelurahan*, respectively). Each province, district, and municipality has its own elected head of government (governor, *bupati,* and mayor, respectively) and elected DPDs. The subdistricts (*kecamatan*) are administrative arms of the districts and municipalities, while the villages operate at the community level with elected heads.

Figure 11.1: Structure of the Regional Government System in Indonesia

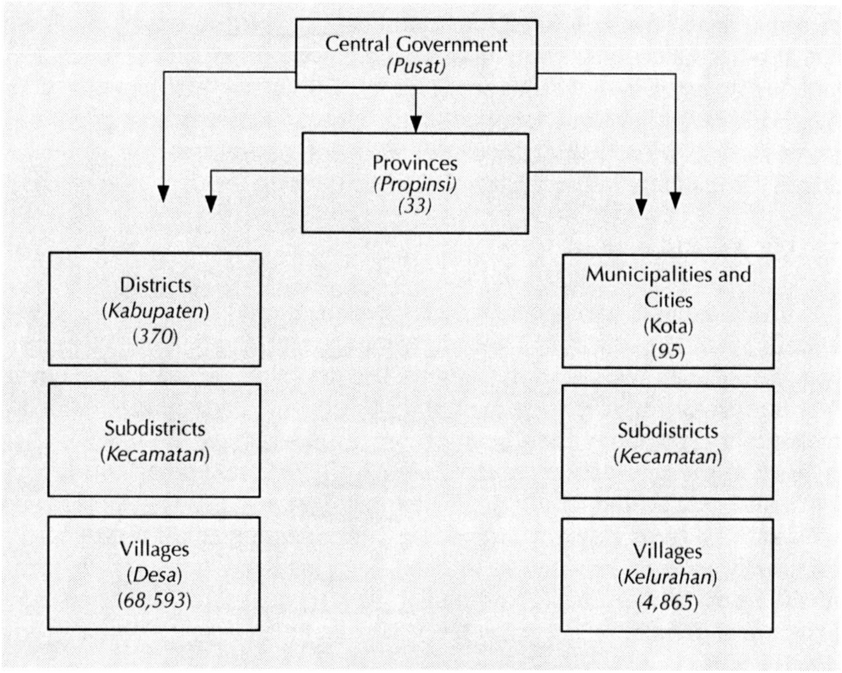

A total of 635 subdistricts (kecamatan) are under districts and municipalities/cities.
Source: Data from BPS (2009).

Initial administrative and political legislation in Law 22 of 1999 on regional administration provided highly autonomous powers to the cities, municipalities, and districts with no clear hierarchical links to the provinces, which thus had limited powers to direct or supervise lower level governments within them. For a couple of years after 1999, provincial governors were appointed by the CG, but then they also came to be elected by the people. The change lessened the extent of direct legislated power the CG had over the provincial governors, though indirect forms of influence remained (e.g., through political parties). Administrative, political, and financial reforms enacted in Law 32 of 2004 to some extent introduced additional hierarchical linkages between the CG and provinces and between the provinces and their municipalities and cities. Examples include the power given to higher level governments to approve (and in some cases veto) the budgets of lower tiers and to impose certain accountability and supervision measures on the lower levels' performance. The role of regional heads became somewhat split with some responsibilities to higher level forces above them at provincial and/or central government levels, while still being elected by local populations.

Much of the more recent political debate has related to the roles, accountability, and performance of RG heads, a relatively significant number of whom have been convicted for fraudulent and corrupt activities. There has also been a major push to increase the powers of provincial governors, and one strong school of thought argues for them again being appointed by the President rather than being popularly elected. Other reform advocates argue for less direct (though strong) forms of central control, while yet others favor a more indirect form of election through the DPDs.

11.2.2. Administration

Administrative arrangements for decentralized management were initially set out in Law 22 of 1999 on regional administration, which in turn was significantly revised in the form of the new Law 32 of 2004. A dense and complex array of government and Ministry of Home Affairs (MOHA) ministerial regulations have been prepared under the 2004 law. Further reforms to the core administrative Law 32 of 2004 were being considered by the CG and Parliament in 2010 and may lead to further amendments, with one body of thought suggesting the amendment processes might eventually emerge as three new laws, covering separately (1) elections of RG heads and DPDs; (2) administrative arrangements, especially the assignment of functions between levels of government; and (3) village-level administration.

Institutionally, the law and regulations on the administration of regions are prepared and administered by MOHA, and, reflecting MOHA's broad interests in controlling the management of most decentralized matters, the law covers a very broad range of functions and powers. These go beyond the scope of coverage of similar local administration laws in many countries, reflecting to some extent MOHA's desire to spell out in laws a set of powers and functions that justify MOHA's involvement in affairs that might elsewhere be covered by other agencies. Many matters in Law 32 of 2004 are also covered in competing laws, for example, in cases of the National Development Planning Board (Bappenas), with planning matters; the Ministry of Finance (MOF), with financial matters; and the Ministry of Manpower and related civil service agencies, with civil service and public sector management matters.

Law 32 of 2004 covers a very broad range of matters, including (1) functional responsibilities of different tiers of government; (2) subnational elections of RG heads and DPDs; (3) roles of RG heads; (4) roles and functions of DPDs; (5) RG apparatus and organization structures; (6) civil service administration; (7) intergovernmental financing; (8) regional financial management systems; (9) development of the regions; (10) supervision of regions; (11) coordination of advice on regional autonomy; (12) territorial arrangements and the setting up of new RGs, including special autonomous regions; (13) administration of villages; and (14) a wide range of other administrative matters that apply to RGs, including powers and procedures for making RG laws and regulations.

As set out in more detail in section 11.3, several important issues and constraints have arisen from the many matters addressed by Law 32 of 2004. Some of the issues relate to problems with the law itself (e.g., lack of clarity in the functional assignments and uncertainties as to the roles and functions of RG heads and DPDs). Some issues relate to matters that possibly should have been exclusively dealt with in other laws and by other central agencies (e.g., financial matters and civil service management matters). A third category of issues relates to matters that one would normally expect to be dealt within an LG administration law but that have proved challenging to implement in practice, especially at the RG level, such as the orderly making and management of local regulations (ADB 2008).

11.2.3. Finance and the Economy

The devolution of significant powers and authorities to the RGs meant a need to significantly revamp the previously highly centralized approach to budgeting, financial management, reporting, and audit. Initially, the main financial umbrella law was passed as Law 25 of 1999, which was subsequently revised and reissued as Law 33 of 2004 (eventually backed by detailed government and, in some cases, MOF and MOHA regulations). Law 33 of 2004 is relatively comprehensive and includes

- the principles and basis for funding decentralization;
- RGs' own revenues (*pendapatan asli daerah*—PAD)[2];
- The Balance Fund comprising (1) the revenue sharing fund (Dana Bagi Hasil); (2) the General Allocation Fund (Dana Alokasi Umum—DAU); and (3) the Specific Allocation Fund (Dana Alokasi Khusus—DAK);

---

[2] While basic principles of the PAD are in Law 33 of 2004, more detailed treatment was provided in the Law on Regional Taxes and Fees, initially Law 34 of 2000, which was subsequently revised as Law 28 of 2009.

- other revenues (including domestic and foreign grants, and emergency funds);
- regional borrowing, including the issuance of bonds;
- financial management systems in the RGs;
- financial control and accountability;
- supervision and audit;
- deconcentration funding;[3]
- funding of coadministered tasks (a form of CG deconcentration funding implemented by RGs; and
- the regional financial information system (Sistem Informasi Keuangan Daerah—SIKD).

The DAU has become the predominant form of funding for most RGs, though shared revenues and, to a lesser extent, the specific purpose grants (the DAK) have grown in importance. Own-source revenues (PAD) have been of low significance for most RGs (typically less than 10% of LGs' total revenues), though recently the PADs have shown modest growth.

As set out more fully in section 11.3.4, a wide range of issues and constraints have arisen from the financial arrangements for decentralized government, though the basic model adopted is generally regarded as sound, as it includes at least in theory a number of "best practice" principles. Broadly, some of the issues that have arisen include (1) limited provision of own-revenue raising powers to RGs, with reform to date mainly expenditure driven; (2) policy and technical flaws within the DAU that have limited its role as an equalization grant (for reducing horizontal and vertical fiscal imbalance); (3) inequities in the shared revenue fund that work against the DAU's equalization goals; (4) policy and implementation weaknesses in the DAK that have lessened its impact; (5) major bureaucratic constraints to facilitating on-lending and channeling grants to RGs, in part because of large hangovers of poorly serviced RG debts, often dating back to pre "big bang" times; (6) major abuses by CG ministries in the use of deconcentration funding, in part relating to a lack of legal clarity as to the assignment of functions between levels of government and in part because of insufficient legal powers and budget management strength to stop illegal spending on deconcentration; and (7) excessive complexity and confusion regarding the forms of financial management systems to be adopted at RG levels.

A number of the issues and constraints in relation to financial management matters result because Law 32 of 2004 on the administration of RGs unusually sets out many important financial management arrangements

---

3   Deconcentration covers areas in which the CG, according to Law 32 of 2004 and Government Regulation 38 of 2007, has a legitimate role in providing decentralized service through regional governments (either directly or shared). Illegitimate deconcentration relates to areas of regional activity where the law and government regulations do not allow the CG to provide services but where the central agencies are still operating.

that, in MOHA's eyes, legitimizes it playing a strong role in decentralized financial management matters. Many conflicts in approach relate to the nature of financial management and reporting systems in the RGs, with MOF and MOHA, and at times the Audit Board (Badan Pemeriksa Keuangan—BPK), having somewhat conflicting views as to standards and systems that should apply to budgeting, accounting, and reporting.

11.3. Constraints on Effective Decentralization

11.3.1. Approach Adopted

Section 11.3, which is the main body of this chapter, focuses on issues and policy and draws heavily on recent work (including empirical studies). No major attempt is made to present empirical or financial analysis; rather, the issues and constraints are presented in a succinct policy type of format. Representing the broad nature of the political economy of fiscal decentralization, the section is divided into three general areas: political, administrative, and financial and economic matters. However, most attention is given to financial and economic issues and constraints.

11.3.2. Political Issues and Constraints

11.3.2.1. Role and Election of Provincial Governors

Many policymakers have argued the need for increased clarity in the role of provincial governors and that they not be popularly elected in the future. These issues continue to be debated as part of the proposed revisions to Law 32 of 2004 on the administration of RGs. The centralist forces within the government, particularly in MOHA and the Office of the President, favor a return to the appointment of governors by the President. Under this approach, the currently split roles of governors would be changed, with governors being seen as solely representing the CG, which in turn would allow the CG to pursue its national objectives more clearly, with strong governors forcing through national reforms.

Another group of policymakers has argued for enhancing the role of DPDs vis-à-vis governors, including enhanced roles in the election of governors, perhaps through indirect voting for governors through members of local or provincial DPDs. This approach would continue to provide for a fair degree of split accountabilities, with governors finding themselves beholden to both provincial electors and to the CG.

The final model to appear from the current debate remains to be seen, but it seems unlikely that national DPD members will be easily persuaded to move away from popularly elected governors to those appointed by the

President. In terms of participative decentralization principles, such a step would be a retrogressive return to the autocratic system of presidentially appointed governors. Continuation of popular election for governors is worthy of support, but could be more closely linked to the elections of DPD members and the roles of the governor and provincial DPDs could be better integrated. While, over time, provinces are likely to become stronger if they are primarily accountable to and elected by the people, the roles and functions of provinces and their governors should be better clarified and in many respects strengthened (Donor Working Group for Decentralization 2009).

11.3.2.2. Hierarchical Relationships between Provinces and Local Governments

Under the initial arrangements of Law 22 of 1999 there was no significant hierarchical relationship between provincial and local governments. This situation derived in part from the dramatic political events of the time and the clamor from the general populace for very decentralized forms of governance. This left the provinces in a difficult situation in terms of pursuing province-wide development and supervision of the LGs. At the same time, funding available to the provinces was often not sufficient to allow for the provision of major province-wide investments in social or (particularly) physical infrastructure.

The revision of Law 22 of 1999, the administrative Law 32 of 2004 providing for popular election of provincial governors, introduced some additional hierarchical powers for governors. Law 32 of 2004 provided the CG with additional powers and responsibilities to develop and supervise the regions, including coordination of interprovincial affairs; guidance on standards of implementation; and provision for the development of systems and capacities of the regions, including the training and development of regional officials. MOHA was given overall responsibility for these matters at the CG level. In turn, the provincial governor was given the responsibility to coordinate and stimulate development and supervision of the LGs.

Law 32 of 2004 also gave the CG (through MOHA) powers to review and in certain cases reject or seek changes in the annual budgets, tax regulations, and other matters of provincial governments, while the provinces (through the governors) were given identical powers to reject or seek changes in the annual budgets, tax regulations, etc. of LGs. These are potentially significant powers. However, they do not seem to have been widely or strategically used, in part because of lack of capacities of both central and provincial authorities to quickly review (in the short time frames provided by the law) and change the budgets of lower level governments. Issues of hierarchical relationships are also closely related to a lack of clarity in the assignment of functions (both revenue and expenditure) to different levels of government (see section 11.3.3), adding confusion as to the role of provincial governments.

While aspects of the hierarchical relationships could be more clearly defined in a revision of Law 32 of 2004 and even the Constitution, undemocratic provisions that allow budgets of elected heads and assemblies to be overturned by higher level bodies should be removed, though with added attention given to raising the capacities of BPK to undertake comprehensive audits of RGs. Thereafter, most emphasis should be given to significantly improving the legal strength and clarity of functional assignments, particularly with regard to expenditure functions.

11.3.2.3. Developing Capacities of Regional Heads and DPDs

Indonesia started implementing democratic forms of decentralized governance and political arrangements in 2001 and 2002, so the country's experience with new democratic approaches has been limited to 8–9 years. This is a short timeframe to master the new approaches, and longer periods will be needed to develop the experience and capacities of RG heads and DPDs to work effectively to their full potential. Supervision and audit reports, field research, and popular writing in the media all indicate that the performance of the RG heads and DPDs has been very mixed.

At one extreme, there have been a significant number of cases of adverse performance by the political leadership, including (1) actions leading to imprisonment of a large number of RG heads and DPD members for misappropriation, procurement fraud, etc.; (2) inappropriate public financial management (PFM) practices, including failure to prepare budgets in timely and comprehensive ways, ineffective accounting systems, and reporting arrangements that are frequently incomplete and not transparent; (3) major qualifications and adverse findings in external audit reports; and (4) poor performance with the delivery of high-priority services. At the other extreme, a much smaller group (10%–15% of RGs) have adapted very quickly to the new arrangements with strong and effective political leadership leading to low incidences of corrupt practices and adequate and improving performance of PFM, audit results, and service delivery. In a few cases, competent political leadership has led to important innovations in the enhancement of services delivered to the population.

The majority of RGs appear to fit between the extremes of good and bad, with inexperienced RG heads and DPD members often struggling to develop the experience and skills needed to deal with complex bureaucratic, administrative, financial, and service delivery matters. Many RG heads and DPDs rely heavily on more permanent civil service members of local bureaucracies to get things done. This frequently leaves a vacuum of leadership, vision, and direction, as the civil servants come from a tradition of cumbersome bureaucracy and are not well placed to provide dynamic and innovative leadership and improved performance in the enhanced functional responsibilities assigned to RGs.

In the short term, the situation is not helped by the high turnover rates of heads and DPD members at election times. The rapid turnover of elected people frequently means replacing people who have at least a few years of experience with people who commence with little or no experience. The restriction of elected candidates to members of eligible political parties was introduced to limit turnover and gradually lead to an experienced group of politicians emerging, but the restriction also precludes the use of a wider pool and has on balance been a negative feature; thus, there may be a case for opening positions of RG heads and members of DPDs to independent candidates.

Another institutional feature that many believe hampers decentralized political performance is the essential mirroring of the CG presidential system in the regions. These arrangements give significant powers to RG heads but also provide checks and balances often involving joint approvals of both the RG head and the DPD. Preparation and approval of RG budgets is one case in point. Budgets are prepared and eventually approved by the RG head, but require discussion with and approval of the DPD. This often leads to disputes and delays, both in relations between the RG heads and the DPDs and within the party groups in the DPD. Changing the current presidential approach to local-level politics would be a major legal issue. Thus, the easiest route would likely be to enhance the DPD under a head that is more an integral part of the DPD while still being popularly elected by the people.

11.3.2.4. Political Accountability—"Money Politics"

Very closely related to the issues raised in the last section on capacities of RG heads and DPDs are issues relating to political accountability and "money politics." The nature of corruption is thought to have changed in Indonesia over the past decade. During the earlier post-independence era, a narrow base of politically powerful people close to the central political apex is thought to have extracted massive amounts of state resources for personal and political gain. More recently, problems of massive political corruption appear to have spread out more broadly to the line ministries and, increasingly, to the RGs.

To the credit of anticorruption, audit, and other supervisory agencies (particularly the Corruption Eradication Commission,[4] BPK, and Anticorruption Court), many regional heads and DPD members have been prosecuted and found guilty of matters relating to money politics. A significant number of civil service members in the bureaucracy have also been

---

[4]   The Komisi Pemberantasan Korupsi, or KPK.

found guilty of matters linked to money politics as well as broader offences of corruption and financial wrong doing (Suryana 2011).[5] Money politics manifests in many ways at local levels. Many instances are related to political parties, wherein party endorsement for elected positions is frequently linked to patronage arrangements whereby the selected candidate is expected to provide money and other benefits back to the party and/or key officials in return for an appointment. This may also involve invalid procurement procedures that provide contracts to politically or financially preferred bidders. Licensing is also a common area of concern, as is the allocation of rights and permits, for example in the use of natural resources.

As discussed in Chapter 3, control of corruption, though improved, still compares unfavorably with regional (international) averages. Across Indonesia there are disparities. Using a scoring system where zero means massive corruption and 10 means no corruption, Transparency International assessed at about 4.5 the average region in Indonesia between 2004 and 2009, with scores ranging from about 3.0 to 6.0. Over time, the rating trends have remained stable or indicated very modest improvement (TI various years).

An important policy question for the future is whether enough is being done to address relatively high levels of money politics and corruption. Should further measures be considered necessary, then difficult choices will need to be made, including whether to address institutional and legal arrangements determining regional political systems and/or whether to apply further supervisory- and sanctions-based solutions, such as strengthening the regional arms of the Corruption Eradication Commission and BPK. Closer scrutiny and supervision of the role of parties will be needed, including stronger strictures on funding abuses and client–patron relations within political parties. Opening RG elections to independent candidates may also assist.

11.3.3. Administrative Issues and Constraints

11.3.3.1. High-Level Coordination of Decentralization Matters— Weaknesses of the Regional Antonomy Advisory Council

Given the size, geographical diversity, and very bureaucratic traditions of Indonesia, it is not surprising that coordination of decentralization is fraught with challenges and difficulties and at times unfavorable outcomes. The main three CG ministries involved in decentralization matters are Bappenas, MOF, and MOHA. While coordination among the three ministries has

---

[5] The Jakarta Post reported that 155 heads of regional governments, 17 of them governors, have been prosecuted for corruption since 2004. Corruption cases involving regional heads have occurred in all but 5 of the country's 33 provinces (Suryana 2011).

improved from time to time since 2001, the institutions for and the outcomes of coordination have remained disappointing and weak, not only among the key CG ministries but also between the CG and the provinces and LGs.

Law 32 of 2004 sets out the arrangements for the key decentralization coordinating body, the Regional Autonomy Advisory Council (Dewan Pertimbangan Otonomi Daerah—DPOD). The DPOD is chaired by the minister for MOHA and is composed of a high-level (mainly political) Board and lower level technical teams and working groups. The DPOD's key stated functions are to generate policy advice and performance and evaluation information and to channel such matters up through the Board to the President. Lower level technical teams (and their related working groups) are essentially split into two streams covering (1) administrative, political, and broad regional autonomy matters (formation, dissolution, and combination of new regions and special regions); and (2) financial and economic matters, especially intergovernmental financing arrangements (DAU, DAK, and shared revenues). Serious constraints that have prevented DPOD from successfully achieving its role include the following:

- The DPOD Secretariat lacks the professional capacity to undertake policy and/or evaluation work or to even administratively coordinate the provision of such matters to the Board.
- The technical teams and related working groups were intended to undertake most of the policy formulation and evaluation work, and submit information and recommendations for the Board's consideration and for raising to the President. However, outputs have been relatively limited in terms of both quality and quantity.
- Because the Board comprises mainly ministers, it has had difficulty convening meetings; in several years, the four required annual meetings could not be held due to a lack of quorum.

The ongoing review of Law 32 of 2004 has given close consideration to possible changes to the structure and role of DPOD, including relocating DPOD away from MOHA and placing it under the office of either the Vice President or President. While a more neutral venue might generate increased activity from part-time public service members, constraints of time and interorganizational rivalries may continue to limit DPOD's effectiveness. Alternative solutions include providing a core of skilled decentralization research and policy staff within the restructured DPOD to provide direct advice to the Board, including on matters coming through the core government ministries. Furthermore, institutional arrangements for coordinating matters between and among the three levels of government are not strong. An adequate formal forum that is broadly inclusive of the RGs is needed to discuss and agree on important policy matters; this merits further consideration in the review of options for DPOD.

11.3.3.2. Proliferation of Regional Governments

The rapid fragmentation of RGs (termed *"pemekaran"*) in Indonesia after the "big bang" has emerged as an important issue for decentralization reform. Territorial arrangements, including the emergence of significant fragmentation, generate complex issues for any country to address. Much of the initial analysis in Indonesia suggested that the creation of most new subnational governments was politically driven and universally financially and economically inefficient and thus almost always unfavorable. However, more recent work has helped to explain the processes and to confirm that, despite recent proliferation, Indonesia's provincial and local governments remain among the largest in the world and that, at least in some cases, proliferation is understandable or even favorable. Despite the more balanced recent debate, views of policymakers remain disparate, and a consensus is needed on a suitable set of policies pertaining to the formation of new LGs in future.

Recent empirical study suggests several major determinants can explain intensification of the fragmentation process (Niazi, Imansyah, and Martinez 2009). First, (and other things being equal), regions that are sparsely populated with large land areas and populations, and those with more heterogeneous populations, are more likely to undergo fragmentation. Second, the regime of fiscal incentives tends to support fragmentation, and the main levers of intergovernmental financing require ongoing review and fine tuning to address distortions. Finally, the study found a political drive behind fragmentation, though it is not as noticeable in statistical terms as economic fundamentals or the fiscal incentives regime. The study also sought to assess the impact of fragmentation on local government performance with public service delivery and found mixed results. Although some negative experiences were found (e.g., in health), there were also positive experiences, such as the fast action new districts took to improve education and local physical infrastructure.

Indonesia's RGs continue to have very large populations, with the average LGs large enough to take advantage of economies of scale. Nevertheless, the process of fragmentation cannot continue unabated without proper regulation and procedures. Improving procedures for processing applications to establish new RGs is now at the center of the policy debate in Indonesia. Important policy and procedural areas include the following:

- The role of the Parliament has often been disruptive due to lobbying by members to promote new LGs. The Parliament should follow strict and consistent processing procedures that should be set out in a law and not in a general regulation (GR), as is now the case.
- The multiple and unwieldy criteria for assessing applications for forming new RGs now in GR 78 of 2007 should be rationalized to

a much smaller number of core criteria regarding (1) minimum population levels, (2) representation and accountability, (3) financial and fiscal capacity and sustainability, and (4) administrative capacity.

- In the formulation of policy, other instruments that have proved successful internationally could be considered, including introducing incentives to encourage the voluntary amalgamation of LGs; the redesign of expenditure assignments by strengthening the role of provincial governments for services with significant economies of scale and externalities across LGs; the promotion of different forms of cooperation among LGs in providing local public services; the creation of special enlarged service districts (for example, for water or transport); and the privatization of some services.

11.3.3.3. Clarity in Assigning Expenditure Functions

As in many countries, Indonesia has considerable work to do to improve the clarity with which the functions are assigned between levels of government. While there is some lack of clarity related to revenue assignments, most clarity problems are on the expenditure side, which is the focus of this section. The assignment of functions has been dealt with under administrative laws, initially Law 22 of 1999 and subsequently Law 32 of 2004. The important (though controversial) GR 38 of 2007 sets out in significant detail assignments of functions, subfunctions, and sub-subfunctions between tiers of government. The GR is divided into 32 sectors that are broadly equivalent to the structure of Indonesia's CG ministries.[6]

Since 1999, new legal instruments have tended to increasingly return responsibilities to the CG. Whereas Law 22 of 1999 gave very broad autonomous powers to the regions (particularly LGs), this has since been progressively watered down. The 1999 law listed 11 broad obligatory RG functions. GR 38 of 2007 complicated the arrangements in at least two areas. First, it gave greater attention to the concept of concurrent or shared functions between all levels of government, effectively providing that all functions of government are shared, with any functions allocated to RGs being on a shared and not a unilateral basis. Second, it introduced considerably more obligatory functions: 26, compared with the 16 provided for in Law 32 of 2004. GR 38 of 2007 thus aimed to emphasize a new role for the CG as a regulator and policymaker in a system where all functions of government are shared. Key reform areas still to be addressed with regard to

---

[6] The sectors are also broadly equivalent to past classifications of 32 sectors used by Bappenas for national planning and budgeting, though this system has been replaced by the more widely used international system of Government Finance Statistics functional classifications for budgetary and accounting purposes of the CG.

functional assignments include the following:

- Greater legal certainty about and clout are needed regarding the assignments contained in GR 38, possibly elevating its status to an Organic Law directly under the Constitution. However, the content of GR 38 needs significant rewriting to address the lack of clarity and inconsistencies in many areas. The rewriting should not be confined to MOHA but should involve all key units of government, perhaps under the leadership of a special commission reporting directly to the President.
- More effective ways are needed to address inconsistencies between sector and decentralization laws and regulations. Past efforts at doing this through detailed reviews of both sets of laws and the development of minimum physical norms have left many inconsistencies unresolved.
- Budget preparation should adhere more closely to the legal assignment of functions. This largely involves identifying and weeding out illegitimate forms of deconcentration expenditures that pervade the budgets of many CG ministries.
- The appropriate role for the public sector vis-à-vis the private sector needs to be clarified and regulated. This is important, as many RGs continue to participate in activities that are not on their obligatory list and that would appear better left to the private sector (e.g., banking, transport, trading, media, and football).

11.3.4. Financial and Economic Issues and Constraints

11.3.4.1. Challenges to Attaining Vertical Balance

Vertical balance relates to whether the system ensures adequate funding to enable the different levels of government to perform their assigned tasks (Figure 11.2). Ideally, money should be provided per the functions that have been assigned to different levels of government. Measurement of vertical balance is never a straightforward task, as (1) resources are scarce and wants unlimited, so the functions of any level of government are rarely funded to the needed levels (thus, Indonesia's minimum service standards are yet to be effectively finalized); (2) all countries have different assignments of expenditures, making international comparisons difficult; and (3) the ways that functional responsibilities are assigned are often unclear, with high levels of deconcentrated expenditures of the CG on matters that should be funded by the RGs.

While further empirical work is needed on the nature of vertical imbalance, some indicators of its current extent in the Indonesian context are as follows:

Figure 11.2: Subnational Government Vertical Structure

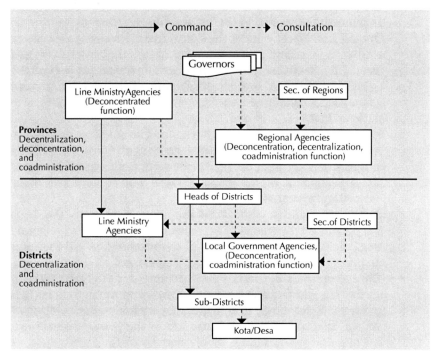

Source: Sidik (2006).

- In aggregate, RGs in recent years have run fiscal surpluses (3% of gross domestic product [GDP]) and accumulated surplus funds in regional banks and indirectly through deposits in Bank Indonesia, the central bank. Although many RGs have large surpluses, their service delivery is widely seen to have major deficiencies, as typified by the inability of most RGs to fully fund key areas such as health, education, and other social and physical infrastructure development to comply with their minimum service standards.

- The CG has in recent years run modest deficits (1%–2% of GDP) after providing significant transfers to the RGs and providing for significant expenditure by key CG ministries on deconcentration matters that they should not be funding—that is, "illegitimate deconcentration expenditures." The CG budget contains significant outlays on matters considered to be low priority for pursuing broad-based growth and poverty reduction. Examples include fuel and energy subsidies, the military, illegitimate deconcentration expenditures, and very large administrative and bureaucratic costs. Figure 11.2 captures the subnational government vertical structure (Sidik 2006).

- Total public resources spent by RGs are high by international standards (about 38% of general government spending recently). Offsetting this are the significant numbers of responsibilities that have been assigned to the regional levels.

Overall, the general observation is that Indonesia's fiscal arrangements demonstrate reasonable vertical balance. However, there is scope for restructuring about 6%–8% of the total CG general budget, or about 1%–2% of GDP. If this were achieved and the benefits were passed to the RGs, about 45% of total general expenditures would be the responsibility of RGs. For successful restructuring, the absorptive capacities of RGs need to be improved to greatly reduce recent tendencies toward surpluses. Improved budgeting, particularly redirecting resources away from low productivity administrative expenditures, would also have to be pursued (World Bank and Government of Indonesia 2007).

11.3.4.2. Challenges to Attaining Horizontal Balance

Horizontal balance relates to whether there is balance or equity between RGs at the same level of government. These are difficult matters to measure and compare, depending on (among other things) what dimensions of balance are being targeted. In some countries, balance relates to equity in per capita expenditure levels between like governments; in other countries it relates to per capita equality in physical and social infrastructure between like governments.

The general provisions of Law 32 of 2004 address horizontal balance through the use of the Balance Fund, which aims to "close the fiscal gap between the government and RGs and among the RGs." Fiscal gap is defined as the difference between fiscal need and the fiscal capacity of a region. However, while the DAU formula in part introduced variables that try to measure the fiscal gap based on horizontal equity, it also introduced matters that were not equalizing, including (1) a "hold harmless provision"[7] protecting better-off regions (since converted to a less costly balance fund); and (2) a basic allocation based on total salaries of the civil service in the region. Other elements of fiscal balance funding, particularly shared revenues, are significantly inequitable, generally favoring resource-rich locations and larger cities.

Whether one measures horizontal balance in terms of access to physical and social infrastructure, per capita expenditures, or the fiscal gap approach adopted by Indonesia, the general conclusion of most empirical work is that there is significant inequity among regions (ADB 2008). Data on total

---

[7]   Under the "hold harmless" provision, the DAU allocation to a region could not be lower than the previous year's allocation.

per capita resources and per capita expenditures show sizeable differences among regions. As shown in Table 11.1, at the extremes, Papua province spent about 17 times more per capita than the lowest spending province, Central Java (World Bank 2006). This also shows that policies toward equalization are working only marginally well and need a major revamp to improve equalization. The elements of a revamped equalization policy are addressed further in the following text.

11.3.4.3. Revenue Assignments

Many of Indonesia's "big bang" reforms occurred on the expenditure side, with limited attention to revenue reforms, particularly to boost the RGs' own-source revenues. Some policymakers during the reform time indicated that this decision was taken partly because local revenue collection agencies were perceived as having low capacities and partly because most of Indonesia's key high-yielding taxes were better suited for collection by the CG. A trade-off was in the sharing arrangements for key taxes, including natural resource revenues, property and transfer taxes, and income taxes.

Law 34 of 2000 listed the own-source taxes and charges that could be levied by different levels of government and introduced good principles of taxation policy that provided some scope for RGs to design new taxes providing principles were met, though this led to concerns about the proliferation of a range of "nuisance taxes" that might hinder private business investment and activity. Own-source revenues (PAD) have shown some modest real growth in the decade leading up to 2011 and have proven more robust at provincial than at district levels. Recently, provincial PADs have averaged about 45% of total budget resources, while those for districts have been much lower, at about 7%. Law 28 of 2009 replaced the earlier 2000 law and provided some additional own-source revenues to RGs. Law 28 of 2009 provided for, among other things, (1) movement from an open to a closed list approach; and (2) introduction of six new taxes and six new charges, including urban and rural property taxes and the transfers tax (which previously were shared taxes).

Other broader policy work is being undertaken to assess the feasibility of shifting other major CG taxes to the RGs, including possibilities of the value-added tax (VAT) and personal income tax. A number of RG taxes (hotels, entertainment, and restaurants) are similar to the VAT. Some policymakers are also reviewing the tax sharing arrangements in place, particularly to see if current extreme disequalization effects can be lessened—perhaps in the context of building these taxes more into the DAU formula, which itself is a revenue-sharing approach. These are all difficult political and administrative policy matters to address, and major further taxation amendments are not likely to be made in these areas in the near future. Immediate areas of importance for further reform include

Table 11.1: Extremes in Per Capita Expenditures, by Province and District (2001, 2004, and 2006; Rp)

	2001	2004	2006
Provincial Extremes			
Mean Expenditure Per Capita	150,600	288,800	465,600
Median Per Capita Expenditure	92,400	185,500	300,700
Minimum Per Capita Expenditure	40,600	78,000	116,500
	(Banten)	(Central Java)	(Central Java)
Maximum Per Capita Expenditure	769,000	1,269,800	1,984,800
	(Jakarta)	(Papua)	(Papua)
Ratio of Maximum to Minimum	18.9	16.3	17.0
District /City/Extremes			
Mean Expenditure Per Capita	641,000	987,400	1,503,400
Median Per Capita Expenditure	460,000	741,300	1,122,200
Minimum Per Capita Expenditure	147,300	135,600	315,100
	(Bogor District)	(North Halmahara District)	(Bogor District)
	(West Java)]	(North Maluku)	(West Java)
Maximum Per Capita Expenditure	4,360,700	8,484,200	15,634,300
	(Sabang District)	(Malinau District)	(Sarmi District)
	(Aceh)	(East Kalimantan)	(Papua)
Ratio of Maximum to Minimum	29.6	62.6	49.6

Sources: Author's information and data from Badan Pusat Statistik (BPS); Audit Board (BPK); Regional Financial Information System (SIKD, MOF); unaudited government financial reports—Lapunan Keuangan Pemerintah Pusat (LKPP); and the Ministry of Finance.

- successfully implementing the devolution of the property and transfer taxes and devolving further parts of the property tax, particularly mining, plantation, and forestry (Niazi, Gyat, and McDermott 2009);
- simplifying tax classification codes and systems at RG levels; and
- improving RG systems and capacities for better local collection yields.

11.3.4.4. Deconcentration Expenditures

Policy on deconcentration expenditure has been a significant recent issue of debate in Indonesia.[8] The debate distinguishes two forms of deconcentration expenditure: (1) legitimate deconcentration expenditure, when a CG ministry uses an RG for facilitating goods or services for matters that are assigned as uniquely CG responsibilities; and (2) illegitimate deconcentration expenditure, when a CG ministry funds an RG to undertake tasks that are already assigned to the RGs.

Deconcentration expenditures are of significant value in Indonesia, though their precise dimensions are difficult to measure because (1) those that are included in the deconcentration parts of the budget are typically argued to be legitimate deconcentration expenditures, but on deeper investigation they are often found to be illegitimate; and (2) many items that are actually of an illegitimate deconcentration nature are often disguised in nondeconcentration segments of the budget and are often implemented directly by the ministry in question.

Estimates for the Ministry of National Education budget for 2008 indicate the deconcentration segment of its budget contained about Rp19 trillion ($1.960 billion) in illegitimate expenditures and that they made up 38% of the ministry's total budget (Niazi and Oosterman 2009).[9] Furthermore, while the MOF was preparing the 2010 CG budget, it identified about Rp7 trillion ($770 million) in illegitimate deconcentration expenditures across about 13 ministries (excluding the Ministry of National Education), which the MOF transferred to its control and reappropriated to about 320 RGs as conditional grants under a newly established grant scheme (Hibah).

Estimates suggest that illegitimate deconcentration expenses are as high as Rp120 trillion ($13.201 billion) or about 12% of the CG expenditures.

---

[8] A scheme of coadministered expenditures also exists in Indonesia, which is a form of CG deconcentrated funding managed by an RG head. This is confined to physical expenditures, whereas deconcentration expenditures are confined to nonphysical expenditures. Significantly more funding goes to deconcentration than to coadministered expenditures.

[9] Exchange rates from the rupiah to the dollar for 2001, 2008, 2009, and 2010 are from ADB (2011).

Accordingly, sorting out deconcentration policy is an important matter for administrative aspects of decentralization and for central fiscal policy. To date, senior officials in the MOF and Bappenas have not been prepared to seriously address illegitimate deconcentration expenditure, in part because of poor information regarding what ministries actually spend their budgets on. As budget reforms take hold and as the Medium Term Expenditure Framework comes to be more broadly introduced, more serious budget restructuring may occur. Important policy issues raised in the subsection, "Clarity on Assuring Expenditure Functions," are also relevant in the financial context, with lack of clarity on functional assignments being one of the main causes of illegitimate deconcentration expenditure.

11.3.4.5. Intergovernmental Transfers (DAU, DAK, Shared Revenues, and Grants)

Much recent policy debate has concerned key intergovernmental transfers. While the overall framework for intergovernmental financing is likely to remain broadly in place, reforms to individual parts of the overall system need to be considered for continued fine tuning.

General Allocation Grant—the DAU. The main way that the CG finances RGs is through the DAU, which currently provides a grant pool equivalent to 26% of net CG revenues for redistribution to the RGs on a nonspecific basis. The DAU grew from Rp60.7 trillion ($5.916 billion) in 2001 to Rp186.4 trillion ($17.940 billion) in 2009, while remaining at about 4.0% of GDP in most years (Table 11.2). In terms of total resources available to RGs, the share of the DAU declined somewhat, from 59% of total RG resources in 2001 to about 50% in recent years. This does not reflect declining real values of the DAU but rather rapid growth in real values of shared revenues and the DAK, and, in very recent periods, rapid real growth of the Hibah (grants). The DAU has equalization as its core stated objective and in part (excluding the general allocation) is determined according to a fiscal gap formula where the gap is determined by fiscal capacities minus fiscal needs.

Access to physical and social infrastructure varies very widely between regions in Indonesia. The fiscal gap part of the DAU contributes to lessening such inequalities but it can only make a slow contribution over time. Per capita expenditures vary widely between RGs (Table 11.3). Recent data suggest the variations are about 50-fold between the highest and lowest spending districts. Differentials in part reflect the equalizing effects of the DAU (e.g., Papua and its LGs are among the poorest provinces and districts but have among the highest per capita expenditures of any region). However, these are not simply DAU effects. They also relate to the inequitable distribution of shared revenues, DAK, other grants, and local PAD collections—and, in the case of Papua and Aceh, special autonomy grants.

Table 11.2: Actual DAU Transfers to Provinces, Districts, and Cities, 2001–2008

Item	2001	2002I	2003	2004	2005	2006	2007	2008
(In Rp Billion)								
Transfers to Provinces	6,462.9	7,351.3	8,288.4	8,698.6	9,183.0	14,571.4	16,478.7	17,980.7
Transfers to Districts and Cities	54,279.1	62,202.7	70,230.4	73,328.9	80,170.4	131,114.1	148,308.7	161,769.3
Total DAU	**60,742.0**	**69,554.0**	**78,518.8**	**82,027.5**	**89,353.3**	**145,685.4**	**164,787.4**	**179,750.0**
% Growth		14.5	12.9	4.5	8.9	63.0	13.1	9.1
(As % of Total GDP)								
Transfers to Provinces	0.43	0.40	0.41	0.38	0.33	0.44	0.42	0.40
Transfers to Districts and Cities	3.6	3.4	3.5	3.2	2.9	3.9	3.7	3.6
Total DAU	**4.1**	**3.8**	**3.9**	**3.6**	**3.2**	**4.4**	**4.2**	**4.0**

DAU = general allocation fund, GDP = gross domestic product.
Note: Exchange rates for the rupiah to the dollar are as follows: 2001: 10,261; 2002: 9,311; 2003: 8,577; 2004: 8,939; 2005: 9,705; 2006: 9,159; 2007: 9,141; 2008: 9,699; 2009: 10,390; 2010: 9,090 (ADB 2011).
Sources: Author secured data from Badan Pusat Statistik (BPS); Audit Board (BPK); Ministry of Finance regional financial information system (SIKD); unaudited government financial reports—Lapunan Keuangan Pemerintah Pusat (LKPP).

Particular reform issues with the DAU that merit addressing include the following:

- About 40% of the DAU is composed of a basic allocation that meets the wages and salaries bills of RGs on a relatively standardized basis. This has produced perverse incentives for RGs to employ additional staff in the belief that the CG is picking up the total wages bill. Such funding occurs despite widespread evidence and views that RGs spend too much on nonproductive administration. Staffing levels per population vary widely between RGs—recent data suggest the range is from 0.44 staff members per 1,000 people in the lowest staffed RG to 111.7 per 1,000 in the highest (ADB 2008). There is much scope to remove negative signals coming from the Basic Allocation, preferably by removing it altogether, or by increasing flexibility in ways it can be used and in staff numbers that can be employed.
  - While the "hold harmless clause" that protected better-off RGs has now been removed, it has now been partly replaced by special

Table 11.3: DAU as a Share of Subnational Government Revenues (2001–2006, %, by province)

Province	2001	2002	2003	2004	2005	2006
Aceh	33.18	9.93	3.99	3.37	7.13	11.33
Bali	30.49	24.84	29.40	23.90	19.73	30.70
Bangka-Belitung	59.53	64.30	...	51.95	42.90	51.61
Banten	32.99	16.76	15.37	13.96	12.39	15.45
Bengkulu	77.47	74.20	70.94	62.85	58.94	67.96
Gorontalo	58.37	80.69	79.18	82.28	78.08	84.94
West Papua	xxx	xxx	xxx	90.02	43.77	...
Jambi	53.41	47.55	40.15	35.44	32.53	37.06
West Java	25.64	15.50	17.64	14.19	11.83	11.21
Central Java	44.27	26.02	32.13	19.18	15.59	23.32
East Java	18.56	16.40	12.72	11.72	9.86	16.07
West Kalimantan	53.21	52.27	...	47.48	45.85	55.97
South Kalimantan	33.17	32.52	36.32	31.48	25.80	32.09
Central Kalimantan	52.46	61.17	61.55	49.84	50.72	62.06
East Kalimantan	14.01	13.04	11.28	10.53	7.20	1.50
Riau Islands	xxx	xxx	xxx	29.86	5.26	15.76
Lampung	42.76	37.35	37.62	34.92	29.72	35.59
Maluku	N/A	81.78	72.02	69.17	54.11	...
North Maluku	48.87	76.13	80.65	...	...	...
West Nusa Tenggara	36.00	55.30	52.32	49.02	47.24	54.55
East Nusa Tenggara	45.73	66.67	68.25	65.32	61.31	...
Papua	41.45	16.99	45.46	15.16	15.66	16.55
Riau	16.81	6.61	3.72	2.92	3.45	2.57
West Sulawesi	xxx	xxx	xxx	xxx	0.00	78.39
South Sulawesi	46.96	39.08	36.24	30.59	28.55	34.43
Central Sulawesi	57.39	65.92	64.44	62.24	59.26	70.10
Southeast Sulawesi	52.15	71.51	67.76	65.10	64.77	71.25
North Sulawesi	24.16	68.71	61.94	58.54	50.79	61.86
West Sumatra	56.31	40.06	41.77	34.25	31.73	...
South Sumatra	30.49	29.06	25.32	20.66	17.48	22.58
North Sumatra	31.51	25.32	21.35	19.21	16.46	...
Yogyakarta	28.53	47.69	38.10	38.42	34.12	45.68
Indonesia	32.01	22.29	21.88	18.72	16.13	21.95

... = not available, xxx = not applicable.
Source: Data from the regional financial information system (SIKD) of the Ministry of Finance.

balance funds to provide some continuing (but lower) support to partly protect the positions of better-off RGs. These special balance funds should be phased out.

○ The main variable making up the fiscal gap formula has technical problems: (1) While the fiscal capacity formula is meant to be based on revenue potentials of particular RGs, for most years it has been based on actual historical revenue collections. This acts as a disincentive for RGs to report and collect own-source revenues, as higher collected revenues equate to lower fiscal gap allocations under the DAU. (2) Debate continues as to whether the "expenditure needs" components and weights of the formula adequately measure expenditure needs. Regular and transparent studies are needed to assess and update the suitability of variables and weights used in the expenditure needs part of the formula. (3) The use of the "fiscal gap" formula has lacked transparency, and weights and methodologies have not been published regularly. These should be fully disclosed annually in the CG budget papers.

Specific Allocation Grants (DAK). The DAK has increased in absolute and relative importance over the past decade (from Rp1.1 trillion [$107 million] in 2001 to Rp24.8 trillion [$2.386 billion] in 2009, or from 0.1% of GDP in 2001 to 0.5% of GDP in 2009). However, DAK grants remain a small part of the total resources available to RGs (about 5% of LG financing in 2008, with negligible funding going to the provinces). There is widespread dissatisfaction with performance of the DAK, and its policies and procedures have been undergoing close review since 2008. A major revamp of DAK arrangements is expected starting in 2011. Important matters that need to be considered in the reform context include the following:

- The current single-year timeframe hampers the management of capital projects. Movement toward a medium-term budgeting approach (the Medium Term Expenditure Framework), with scope to carry forward unspent funds at year-end, would be beneficial.
- Sector specialization has dissipated from a handful of high priority sectors in the early years of the DAK to about 14 sectors. The selection criteria set out in GR 5 of 2005 have not worked well in practice and require review and revision.
- Technical guidelines developed by the CG technical ministries are often not suitable to the needs or interests of RGs. Movement to a less specific block form of funding with more discretion to RGs within broad guidelines merits consideration.
- The CG's inability to monitor the performance of DAK projects needs to be addressed. This includes poor reporting on finances and performance of DAK projects by RGs and the CG's inability to follow

up on financial and nonfinancial performance issues. An enhanced role for the Audit Board, BPK, is needed;

- Technical difficulties exist in the required switching of illegitimate deconcentration spending to DAK, including criteria limiting deconcentration to nonphysical expenditures, while DAK is limited to physical expenditures (this could be addressed by either clarifying that deconcentration funds, not projects, are being targeted or by allowing both capital and recurrent outlays in DAK).
- Policy should address disincentives stopping better-off RGs from borrowing for capital funding due to the availability of CG grants. This would involve grading RGs into those that are and are not capable of borrowing for capital spending (and those that may have limited capacities where a blend of debt and grant financing is appropriate).

Shared Revenues. Revenue sharing has grown rapidly in the decade leading to 2011, to the point where it is now a significant part of the CG funding mix for RGs. CG revenue sharing rose sharply, from Rp21.7 trillion ($2.115 billion) in 2001 to Rp86.7 trillion ($8.345 billion) in 2009, and relatively, from 1.3% of GDP to about 1.8% of GDP during the same period. The main revenues shared include income taxes, property and transfer taxes, and a variety of resource-related taxes (mining, oil, gas, forestry, and fisheries). Following introduction of the new Law 28 of 2009 on regional taxes and charges, the property and transfer taxes for urban and rural areas (but not for mining, plantations, and forestry) are to be gradually devolved.

Revenue sharing comprises approximately half of the DAU, but is distributed very inequitably, mainly going to areas providing the source of the revenue, thus favoring resource-rich regions and (in the case of the income tax) large, populous cities. Some important reform areas need to be addressed:

- Distribution arrangements for resource-based revenues have largely been politically determined to support areas where major resource developments occur. Although politically difficult, consideration needs to be given to a broader sharing of resource revenues in line with the equalization concept of the DAU.
- Property taxes for mining, plantations, and forestry remain solely CG taxes, with sharing arrangements heavily favoring resource-rich regions. These taxes do not follow international norms, as they contain two separate components: (1) a royalty type turnover tax based on production levels, and (2) a more conventional property tax applying to property assets at resource development sites. There is a case for splitting the two forms of taxes, treating the former as CG taxes but still subject to sharing, and treating the latter as devolved taxes of the RGs.

- A number of other higher yielding CG taxes are currently under review for either full or partial devolution to RGs and/or to add to the mix of taxes that are shared by the CG with the RGs. One such tax is the VAT, which is currently solely a CG tax. Policy work in this area is rife with political and bureaucratic challenges, and major decisions on reform are not likely to be made in the foreseeable future.

Grants (Hibah). Although not originally envisioned to be a major part of the intergovernmental financing arrangements as set out in Law 33 of 2004, the Hibah system of grants has taken on new and significant funding dimensions commencing from about 2009–2010, with significant further funding possibly to be channeled through this mechanism in future years. The two emerging dimensions to the Hibah are the "on-granting"[10] of foreign-funded grant project funds and the domestic financing of projects in the RGs.

Development partners have been trying for some years to open channels for on-granting. This was facilitated in part by GR 57 of 2005 regarding on-granting and related MOF Regulations 168 and 169 of 2008. Work is now proceeding to rewrite the 2005 GR to, among other things, make processing of foreign grants more practical and efficient. A relatively significant number of foreign-funded projects are in the pipeline, including those relating to (1) regional hospitals (from the World Health Organization); (2) education infrastructure (the European Union and the World Bank); and (3) water supply, roads, and education facilities (the Australian Agency for International Development). Many of these projects seem to be establishing forms of assistance parallel to the government's main funding mechanism for capital projects, the DAK scheme.

In 2010, the government decided to channel approximately Rp7 trillion ($770 million) through the Hibah mechanism using MOF as the conduit with funds thought to have been sourced from identification of illegitimate deconcentration expenditures in the budgets of about 13 key line ministries (the Ministry of National Education was excluded from the list for 2010, despite having considerable sources of illegitimate deconcentration funding). Projects are currently being identified and prepared to allow spending of these funds. Performance-based contracts are likely to be developed between MOF and participating RGs (about 320 RGs).

There are a number of concerns about these Hibah projects, including (1) overlap and duplication with the DAK scheme; (2) establishment of new institutional structures (in a different directorate of the Directorate General for Fiscal Balance, MOF) when existing (DAK) structures and procedures are not working well; and (3) many of the LGs and projects appear to have been

---

[10]   "On-granting" refers to the CG receiving funds and providing them to RGs as grants.

selected on political bases rather than through rigorous selection methods. The emerging Hibah scheme needs to be closely watched and reviewed to ensure that problems such as those just listed do not eventuate.

11.3.4.6. RG Borrowing and the Financing of Investment

Despite massive shortfalls of physical infrastructure in the regions, RGs have borrowed only insignificant amounts since 2001. This in part relates to longstanding problems with RG arrears on their debts raised in earlier periods through the CG, including debts related indirectly to the RGs through water supply companies and other RG-owned enterprises. Recently, efforts have been made (including the issue of MOF Regulation 120 of 2008 on the restructuring of water supply companies' debts) to restructure past debts, including (1) separating out debt incurred prior to the "big bang" reform; (2) applying restructuring incentives, including, for example, forgiving part of the debt, to support a return to regular repayments; and (3) providing arrangements for DAU transfers to be redeployable to service RG debt that is not being satisfactorily repaid.

A related complicating factor is that many RGs are holding excess cash reserves (equivalent to about 3% of GDP), which could be a source of investment financing, but have not been used for productive purposes. Recent anticorruption cases have revealed that a number of RG officials have been receiving commissions for holding large deposits with regional banks. Also, RGs have mixed capacities to borrow and service debt. A large number of RGs may have quite low capacities to service debt, and only a few have viable debt-servicing capacities, while a sizeable group in the middle may have the capacity to service debt if it comes in a blend of grants and loans.

Law 33 of 2004 and MOF Regulation 147 of 2006 provide for RGs to raise debt financing by issuing RG bonds. While a number of possible bond issues are being studied in selected pilot locations (Bandung, Jakarta, and Surabaya), no successful bond raisings have been finalized. Progress on this front is likely to be slow, and many years may elapse before RGs achieve significant borrowing through bond issues.

Future reform needs in relation to debt matters include (1) satisfactory progress on the proper restructuring of the large overhang of past debt and the servicing of legitimate debts that remain, including CG use of the "DAU intercept mechanism"[11] in suitable cases; (2) improved financial management and reporting by RGs, including increased issuance of unqualified audit opinions to support the issuance of independent ratings to facilitate bond raisings; (3) CG willingness to remove bureaucratic complexities from the

---

[11]   The government is testing a performance-related mechanism for fiscal transfers—DAU can be withheld due to late submission of budgets and financial reports.

on-lending of funds from multilateral lenders willing to lend to the RGs for infrastructure development; and (4) development of appropriate mixes of grant and debt funding for investment spending, including development of more appropriately financed DAK and/or Hibah arrangements.

11.3.4.7. RG PFM Systems and Improved Service Delivery

Broad reforms in the RG PFM systems (planning, budget formulation, budget execution, accounting, reporting, and audit) are being addressed, with goals for ultimate outcomes being improved governance, better budgets, and improved quantities and qualities in the delivery of goods and services to local communities. Since 2001, major changes have been made to the regulatory and systems regimes for PFM at both CG and RG levels. Given that Indonesia is a unitary state, these changes have been broadly consistent, though important inconsistencies exist, mainly due to differing views between MOF and MOHA in the design of RG regulations and systems. Correcting inconsistencies over time will be important. The main legal reforms that have impacted PFM over the decade have been as follows (MOF 2008, 2009):

- new national laws with RG implications issued between 2003 and 2005, covering public finance, treasury, national planning, and external audit; and
- a raft of lower level regulations (below the laws) with implications for PFM systems, importantly including (1) national (and RG) accounting standards (2004); (2) GR 58 of 2005 on RG PFM systems (as updated by GR 39 of 2007); and (3) MOHA Regulation 13 of 2006 on RG PFM systems (as updated by MOHA Regulation 59 of 2007).

The detailed RG PFM systems developed largely in new regulations between 2005 and 2006 came rather soon on top of earlier transformational changes as set out in MOHA Decree 29 of 2002. Taken together, the two sets of changes represented revolutionary transformations in the largely centralized Dutch systems of budgeting and accounting that had prevailed prior to the "big bang" reforms. A common complaint at the time of the 2006 reforms was that they came too quickly on top of the 2002 reforms and that they provided systems that were too new, complex, and comprehensive for RG officials to grasp. To some extent, such criticisms still abound today, though increasingly, RG officials have started to absorb the new systems; at least the basic elements of the new systems have now been introduced almost universally in all RGs, though with varying degrees of implementation quality and completeness.

The new PFM systems are relatively modern in nature, providing for accountable, medium-term, performance-based approaches to PFM. They take a comprehensive approach to PFM with provisions relating to (1) designation of key officials and their authorities, including the RG heads and the DPDs; (2) effective medium-term planning linked to budgeting; (3) unified and comprehensive performance-based budget formulation and approval; (4) efficient budget execution; (5) regular reporting and monitoring in transparent ways; (6) accounting systems and charts of account that meet national accounting standards; and (7) strong internal and external audit and supervision requirements.

Most field-based reviews and experience suggest that, while Indonesia's PFM systems are relatively sound, challenges remain in the practical implementation of systems. Some of the challenging areas for reform include the following:

- Approaches to planning are ineffective and nonconsultative, with plans still not strategically prepared and not well linked to budgets.
- Budgets are frequently prepared too late and do not secure effective reforms to resource allocation, with excessive amounts commonly provided for staffing and low productivity administrative costs. Performance-based budgeting has proved very difficult to implement but merits continuing practical effort and support (OECD 2009).
- Classifications for budget preparation and reporting on budget realization are inconsistent, and it is difficult to extract useful information by entity, function, and subfunction due to unusual approaches taken to direct, indirect, and apparatus costs in the MOHA regulations.
- The payments system is complex and cumbersome, which slows implementation without ensuring good quality internal control. The lack of a strong internal audit system has hampered implementation of strong internal controls. Implementing the new GR 60 of 2008 on internal control will be important, but will require a lot of capacity building.
- Major difficulties have been experienced with valuations, accounting, and reporting of assets and liabilities, and are the most common reasons for external audit qualifications. While adherence to the legally required move to full accrual accounting from fiscal year 2007/08 has slipped far into the future, mixed cash and accrual requirements persist, including partial balance sheet preparation, which are proving difficult to manage.
- Financial information flows within RGs remain poor (including down to the sector management work units), so little use is made of budget and budget realization data as a means for improving future work. Computerized financial management information systems have not been standardized, though MOHA (with Asian Development Bank [ADB] support) is now trying (in over 100

RGs) what might become the basis for a standardized approach over time.

Many of the issues pertaining to improving PFM in the RGs must be seen in the light of a need for long-term capacity development of RG systems and staff. This relates to staff in the centralized planning, budget, and accounting work units, and to managers, submanagers, and related financial officials in the sector work units.

11.3.4.8. Monitoring and Evaluation of RG Performance

One of the difficulties with policy formulation in RG matters, especially from a CG policy perspective, has been the lack of timely and good quality information on the performance of RGs. Some improvements have been evident recently, though considerable work remains to be done. Work is proceeding on two broad fronts:

- The SIKD Directorate in the DG Fiscal Balance in MOF[12] is responsible for receiving and processing financial information from the RGs, mainly in terms of budget and budget realization reports. Preparation of consolidated reports has been hampered by manual transmission of bulky data in unedited formats, late or no transmissions, and widely differing formats used for data submission. Many of the data prior to 2007 are very problematic due to widely differing formats and incompleteness. Some improvements have occurred since 2007 with better standardization of accounting classifications, though manual submission and entry of data means that data consolidation remains slow. MOF with the support of development partners (ADB and the World Bank) is pursuing both longer term solutions to the problem (standardized computerization of financial management information systems in all RGs) and shorter term ones (electronic submission of standardized pro forma reports by the RGs).
- The Capacity Development and Performance Evaluation Directorate of the DG Regional Autonomy in MOHA is pursuing a broadly based computerized monitoring system to collect information on wider governance and service delivery aspects of RG performance. Initially, a computer database has generated data on a range of performance indicators from 40 RGs. Attempts are now being made to spread coverage to all RGs over time, while the number of indicators to be monitored is under review. The relevant MOHA regulation provides for more than 100 indicators, but a smaller number of indicators is being considered to make management, maintenance, and use of the system more efficient.

---

[12]   SIKD is the Sistem Informasi Keuangan Daerah (Regional Financial Information System).

11.3.4.9. Development of Capacities of CG and RGs (especially in PFM)

Broadly based capacities (institutions, systems, and people) need to be widely developed, including political, administrative, and financial and economic aspects of decentralization. With much of the political and legislative reform program now complete, the attention everywhere is turning to capacity development, especially in the regions. This subsection concentrates mainly on issues relating to capacity development in PFM–related areas. However, broader efforts at capacity development on all fronts are needed.

PFM capacity development efforts in the regions currently come from a wide array of sources, including the central ministries (especially Bappenas, MOF, and MOHA); the provinces (in support of LGs); regional associations of RGs; and the RGs themselves, as initiatives in capacity development, often with the support of private accountants and regionally based software developers. There is also a significant presence of development partners in supporting RG PFM capacity development through centralized preparation of regulations, manuals, training materials, etc., and through direct capacity development projects in a large number of RGs throughout the country. The CG has particular responsibilities to support the provinces' capacity development while the provinces have important roles in coordinating support for capacity development in LGs. The current National Action Plan for Fiscal Decentralization (NAPFD) envisaged development of a nationwide plan to facilitate PFM capacity development at different levels of government, but this has not yet been finalized.

The broad framework for capacity development in the regions was set out in the MOHA Guideline of 2002, the National Framework for Capacity Building to Support Decentralization. The framework postulates capacity development interventions at three levels: (1) strengthening policies and regulatory frameworks at the systems level; (2) improving organizational structures and decision-making procedures to facilitate more participation of civil society, and management systems to deliver results at the institutional level; and (3) upgrading individuals' professional skills and attitudes, and motivational changes as needed. Significant work has been undertaken since 2008 to upgrade this framework to the level of a presidential regulation, and it is hoped that this regulation, after much delay, will soon be released.

The CG increasingly seeks to support capacity development in the regions to assist effective implementation of new systems. Some recent CG initiatives have included the following:
- Bappenas has prepared materials and courses to improve planning skills.
- MOF and MOHA have provided familiarization and training on new PFM laws and regulations, including preparation of central manuals and training materials.

- Specialized PFM courses have been convened, especially by MOF, through long-term contracts with eight regional universities to train about 1,600 RG officials per year. MOF is currently preparing plans to expand these courses through additional universities and web-based learning.
- Standardized computerized financial management information systems are being developed for RGs under MOHA and MOF leadership (with support of ADB, the Canadian International Development Agency, and the United States Agency for International Development).
- Regionally based CG treasury officials are receiving professional development and certification. MOF (DG Treasury) is designing documentation for a staff development scheme that will allow for certification of new functional positions for key regional treasury officials. Certification will depend in part on upgrading professional qualifications through professional training and examinations. Preliminary design work is also being undertaken to see if such approaches might be extended to PFM officials employed within the RGs.

One area of concern is that a significant amount of training and capacity building being conducted is ill informed and inconsistent with the laws and regulations (including some support by development partners). Some form of accreditation of PFM trainers may be needed to ensure consistency and quality—a concerted effort to fully train and properly accredit private sector trainers may well bear fruit. The provinces could play a larger coordination and facilitation role in this regard. While noting the challenges, the range of CG, RG, and development partner efforts appears broadly appropriate. However, improved planning, coordination, and financing of all efforts is needed. Without significant intensification of effort at all levels, capacities are not likely to be developed to the extent and at the speed needed.

11.3.4.10. General Performance Indicators

In the new decentralization era since 2001, regional governments have played a key role in delivering social services in education and health, as well as in developing infrastructure for basic services such as clean running water and roads. An important question is what has been the impact of decentralization on the quantity and quality of those services. Decentralization is a relatively new experience for Indonesia, and in some ways it may be too soon to make a full account of its performance. But at least a preliminary assessment is possible. The RGs' performance can be evaluated from a service delivery perspective—such as, whether the quality of services has improved (World Bank 2008).

Stakeholders widely believe that the quality of local public services continues to be poor after decentralization.[13] However, overall, the little evidence available gives a mixed picture of service performance and in some cases indicates an improved quality of services. For example, a study sponsored by the World Bank concluded, based on survey data, that decentralized government services in education, health, and general administration had improved while the quality of a CG service that has not been decentralized (the police) had deteriorated (Kaiser, Pattinasarany, and Schultze 2006). Survey evidence, of course, can only be taken as suggestive and to be corroborated by objective indicators.

In addition, there are large regional disparities in income distribution and service delivery. Poverty in Indonesia fell from 16.6% in 2007 to 13.3% in 2010; however, Maluku Province has a poverty rate of 27.7% compared with 3.5% in Jakarta and 4.3% in Bali (BPS 2011). Inequalities extend to other human development dimensions. East Maluku had a human development index of 70.96 in 2009, below Jakarta at 77.36. Of households in Yogyakarta, 75% had improved sanitation, compared with 25% in Papua or Central Kalimantan. In at least 12 provinces, fewer than 70% of households have access to electricity; a similar number of provinces have full coverage (World Bank 2009).

11.4. Institutional Framework for Policy Reform and Program Support

This section focuses mainly on the institutional framework for reforming fiscal aspects of decentralization, though aspects of broader political and administrative reform are also touched on, particularly with regard to the role of MOHA and the development partners. Reform efforts remain somewhat disjointed in Indonesia, with many players (both in and outside government) running their own race with regard to the development of policy, legal, and other reforms and with the development and management of financial programs of support. Attempts at better coordination and harmonization are being made, but at present there is no single government decentralization reform program and no single well-harmonized package of development partner support for decentralization reform.

---

[13] The counterfactual scenario for the current situation (or the quality of services that would have been delivered now if decentralization had not taken place) is not an efficient decentralized system with glowing performance indicators but rather the centralized system of service delivery before the 2001 decentralization reforms. Under the centralized system, the quality of most services was rather poor.

11.4.1. Institutional Evolution of Fiscal Decentralization Reform Efforts

When the national white paper on PFM reform was prepared in 2001, responsibilities for CG coordination of fiscal aspects of decentralization reform were perceived to come under the Financial Management Reform Committee. However, as the committee became largely dormant in 2005–2006, new institutional arrangements came to the fore for coordinating CG fiscal decentralization reforms. These were based mainly around the following:

- An independent DG Fiscal Balance in MOF was reestablished in 2005, with responsibilities for policy and day-to-day management of fiscal aspects of decentralization, including capacity development.
- Law 32 of 2004 established the President's advisory body on decentralization (DPOD), with wide representation, including from Bappenas, MOF, MOHA, and the regions.
- In 2007, the MOF appointed a special team to work for the MOF minister and the DG of Fiscal Balance in the MOF, to support development of the reform model for fiscal decentralization, including preparation of a long-term grand design for fiscal decentralization reform to 2030. This aims to provide a longer term strategic framework for the 5-year National Action Plan for Fiscal Decentralization (NAPDF) 2005–2009, which is being updated for the period 2010–2014.
- Within MOHA, a new DG for Regional Financial Management was formed in 2003 to become the focal point for PFM reform in MOHA (though some important matters, particularly policies relating to the assignment of expenditure functions between levels of government, formation of new subnational governments *(pemekaran)*, and RG performance evaluations, were to remain in the MOHA DG for Regional Autonomy.
- Partly because of continuing weaknesses in making DPOD operationally effective, Bappenas has come to play an increasingly important role in coordinating fiscal aspects of decentralization through the deputy minister for regional development and autonomy and the director for regional autonomy. This role included responsibility for preparing and monitoring performance against the NAPFD, preparing decentralization components of the new National Development Plan 2010–2014, and preparing a new NAPFD 2010–2014.
- A range of institutional structures are in place to support PFM reforms at the decentralized levels. In many places, the provinces play an active role in trying to provide incentives to stimulate

improved management and PFM practices (e.g., Gorontalo and Papua). In other places, regional associations of RGs play education, training, and coordination roles. However, in many places, RGs need to rely heavily on their own resources to improve management (often with the help of local academics, private accountants, and software developers) to get things done.

11.4.2. Grand Design for Fiscal Decentralization

Since 2008, a special team in MOF appointed by and reporting to the minister (through the DG Fiscal Balance of MOF) has been preparing the long-term Grand Design of Fiscal Decentralization. The team published an initial draft strategy concept paper in late 2009, though it is not yet endorsed by the CG. The timeframe of the strategy being prepared is approximately 20 years, to 2030, though shorter term actions to 2015 are provided. This work is intended to provide longer term strategic direction to the more medium-term and practical action-oriented NAPFD. The strategy work is expected to be finalized in 2011 and to be formally endorsed as a government document, perhaps by way of a regulation. The Grand Design is likely to be high-level and strategic in nature, with limited detail on strategies or actions. It is expected to contain (1) a long-term vision and mission; (2) key pillars—human resources, institutions, information systems, regulatory regime, and expertise; (3) goals—vertical and horizontal balance, effective revenue systems, appropriate expenditure assignments, harmonization in expenditure between levels of government, and strong national and regional economic development; and (4) a framework for implementing the strategy and monitoring progress over time.

11.4.3. The NAPFD, 2005–2009

The NAPFD was first prepared in 2005 and was published by Bappenas under the signed agreement of the ministers of Bappenas, MOF, and MOHA. An important test for the longer term viability of the NAPFD is now being played out as Bappenas, MOF, and MOHA have commenced writing a new version of it to cover 2010–2014. This writing is occurring in relation to decentralization sections of the newly issued National Development Plan, 2010–2014. More inclusive approaches to preparing the new NAPFD are being pursued in the hope that final actions prepared by the government might lead to broader consensus on medium-term reform directions, which most development partners that are backing fiscal decentralization might be willing to support with flexible financing and technical arrangements for the future. The NAPFD's scope is somewhat broader than simply PFM or fiscal decentralization, as it includes aspects of political and administrative decentralization. The main broad strategic areas set forward in the NAPFD 2005–2009 are as follows:

- clarifying administrative arrangements impinging on fiscal management:
  ◦ providing functional assignments,
  ◦ ensuring money follows function, and
  ◦ strengthening DPOD to lead functional assignment and coordination;
- improving the effectiveness of RG spending:
  ◦ reviewing and monitoring expenditures,
  ◦ preparing and implementing minimum service standards, and
  ◦ restructuring and improving the efficiency of RG organizations;
- ensuring the efficiency and equity of local resource availability:
  ◦ enhancing local revenue collections;
  ◦ improving the horizontal and vertical equity of CG transfers (DAU, DAK, etc.); and
  ◦ developing effective policies for RG borrowing;
- reforming and strengthening RG PFM:
  ◦ strengthening assets and liabilities management;
  ◦ using consistent approaches to budgeting, accounting, and reporting; and
  ◦ improving financial accountability (including internal control and external audit);
- developing national and local capacities in PFM, monitoring, and evaluation:
  ◦ developing systems and institutional capacities, and
  ◦ developing human capacities; and
- improving coordination, monitoring, and evaluation of fiscal decentralization reform efforts:
  ◦ enhancing the role of a strengthened DPOD; and
  ◦ enhancing coordination roles for Bappenas, MOF, and MOHA.

In late 2008, Bappenas assessed progress made in implementing the NAPFD. Some of the main conclusions were that (1) much of the emphasis when the NAPFD was written in 2004–2005 had been on finalizing the legal and regulatory framework, and by late 2008 about 75% of the new laws and regulations that had been envisaged had been passed; (2) while Bappenas, MOF, and MOHA had all made important contributions to RG capacity development, they had been inadequate to meet the very significant needs and greater CG effort to support RG capacity development efforts that would be required in the next phase; and (3) the DPOD has continued to be quite weak in leading the RG reform effort from the center, and decisions will be needed in the next phase as to whether to continue coordination through the DPOD or make less formal arrangements between the relevant parts of Bappenas, MOF, and MOHA (Bappenas 2008). Some matters left over from the first NAPFD are likely to be included in the second, but the second NAPFD document may end up looking rather different from the first, with a smaller number of better prioritized actions to be developed.

11.4.4. The Framework for Reform and Capacity Development

The foregoing shows that responsibilities for decentralization reform and capacity development come from a wide array of sometimes conflicting sources, including the central ministries (especially Bappenas, MOF, and MOHA); the provinces (in support of LGs); regional associations of RGs; and the LGs themselves, in terms of local regulatory reforms and initiatives in capacity development, often with support of the private sector. There is also a significant presence of development partners, mainly supporting a broad range of CG and RG policy reform and capacity development initiatives.

The CG has particular responsibilities to support the provinces in their policy development and capacity building, while the provinces have important roles in coordinating support for policy and regulatory reform and capacity development in LGs. While the NAPFD 2005–2009 envisaged a nationwide plan to facilitate fiscal capacity development at different levels of government, this has not yet been finalized, though further work is proceeding in an effort to prepare such a plan. While the various longer term Grand Strategy documents being prepared either implicitly or explicitly assume that decentralization reforms and capacity development will be well coordinated, this is often not the case.

Given the tumultuous history of coordination among the three main CG ministries, some observers are of the view that reform coordination efforts may never be entirely satisfactory and that the best hope lies in designing distinctly different roles for different institutions. For example, one key issue is whether responsibilities for fiscal and PFM aspects of decentralization could be excised completely from MOHA or should become the sole responsibility of MOF. Another example is whether matters relating to the assignment of functions between levels of government have been correctly placed within the DG Regional Autonomy of MOHA. While such a single location potentially removes problems of coordination, it seems that MOHA operating alone lacks the capacity to perform this complex role adequately, including taking into account national planning and national budget views of Bappenas and MOF. Thus, moving the assignment of functions to a single higher body capable of considering the views of multiple levels of stakeholders inside and outside government may be needed, through a specially convened form of constitutional commission with a brief to finalize functional assignments and to be given strong backing of the Constitution and law.

This chapter has argued for further reform and capacity development in key strategic areas; however, strategically unified approaches to implementation will not always be possible under the existing institutional framework. While it is possible to recommend alternative structures for managing reform and capacity development efforts, the completely new structures are unlikely to emerge suddenly. Suggestions for future reforms should bear these realities in mind.

11.5. Conclusions

In the first decade of Indonesia's decentralization reform efforts, the country has made solid progress, but there is significant ongoing debate as to whether the glass is currently half full or half empty. Certainly no one denies that progress has been made, but few people suggest there is not a considerable way to go before a more satisfactory situation can be achieved, particularly in the more effective delivery of high priority goods and services that have become the assigned responsibilities of Indonesia's provincial and local governments.

A complex array of constraints and issues needs to be addressed on political, administrative, and financial fronts if the RGs are to move closer to attaining their full potential. Clearly, the future path for reform will be complex and challenging, and other observers and policymakers with differing perspectives may add other important issues. Policymakers and practitioners in Indonesia are thus continually confronted with a vast and at times seemingly insurmountable range of tasks that many people observing from the sidelines would have them address all at once.

The "big bang" has been a useful approach to usher in revolutionary reforms to decentralized democratic governance at the overall level. However, much of the hard work and fine detail of implementation will need to be addressed during decades to come, and further progress will be largely incremental rather than of a revolutionary nature. This should not come as a surprise, as much of the developed world continues to struggle with systems of functional assignments, intergovernmental financing arrangements, and the like, the basic elements of which were often designed centuries ago, with many remaining just as controversial now as they were then.

How Indonesia in practice will prioritize its issues and actions in the decade or two ahead remains to be seen, as it works gradually but surely toward a better performing system of decentralization. The issues and possible reform responses set out in this chapter are by no means new and have been the subject of discussion among Indonesian policymakers for

426

several years. Most of the issues will continue to be worked on during the coming years in one form or another, and steady progress will likely be broadly made to the benefit of communities receiving goods and services from their democratically elected provincial and local governments.

References

Asian Development Bank (ADB). 2008. *Report and Recommendations of the President, Local Government Finance and Governance Reform Program 2 (LGFGR 2)*. Manila.

———. 2011. *Key Indicators for Asia and the Pacific*. Manila.

Badan Perencanaan Pembangunan Nasional (Bappenas—National Development Planning Board). 2008. *Review of Progress in Implementing the NAPFD, 2005–2009*. Jakarta.

Badan Pusat Statistik (Statistics Indonesia—BPS). 2009. *Statistical Yearbook of Indonesia 2009*. Jakarta.

———. 2011. BPS Website. www.bps.go.id

Donor Working Group for Decentralization. 2009. *Stocktaking on Indonesia's Recent Decentralization Reforms, Update 2009*, Jakarta.

Kaiser, K., D. Pattinasarany, and G. Schulze. 2006. *Decentralization, Governance and Public Services in Indonesia*. World Bank: Jakarta.

Ministry of Finance (MOF). 2008. PFM Reform Strategy Note. Jakarta.

———. 2009. PFM Reform Strategy Note. Jakarta.

Niazi, T., N. Gyat, and M. McDermott. 2009. Strategy and Roadmap for Devolving the Property Tax. Jakarta: Ministry of Finance, Government of Indonesia and ADB.

Niazi, T., H. Imansyah, and J. Martinez. 2009, Understanding Sub-national Government Fragmentation in Indonesia and Options for Reform: Background for a Grand Strategy for Pemekaran. Jakarta: Ministry of Finance, Government of Indonesia and ADB.

Niazi, T. and A. Oosterman. 2009. An Analysis of Deconcentrated Expenditure by the Ministries of Environment and National Education. Jakarta: Ministry of Finance, Government of Indonesia and ADB.

Organisation for Economic Co-operation and Development (OECD). 2009. *Budgeting in Indonesia*. Bangkok.

Sidik, M. 2006. *A New Perspective of Intergovernmental Fiscal Relations, Lessons from Indonesia's Experience*. Jakarta.

Suryana, A. 2011. Corruption Cases Stall Development. *The Jakarta Post*. 7 February. http://www.thejakartapost.com/news/2011/02/07/corruption-cases-stall-development.html

Transparency International (TI). various years, 2003–2009. *Corruption Perception index*. http://www.transparency.org/policy_research/surveys_indices/cpi

World Bank. 2006. *Papua Public Expenditure Analysis—Overview Report.* Jakarta.

———. 2008. *Summary of the 2006 GDS Survey.* Jakarta.

———. 2009. *An Analysis of Regional Public Expenditure and Financial Management.* Jakarta.

World Bank and Government of Indonesia. 2007. *Indonesia Public Expenditure Review—Spending for Development.* Jakarta and Washington, DC.

12. Making Indonesia's Growth Green and Resilient

Suphachol Suphachalasai, Juzhong Zhuang, Jindra Nuella Samson, Rizaldi Boer, and Chris Hope

12.1. Introduction

The current climate, food, fuel, and water crises have convinced many countries, including Indonesia, that a different model of economic growth is needed. "Green growth"—a growth path that places long-term developmental and environmental sustainability at its core—has emerged as a desirable paradigm in Indonesia, and the concept of a low carbon, green economy has moved into the mainstream of the country's policy discourse over the recent years. Indonesia's green growth strategy rightly recognizes that the country's sustainability depends not only on the pace of physical and human capital accumulation, but also on its natural capital.

However, transforming the growth trajectory to one that is green, resilient, and sustainable is by no means an easy task. This is because of the multiple and simultaneous challenges of dealing with unavoidable and uncertain climate risks; attaining energy security; improving access to energy; managing scarce resources, particularly forests, land, and water; and finding ways to reduce greenhouse gas (GHG) emissions while creating new economic opportunities and minimizing adverse social consequences. A number of barriers stand in the way of achieving these goals.

As in other developing countries, natural capital is a significant share of total wealth in Indonesia, greater than the share of physical capital (World Bank 2006b). Green growth is therefore essential for Indonesia's long-term sustainability. Broadly, environmentally unsustainable growth may be attributed to two sources: (1) global environmental risks, particularly associated with the impacts of climate change; and (2) the degradation of environmental and natural resources that occurs locally (Figure 12.1). A number of factors may contribute to the two sources of unsustainability, through different sectors, e.g., power generation; industry; transport; residential, commercial, and agricultural land use; and forests.

Figure 12.1: Diagnosing Environmentally Unsustainable Development

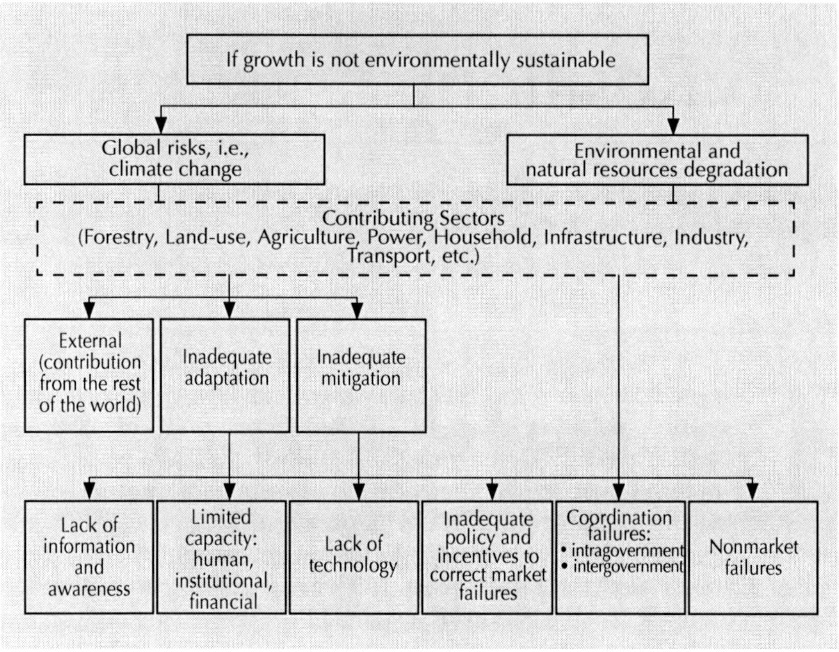

Source: Authors.

Regarding climate change, unsustainability can be caused by inadequate efforts to mitigate and adapt to climate change. Inadequate adaptation efforts can be due to lack of information about and awareness of potential climate impacts, such as on agriculture production and coastal infrastructure. People and governments in developing countries are often not capable of effectively responding to climate change due to limited human, financial, and institutional capacity. At times, the market fails to provide measures that have local public good characteristics, such as early warning, irrigation, and water storage systems. Some issues are cross-sectoral and are not properly addressed due to the lack of a coordinated effort among agencies, while other issues are transboundary and need regional cooperation. In the context of mitigation, technologies needed may simply not be available. They are usually found to be costly, and access to international assistance is limited. Externalities associated with energy and resource use are often not reflected in the market. Moreover, many low-cost options are not being implemented because of the lack of awareness about their availability, a traditional carbon-intensive lifestyle, and so on.

Climate change and natural resource degradation are interconnected, and there are synergies between the two. For example, if the right incentives are provided, large areas of mangroves can be preserved to protect coastal communities from extreme weather events (through adaptation). Mangroves also act as carbon sinks (through mitigation) and help maintain rich ecosystems that provide ecological services and life-support functions (protecting natural capital). In a hotter climate, energy conservation reduces both the cost of energy for cooling (adaptation) and GHG emissions (mitigation). Lifting constraints to implementing such measures will have dual benefits, reducing the global risks and local damage simultaneously.

This chapter assesses Indonesia's current status and discusses the nexus of challenges the country faces in moving toward a green development model, based on the conceptual framework in Figure 12.1. The chapter also points to key policy directions that could facilitate the transition to green growth and relax the constraints on the transition.

12.2. Global Challenges: Climate Risks and Vulnerabilities

Climate change is likely to be one of the most significant developmental challenges Indonesia will confront in the 21st century. Indonesia is one of the most vulnerable countries to climate change, partly due to its geography. The impact of temperature rise on crop yields and water resources tends to be more severe in tropical zones than in other regions. The Indonesian archipelago, with about 17,500 islands and long coastlines, is susceptible to sea level rise and weather-related disasters, and Indonesia has low-lying coastal areas that are densely populated. Millions of Indonesians are still trapped in extreme poverty and are employed in sectors that depend on the climate, particularly agriculture. Most of the energy and transport infrastructure—key to economic development and poverty reduction—is not climate-proof.

12.2.1. Climate Trends

Indonesia's climate has been changing during the last century. During 1865–1990, mean temperatures in Jakarta increased by 1.04°C in January, during the wet season, and about 1.40°C in July, during the dry season (MOE 2010). Observations from 33 stations in Indonesia indicate that the minimum and maximum temperatures have increased at the average rate of 1.7°C and 4.7°C, respectively, during the last century (Boer et. al 2009). The high rates were observed mainly in stations located in urban areas. Annual and seasonal rainfall has also been declining at many stations, particularly those located south of the equator (Boer and Dewi 2008; Figure 12.2). The sea level has risen 0.2–1.0 centimeters (cm) yearly (averaging 0.6 cm/year), based on an altimeter data analysis during 1993–2008 (MOE 2010). This is consistent with earlier reports from many port stations (MOE 2007).

Figure 12.2: Annual Rainfall in Bengkulu, Sumatra, and Ketapang, Kalimantan (1968–1996)

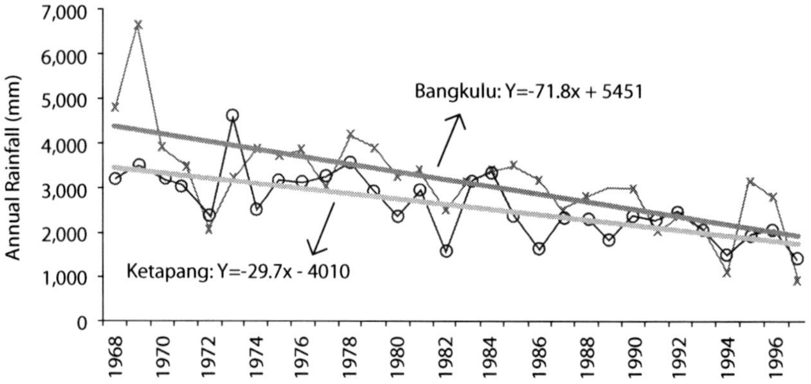

Source: Aldrian (2007) cited in Boer and Dewi (2008).

The frequency with which extreme weather events occur is increasing in Indonesia and is normally associated with the El Niño Southern Oscillation. This has a very strong impact in Indonesia, particularly in the regions that have a monsoonal climate (Java and Bali, and Nusa Tenggara). Since 1953, extreme events have been occurring with increasing frequency (Figure 12.3a). The incidence of frequent flooding, followed by landslides, has increased health risks from vector-borne diseases such as malaria and dengue. Wind storms, forest fires, droughts, and high tides and storm surges are among the climate-related hazards frequently reported (Figure 12.3b).

12.2.2. Future Climate

While great uncertainties are associated with climate change projections, existing models agree that the temperature in Indonesia will rise if the world continues a "business-as-usual" path. The annual mean temperature in Indonesia, under the A1F1 scenario (wherein economic growth is very

Figure 12.3: Frequency and Number of Climate-Related Hazardous Events

a. Frequency (1953–2005)

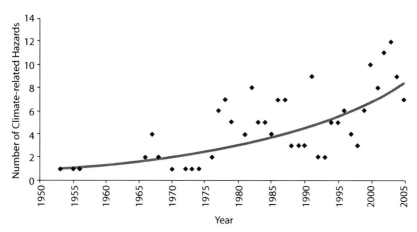

b. Type and Number

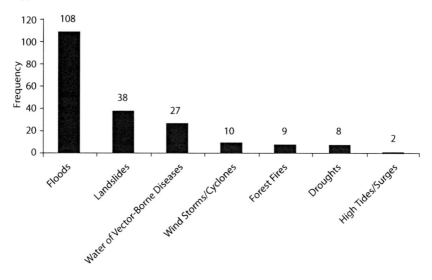

Sources: Boer and Perdinan (2008), MOE (2010, Figure 1.3).

rapid and intensively uses fossil fuels), [1] will likely rise above 4.5°C by 2100 from the 1990 level (Figure 12.4), and the global mean sea level is projected to rise more than 50 cm during the same period.[2]

Figure 12.4: Projected Average Annual Temperature Change in Indonesia

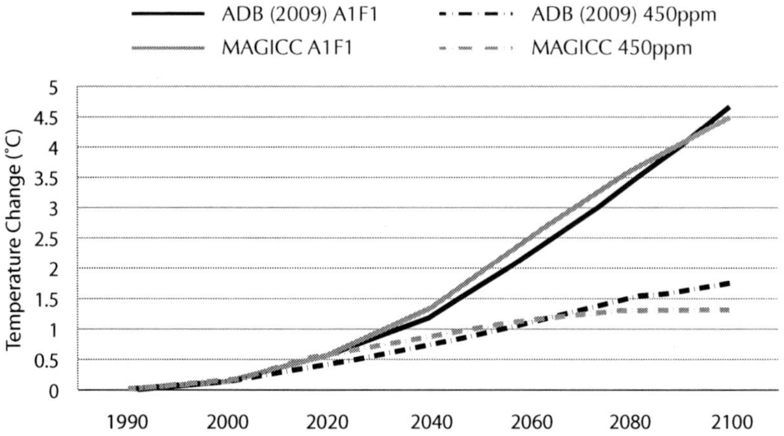

Sources: Authors, based on MAGICC/SCENGEN default runs of 20 general circulation models; ADB (2009).

Indonesia is also projected to experience an increase of extreme weather conditions: dry seasons will become drier and rainy seasons shorter and with greater intensity of rainfall and risk of flooding. The impact of warming will be felt across economic sectors. Based on 14 general circulation models, it appears that wet seasonal rainfall (December to February) will increase in Bali, Java, Nusa Tenggara Barat, Nusa Tenggara Timur, and Papua in 2025 under the A2 scenario (MOE 2010). By 2080, heavier rainfall would be experienced in most parts of the country, except in the northern part of Sumatra and Kalimantan. Under the same scenario, dry seasonal rainfall (June to August) in West Java and South Sumatra is predicted to be declining during 2025–2080 (Boer et al. 2009).

---

1   "The A1 storyline and scenario family describes a future world of very rapid economic growth, global population that peaks in mid-century and declines thereafter, and the rapid introduction of new and more efficient technologies.... The A2 storyline and scenario family describes a very heterogeneous world. The underlying theme is self-reliance and preservation of local identities. Fertility patterns across regions converge very slowly, which results in continuously increasing global population. Economic development is primarily regionally oriented and per capita economic growth and technological change are more fragmented and slower than in other [scenarios]." (IPCC 2000: 4).

2   Results based on MAGICC/SCENGEN (http://www.cgd.ucar.edu/cas/wigley/magicc/). Under the 450 parts per million (ppm) scenario (wherein the global GHG emissions are cut back significantly and the level of GHG concentration is stabilized at 450 ppm), annual mean temperature increases would be much lower, at about 1.4°C by 2100.

Naylor et al. (2007) found a similar pattern using 15 general circulation models and empirical downscaling techniques to study the impact of global warming on the monsoon onset in Java and Bali. Under the A2 scenario, they found that the total rainfall in Java and Bali would decrease in July–September by about 10%–25%. The decline could be up to 50% in West and Central Java and 75% in Bali and East Java at the tail end of the distributions. In Bali and East Java, some models project that total rainfall would even drop close to zero during July–September.

12.2.3. Climate Change Impacts

Indonesia is already being affected by climate change, as shown by the increasing frequency and intensity of extreme weather events such as droughts, floods, and storms in recent decades (Figure 12.5). Rising temperature is exacerbating water stress, constraining agricultural production, causing forest degradation, and increasing health risks. The poor, with low capacity to adapt to these impacts, will be hit soonest and hardest.

Figure 12.5: Drought and Flood Risks in Indonesia

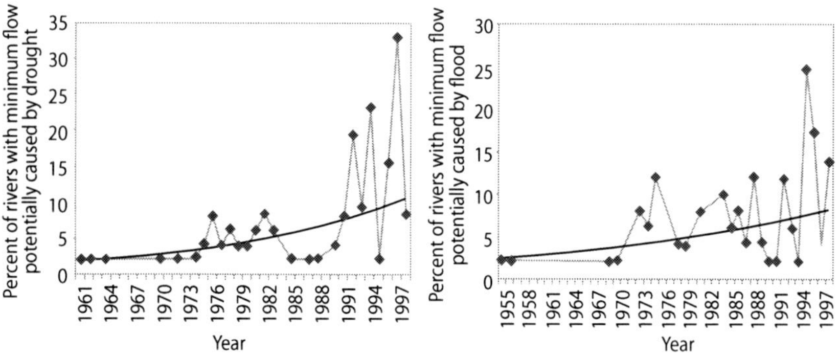

Source: Boer and Dewi (2008).

Water Resources. The large variation in rainfall due to the El Niño Southern Oscillation has a significant impact on river flows and water storage in reservoirs (MOE 2010). In the dry season, the water level in many dams decreases significantly, causing drought problems, shortage of drinking water, and a drop in electricity production. Drought and flood risks increased during 1960–1997 in river systems. Flow data from 52 rivers across Indonesia show that the number of rivers in which the minimum flow potentially caused drought increased significantly; the number of rivers in which the peak flow potentially caused flood also increased significantly.

In terms of water availability, a river area unit analysis suggested that the number of months with surplus water is close to zero in most districts in Bali, Northern Java, Lampung, East and West Nusa Tenggara, South Sumatra, and parts of Sulawesi (Heriensyah et al. 2009). Water deficits in some districts last up to 12 months, particularly in eastern Indonesia, such as East and West Nusa Tenggara. In East Nusa Tenggara, even one planting is not possible during El Niño years without irrigation. With future climate change, the water supply situation is likely to worsen.

In 2010, 14% of Indonesia's 452 districts were already experiencing no months with water surplus (Table 12.1). The water deficit is likely to increase significantly under the projected climate change scenarios. Under the A2 scenario, the percentage of districts with no months of surplus water is expected to increase from 14% to 21% in 2025 and to 31% in 2050 (Heriensyah et al. 2009).

Table 12.1: Districts without Surplus Water in Any Month

Location	Baseline # Districts	A2, 2025	A2, 2050	Total Districts
Bali	7	8	9	9
Java	22	26	23	120
Kalimantan	7	11	15	54
Maluku	1	1	2	16
West Nusa Tenggara	3	6	9	10
East Nusa Tenggara	1	2	6	16
Papua	0	0	3	29
Sulawesi	10	22	40	63
Sumatra	14	20	32	135
Total	65	96	139	452

Source: Heriensyah et al. (2009), MOE (2010)

Agriculture. Climate change can adversely affect crop productivity, both directly through temperature rise and indirectly due to changes in rainfall patterns, water availability, soil quality, drought, and flood. Naylor et al. (2007) showed that a 1-month delay at the start of the rainy season during El Niño years can negatively affect wet season rice (January–April). Data showed that a 1-month delay decreased production by about 6.5% in Central and West Java and by 11% in Bali and East Java. Other studies also consistently observed that a severe delay in the first rice crop would push back the second cropping season (dry season), exposing the second crop to higher drought risks (Boer and Subbiah 2005).

Similarly, Boer et al. (2009) estimated that, under the current farm practices and not considering the effect of carbon dioxide (CO_2) fertilization, total rice production in Java would decrease by 1.8 million tons in 2025 and 3.6 million tons in 2050 under the A2 scenario. However, if the effects of CO_2 fertilization were taken into account, the decrease in rice production would be lower (33,964 tons in 2025 and 59,584 tons in 2050). Rice production in Indonesia also faces other challenges, such as conversion of rice land to other uses. To improve productivity in rice cultivation, some adaptation measures were identified to at least partly cope with these impacts, including increasing the number of crops grown per year and introducing technology improvements such as improved rice varieties.

Forest and Biodiversity. An important threat that climate change poses to Indonesia is the increased risk of forest fires due to decreasing rainfall during the dry season and shortening of the wet season in some areas. Kalimantan and Sumatra are already exposed to a high risk of forest fire. Hotspot densities in these two islands increase rapidly during the shortened wet season and prolonged dry season in El Niño years (Ardiansyah and Boer 2009).

The total area burned by wildfire has increased in the recent El Niño years. During the 1982 El Niño, the total reached 3.5 million hectares (ha) in East Kalimantan alone (Lennertz and Panzer 1984). In the 1994 El Niño, about 5 million ha burned (Goldammer et al. 1998), and the worst El Niño, in 1997, caused massive land and forest fires and affected approximately 11.7 million ha (Bappenas and ADB 1999). The regions most affected were Kalimantan and Sumatra (Table 12.2). Economic loss as a consequence of the 1997 fire was tremendous and may have reached $1.056 billion (MOE 2010).

Table 12.2: Area Affected by Forest Fires in 1997/1998 (hectares)

Vegetation	Sumatra	Java	Kalimantan	Sulawesi	West Papua	Total
Montane Forest	...	...	213,194	...	100,000	313,194
Lowland Forest	383,000	25,000	2,690,880	200,000	300,000	3,598,800
Peat and Swamp Forest	624,000	...	1,100,000	...	400,000	2,124,000
Dry Scrub and Grass	263,000	25,000	375,000	...	100,000	763,000
Timber Plantation	72,000	...	883,988	...	...	955,988
Estate Crops	60,000	...	382,509	1,000	3,000	446,509
Agriculture	669,000	50,000	2,481,808	199,000	97,000	3,496,808
Total	2,071,000	100,000	8,17,379	400,000	1,000,000	11,698,379

... = data not available.
Sources: MOE (2010, Table 4.7); Bappenas and ADB (1999).

Coastal and Marine Resources. Approximately 40% of Indonesia's 81,000 kilometer (km) coastline is prone to coastal erosion and damage, caused largely by sea level rise and climate-related hazards. This will affect a large number of people and settlements and much infrastructure and could contribute to the destruction of many agriculturally productive areas. Along the northern coast of Java, about 5,500 ha have been eroded. If the sea level rises by half a meter by 2100, as projected by several climate models, significant areas of coastal Indonesia will be affected (MOE 2010). Land subsidence will exacerbate this effect, increasing the area that will face permanent inundation.

In Jakarta, a sea level rise of just 25 centimeters (cm) will inundate part of the city, with Sunter Agung and Papango of Tanjung Priok subdistricts experiencing the worst impacts. A 25 cm sea level rise will also result in (1) flood depths of 11–20 cm in some locations, and (2) movement of the coastline inland by approximately 1.5 km. If the sea level rises 1 meter, more districts in North Jakarta (Koja and Tanjung Priok) and West Jakarta (Kalideres and Penjaringan) will be affected, and inundated areas will significantly increase due to an increased flood depth of approximately 30 cm. With the combined effects of high tide, the total area inundated will be much larger still—an estimated 25%–50% of the total area of the coastal cities Jakarta, Medan, Semarang, and Surabaya will be permanently under water (Hariati et al. 2009). In the worst-case scenario, 2.6 million people along the coast of the four cities would be affected and the total economic loss would amount to about Rp9,056 billion (equivalent to $871 million in 2009) due to damage to settlements, infrastructure, and agriculture (Table 12.3). Among the four cities, the largest economic losses would be in Jakarta.

The disappearance of small islands due to sea level rise will also have serious implications for Indonesia's borders. At least 8 of 92 outermost small islands that serve as a baseline for the Indonesian sea territory (Brass, Dolangan, Fani, Fanildo, Kepala, Laag, Manterawu, and Nipah islands) are

Table 12.3: Impact of a 1 Meter Sea Level Rise and High Tides in Coastal Indonesian Cities

Area	No. of People Affected ('000)	Economic Loss (Rp billion)			
		Settlements	Rice	Ponds	Harbors, Airports	Total
Jakarta	381	2.15	11.05	1.71	8,622.76	8,637.67
Medan	998	0	46.02	22.73	0	68.75
Semarang	443	2.08	0.01	2.15	8.76	13
Surabaya	751	0.68	5.18	13.56	316.61	336.03

Source: Hariati et al. (2009)

highly vulnerable to sea level rise (Hendiarti 2007). A 0.5 meter sea level rise, combined with tidal patterns in the region, would temporarily submerge five of the outer islands.

The increase in sea temperature level can also result in serious problems for coral ecosystems. Burke, Selig, and Spalding (2002) reported that the 1982 and 1997 El Niño events caused massive coral damage in the coasts of Bali, Java, Lombok, and East Sumatra. They noted that, in the "thousand islands" (north of the Jakarta coast), about 90%–95% of the coral 25 meters below the sea surface had been bleached, and coral bleaching had affected over 75% of Bali's coral reefs.

Human Health. Particularly in tropical areas, climate change can increase risks associated with vector- and water-borne diseases. Hidayati et al. (2009) found that incidences of malaria and dengue fever are likely to increase under the future climate scenarios, with the potential for malaria transmission predicted to rise much higher than that for dengue fever.

Economic Cost of Climate Change. Climate change impacts manifest across many economic sectors. To put climate change impacts into perspective, work for this chapter simulated PAGE2002, an integrated assessment model, to calculate the total cost of climate change. The model covers two types of impact: market impact, on the agriculture sector and coastal zones, and nonmarket impact, on health and ecosystems. (See Hope [2006] for a description of PAGE2002.) The possibility of future large-scale discontinuity is also incorporated to reflect the increased risk of climate catastrophes, such as melting of the West Antarctic ice sheet. The assumptions adopted in this analysis are consistent with those used in the Stern Review (Stern 2007).

The PAGE2002 simulation suggests that Indonesia is likely to suffer severely from climate change in the future. The impact of climate change on the country—if the world continues its business-as-usual—could be equivalent to Indonesia losing 7% of its annual gross domestic product (GDP) by 2100 on average (Figure 12.6). Taking into account the uncertainties associated with the way climate systems function and the sensitivity of potential impacts, the model indicates a 5% chance of Indonesia losing nearly 20% equivalent of its annual GDP by 2100.

This modeling exercise is based on the scientific knowledge from the Intergovernmental Panel on Climate Change (IPCC) Third Assessment Report published in 2000. Most recent climate science suggests, however, that the impact will be more severe and will happen decades earlier than previously projected (see Pew Center 2009). The analysis does not cover extreme events such as flashfloods and tropical storms. If not addressed, the effects of climate change will seriously hinder Indonesia's growth and poverty reduction efforts. Sustainability cannot be achieved unless Indonesia moves to a climate-resilient development path. Although this seems to be a long-term sustainability issue, the preparation needs to start today.

Figure 12.6: Mean Climate Cost in Indonesia under the A2 Scenario (% of GDP)

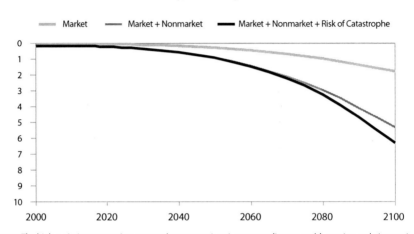

Note: The high emissions scenario assumes the current situation: a very diverse world, continuously increasing population, regionally oriented economic development, and fragmented technological change.
Source: Authors.

12.3. Local Challenges: Environmental and Natural Resources

12.3.1. Natural Resource Degradation

Indonesia is one of the world's richest countries in natural resources and biodiversity (Table 12.4). Studies and data, however, suggest that the sustainability of these resources is under serious threat. The country's increasing population and fast economic growth are placing intense pressure on its natural resources. In addition, global threats such as climate change and rising temperatures will have adverse impacts on crop yields and water resources. Rising sea levels are a serious threat, given Indonesia's 17,500 islands and extensive coastlines.

Studies and data indicate that Indonesia's natural capital and environment are being degraded rapidly. Major issues related to environment and natural resources include (1) loss of forest and terrestrial biodiversity, (2) deterioration of coastal and fisheries resources, (3) degradation of water resources, and (4) wastes and pollution (ADB 2005).

Loss of Forest and Terrestrial Biodiversity. Forests comprise 191 million ha—more than 60%—of the country's land area. The country's vast rainforest is habitat for a wide diversity of species. The rich natural ecosystem and biodiversity provide goods and services that are important in sustaining the country's water supply, agriculture, coastal fisheries, and tourism, and the livelihoods of the country's people.

Table 12.4: Selected Environmental Indicators in Indonesia

A. Land Area and Use[a], 2004	
Total land area (million ha)	190.9
Land use (% to total land area)	
Non Agriculture	2.3
Wetland	4.5
Dryland	8.0
Plantation	8.7
Forest	62.9
Others	13.6
Protected Area (% of total land area)[b],2008	13.1
B Biodiversity[b]	
Number of species	17,157
Number of endemic species	8,537
Number of endangered species	976
C. Water resources	
Internal renewable freshwater resources (billion m^3)[b],2007	2,838
Freshwater water consumption rate[c] (million liters/day)	766,145
Water use by sector (% share to total consumption)[b]	
Domestic	3.9
Industry	5.2
Agriculture	58.5
Others	32.4
Water use intensity (m^3/ha/y)[e],2000	2,250.0
Industrial water pollution (t/day)[e],1997-2000	662.0
D. Marine and Coastal Resources	
Length of coastal line (km)[b],2009	108,000
Coral reef area (km^2)[f], 2002	51,000
Mangrove area (ha)[d], 2007	1,229,117
No. of mangrove species[d]	45

No. of seagrass species[d]	13
Quantity of captured fisheries(t)[a] ,2006	
Sources: River	175,794
Lake	42,276
Reservoir	12,159
Swamp	62,480
Marine	795,019
E. Air Pollution from Transport (million t/y)[a], **2007**	
CO	39.2
NOx	1.9
SOx	0.1
Hydrocarbons	3.4
Suspended particles	0.2
F. Others	
Fertilizer consumption ('000 t), 2006	4,062.2
Fertilizer use intensity (kg/ha), 2007	99.5
Pesticide use intensity (kg/ha), 1993	0.1

CO = carbon monoxide, ha = hectare, kg = kilogram, km = kilometer, km² = square kilometer, m³ = cubic meter, NOx = nitrogen oxides, SOx = sulfur oxides, t = ton, y = year.
Sources: [a] BPS (2008),
[b] ASEAN Secretariat (2009),
[c] MOE (2004)
[d] Burke, Selig, and Spalding (2002),
[e] WRI (2009b).
[f] Leitman et al. (2009).

Deforestation is a critical problem—its far-reaching effects have led to a loss of biodiversity, desertification, flooding, food insecurity, and the increased impoverishment of local communities whose existence depends critically on the use of forest resources. The rate of deforestation rose from about 200,000 ha/year during 1982−1997 to 500,000 ha/year during 1997−2005 (Ministry of Forestry 2007) and, during 2000–2005, the deforestation rate accelerated to 1.1 million ha/year (Table 12.5).

About 26% of Sumatra's forest was lost during 1990−2000. Similarly, since 1950, tropical lowland and highland forests have contracted rapidly in Kalimantan (Figure 12.7). The primary causes of deforestation in Indonesia include illegal logging, conversion for agricultural use, forest fires, and mining (ADB 2005). If the situation is not reversed, significant forest loss will continue.

Table 12.5: Deforestation in Indonesia's Main Islands (2000–2005)

Location	Total Deforested Area (hectares)	Annual Average Loss (hectares)
Bali and Nusa Tenggara	359,800	71,960
Java	712,800	142,560
Kalimantan	1,230,100	246,020
Maluku	214,900	42,980
Papua	718,400	143,680
Sulawesi	866,300	173,260
Sumatra	1,345,500	269,100
Indonesia	5,447,800	1,089,560

Source: Ministry of Forestry (2007).

Figure 12.7: Deforestation in Kalimantan—Actual and Projected

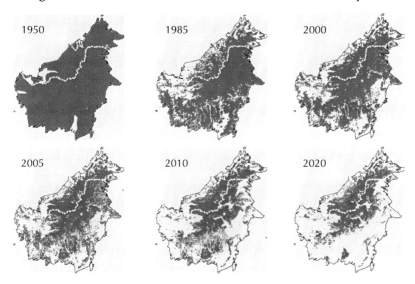

Source: UNEP/GRID-Arendal (2007).

Large-scale land conversion was the biggest single cause of the 1997–1998 forest fires that destroyed nearly 5 million ha of forest and resulted in $8 billion in economic losses to Indonesia (ADB 2005). As Figure 12.8 indicates, the country's palm oil production area grew by a multiple of 314 during 1995–2008 (BPS 2008). In 2006 alone, approximately 816,000 ha of the forest area in Central Kalimantan were released for palm oil development—the most rapid expansion of palm oil plantation in the country (Forest Watch Indonesia 2007).

Figure 12.8: Expansion of Plantations (1995–2008)

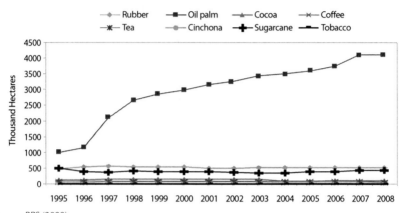

Source: BPS (2008).

Factors such as forest destruction, land-use change and intensification, and rampant forest fires have led to a sizeable loss of Indonesia's important ecological and forest ecosystems. Deforestation alone has destroyed many species' habitats and has threatened or led to the extinction of many endemic species. In fact, Indonesia has one of the highest numbers of threatened species in the region (ASEAN Secretariat 2009).

Loss of Coastal and Marine Resources and Biodiversity. Indonesia has 108,000 km of coastline and the world's 6th most extensive exclusive economic zone. The country is guardian to about 2.7 million square kilometers of coastal and marine ecosystems that contain some of the world's richest and most diverse natural resources (FAO Fisheries and Aquaculture Department). However, these resources are being endangered due to inland activities that have increased the discharge of sediments onto the reefs, pollution from agricultural and industrial activities, and damaging harvesting practices.

The cumulative pressures have significantly degraded Indonesia's reefs over time, affecting most of the breeding grounds and habitats of important marine species. Suharsono (2005) revealed that only about one-third of Indonesia's coral reefs were in excellent to good condition—the remaining two-thirds were assessed to have lost half their living coral cover (Table 12.6).[3]

Indiscriminate harvesting of fishery and marine resources in return for short-term profits and growing competition among fishers have resulted in unsustainable fishing practices such as cyanide and blast fishing in

---

[3]   Coral reefs were monitored at 648 stations of 58 localities throughout Indonesian waters during 1993–2003.

Table 12.6: Status of Coral Reefs in Indonesia (%)

Area	No. of Locations	Excellent	Good	Fair	Poor
West	243	5.76	20.99	33.33	39.92
Central	210	6.19	31.43	45.24	17.14
East	195	9.23	29.23	33.08	28.46
Indonesia	648	6.69	26.59	37.56	29.16

Note: Excellent = 75%–100% living coral cover; Good = 50%–74%; Fair:= 25%–49%; Poor = 0%–24%.
Source: Suharsono (2005).

many locations.[4] Burke, Selig, and Spalding (2002) estimated that, if left unregulated, the net economic loss to Indonesia from blast fishing over a period of 20 years would reach $570 million, while loss from cyanide fishing is estimated to cost the country $46 million annually.

Important coastal and inland wetlands include peat marshes and mangrove systems that are essential breeding grounds for fish and wildlife. At the same time, they are buffers to flooding, storm surges, and sea level rise. Indonesia had an estimated 3.5 million ha of mangroves in 1988 (Wilkie, Fortuna, and Souksavat 2002). In 2007, however, the Ministry of Forestry reported only about 1.2 million ha of mangroves (BPS 2008). Numerous benefits from this ecosystem were lost as a result of agricultural expansion, urbanization, and increased economic activity along the coast. Indonesia had 65% of the total mangrove area in Southeast Asia in 2007 (ASEAN Secretariat 2009).

Degradation of Water Resources. Indonesia holds approximately 6% of the world's and 21% of the Asia and Pacific region's freshwater reserves (MOE 2004). However, Indonesia struggles to supply enough water for its industry and agriculture, and adequate clean water for human consumption. In agriculture alone, water intensity is estimated to be 2,250 cubic meters per hectare per year, higher than in other agricultural countries, such as Cambodia and the Philippines (WRI 2009b). Agriculture consumes the largest portion (58.5%) of Indonesia's available water supply, followed by industry (5.2%), domestic use (3.9%), and others (32.4%). Sources of freshwater, including river basins, groundwater reserves, lakes, and manmade reservoirs, are under increasing pressure to meet the growing demand of the economy and population. Water use was estimated at 591 billion liters per day in 2005, and was projected to increase to 817 billion liters by 2010 and 1,131 billion liters by 2015.

Wastes and Pollution. Many of the country's water resources are exploited unsustainably. Rivers are often used as catchments for wastewater disposal from industries and waste from households, and intensive

---

[4]   About 65% of surveys conducted in the Malaku islands found evidence of blast damage (Hopley and Suharsono 2000).

extraction of groundwater has resulted in seawater intrusion to aquifers. Of the 33 rivers monitored in 2008, over half (about 54%) were polluted (ASEAN Secretariat 2009). Some groundwater wells monitored in Jakarta also showed contamination with *Escherichia coli* and other fecal coliform bacteria (MOE 2004).

The levels of air pollutants, such as suspended particulate matter, sulfur dioxide (SO_2), and nitrogen dioxide, are already over safe limits in many cities (BPS 2008), increasing the health risks to society and causing acid rain that damages infrastructure. Although outdoor sources are often the dominant pollutants, indoor air pollution is also a major health threat to many poor Indonesians, as 44% of the country's households continue to use biomass fuel for cooking. Acidic rainwater, due the increased concentration of SO_2 in the air, adversely impacts forests, freshwater, soil, plants, animals (including humans), buildings, and infrastructure.

Economic Cost of Environmental Degradation. Environmental degradation brings significant economic costs in terms of income and health. Leitman et al. (2009) estimated that inadequate water and sanitation cause the country a short-term economic loss of about 2% of its GDP (Table 12.7). Thus, water and sanitation rank among the country's highest priority environmental challenges. In addition, health impacts from outdoor pollution and household exposure to indoor pollution can cost the country a GDP loss of 0.9% and 0.4%, respectively.

Table 12.7: Estimated Economic Costs of Environmental Degradation in Indonesia

Source of Degradation	Economic Cost (%of GDP)	Preliminary Ranking of Environmental Challenges	
		Impact Potential	Financial Resources
Water, Sanitation, and Hygiene	2+	+++	++
Outdoor Air Pollution	0.9	++	+
Indoor Air Pollution	0.4	++	+
Forest Degradation	n/a	++	++
Soil Degradation	n/a	++	+
Coastal and Marine Environment	n/a	++	++

Source: World Bank (2009b).

Overall, the country's Environmental Performance Index[5] scored 44.6, ranking Indonesia 134th of 163 countries in terms of environmental sustainability and performance (Emerson et al. 2010). Among the 13 Southeast Asian countries, Indonesia ranked 12th—showing that more attention and high priority should be given to protecting, preserving, and improving the country's environment for sustained development.

While national savings seems highly positive and resilient, adjusted net savings is in decline—a sign of environmentally unsustainable growth. From a macroeconomic perspective, the gross national savings rate—gross national income less consumption—stayed well above zero during 1990–2006 and seemed to bounce back and remain stable after the 1997 Asian financial crisis (Figure 12.9). As expected, net national savings, which takes into account depreciation of fixed capital, had followed the same trend. What deserves attention is adjusted net savings (sometimes referred to as "genuine savings"), which takes into account natural resource and mineral depletion, and damage from pollution. To maintain peoples' welfare and capital accumulation, an economy's savings can not be negative over time. The downward trend of genuine savings[6] is an initial sign of environmentally unsustainable growth.

While Indonesia's gross national savings rate in 2006 is comparable to that of many countries in Asia, its genuine savings rate is relatively low (Figure 12.10). The large savings gap in Indonesia is as a result of relatively high rate of natural resource depletion (World Bank 2009a). Declining trends in net adjusted savings and a large savings gap are an initial sign that growth is environmentally not sustainable.[7]

---

[5] The 2010 Environmental Performance Index measures the effectiveness of national environmental protection efforts in 163 countries. The index considers 25 indicators that capture the best worldwide environmental data available on the country scale and incorporates criteria from other policy assessments such as the Millennium Ecosystem Assessment, the IPCC, the Biodiversity Indicator Partnership, and the Global Environmental Outlook-4.

[6] The genuine savings measure is a good starting point for measuring sustainability, but there are limitations. For example, positive genuine savings does not necessarily imply sustainability, since the economy can still be prone to external shocks such as financial crisis and extreme climate impacts. There are also measurement problems, particularly of natural resource depletion and pollution damage, normally leading to overestimation of genuine savings. Also, the measure indicates whether total wealth rises or falls, but fails to account for population growth.

[7] Alisjahbana and Yusuf (2003) found similar evidence and suggested that the Indonesian economy had not been on a sustainable path during 1980–2000.

Figure 12.9: Savings Rate in Indonesia (% of GNI)

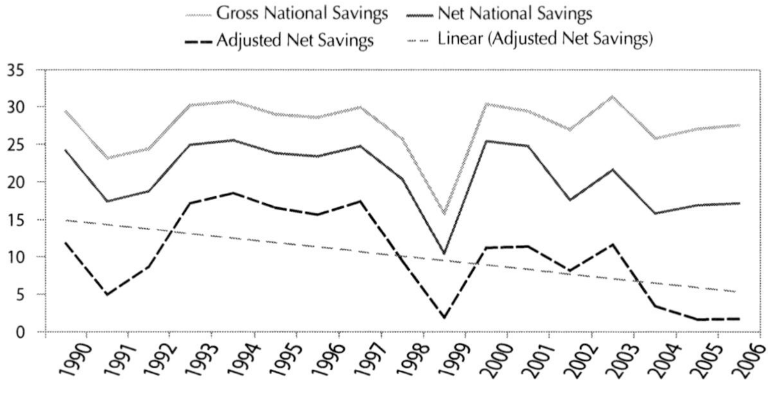

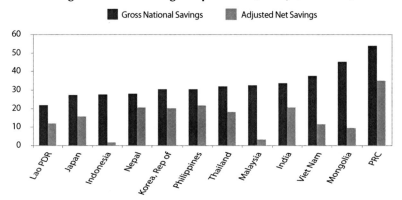

GNI = gross national income.
Source: World Bank, WDI, accessed 25 March 2010.

Figure 12.10: Savings Gap in Asia (2006, % of GNI)

GNI = gross national income, Lao PDR = Lao People's Democratic Republic, PRC = People's Republic of China.
Source: World Bank, WDI, accessed 25 March 2010.

12.3.2. Energy Challenges

As in other countries, energy has been a key driving factor behind Indonesia's economic development. However, the historical and current patterns of energy consumption and production, together with rapid urbanization, have placed enormous pressure on the country's energy resources and have led to adverse environmental and climate consequences. This could in turn undermine Indonesia's natural resource base and human productivity, and jeopardize its growth potential. Looking ahead, Indonesia needs to ensure that it has the energy supplies required to push its economy forward, while making additional efforts to decouple emissions from energy use in order to achieve environmental sustainability and contribute to the global effort to combat climate change.

Indonesia is the world's 4th most populous country. In 2008, the people of Indonesia consumed nearly 200 million tons of oil equivalent (Mtoe) of total energy (IEA 2009), five times more than the 29 Mtoe in 1980, and the highest in the Association of Southeast Asian Nations (ASEAN) region. Energy consumption in the country has remained heavily dependent on fossil fuel, particularly imported crude oil products and domestic coal. In 2008, Indonesia added about 434 million tons of CO_2—a GHG—to the atmosphere.

With continued economic and population growth, together with a switch to urban lifestyle as millions of people acquire cars and household appliances, energy demand will increase significantly and rapidly in the future. Although good progress has been made on rural electrification in recent years, over 80 million people still live without electricity (IEA 2009). Making energy supply available, secure, and green at the same time poses a serious challenge for Indonesia.

Under the IEA (2009) Reference Scenario, Indonesia's primary energy demand is projected to grow at an average annual rate of 2.4%, from 191 Mtoe in 2007 to 330 Mtoe in 2030 (Figure 12.11). Under this scenario, the

Figure 12.11: Indonesia's Primary Energy Demand, by Fuel, in the Reference Scenario

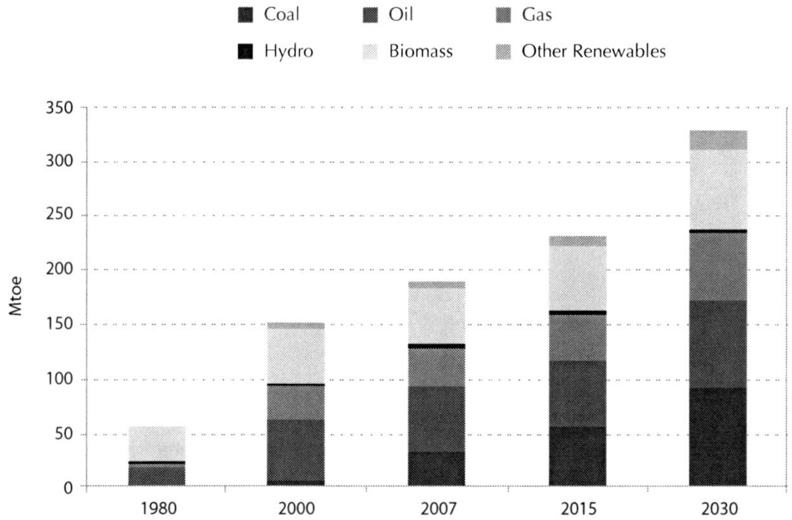

Mtoe = million tons of oil equivalent.
Source: IEA (2009).

449

share of fossil fuels in the primary energy mix will rise from 69% in 2007 to 72% in 2030; coal demand, driven mainly by power generation and industry, will grow at 4.2% per year, the fastest among fossil fuels; and, by 2030, coal's share of primary demand will reach 29%, to become the leading fuel in the energy mix.

Oil. Indonesia is the largest oil producer in the ASEAN and the second largest in Asia, next to the People's Republic of China (PRC). Recoverable resources from discovered fields are estimated at 44 billion barrels (USGS 2000). Indonesia has proven reserves of 4 billion barrels (*Oil and Gas Journal* 2008) in 16 producing basins. The bulk of Indonesia's oil and gas reserves are onshore and offshore in Central Sumatra and Kalimantan. At current levels of production, Indonesia's proven reserves would sustain production for another 12 years.

Indonesian oil production averaged about 1.0 million barrels per day (mb/d) in 2008 (WEC 2010). Output has been declining rapidly since peaking at just over 1.6 mb/d in the early 1990s, as the majority of the fields are maturing. With rapidly rising oil demand and declining production, Indonesia became a net importer of crude oil and petroleum products in 2004 (Figure 12.12). The country imported about 320 thousand barrels per day (kb/d) of oil in 2008. In the Reference Scenario, Indonesia's oil production is projected to fall to about 800 kb/d in 2015 and 300 kb/d in 2030 (Figure 12.13). As a result, the country would rely on imports (1.3 mb/d) to meet 80% of its crude oil requirements by 2030, raising concern about oil security.

Figure 12.12: Trends of Supply of and Demand for Petroleum Products

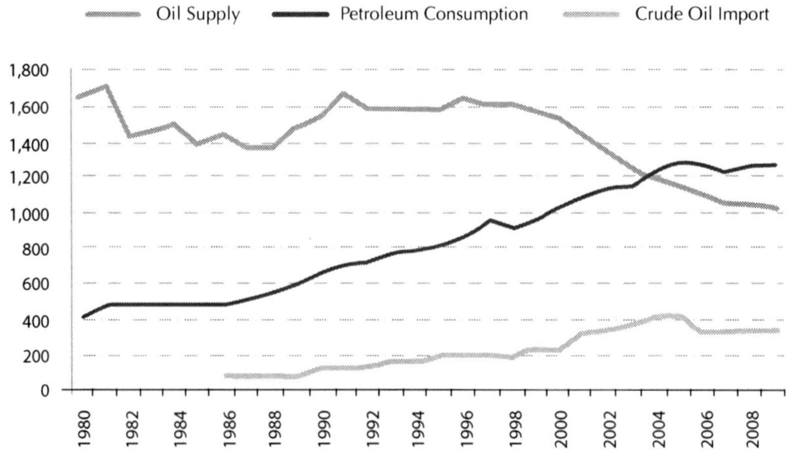

Source: IEA (2009).

Figure 12.13: Indonesia's Oil Balance, in the Reference Scenario

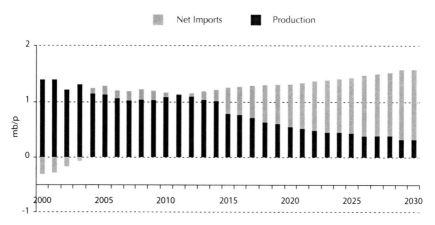

mb/d = million barrels per day.
Note: Negative numbers denote net exports.
Source: IEA (2009).

Coal. Indonesia has 5.5 billion tons of economically recoverable reserves of coal and 105 billion tons of total coal resources (WEC 2010). The country's known potential coal resources have grown by 34.4 billion tons since 2007, with 95% of the growth being anthracite, also known as hard coal (BGR 2009). Combining both anthracite and lignite (also known as brown coal), Indonesia has a potential 92 billion tons of coal, which would suffice for nearly 350 years at the current rate of production.[8] In 2007, Indonesian coal production reached 230 million tons of carbon equivalent (Mtce), more than four times that in 1998.

In the Reference Scenario, Indonesia's coal production is projected to rise to 282 Mtce in 2015 and nearly 400 Mtce in 2030, an increase of nearly three-quarters from current levels (Figure 12.14). However, to achieve this and meet increasing demand, especially from the emerging markets of the PRC and India, substantial investment is required to further develop and improve coal production and transport infrastructure.

Renewables. Despite Indonesia's significant hydroelectric potential, especially in Irian Jaya and Kalimantan, hydropower is not well developed due to geographical barriers. Indonesia is also rich in geothermal energy. Its production of 7 terawatt-hours of electricity from geothermal sources in 2007 was the third largest in the world, after the United States and the Philippines (REN21 2009). Although these clean energy resources could

---

[8]   Most of Indonesia's coal reserves are in East Kalimantan and South Sumatra; smaller deposits are found in West Java and Sulawesi. Indonesian coal has a low ash and sulfur content (typically less than 1%), making it among the cleanest coal in the world. But it is high in moisture and has a low average heating value.

Figure 12.14: Indonesian Coal Production by Type and Hard Coal Net Exports, in the Reference Scenario

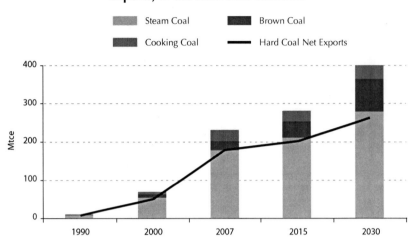

Mtce = metric tons of carbon equivalent
Source: IEA (2009).

help serve future demand and replace some fossil fuels, their development and production in Indonesia remain low due to constraints in technology, research and development, infrastructure, and institutional and financing mechanisms.

12.4. Nexus of Local and Global Challenges

Just as global environmental problems such as climate change have an impact on Indonesia, environmental sustainability or lack of it in Indonesia can have major impacts at the global level, too. Indonesia is currently the world's third largest emitter of GHGs, with 71% of its GHG emissions in 2005 due to deforestation and land-use changes (WRI 2011). The "National Strategy Study for Clean Development Mechanism (CDM) in Forestry Sector," formulated by the Ministry of Environment, estimated Indonesia's total potential carbon stock in 2000 at 90 billion tons of CO_2 equivalent, more than two times the total world GHG emissions in the same year (MOE 2003).

About 80% of the carbon stock is stored in the standing forest, which will release large amounts of CO_2 into the atmosphere if disturbed. Indonesia has placed a high priority on reducing emissions from deforestation and forest degradation (known as "REDD"). Efforts toward sustainable forest management, rehabilitation of degraded forest and nonforest land, and protected area management have multiple benefits. They help preserve rich ecosystems that support and serve communities and the economy, and they reduce CO_2 emissions and thus global climate risks. However, it is important to recognize that carbon stock is a global public good that comes with a high opportunity cost to Indonesia.

Indonesia's primary energy demand is projected to grow rapidly and, under a business-as-usual scenario, its energy sector will continue to be dominated by dirty fossil fuel (ADB 2009, IEA 2009). Indonesia's power generation will largely be coal-based. Gasoline-powered internal combustion engine vehicles will continue to dominate the transport sector, and the numbers will increase dramatically during the next few decades. This could result in a rapid growth of CO_2 emissions (Figure 12.15) as well as local pollution that could have serious negative impacts on human health and natural systems. Indonesia's emissions are estimated to grow from 2.1 gigatons of CO_2 equivalent in 2005 to 3.3 gigatons in 2030 (NCCC 2010). "Green" policy and technology options are available, and Indonesia could switch to a low carbon growth trajectory, while at the same time improving its local environmental sustainability. Improving energy efficiency and moving toward cleaner energy sources and technologies, particularly in power generation, are expected to be key elements of the green growth strategy in Indonesia during the coming decades.

Figure 12.15: Projected Emission Increases in Indonesia (2020 and 2030; gigatons)

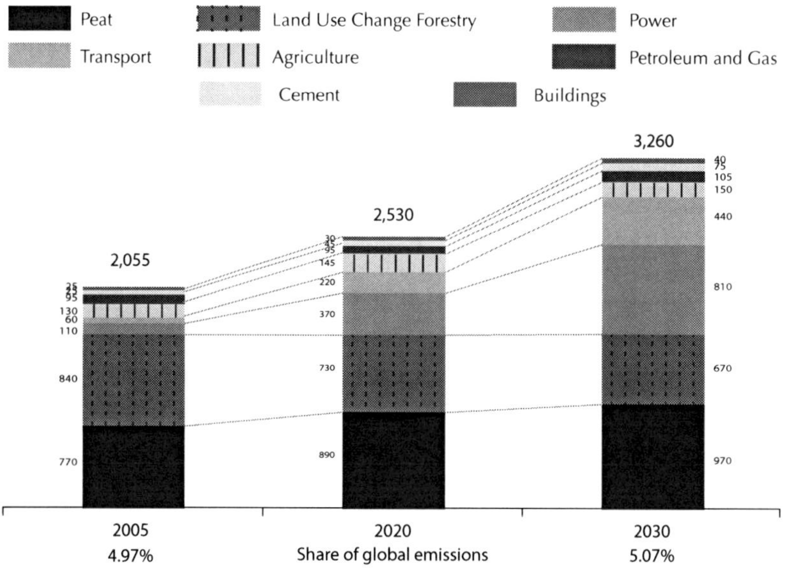

Notes: Includes only direct emissions from each sector. Emissions from land use change in forestry are based on a net emission approach, i.e., including absorption.
Source: NCCC (2010).

453

12.5. Challenges to and Opportunities for Transformation

Transformation from business-as-usual to a cleaner and more efficient scenario is a real challenge. Substantial investment is needed in energy supply infrastructure; in demand-side options, such as more efficient electrical household appliances, motor vehicles, and industrial equipment; and in REDD measures. Another major challenge is to find effective ways to remove the barriers to the adoption of such measures. The barriers range from lack of information and awareness, habits and lifestyle, limited capacity (human, technical, and financial), and lack of technology, to inadequate policy and incentives to correct market failures and price distortions.

Moving to a green pattern of development would completely restructure the economy and create new sectors and business opportunities that can become new engines of Indonesia's economic growth, while ensuring resource and environmental sustainability. The policy making process is also a critical consideration, as the country's environmental policy making process is highly dispersed and climate change issues cut across sectors. Strong leadership at the highest level of government in terms of strategic direction and policy framework is of utmost importance, while a solid partnership among the stakeholders and coordination among the agencies involved are also needed.

12.6. Policy Options

Despite the tremendous effort to put in place a wide range of environmental and climate change policies, there is evidence of environmental unsustainability in Indonesia. To make growth green and sustainable, barriers to it must be identified and relaxed to permit the beginning of the transition process. Indeed, the underlying constraint to Indonesia's environmentally sustainable growth is inadequate mainstreaming of "green" elements into development planning. However, based on the diagnostic framework (Figure 12.1), this section focuses on three specific constraints: (1) limited financial and technical capacity to mitigate and adapt to climate change, (2) lack of awareness and information about future climate change impacts and options, and (3) inadequate policy and incentives to address market failure.

12.6.1. Limited Financial and Technical Capacity to Mitigate and Adapt to Climate Change

Strengthen Indonesia's Capacity through International Mechanisms. Many measures with substantial mitigation potential that come with high returns and low costs, and will simultaneously bring co-benefits, such as energy security and better environmental quality, are available (ADB 2009, NCCC 2010). Nevertheless, implementing climate change mitigation and adaptation measures requires investment, technology and know-how, and financial resources. For Indonesia, many mitigation and adaptation options are still relatively costly to deploy, posing a considerable challenge. Given equity issues, Indonesia's technical and financial capacity will have to be supported by the international community for the country to exploit significant untapped opportunities.

Support Up-Front Investment to Tap "Win–Win" Opportunities. Indonedia's "win-win" potentials are concentrated in energy-related sectors (NCCC 2010). ADB (2009) estimated that more than half of total CO_2 reduction potential in these sectors can be achieved through "win-win" options, which would bring about both a large reduction in CO_2 emissions and energy cost savings (i.e., due to more efficient use of energy, the implementation cost would be outweighed by the savings), as well as co-benefits. The "win–win" potential primarily includes efficiency improvement in existing power plants, industrial processes, motor vehicles, and residential and commercial buildings. However, capturing the potential entails large up-front investment, which is among the most critical constraints to implementing mitigation and adaptation measures in Indonesia. Like other fiscally constrained developing countries, the high up-front capital cost is a significant disincentive to investing in low carbon technologies and adaptive options. Therefore, this issue needs to be addressed for Indonesia to move further toward a climate-resilient and low carbon economy.

By 2020, the total energy-related CO_2 reduction potential in Indonesia is projected to be about 344 metric tons of CO_2 ($MtCO_2$). The CO_2 reduction potential from improving the efficiency of coal and gas power plants is projected to be 97 $MtCO_2$ in 2020, while improving energy efficiency in the industry, transport, and residential sectors together could save as much as 93 $MtCO_2$ (ADB 2009). However, the carbon capture and storage potential would come at a price of at least $20/t$CO_2$. There would be very little potential to reduce CO_2 at a carbon price below $10/t$CO_2$. Capturing Indonesia's total CO_2 reduction potential at a positive cost (below $50t/$CO_2$) in 2020 would require the country to invest $4.3 billion in clean technologies, amounting to about 1% of GDP in 2020.

Leverage Private Finance for Climate Change Adaptation and Mitigation. The funding required for climate change adaptation and mitigation is substantial, and existing financing instruments have limits and inefficiencies (World Bank 2009b). The current levels of climate finance fall far short of estimated needs. Filling the gap requires reforming carbon markets and tapping new sources. Funding by multi- and bilateral agencies will be small relative to private investment in energy sector development, infrastructure, and housing, so Indonesia will continue to need sound policies and incentives to attract and leverage private investment toward sustainable development and lower carbon outcomes. The government needs to step in, but it will be equally important to leverage private finance. The private sector has an important role in financing mitigation through carbon markets and related instruments, while official flows and international funding are crucial complements to target areas overlooked by the market, to build capacity, and to correct market imperfections. Private finance will also be important for adaptation, although public finance will have a key role.

More Closely Integrate Climate Change Concerns into Development Planning. While significant efforts have been made in Indonesia, coordination of planning still needs enhancement across levels of government and ministries, ranging from energy, industry, transport, environment, agriculture, health, tourism, finance, and education, to foreign affairs. Climate change and environment issues cut across many sectors and should be integrated into central and sector planning. Funding for environmental improvement, which includes climate change activities, has increased recently, although it remains modest at about 0.5% of Indonesia's national budget (PEACE 2007). Streamlining climate change issues into planning will have direct consequences on budget, technology, and human resource requirements. In parallel, the capacity of sectors to use financial sources and technology support under the United Nations Framework Convention on Climate Change (UNFCCC) processes should be enhanced. Tools and methods to evaluate and assess mitigation and adaptation options should also be made available to policymakers.

Make Better Use of International Funding Sources. Several international funding sources and mechanisms are available for climate change mitigation and adaptation in developing countries, but Indonesia has barely tapped into these sources (ADB 2009, World Bank 2009b). In addition to raising new funds, using available resources more effectively is crucial. Indonesia has made very little use of the CDM. In the number of CDM projects registered, Indonesia is far below other Asian developing countries such as the PRC and India, and is even behind Malaysia and the Philippines (UNFCCC, CDM in Numbers). Indonesia should increase its use of the CDM and other financing mechanisms. Existing funding sources, albeit far short of what is required, provide initial support and can catalyze cofinancing. In addition, the government needs to facilitate access to these sources through better information dissemination and technical assistance.

12.6.2. Lack of Awareness and Information about Future Climate Change Impacts and Options

Step Up Research Efforts on Climate Change and its Future Impact, Particularly at the Local Level. Inadequate adaptation efforts can result from a lack of information and awareness of potential climate change effects (such as temperature increase, change in rainfall patterns, sea level rise, and extreme events) and their impacts (such as on water resources, agriculture production, coastal infrastructure, human health, and ecosystems). Evidence of historical climate change is relatively well documented in Indonesia, but assessments of future weather and climate conditions and the potential impacts are scarce. Future climate projections exist only for limited sectors, and are not available at the local levels. Thus, research is needed to fill the gaps and increase the understanding of climate variability and changes and their implications across sectors of the economy. Since climate change disproportionately impacts the poor, assessing the impact on the livelihood of rural communities and how it relates to economic development and poverty reduction is also merited.

Projections indicate that Indonesia's agriculture sector will suffer greatly from rising temperatures; changes in rainfall patterns; and an increased frequency and intensity of extreme events such as droughts, floods, and storms. Forecasts of these weather and climate conditions are limited, but would help farmers adapt to the changes by adjusting their cropping practices. Most existing studies use general circulation models of a coarse resolution that is not suitable for projecting local weather. Boer and Faqih (2005) also suggest that there are inconsistencies between the results generated by different general circulation models. To assess future climate change requires models that are downscaled to the local level. Furthermore, many of the present and anticipated impacts of climate change are related to water resources, but the knowledge base for and data on resources are insufficient to predict the impacts.

Raise Public Awareness and Provide Better Climate Education and Information. While societies have a long record of adapting to the impacts of weather, future climate change poses risks that are often outside the range of historical experience. There are examples of adaptation practices that incorporate considerations of climate change, but progress with increasing their use in Indonesia remains limited. Adaptation decisions are largely decentralized and will mostly be taken by private agents, including individuals, households, and firms. Therefore, the government should extend its awareness raising programs to share information on potential impacts and available coping options with private households and local communities. A good example is the Climate Field School experiment in West

Java, which aims to increase farmers' knowledge about applying climate information in their decision making. The experiment should be scaled up and supplemented by other initiatives. Awareness regarding climate adaptation, energy conservation, and other environmental protection matters should also be raised in schools and through media.

Incorporate Climate Information into Planning and Adopt Forward-Looking Approaches. Indonesia has started encouraging adaptation action in key sectors, but most of the measures have been reactive rather than proactive, dispersed, and not well planned. Also, current adaptive measures may not work in the future as climate patterns change. For example, the wet season is expected to shorten in Java due to climate change, exposing the second yearly rice crop to higher drought risk. Without assistance, such as new irrigation facilities or interbasin water transfer, farmers could suffer significant losses. Therefore, the government needs to develop plans to adapt to less water in view of predicted future changes. A number of sectors have identified programs for adaptation, but they were not developed based on quantitative assessment of climate risk (MOE 2007). The adaptation programs may have to be updated when new information on climate risks becomes available.

Information on Costs and Benefits of Adaptation Is Very Limited. Planning for coping with the observed and anticipated climate change impacts requires decisions based on sound economic considerations. It is important to know what adaptation could cost, and to what extent it could help avoid damage due to climate change. Information on costs and benefits would help policymakers decide on whether to make specific adaptation investments, how to prioritize them, what levels of investment and funding are needed, and so on. However, studies of adaptation costs and benefits in Indonesia are very limited. Although broad estimates of adaptation costs and benefits exist at global and regional scales, there is an urgent need for detailed assessment of specific adaptation options in key sectors in Indonesia.

Government Has a Major Role in Providing Public Infrastructure and Services. Farm-level adaptation practices help cope with climate variability, and their effectiveness can be enhanced significantly with government support (OECD 2008). Government interventions may include developing early warning infrastructure and providing weather information forecasting. Crops are very sensitive to temperature and precipitation, and farmers need to be able to plan according to localized, time-specific information. The effectiveness of farm-level adaptation depends on whether relevant information is given to farmers, and whether they know how to use it. Other public goods and services the government can provide include, for example, extension and improvement of irrigation infrastructure and provision of drought- and heat-resistant crop varieties; appropriate fertilizers and pesticides; and rain harvesting facilities, which have already been employed in some drought-prone districts of Indonesia. For example, the consistent use of the Southern Oscillation Index information in designing cropping strategy helps improve rice-based farm income during El Niño years by letting farmers know when to switch from rice to other crops for the second planting (Boer and Surmaini 2006). The government can also help farmers by establishing an information sharing network and training programs. Indonesia's main challenge is to encourage farmers to use climate information consistently in making cropping decisions, and local authorities to mobilize the resources needed to support farmers in implementing their decisions.

12.6.3. Inadequate Policy and Incentives to Address Market Failure

Climate change is the most serious market failure the world has ever witnessed, and it cannot be resolved without the intervention of public policy. This requires involving national governments and the global community. Indonesia has voluntarily set the target to reduce GHG emissions by 26% relative to business-as-usual emissions by 2020 as part of the Copenhagen Accord of the UNFCCC, and has developed plans and designated key agencies to implement them (Witoelar 2010).

Furthermore, Indonesia has taken steps to (1) rationalize energy pricing by reducing fossil fuel subsidies, (2) reduce deforestation through improved enforcement and monitoring programs, (3) provide incentives for energy efficiency and conservation, (4) promote development of renewable energy, and (5) provide incentives for importing and installing pollution control equipment (Ministry of Finance 2008). The finance and development planning ministries have developed a national blueprint and budget priorities for integrating climate change into the national development process. The Ministry of Finance is also examining fiscal and financial policies to stimulate climate-friendly investment; move toward lower carbon energy options, including renewable and geothermal energy; and improve fiscal incentives in the forestry sector.

Policy Gaps Need to be Bridged, and Policy Conflicts Reconciled. Although Indonesia has made significant progress on energy efficiency and conservation policies, the development of renewable energy and investment in clean technology, particularly in power generation, have been relatively limited and need additional policy support. Renewable energy policies exist, but supporting instruments, such as financial incentives, have not been adequately developed. The National Resilience Institute has identified several instruments that could help improve the environment for investment in renewable energy in Indonesia. They include soft loans for renewable energy investment, tax incentives in the form of value-added tax reduction, and tax exemption for energy and energy conservation companies (PEACE 2007). Cost is a major barrier to the adoption of renewable energy and new options such as clean coal technology. The government has a vital role to play in providing incentives and an effective policy framework that are compatible with the international mechanisms.

Energy initiatives could adversely affect land use and forest cover. Presidential Decree No. 5 of 2006 on National Energy Law intends to increase the use of coal and to quadruple the use of biofuels within 20 years. This initiative could lead to extensive strip mining, threatening forests in Kalimantan and Sumatra and increasing GHG emissions (World Bank 2006a). While biofuel is renewable, the production process often involves forest clearing. Such policy conflicts need to be reconciled.

Strengthen Governance and Enforcement to Translate Good Policy into Good Practice. Clear goals have been established for the forestry sector, including economic output, equitable distribution of benefits to improve people's welfare, watershed protection, and conservation. These are intended to build on interrelated objectives: harnessing the potential of forests to reduce poverty, integrating forests in sustainable economic development, and protecting global forest values. In Indonesia, many good policies are already in place, and support for sustainable forest management is available. But, in terms of implementation, enforcement and governance issues remain. The effectiveness of existing policies depends very much on how they are interpreted into measures and regulations that are implemented at the provincial and district levels. Many laws and legislations on fire and illegal logging have been issued, but weak law enforcement renders them ineffective. Conflicts among sectoral government institutions and the emerging conflicts due to decentralization also slow the efforts to find a solution to deforestation in Indonesia (World Bank 2006a).

Address Uncertainty of Land Tenure for Better Forest Management. Among the most significant causes of deforestation in Indonesia is the uncertainty of land tenure. This uncertainty has led to conflicts in many areas. Disagreement over who should manage the country's forests and forest lands results in the tensions and the structure of incentives that lead to ways of operation that are detrimental to forest management. Many local communities plant agroforests on their customary lands, and find their rights to access and use these lands greatly restricted by forest regulations. They face disincentives to increase land productivity and to manage resources in a sustainable manner. In many cases, they have been unfairly forced off their customary lands, thus creating social conflicts that raise obstacles to better management. Conflict takes place not only between the government and the local people, but also among sectors, between central and local government, and among the people themselves (Panjiwibowo et al. 2003). As a result, land degradation continues. The conflicts over control of land and natural resources due to uncertainty of ownership will persist unless the state forest zone is rationalized with a clear action strategy (Contreras-Hermosilla and Fay 2005).

12.7. Conclusion

The progress to sustainable green growth in Indonesia faces numerous impediments. Realizing Indonesia's vision to move toward a green growth pattern will require considerable investment and removing the many barriers that stand in the way of adopting the necessary policies and technologies. In the coming years, Indonesia will build new power plants, new industrial plants, and new commercial and residential buildings, and will continue to use land and natural resources for development purposes.

Swift action is needed to capture the full potential of green measures and avoid infrastructure "lock-ins." The window of opportunity to move to sustainable green growth is limited, because once infrastructure is built, it is in place for many decades, so a major push is merited to build "green" now rather than building environmentally unfriendly and costly infrastructure. Rapid action will allow Indonesia to successfully transform to a green and efficient economy, and ultimately move the country on a sustainable growth trajectory.

This chapter argues that synergies exist between protecting local and global environments. A number of good policies and practices should be scaled up and strengthened, and there is an urgent need for mainstreaming "green elements" into development planning. Policy and planning coordination across ministries and levels of government needs to be enhanced. Indonesia can benefit from international and regional initiatives on climate change, and the international climate change regime will need to do more to facilitate the transfer of finance, knowledge, and technology to Indonesia. A framework should be established to support South–South cooperation and information sharing among neighboring countries. Moreover, Indonesia should leverage private finance for climate change mitigation and explore innovative forms for financing adaptation through partnerships with the private sector.

References

Alisjahbana, A. and A. Yusuf. 2003. Assessing Indonesia's Sustainable Development: Long-Run Trend, Impact of the Crisis, and Adjustment During the Recovery Period. *MPRA Paper* No. 1736, November 2007.

Ardiansyah, M. and R. Boer. 2009. Forestry Sector. In MoE. Technical Report on Vulnerability and Adaptation Assessment to Climate Change for Indonesia's Second National Communication. Ministry of Environment and United Nations Development Programme.

ASEAN Secretariat. 2009. *Fourth ASEAN State of the Environment Report 2009*. Malaysia. ISBN 978-602-8411-27-1

Asian Development Bank (ADB). 2005. *Country Environmental Analysis: Indonesia.* Manila

———. 2009. The Economics of Climate Change in Southeast Asia: A Regional Review. Manila.

Badan Perencanaan Pembangunan Nasional (Bappenas—National Development Planning Board) and ADB. 1999. *Causes, Extent, Impact and Costs of 1997/98 Fires and Drought* Final Report, Annex 1 and 2, *Planning for Fire Prevention and Drought Management Project* (Asian Development Bank TA 2999-INO). Jakarta.

Badan Pusat Statistik (BPS—Statistics Indonesia). 2008. Statistik Lingkungan Hidup Indonesia (Environment Statistics of Indonesia). Katalog BPS:3305001. ISSN: 02166224. Jakarta

Boer, R., A. Buono, A. Rakhman, and A. Turyanti. 2009. Historical and Future Change of Indonesian Climate. In Ministry of the Environment, Technical Report on Vulnerability and Adaptation. Jakarta.

Boer, R. and R. Dewi. 2008. Indonesia Country Report – A Regional Review on the Economics of Climate Change in Southeast Asia. Manila: ADB. Unpublished.

Boer, R. and A. Faqih. 2005. Current and Future Rainfall Variability in Indonesia. Technical Report of AIACC Project Integrated Assessment of Climate Change Impacts, Adaptation and Vulnerability In Watershed Areas and Communities in Southeast Asia (AIACC AS21): Indonesia Component. Washington, DC: International START Secretariat.

Boer, R. and Perdinan. 2008. Adaptation to Climate Variability and Climate Change: Its Socioeconomic Aspect. Paper presented in the EEPSEA Conference on Climate Change: Impacts, Adaptation, and Policy in South East Asia with a Focus on Economics, Socio-Economics and Institutional Aspects, 13-15 February 2008, Bali.

Boer, R. and A. Subbiah. 2005. Agriculture Drought in Indonesia. In V.K. Boken, A.P. Cracknell, and R.L. Heathcote (eds). *Monitoring and Predicting Agriculture Drought: A Global Study.* New York: Oxford University Press.

Boer, R. and E. Surmaini. 2006. Economic Benefits of Using SOI Phase Information for Crop Management Decision in Rice-Base Farming System of West Java, Indonesia. Technical Report APN Project. Bogor: Bogor Agricultural University.

Bundesanstalt für Geowissenschaften und Rohstoffe (BGR—German Federal Institute for Geosciences and Natural Resources). 2009. *Reserves, Resources and Availability of Energy Resources in 2009.* Hannover.

Burke, L., E. Selig and M. Spalding. 2002. *Reefs at Risk in Southeast Asia.* Washington, DC: World Resources Institute. http://www.wri.org/publication/publication/content/8135

Contreras-Hermosilla, A. and C. Fay. 2005. Strengthening Forest Management in Indonesia through Land Tenure Reform: Issues and Framework for Action. http://www.rightsandresources.org/publication_details.php? (accessed 28 March 2010).

Emerson, J., D. Esty, M. Levy, C.H. Kim, V. Mara, A. De Sherbin, and T. Srebotnjak. 2010. 2010 Environmental Performance Index. New Haven: Yale Center for Environmental Law and Policy.

Food and Agriculture Organization (FAO). Fisheries and Aquaculture Department. http://www.fao.org/fishery/country sector/FI-CP_ID/en

Forest Watch Indonesia. 2007. Palm Oil Threats: Deforestation and Peat Land Degradation in Central Kalimantan. (http:/fwi.or.id/English/?p=140)

Goldammer, J., H. Rufelds, J-P. Malingreau, R. Yokelson, H. Abberger, and A. Manila. 1998. The ASEAN FireForum: Results of the Working Group Discussions. In: Proceedings, AIFM Conference on Transboundary Pollution and the Sustainability of Tropical Forests: Towards Wise Forest Fire Management, 2-4 December 1996, Kuala Lumpur. Kuala Lumpur: ASEAN Institute for Forest Management.

Hariati, F., B. Dasanto, R. Boer, A. Heriensyah, Fitriyani, and D. Octavariani. 2009. Marine and Coastal. In Minostry of Environment Technical Report on Vulnerability and Adaptation Assessment to Climate Change for Indonesia's Second National Communication. Jakarta: Ministry of Environment and United Nations Development Programme.

Hendiarti, N. 2007. Potrets Pulau Nipah. Round table discussion: Pemanasan Global dan dampak SLR dan hilangnya pulau-pulau kecil, Kementrian Negara Lingkungan Hidup, Jakarta, 9 April 2007.

Heriensyah, A., R. Boer, Yanuar, and B. Dasanto. 2009. Water Resources. In Ministry of Environment Technical Report on Vulnerability and Adaptation Assessment to Climate Change for Indonesia's Second National Communication. Jakarta: Ministry of Environment and United Nations Development Programme.

Hidayati, R., A. Buono, A. Rakhman, Fitriyani, and R. Boer. 2009. Health Sector. Technical Report on Vulnerability and Adaptation Assessment to Climate Change for Indonesia's Second National Communication. Jakarta: Ministry of Environment and United Nations Development Programme.

Hope, C. 2006. The Marginal Impact of CO_2 from PAGE2002: An Integrated Assessment Model Incorporating the IPCC's Five Reasons for Concern. The Integrated Assessment Journal 6(1):19–56.

Hopley, D. and Suharsono. 2000. The Status of Coral Reefs in Eastern Indonesia. Townsville, Australia: Australian Institute of Marine Science.

International Energy Agency (IEA). 2009. 2009 World Energy Outlook. Paris.

Intergovernmental Panel on Climate Change (IPCC). 2000. *Special Report Emissions Scenarios: Summary for Policymanters.* Geneva: World Meteorological Organization and UNEP. http://www.ipcc.ch/pdf/special-reports/spm/sres-en.pdf

Leitman, J. et. al .2009. Investing in a More Sustainable Indonesia. Country Environmental Analysis. CEA Series, East Asia and Pacific Region. Washington DC: World Bank.

Lennertz, R. and K. Panzer. 1984. Preliminary Assessment of the Drought and Forest Fire Damage in Kalimantan Timur. East Kalimantan Transmigration Area Development, Project PN 76.2010.7 sponsored by the DFS German Forest Inventory Services for German Agency for Technical Cooperation, Jakarta.

MAGICC/SCENGEN. http://www.cgd.ucar.edu/cas/wigley/magicc

Ministry of Environment (MOE). 2003. *National Strategy Study on CDM in Forestry Sector.* Jakarta.

———. 2004. *Indonesia State of the Environment Report.* Jakarta.

———. 2007. *Indonesia Country Report: Climate Variability and Climate Change, and Their Implications.* Jakarta

———. 2010. *Indonesia Second National Communication under the United Nations Framework Convention on Climate Change.* Jakarta.

Ministry of Finance. 2008. Climate Change and Fiscal Policy Issues: 2008 Initiatives. Working Group on Fiscal Policy for Climate Change. Jakarta.

Ministry of Forestry. 2007. Forestry Statistics of Indonesia. Jakarta

National Council on Climate Change (NCCC). 2010. Indonesia's Greenhouse Gas Abatement Cost Curve. National Council on Climate Change. Jakarta.

Naylor, R., D. Battisti, D. Vimont, W. Falcon, and M. Burke. 2007. Assessing Risks of Climate Variability and Climate Change for Indonesian Rice Agriculture. Proceeding of the National Academic of Science 114:7752–57.

Oil and Gas Journal. 2008. Worldwide Look at Reserves and Production. *Oil and Gas Journal 107*(22). December 2008, PennWell Corporation, Oklahoma City, OK.

Organisation for Economic Co-operation and Development (OECD). 2008. *Economic Aspects of Adaptation to Climate Chage: Costs, Benefits and Policy Instruments.* Paris.

Panjiwibowo, C., M. Soejachmoen,, O. Tanujaya, and W. Rusmantoro. 2003. Mencari Pohon Uang:CDM Kehutanan di Indonesia. Pelangi, Jakarta.

PEACE. 2007. Indonesia and Climate Charge: Current Status and Policies. Jakarta.

Pew Center on Global Climate Change. 2009. Key Scientific Developments since the IPCC Fourth Assessment Report. Science Brief 2, June 2009. Arlington, VA.

REN21 (Renewable Energy Policy Network for the 21st Century). 2009. *REN21 Renewables Global Status Report: Energy Transformation Continues Despite Economic Slowdown,* Press release. Paris. www.iea.org/fi les/REN21_Press_Release.pdf (accessed September 2009).

Stern, N. 2007. *The Economics of Climate Change: The Stern Review.* Cambridge: Cambridge University Press.

Suharsono. 2005. *Status of Coral Reefs in East Asia Seas Region.* International Coral Reef Research and Monitoring Center. Tokyo: Ministry of Environment of Japan.

United Nations Environment Programme–Global Resource Information Database (UNEP/GRID)-Arendal. 2007. Extent of Deforestation in Borneo 1950--2005 and Projection Toward 2020. UNEP/GRID-Arendal Maps and Graphics Library.

United Nations Framework Convention on climate Change (UNFCCC). CDM in Numbers. http://cdm.unfccc.int/Statistics/index.html (accessed 12 October 2009).

United States Geological Survey (USGS). 2000. World Petroleum Assessment 2000. Washington, DC.

Wilke, M., S. Fortuna, and O. Souksavat. 2002. FAO's Database on Mangrove Area Estimates. Forest Resources Assessment Working Paper No. 62. Rome: Food and Agriculture Organization.

Witoelar, R. 2010. Letter from the Executive Chair, Naltional Council on Climate Change, Indonesia, to the Executive Secretaru, United Nations Framework Convention on Climate Change. http://unfccc.int/files/meetings/cop_15/copenhagen_accord/application/pdf/indonesiacphaccord_app2.pdf

World Bank. 2006a. *At Loggerheads? Agricultural Expansion, Poverty Reduction and Environment in the Tropical Forest.* Washington, DC.

———. 2006b. *Where is the Wealth of Nation? Measuring Capital for the 21ˢᵗ Century.* Washington DC.

———. 2009a. World Development Indicators (WDI). http://data.worldbank.org/data-catalog/world-development-indicators (accessed 25 March 2010).

———. 2009b. World Development Report 2010: Development and Climate Change. World Bank, Washington

World Energy Council (WEC). 2010. Survey of Energy Resources 2010. London. www.worldenergy.org

World Resources Institute (WRI). 2009a. Climate Analysis Indicators Tool (CAIT). 2009. Version 6.0. Washington, D.C.

———. 2009b. Earthtrends Database. http://earthtrends.wri.org (10 March 2010).

———. 2011. Climate Analysis Indicators Tool (CAIT). 2009. Version 8.0. Washington, D.C.

Index

15–16; regulatory environment and 204–7; spatial dimensions of 202–4; structural changes in 186–94; trade policies and 199–201; trends and patterns in 184–95

inequality: constraints on reduction of 7–10, 87–143; employment opportunities and 92–7; health status and 115–22; in income distribution 324–5; international comparisons of 92; social services access and 122–8, 141–3

infant and child mortality 115–22

infectious disease 116–22

inflation: economic growth and reduction of 168–73; employment slowdown and 311–12; macroeconomic risk and 56, 58, 152–3; Suharto era management of 15. *See also* hyperinflation

informal employment, education and 326–8

infrastructure: airports 248–51; climate change management and 457–8; development of 8, 227–71; electricity 251–5; employment and investment in 312–13; financing shortages 270–1; governance constraints 268–70; growth diagnostic approach to development of 231–4; human and institutional capacity constraints 265–8; investment constraints 237–8; land acquisition difficulties 262–5; private and public-private partnerships 250–1, 254. 256–7; project implementation delays and 267–8; public investment constraints 249–50, 252–3; railways 246–8; regional disparities in development of 229–31; resource allocation for 135–8; seaports 242–6; social services access and 122–8; survey of stakeholders in 235–6, 258–62; telecommunications 255–8; transport and electricity constraints 236–7, 238–42; unequal access to 129–40

Inpres Desa Tertinggal 365–7

institutional capacity: development of 21–2; employment creation and 320–4; infrastructure development and weaknesses in 261–2, 265–8; poverty reduction and 351–2, 371–3; regional governments 421–6; telecommunications infrastructure and weaknesses in 256; weaknesses in 55

intensive margin goods, export of 198–9

Interim Poverty Reduction Strategy Paper (IPRSP) 345–8

international capital account 15

international direct dialling (IDD) business, telecommunications infrastructure and 258

international finance organizations, democratic transition and role of 20–1

international mechanisms for capacity development 454–60

International Monetary Fund (IMF) 15, 18; trade policies and 199–201

international trade, seaport infrastructure and 242–6

investment: economic growth and 161–2; employment creation and 320–4; in human capital development 288–91; infrastructure development 227–31, 237–8; regional government borrowing and financing of 415–16; "win-win" opportunities for 455

Islamic Development Bank (IDB) survey of infrastructure development 235–6, 267–8

J

Jamkesmas social health insurance 356–7, 361–5

Japan, relations with 15

Jaring Pengaman Sosial (JPS) 343–5, 360–5

Java-Bali: deforestation of 440–4; economic dominance of 28–9;

Lightning Source UK Ltd.
Milton Keynes UK
UKOW050739160312

189073UK00001B/83/P